ENDEAVORS IN PSYCHOLOGY

HENRY A. MURRAY

ENDEAVORS
IN PSYCHOLOGY

Selections from the Personology of
HENRY A. MURRAY

Edited by
Edwin S. Shneidman

HARPER & ROW, PUBLISHERS
NEW YORK

Cambridge
Hagerstown
Philadelphia
San Francisco

1817

London
Mexico City
São Paulo
Sydney

Copyright acknowledgments are to be found on pages 625-27, which constitute a continuation of this copyright page.

ENDEAVORS IN PSYCHOLOGY: SELECTIONS FROM THE PERSONOLOGY OF HENRY A. MURRAY. Copyright © 1981 by Edwin S. Shneidman. All rights reserved. Printed in the United States of America. No part of this book may be used or reproduced in any manner whatsoever without written permission except in the case of brief quotations embodied in critical articles and reviews. For information address Harper & Row, Publishers, Inc., 10 East 53rd Street, New York, N.Y. 10022. Published simultaneously in Canada by Fitzhenry & Whiteside Limited, Toronto.

FIRST EDITION

Designer: *C. Linda Dingler*

Library of Congress Cataloging in Publication Data

Murray, Henry Alexander, 1893–
  Endeavors in psychology.

  Bibliography: p.
  Includes index.
  1. Psychology—Addresses, essays, lectures.
2. Personality—Addresses, essays, lectures.
I. Shneidman, Edwin S.   II. Title.
BF149.M864   1980   150   80–7598
ISBN 0–06–014039–9

81 82 83 84 85 10 9 8 7 6 5 4 3 2 1

CONTENTS

"Upon my soul, he's been studying Murray's Grammar! Improving his mind . . ."

HERMAN MELVILLE
Moby-Dick
Chapter 99

So that there are instances among them of men, who, named with Scripture names—a singularly common fashion on the island—and in childhood naturally imbibing the stately dramatic thee and thou of the Quaker idiom; still, from the audacious, daring, and boundless adventure of their subsequent lives, strangely blend with these unoutgrown peculiarities, a thousand bold dashes of character, not unworthy a Scandinavian sea-king, or a poetical Pagan Roman. And when these things unite in a man of greatly superior natural force, with a globular brain and a ponderous heart; who has also by the stillness and seclusion of many long night-watches in the remotest waters, and beneath constellations never seen here at the north, been led to think untraditionally and independently; receiving all Nature's sweet or savage impressions fresh from her own virgin voluntary and confiding breast, and thereby chiefly, but with some help from accidental advantages, to learn a bold and nervous lofty language—that man makes one in a whole nation's census—a mighty pageant creature, formed for noble tragedies.

HERMAN MELVILLE
Moby-Dick
Chapter 16

PREFACE

Whatever faults or mistakes of mine that appear in this book are probably due to the fact that, for me, it has been a labor of love and, as is well known, such a passion can lead a man into error. This enterprise, which has been urged on Dr. Henry A. Murray for the past several years, finally had his approval early in 1979, but when that agreement came, it seemed such a heavy responsibility for me to assume singly that I immediately asked four former students of his (and friends of mine) to assist me by constituting themselves an informal "committee" to help make the final selections and to edit my interstitial materials. Fortunately, they all live in California and so we—Gardner Lindzey, Donald MacKinnon, Nevitt Sanford, Brewster Smith, and I—met in April 1979 at the Center for Advanced Study in the Behavioral Sciences at Stanford (where Lindzey, who is director there, was our host). We subsequently corresponded several times on major and detailed issues. The sharpening and shaping of this book reflects their efforts, and I am grateful to each of them.

Dr. Murray was, of course, ex officio chairman of this group. No item was included or excluded without his knowledge and approval—keeping in mind that the final table of contents represents a series of difficult compromises between our press for greater inclusion and the restrictions of publishing realities. The title of this volume was his selection. The sixth member of the committee was Nina Murray. It is no exaggeration to say that her efforts were invaluable. She was the *sine qua non* for this volume. For these reasons, and because of my deep affection for her, I dedicate my efforts in this book to her.

I first met Dr. Murray in 1951, when he wrote the foreword to a book of mine. I am proud to state that he has been the most important intellectual influence in my life. I am honored now again to have this opportunity to bring a selection of his magnificent works before a new and wider audience.

E. S. S.

University of California at Los Angeles
May 13, 1980

I

Personology
(as well as the personologist)
is shaped by numerous
and various forces

Numerous forces help to create an individual personality, even—or especially—that of Henry A. Murray. In an essay on Dr. Morton Prince, the man with whom he worked at Harvard, Murray speaks of "genes and fortune," a phrase which seems to include almost everything. But if we know anything about Murray's work, we are aware that it focuses on taxonomy and explication, so obviously there is much more than those two simple factors.

In discussing "fortune," many forces that shape personality can be cited. There is the role of planful choice, those turns in life when one makes a conscious decision, as Murray did when he elected to attend medical school in New York, specifically in order to detach himself from his "playboy and athletic friends in the Harvard-Boston area." There are vast underground currents—the unconscious psychic processes—which are enormously important in the swaying and shaping of any life. And there are, to use Pasteur's felicitous phrase, "chance and the prepared mind"—terms which could be used to describe Murray's meeting with Moby-Dick *aboard a ship or his reading Jung's* Psychological Types *at just the propitious moment in his life or his being offered the post at the Harvard Psychological Clinic seemingly against all odds.*

And naturally, there is chance alone, what Murray calls Fate, defined as "the epigenetical program plus other factors." There is, to use Otto Rank's phrase, "willing the obligatory" or acceding to the inevitable or gracefully accepting the immutable. And, idiosyncratically for Murray, there is what he calls his "sanguine surplus," by which he means his penchant for adventurously embracing the largest ideas and conceptualizations. And there are many more.

Herman Melville—Murray's lifelong obsession—said, "Like a frigate I am filled with a thousand souls." In this present context, we can understand this to mean that I, a human personality, bear within me the cargo of a thousand influences. Some of these influences were laid down with the keel of my hull and some others were taken on board every league of every trip since I was first launched and first embarked.

As one reads the lives of interesting persons, one notes how often

3

such individuals will have known and interacted with a substantial number of other noteworthy persons of that same era. It is not at all surprising then that Murray would have followed this same pattern. His friends and acquaintances included scientists L. J. Henderson, J. B. S. Haldane; Nobel Laureate F. Gowland Hopkins; Jacques Loeb, Alexis Carrel, Talcott Parsons, Kurt Lewin, Hans Zinsser, and Clyde Kluck-hohn; the sculptor Gaston Lachaise—who sculpted a bust for him; poets Edwin Arlington Robinson and Conrad Aiken; the actress Katharine Cornell; Felix Frankfurter; Sigmund Freud and Carl Gustav Jung. As a young surgeon in New York City and as a psychoanalyst in Boston, Murray met and developed, as he says, "varied, intimate relations with hospital patients, ranging from a notorious gangster and dope addict to a champion world politician with infantile paralysis."

Murray is a dynamically oriented "man-watching naturalist." The two giants of psychoanalysis, Freud and Jung, were enormous personal influences in his life. Murray met Freud, and although there was not an intense personal relationship between them, he never lost sight of the fact that much essential sense and wisdom necessary for a meaningful —not to say profound—understanding of man came from Freud's writings.

For Murray, Jung was a different story. The impact was not only from writings but also from the man himself. Simply put, Jung was probably the most influential person in Murray's life; although Murray never was, strictly speaking, a "Jungian." In his two autobiographical essays, Murray tells us again and again of Jung's charismatic effect on him. He never forgot the impact of his first electrifying session with Jung, "from which explosive experience he emerged a reborn man." One important result of this critical experience was that Murray would never again in his life give picayune statistical details, no matter how precise or "accurate," priority over meaningful relevance in the study of himself or others.

Another major influence on Murray was Herman Melville. Among his idiosyncrasies is a special quest for perfection, particularly as it touched a topic in which he was especially invested: his abiding passion for the life and works of Melville. It was difficult for him to feel that anything he wrote on Melville was finally fit for print. There was in him, figuratively speaking (he never wore any personal jewelry), a keen disdain for lesser gems than flawless diamonds. In practice, this meant that in relation to Melville every word of every essay, every phrasing of every thought, every facet of every word had to reflect just the right light, to gleam in just the right way. It is a lofty standard that certainly does not

*make for rushing into print. Thus, during over half a century of inten-
sive creative thought and after many pages of carefully crafted manuscript about Melville, Murray regrettably published only four relatively
short pieces on the man who had almost obsessively colored his entire
intellectual and psychological life. They are published together for the
first time in this volume.*

*Early in the 1920s, Murray, then a young doctor, was on his annual
trip to England and the Continent on one of the Cunard liners when,
three days out to sea, the captain of the ship developed acute appendicitis
necessitating an emergency-at-sea operation. The ship's surgeon invited
Murray, inasmuch as he was also a physician, to assist him by administering the chloroform and, in their conversation, mentioned his admiration of Herman Melville. Indeed, on this trip to the States the surgeon
had taken special pains to go to New Bedford to see the Whaleman's
Chapel. By pleasant coincidence, Murray had had a copy of* Moby-Dick
*"forced upon" him by a friend and had begun to read it on that voyage.
Thus, during the decade of the Melville Revival, an Englishman and a
Boston Brahmin, almost literally over their captain's anesthetized body,
discussed America's masterpiece. Appropriately, while at sea, Murray
finished this great oceanic book.*

The effect of Murray's first reading of Moby-Dick *was magical. In
one elevating and insightful experience, Melville's book revealed to
Henry Murray the vast mysterious world of the unconscious—a topic
that had previously never occupied his mind and subsequently never left
it.*

*Thus began Murray's central lifelong interest—soon thereafter
made alive by his contact with Freud and his intense relationship with
Jung—in the workings and wonders of the unconscious elements of the
human mind.*

*The title of Murray's paper "In Nomine Diaboli" comes from Chap-
ter 113, "The Forge," of* Moby-Dick, *in which Captain Ahab deliriously
howls, "Ego non baptizo te in nomine patris, sed in nomine diaboli." (I
do not baptize you in the name of the father, but in the name of the
devil.) When it appeared in* The New England Quarterly *in 1951, it was
a bomb-burst. Murray was an outsider to literary criticism, yet he
brought to his work on Melville impeccable scholarship and, what no
professional student of literature seemed then to possess, profound psychoanalytic insights. "In Nomine Diaboli" transformed Melville scholarship. It dared to grapple with the demonic powers in Melville's book,
providing deep understandings of the psychodynamics of Ahab's mono-
mania and, indirectly, of Melville's core interests and conflicts. In this*

one brief essay, Murray became one of the few writers since the 1920s to testify to the epic proportions of Moby-Dick *and to recount the awful price that it cost Melville to write it.*

James Grier Miller, an eminent psychologist/psychiatrist and systems theorist, paying homage to Murray and citing him among the major influences in his life in the preface to his recent monumental book, Living Systems, *characterizes Murray in these ways: "a sociotropic biochemist, a psychologist physician, a clinician, an imaginative humanist and scientist, and an exciting mind capable of stimulating others to concern themselves with central issues." Murray himself, in his own autobiographical essays, indicated a large number of the influences—the books, the people, the events and situations, the challenges—that touched and moved him and played variously weighted roles in shaping the components of his own complex personality.*

1

PREPARATIONS FOR THE SCAFFOLD
OF A COMPREHENSIVE SYSTEM

INTRODUCTION

It seems that the majority of my voices are in favor of this enterprise, for here I am, pen in hand, intending to comply so far as possible with the editorial suggestions.

But a minority of me—and now surely, at the outset, is the moment to give vent to it—believes that certain of the analyses invited by the discussion outline are premature, not for all psychologists perhaps, but for those who are concerned with human lives and personalities. The topics suggested for discursive treatment are broadly defined; but, even when taken with a grain of salt, the task calls for meticulous criticism of one's own speech, semantic niceties, overelegant definitions. Should not criticism and refinement be in balance with spontaneity, exploration, and invention if a science is to grow in a way and at a pace appropriate to its age? Also, do we have sufficient data or sufficient organization of the data to arrive at anything more than a miniature system for a tiny region of transactions? Systematic psychology, being very young, has occupied only a small portion of its legitimate terrain. Its contemporary schools are like our thirteen colonies along the Atlantic coast line, a narrow strip of provincial culture. Their manifest destiny is to move West, order the wilderness with the best available tools, crude as they now are, and eventually achieve a more refined and comprehensive system which embraces all parts and functions of the whole, the total personality. At this stage I should hate to see our center of gravity move any further to the side of perfectionistic rituals, a hair-splitting fussy Conscience.

No doubt this large endeavor will bear fruit; but despite its promise, it is not applauded at this moment by some members of my household because of their suspicion that it is liable to seduce some promising psychologists away from the study of personalities—the domain that is theirs, and only theirs, to explore, survey, and map—away from the

From S. Koch, Ed., *Psychology: A Study of a Science.* Vol. 3. New York: McGraw-Hill, 1959, pp. 7–54.

humanistically important riddles which we should be creeping up on gradually and craftily.

Another reason for my hesitation in joining this enterprise is the impossibility of my adhering to the suggested ordinance of discourse. It is evident that certain of its terms could be met only by psychologists with other aims than mine. It is an admirable mold—straightedged and nicely shaped—for exclusively experimental specialists, observers of closely restricted animal activities, peripheralists, and positivists; but literal adherence at all points is scarcely possible for naturalists, generalists, and centralists, who study gradual transformations of the dispositions, beliefs, and modes of action of human beings as they manifest themselves in different social settings.

Despite the above reservations, twenty months ago it was decided somehow that I accept the challenge as an adventure in self-discipline; and, in conformity with the committee's outline, I went ahead with what amounts to an intellectual autobiography in so far as this relates to the development of my present scaffold for a theory of personality. This part of the assignment was easier than I anticipated; but the second part— setting up a logically articulated skeleton of the whole—was so much more difficult that, despite an extension of time as well as every possible guidance and encouragement from a most charitable Director, I was unable to arrive at a satisfactory set of basic propositions before the date line. In short, I proved unequal to the set standard. It happened, however, that more than half of the matter to be ordered in Part 2 has been included in Part 1, and so, the Director, pressed by generosity, decided that the peculiar fragment which lies before you might serve as a kind of substitute contribution. Its title might be this: certain orienting dispositions, impressive observations, and influential theories as determinants of scientific aims, assumptions, methods, and conceptions.

INTEREST IN SIGNIFICANT HUMAN FEELINGS, THOUGHTS, AND ACTIONS. INFLUENCE OF MEDICINE

It is generally assumed by the uninformed and innocent that all psychologists must have at least one "orienting attitude" in common: a stout affection for human beings coupled with a consuming interest in their emotions and evaluations, their imaginations and beliefs, their purposes and plans, their endeavors, failures, and achievements. But this assumption, it appears, is not correct. A psychologist who has been constantly prodded and goaded by these propulsions, as I have been, belongs to a once small and feeble, though now expanding and more capable, minority. Anyhow, this bent of empathy and curiosity toward all profound experiences of individual men and women should be set down as one of the prime determinants of several definitive decisions, which shall be mentioned, respecting the scope of my scientific concern and of a methodology to fit. This is a crucial point because, if my interest in events of this sort had been less steadfast, I might have turned to more manageable phenomena.

My interest in people, their doings and their ills, must have had something to do with my choice at college of history as field of concentration and of medicine as career for later life.

The study of history implanted the idea of the time dimension as an essential part of the very definition of reality as well as a miscellany of coarse facts to support my speculations when I dipped, three decades later, in the stream of sociology and anthropology. But the study of medicine was more influential: it led to two years of surgery and five years of research in physiology and in the chemistry of embryology, with a Ph.D. from Cambridge University in physiological chemistry.

The practice of medicine taught me a lot of commonsensical things, one of which was that among the few almost indispensable methods of arriving at valid diagnoses (apperceptions, inferences) is that of inquiry —the thorough detailed recording of the patient's memories of interior sensations and pertinent emotional experiences. We were taught to distinguish perceptible *physical signs* (overt sense data) and imperceptible *symptoms* (reports of covert psychic processes) and to value both. The proof obtained on the operating table, time and time again, that a correct diagnosis of an abdominal condition could be made solely on the basis of a patient's reported symptoms was so firmly imprinted on the entablatures of my cortex that when, in later years, I was confronted by Watson's dogma—his radical repudiation of subjective experiences as material for psychology—my head assigned it to the category of eccentric foibles. I was an empirical behaviorist, born, bred, and trained, in the sense that every physicist, chemist, and biologist is necessarily a behaviorist. But when it came to dealing with human beings, I could see no advantage in allowing myself to be converted into an exclusive half-paralyzed behaviorist who, on metaphysical grounds, elects to deny himself an invaluable source of data. (This does not apply to the current cultural situation: today, after a complete semantic somersault, every psychological process—perception, emotion, dreaming—is called "behavior.")

My above-mentioned interest in people was not at all confined to their physical activities—say, to the routes they chose and the muscles they used in locomoting to the restaurants they preferred to ingest the food that was most appealing to their senses. I was much more interested in their feelings, evaluations, and conceptions relative to other matters, and for the most part, so were they—and so were my militantly behavioristic friends of later years—more interested in the valued products of their intellections than in their own muscular accomplishments. In due course, assured that correctness of prediction is the best index of the relative worth of different methods, I did a few impromptu experiments and found empirically that the most dependable single operation I could perform in attempting to foretell what a behaviorist would do next or in the near future was to ask him. But the commonsensical avowal I wish to make here is this: that first as a doctor and second as a psychologist I have never ceased to elicit direct expressions and reports of interior experiences—somatic, emotional, and intellectual—not only as sources of indications of overt actions to be executed in the future, but as indications of occurrences that are intrinsically important. For example, the occurrence of anxiety, or the persistence of unhappiness, or the generation of a new theory is as important to me when taken as a dependent variable (something to be predicted) as it is when taken as a hypothetical or intervening variable (an aid in the prediction of something else). Though imperceptible to us and therefore inferential, covert mental processes and products, some with and some without the property of consciousness, happen to be intrinsically attractive to a cogitator of my persuasion, and I see no insuperable barrier to their being incorporated in a unified body of scientific facts and propositions. If the heavenly bodies had memories reaching back to the Big Bang and words intelligible to us, what astronomer would shut his ears to them on principle? Anyhow, this concern of mine, this reliance on a multiplicity of inferences, checked and rechecked, this vision of a theoretical system largely composed of psychological, rather than physical, variables, makes it necessary for me to leave exclusive positivism to those who deal with entities that are incapable of supplying us with valuable verbal representations of what has occurred and is occurring behind their surfaces. But enough said; I must return to my surgical internship and finish listing what I learned that influenced subsequent decisions respecting procedures and objectives in the field of psychology.

From medical practice I derived the "multiform method" of assessment, coupled with the belief that it should be possible for a group of trained collaborators using a wide variety of methods to make a reasonably complete examination, formulation, and appraisal of a whole person as an ongoing order of differentiated functional activities. This objective is achieved over and over again on the physiological level by practitioners of medicine but when transferred to the psychological level its attainment is impeded by innumerable special difficulties. To cut down my hope to size—to make it congruent with what can feasibly be undertaken under existing conditions, with available personnel, with existing concepts and existing methods—has been my enduring but never sufficiently successful resolution.

Also derived from medicine were consequential convictions respecting (1) the determining importance of biochemical occurrences—say digestion, assimilation, metabolism, excretion—after the organism has finished eating and the interest of the average psychologist has faded; (2) the ultimate scientific value of systematic, thorough, and detailed case histories; and (3) the necessity of an adequate classification of the entities and processes within the domain of one's elected discipline.

I have nothing more to say under the present heading except to avow that my special interest in the dispositions and thoughts (rather than the bodies) of human beings was one determinant of the rather sudden decision I made to shift from physiology to psychology. Also influential in some degree were the impressions (1) that human personality, because of its present sorry state, had become *the* problem of our time—a hive of conflicts, lonely, half-hollow, half-faithless, half-lost, half-neurotic, half-delinquent, not equal to the problems that confronted it, not very far from proving itself an evolutionary failure; (2) that psychoanalysis had already made appreciable progress in exposing and interpreting the deeper processions of the mind; and (3) that my temperament was more suited to the making of coarse maps of newly explored areas than to the refinement of relatively precise maps of familiar ground.

INTEREST IN THE EARLIEST
AND INNERMOST ORIGINS OF THINGS

It seems that I was scarcely four years old when, like a cornerstone, the law was laid in me that storytellers should begin at the beginning. The beginning was not only engaging in itself, but necessary to an appreciation of the rest—all succeeding adventures, stratagems, conflicts, loves, and triumphs of the hero. I felt with Aristotle: no beginning, no excitement at the climax, no catharsis. And so, if my father or my mother failed to start a fairy tale with "In the beginning," or its equivalent, "Once upon a time," I knew that I was about to be deprived of essential information and this, in my book of rules and regulations, was ground for protest.

But more consequential than this early requirement for a good fairy tale was my first down-to-earth attempt to latch on to the beginning of a course of actual events. The attempt was prompted by a sudden bellow that originated, I soon discovered, from a strange baby in my parents' room. Puzzled, I was told that this noisy creature was my brother and perfectly adorable. Here surely was a notable beginner; but what was the beginning of this beginner? My inquiry ended with the answer that Dr. Anderton, my mother's red-bearded physician, had brought him in his bag, the very bag from which I had so often seen him lift spatula, swabs, and stethoscope.

That I should have rested—I won't say comfortably—with the words "doctor's bag," that I should have abandoned my quest for basic knowledge after one essay, not followed the path of my intent, the path of infinite regressions, one leg further at the least, a step which would have taken me to the place where Dr. Anderton obtained the babe, that I should have quit so soon, is evidence of a docility or squeamishness so unsuited to the career of science that even now I blush to acknowledge it in print. If all along I have been stopped at the very verge of the unknown by some constitutional timidity, it is possible, yes probable, that I have failed to see, or to interpret properly, or to report candidly occurrences that were beyond the stretch of well-established scientific theories or beyond the bounds of embedded moral sentiments.

I have mentioned my halt at the "doctor's bag" conception of the fount of life—suggesting parenthetically that I might not have lain down too happily with this solution—I have mentioned this defeat of curiosity as a possible indirect determinant of what eventually became a confirmed interest in the earliest and innermost origins of things. This hypothesis might help to explain why, twenty-five years later, I elected to spend the greater part of three years in an incubator with several dozen eggs, observing and measuring the chick embryo's earliest manifestations of vitality. The point is that I managed at long last to get inside the doctor's bag, or, better still, at 103.6° F, almost within the womb of the beginning of a beginner. Peering through a microscope, through a little fabricated window in the egg's shell, spellbound as any libidinous voyeur, I witnessed the procession of momentous transformations that mark the hours when the embryo is no bigger than an angel perching on a pin point. Here, it seemed, were occurrences of great significance which led into concepts no contemporary intelligence could digest.

The same hypothesis might serve, in some measure, to account for my disappointment, if not aversion, when I encountered the science of psychology at college and listened for a while to what was considered worth announcing about the perceptual processes of the adult mind, the mind of a Western intellectual, a mind without a history, strapped to a piece of apparatus in the laboratory. Also in keeping with this hypothesis was my subsequent embrace of Freud with all his facts and legends respecting the earliest months and years of life. Freud kept my first commandment: he began at the beginning. In my initial enthusiasm I hardly noticed that he never reached the consummation of the allegory, the heroic adult and his tragic end.

Depth psychology was obviously my meat. In the depths one came upon the earliest and most determining dispositions. Whatever initial doubts I had respecting unconscious psychic processes were soon enough dispelled. Several weeks with Dr. Jung at different times, three years with Dr. Morton Prince, an orthodox Freudian psychoanalysis, and a period of training with Dr. Franz Alexander and Dr. Hanns Sachs, ten years of therapeutic practice—these experiences were hugely influential in shaping my personality and my thought. But at no time, to the annoyance of my friends, was I a good Jungian, a good Freudian, a good Adlerian, or a good schoolman of any breed. I held all my teachers in high esteem, but judged that each of them—necessarily at this stage of theoretical development—was more or less one-sided. The notion which invited me was that of attempting, with the aid of additional ideas culled from the writings of McDougall, of Lewin, and of my colleagues at Harvard, a preliminary revision and integration of current academic and psychoanalytic theories to accord with a large collection of reasonably solid facts obtained by the multiform method of assessment. This effort resulted in the crude blueprint for a system which a number of us submitted in *Explorations in Personality,* [1] a blueprint which stressed the earliest and least accessible determinants of behavior. We did not do this to the satisfaction of the psychoanalysts, first, because *all* behavior was not traced to infantile sexuality and aggression and second, because we classified overt actions as they occurred, whether or not we had reasons to believe that they were subsidiary to deeper, hidden aims.

But now, if I may, I shall mention another disgrace of childhood which seems relevant to this topic—what I have called my interest in origins and beginnings. If, a while back, I almost disqualified my childhood self as a potential truth seeker, by mentioning that moment of scarcely pardonable poltroonery in the face of the Great Riddle, what I now have to confess is evidence of something bordering on complete damnation in the scales of science. Not going beyond Dr. Anderton and his bag signalized a defect in daring and determination to solve problems; but worse than this is the inability to know a pithy problem when you see it. So far as I can recall, if truth will out, I was never prompted to ask about the *very* beginning, the beginning of mankind or the beginning of the world. Passively and without suspicion or comment I received the news that some six thousand years ago God—who, in pictures I was shown, had a big beard, not red like Dr. Anderton's, but white as my venerable and remote grandfather's—that God had constructed the first man in a single day, and, a little later, molded from one of this man's ribs the first woman, et cetera, et cetera.

I suspect that it was the swallowing and digesting of this fable, trustfully and without complaint, which determined, to some degree, my gust for Darwin and the evolutionists who succeeded him, as well as the joy I felt in shedding the constraining creeds of orthodox religion. It was as though a strait jacket had been unfastened and I stepped out to breathe and move and think for the first time without embarrassment.

It was from biology and chemistry that I received the exciting notion that man is descended from the very humblest of parents, a more or less fortuitous combination of chemical elements—such low-caste stuff as hydrogen, oxygen, carbon, and nitrogen—and that, instead of a day, it took two billion years or more to shape him. Also noteworthy was the evidence that the wondrous evolutions of man and of his productions may be credited, in some measure, to the very tendency which in the Garden of Eden version led to his disgrace and fall, that is, the inborn tendency to explore and to experiment among forbidden things.

My enthusiasm for this theory becomes more intelligible when viewed in conjunction with the next orienting disposition to be listed.

INTEREST IN PROCESS, CHANGE, DIFFERENTIAL DEVELOPMENT, CREATIVITY. INFLUENCE OF CHEMICAL EMBRYOLOGY

It is hard to decide: should I speak here of a predisposition that sensitized me to a certain class of facts or should I speak of a certain class of facts which engendered a disposition to accept them and look for more of the same kind? I have always thought it good emotional policy not only to enjoy, so far as possible, the inevitable, but to will the obligatory. In this case, however, I am inclined to stress the inner bent ahead of the compelling facts because to the majority of psychological theorists these facts are not particularly compelling.

I am referring to facts which particularly attracted me during my studies at the Rockefeller Institute of the physiological ontogeny of chicken embryos. To summarize a long story, what seemed both most obvious and most important about the interior of the embryo were (a) the givenness, the inherent spontaneity, of its cellular activities and (b) the continuous sequence of orderly metamorphoses (clearly perceptible under the microscope) which resulted from these activities, and hence the necessity of including formative (constructive) processes in one's scheme of variables.

Unintrusive observation was enough to nail down the self-evident proposition that chemical and physical activity, metabolism and movement, are integral properties of every animate body, things to be included in the very definition of life. Also, it appeared that organic processes are not only primarily endogenous, autonomous, and *proactive* (initiated and sustained from within, rather than being *merely* reactive to external stimuli) but especially in the early stages of development are, so far as one can see, not perfectly coordinated with other processes, not constantly directed toward the achievement of effects *extrinsic* to themselves. This view of things was initially implanted by observing, time after time, the very first beat of the uncompleted embryonic heart and noting that it contracted irregularly and then regularly for quite a while —I forget how long precisely—before the blood vessels and the corpuscles were far enough along in their development to make it possible for this organ to perform its predestined function, namely, to pump oxygen-refreshed blood through the arteries of the body. The primitive heart was merely exhibiting its emergent capacity to contract, like a playful child or puppy, achieving for a period no effects outside its own growth of form and potency.

This notion of endogenous, initially undirected and uncoordinated, *process-activity* constrained me, in later years, on the one hand, to qualify my acceptance of the fashionable stimulus-response formula, with its implicit assumption of a nothing-but-reactive organism and, on the other hand, to qualify my acceptance of the proposition that all activities are motivated. In short, I take "life"—say, the ceaseless processes of metabolism—as *given*, just as Newton took motion as given, and do not look for something antecedent to it, except in an evolutionary sense.

The other influential impression I received from my studies of embryonic physiology was that, during the first phases of its career, a relatively large proportion of the totality of processes within a living organism is involved in the development of somatic substance, in the work, let us say, of anabolism, of incorporating and combining new elements, and so of constructing and of reconstructing parts unexampled in the history of that particular unity of animation. In other words, the most significant characteristic of the embryo is not so much the arrangement of its perceptible component forms of matter at this or that moment, as its activity in forming and transforming forms of matter. Defining "energy" as the capacity to produce change, change of relations, we can say that most of the energy of the embryo is devoted to generative changes, that a host of processes *precede* forms, one of the effects, or "functions," of some processes being to build and to rebuild them. That is, the organism, being an open system (as Bertalanffy showed me later), selects from its environment, incorporates and synthesizes, potentially energic matter, and thereby increases its resources, taking a course opposite to that defined by the second law of thermodynamics (which applies to closed systems). Furthermore, clearly perceptible under the microscope were divisions of the soma into regions and in each region the production of distinctive structures, in short, morphological differentiation, preparatory to specialization of functions.

It was these observations of embryonic developments, besides what I could understand about the science of energetics, which initially predisposed me to stress "mythologies" of energy, process, change, function, more than "mythologies" of matter, structure, permanence, and to regard the organism as ordered successions of different kinds of processes, the effects of some of them being primarily internal—formations and re-formations of component structures—with a re-ordering of the processes occurring consequentially. In short, according to this way of thinking, creativity is an inherent property of the organism and stability is another.

Four of the ultimate resultants of my interest in process, development, and creativity were (1) the adoption of the whole history of an organism, the entire life span of a personality, as the macro-temporal unit that requires formulation (although it may be half a century before a satisfactory way of doing this—an adequate conceptual scheme and an adequate methodology—is devised); (2) an interest in all manifestations of significant changes of personalities—progressive transformations, eliminations, and reconstructions, learnings, extinctions, and relearn-ings, regressions and deteriorations—and in the determinants of such changes, and hence a special, but by no means exclusive, emphasis upon the influential experiences of childhood; (3) a devotion to all forms of the imagination—dreams, fantasies, prospections, ordinations (plans), plays, story-constructions, myths, rituals, religious conceptions, works of art, and scientific speculations—as manifestations of involuntary and largely unconscious process-activities which, when influenced by a strong and continuing intention, may, in some cases, have a definitely creative out-come; and (4) the construction of a large number of methods (most of them unpublished) for the education and exposure of imaginal processes and products (so-called projective tests).

Imaginal processes and products appeal to me not only because of their intrinsic interest, but because they have been shown to be the best source of dependable clues of underlying (and often unconscious) disposi-tions and conflicts of dispositions. An often verified hypothesis is that some of these inferable dispositions are residua of deformative infantile experiences and that a few of them are prodromes of conditions in the offing.

OBSERVATIONS OF THE INTERDEPENDENCE AND HIERARCHICAL INTEGRATION OF FUNCTIONAL PROCESSES: ADOPTION OF THE ORGANISMIC CONCEPT. INFLUENCE OF L. J. HENDERSON

It was in 1920, during my studies of oscillations of the physicochemi-cal equilibria in the blood, under the tutelage of Lawrence J. Henderson, author of *The Order of Nature*,[2] that I first became familiar with the organismic, or organismal, proposition, as formulated by E. S. Russell in 1916 and elaborated by W. E. Ritter in 1919. Belief in its essential validity was confirmed a little later (sometime before I heard anything about gestalt psychology) by observations of the embryo—perceiving the se-quential effects of Spemann's genetical "organizers"—and by studies of the regulatory functions of the autonomic nervous system in conjunction with the endocrines. Clearly demonstrable in higher animals are *vertical* integrations of superordinate and subordinate loci of control, levels of directors and coordinators, "lines of command" starting from some cen-ter in the segmented neuraxis, or lower brain, and ending in regional plexuses and local nervous networks, a hierarchical *system,* depending on "feedbacks" (as we say today), which executes the genetically deter-mined "domestic policy" of the organism.

Here it might be appropriate to refer to Cannon's principle of ho-meostasis, and to the fact that consideration of the radical developments during the embryonic period led me to stress the concept of progressive disequilibrium, continuity through expansive, constructive change, as a supplement to that of homeostasis (which is more applicable to the interior activities of adult organisms). The concept of homeostasis (the maintenance and, if disturbed, the restoration of the *same* state of equilibrium) is a basic scientific induction, defining as it does the measurable relationships of multifarious interdependent elements and processes, relationships which either persist unchanged, or, if modified by some intruding element of exigency, are in due course re-established. But it should be noted that this principle, as commonly defined, is valid only within a certain time span. The time span varies with the age of the organism as well as with the system (physiological, psychological, or sociological) that is under consideration. In the body of a healthy adult, the morphological, physicochemical, and physiological relationships are quite stable, or soon restabilized, over a period of many years despite the slow changes which eventually result in the signs and symptoms of senescence. But in the embryo homeostasis has virtually no span at all, or an extremely short one: the organism as a system being characterized in all its manifestations by perpetually changing states of equilibria, states that move in an *irreversible* direction. In short, the embryo is in disequilibrium or, at most, transitional equilibrium from first to last. Comparable, I thought later, though less striking to the eye and less susceptible to precise measurement, are the seasons of transitional equilibrium on the psychological level, which occur most obviously in childhood but also later, during the early phases of some new enterprise, let us say, or when the creative imagination is steadily advancing. At such times psychological processes are transformative, and when they terminate, the person is a different person, or his sphere of relationships is different, and there is a different equilibrium to be sustained.

Although I came away from my embryological studies with a firm belief in the unity of the organism through change, in orderly differentiations and integrations, my medical training had established a special vigilance in respect to signs and symptoms of functional imperfection, and I soon discovered how normally abundant are such evidences on the psychological level, evidences of disunity, of retardation, deviation, deformation, and retrogression. It appears that millions of years of evolution have resulted, on the one hand, in an almost perfect system, let us say, of somatic operations, and on the other hand, in a human brain which contains at birth no comparably ordered system of dependable proactions and reactions, but instead, a matrix of potentialities in a relatively amorphous state, potentialities for unprecedented developments of talent, at one extreme, and for idiocy and lunacy, at the other. Hence, especially for human beings, life is a continuous procession of explorations, surmises, hunches, guesses, and experiments, failures and successes, of learnings and relearnings—aging consisting of a sequence of gradual and occasionally abrupt *indurations* (rigidifications, solidifications, fixations, hardenings), both of forms and functions. Consequently, a psychologist has to deal conceptually with doubt, distrust, indecision, and postponement of behavior among his subjects, together with occurrences and continuities of competition and paralyzing conflict between their dispositions.

My bent toward organismic, holistic, molar, or "gestalt" conceptions of the personality and its activities scarcely fitted me to wax avid when I encountered, later on, the then dominant elementalistic, connectionistic, chained-reflex, molecular theories of learning, theories that were being hungrily ingested by all who cared on what side their academic bread was buttered. Of the two fallacies, reductive and seductive, so nicely discriminated by Herbert Feigl, I was more liable to the second, though I had no use for those lazy white elephants of the mind—huge catchall global concepts signifying nothing. Eventually I was persuaded by Professor Boring—more generous of his time than any teacher I ever had—that the principles of elementalism and associationism are applicable under many circumstances, especially, let us say, to the establishment of certain neurotic symptoms as well as to conditionings that occur below the level of conscious control or when the mind is tired or confused and functioning below par. In short, elementalism (emphasis on parts, integrants, components) and holism (emphasis on wholes, integrates, ordinations of components) are necessary complements.

INTEREST IN THE DIRECTIONALITIES
AND EFFECTS OF OVERT BEHAVIORS

One passes by inseparable gradations from an interest in the autonomic-endocrinal coordination of the multifarious somatic processes of the body and in the local effects of their different operations, to an interest in the cortical ordination of sensory, muscular, and verbal processes toward successive achievements of different overt effects, most of which endeavors, if successful, contributing in some way or other to the well-being of the total organism.

Hence, it was already in the cards I held that, on entering the domain of psychology, I should very soon become concerned, not so much with reflexes and patterns of muscular movements, as with the various changes effected by such movements and the changes in the states and thoughts of other people effected by spoken words and sentences.

The fundamental fact, it seemed to me, is the survival of the living organism, the continuation of its metabolic processes, and the dependence of this procession upon the periodic attainment of a number of distinct effects, such as the inspiration of oxygen, the expiration of carbon dioxide, the ingestion of water and food, and the excretion of waste products. The different processes, modes, and subeffects whereby the same kind of terminal effect is achievable in different species of organisms or even in the same organism at different times were, at the start, a matter of considerable, but subsidiary, importance. A man shivering with cold may restore optimal body temperature by moving to a warm place, putting on an overcoat, closing doors and windows, lighting a fire, turning on the radiator, taking a hot drink, or exercising strenuously. Defined in terms of physical vectors (locomotions or manipulations in space) these are different actions, but the beneficent effect in all cases is the same. Indeed, a person may obtain all necessary "goods" with the minimum of activity on his part: they may be furnished providentially by nature, gratuitously by parents or friends, or in exchange for money, by domestic servants or employees. I had a good friend who lay in bed, blind and completely immobilized from his neck down, for twenty years. He had a sensitive and brilliant mind that was bubbling over with unimpaired effectiveness and charm until his death, and yet he saw nothing and never moved a muscle. Every act necessary to his survival, to the stimulation of his feelings, and to the increase of his knowledge had to be performed by someone else. This was but one of countless observations which persuaded me of the necessity of providing concepts for the analytical dissection, whenever necessary, of any short segment of activity into (1) kinds of exciting *initial situations*, (2) kinds of *processes* (e.g., covert psychic processes, overt psychomotor or psychoverbal processes) with or without kinds of utilities (e.g., tools, weapons, conveyances, telephone, typewriter, etc.), (3) kinds of *modes*, or styles, of processional activity, kinds of psycho-expressive processes (e.g., speed, grace, gestures or tone of voice expressive of uncertainty, anxiety, self-confidence, anger, good will, deference, compassion, etc.), and (4) kind of *effect* (*change* from the initial exciting to the terminal gratifying situation).

In my persistent efforts to move, step by step, toward an adequate solution to such problems, I was greatly assisted by the reported observations and formulations (1) of biologists from Darwin on, and of others, particularly McDougall, who had used the concept of instinct as their tool; (2) of Freud relative to the sex instinct, aggression, and anxiety, and of Adler relative to the craving for superiority; (3) of Tolman and other animal psychologists who had carried forward the endeavor to define and measure rigorously different drives; (4) of Lewin with his constructs of tension system and of quasi need; and (5) of sociologists regarding the wants of men for status and for power.

In *Explorations of Personality* I attempted to define a number of actional dispositions which, in the absence of a less objectionable designation, were termed "needs" (or "drives"). These constructs proved useful in categorizing inferentially the overt behaviors of the subjects we studied as well as the behaviors of the characters in the stories they composed. But this particular working inventory of human drives (kinds of motivations, purposes, intended effects, goals) was, in several respects, deficient, and ever since, these deficiencies have kept provoking me to prolonged efforts to conceive of fitting remedies. An account of today's resultant of my arduous and still continuing endeavor to arrive at a more comprehensive and integrated system will be presented in a later work.

Before leaving this topic I should say that I have not been satisfied to limit my objective to the formulation of overt behaviors, certainly not to the formulation of purely physical behaviors. Indeed, after perceiving that the food-ingesting activities of animals and of men are not at all representative of the majority of human actions (as Maslow has pointed out) but, being most readily formulated in physical terms, are repeatedly used nonetheless to illustrate this and that concept or generalization or to serve as foundation for this and that postulational system, and that they thus constitute an alluring conceptual trap for the unwary theorist— perceiving all this, I established in myself a prohibition (which I guiltily break occasionally) against using the hunger drive and its ensuing motor patterns and effects as paradigm of directional behaviors or even as a reliable reference point for speculation.

As I see it, a psychologist should be concerned not only with the formulation of overt interpersonal verbal communications, the immediate (intended) effects of which are changes of some kind among the dispositions, evaluations, represented facts, interpretations, or commitments of the other person, but also with the formulation of covert intraverted mental activities, the immediate (intended) effects of which are such things as: a better interpretation and explanation of some recalled event or of some current physical symptom, a re-evaluation of one's own enactions (past behaviors) or present abilities, the definition of the content and boundaries of a required concept, the composition of the plot of a story to be written, the resolution of a conflict between two purposes, or the ordination of a plan of action (tactics) to be executed at some future date.

INFLUENCE OF WHITEHEAD AND LEWIN: CONCEPTS OF PHYSICAL FIELD, CATHEXIS, PROCEEDING, SERIAL, ETC.

I owe much to the incomparable Alfred North Whitehead and the incomparable Kurt Lewin, nothing less than the conviction that concrete reality is to be found only in the momentary. With theoretical physics in mind, Lewin devoted a good deal of his unusual imaginative powers to the definition of space constructs, topological and hodological, the *momentary field;* whereas Whitehead, founding his penetrating reflections on organic and mental phenomena, emphasized the *momentary process,* the perpetual becoming and perishing of "actual occasions" and the historic continuity or progression of these occasions. Although I have never gained sufficient understanding of Whitehead's terminology to apply the categorial scheme of his philosophy of organism to the realm of ordinary human experience and behavior, I am indebted to him for a number of conceptions which I have revised to suit the purposes of a psychologist. First among these is the concept of an *event,* or fact, as a participation of processes in which two or more interdependent entities are involved occurring in a certain place or along a certain path, within a certain medium, through a certain segment of time, and resulting in a certain kind of change. I conceive of a range of events of different molarities. Theoretically, an ultimate *submicro event* would have the smallest *spatial scope* (smallest containing field), the smallest *entity scope* (fewest component particles), smallest *process scope* (fewest distinguishable changes), and shortest *temporal span* (duration). (For example, it is estimated that tau and theta mesons are composed and decomposed in about a hundred-millionth of a second.) Some micro events occur within the boundaries of solids, i.e., entities that can be treated as solids under most conditions (anything from a crystal to a planet), but others are integrated, synchronously and sequentially in time, in such a way as to constitute an event of greater scope and span, and this event, in turn, can be seen to constitute a necessary part, or phase, of an event of still greater scope and span, something that can be defined in terms of a single resultant process—secretion of a hormone by one cell, a single color sensation, influxion of a single image, contraction of a single muscle fiber —or in terms of a longer or more massive process—secretion of saliva, contraction of the heart, perception of a configuration, momentary feeling, evaluation of an object, movement of a limb, etc. Such an event may be a part of a yet larger, longer whole—say, a stimulus-response unit (perception, apperception, and evaluation of a pertinent entity, concurrent emotion, actuation of a pattern of muscular movements against resistance, production of an effect, perception, apperception, and evaluation of this effect). Thus, by increasing step by step one's scope and span of concern, one arrives at the largest and longest definable unit of activity, a *macro event.* A personologist usually has to deal with macro events, or *proceedings;* and from the fullness of each of these he abstracts those variables which are relevant to his purpose, in the knowledge that numberless other variables will be unrecorded and hence omitted from his formulation. Thus, the major concepts of the scaffold to be built—such as need, entity, configuration, process, succession, effect, place, route, time—are all considered to be abstractions from an event or progression of events.

As twentieth-century inhabitants of the Western world, we seem to be living and acting—partly as a consequence of our acquired Indo-European language—in Euclidean space, moving about on the supporting surface of an assumptively permanent material planet amid a great variety of substantial objects, inanimate and animate, natural and artificial (man-made), some transient, some relatively permanent, each with its distinguishing physical attributes. "Such presumptions," as Whitehead says, "are imperative in experience," and "in despite of criticism," we still employ them "for the regulation of our lives." And so, for better or for worse, I too have employed them, not only in the regulation of my life but, with certain qualifications, in the regulation of my theorizings.

If I were forced to choose one side of the age-old antinomy between the "metaphysics of substance" and the "metaphysics of flux," my temperament would decide in favor of the latter, the version of the universe that is linked in our minds with some vivid sentences attributed to Heraclitus. But, as I see things and events, it is not necessary to go to one side or the other, either of this classical division between different aspects of nature or of other dichotomies, such as that between matter in space and motion in time, or between instantaneous configurations of material bodies and modifications of these configurations, or between chemical structure and chemical properties and processes, or between form and function, or between anatomy and physiology, or between entity and activity, or between actor and action, or between noun and verb. It is possible to choose both sides and combine them in single propositions.

Perhaps my most influential basic model is that of biochemical metabolism, repetitive and restorative as well as progressively and irreversibly transformative: the lifelong succession of *compositions, decompositions, and recompositions* of concrescences and perishings, of vital chemical substances. Here is incessant *flux* certainly, with the catabolism of anabolized materials liberating the energy for every manifestation of vitality (thermal, chemical, electrical, mechanical—emotional, dispositional, mental, and muscular); and here also are countless instantaneous configurations of *substances* within cells, of cells within organs, and of organs within a body, some parts of which (skeleton, ligaments, connective tissue, skin) are relatively solid and enduring like the framework of a house. Consideration of anabolisms, in which two or more chemical entities combine to form or to re-form a more complex entity, where one can attribute the course of events to no single actor and his act, has led me to conceptualize, in many cases, *systems of participant entities and participating processes* rather than placing the major burden of determination on one person or on one person's conscious purpose. Here one might think of the mental participations involved in creative activity, with conscious intention playing but a minor role, or of the emotional, verbal, and actional participations of two lovers.

At this point let me explain for clarity's sake that in view of the mind's tendency to "spatialize" everything, as Bergson pointed out, and in view of the ambiguous usages in the social sciences of such words as structure, configuration, form, pattern, integration, etc., I prefer to restrict the word *configuration* to the instantaneous (transient), and the word *structure* to the enduring, *spatial relations* of the *substantial com-*

ponents of an entity, assemblage of entities, or region (extended surface area), and to use the word *succession* to designate the once-occurring, and the word *integration* to designate the recurrent *temporal relations* of the *component processes* of a *proceeding* (uninterrupted activity, endeavor, interaction). According to this terminology it would be proper to speak of the structure of a house, of a painting, of an organism, of a chemical compound, of a crystal, or of an atom; and it would be proper to speak of the integration of mechanical, electrical, chemical, mental, verbal, or musical processes, through a certain period of time. One could also speak, in a highly abstract way, of the hypothetical structure of the mind or of the personality, although mind and personality are known to us only through successions of covert (subjective) and overt (objective) processes. You see I am wary of the word *structure,* because, if used to describe concatenations of activities one gets that impression of permanence, regularity, and lawfulness which is so dear to the hearts of scientists and yet so incongruent with the facts in many instances.

The debt I owe to Lewin can be most simply set forth if we restrict thought, for the time being, to the motor activities of one person from the beginning to the end of a single simple *proceeding*, or endeavor, a goal-directed and goal-attaining course of action. In such a case the "whole" effect (attained goal) of the pattern of muscular processes can be defined by designating the relevant differences between the structure of the physical field at the initiation of the activity and the structure of the physical field at its termination. This will tell us what the person "did" —he moved, let us say roughly, from one location to another, or moved an object from a table to his mouth, or put a new tire on his car, or hung a picture over his desk, etc. But more than this, ideally considered—and here is where Lewin comes in—a sufficient characterization of the field at the start of the activity, and at every instant from then on, would set forth the immediate determinants of the over-all direction of the activity as well as of each successive part, or unit, of the whole. As Lewin put it, "the behavior b at the time t is a function of the situation S at the time t only," where S denotes the total situation (field)—the field of forces within the person (internal situation) as well as the field of forces exterior to the person (external situation), as apperceived and evaluated by the S. The initiating total field (a momentary cross section, or time-slice, through everything that is influential) determines the behavior resulting in the next field, which, in turn, determines the behavior resulting in the subsequent field, and so on, until the occurrence of an act resulting in a field which determines the cessation of that variety of endeavor. In Lewin's scheme of constructs, as in mine, the major variable of the internal situation (internal field) is some kind of excitation (with direction and magnitude)—a quasi need, need-aim, or drive; but here I am stressing the external situation.

It should be noted in passing that an adequate formulation of the immediate, or antecedent, determinants of behavior can never be given in terms of the *instantaneous* external situation (configuration of space or of objects or of forces in space). Even in the extreme case of a wholly stationary external environment one must take account of the process through time of the subject's perception, apperception, and evaluation of the situation; and this brings us to Whitehead's actual occasion, the "real thing." In most cases, the so-called momentary external situation (set of antecedent determinants) is likely to consist, not so much of a spatial configuration, as of a rather long pattern of symbolic processes, such as a paragraph of instructions read to the subject by an experimenter. But, let us return to the simple case of a stationary physical field in which a mobile person is positioned and consider what kind of map should be made of this so-called momentary situation.

Man being a terrestrial organism for the most part—for the duration of this discussion, anyhow—the space to be represented will be a two-dimensional flat surface, natural or artificial—either a circumscribed area of ground (composed of rock, soil, or sand) or a floor area within a building. This area we shall call the *territory* (the total spatial scope of our concern), and this territory (say, a sparsely settled rural area) we shall divide into *regions,* and these regions into subregions, and so on indefinitely, if necessary, until we arrive at a multiplicity of *places.* Each region will have a certain area and shape and will be distinguishable from other regions by the number, position, and physical attributes (size, shape, color, etc.) of its *occupants* (say, an assemblage of trees, of potato plants, of weeds, or of buildings), or by the absence of occupants, and/or by boundaries (walls, fences, hedges), not to speak of brooks and rivers. Furthermore, there will be strips with smooth surfaces connecting some of the differentiated regions, which I shall call *routes,* one of which will run through a subregion occupied by buildings, each marked by sets of symbols, one set indicating that food may be purchased there, another indicating tools, another drugs, and another clothes. Let this suffice as an account of the structure of the space relevant to our problem. Now Lewin was shrewd enough to see that a map of such a territory showing the location of physical objects and their attributes, *mere* patterns of sense data, or *mere* primitive perceptions, is of little relevance to psychology. A modern artist, by a conscious effort, might view his environment in this way, or possibly a visitor from Mars; but even in the above-given bare description of the territory I could not without misunderstanding omit such words as trees, potato plants, buildings, fences, routes, food, tools, drugs, and clothes, all of which words refer in a rough way to objects which not only make themselves known to our senses by means of their physical attributes, but which, under certain conditions, are capable of contributing to (or, in other cases, subtracting from) our welfare. Hence, it is not so much the physical attributes as such but the known or supposed man-pertinent capacities of objects which influence behavior (including the capacity of some objects to delight the aesthetic sensibilities of the subject). It was these pertinent capacities that Koffka and Lewin had in mind when they spoke of the "behavioral" or "psychological" environment, the environment of meanings or significations.

This point of view was congenial to the one at which I had arrived with the help of Uexküll. Accustomed to the distinction between the attributes and properties of chemical compounds, I had made a comparable distinction between what a human object "looks like" and what he "does" under specified conditions. Here I am leaving out, for the moment, what an alter does to the subject solely by virtue of her or his physical attributes (beauty, ugliness). What an alter does, the kind of thing he does, *to the subject,* I called a *press* (plural: *press*). For example, the press of Mr. X vis-à-vis a given subject might be "to animate him (the subject) intellectually," just as the usual press of the drug Benzedrine when taken by mouth is "to stimulate mental processes." The *capacity* to stimulate is one of the biochemical *properties* (latent press) of Benzedrine, and when Benzedrine passes into the blood stream the property becomes manifest as a process distinguished by its effect. Similarly, a known alter, regarded from the subject's point of view, can be represented as an assemblage of *subject-pertinent properties,* or latent press, which will be manifested as processional effects (operative press) either spontaneously or after appropriate stimulation, when the subject and the alter meet. Thus, as I saw it, the physical structure of the environment was representable in terms of the geometric configuration of regions, places, and objects, each with its potentially effective subject-pertinent properties (latent press). That strip of smooth surface over there is called a *route* because from position A to position B it has the property of supporting a human body or a conveyance and of facilitating locomotion; and boards cut from those trees have properties suitable for the excluding walls and supporting floors of houses, etc., etc. As a consequence of countless past experiences, such properties seem to be revealed to us immediately by *mere* perception, but at this point I prefer to speak of apperception, or apperceptive perception, since it is convenient and often important to distinguish verbally between the clear impression and identification of a particular kind of object—say, a hickory tree—and the realization of its properties—say, the properties of hickory which make the wood especially suitable for ax handles. The chief difference between the conceptualization of a pertinent property of an inanimate object, such as a drug, and a pertinent property of a person (alter) is that, in the case of the latter, one is dealing with a mobile object whose activity may be unprovoked by the subject, and one must distinguish between an endeavor that fails (through incapacity) and an endeavor that succeeds. It is the difference between a pressive disposition without ability and a pressive disposition with ability. But more of this later; I must return to my topic.

There was a wide gap, it always seemed to me, between Lewin's symbolic constructs on the level of physics (representative of public physical events) and his constant references to a miscellany of wholly private psychic processes in his subjects which he cleverly distinguished by intuition, but which he spoke about as if they were overt and obvious to everyone, or could be reliably inferred on the basis of observed behaviors. Not many psychologists realized so clearly as did Egon Brunswik, that for Lewin the exterior field (the environment) was within the subject's head. What Lewin called the "psychological environment" is the subject's apperceptions of the environment—a necessary construct; but it stood alone, no place having been provided for a more "objective" definition of the environment, say, as apperceived by the psychologist, by selected judges, or by the conventional majority. Thus by Lewin's scheme it is not possible to distinguish between a morbid delusion and a realistic, or congruent, estimation of the external situation: the situation is exactly what the subject thinks it is, or more accurately—since Lewin rarely, if ever, asked a subject—it is what you think the subject thinks it is as you empathically perspect his thoughts during the course of his behavior. Furthermore, if the humanly pertinent properties of other environmental objects (as estimated by the psychologist) are never mentioned, we shall never know how much of the external situation was rejected by the subject.

As a step toward the clarification of this issue, a number of us, stimulated by an extended definition of Freud's important concept of projection, conducted numerous investigations of differences between the external situation as carefully and systematically perceived and apperceived, say, by a consensus of trained observers (the *alpha* situation), and the same situation as perceived and apperceived (under conditions less favorable to accuracy) by subjects with different personalities (each a *beta* situation), or by subjects in a certain experimentally engendered temporary state. This is the sphere of concern which is now called "personality and perception."*

*In this and in other related enterprises, fortune favored me with early colleagues of the stature of Erik H. Erikson, Donald W. MacKinnon, Saul Rosenzweig, R. Nevitt Sanford, and Robert W. White, of William G. Barrett, Kenneth Diven, Isabelle V. Kendig, Walter C. Langer, Christiana D. Morgan, and Carl E. Smith; later of Thelma G. Alper, Leo Bellak, Vera V. French, Elliott Jaques, Robert R. Holt, Daniel Horn, Morris I. Stein, Silvan Tomkins, and Frederick Wyatt; and, more recently, of Gardner Lindzey, of Anthony Davids, Richard V. McCann, and Robert N. Wilson. I have also been advantaged by collaborations, all too short, with Freed Bales, Tamara Dembo, Cora DuBois, Walter Dyk, Jerome D. Frank, Christopher Fried, Äsa Koht, Philip Lichtenberg, Goodhue Livingston, Charles C. McArthur, H. Scudder McKeel, James G. Miller, Merrill Moore, Hobart Mowrer, Benjamin J. Murawski, and Henry W. Riecken, as well as with a host of others on the OSS assessment staff during the war years, of whom Edward Tolman and John Gardner have, in interior dialogues, admonished me most often. Among these warm friends and co-workers I have no reliable way of apportioning the credit for leading me to relatively valid concepts and for canceling many of my least propitious errant speculations, and no reliable way of apportioning the blame for withholding criticism at moments when I might have been deterred from this or that cognitive folly. Anyhow, I am grateful for the opportunities I

The bulk of our experimental findings were unanimous in their verdict respecting the importance of dispositions (interests, evaluations, and needful tensions) in determining the outcome of perceptual, apperceptual, conceptual, compositional, and ordinational (planning) processes. In short, as antecedent determinants of overt behavior, one must include, not only the structure of properties and processes of the confronting exterior situations as arranged by the experimenter (cluster of independent variables, or alpha situation), but perceptions and apperceptions of certain of these things (beta situation) as determined by the dispositional state of a given personality or type of personality (cluster of intervening, hypothetical, or conventional variables).

Besides many other things, this meant to me (with my memories of chemistry) that a psychologist will bring in less knowledge by viewing a person as a mass-point of indifferent constitution in a field of forces, as Lewin (with his interest in physics and his image of Galileo at the tower) was tempted to do, than he will by viewing him as an entity with a particular conjunction of distinguishable properties. It is, of course, true that in establishing some sorts of lawful relationships between entities it is possible to disregard differences of constitution, but even in physics, how often can one predict the outcome of an experiment without taking into account the internal structure of the molecules, or such properties of substances as conductivity or melting point? In short, on the down-to-earth empirical level (as contrasted with the sphere of transcendent, or purely hypothetical, entities) one must include in one's formulations the properties (in specified states) of the entities engaged in the observed transaction. For example, some material entities are nourishing to human organisms, others stimulating, others soporific, and others lethal, and one property of some human organisms in a certain (suicidal) state is to select a lethal rather than a nutritive entity for incorporation. I would delete these references to the obvious, if it were not for the fact that most of us, in our endeavors to be objective, to formulate behavior in terms of perceptible movements—say approach and ingestion for survival—forget, for example, that poison is attractive to persons in a certain state. In short, we cannot throw Aristotle to the dogs and restrict our diet to the more elegant formulas of Galileo: chemistry is still among the reputable sciences and closer to psychology—think of oxygen, digestion, metabolism, and endocrines—than is its more admired older brother.

Another related conclusion supported by our findings was that the historic succession of the dispositions and experiences of a scientist has

---

have had to serve as one of many channels for the ebullient ideas that have swirled and eddied round the table at the Harvard Psychological Clinic. And here I must make public my profound indebtedness to my good friend and critic, Gordon W. Allport, staunch champion of minorities, without whose timely advocacy the Clinic might have been dissolved and left no wrack behind.

a great deal to do with the concepts and theories that he comes out with, and largely because of this conviction, I have often taken pains, as by request I am taking now, to expose my inborn and acquired bents and biases, rather than to make a great to-do about my exemplary scientific objectivity. It happens that one of my inductions from experience is that many of those who spend most type asserting their immaculate empiricism are somewhat below average in their awareness of the distorting operation of their own preferences and ambitions and, therefore, are more liable than others to sally forth with reductively incongruent versions of reality.

Additional Concepts for the Present Scaffold

Among the other conceptual consequences of our studies of personalities and their apperceptions of other personalities and of my attempts to analyze single proceedings, six may merit definition.

Cathexis. From Freud I gratefully accepted the concept of cathexis (value, valence) as a useful variable in formulating personalities as well as single interactions of personalities. But instead of limiting its application to a loved person (the power of an alter to attract, enchant, and bind the affections of a person), I defined it as a possible disposition-evoking capacity of *any* kind of entity, or of any kind of activity of an entity, chiefly the capacity (1) to excite attention (interest, concern, thought, talk), or (2) to excite attention plus evaluation, either positive (favorable —say, gust, wonder, admiration, love, approval) or negative (unfavorable —say, disgust, contempt, disapproval, distrust, resentment, fear), or (3) to excite attention plus evaluation plus pertinent activity. All types of entities seem to be capable of such evocation—a certain kind of food, a homestead, a utility, a person, a social institution, a novel, a moral code, a scientific theory, a philosophy of life—and similarly capable are all types of activities of entities. Not only a total entity, but any part, integrant, or component activity of an entity may have the power to attract attention, to please or to displease, to instigate activity. You may like a person as a whole but not like certain things he does, or you may like certain things he does but dislike him as a whole. A father spanks the boy he loves because he hates lying and hopes to spank this habit out of him, and so forth. The same might be said of the negatively cathected (and hence deleted) parts of a book in process of composition, a book which, taken as a whole, may be highly cathected by its author.

My present notion of cathexis is not far from the elaborate definitions of it that were published in *A Clinical Study of Sentiments,*[3] except now the more favored term is "value" and the concept has been incorporated in a larger system. The term "sentiment," "attitude," or "established evaluation" points to dispositional property of a personality which corresponds to the cathexis of an entity. One can say that subject A has a strong sentiment or attitude (established disposition) *pro* X, or that his consistent evaluation of X is highly positive, or that X has a high positive cathexis or value for A. Both terminologies are useful. The concept of cathexis is also useful, perhaps most useful, in indicating the *subject's* effect on other people: in what quarters and to what extent he will evoke positive evaluations, based, say, on affection, erotic love, admiration, or compassion, and leading to accessions or invitations, associations and conjugations, compliances, services, or donations, etc., in what quarters and to what extent he will evoke negative evaluations, engendered by disgust, contempt, moral condemnation, or envious resentment, and leading to rejections, exclusions, decessions, expulsions, or inflictions, etc. It is not sufficiently acknowledged, I surmise, that a full characterization of a personality should include, as does the characterization of a chemical compound, the varieties of dispositional effects the subject has on different kinds of alters.

Dyadic System. The notion came and stuck that a dyadic (two-person) relationship, whether transient or enduring, should be formulated as a single system, equal analytic attention being devoted to each participant. Although I have never been inclined to accept Harry Stack Sullivan's restriction of the domain of psychology to the sphere of interpersonal relations, I use dyadic interactions as a test of every formulation or theoretical system I encounter in the literature. If the proposed set of antecedent environmental variables does not provide for the definition of an alter's subject-oriented verbal or physical behavior (e.g., such kinds of "stimulation" from the alter as petition or command, praise or reprimand, inquiry or offering of information, expression of good will, and so forth), if it does not provide tools of this sort, then the system is not suited to the representation of the great bulk of human reactions. It may, of course, have other virtues, but not those I require: variables appropriate to the prediction of concrete social episodes.

Thema. The idea matured that the basic pattern of a single dyadic interaction might be most simply represented by *i*, a symbol denoting the immediate direction, the need-generated orientation (goal), of the proactivity emanating from the first interactor, followed by *ii*, a symbol denoting the emotional response of the second interactor, and when indicated, a symbol denoting the need-generated orientation (goal) of his reactivity. Whether the goal of the first interactor's (subject's) activity is the aim of an independent need (and hence intrinsically satisfying if achieved), or the aim of a subneed (satisfying if achieved although it is no more than a subordinate component of a large system of need-aims), or the aim of a quasi need (merely instrumental and hence not intrinsically satisfying) would be a question for further investigation. Months of antecedent study and subsequent exploration might be required to determine the probable status, or relative potency, of all the needs involved in a single sentence. The same applies to the need-determined response of the alter. On this level of formulation (the formulation of a single proceeding), it would be sufficient to represent the immediate need-aim of the subject (proactor) and the need-response of the alter (reactor). The need-response of the reactor, viewed from the subject's standpoint, has been termed a *press,* the *alpha press* being the alter's actual response and orientation (in so far as he and the psychologist can define it) and the *beta press* being the subject's apperception of the alter's response and orientation. The simplest formula, then, would be either an N-P (if the subject initiated the interaction) or a P-N (if the alter acted first). This I termed a *simple micro thema,* a *simple macro thema* being an over-all, and hence much coarser, formulation of a longer transaction, and a *serial thema* being an articulated procession of simple micro themas, which might or might not be representable as a macro thema.

I might clarify this a bit by illustrating *complementation,* the simplest type of dyadic thema (others being reciprocation, cooperation, competition, opposition). Let us assume two interactors: X a confirmed *transmittor* and Y a confirmed *receptor;* and then, out of a large number of complementary needs, let us choose the following pairs, and finally, let us assume that in each case the episode is completed to the satisfaction of both parties (criterion of a veritable complementation).

SUBJECT X, TRANSMITTOR	SUBJECT Y, RECEPTOR
Need to inform (to relate facts, rumors)	Need for information (state of interest, curiosity)
Need to explain (to interpret events)	Need for explanation (state of perplexity)
Need to counsel (to give advice)	Need for counsel (state of indecision)
Need to amuse (to tell a funny story)	Need for amusement (readiness for mirth)
Need to console (to express sympathy)	Need for consolation (state of distress)

These pairs can be taken to represent the state of affairs in a dyadic system, at the start of five different proceedings. The transmittor is characterized by the tension of a valued fullness (*pleni-tension*)—he has a mental possession and the need *to* impart it—whereas the receptor is characterized by *lack-tension,* that is, by a need *for* something, something which, in this case, the other person is capable of giving him. Assume, for example, X has a mental possession (a funny story) which he is keen to communicate and Y is keen to hear a funny story. As a rule, there will be mutual satisfaction if the story strikes Y as funny and he responds with a hearty laugh. Further analysis may reveal that the apparently pleni-tensive transmittor has nothing very interesting to say but merely a strong (processional) disposition to babble (verbosity), and/or a lack-tensive need for attention and appreciation. Similar is the next type of dyadic pattern, *reciprocation,* except in this case we have a reciprocal complementarity, the second phase being marked by a reversal of roles —the former receptor transmits with an appropriate degree of zest and the former transmittor receives with due appreciation.

Consideration of long sequences of interpersonal themes of this sort has pretty much confused me respecting the proper usage of the venerable S-R concept. The intended effect (need-aim) of much proactive talk (reactive to the mere sight of another person) is an appropriate kind of sympathetic response (press) from the alter (e.g., expression of agreement, compliance, interest, mirth, affection, admiration, gratitude, and so forth), and there seem to be a good many hypomanic (chemically stimulated) self-starters and transmittors in the world who, instead of predominantly *responding* to other persons, sail forth each day full-freighted with a miscellany of impatient stimulations for any acquaintance (releasor) who might be capable of the complementary responses; and when a conversation is once launched, every response is a stimulus to a response which is a stimulus to a further response, and so forth, until the tidy S-R model has been so thoroughly rolled through all things that it looks as if it needed treatment, some sort of radical rehabilitation. Perhaps it has already been rehabilitated, without my knowledge, by the more advanced S-R theorists.

It became evident in due course that a simple thema, whether micro or macro, is no more than a very coarse, though often meaningful and convenient, classification of an episode. To formulate an episode in a more refined way numerous other variables must be included until one's initially simple representation of its major dynamic components has been transformed into a *complex thema.* Among the immediate determinants, for example, of Y's positive or negative reaction to a "funny story" told by X, might be the "appropriateness" of the situation (never mind now how this is judged), the relative status and degree of intimacy of X and Y, the mirth-potency of the story, whether it is new or stale to Y, how well it is told by X, whether Y is momentarily at odds with X, the current mood or state of Y, the acuteness of Y's sense of humor in general and for this kind of story in particular, how fastidious is his standard of wit, to what extent is Y's system of values susceptible to offense by this kind of story, and so forth. Just as some psychologists have profitably devoted a professional lifetime to the study of a hungry animal in a maze containing food, so might others spend rewarding years in investigating the interior and exterior determinants of any one of a hundred other common types of themas, say, a thema with an unsuccessful or unexpected outcome, such as "the joke that fails," "the command that is defied," "the conjugal proposal that is rejected," "the injury that is forgiven," and in each case, why?

My own attempts to practice what I am now preaching—to explain in some detail the course of a single type of interaction—have been spotty and rather crude, and, for the most part, this side of publication. Christopher Fried, Philip Lichtenberg, and I have separately spent two years or more investigating a few of the determinants of the dyadic themas that occur during film-recorded competitive and cooperative attempts to arrive at a common plan of action; and, of course, there have been countless "clinical" occasions for minute perceptions of other common patterns. But, on the whole, the facts compel me to acknowledge that, except for resolute endeavors over the last twenty years to analyze and formulate the apperceptible processes and products that occur during impromptu compositions of dramatic stories, I have not focused long enough on any single type of thema or on any single method of observation and measurement to come out at last with a brilliant cluster of decisive findings. Decision has been difficult, because if a would-be personologist should elect to devote his energies to the building of a miniature system of postulates and theorems applicable to the understanding of one kind of thematic unit, he would have no time for the observation of other varieties of behavior; hence he would never get around to the practice of his profession, namely, the investigation of the *interrelations* of the more determining gross components of personality.

Thematic Dispositions. It has become more and more apparent to me that the energic components of personality can be better defined as thematic dispositions than as general actional dispositions. For example, instead of saying that X possesses the trait of aggressivity, or that he has a ready and intense need for aggression, one should, if possible, specify the nature of the pertinent press (stimulus) and say with more precision that two of the properties of his personality (I won't translate this into symbolic shorthand) are supersensitive dispositions to react with resentment and aggressive words (1) to apperceived insults to his self-respect and (2) to apperceived vainglorious boastings by an alter.

Serials. I was slow to perceive that current psychological theories of behavior were almost wholly concerned with actions of relatively short duration, reflexes and consecutive instrumental acts which reach their terminus within one experimental session, rather than with long-range enterprises which take weeks, months, or years of effort to complete. Here, it seemed, was one of the most striking differences between men and animals, namely, the capacity for time-binding (Korzybski) or the span of time-perspective (Frank, Lewin). The behavior of animals can be explained so largely by reference to attractive or repellent presentations in their immediate environment and/or to momentarily urgent and rather quickly reducible states of tension; whereas a great deal of a man's behavior cannot be explained except by reference to persistent "self-stimulation" in accordance with a plan of action, which often involves the subject's commitment to a distal goal or set of goals, as well as to a more or less flexible (or rigid) temporal order (schedule) of subsidiary, or stage, goals. Observing his behavior over several months or years, we see, not only the recurrence of a large number of patterns devoted to the repetition of valued experiences and the prevention of disvalued experiences, patterns with homeostatic effects, but a number of interrupted successions of proceedings (which I am calling *serials,* or long enterprises), each temporal segment of which is progressively related to the last (carrying on from where the other stopped), though separated from it by an interval of time (commonly a day). A successful *serial* is different from many day-by-day reactions in so far as its effects are *transtatic* rather than homeostatic, that is to say, it transforms or transcends the existing steady state by carrying a person from one level or form of equilibrium—dispositional, material, ideational, or social—to another: a new interpersonal relationship (an additional commitment) becomes established; a new house is purchased and furnished (which must hereafter be kept up); knowledge is gradually assimilated, and a new orientation (directing one's efforts toward another target) is acquired; the subject graduates from college, gets a job, and takes on the responsibilities of a new office; a novel is written and published, and so forth. Progressive enterprises of this sort constitute the bulk of a healthy young adult's endeavors in a "civilized" society.

Ordination. It took me years to realize that the psychology of the higher mental processes had been equivalent, in the minds of most psychologists, to the psychology of cognition, and that the psychology of cognition was largely concerned with the processes whereby a person acquires objective knowledge and understanding of his physical environment—the very processes and the very aims which are dominant in us psychologists—and that *i,* the more fundamental and important knowledge of the satisfying and dissatisfying, the beneficial and the harmful properties of the environment and of the self's capacity to cope with them, and *ii,* the still "higher" mental processes involved in the construction of a plan of action, were pretty generally neglected. What should we call the persistent, self-critical, conceptual, and often logical mental processes that continue over several months in the mind of a psychologist until they terminate with the construction of an integrated design for his next experiment? These processes commonly take off from perceptions and explanations of previous experiments and results; but their immediate aim is not so much to conceptualize already observed events (cognition), but to imagine something unobserved—new conditions and new experimental operations—and, by logic or intuition, to predict the outcome. During his months of planning the scientist (or anyone else for that matter) is more frequently thinking, one might say, on the efferent, rather than on the afferent, side of the cortical arc, and some psychologists might, therefore, be disposed to subsume his mental processes (processes which sometimes occur very rapidly—within a few seconds) under conation, on the grounds that their function is to orient and coordinate action. But against this is the fact that they are often very "intellectual" (higher mental processes in the strictest sense), engaged in a most difficult endeavor (since rational prediction is usually harder than rational explanation), and superordinate to other processes, in the sense that the goal and strategy which is ultimately selected will determine behavior for a good many months to come.

For better or for worse I have been calling such mental processes—

processes concerned with the selection and integration of plans of action
—*ordination*. The preliminary processes of the imagination—fantasies
and trial experiments in the mind—I am calling *prospections*. Here,
instead of entertaining recollections (replicative imaginations of past
events), the subject is concerned with the future, prospectively picturing
himself in this and that situation, seeking this or that opportunity for
gratification or for the advancement of his ambitions. Here creativity
may operate to a marked degree. The selection from numerous alternatives of a concrete and specific goal, purpose, or aim to appease one or
more needful dispositions, I am calling *orientation*. It is the subsequent
phase—the selection and temporal articulation of ways-means, strategies, or tactics (represented by images or words)—that I am calling *ordination*. I have found that the word can be used without confusion, both
for the process of constructing (ordinating) a plan and for the construction (ordination) that results from this process. An ordination may have
a very short or very long time span; it may be vague and global or clearly
differentiated into discrete behavioral units; it may be disjunctive or
conjunctive (temporally integrated in a logical manner); it may stand at
any point along the rigidity-flexibility continuum; and it may have more
or less of the property (power) of "imperativeness" (indicated, partly, by
shame or guilt if adherence to the ordination is imperfect); and so forth.
One significance of this concept is its discrimination of a major antecedent determinant of behavior in a "civilized" society, namely, a fixed
schedule, the time set for a certain kind of activity, a prearranged ap-
pointment, a prescribed order of procedure—quite regardless of the
mood, dispositional state, need, or what not, existing at the moment. A
good part of socialization consists in acquiring the capacity to keep promises, and hence, to do something which, *at the appointed time*, you are
not inclined to do. Furthermore, we need a concept of *prospective time*
reaching into an imagined future, some of which is *filled* (committed,
planned) and some of which is still *unfilled* (open, available for use).

INFLUENCE OF FREUD, JUNG, AND OTHER PSYCHOANALYSTS

I came to psychology via Jung's *Psychological Types* and his *Psychology of the Unconscious,* the first of which initiated my professional interest in types of human nature, and the second, my interest in unconscious
processes as revealed by mythologies and religious imagery as well as in
the more central and integral transformations of personality. What I
gained from Freud was somewhat more specific and more applicable in
practice and, in due course, became so much a part of my regular and
irregular modes of thought that there have been times when I forgot my
debt and took his huge gift for granted. In the late twenties and early
thirties when Freud's name and works were anathema to the majority

of academic psychologists, I was a staunch advocate and defender—as I am now—of his greatest contributions: (1) evidences of the theory of unconscious psychic processes and their effects, (2) evidences of the determining importance of early family relations and of the experiences of childhood, of the persistence of complexes established in those years, (3) countless illustrations of the multifarious manifestations of the sex drive, (4) division of the personality into id, ego, and superego (conventional constructs), (5) definition of several mechanisms—repression, isolation, denial, etc.—that operate in the service of adjustment, of self-esteem, and of serenity of consciousness, and a host of other more restricted constructs and theories illustrated by abundant case material.

I was one of the founding members of the Boston Psychoanalytic Society and throughout the thirties was so closely identified with its cause that President Conant decided, primarily on these grounds, that I was not qualified for tenure. Similarly, in the opinion of the psychologists who reviewed it, *Explorations in Personality* was a treatise out of Freud, or, more accurately, an attempted adaptation of psychoanalytic theory to academic standards. In short, what I have seized from Freud is so very obvious that it should not be necessary for me, at this late date, to lay it on the line.

The present situation is entirely different: Freud has conquered. He has captured a large portion of the Western mind, his revolutionary theories are learnedly and respectfully discussed in General Education courses, he is now an indispensable fixture in the domain of psychology, and so venerated by his professional disciples that his most casual comments are repeated ritualistically as absolutes. Clearly his position is assured and what we all owe to him is plain. The danger now is precisely the opposite of what it was in the twenties, when it looked as if professors were built to shut their minds to him. Caught up as we are today in a great wave of Freudiolatry we are inclined to take it all as gospel, to feel that the greater part of what the Master said is so astute that the gestalt which he created should not be spoilt by calling attention to a few trivial defects. This attitude would have been impossible to Freud himself, and if continued its only consequence can be sclerosis of the mind and rigor mortis.

As I weigh it, Freud's contribution to man's conceptualized knowledge of himself is the greatest since the works of Aristotle; but that his view of human nature is exceptionally—perhaps projectively and inevitably—one-sided, an extraordinary abstraction from the abundant facts of life, facts which may have little bearing on the etiology of neurotic symptoms but great relevance to other issues. My chief objection is the commonplace that in his system the libido has digested all the needs contributing to self-preservation, self-regard, and self-advancement, together with a host of others, and rebaptized them in the name of Sex; and that sex itself is never given either its profound evolutionary status or its interpersonally creative status. In the last analysis, it is reduced to transient, superficial, localized sensations. But then, who at this preliminary stage of knowledge can cover everything and be right?

INFLUENCE OF DARWIN, BERGSON, AND OTHER EVOLUTIONISTS: ADOPTION OF THE CONCEPT OF CREATIVITY

My Heraclitean concern with process, change, and transformation, dating from incubator years at the Rockefeller Institute, did not gain the impetus of a possession until, with Lucretius vastly and vaguely in the background, I came upon Bergson's theory of creative evolution, Lloyd Morgan's concept of emergence, Whitehead's philosophy of organism, Leibniz's monad, and the speculations of L. L. Whyte, Oparin, Wald, and others, respecting biochemical evolutions. What I abstracted from these authors, in conjunction with a few miscellaneous influxions from the "unconscious," brought me to the conclusion that creativity—the formation of new and consequential entities and of new and consequential patterns of activity—is a centrally determining capacity of nature, more especially of human nature. I had observed the progress of morphological maturations in the embryo and later the establishment of new ordinations of serial enterprises and of new tactical patterns and skills in personalities; but not until I paid attention to analogous proceedings on the physicochemical, sex-genetical, societal, and symbolic-representational levels and in the sphere of technology, did I arrive at a general conception of formative, or constructive, processes operating throughout nature.

What does this amount to? First, a comprehensive generalization respecting a widely distributed capacity of entities, namely, under favorable conditions to associate and remain associated, to combine and remain combined, to become involved in the creation of new entities with previously unexampled properties, and thereby to participate in the making of an irreversible route of events. Finding manifestations of such formative capacities at all integrative levels, we become more assured of their importance, more convinced that they deserve a place in our catalogue of fundamental dispositions. Also, we are invited by the possibility that detailed investigations of new productions at one level may suggest analogies, correspondences, and hypotheses to be tested at another. Second, the observation that matter has formative capacities makes us realize that creativity is *immanent* in nature, not the prerogative of some transcendent craftsman, such as Plato's Demiurge or the Yahweh of Genesis, nor imposed on nature by the will of man. On the one hand, it permits a natural explanation of some of the phenomena on which the doctrine of vitalism once built its case, and, on the other hand, it shows us why the term "mechanism" (with its implicit reference to a man-made machine as model) was not the happiest choice to characterize the procession of open systems under natural conditions. Our conviction that the old vitalist-mechanist opposition is a dead issue is supported, I believe, by the abandonment of classical mechanics by physicists and chemists as basis for their theoretical inventions. Third, the addition of the formation (creation, construction, reconstruction) process and effect to our inventory of dispositional properties of personality provides us with the otherwise missing necessary factor not only for an adequate conception of the liveliest course of mental processes through time (the work of the imagination), but for the systematic representation of the functional interdependence of other members of the inventory during the growing, expanding, and developing phases of a person's life.

The concept of survival in one or another guise—self-preservation, continuation, maintenance, homeostasis, and so forth—can fulfill the same construct-integrating function in a theoretical system that is designed to apply to mature lower organisms, since the great majority of their activities may be partly understood historically, in terms of their generally beneficent contributions to the continuation or the restoration of a steady state. But the principle of survival is applicable only to the status quo, not to mutation resulting in ontogenetic and phylogenetic emergent evolutions. In my view of affairs, anyhow, it is necessary to put the processes of composition and decomposition at the center of things, between the terminus of the afferent side and the initiation of the efferent side of the energy conversion arc of personality.

But this is not the accepted view today—despite our great concern with learning, with developments of personality, and, very recently, with some forms of mental creativity. The Freudian inventory of drives, for example, includes sex, aggression (destruction), and anxiety-avoidance, but *not* construction. Construction—which, being exemplified on the chemical level, is more fundamental, in my view, than any of these instincts as operationally defined by psychoanalysts—is subsumed, in a vague and general way, under the concept of sublimation of infantile eroticisms. Similarly in other special fields—sociology as well as experimental psychology. It may be a matter of time-perspective. If we are in the habit of performing short experiments with a peripheral subsystem of personality, no products of formative energies may strike our apprehensive mass; but if we take a longer view we are struck by nothing else.

Let us assume a comfortable position on Ganymede, satellite of Jupiter, about two billion years ago, and with supernatural eyes take a morning look at the surface of this planet. We shall perspect, according to those who are entitled to a guess, nothing save a fairly hot solution of inorganic salts keeping company with the simplest carbon compounds and enveloping this broth an atmosphere of gases from which oxygen is absent. In the evening let us take another look. Since we have temporarily assumed the power of a celestial being, a thousand ages in our sight is as a day gone by and we shall now be in the twentieth century gazing, I should hope with wonder, at a tremendous miscellany of natural productions—500,000 kinds of organic compounds, over 250,000 species of plants, over 1,000,000 species of animals already identified by man. We shall perceive numberless societal formations: human beings almost everywhere, behaving rather regularly as members of a family, clan, tribe, state, or nation, small or great, with fairly consistent governments, laws, and policies. More obvious will be the territorial and habitational constructions: land masses studded with settlements, villages, towns, and cities, surrounded by cultivated fields and connected by paths, roads, boulevards, and iron rails running through tunnels and over bridges. How long would be a catalogue of man's material manufactions, architectural, mechanical, electrical! Think of the palaces and temples, tools and armaments, machines and dynamos, waterworks, heating systems, lighting systems, automobiles and airplanes, and gadgets by the millions. Enough said. In the name of brevity, let's skip the rest and consider the manifold combinations of sounds—the songs and symphonies—and the combinations of images and imagined episodes—the mythologies and dramas, sonnets and heroic epics, histories and novels, and their representations in paint, wood, and marble—and the combination of concepts and reflections—the ethical philosophies, mathematical formulations, and scientific systems—which engage the minds of men; and with these let's end our swift survey of entities and activities on the earth's skin. All these things, all varieties of social governments, material conveyances and utilities, symbolisms and ideas, are productions of the human part of nature, and in all probability, the vast majority of them had their genesis in the imaginations of a single individual or of a cluster of individuals.

And yet, the word "imagination" has been absent from the index of most textbooks of psychology, and one has to search diligently to find a little reference here and there to planning processes (prospection and ordination), and despite the emergent interest in creativity, only a few authors have seen fit to include, in some indefinite guise or other, a formative disposition—habitational, implemental, interpersonal, social, or symbolic—among the properties of human personality.

Darwin was primarily concerned with the occurrence of successively more effective variations of mature morphologies from generation to generation. In his day, biochemical science was not so far advanced as to assist him with suggestions of plausible hypotheses respecting the determination of these gross changes. Knowing nothing of the role of chromosomes and genes, of nucleoproteins and DNA, it could hardly be realized that chemistry is the instrument of heredity. Today, however, we can reasonably postulate the creation of new genes along the route of evolution, the mutation (by the transposition of a single atom within a molecule) of a gene, and a stupendous variety of possible combinations of genetical clusters from male and female. The chemists of Darwin's time were not prepared to cope with the problem of the emergence of living entities from nonliving entities, the virus was unknown; and the physicists were speculating about matters other than the possibility of the evolution of increasingly complex chemical elements and compounds, say, out of light atomic nuclei. No one had yet suggested that as the universe expanded new matter was constantly coming into being. In psychology, prevalent interests and conceptions were far from the idea that formative (gestalt-making) processes were involved in perception and apperception, not to speak of their engagement in the psychologist's own business of making concepts and formulating propositions. In short, the data necessary for a systematic representation of constructive processes on different levels of integration were not available in the nineteenth century. Today, however, a multiplicity of facts and of reflections are at hand, enough, it seems to me, for a rough preliminary draft of meaningful analogies.

The very briefest outline I can devise, omitting several important vectors and all details, includes the *movement* (motility, exploration), and hence, by *chance,* the inevitable *contiguity* of different entities, one or each of which is inherently attractive to the other—*attraction* (gravitation, valence, cathexis) being one of the ever-present forces of the universe—and, consequently, either symmetrical or asymmetrical *accession* (approach) resulting in an *association* or structural *formation* (creation, construction, synthesis, conjugation, or incorporation of a smaller by a larger entity) new to this planet, and the *cohesion,* the sticking and staying power, and hence the relative stability and longevity of this unprecedented form of whatever category—organic compound, genetical configuration, family relationship, tribal federation, governmental law, religious belief, creed, or rite. If the established form is to have further evolutionary value it must have the attribute of *plasticity,* or flexibility, the capacity, that is, to play a part or to become involved in subsequent *transformations* or reconstructions. The picture is one of continuity through change. Only by losing its particular identity, by perishing as such, can a variation become a link, stage, or episode in an evolutionary sequence, such as the one and only sequence that led to the human species.

Some of my more earnest and literal-minded friends remind me that a psychologist should abjure fantasies of temporal omniscience and keep off of Ganymede. Formative processes lie outside the sphere of psychology: they occur in the "depths," behind the scenes, take a long time to get worked out, and are wholly unpredictable. A psychologist should attend to the precise particulars of today's circumscribed field of observation. Agreed, but suppose I ask one of these friendly critics to serve as a subject and request him at the first session to demonstrate his ability to design an experiment which will confirm or unconfirm a hypothesis that is unfamiliar to him. In the second session he might be asked to invent two different parables to illustrate the evil effects of fanaticism, and in the third to outline a course of action that might happily settle a specifically defined dissension among four members of an academic group. If, in each case, my friend gives voice to the thoughts that successively come to mind, the chances are that we shall apperceive the components of a constructive process operating before our ears from the beginning to the end of the experiment—influxions of ideas from the "well" of mind (What are they? How fast do they come? How varied are they? How definite? How appropriate to the given task?), interspersed with evaluations of these influxions, the rejection of some and the acceptance of others (How much consideration is given to each idea? How exacting is the standard of assessment? How excellent are the judgments in the opinion of experts? How much inhibition, hesitation, censorship, self-criticism occurs along the route? How quick are the acceptances? How decisive?), and then, to make a long story shorter, the temporal allocations, or ordinations, of the accepted components of the design, the parable, or the plan (Are the concatenations actually logical? Clearly expressed? Have all probable contingencies been met? Has anything essential been omitted? How superficial or profound is the offered solution or composition, and so forth). In every such experiment I submit we shall obtain a unique mental composition which, at one extreme and perhaps in the majority of cases, may be socially worthless in the estimation of qualified judges and advisedly forgotten but, at the other, might be a rare gem of creativity, something memorable that may eventually find a place in the great body of cultural transmissions. We may, for instance, be dealing with a Whitehead equal to such utterances as these:

Insistence on clarity at all costs is based on sheer superstition as to the mode in which human intelligence functions.

No science can be more secure than the unconscious metaphysics which it tacitly presupposes.

Murder is a prerequisite for the absorption of biology into physics as expressed in [its] traditional concepts.

A self-satisfied rationalism is in effect a form of anti-rationalism. It means an arbitrary halt at a particular set of abstractions.

A science which hesitates to forget its founders is lost.

Scientists animated by the purpose of proving themselves purposeless constitute an interesting subject for study.

Of course, creativity—the real thing—is an autonomous and capricious process which rarely shows itself when called upon; hence, impromptu tests are not likely to bring forth anything but rather shallow forms of originality and inventiveness. Nevertheless, to my way of thinking, there are compositional processes at work, ordering ideas and shaping sentences—sometimes brilliantly—in the course of every communication. Most of us, to be sure, make use of the same worn words and trite phrases time and time again, and integrativeness in speech or writing is limited to the joining of one commonplace to the next; but were we to abide by the current laws of learning and in talks with friend or spouse repeat tomorrow the response—the bit of news, the joke, the idea—that was reinforced today, we would be heading for press rejection or divorce. What we have to learn is to break a specific speech-reward connection and on a subsequent occasion substitute some variation. In short we will be rewarded only for saying something different from, but as stimulating as, that for which we were rewarded last. Conclusion: a gust for novelty and emergent forms is widely distributed among members of our breed.

For the present, we may define participant creative processes in terms of their effect, result, achievement, namely, an unprecedented form, and confine our attention to stable forms which are retrospectively apperceived as valuable and as having further consequences in an evolutionary context. Striking to many of us is the blindness of these processes, their experimental character, and their resistance to the coercions of conscious purpose, which is something that is worth considering in connection with human imaginations, and the occurrence in some people of a strong disposition to create: to combine sounds, images, words, concepts, propositions, ideas, ordinances, people, things, strategies, or techniques in new and significant forms which express something that is worth expressing, order things that are worth ordering, build something that is worth building, or solve a problem that is worth solving. Mobilized by a need of any other class than this, a human subject is likely to have a picture in his mind's eye of what he wants—water, sexual intercourse, a habitation, an automobile, world news, membership in a certain group, promotion, prestige, or what not. Under most circumstances, what he wants already exists somewhere, actually or potentially, in the environment, and he must take it pretty much as it is or as it comes. There is food in that restaurant, information he requires in that book, a person over there whose friendship he might win, a job to be had and money to be earned, et cetera, et cetera. But the aim of creativity—say, a design for a more efficient machine, an architectural innovation, a symbolic plot for a drama to be written, the explanation of an enigmatic phenomenon, a more enlightened foreign policy—has no existence anywhere. A person with this need must work, think, brood, daydream, rest, sleep, turn his thoughts to other things—perhaps drink and read detective stories—until his mind will favor him with a representation which possesses, in his prospecting eye, the attributes that he seeks, and then he must be favored further by representations of suitable embodiments. A man may rack his brains throughout a lifetime without receiving the vision or idea for which he longs, or if the idea has come to him, he may labor for years without finding the way to expound it in a persuasive manner or to implement it in an actional endeavor. That is to say, we are dealing here with energies of the human mind that do not respond directly to voluntary efforts. Voluntary efforts can influence their direction, defining, so far as possible, the target of their endeavor, but they cannot force them to render up the desired form or answer.

Nowadays it is pretty generally agreed, I would suppose, that imaginations of any real consequence are generated outside, or "below," the stream of awareness, after a more or less prolonged period of incubation, and they are apt to leap to consciousness abruptly at the most unexpected moments. Sometimes, like a dream, they seem to come from without rather than from within the mind. A vision has been called a vision because it is a visual presentation, a present, a gift, to the inner eye, just as the heavenly constellations at night are a presentation, or gift, to the outer eye. It was partly on this ground, we may surmise, that the ancients believed that visions of import came from the gods, as best among their blessings to deserving men. Today we are disposed to say that they come from the unconscious. But the proposition I am submitting here is that the witting purpose to create something with certain valued properties is almost wholly blind, its goal being to conceive a goal; and though voluntary effort is one determinant of success, the processes on which creativity depends proceed, for the most part, spontaneously and autonomously outside of consciousness and give rise to hundreds of influxions which do not survive because consciousness rejects them, and if a certain influxion is considered worthy of survival it may not be what consciousness was seeking, but something else entirely.

Facts of this order constitute the basis for the not uncommon experience among creative men of serving as a vehicle or mouthpiece of some supernatural or superpersonal imperative, of being an agent of evolution instead of a feverish egoistic little self. "This is the true joy in life," Bernard Shaw has written, "the being used for a purpose recognized by yourself as a mighty one."

INFLUENCE OF SOCIAL EVOLUTIONISTS, CULTURAL ANTHROPOLOGISTS, AND SOCIOLOGISTS

As one of the charter members of the Department of Social Relations at Harvard, I could hardly fail to be inspired and directed in my thinking by our largely shared ambitious aim to advance by successive trials toward a common theoretical system for basic social science. If it had not been for this association, for the continuous influence of such learned and persuasive colleagues as Clyde Kluckhohn and Talcott Parsons, I might still be representing personalities in so near a social vacuum as we did in *Explorations.* As a biologist I had been attached to the concept of the herd instinct, as elaborated, say, by Trotter, and as a psychoanalyst, to the concept of identification in each of its different meanings, as well as to the several propositions respecting the internalization of the parental superego. Nothing is more apparent as we look at others and ourselves, especially in the United States—despite or because of our loudly avowed ideology of freedom and individuality—than the tremendous prevalence of unconscious imitation and conformity, of the educing and constraining force of public opinion and behavior. But I did not become aware of the numerous cultural differentiations one had to make, differentiations of socioeconomic classes, of special subgroups, of rank in the decision-making hierarchy, of role and function, until I gave a joint seminar with the encyclopedic Kluckhohn, who consented to the office of tutor in these matters. There I once again experienced the truth of the old adage: the best way to learn a subject is to teach it, in this case in conjunction with an expert. Besides my indebtedness to the elaborate classifications and generalizations of Talcott Parsons, I should mention among other respected instructors in the social sciences: Pareto as expounded by L. J. Henderson in a memorable seminar, Malinowski, Sapir, Margaret Mead, Ralph Linton, John Dollard, Florence Kluckhohn, Edward Shils, Robert Merton, Harold Laswell, Ernest Cassirer—the list is long; many congenial influences have necessarily been omitted.

Since the anthropological and sociological concepts that I employ are pretty nearly all derivative, I need not say much on this score. Here again I have been influenced by Darwin, specifically by the theory that the group more than the individual has been the evolutionary unit. Being of this persuasion, I have come to think that no theoretical system constructed on the psychological level will be adequate until it has been embraced by and intermeshed with a cultural-sociological system. Although every individual has some measure of inner life, a host of private and largely secret feelings, fantasies, beliefs, and aspirations, and has some extent of free play outside the coercions and restraints of the social system, the great bulk of his overt behaviors are regulated by the memberships and roles to which he is committed, his actual behavior being the resultant of a fusion or compromise between cultural specifications and standards and his own dispositions and abilities. Such is the conventional doctrine of our time, in one guise or another, and I have little to add to it. But, since the group theory of evolution is rarely mentioned today and since, for better or for worse, it has strongly influenced my speculations, I am yielding to the temptation of quoting a few paragraphs from a recent attempt I made to expound it in a condensed form.

Surveying the evidences of man's development on earth, the later Darwin concluded: first, that the survival of the fittest is a principle which applies decisively not so much to individuals as to rival groups—tribes, states, or nations—and second, that mutual sympathy, aid, and collaboration among members of a group are conducive to its solidarity, and hence to its combative power and survival. To put it another way, one of the critical variations established long ago was a clannish combination of families more powerful than any single person, a flexible yet stable social system with some differentiation of functions and consequently with an enhanced capacity to cope with various tasks and crises.

From the beginning, if we follow Sir Arthur Keith's composition of the evidence, every successful group has adhered to a double code of conduct, a Janus-faced mortality: one face preaching submission to authority, reverence, cooperation, loyalty, good will, and generosity within the group, and the other more contorted face shouting with rage and murderous aggression toward members of opposing groups. Other things being equal, it must have been the clans or tribes which embodied this dual standard in the best balance that triumphed and endured, and passed on to their descendants down to the present day the dispositions which sustained it.

This theory of group evolution helps us to understand why man is a social, rather than a solitary, self-sufficient creature and why, as a social creature, he is both humane and brutal. Illustrative of his *social* properties are such familiar facts as these: that the vast majority of men are reared in one particular society, a society that is prejudiced in its own favor, and are satisfied to be lifelong interdependent members of this society, that the bulk of their enjoyments come from interacting with its members, that they are at peace with themselves only when they feel and act in accord with its customs and ideals, and that, even in their furthest reaches of self-forwarding ambition, they choose for their most delectable final prize the applause of their fellow beings, and after death, fame, "that last infirmity of noble mind." The dual morality of groups—tribes and nations—accounts in some measure for the failure, the half-heartedness and insincerity, of all attempts to abolish war and for the fact that human beings have been generally so willing, even eager, to suppress their fears of self-extinction and fight for their country to the tragic end, as well as for the fact that a man who kills a hundred members of an enemy society is declared glorious, but is condemned to the severest punishment if he stops the life of a single fellow citizen.

It is supposed that the generally victorious groups were those which most fully incorporated and exploited the vaingloriousness and pride, the greed and will to power, of their individual members. But what is the significance of the will to power? Power, intoxicating as it may be to some men and to some nations, is a means to something, not an end. Power for what? To this question the response of a creative evolutionist might be: power to construct ever larger and less vulnerable social systems controlling ever larger areas of the earth's resources, or in other words, power, spurred on by greed, to grow and to develop, by invading, conquering, subjugating, and assimilating weaker units, or more peacefully and happily in some cases, by federating with other units. History reports a great number of such sequences: the integration of primal groups into clans, and of clans into tribes, and of tribes into small nations, and the integration of small nations into great nations that subsequently broke apart, the rise and decline, the evolution and involution, of mighty civilizations, as Toynbee has shown us, but as yet no orchestration of state sovereignties into a world order, no political embodiment of that dream of universal fellowship which centuries of idealistic men have recommended to our hearts.

In short, everything I have said relative to formations, transformations, malformations, and deteriorations on the psychological level is applicable in a general, though not specific, way to the level of group dynamics.

COMPELLING NEED FOR COMPREHENSIVENESS

Although I was educated on the principle that limitation of aim is the secret of success in science, and that the scientist is responsible for particulars, it must be only too apparent to you that I have been tempted to depart from the wisdom of this strategy by the dream of an all-embracing scheme, a unified science, not, of course, to be achieved in my own lifetime but in the distant future, if there is to be a future for our species.

I suppose it would be proper to speak of:

1. A comprehensive concept (such as energy, process, matter, form, motion) which refers to something that is always and everywhere observable or inferable.

2. A comprehensive conceptual scheme (such as the periodic table, classifications of botanical and zoological forms) which differentiates relationally all entities and all attributes and properties of entities within the domain of a single discipline.

3. A comprehensive formulation, theory, or law (such as $e = mc^2$, the laws of thermodynamics, the theory of evolution) which is applicable over a wide range of phenomena.

4. A comprehensive spatial scope of individual concern within a single discipline, such as (to limit consideration to the biological and social sciences) that of a physiologist who takes the total organism as his province (rather than specializing in kidney function), that of a psychologist who takes the whole personality (rather than specializing in cognition), or that of a sociologist who takes the total community (rather than specializing in family structure). Scope of data.

5. A comprehensive temporal span of individual concern within a single discipline, such as that of a biologist who is interested in genetics and heredity, that of a psychologist who is occupied with parental as well as subsequent determinants of personality, or that of a sociologist or anthropologist who studies historic transformations. Span of data.

Now, one of the best appraisers of the status of psychological theory in this country, the wisely chosen Director of this project, stated not so long ago that the development of our science had been more retarded in recent years by straining after comprehensiveness than by any other variety of ambition. But since it is not clear to me which of the above forms of comprehensiveness he had in mind, I have not yet had to square my shoulders to the verdict *guilty*. There is at least one form of comprehensiveness for which I have not reached, the comprehensiveness of a neat net of postulates and theorems that is expected to catch every kind of fish that swims in the stream of human experience and behavior. I have never been so optimistic as to think that we psychologists were anywhere near the day when some master mind might achieve so much. Instead I have been a perpetual catcher and collector of facts and figures, a perpetual classifier of concepts, and a promoter, in a little way, of marriages of concepts, believing that these pedestrian occupations were appropriate to the stage of conceptual evolution at which psychology has arrived. Here I am not speaking for the psychobiologists who study the ways-means learning processes of imprisoned animals. They, so far as I can see, have already arrived at that state of knowledge and mastery of their variables from which lawmaking for their territory makes sense.

The forms of comprehensiveness of which I am most surely guilty are comprehensiveness of territory in space and time. I have spoken of my interest in creative evolution down the ages and in developments of personalities from birth on (temporal comprehensiveness); and I have indicated how I was forced, to put it bluntly, by my colleagues at Harvard to become socio-spatially comprehensive, concerned with the supraorganism of which every personality is imperatively a functioning component. Nor can other groups—out-groups and foreign nations—be excluded from the picture, it being all too evident these days that a little shooting incident on some distant surface of our planet might initiate a global conflict which would change the roles, the activities, and the effects of millions of human beings. Belief in the imminence of a catastrophic war is currently one of the determinants of anxiety in a large number of people occupying statuses of responsibility. And then, beyond the earth and its contentious nationalities, revolve the sun, the moon, the planets, stars, and Milky Way, all of which have influenced the minds of countless individuals and collectivities, not as the Chaldean astrologers surmised, but by drawing aspirations and cognitions upward, by engendering images and stories of celestial divinities and powers, of resurrections and ascensions to a heavenly paradise beyond the grave, and of life everlasting in a society of musical winged beings, not to speak of the attraction by cosmic bodies of astronomers and poets.

TOLERANCE OF UNCERTAINTY

From what I have confessed so far it must seem as if the need for certainty, powerful in most scientists, is very weak in me. But, as I weigh them, my hopes and expectations in this regard are no higher and no lower than they legitimately can be nowadays in the sphere of endeavor to which I am committed. Were my demands greater, I either would be perpetually defeated or, to escape from this, would be impelled to quit personology and return to chemistry for peace. I take heart from Aristotle: "It is the mark of an educated man to look for precision in each class of things."

But this is not the whole story. There is something more in me which is not irrelevant to this issue: the induction from experience that a compulsive need for intellectual certainty—abetted, I would suppose, by longings for personal security—is very apt to lead to deadly falsifications and distortions of reality. Leaving aside the changeless eternal forms and absolutes of philosophers and theologians, and confining ourselves to scientists, we can find innumerable examples of the operations of this need: the selection of the most fixed, permanent, or recurrent things to study; the unnatural stabilization of the experimental environment; the prevention of all but two or three possibilities of response; the circumscription of the area of observation to a small part of the total field of influential forces; et cetera, et cetera. Such choices and constraints are valid parts of the strategy of science and not criticizable as such. They are to be criticized only when the results obtained in highly focused studies of this sort are generalized across the board and the notion propagated that the entities with which we are concerned are far more structured, rigid, stable, orderly, consistent, and predictable than they really are.

In my philosophy there are no absolute or inevitable laws, no enduring certainties: every observation, every inference, every explanation, and every prediction is a matter of less or greater probability. To this most psychologists, I trust, would be ready to assent.

INTEREST IN SYSTEMS

My interest in systems was confined at first to shifts of equilibria, as a function of oxygen tension, among the electrolytes of blood within the walls of a glass vessel. The scope of the next system I studied with some care was a volume bounded by an eggshell, closed to material substances but open to intakes and outputs of gases. Here my chief source of illumination was *Elements of Physical Biology* by Lotka.[4] But the relevance of these investigations and formulations to psychology was not apparent to me until the thirties, when I was introduced to Pareto's representation of society as a system, and somewhat later to the conceptualizations of the Chicago group as set forth, say, in *Levels of Integration in Biological and Social Systems,* edited by Robert Redfield.[5] Ever since, encouraged by Whitehead's speculations, I have been addicted to the perilous practice of discovering analogies among events at different levels. This hobby, once private and covert, has become more articulate of late, partly owing to parallels discovered in the writings of L. von Berta-lanffy, A. E. Emerson, R. W. Gerard, and other men who are concerned with correspondences and differences between various kinds of systems —what is now known as General System Theory.

I am wary of the word "system," because social scientists use it very frequently without specifying which of several possible different denotations they have in mind; but more particularly because, today, "system" is a highly cathected term, loaded with prestige; hence, we are all strongly tempted to employ it even when we have nothing definite in mind and its only service is to indicate that we subscribe to the general premise respecting the interdependence of things—basic to organismic theory, holism, field theory, interactionism, transactionism, etc. For example, the terms "personality-as-a-whole" and "personality system" have been very popular in recent years; but no writer, so far as I know, has explicitly defined the components of a "whole personality" or of a "system of personality." When definitions of the units of a system are lacking, the term stands for no more than an article of faith, and is misleading to boot, in so far as it suggests a condition of affairs that may not actually exist. It suggests not only that one is dealing with a set of recurrent, orderly, lawful interactions, but that the number, constitution, position, and effects of the interacting units remain relatively constant. That is, it is usually taken for granted that "system" refers to a homeostatic, boundary-maintaining system. Finally, overtones convey the impression that the speaker has a steady coherent theoretical system in his head which conforms to the steady coherent system he is studying. Hence I am wary of the word. But, having found that I cannot get along without it, I must do my best, when the time comes, to define my restricted usages of this term.

I might say, in a general way, that, for me, system applies to a more or less uniform integration of *reciprocating* and/or *cooperating* functional activities, each of which, under favorable conditions, contributes to the continuation of the entire cycle of activities which constitute the system. As a rule, such a system is boundary-maintaining. According to this view, each entity (form of matter) involved in a cooperating system may be called an organ, relative to that system, each organ being defined in terms of process and its contributing effect, or since organ processes are not always capable of achieving a contributing effect, in terms of their direction, *endeavor,* or intended effect. Thus, each unified boundary-maintaining system may be partially defined by representing the integration of successive processes and effects which are required to keep it growing and/or to keep it going as a unique and vital whole. The major unitary functional systems with which a social scientist is concerned are these: personality systems, dyadic social systems, polyadic social systems, representational (symbolic) systems, each of which may be divided—

according to different spheres of concern—into large subsystems. For example, a personality system may be divided into:

1. A psychosomatic system, consisting of all needs and activities concerned with the growth and welfare of the body: procurement and incorporation of water and food, transposition and allocation of food particles, differential construction of frame and organs, excorporation of water and waste, actuation and integration of muscular patterns, development of manual and athletic skills, defense of the integrity of the body, etc.

2. A psycho-material system, consisting of all needs and activities concerned with the acquisition, restoration, or construction of a territory and/or of a habitation (stead and shell), as well as with the acquisition, restoration, or construction of implements or machines, utilization of these implements, development of technical skills, defense of property, etc.

3. A psychosexual system, consisting of all needs and activities concerned with erotic love: stimulations and interactions, the formation and continuation of an erotic dyad, conjugations, and the conception of offspring, etc.

4. A psychosocial system, consisting of all needs and activities concerned with nonerotic social reciprocations: transmissions and receptions of affection, of food, money, and material entities, of information and evaluations, of orientations and ordinations, directions and compliances, development of social skills, etc.

5. A psycho-representational system, consisting of all mental (cognitive and ordinative) needs and activities associated with the above-mentioned systems—acquisition of knowledge, explanations, and postulations —as well as mental needs and activities concerned with impersonal symbolic systems (explicit culture), with law, art, science, morals, ideology, and religion, development of mental skills.

The personality system, as such, is concerned with the allocation of time and energy among these different subsystems and sub-subsystems, the ordination of their component serial endeavors, the repression of unacceptable emotions and impulses, and the reduction of conflicts and strain.

A dyadic system consists of the interplay of two personality systems, each of which is given equivalent attention. This is enough to indicate, very roughly, the way the term "system" is applied in the scaffold as now constituted.

APOLOGIA

When, after finishing part 1 of this assignment—my autobiography of somewhat relevant cerebrations—I got round to a closer examination of the scheme provided us, I discovered that it was even more exacting than I had initially believed. It was definitely beyond my reach, beyond the reach, I judged, of anyone who is primarily concerned, at this stage of things, with the formulation of different types of personalities as manifested, say, by different classes of reactions to a variety of similar situations, rather than with the reactions of most people, say, to modifications of one particular experimental situation.

I might have profited by the moral of the Icarian thema, as represented in the careers of several young persons assessed at the Baleen, annex of the Harvard Psychological Clinic. Its moral is that of the inevitable fall of overreaching aspiration, the nemesis of *hubris,* so familiar to the Greeks. But the prospect of this outcome did not bring about a reasonable abandonment of the project. It merely served to check me to the point of regarding the committee's standard as an unrealizable ideal, but yet something to be held in view while I labored over the development of the scaffold. As it turned out, the effect of this ideal was an almost continuous procession of very general as well as of very particular conceptual compositions, decompositions, and recompositions, which kept informing me of the intricate influence of more and more variables in the determination of the course and outcome of almost every unit of behavior that could interest a personologist. Thus, I was led on from complication to complication, and though many were resolvable, the resolutions served only to increase the number of aspects to be considered and of discriminations to be made in analyzing, explaining, or predicting any sequence of significant transactions. After a year or more of this sort of thing, the produce of variables had reached an unmanageable degree of refinement and of magnitude; and, approaching the deadline, I was reminded of the judgment of Hippocrates: life is short, the art long, occasion instant, decision difficult.

REFERENCES

It is not possible to pinpoint in the vast libraries of books and periodicals the precise source of each assumption, concept, method that has been mentioned in this paper. I have included the names—all well known—of the more influential theorists, but what I have acquired from some of these—Henderson, Jung, Prince, Alexander, Whitehead, Lewin, Kluckhohn, Allport, Parsons, and others —came very largely through conversations and discussions, and what I have acquired from the writings of these and others came not from one article or book but from pretty nearly all their works. This is not the place, it seems to me, to list the relevant works of Aristotle, Darwin, William James, Bergson, Lloyd Morgan, Santayana, Whitehead, or Cassirer, or of such social scientists as Pareto, Parsons, Laswell, Malinowski, Sapir, or Kluckhohn, or of such authors as Janet, Freud, Jung, Adler, Rank, Alexander, Horney, Sullivan, Kris, or Erikson, or of those psychologists who are concerned with personality, such as McDougall, Allport, Murphy, Maslow, Adams, or McClelland.

My constant disposition has been to select new fields of investigation and to avoid those which have already been occupied, if not packed, by competent experimentalists. For example, I have had no firsthand experience in dealing with the intricate problems of perception or of animal learning, and hence I have mentioned but few names of psychologists who have contributed to our understanding of these phenomena. Many of these have influenced me directly as well as indirectly. But it would hardly be appropriate in this place to list the works of such men as Pavlov, Thorndike, Watson, Hull, Tolman, Dollard, Mowrer, Neal Miller, or Skinner, or of those who have been concerned with the philosophy, logic, or semantics of theory building, such authors as Bridgman, Stevens, Hull, Lewin, Koch, Egon Brunswik, Else Frankel-Brunswik, Bergmann, Meehl, or Feigl.

So far as my own bibliography is concerned, the latest edition of it can be found in C. S. Hall and G. Lindzey, *Theories of Personality* (1957), published since the completion of all that I have written here.

The works referred to in the text are these:

1. Murray, H. A., et al. *Explorations in Personality.* New York: Oxford Univer. Press, 1938.

2. Henderson, L. J. *The Order of Nature.* Cambridge, Mass.: Harvard Univer. Press, 1917.

3. Murray, H. A., and Morgan, Christiana D. *A Clinical Study of Sentiments.* Published separately and in *Genet. Psychol. Monogr.,* 1945, No. 32.

4. Lotka, A. J. *Elements of Physical Biology.* Baltimore, Md.: Williams & Wilkins, 1925.

5. Redfield, R. (Ed.) *Levels of Integration in Biological and Social Systems.* Lancaster, Pa.: Jaques Cattell, 1942.

2

THE CASE OF MURR

PROLOGUE

It occurred to me that the easiest way for a veteran examiner of men to cope with this present assignment would be to hold the mirror up to the manifestations of his own nature pretty much as he would do in the case of any individual who volunteered as subject for exposure to the threatening and dubious procedures of assessment. This notion was particularly inviting at this moment since it offered me a chance to illustrate the applicability of some unfamiliar ideas to which I am nowadays attached, and since, by so doing, I might alleviate to some extent the tedium of a long parade of unexciting and unilluminated facts. Full of enthusiasm, I embarked on the execution of this plan with the special purpose of representing and explaining the professional mentational history of my subject, whose pseudonym is Murr, in terms of the theoretical system to which I currently subscribe; but in due course I found myself involved in the conceptualization of the *concrete* system of mental operations by which Murr had arrived at the *theoretical* system, the very terms of which I was then using to conceptualize the concrete system which produced them. It was not till I arrived at these complications that I concluded that this mode of coping with the task would be impossible within the space that was fittingly allotted us. I had been yielding, once again, to an expansive, omnivorous, sanguine disposition (the "sanguine surplus," let us say for short) which leads me to start by envisaging every new, appealing undertaking in the most voluminous dimensions, huge and teeming with every possibility of adventure and achievement. I have illustrated this impediment to sound science at the outset because it is one of those temperamental forces which, however exhilarating and fructifying, has rocked or wrecked a whole procession of enterprises, despite the continued existence in my head of the corrective maxim: limitation of aim is the secret of success.

The functionally autonomous governor of my conscious ego system (the little self) is now definitely resolved to ostracize theory and the sanguine surplus (from the larger Self) and cleave to the corrective

From E.G. Boring and G. Lindzey, eds., *A History of Psychology in Autobiography.* New York: Appleton-Century-Crofts, 1967. Vol. V, pp. 285–310.

maxim. And so, in order to improve its chances of carrying out this resolution I have decided: (1) to omit those experiences and activities and those components of personality which Murr has shared with the majority of his colleagues and, at the risk of portraying him as a repellent freak, focus on his peculiarities and eccentricities; and (2) from these peculiarities select those that are pertinent to one or more of these four topics: (i) Murr's discovery of psychology as his vocation, (ii) his conception of his role in this domain, (iii) his accomplishments, and (iv) his retrospective critical evaluation of his professional endeavors. (To facilitate the victory of the corrective maxim, there is the presence in the bibliography of two papers written by Murr which taken together constitute a sizable chunk of what could be termed his intellectual autobiography. When necessary in the ensuing text the first of these papers will be referred to as Auto. 1, the second as Auto. 2.) Finally there is the task of steering a fitting course for Murr between the Scylla of concealment and mendacity and the Charybdis of the "meanest mortal's scorn."

THE CASE OF MURR

Murr's Vocational Choice

The Improbability of Murr's Vocational Choice. The first question relevant to the purposes of this volume is: what were the determinants of Murr's exultant selection of academic psychology in 1926 as the domain for his vocational life from then on? Could his decision have been anticipated by the experts? In 1926, when Murr was admitted to the Harvard Department of Philosophy and Psychology, his past history differed from all but a small fraction of one per cent (as a crude estimate) of the membership of the American Psychological Association (as it was then and as it has been over the years, so far as I can tell) in *most* of ten respects. In view of the compounding of these peculiarities, what could an actuarial psychologist have said except that the probability of Murr's making this decision was virtually nil. In an actuarial sense, there were no empirical, positive determinants: his record consisted of nothing but items which correlated negatively, to a highly significant degree, with the records of the vast majority of professional psychologists. For instance: (1) Murr's experience was restricted by his never having studied at a public school. For his first six years of education he went to two small private schools in New York City and for the next five years attended boarding school at Groton, Massachusetts. (2) Throughout those eleven years at school and throughout the four subsequent years at Harvard College, where he received below average grades, none of his scholastic records were indicative of intellectual interests or aptitudes; even less promising was the decline of his marks from year to year in each of the institutions he attended. (3) One of the several determinants of Murr's continuously low academic standing at school and at college was his unremitting youthful passion for athletic achievement, an ambition which was thwarted in most areas of endeavor partly by a basic sensori-motor defect, but not in rowing, a sport in which endurance, not speed, is at a premium; and, by sweat and luck, he managed to "make" the crew at Harvard. (4) After medical school, Murr enjoyed a two-year surgical internship at the Presbyterian Hospital in New York. (5) This surgical experience was preceded and followed by what amounted to five years of experimentation and research relating to the biochemical aspects of various phenomena, for example: blood as a physicochemical system; changes in the chemistry of the blood as found in various diseases and as experimentally produced by parathyroidectomy and pyloric occlu-sion; biochemical, metabolic, and tissue changes as a function of age in chicken embryos—researches which were conducted in this country at Harvard, at Columbia, and at the Rockefeller Institute for Medical Re-search, and in England at Cambridge, from which university he received a Ph.D. in biochemistry. (6) Instead of mathematics or physics, Murr's earliest avenue of approach to psychology was history (his field of concen-tration) and biography, with an emphasis on alienated rebels, I suspect, since he won the history prize at Groton with a short life of John Brown of Osawatomie; and much later, a year before he reached psychology—after discursive readings in the world's literature which found their peak in the works of Herman Melville—Murr, regardless of the unpropitious fact that at school he had received his consistently worst marks in English composition, zestfully embarked on a biography of that alienated genius. (7) In the Easter vacation of his year at Cambridge University—working next to Joseph Needham and J. B. S. Haldane in the laboratory of the Nobel prizewinner F. Gowland Hopkins—Murr spent three weeks of daily sessions and long weekends with Dr. Jung in Zurich, from which explosive experience (already described in Auto. 1) he emerged a reborn man. (8) Having been for twenty-four years an incurable stutterer with a very-seldom-overcome repugnance to public speaking, and (9) having never taken a single course in psychology, Murr was clearly an extremely reckless applicant and an extremely risky choice for a lifelong job as lecturer in this complex domain of knowledge when, at the late age of thirty-three, he was squeezed into the Harvard faculty by some sort of high-hushed finaglings engineered by Professor L. J. Henderson. (10) Murr was advantaged by having an independent income which allowed him to accept the offer of a meager $1,800 to serve as the assistant of the famous psychopathologist Dr. Morton Prince in inaugurating and carry-ing on research and teaching at the Harvard Psychological Clinic.

The Determinants of Murr's Vocational Choice. A few of the items which I have listed as actuarial negative determinants of Murr's voca-tional choice were, in fact, positive determinants. This discrepancy is readily explained by the fact that Murr's initial intention was to combine experimentation and psychotherapy in an institutional setting, such as might presumably be found in the clinic of a mental hospital. As it happened, Dr. Prince had had the wisdom to foresee that if in 1926 the clinic (for the running of which he had raised barely enough funds) were attached to a hospital, research would inevitably give way to the more urgent demands of therapy. The establishment of a clinic for the treatment of psychoneurotics under the auspices of a college department of philosophy and psychology was, so far as I know, an innovation, not only in America but in the world. And so it is to the occurrence of this highly improbable arrangement that one may attribute Murr's enrollment as a member of an understandably reluctant academic department. This being the case, my part, at this point, is to list the more probable determinants of Murr's analytic interest in people, his curiosity regarding the "causes" of normal and abnormal human states, thoughts, and actions, and of his hopeful resolution to reveal them by suitable scientific means. The determinants that stand out are as follows: (1) Murr's first shadowy memory is that of experiencing what he calls the "marrow of his being," the nature of which will be described in a later section. Suffice it to say here that it seems to have sensitized the boy to the sufferings of other people and to have played a part in his decision first to become a surgeon and subsequently a psychotherapist. (2) Murr was exposed to and may have been somewhat moved by the presence in his environment of two neuropsychiatric sufferers, younger sisters of his mother: one the victim of seasonal psychotic depressions, and the other, a sweet hysterectomized hysteric, whose daily state of quavering health was, for forty years, the focus of her four healthy sisters' dutiful and compassionate regard, each of them vying with the rest for the crown of exemplary charity. (3) Murr was intrigued by what he saw of the patients in mental hospitals whose expressions of emotion struck him as more naturally human and appealing than the perfunctory official behavior of the tired doctors whose role it was to label them. (4) At medical school and later, there were many occasions to be astonished, stimulated, and instructed by Dr. George Draper's pinpoint observations and brilliant intuitive diagnoses of patients with what was later to be called psychosomatic illness. For some years he was Murr's most uniquely influential teacher, both by exhibiting these talents and by expounding his very original conceptions respecting varieties of human constitution, many of which would eventually be more systematically set forth by W. H. Sheldon. (5) While working at the Rockefeller Institute, Murr was repeatedly confounded by a radical theoretical (if not metaphysical) opposition between the Institute's then-most-famous members, Jacques Loeb, who stood for an extreme version of mechanism, and Alexis Carrel, the defender of some type of vitalism. How, Murr asked himself, can one account for such irreconcilable interpretations of identical phenomena? The notion that science is the creative product of an engagement between the scientist's psyche and the events to which he is attentive prepared Murr for an enthusiastic embracement of Jung's *Psychological Types* on the very day of its timely publication in New York (1923). Except for Herbert Spencer and the admirable William James, no theorists in the realm of subjective events were known to Murr; and this book by Jung came to him as a gratuitous answer to an unspoken prayer. Among other things, it planted in his soil two permanent centers of preoccupation: the question of varieties of human beings and in what terms they can be most significantly represented and discriminated, and the question of what variables of personality are chiefly involved in the production of dissonant theoretical systems. These questions were at the root of Murr's first spurt of veritable intellectual interest in the direction of psychology. The transaction with Jung led to an omnivorous and nourishing procession of readings through the revolutionary and astonishing works of Freud and his disciples, heady liquor for the young chemist.

(6) I am venturing the hypothesis that from 1915 to 1923 the chronological order of the classes of phenomena and of applicable concepts to which Murr was successively attracted corresponded to the emergent phases of an epigenetically determined program of mental maturations. It is chiefly to the slow pace of this program from birth on that one must attribute the protracted sleeping span of his intellectual potentials (he was a slow developer physically and sexually as well); and now I am proposing that, once awakened, the temporal order of his mental preoccupations was determined in part by the sequence of objects and events to which he was exposed at medical school and in part by the recurrence, on a theoretical level, of a sequence of cortical developments, such as those (as Piaget has shown) that are manifested in early years by the chronological order in which certain abstract concepts (of increasing difficulty) become comprehensible to the child. In Murr's case, the sequence of his devotions was as follows: a staunch affectionate affair with anatomy and surgery was succeeded by a brief flirtation with physiology, which led to a fairly stable amorous dyad with biochemistry, a relationship that deepened when the two of them became involved with the wonders of embryological metabolism; but, as Fate (the epigenetical program plus other factors) would have it, this amicable union ended in a separation when Murr contracted a responsible marriage with psychology until death them do part. What calls for an explanation is the fact that although at the start of medical school Murr was simultaneously exposed to three distinguished sister disciplines, two of them, biochemistry and physiology, were wallflowers so far as he was concerned, and anatomy, a subject that is nonseductive to the majority of students, immediately became the target of his libido. And then in need of explanation is the fact that it was not until Murr arrived at surgery and visualized his role as that of an emergency carpenter manipulating visible macro structures

that he began wondering with serious intent about the invisible micro events that were pumping along in the tissues he was grossly handling and turned for answers to physiology, then to biochemistry (the only subject in which he got a B in medical school), then to physical chemistry (including a course in calculus!) and finally to chemical ontogeny. In shifting his focus of attention in this manner Murr was both descending into the hidden and obscure depths and genesis of living creatures (in compliance with a disposition described in Auto. 2) and ascending the Jacob's pecking ladder of the angelic sciences, although not to a point that was within earshot of the trumpet of the seraphic physicists. And besides all this, what struck me as indicative of epigenetical cortical developments was Murr's apparent repetition of certain trends of conceptual emphasis that have characterized the history of the sciences, such as from macro to micro, from matter to energy, from structure to process, from single entities and processes to systems of entities and processes, from permanence to change, and so forth; and, generally speaking, in the case of each of these pairs of complementary aspects of natural phenomena, it is easier to comprehend and deal conceptually with the earlier than with the later emphasis.

Finally, there remains to be explained, by reference to another part of the epigenetical program of interior developments, the fact that up to 1923 Murr had been immune to the enticements of all encountered versions of the science of psychology: a single lecture at Harvard by Professor Münsterberg, the course in psychiatry at the Columbia College of Physicians and Surgeons, and a single hour at the hospital with Freud's *Interpretation of Dreams* had been enough to cancel whatever potential gust for that sort of thing was in the offing. But then suddenly Murr was in a blaze, a blaze which would go on for three years and eventually pressure him to embrace psychiatry and psychology, and so to take the last step in his slow and devoted recapitulation of the order in which the disciplines pertinent to modern medicine were founded: anatomy (Vesalius), physiology (Harvey), biochemistry (Claude Bernard), and psychiatry (Kraepelin), with the significant omission of biophysics, and with evolutions to be subsequently experienced in the realms of sociology and culturology. All that I have said so far is in behalf of my thesis that the publication of Jung's book at just that moment in the course of Murr's mental and emotional metamorphoses is an example of what Pasteur called chance and the prepared mind.

(7) The actualizations of the genetical program may be mentational in nature, as I believe they were in Murr's psyche from 1915 to 1923, or they may be emotional, or both mentational and emotional. From 1923 to 1926, during which span Murr's bonds of affinity with the creative processes in chicken embryos were step-wise disengaged and attached to the germinal affects of human beings, the actualizations he experienced were in part mentational but predominantly emotional.

Throughout his hospital activities, his emotions had been engaged in empathizing with the somatic discomforts and anxieties of each patient, especially on the female ward; but these involvements were necessarily brief and superficial, and when it came to chicken embryos, lovely as they were, the opportunities for empathy were critically curtailed. In short, in view of the profound affectional upheaval that swept Murr into the unruly domain of psychology—and thereby down the pecking order of the sciences—I am assuming, first of all, that up to that time an assemblage of emotional potentialities had been denied adequate participation in his work, and, secondly, that the evolving genetical program had arrived at a new stage, comparable in a way to that of puberty, because what surged up was not merely what had been previously excluded, as in the "return of the repressed," but something wholly novel and astonishing, never dreamt of in his philosophy, with a dimension of depth and elevation which landed him in a vast brew outside the husk of his contemporary world. Instrumental in effecting and reinforcing this transition were influences emanating from the up-to-then-neglected realm of art, from artists and art-sensitive associates: a galaxy of seminal books, especially the works of Nietzsche, Dostoevski, Tolstoy, Proust, and Hardy; the music of Beethoven, Wagner, and Puccini; the poetry of E. A. Robinson and the plays of Eugene O'Neill, meeting both of them as well as a number of other poets and dramatists, actors and actresses, and attending rehearsals of their plays; endeavoring to sculpture in clay a head of his beautifully featured wife in their back yard; communing with a circle of kindred spirits, including Dr. Alfred E. Cohn, his boss at the Institute, Robert Edmond Jones, Dr. Carl Binger, who was about ready to shift from experimental physiology to psychiatry, and Christiana D. Morgan, who was destined to experience visions which would occupy the attention of Dr. Jung for twelve memorable seminars and then to join Murr at the Harvard Psychological Clinic; attending thought-kindling lectures at the New School for Social Research; and more besides, in this country and in Europe, not to speak of a *femme inspiratrice* here and there along the way. (8) As I have said already, Melville was a very potent factor, not only like Beethoven as a deep prime mover from the sphere of art and a model of powerful metaphorical speech, but as an illustrator of nearly everything that Murr was finding and about to find in Freud and Jung. (9) The revolutionary sessions with Dr. Jung in Zurich in 1925 (described in Auto. 1) have been mentioned earlier. This first encounter with an analytical psychiatrist of the new order provided Murr with an exemplar of genius that settled the question of his identity to come. (10) Murr's unswerving addiction to scientific research canceled the possibility of his devoting the bulk of his time and energy to private practice, and so (11) when Dr. Morton Prince made the unprecedented offer of a position as his research assistant in founding a clinic at Harvard College, this struck Murr as another glorious instance of chance and the prepared mind.

Murr's Conception of His Role
and Some Determinants Thereof

I have pointed out that Murr was an eccentric in about ten respects when he became an academic psychologist at Harvard in 1926, and now is the moment for me to add that within the next few years it became all too obvious that he was a deviant in other respects besides those already mentioned, such as his being woefully ignorant of the content of academic psychology, which at that time consisted mostly of psychophysics and animal conditioning. In the first place, as I have said, Murr was vitally interested in persons, intent on understanding each of them as a unit operating in his or her environment. And then, coming from medicine, he was at first especially attentive to abnormalities of functioning, the psychoneuroses, no sufficient explanations of which are possible (as he learnt from Dr. Prince and from all breeds of psychoanalysts) without the concept of unconscious psychic processes. Believing in addition (against the sturdy opposition of Dr. Prince) that Freud's theoretical system was more applicable than any other to an understanding of dysfunctionings, Murr became one of the founders of the Boston Psychoanalytical Society, went through the then-existing course of formal Freudian training, including an analysis by Dr. Franz Alexander (described in Auto. 1) and several control analyses supervised by Dr. Sachs, and for a number of years practiced orthodox psychoanalysis, modified by ideas derived from Jung, Adler, and Rank. These were the activities which incurred the disapproval of Karl Lashley and through him of President Conant, whose inclination to fire Murr was eventually overruled by various considerations advanced by Gordon Allport, Whitehead, and several other brave supporters.

As time went on, Murr became more interested in normal than in abnormal personalities, partly because there was no existing theoretical system which was anywhere near as applicable to the representation and understanding of the activities and achievements of healthy and supernormal human beings as the Freudian system was in dealing with the fears, fixations, and regressions of neurotics. As a starting point, Murr turned to what seemed most self-evident to him, in the light of common human experience, namely, that the most critical of all the variables involved in the determination of situational reactions and proactions was the nature of the goal-directed motive force (the subject's needful aim). As it happened at that juncture, this concept was not acceptable to the leading lights of Murr's department. McDougall, who had called the motive force "instinct," had been knocked out of the ring by Watson, and the triumphant champion had managed to persuade the brethren that they could get along without this imperceptible energizing and orienting factor. Watson's proposal to limit the science of psychology to concepts that pointed only to perceptibles struck the former biochemist—all of whose critical concepts had referred to imperceptibles—as a naive, juvenile perversity, even though it succeeded in rescuing psychology from the meanderings of the traditional form of introspectionism. A budding psychologist who was devoting fruitful hours listening to reports of the ongoing stream of consciousness—dreams, fantasies, memories, feelings, and thoughts—of other people (experiential psychology, as Murr would call it) could scarcely have been disposed to adopt with zest the dogmas of those whose avowed conscious purpose was to convince us that consciousness and purpose were nonexistent, or—considering that life is short and the art long—to pay close attention to the latest advances in psychophysics. William James (who was said by a later member of the Harvard department to have done unparalleled harm to psychology) had become one of Murr's major exemplars by that time, and the young man found himself agreeing with almost everything his hero had to say—completely, for example, with the heretical statement that "Individuality is founded in feeling; and the recesses of feeling, the darker, blinder strata of character, are the only places in the world in which we catch real fact in the making, and directly perceive how events happen and how work is actually done." (James, 1903, p. 501)

This idea that the "real facts" are to be found not on the surface of the body or in the full light of consciousness but in the darker, blinder recesses of the psyche was of course anathema to the majority of academic psychologists, who were militantly engaged in a competitive endeavor to mold psychology in the image of physics, a competition in which positive reinforcements would be reserved for those who could bring forth experimental findings with the highest degree of face-validity, statistical significance, and verifiability in all cases, obtained by the most reliable and precise methods. To be among the leaders in this race it was necessary to legislate against the "blinder strata," to keep away from those events which intellectuals at large assumed to be the subject matter of psychology, to disregard individual and typological differences, and to approximate universality and certainty by measuring the lawful relationships of narrowly restricted forms of animal behavior, of physiological processes in general, and of the simplest sensory and sensorimotor processes of human beings in particular. In short, methodological excellence was dictating (more than it did in any other science) the phenomena to be investigated, with the result that in those days psychologists were not the experts to be consulted about problems involving varieties of human nature, as biochemists, botanists, and ornithologists, for example, are consulted about problems involving varieties of chemicals, plants, and birds. On this general issue Murr, at variance with his contemporaries, was facing in the opposite direction with the hope of devising the best possible methods for the investigation of obscure phenomena, realizing that it is the part of an educated man, as Aristotle said, to know what degree of precision is appropriate at each stage in the development of each discipline. Although, for various reasons, Murr did not attempt any direct exposures of the blinder strata of feelings, he would in due course find ways of eliciting feelingful imagery and fantasies from which one could infer the nature of some of the components of the blinder strata.

The chief determinants of all these eccentricities of Murr have been listed in the previous section. What remains to be presented here are the reasons why it took no courage on his part to stick to views which were diametrically opposed to those that were winning all the prizes: (1) Having been trained in a more exact science, he did not feel compelled for the sake of self-esteem to put exemplary technical competence in a less exact science at the top of his hierarchy of aims. (2) He had come to psychology with the hope of advancing current knowledge about human beings, not to raise his status on the totem pole of scientists. (3) There was nothing original about his ideas: they were derived from a score of world-famous medical psychologists whose practical aims had kept them far closer to the raw facts than occupants of the groves of academe had ever got. (4) Murr's varied, intimate relations with hospital patients, ranging from a notorious gangster and dope addict to a champion world politician with infantile paralysis, together with privately experienced emotional revolutions, upsurges from below consciousness, had given him a sense of functional fitness, the feeling that all parts of his self were in unison with his professional identity as he defined it, and that he was more advantaged in these ways than were many of the book-made academics who talked as if they had lost contact with the springs of their own natures. (5) Despite his obnoxious behavior now and then (after Dr. Prince retired and Murr took over the running of the Clinic), the permanent members of the department, Professor Boring and Professor Pratt, were invariably friendly, helpful, and indulgent: they included him in all official and unofficial gatherings, yet let him go his independent way uncriticized, except for a rare paternal hint, such as the warning after he had written one of his first papers, "Psychology and the University," that if he published it he would be *persona non grata* in the APA. (6) He was not much of a teacher, but because of the drawing power of psychoanalysis he was reinforced from the beginning of his career by having a number of promising graduate students—such as Donald MacKinnon, Saul Rosenzweig, Nevitt Sanford, Isabelle Kendig, Kenneth Diven, and Robert White—come his way to get their Ph.D.'s. (7) He was not tempted to toe the line of rewarded theories and experiments, as some others were, by economic need or even by any continuing unrealistic want for recognition from the elite of his profession. (The reward of tenure, for example, was not granted until he had arrived at the seldom-equaled late age of fifty-five.) The scientific reference group whose standards had shaped his aspirations in the past—composed of men who were both specialists and generalists, such as his teachers and good friends L. J.

Henderson, Hans Zinsser, Raymond Pearl, and others I have mentioned —was now marginal to the line of his vision, and at the focus there were no equivalent replacements, except perhaps the next generation or a shadowy posterity, because I am sure that Murr was confident that the ideas and values he supported were slanted toward an allied future.

In due course the practice of introspection and the concept of motive force, in altered forms and disguised by fresh labels, surreptitiously regained their lost respectability; and after World War II, Freudian theory *in toto* overran large areas of American psychology as Napoleon overran Europe. In short, much that was pretty generally tabooed in academic circles between 1926 and 1936—the ideas and practices that gave Murr the brand of a dispensable eccentric on the Harvard faculty —became popular commonplaces within a single generation, things to be taught in general education courses, and as a consequence of this cultural expansion, Murr found himself occupying a position of discomforting respectability. He was not the real McCoy, however, because of his conception of his role as that of an unstatistical naturalist and differentiating generalist who believed that all members of the human species were not birds of the same feather.

Flashback

Apologia. The corrective maxim dictated that no space be devoted to an account of the parents and the childhood of my subject because there is nothing back there that qualifies as an aid to our understanding of his mind when it came to wrestling with the problems of psychology. In his twenties, so far as I can see, Murr's headpiece was like the island of Nantucket, standing off shore, "all beach, without a background." But, sad to say, the protests of the caucus of friends who frequent my boardinghouse drowned out the feeble voice of conscience and pressured me to cancel the corrective maxim for the nonce. And so, with suppressed scruples, I shall offer some passages extracted from the autobiography that Murr wrote in performing the first task in the usual order of assessment procedures. Here is his potpourri of sheer facts dished out for those who have a taste for them.

Parents. "My father was a Scot, born near Melbourne, Australia, where his father, a British Army officer, was sent and stationed until he died a few years after his fourth son's birth. This son, my father, was about nine when he and his mother rounded the tempestuous Cape in a schooner, with cascades of ocean pouring into their cabin, and eventually arrived in England as destitute relatives of some studbook uncles and cousins who were not inclined to be disturbed beyond using their influence to get my father entered at the famous "bluecoat" charity school in London, Christ's Hospital, where Coleridge, Leigh Hunt, and Lamb had studied. And so, to keep the home pot boiling, my grandmother—

who was equipped with French and Irish genes as well as British—called on whatever talents for artistic compositions she could muster. In view of the attractive portrait by her brush that I now have in my possession, I shall gladly ascribe to her the honor of the A's in drawing I received in primary school. As for the uninspired novels of the then-current feminine brand which she managed to get published (one entitled *Ella Norman, or a Lady's Perils*), the genetical potential for creative writing they exhibit could not have been enough to count for anything in later generations.

"After his mother's premature death my father, a penniless orphan without a college education, came by way of Toronto to New York City. His anonymous arrival must have been as different as it could have been from that of his great-grandfather, the flamboyant and irascible Earl of Dunmore, who a hundred years earlier, being sent there to serve as Governor of the State, seems to have done more than he should have done to antagonize the citizens of Manhattan and was soon removed to become the last Royal Governor of Virginia, where he lived in that grand mansion at Williamsburg which we can see today in a restored state. In no obvious way resembling this ancestor, my father came to New York as an unknown and unassuming young man, presumably to seek his fortune, an outcome which looked dubious when he was given his first job cleaning ink-pots in the offices of a stock company. Inevitably he went up as time went on, though he proved less fortunate in making money than in making friends, and not so fortunate in making friends as he was in courting the liveliest of the six daughters of a highly respected merchant, president-to-be of the Mutual Life Insurance Company, whose fortune was both ample and secure for succeeding generations. My father and his bride actually lived happily ever after.

"All my mother's near ancestors were made out of English seeds transported to this country in the seventeenth century, the original American population of them being distributed in Connecticut, Rhode Island, and Pennsylvania; but eventually a number of their carriers converged and united in the City of New York. On the way down from the first immigrants, these seeds produced a doctor and jurist, his son, an Eli and Revolutionary colonel whose mind became unhinged, a minister, a sea captain, and a score of merchants of one sort or another, and a wife for each of them whose merits and demerits are matters of conjecture. Of all these progenitors I was acquainted only with my daughter-venerated grandfather, aloof toward me, but a kindly gent whose white-bearded visage resembled God's as painted, say, by Tintoretto. Remembering him I have been led to surmise that the image and concept of Jahveh must have come not from the all-too-familiar father figure, but from the more remote and lordly grandfather, the overruling patriarch of the clan.

"If, as countless philosophers have held, happiness, resulting from this or that variety of conduct, is the only state that a rational man will endeavor to secure, then my father was as successful as anybody I could name, provided one correlates happiness with a continuing state of unperturbed serenity, cheerfulness, enjoyment of sheer being, trust, and mutual affection, or, in other words, a life of moderate, solid, predictable satisfactions, free from choler, anxiety, guilt, and shame. In Aristotelian terms, the key to it all was his adherence to the *res media;* and in William James's somewhat comparable terms, the secret lay in the willingness of this man (who was no great shakes as a businessman and banker) to renounce in good faith unrealizable ambitions: 'With no attempt there can be no failure; with no failure no humiliation.' (James, 1890)

"As for Freud, he seems to have had no concepts at all to represent such an unself-centered, even-tempered, unpretentious, undemanding, acquiescent, firm yet nonauthoritarian, jolly father who is scarcely capable of a veritable splurge of anger, even when he breaks the door down to put a stop to a voyeuristic-exhibitionistic party of mixed doubles initiated by his little daughter and her younger brother. Anyhow, in the analysis of my life's course conducted by Dr. Alexander, no indications of any hidden resentment against my father nor any memories of a persisting rage reaction—following, say, one of the two just spankings I received from him—were ever brought to light. In short, so far as I recall, my father, though not installed as a charismatic hero, was always a positive univalent figure in my mind, a dependable guide and teacher in the Hellenic mode rather than a threatening, awesome, high and mighty judge. Consequently, in later life when I came upon Freud's conception of the father-son side of the oedipus complex, it did not strike home with any vibrant shock of recognition. Furthermore, in my case there was no confirmation of the tenet that antagonisms to authority figures in later life (several in my history) can invariably be traced to the person's original hostility to his father.

"It was my mother who was the ambivalent parent: more often the focus of attention, affection, and concern than my father was, year in and year out, but also more resented now and then, mostly for correcting my abominable manners, for nagging about minutiae, or for enforcing duties or requesting services which interrupted my activities. Of the two, she was the more energetic, restless, enthusiastic, enterprising, and talkative —giving us daily reports of her personal preoccupations, her doings, encounters, worries, and frustrations—also the more changeable, moody, and susceptible to melancholy. I resemble my mother in all but one of these respects: like my fortunate father, I have never been plagued by endogenous anxieties and worries, and, like him again, I adopted at a very early age the role of physician to these perturbations in my mother and later to comparable but slighter perturbations in my more rational and steady wife.

"My mother was an effective, though overexacting, administrator of the household, and I'm afraid there was good ground for her imbedded feeling that her unusual industry, thrift, and competence in carrying out these functions—keeping the seven domestics busy as could be—were not duly appreciated by her children, but taken for granted as the given order of nature. My mother was even more sedulous in the performance of her role as supervisor of the health and of the social development of her three children more than three years apart in age: a fascinating, mischievous daughter with flashes of ungovernable temper, followed by two more easily manageable sons, me in the middle and my brother, the cute kid, with a repertoire of precocious tricks indicative of real brilliance in the future."

Past History. Memories. Here again I will have Murr speak for himself. But since he cannot recall his birth, nor anything of his sojourn in the maternal claustrum, nor earlier when the particles that made him were located in two places, neither one of these in heaven, it is up to me to announce that on May 13, 1893, in a brownstone residence, where nowadays the Rockefeller Center's sky-assaulting piles of concrete blocks irreverently stand, the little cherub, trailing humors of the original sin of selfishness, came from darkness into light in a shorter time, I wager, than it has taken me to reach this beginning of his life. In addition let me say that this was the location in New York City of his first and second winter homes up to the time of his marriage at the age of twenty-three. His summers were spent on Long Island near the seashore, with visits to boyhood friends in other places, except for four longish trips to Europe (his father loved England, his mother was a fervent Francophile and had her children learn French), during the course of which Murr compliantly dragged his feet through most of the great museums, cathedrals, and historic buildings between Naples and the Highlands of Scotland. At home on Long Island he built sand fortresses and claustra of barrel stays (his mother fantasied that he was cut out to be an architect) until his father taught him how to swim, fish, and sail, and later to play tennis, golf, and baseball with limited proficiency. More enticing than those games, however, were his animals—goat, dog, and hens—and the woods back of the house where he could climb trees, put up a tepee, and pretend he was an Indian. He read every accessible French and English fairy tale, all about the Knights of the Round Table, and boys' books about animals, Indians, frontiersmen, and the American Civil War. His father, who was steeped in the British classics, encouraged him to extend his range to a few of the works of Scott and Dickens. But almost invariably the greater lure was outdoor physical activity, and, on the whole, he seems to have grown up as an average privileged American boy of that era (before the days of automobiles, motorboats, movies, and all that), with an identity in the eyes of his miniature social surround which could not be captured in terms of either docile or rebellious, timid or reckless, awkward or agile, dull or bright, hopeless or promising, in or out. He got on famously with his younger brother but infamously with his older sister until he was nine and had gathered up enough muscle to subdue her. Despite the experience gained in coping with this tempestuous sibling, come puberty he was shy in his approach to girls and did not know the pangs of calf love until he was sixteen. In college there was a three-year period of devoted courtship of Josephine L. Rantoul of Boston before he got around to the long-since-predetermined question and answer the day after the Harvard-Yale boat race. Since I have already called attention to Murr's mediocre scholarship record up to the age of twenty-two, I have only two items to add: one, that no bona fide intellectual ever crossed the threshold of his home, and two, that his parents were Episcopalians and Republicans, his father being a great admirer of Disraeli, his character, his policies, and his novels. So much as a prelude to the memories that follow. Here is Murr speaking.

"*The Marrow of My Being. Memory* (about four years of age): Absorbed in looking at a fairy-book picture of a sad-faced queen sitting with her sad-faced son, I learn from my mother that it is the prospect of death that has made them sad. Translated briefly into today's words, my melancholy feelings and thoughts were of this nature: 'death . . . sad for the queen if her son is going to die, sad for the son if his mother is going to die . . . pitiful that this must be and nothing can be done about it.' My present free associations, starting from this first recalled encounter with the idea of death and its severance of affectional bonds between mother and son, have carried me back in time to a few items which suggest that one crucial affectional bond between mother and child had already been severed: (i) the fact that I was abruptly weaned at two months because my mother, for some reason, was too upset to continue nursing me (the possibility that sucking interfered with breathing and that I 'fought' the stifling breast as some infants do to the great discomfort of their mothers), (ii) the fact that I was a feeding problem for a year or more and in my earliest photograph look decidedly undernourished and forlorn, and (iii) the fact that my mother was at most times far more occupied with my older sister, her favorite child however troublesome, and at this time was especially occupied with my cunning baby brother. These facts and a score of other consonant filaments from the remembered past have led me to the following hypothetical *Chronology of Events:* Quite a while before the traditional oedipus hunting season, that infant had come to the grievous (and valid) realization that he could count on only a limited third-best portion of his mother's love; and since his spectacles of hypersensitive grief and his petitions for an ample supply of reassuring consolation—such as his tearfully saying, 'You make my feelings hurt me'—since these led only to frustration and shame, he proudly withdrew, with some of the murderous resentment of an abandoned child ('You'll be sorry if I die'), into a private, maternallike claustrum of his own making, where, bathed in narcissistic self-pity for a while, he could lick his own wounds until nature healed them. In this way, that special bond of mutual affinity, which depends, in an extremity, on a child's need to receive and his mother's capacity to bestow a sufficiency of emotional nurturance, was forever severed; in this one respect they were now dead to each other, an outcome which was once in a while tragically experienced by the child (as in the memory), despite his early gain in emotional self-sufficiency ('I can get along without you') and in venturesome autonomy, coupled with the repression of the residues of suffering, the abatement of his resentment, and the displacement of pity from the self to some sufferer in his environment. Needless to say, the pitied sufferer was none other than his mother, who took to her couch periodically with a sick headache; and being given to understand that if he made a noise or misbehaved in any way, his mother's headache would become unbearable ('You'll be sorry if I die'), pity soon became one of the most influential ingredients of his conscience. This reversal of roles was vividly illustrated in the one really astonishing (and uninterpreted) dream I had in my analysis with Dr. Alexander: I was comforting my mother in my arms as if she were a baby while she was vomiting over my left shoulder. All this is susceptible to a great deal more analysis; but let this much suffice because the determinants of this complex are of less interest than some of its *Consequences.* These included (i) a marrow of misery and melancholy repressed by pride and practically extinguished in everyday life by a counteracting disposition of sanguine and expansive buoyancy [described in the Prologue]; (ii) a profound attraction, coming from the marrow, for tragic themes in literature, which drew me to Herman Melville, Shakespeare, and other authors (the saddest of all circumstances being the loss of a beloved person), and incidentally disposed me to select many gloomy pictures for the TAT [Thematic Apperception Test]; (iii) also coming from the marrow, an affinity for the darker, blinder strata of feeling (as mentioned in connection with William James), this being a representative of the feminine component of my nature which, evoked by art, was influential in converting me to psychology; (iv) for some thirty years of my life, also coming from the marrow, a hypersensitivity to the sufferings of other individuals, especially women, which inclined me toward medicine and psychotherapy with the sanguine confidence that I could restore their health and joy; (v) coming out of pride, denial, and repression, the conviction that I could get along well enough with a minimum amount of aid, support, appreciation, recognition, or consolation from others; anyhow, I could never depend on it and should never seek it; in solitude and privacy I could be happily independent of all that; (vi) the (unnoticed) concept of inviolacy in *Explorations;* (vii) the concept of nurturance, of receiving and transmitting it; and finally (viii) later when new ideas began bubbling autonomously in my head, these became the foci of my nurturant disposition and there was not much energy left over for the miseries of others.

"Nansen and the Exploration of Remote, Unknown, and Unspoiled Regions of Nature, Solitude and Pantheism. Memory (3.8 years of age): Pacing back and forth one evening in the presence of my parents and saying that I would not go to bed until they promised to give my (one-month-old) brother the name of Nansen. *Explanation:* A few days earlier my parents told me about a lecture at the Metropolitan Opera House by Nansen, the arctic explorer, and this, together with a fine picture of him in the newspaper, was enough to get his figure immediately established as my first grand hero, having been prepared by *Robinson Crusoe* to be captivated by this chance encounter with a venturer into unstaked territory. *Consequences:* (i) choosing Nansen's *Farthest North,* in two volumes, as the first book to read alone from cover to cover; (ii) incorporating later generations of similar exemplars—American Indians, pioneers, woodsmen, explorers, mountain climbers—whose wilderness achievements depended on know-how, endurance, and fortitude; (iii) positive cathection, with pantheistic fervor, of the more remote, less frequented and unspoiled regions of nature, resulting in the development of a major territorial system of my personality exemplified by camping, fishing, and hunting trips in the Adirondacks, New Mexico, California, Oregon, British Columbia, Manitoba, Ontario, Quebec, New Brunswick, Newfoundland, the traverse of Mont Blanc from the Italian side, and the building of solitary hideouts here and there at some distance from 'the madding crowd'; and (iv) a psyche prepared by empathic communions with nature—receiving impressions 'fresh from her own virgin voluntary and confiding breast'—to appreciate nature poetry, the writings of Herman Melville, and the earth, animal, and sky mythologies of our earliest ancestors (closed books to city-dwelling theorists); and on the other hand, prepared to detest all the landscape horrors of commercial advertising. *Later consequences:* (i) the replacement of alluring geographical territories by the more enticing, primitive, mysterious, and unsurveyed regions of the psyche (explorations of personality); (ii) a miniature of nature in the form of a garden next to each of the four Clinic buildings we inhabited; and (iii) the concepts of egression, ingression, ascension, descension, and so forth to represent movements in social and cultural space as well as in territorial space.

"A Sensorimotor Defect. Memory (nine years old): Returning from school innocent as could be one day to find the dining room transformed into an operating room, with two white-gowned surgeons and an anesthetist awaiting my arrival, and my mother confronting me with the option of a pain-eliminating general anesthetic or an aquarium as prize for getting on without it. *Explanation:* Four years earlier, my mother, ever on the lookout for deviations from the norm, detected a slight crossing of my eyes (internal strabismus) which became steadily more accentuated despite the therapeutic efforts of New York's most eminent ophthalmologist, and so now the time had come for this worthy to cut

some of the hyperactive orbital muscles. *Consequences:* Although I was pleasured by an aquarium of enchanting fish, it turned out that I had been somewhat disadvantaged by the expert surgeon's having cut a few more muscle fibers than was necessary to correct the crossing of my vision, and I came forth with the opposite defect, an external strabismus, which, though far less obvious than the previous condition, left me nonetheless as incapable as ever of focusing on a single point with more than one eye at a time, and hence incapable of stereoscopic vision. But I was entirely unconscious of the significance of this defect until as a medical student I went to the office of Dr. Smith Ely Jeliffe, a spectacular New York psychiatrist, to consult him about my stuttering, which had set in shortly after the operation. To my amazement, Dr. Jeliffe's first question was 'Have you found any difficulty in playing games, such as baseball, tennis, or squash, which necessitate catching or hitting a fast-moving ball?' 'Yes, I certainly have,' I said, 'but how did you know?' 'Well,' Dr. Jeliffe replied, 'I noticed that one eye was not looking at me directly but turned out a bit, and that would be enough to unfit you for games of that sort and also for swift, precise manual movements.' The doctor's astonishing powers of observation and of inference succeeded in casting a penetrating ray of illumination into uprushing memories of humiliating incidents, particularly in baseball games, when I had struck out or let an easy one slip through my fingers, and so forth and so forth. Dr. Jeliffe went on to relate this elementary sensorimotor defect to my stuttering, but whatever wisdom he had to offer on that issue has long since passed beyond recall. Today I am partial to the notion that a primary suffocation experience which, as mentioned earlier, involves a panicky incoordination of sucking, breathing, an inturned eye, and hands lunging at the breast could have established a predisposition to all three of the disabilities I have mentioned. But to return to Dr. Jeliffe's office, what surprises me now is that it never occurred to me that the revelation I had been vouchsafed had any bearing on my intention to become a surgeon; and it was not until three years later that the realization that my manual dexterity was definitely limited became clear enough to fortify my decision to devote myself exclusively to research."

Murr is so convinced that personality is revealed only vaguely in the empty abstractions derived from questionnaires and factor analyses, but substantially in the minute, concrete details of critical and typical episodes in the life history of an individual, that even after deleting most of the detail in the three memories I have offered you, I find that these have already usurped more than the allotted space. Consequently, instead of allowing him to go on in this fashion, I shall give the bare gist of three of the last dozen clusters of memories that he submitted. (1) *A non-Freudian child.* Murr tells of Dr. Alexander's boredom when his analysand, despite continuous scratching at his unconscious, failed to bring forth the expected array of polymorphic episodes. With the advent of passionate love in post-adolescence, Murr exultantly experienced and reciprocally expressed, as related in one of his papers, pretty nearly every Freudian component of the sex instinct, showing that none of these dispositions were absent in his constitution and, incidentally, that Freud erred in affirming that men of our civilization are necessarily doomed to renunciation and incurable discontent. But, except for a few banal universals, there were no veritable exhibitions of these tendencies in his early dreams and memories, either, perhaps, because of the rarity in his protected environment of suitable stimulations and opportunities, or perhaps because of a too firmly established barrier of repression. (2) *Possibly an Adlerian boy.* Freud's theories are consistent with a concept of the child as an armless and legless torso and head, with three cathected orifices in constant need of stimulation, a concept which offered Murr another possible reason for his failure to qualify as a typical Freudian child. Perhaps the locomotive and manipulative activity of his append-ages were functionally more important to him than the superficial sensi-tivity of the orifices per se. Anyhow, from nine to eighteen, football heroes (which excluded his father) and playing football were at the top of his system of values, which suggests that an Adlerian factor was at work, because he, a confirmed stutterer, always played quarterback—not too well, but he persisted and, for some reason, never stuttered when he gave the signals. Another Adlerian story that Murr related with some pride was of being licked in a fight during recess at primary school and then taking up boxing until he won the featherweight championship. (3) *Egression from the husk of his youth.* Murr had been brought up on the conservative Republican Episcopalian side of the traditions of a rela-tively stable society, with a moral code, cluster of tastes, and privileged status that were taken for granted by his parents and unobtrusively exemplified. Molded by these values, which had been reinforced by the Rev. Endicott Peabody of Groton, Murr arrived at medical school not suspecting that in due course his analytical mind would identify their ethnocentric determinants, and that before he graduated he would re-fute a basic Marxian theorem by saying goodbye to his implanted preju-dices in favor of Christianity, the Republican Party, and the class of people with whom he had been reared. Foremost among his redeemers was a brilliant classmate, Alvan Barach, his first intimate (and lifelong) Jewish friend, who was headed for a distinguished career as a practitioner and scientific innovator. Murr had chosen to go to the P & S [Columbia University College of Physicians and Surgeons] in New York with the express purpose of detaching himself from his playboy and athletic friends in the Harvard-Boston area; but the separation that was intended to be temporary turned out to be a permanent divorce of interests and viewpoints with no remaining valid bridges of communication. But not so in his own family, since they had found a way of getting along happily together, all talking at the same time, without more than an occasional reference to basic issues.

Murr's Accomplishments

Murr is known here and there in professional circles as an imprecision instrument maker because of his part in the fashioning of the Thematic Apperception Test (1935), and as a theorist because of his part in the building of the edifice of principles, concepts, methods, case material, and experiments entitled *Explorations in Personality* (1938). And here let me immediately record that in Murr's opinion the major determinant of the volume, quality, and pre-timeliness of that cooperative book was the exceptional spirit, character, competence, and imaginative scope of the students and colleagues who worked in companionship with him at the Harvard Psychological Clinic from 1934 through 1936. In Auto. 2 Murr gratefully named each member of that body and of later bodies of congenial and talented collaborators (some forty in all), so many of whom went on to surpass him, each in his own way as a productive contributor to the science of psychology, that, in some quarters, Murr is thought of not as an author so much as an author of authors, a diversity of them, none bound to his ideas.

Murr, with modesty in abeyance, is disposed to claim more than half the credit for the following endeavors to advance the science of human nature in 1938: (1) *Methodological:* the *multiform system of assessment,* the more practical part of which consists of multifarious procedures administered by multifarious specialists to each of a number of subjects, followed by staff meetings in which the data obtained from one assessee are presented, discussed, interpreted, and organized (by an appointed personographer) into an explanatory formulation of the history of that assessee's personality. The general design of this system of operations was determined by a mere transfer of learning from medicine to psychology, with the crucial difference that the terminal process is not simply the assignment of each subject to a known diagnostic category, as it commonly is in medicine, but a novel, creative composition (consisting of universal, typological, and unique features) the validity of which is susceptible to judgments in terms of various criteria. These lengthy personographies based on data obtained from some forty procedures and revised to take account of the diverse judgments of other generalist assessors canceled for Murr all further confidence in the rating of any variable by a single test or in the representation of a personality by a list of traits or, indeed, in any representation (except a truly creative one) that has escaped exposure to a variety of insights. But the point overlooked by most readers is that the superordinate purpose of these assessment procedures, repeated in modified versions with other assemblages of subjects, is to permit the periodic exemplification, testing, correction, expansion, and reconstruction (and hence the continuous evolution) of a personological system of concepts and theories. (2) *Technical: special methods,* several of which, like the TAT (better named "eductors" than "projection tests"), were designed to educe (draw forth) words, sentences, or stories as ground for verifiable or plausible inferences in regard to influential components of the personality which the subject is either unable or unwilling to report. (3) *Synthetical:* the incorporation into the sphere of academic concern of a large portion of Freud's theoretical system integrated with contributions from Jung, Adler, McDougall, Lewin, and others. (4) *Conceptual:* (i) the first version of a reasonably comprehensive classification of aimed motive forces (needs, wants, drives) as a necessary revision and extension of Freud's irrational, sentimental, and inadequately differentiated division of instincts into Eros and Thanatos, and so forth; (ii) the first version of a classification of the salient properties of the "behavioral environment" (Koffka, Lewin) into varieties of *press,* and (iii) a number of concepts which define different dynamic relationships between needs and between needs and press. The chief determinant of these taxonomic endeavors was merely a transfer of learning from chemistry, medicine, and the biological sciences, all of which were launched on their careers as differentiated systems of knowledge by extensive classifications of the entities and phenomena that lay within the circumference of their responsibility.

The absence in *Explorations* of any clearly stated testable propositions contributed by Murr is definitely to his discredit, as Hall and Lindzey have properly pointed out. Of little weight in his defense would be the observation that here and there are passages expressive of tacit propositions which could easily be made explicit, and many of these could be ordered in relation to one theme: the various components of personality (such as interests, emotions, needs, sentiments, defenses, and past experiences) that operate as determinants or modifiers of a person's apprehensions (perceptions, estimations, interpretations, predictions, recollections, conceptualizations, and theoretical explanations) of observed phenomena. Another factor to be considered in this connection is Murr's perverse antipathy to any odor of scientific pretentiousness, any greater methodological refinements than the nature of the data warrants, having too often been a witness of a mountain of ritual bringing forth a mouse of fact more dead than alive. To me this perversity in Murr looks like a willful addiction to foreseeable negative reinforcements.

After editing the manuscript of *Explorations* for delivery to the Oxford University Press (whose consultant argued strongly for rejection), Murr left for an official absence from Harvard that would extend over nine of the subsequent eleven years. The first among other things he did was to sojourn and travel in Europe with his wife and daughter Josephine (who was destined to become a pediatrician). They traveled in Germany, where in 1937 they saw the frenzied Hitler and noted with horrible forebodings the unmistakable premonitory signs of a collective Faustian explosion, then in Switzerland, where they visited Dr. Jung at his Bollingen retreat and listened to his analysis of Hitler's syndrome of symptoms, and finally in Hungary and Austria, where he spent a memorable evening with Dr. and Anna Freud in the room where that astounding corpus of cultural history had been shaped. Four years later, in the fall of 1941, when Murr returned to his cherished workshop in Cambridge—succinctly described in his day as "wisteria outside, hysteria inside," but now progressing on a saner course under the steadier and more competent directorship of the beloved Robert White—he was greeted by the largest and liveliest group of knowledgeable and diversified investigators that had ever gathered there or ever would. Some of these men—Leo Bellak, Elliott Jaques, Silvan Tomkins, Frederick Wyatt, and others—were prepared to engage in the multiform assessment of another aggregate of subjects, but this time with an expanded and improved conceptual system and an elegant statistical design composed by Daniel Horn. There was promise of a considerable advance in both methodology and theory; but Pearl Harbor and its consequences for the staff brought the whole program to a halt after the thorough study of only eleven subjects. Only some of the gathered data was salvaged for publication, some by White, Robert Holt, and others, and some by Murr and Christiana Morgan in a monograph entitled "A Clinical Study of Sentiments" (values), which, finished under pressure amid wartime duties, failed, by an inexcusable oversight, to mention the names of the numerous collaborators to whom they were unequivocally indebted. Between 1943 and 1948 Murr was primarily engaged in the operations of the OSS Assessment Staff, in company with several of his former colleagues, James G. Miller, Morris Stein, and a few previously mentioned, especially Donald MacKinnon, able director of the main assessment station near Washington (not to speak of almost fifty other "behavioral scientists"). After the war was over, Murr was busy with some of the chapters of *Assessment of Men* (1948), which contains a full account of the exciting history and ambiguous results of that wholly absorbing worldwide enterprise. Finally, before returning to Harvard, Murr wrote a 100-page introduction to Melville's bizarre yet profound *Pierre* (1949) and several other pieces.

From 1950 to 1962 Murr was in charge of grants from foundations and from the government (National Institutes of Health), which covered the expenses of four successive assessment programs, each consisting of a three-year examination and analysis of the performances in testing situations and in experiments of twenty or more Harvard undergraduates. One result of all of these endeavors was a collection of eighty-eight copious case histories (including in all about 4,000 story compositions), teeming with grist for whoever has the time, bent, and capability to make scientific sense of it. Of the many collaborators in these projects, some (to whom Murr is especially grateful and indebted)—starting with the dynamo of 1950, the disciplined and effective Gardner Lindzey, and ending with the dynamo of 1962, the contagiously zestful and productive Ed Shneidman (not to speak of many other wonders, such as Gerhard

Nielsen of Copenhagen, in between)—are already notable for their accomplishments along the way; but, except for a sketch of the Icarian
personality and an article on the heart rate in stressful dyadic disputations, Murr's bibliography is mute as regards all the grain-full information
garnered in those years, and unless he has something creditable to exhibit in his sections of the cooperative volume with which he is currently
involved (to be entitled *Aspects of Personality*), there will be no substantial accomplishments to record for those twelve years of industrious
activity.

One determinant of the barrenness of Murr's record in the sphere
of personological research after World War II was the spontaneous pro-
pulsion of his thoughts by the sanguine surplus into other, continuously
expanding regions of concern. For ten years or more he and his wife
would rise at 4:30 A.M., and by 5 Murr was at his desk ready to set down
the bubblings of images and ideas which would invariably invade his
stream of consciousness, sometimes in league with a set task but more
often not. One of the main regions of concern was one which might be
called the world's dilemma. The OSS assessment job had taken Murr
around the world to check up on the errors they had made, and he
happened to be in Kunming, testing officer candidates for the Chinese
Nationalist army, when the news of Hiroshima, announced over the radio
of his jeep, set off a hectic procession of horrendous images of the world's
fate, which ever since have magnetically directed the path of countless
currents of imagination toward some far-off ultimate solution, in the
constant view of which, year by year and month by month, short-range
international strategies and tactics could be more creatively designed.
While others were thinking of ways of reducing momentary tensions and
quieting the anxieties of their fellow citizens, Murr was oriented toward
the total abolition of war. Peace must be insured by a world government
of an unprecedented type, which would never be established or never
last without a radical transformation of ethnocentric sentiments and
values on both sides of our divided world; and a transformation of this
nature would never occur without some degree of synthesis of the best
features of the two opposing cultural systems; and this would not take
place creatively except in sight of an unprecedented vision and conception of world relationship and fellowship, a kind of superordinate natural
religion, or mythologized philosophy. This line of thinking, which
brought Murr to a consideration of the determinants of the genesis and
history of Judeo-Christianity, issued in a number of papers listed in the
bibliography.

Murr's other absorbing region of concern contained potential constituents for a basic revision and expansion of his theoretical system. It
is impossible to summarize 2,000 pages of diagrams, notes, and scrib-
blings; but to deprive those voyages of thought of a little of their strangeness, let me just mention a few of the incorporated components that can

be readily identified: (1) Keith's group theory of evolution; (2) role theory which Murr, as a member of the newly formed Department of Social Relations, learnt from Talcott Parsons in conjunction with much that he received from Clyde Kluckhohn regarding the pervasive influence of culture; (3) general systems theory, the abstract essence of which Murr derived from Whitehead; (4) adoption of the ongoing processes of metabolism (the anabolic composition, Co, and the catabolic decomposition, De, of energy-binding substances) as the *sine qua non* of the givenness of life, the source of psychic energy (psychometabolism), and the *core* (with additional variables) of his basic paradigm for a host of analogous phenomena at different levels; (5) the application of this paradigm to the problem of the genesis of life from non-life, to the theory of the creative (emergent) evolution of genetical systems, to the life cycle of a single individual, and to the compositional activities of the mind, and so forth, and so forth. A little of all this was included in Auto. 2, which Murr wrote for Sigmund Koch, but not enough to give any of the more recent expositors of contemporary theories of personality the impression that Murr had inched his thoughts a measurable distance beyond their original positions some thirty years ago.

Anyhow, the impression he has given others of a stationary mental apparatus is not very likely to be corrected. After being vouchsafed an extremely happy and full-freighted life, with a few trough and many peak experiences, he was confounded in 1962 on the one hand by the sudden death of his superlatively good and loyal wife, and on the other by the fading of the mental energies on which he had been counting to deal with one or two at least of the ten half-finished books that are calling for completion, residual products of his sanguine surplus.

EPILOGUE

I told you at the start of this case portrait that my functionally autonomous will, the conscious governor of my ego system (the little self) had resolved to check the incontinence of the sanguine surplus from the larger Self and adhere to the corrective maxim. But it must have been apparent to you almost from the start that although I was managing to focus pretty well on the eccentricities of Murr, there was more functional autonomy in the Self than in the self: the legs of the portrait came out too long and lanky, the belly of childhood memories was too bloated, and I had hardly stretched above the eyebrows when I found myself simultaneously at both the ordained space limit and the time limit. Down came the blade of the editor's guillotine, and my last section, the forehead and crown of the portrait, which contained whatever retrospective bits of wit and wisdom Murr could muster, rolled into the basket with a thud. In short, I need not have taken a paragraph of the prologue to describe the sanguine surplus, because it was fated to make a disastrous spectacle of itself in the ensuing pages, and to leave Murr and myself, the viewed and the viewer, with one residual query: Would I not have been capable of contributing more substantially to my profession if that eminent ophthalmologist had left my right eye focusing on something just beyond my nose which I could seize and scientifically contain in the hollow of one hand, instead of allowing his own sanguine surplus to take hold of his scalpel and send me off with a right eye that was bound to wander, joyfully but wastefully, beyond the standard circumference of healthy vision?

REFERENCES TO SELECTED PUBLICATIONS BY HENRY A. MURRAY

Autobiographical and Theoretical

What should psychologists do about psychoanalysis? *J. abnorm. soc. Psychol.*, 1950, *35*, 150–175. (Auto. 1)

Preparations for the scaffold of a comprehensive system. In S. Koch (Ed.), *Psychology: A Study of a Science*, vol. 3. New York: McGraw-Hill, 1959. (Auto. 2)

Theoretical

(with staff) *Explorations in Personality.* New York: Oxford, 1938.

(with C. D. Morgan) A clinical study of sentiments. (ch. II) *Genet. Psychol. Monogr.*, 1945, *32*, 3–311.

Toward a classification of interactions. In T. Parsons, E. A. Shils, E. C. Tolman, *et al.* (Eds.), *Toward a General Theory of Action.* Cambridge, Mass.: Harvard, 1951.

(with C. Kluckhohn) Outline of a conception of personality, and Personality formation: the determinants. In C. Kluckhohn, H. A. Murray, and D. M. Schneider (Eds.), *Personality in Nature, Society, and Culture.* New York: Knopf, 1953.

Drive, time, strategy, measurement, and our way of life. In G. Lindzey (Ed.), *Assessment of Human Motives.* New York: Holt, Rinehart and Winston, 1958.

Methodology and Methods

(in addition to *Explorations in Personality* and A clinical study of sentiments, ch. III)

(with C. D. Morgan) A method of investigating fantasies. *Arch. neurol. Psychiat.*, 1935, *34*, 289–306. Reprinted in R. C. Birney and R. C. Teevan (Eds.), *Measuring Human Motivation.* Princeton: Van Nostrand, 1962.

Principles of assessment. In H. A. Murray, D. W. MacKinnon, J. G. Miller, D. W. Fiske, and E. Hanfmann, *Assessment of Men.* New York: Holt, Rinehart and Winston, 1948.

(with A. Davids) Preliminary appraisal of an auditory projective technique for studying personality and cognition. *Amer. J. Orthopsychiat.*, 1955, *25*, 543–554.

Introduction. In G. G. Stern, M. I. Stein, and B. S. Bloom, *Methods in Personality Assessment.* Glencoe, Ill.: Free Press, 1956.

Historical trends in personality research. In H. P. David and J. C. Brengelmann (Eds.), *Perspectives in Personality Research.* New York: Springer, 1960.

Research and Case Studies

The effect of fear upon estimates of the maliciousness of other personalities. *J. Psychol.,* 1933, *4,* 310–329.

(with H. A. Wolff and C. E. Smith) The psychology of humor. *J. abnorm. soc. Psychol.,* 1934, *28,* 341–365.

The psychology of humor. II. Mirth responses to disparagement jokes as a manifestation of an aggressive disposition. *J. abnorm. soc. Psychol.,* 1934, *29,* 66–81.

(with D. R. Wheeler) A note on the possible clairvoyance of dreams. *J. Psychol.,* 1936, *3,* 309–313 (concerned with the kidnapping of the Lindbergh baby).

(with C. D. Morgan) Eleven case studies (chs. IV–VII) in A clinical study of sentiments. *Gen. Psychol. Mono.,* 1945, *32,* 3–149.

Introduction. In A. Burton and R. E. Harris (Eds.), *Clinical Studies in Personality,* Vol. I. New York: Harper & Row, 1947.

American Icarus. In A. Burton and R. E. Harris (Eds.), *Clinical Studies of Personality,* vol. II. New York: Harper & Row, 1955.

Notes on the Icarus syndrome. *Folia psychiatrica, neurologica, et neurochirugica Neelandica,* 1958, *61,* 204–208.

Studies of stressful interpersonal disputations. *Amer. Psychologist,* 1963, *18,* 28–36.

Miscellaneous: State of Man, Evolution, Creativity, and Mythology

Individuality: the meaning and content of individuality in contemporary America. *Daedalus,* 1958, *87,* 25–47. Reprinted in *The American Style,* New York, 1958; and in H. M. Ruitenbeek (Ed.), *Varieties of Modern Social Theory,* New York: Dutton, 1963.

Vicissitudes of creativity. In H. H. Anderson (Ed.), *Creativity and Its Cultivation.* New York: Harper & Row, 1959.

Beyond yesterday's idealisms. Phi Beta Kappa Oration, Harvard Chapter, 1959; printed in C. Brinton (Ed.), *The Fate of Man.* New York: George Braziller, 1961; also in *Man Thinking,* United Chapters of Phi Beta Kappa, Ithaca, N.Y.: Cornell.

Two versions of man. In H. Shapley (Ed.), *Science Ponders Religion.* New York: Appleton-Century-Crofts, 1960.

The possible nature of a "mythology" to come. In H. A. Murray (Ed.), *Myth and Mythmaking.* New York: George Braziller, 1960.

Unprecedented evolutions. *Daedalus,* 1961, *90,* 547–570. Reprinted in H. Hoagland and R. W. Burhoe (Eds.), *Evolution and Man's Progress.* New York: Columbia, 1962.

Prospect for psychology. *International Congress of Applied Psychology,* Copenhagen, 1961. Reprinted in *Science,* 1962, *136,* 483–488.

The personality and career of Satan. *J. soc. Issues,* XVIII, 1962, *28,* 36–54.

Herman Melville

Introduction with footnotes. In H. A. Murray (Ed.), *Pierre or the Ambiguities.* (H. Melville) New York: Farrar, Straus, Hendricks House, 1949.

In nomine diaboli. *The New England Quart.*, 1951, *XXIV*, 435–452. Reprinted in *Moby-Dick Centennial Essays*, Melville Society (Ed.), 1953; also in *Discussions of Moby-Dick*, M. R. Stern (Ed.), Boston, 1960; and in *Melville: A Collection of Critical Essays*, R. Chase (Ed.), New York: Prentice-Hall, 1962.

Other Publications Cited
James, William. *The Varieties of Religious Experience.* New York: Longmans, 1903.
———. *The Principles of Psychology*, vol. I. New York: Dover, 1950 (originally published in 1890).
Jung, C. G. *Psychological Types.* New York: Harcourt, Brace & World, 1923.

3

JUNG: BEYOND THE HOUR'S MOST EXACTING EXPECTATION

Carl G. Jung's life and works have given all mankind multiple causes for wonder, gratitude, and homage, and a galaxy of qualities to celebrate. Certainly in the coming years—if there are any for our species—a procession of biographies and commentaries will be published, mostly in praise —in praise of the generative power of his ideas and of the wholeness of his charismatic personality—but also to some extent in opposition, for Jung was fearlessly, even recklessly, outspoken—a distinctively controversial genius. Here it will be my part and pleasure to portray one hour of the Old Man in action, as experienced by countless individuals in quest of help.

For forty years or more, men and women in distress, persons with blocked horizons, emotionally impoverished or crippled, were lured to Küsnacht from all parts of the earth with their anticipations raised to an extraordinary pitch by reading something Jung had written that excited, baffled, beckoned all at once, or by hearing of his daring intellectual vigor, clairvoyance, and wisdom. Generally speaking, the hopes of these questers were as high as their need-bred fantasies were capable of lifting them, so high indeed that the uninitiated would most naturally assume that disillusionment was inevitable. But instead of disillusionment, instead of encountering the replica or equivalent of what they had fervently envisaged, they were almost invariably astonished: reality outran imagination. As foreseen, they found in Dr. Jung "a river of waters in a dry place and the shadow of a great rock in a weary land," but, in addition, wine from an ageless vineyard which evoked in each of them "an echo and a glimpse of what he thought a phantom or a legend until then." And those with a sufficient apperceptive reach would leave with the conviction "as invisible as music but positive as sound" that what they now knew they could "say thereafter to few men."

Jung was humble before the ineffable mystery of each variant self that faced him for the first time, as he sat at his desk, pipe in hand, with every faculty attuned, brooding on the portent of what was being said to him. And he never hesitated to acknowledge his perplexity in the

Address given at Carl G. Jung Memorial Meeting in New York, December 1962.

presence of a strange and inscrutable phenomenon, never hesitated to admit the provisional nature of the comments he had to make or to emphasize the difficulties and limitations of possible achievement in the future. "Whoever comes to me," he would say, "takes his life in his hands." The effect of such statements, the effect of his manner of delivering his avowals of uncertainty and suspense, was not to diminish but to augment the patient's faith in his physician's invincible integrity, as well as to make plain that the patient must take the burden of responsibility for whatever decisions he might make.

There have been scholars in our time whose erudition was more extensive and precise than Jung's. There have been doctors and priests who were capable of bringing their whole devoted minds to an equally sharp focus on the immediate plight of a suffering individual. There have been poets who could digest into more captivating metaphors the essence of an enduring verity. And there have been other creative moralists notable for their discernment and sagacity. But who can we name who has combined these powers with such beneficent and transformative effects? Who—hour after hour, day after day—has been so acutely perceptive of the unique particularities of feeling, thought, and action manifested by the individual confronting him? and also so penetrating and infallible in putting his finger on the crux of that individual's dilemma? and also so imaginative at the timely moment in culling from so vast a store of knowledge, personal experience, and reflection whatever was most pertinent to the understanding of that dilemma? and also such a master of apt and pithy utterance that he could transmute his understanding into words which at their best would memorably convey not only a new and startling revelation of the existential difficulty, but a clue to its solution, an intimation of the saving way and the courage to embark on it? Emily Dickinson must have had somebody in mind with powers similar to Jung's when she wrote:

> He found my Being—set it up—
> Adjusted it to place—
> Then carved his name upon it
> And bade it to the East.

In the words of one young man who went to Küsnacht for the first time: "Dr. Jung was the first full-blooded, all-encompassing, spherical human being I had ever met and I knew of no fit standards, no adequate operations by which to measure his circumference and diameters. I had only the touchstone of my own peculiar tribulation to apply to his intelligence with the importunate demand that he interpret what I presumably knew best—myself. He proved more than equal to this exacting test and within an hour my life was permanently set on a new course. In the next few days 'the great flood-gates of the wonder-world swung open' and I experienced the unconscious in that immediate and moving way that cannot be drawn out of books. I came to see that my on-going life was small adventure and the world as I had known it no conclusion. Instead of remaining framed by the standard judgments of my locality and time, I saw myself as the inheritor and potential bearer and promoter of mute historic forces struggling for emergence, consciousness, fulfillment, and communication. All this and more I owe to Dr. Jung." For any number of us, no doubt, memories of comparable occasions will keep the heart and mind of this great man throbbing somewhere in our souls as vitally as ever.

And now, looking beyond us to prospected generations, we have abundant reasons to predict that:

> Despite what current science disavows
> Of his deep wisdom and physician's skill,
> There's ample truth that fashion cannot kill,
> To which posterity will cleave as time allows.
>
> Whether or not they read him they shall feel
> At crucial times the vigor of his name
> Against them like a finger for the shame
> And emptiness of what their souls reveal
> In values prized as altars where they kneel
> To consecrate the flicker, not the flame.*

---

*EDITOR'S NOTE: The above is Dr. Murray's modification of a portion of Edwin Arlington Robinson's poem "George Crabbe." The original poem, reproduced in its entirety below, is reprinted from Robinson's *Children of the Night* with the permission of Charles Scribner's Sons, publishers.

> Give him the darkest inch your shelf allows,
> Hide him in lonely garrets, if you will,
> But his hard, human pulse is throbbing still
> With the sure strength that fearless truth endows.
> In spite of all fine science disavows,
> Of his plain excellence and stubborn skill
> There yet remains what fashion cannot kill,
> Though years have thinned the laurel from his brows.
>
> Whether or not we read him, we can feel
> From time to time the vigor of his name
> Against us like a finger for the shame
> And emptiness of what our souls reveal
> In books that are as altars where we kneel
> To consecrate the flicker, not the flame.

4

IN NOMINE DIABOLI

Next to the seizures and shapings of creative thought—the thing itself—
no comparable experience is more thrilling than being witched, illumined, and transfigured by the magic of another's art. This is a trance
from which one returns refreshed and quickened, and bubbling with
unenvious praise of the exciting cause, much as Melville bubbled after
his first reading of Hawthorne's *Mosses*. In describing *his* experience
Melville chose a phrase so apt—"the shock of recognition"—that in the
thirties Edmund Wilson took it as the irresistibly perfect title for his
anthology of literary appreciations. Acknowledging a shock of recognition and paying homage to the delivering genius is singularly exhilarating, even today—or especially today—when every waxing enthusiasm
must confront an outgoing tide of culture.

In our time, the capacities for wonder and reverence, for generous
judgments and trustful affirmations, have largely given way, though not
without cause surely, to their antitheses, the humors of a waning ethos:
disillusionment, cynicism, disgust, and gnawing envy. These states have
bred in us the inclination to dissect the subtlest orders of man's wit with
ever sharper instruments of depreciation, to pour all values, the best
confounded by the worst, into one mocking-pot, to sneer "realistically,"
and, as we say today, to "assassinate" character. These same humors have
disposed writers to spend immortal talent in snickering exhibitions of
vulgarity and spiritual emptiness, or in making delicate picture puzzles
out of the butt ends of life.

In the face of these current trends and tempers, I, coming out of
years of brimming gratefulness for the gift of *Moby-Dick*, would like to
praise Herman Melville worthily, not to bury him in a winding sheet of
scientific terminology. But the odds are not favorable to my ambition. A
commitment of thirty years to analytic modes of thought and concepts
lethal to emotion has built such habits in me that were I to be waked in
the night by a cry of "Help!" I fear I would respond in the lingo of
psychology. I am suffering from one of the commonest ailments of our
age—trained disability.

From *The New England Quarterly*, 1951, XXIV, 435–452. Reprinted in *Moby-Dick Centennial Essays*, edited for the Melville Society, Dallas: Southern Methodist University
Press, 1953; and in M.R. Stern, Ed., *Melville, A Collection of Critical Essays*, Engle-
wood Cliffs, N.J.: Prentice-Hall, 1962.

The habit of a psychologist is to break down the structure of each personality he studies into elements, and so in a few strokes to bring to earth whatever merit that structure, as a structure, may possess. Furthermore, for reasons I need not mention here, the technical terms for the majority of these elements have derogatory connotations. Consequently, it is difficult to open one's professional mouth without disparaging a fellow being. Were an analyst to be confronted by that much heralded but still missing specimen of the human race—the normal man—he would be struck dumb, for once, through lack of appropriate ideas.

If I am able to surmount to some extent any impediments of this origin, you may attribute my good fortune to a providential circumstance. In the procession of my experiences *Moby-Dick* anteceded psychology; that is, I was swept by Melville's gale and shaken by his appalling sea dragon before I had acquired the all-leveling academic oil that is poured on brewed-up waters, and before I possessed the weapons and tools of science—the conceptual lance, harpoons, cutting irons, and whatnots—which might have reduced the "grand hooded phantom" to mere blubber. Lacking these defenses I was whelmed. Instead of my changing this book, this book changed me.

To me, *Moby-Dick* was Beethoven's *Eroica* in words: first of all, a masterly orchestration of harmonic and melodic language, of resonating images and thoughts in varied meters. Equally compelling were the spacious sea setting of the story; the cast of characters and their prodigious common target; the sorrow, the fury, and the terror, together with all those frequent touches, those subtle interminglings of unexampled humor, quizzical, and, in the American way, extravagant; and finally the fated closure, the crown and tragic consummation of the immense yet firmly welded whole. But still more extraordinary and portentous were the penetration and scope, the sheer audacity of the author's imagination. Here was a man who did not fly away with his surprising fantasies to some unbelievable dreamland, pale or florid, shunning the stubborn objects and gritty facts, the prosaic routines and practicalities of everyday existence. Here was a man, who, on the contrary, chose these very things as vessels for his procreative powers—the whale as a naturalist, a Hunter or a Cuvier, would perceive him, the business of killing whales, the whale ship running as an oil factory, stowing down—in fact, every mechanism and technique, each tool and gadget, that was integral to the money-minded industry of whaling. Here was a man who could describe the appearance, the concrete matter-of-factness, and the utility of each one of these natural objects, implements, and tools with the fidelity of a scientist, and while doing this, explore it as a conceivable repository of some aspect of the human drama; then, by an imaginative tour de force, deliver a vital essence, some humorous or profound idea, coalescing with its embodiment. But still more. Differing from the symbolists of our time, here was a man who offered us essences and meanings which did not level or depreciate the objects of his contemplation. On the contrary, this

loving man exalted all creatures—the mariners, renegades, and castaways on board the *Pequod*—by ascribing to them "high qualities, though
dark" and weaving round them "tragic graces." Here, in short, was a man
with the mythmaking powers of a Blake, a hive of significant associations,
who was capable of reuniting what science had put asunder—pure perception and relevant emotion—and doing it in an exultant way that was
acceptable to skepticism.

Not at first, but later, I perceived the crucial difference between
Melville's dramatic animations of nature and those of primitive religion
makers; both were spontaneous and uncalculated projections, but Melville's were in harmony, for the most part, with scientific knowledge,
because they had been recognized as projections, checked, and modified.
Here, then, was a man who might redeem us from the virtue of an
incredible subjective belief, on the one side, and from the virtue of a
deadly objective rationality, on the other.

For these and other reasons the reading of *Moby-Dick*—coming
before psychology—left a stupendous imprint, too vivid to be dimmed
by the long series of relentless analytical operations to which I subsequently subjected it. Today, after twenty-five years of such experiments,
The Whale is still *the* whale, more magnificent, if anything, than before.

Before coming to grips with the "mystery" of *Moby-Dick* I should
mention another providential circumstance to which all psychologists
are, or should be, forever grateful—and literary critics too, since without
it no complete understanding of books like *Moby-Dick* would be possible
today. Ahead of us were two greatly gifted pioneers, Freud and Jung,
who, with others, explored the manifold vagaries of unconscious mental
processes and left for our inheritance their finely written works. The
discoveries of these adventurers advantaged me in a special way: they
gave, I thought, support to one of Santayana's early convictions, that in
the human being imagination is more fundamental than perception.
Anyhow, adopting this position, some of us psychologists have been devoting ourselves to the study of dreams, fantasies, creative productions,
and projections—all of which are primarily and essentially emotional and
dramatic, such stuff as myths are made of. Thus, by chance or otherwise,
this branch of the tree of psychology is growing in the direction of
Herman Melville.

To be explicit: psychologists have been recognizing in the dream
figures and fantasy figures of today's children and adolescents more and
more family likenesses of the heroes and heroines of primitive myths,
legends, and fables—figures, in other words, who are engaged in comparable heroic strivings and conflicts and are experiencing comparable
heroic triumphs and fatalities. Our ancestors, yielding to an inherent
propensity of the mind, projected the more relevant of these figures into
objects of their environment, into sun, moon, and stars, into the unknown
deeps of the sea and of the earth, and into the boundless void of heaven;

and they worshiped the most potent of these projected images, whether animal or human, as superbeings, gods, or goddesses. On any clear night one can see scores of the more luminous of such divinities parading up and down the firmament. For example, in fall and winter, one looks with admiration on that resplendent hero Perseus and above him the chained beauty Andromeda, whom he saved from a devouring monster, ferocious as Moby-Dick. Now, what psychologists have been learning by degrees is that Perseus is in the unconscious mind of every man and Andromeda in every woman—not, let me hasten to say, as an inherited fixed image, but as a potential set of dispositions which may be constellated in the personality by the occurrence of a certain kind of situation. Herman Melville arrived at this conclusion in his own way a hundred years ago, sooner and, I believe, with more genuine comprehension than any other writer.

An explanation of all this in scientific terms would require all the space permitted me and more. Suffice it to say here that the psychologists who are studying the elementary mythmakings of the mind are dealing with the germy sources of poetry and drama, the fecundities out of which great literature is fashioned. Furthermore, in attempting to formulate and classify these multifarious productions of the imagination, the psychologist uses modes of analysis and synthesis very similar to those that Aristotle used in setting forth the dynamics of Greek tragedy. In these and other trends I find much encouragement for the view that a rapprochement of psychology and literary criticism is in progress, and that it will prove fruitful to both callings. As an ideal meeting ground I would propose Melville's world of "wondrous depths."

To this Columbus of the mind, the great archetypal figures of myth, drama, and epic were not pieces of intellectual Dresden china, heirlooms of a classical education, ornamental bric-a-brac to be put here and there for the pleasure of genteel readers. Many of the more significant of these constellations were inwardly experienced by Melville, one after the other, as each was given vent to blossom and assert itself. Thus we are offered a spectacle of spiritual development through passionate identifications. Only by proceeding in this way could Melville have learned on his pulses what it was to be Narcissus, Orestes, Oedipus, Ishmael, Apollo, Lucifer. "Like a frigate," he said, "I am full with a thousand souls."

This brings me to the problem of interpreting *Moby-Dick*. Some writers have said that there is nothing to interpret: it is a plain sea story marred here and there by irrelevant ruminations. But I shall not cite the abundant proof for the now generally accepted proposition that in *Moby-Dick* Melville "meant" something—something, I should add, which he considered "terrifically true" but which, in the world's judgment, was so harmful "that it were all but madness for any good man, in his own proper character, to utter or even hint of." What seems decisive here is the passage in Melville's celebrated letter to Hawthorne: "A sense of unspeakable security is in me this moment, on account of your having understood the book." From this we can conclude that there *are* meanings to be understood in *Moby-Dick,* and also—may we say for our own encouragement?—that Melville's ghost will feel secure forever if modern critics can find them and, since Hawthorne remained silent, set them forth in print. Here it might be well to remind ourselves of a crucial statement which follows the just quoted passage from Melville's letter: "I have written a wicked book." The implication is clear: all interpretations which fail to show that *Moby-Dick* is, in some sense, wicked have missed the author's avowed intention.

A few critics have scouted all attempts to fish Melville's own meaning out of *The Whale,* on the ground that an interpretation of a work of art so vast and so complex is bound to be composed in large measure of projections from the mind of the interpreter. It must be granted that preposterous projections often do occur in the course of such an effort. But these are not inevitable. Self-knowledge and discipline may reduce projections to a minimum. Anyhow, in the case of *Moby-Dick,* the facts do not sustain the proposition that a critic can see nothing in this book but his own reflected image. The interpretations which have been published over the last thirty years exhibit an unmistakable trend toward consensus in respect to the drama as a whole as well as to many of its subordinate parts. Moreover, so far as I can judge, the critics who, with hints from their predecessors, applied their intuitions most recently to the exegesis of *The Whale* can be said to have arrived, if taken together, at Melville's essential meaning. Since one or another of these authors has deftly said what I clumsily thought, my prejudices are strongly in favor of their conclusions, and I am wholehearted in applauding them—Newton Arvin's most especially—despite their having left me with nothing fresh to say. Since this is how things stand, my version of the main theme of *Moby-Dick* can be presented in a briefer form, and limited to two hypotheses.

The first of them is this: Captain Ahab is an embodiment of that fallen angel or demi-god who in Christendom was variously named Lucifer, Devil, Adversary, Satan. The Church Fathers would have called Captain Ahab "Antichrist" because he was not Satan himself, but a human creature possessed of all Satan's pride and energy, "summing up within himself," as Irenaeus said, "the apostasy of the devil."

That it was Melville's intention to beget Ahab in Satan's image can hardly be doubted. He told Hawthorne that his book had been broiled in hellfire and secretly baptized not in the name of God but in the name of the Devil. He named his tragic hero after the Old Testament ruler who "did more to provoke the Lord God of Israel to anger than all the Kings of Israel that were before him." King Ahab's accuser, the prophet Elijah, is also resurrected to play his original role, though very briefly, in Melville's testament. We are told that Captain Ahab is an "ungodly, godlike" man who is spiritually outside Christendom. He is a well of blasphemy and defiance, of scorn and mockery for the gods—"cricket-players and pugilists" in his eyes. Rumor has it that he once spat in the holy goblet on the altar of the Catholic Church at Santa. "I never saw him kneel," says Stubb. He is associated in the text with scores of references to the Devil. He is an "anaconda of an old man." His self-assertive sadism is the linked antithesis of the masochistic submission preached by Father Mapple.

Captain Ahab-Lucifer is also related to a sun god, like Christ, but in reverse. Instead of being light leaping out of darkness, he is "darkness leaping out of light." The *Pequod* sails on Christmas Day. *This* new year's sun will be the god of Wrath rather than the god of Love. Ahab does not emerge from his subterranean abode until his ship is "rolling through the bright Quito spring" (Eastertide, symbolically, when the all-fertilizing sun god is resurrected). The frenzied ceremony in which Ahab's followers are sworn to the pursuit of the White Whale—"Commend the murderous chalices!"—is suggestive of the Black Mass; the lurid operations at the tryworks is a scene out of Hell.

There is some evidence that Melville was rereading *Paradise Lost* in the summer of 1850, shortly after, let us guess, he got the idea of transforming the captain of his whale ship into the first of all cardinal sinners who fell by pride. Anyhow, Melville's Satan is the spitting image of Milton's hero, but portrayed with deeper and subtler psychological insight, and placed where he belongs, in the heart of an enraged man.

Melville may have been persuaded by Goethe's Mephistopheles, or even by some of Hawthorne's bloodless abstracts of humanity, to add Fedallah to his cast of characters. Evidently he wanted to make certain that no reader would fail to recognize that Ahab had been possessed by, or had sold his soul to, the Devil. Personally, I think Fedallah's role is superfluous, and I regret that Melville made room for him and his unbelievable boat crew on the ship *Pequod.* Still, he is not wholly without interest. He represents the cool, heartless, cunning, calculating, intellectual Devil of the medieval mythmakers, in contrast to the stricken, passionate, indignant, and often eloquent rebel angel of *Paradise Lost,* whose role is played by Ahab.

The Arabic name "Fedallah" suggests "dev(il) Allah," that is, the Mohammedans' god as he appeared in the mind's eye of a Crusader. But we are told that Fedallah is a Parsee—a Persian fire worshiper, or Zoroastrian, who lives in India. Thus, Ahab, named after the Semitic apostate who was converted to the orgiastic cult of Baal, or Bel, originally a Babylonian fertility god, has formed a compact with a Zoroastrian whose name reminds us of still another Oriental religion. In addition, Captain Ahab's whaleboat is manned by a crew of unregenerated infidels, as defined by orthodox Christianity; and each of his three harpooners, Queequeg, Tashtego, and Daggoo, is a member of a race which believed in other gods than the one god of the Hebraic-Christian Bible.

Speaking roughly, it might be said that Captain Ahab, incarnation of the Adversary and master of the ship *Pequod* (named after the aggressive Indian tribe that was exterminated by the Puritans of New England), has summoned the various religions of the East to combat the one dominant religion of the West. Or, in other terms, that he and his followers, Starbuck excepted, represent the horde of primitive drives, values, beliefs, and practices which the Hebraic-Christian religionists rejected and excluded, and by threats, punishments, and inquisitions forced into the unconscious mind of Western man.

Stated in psychological concepts, Ahab is captain of the culturally repressed dispositions of human nature, that part of personality which psychoanalysts have termed the "Id." If this is true, his opponent, the White Whale, can be none other than the internal institution which is responsible for these repressions, namely the Freudian Superego. This, then, is my second hypothesis; Moby-Dick is a veritable spouting, breaching, sounding whale, a whale who, because of his whiteness, his mighty bulk and beauty, and because of one instinctive act that happened to dismember his assailant, has received the projection of Captain Ahab's Presbyterian conscience, and so may be said to embody the Old Testament Calvinistic conception of an affrighting Deity and his strict commandments, the derivative Puritan ethic of nineteenth-century America and the society that defended this ethic. Also, and most specifically, he symbolizes the zealous parents whose righteous sermonizings and corrections drove the prohibitions in so hard that a serious young man could hardly reach outside the barrier, except possibly far away among some tolerant, gracious Polynesian peoples. The emphasis should be placed on that unconscious (and hence inscrutable) wall of inhibition which imprisoned the Puritan's thrusting passions. "How can the prisoner reach outside," cries Ahab, "except by thrusting through the wall? To me, the white whale is that wall, shoved near to me . . . I see in him outrageous strength, with an inscrutable malice sinewing it." As a symbol of a sounding, breaching, white-dark, unconquerable New England conscience what could be better than a sounding, breaching, white-dark, unconquerable sperm whale?

Who is the psychoanalyst who could resist the immediate inference that the *imago* of the mother as well as the *imago* of the father is contained in the Whale? In the present case there happens to be a host of biographical facts and written passages which support this proposition. Luckily, I need not review them, because Mr. Arvin and others have come to the same conclusion. I shall confine myself to one reference. It exhibits Melville's keen and sympathetic insight into the cultural determinants of his mother's prohibiting dispositions. In *Pierre*, it is the "high-up, and towering and all-forbidding . . . edifice of his mother's immense pride . . . her pride of birth . . . her pride of purity," that is the "wall shoved near," the wall that stands between the hero and the realization of his heart's resolve. But instead of expending the fury of frustration upon his mother, he directs it at Fate, or, more specifically, at his mother's God and the society that shaped her. For he sees "that not his mother has made his mother; but the Infinite Haughtiness had first fashioned her; and then the haughty world had further molded her; nor had a haughty Ritual omitted to finish her."

Given this penetrating apprehension, we are in a position to say that Melville's target in *Moby-Dick* was the upper-middle-class culture of his time. It was *this* culture which was defended with righteous indignation by what he was apt to call "the world" or "the public," and Melville had very little respect for "the world" or "the public." The "public," or men operating as a social system, was something quite distinct from "the people." In *White-Jacket* he wrote: "The public and the people! . . . let us hate the one, and cleave to the other." "The public is a monster," says Lemsford. Still earlier Melville had said: "I fight against the armed and crested lies of Mardi (the world)." "Mardi is a monster whose eyes are fixed in its head, like a whale." Many other writers have used similar imagery. Sir Thomas Browne referred to the multitude as "that numerous piece of monstrosity." Keats spoke of "the dragon world." But closest of all was Hobbes: "By art is created that great Leviathan, called a commonwealth or state." It is in the laws of this Leviathan, Hobbes made clear, that the sources of right and wrong reside. To summarize: the giant mass of Melville's whale is the same as Melville's man-of-war world, the *Neversink*, in *White-Jacket*, which in turn is an epitome of Melville's Mardi. The Whale's white forehead and hump should be reserved for the world's heavenly King.

That God is incarnate in the Whale has been perceived by Geoffrey Stone, and, as far as I know, by every other Catholic critic of Melville's work, as well as by several Protestant critics. In fact, Richard Chase has marshaled so fair a portion of the large bulk of evidence on this point that any more from me would be superfluous. Of course, what Ahab projects into the Whale is not the image of a loving Father, but the God of the Old Dispensation, the God who brought Jeremiah into darkness, hedged him about, and made his path crooked; the God adopted by the fire-and-brimstone Puritans, who said: "With fury poured out I will rule over you." "The sword without and the terror within, shall destroy both the young man and the virgin." "I will also send the teeth of beasts upon them." "I will heap mischiefs upon them." "To me belongeth vengeance and recompense."

Since the society's vision of deity, and the society's morality, and the parents and ministers who implant these conceptions, are represented in a fully socialized personality by an establishment that is called the Superego—conscience as Freud defined it—and since Ahab has been proclaimed the "Captain of the Id," the simplest psychological formula for Melville's dramatic epic is this: an insurgent Id in mortal conflict with an oppressive cultural Superego. Starbuck, the first mate, stands for the rational realistic Ego, which is overpowered by the fanatical compulsiveness of the Id and dispossessed of its normal regulating functions.

If this is approximately correct, it appears that while writing his greatest work Melville abandoned his detached position in the Ego from time to time, hailed "the realm of shades," as his hero Taji had, and, through the mediumship of Ahab, "burst his hot heart's shell" upon the sacrosanct Almighty and the sacrosanct sentiments of Christendom. Since in the world's judgment, in 1851, nothing could be more reproachable than this, it would be unjust, if not treacherous, of us to reason *Moby-Dick* into some comforting morality play for which no boldness was required. This would be depriving Melville of the ground he gained for self-respect by having dared to abide by his own subjective truth and write a "wicked book," the kind of book that Pierre's publishers, Steel, Flint, and Asbestos, would have called "a blasphemous rhapsody filched from the vile Atheists, Lucian and Voltaire."

Some may wonder how it was that Melville, a fundamentally good, affectionate, noble, idealistic, and reverential man, should have felt impelled to write a wicked book. Why did he aggress so furiously against Western orthodoxy, as furiously as Byron and Shelley, or any Satanic writer who preceded him, as furiously as Nietzsche or the most radical of his successors in our day?

In *Civilization and Its Discontents* Freud, out of the ripeness of his full experience, wrote that when one finds deep-seated aggression—and by this he meant aggression of the sort that Melville voiced—one can safely attribute it to the frustration of Eros. In my opinion this generalization does not hold for all men of all cultures of all times, but the probability of its being valid is extremely high in the case of an earnest, moralistic nineteenth-century American, a Presbyterian to boot, whose anger is born of suffering—especially if this man spent an impressionable year of his life in Polynesia and returned to marry the very proper little daughter of the chief justice of Massachusetts, and if, in addition, he is a profoundly creative man in whose androgynic personality masculine and feminine components are integrally blended.

If it were concerned with *Moby-Dick,* the book, rather than with its author, I would call *this* my third hypothesis: Ahab-Melville's aggression was directed against the object that once harmed Eros with apparent malice and was still thwarting it with presentiments of further retaliations. The correctness of this inference is indicated by the nature of the injury—a symbolic emasculation—that excited Ahab's ire. Initially, this threatening object was, in all likelihood, the father; later, possibly, the mother. But, as Melville plainly saw, both his parents had been fashioned by the Hebraic-Christian, American Calvinistic tradition, the tradition which conceived of a deity in whose eyes Eros was depravity. It was the first Biblical mythmakers who dismissed from heaven and from earth the Great Goddess of the Oriental and primitive religions, and so rejected the feminine principle as a spiritual force. Ahab, protagonist of those rejected religions, in addressing heaven's fire and lightning, what he calls "the personified impersonal," cries: "but thou art my fiery father; my sweet mother I know not. Oh, cruel! What hast thou done with her?" He calls this god a foundling, a "hermit immemorial," who does not know his own origin. Again, it was the Hebraic authors, sustained later by the Church Fathers, who propagated the legend that a woman was the cause of Adam's exile from Paradise, and that the original sin was concupiscence. Melville says that Ahab, spokesman of all exiled princes, "piled upon the whale's white hump the sum of all the general rage and hate felt by his whole race from Adam down." Remember also that it was the lure of Jezebel that drew King Ahab of Israel outside the orthodoxy of his religion and persuaded him to worship the Phoenician Astarte, goddess of love and fruitful increase. "Jezebel" was the worst tongue-lash a Puritan could give a woman. She was sex, and sex was Sin, spelled with a capital. It was the church periodicals of Melville's day that denounced *Typee,* called the author a sensualist, and influenced the publishers to delete suggestive passages from the second edition. It was this long heritage of aversion and animosity, so accentuated in this country, which banned sex relations as a topic of discourse and condemned divorce as an unpardonable offense. All this has been changed, for better and for worse, by the moral revolutionaries of our own time who, feeling as Melville felt but finding the currents of sentiment less strongly opposite, spoke out, and with their wit, indignation, and logic, reinforced by the findings of psychoanalysis, disgraced the stern-faced idols of their forebears. One result is this: today an incompatible marriage is not a prison-house, as it was for Melville, "with wall shoved near."

In *Pierre* Melville confessed his own faith when he said that Eros is god of all, and Love "the loftiest religion on this earth." To the romantic Pierre the image of Isabel was "a silent and tyrannical call, challenging him in his deepest moral being, and summoning Truth, Love, Pity, Conscience to the stand." Here he seems to have had in mind the redeeming and inspiriting Eros of courtly love, a heresy which the medieval church had done its utmost to stamp out. *This,* he felt convinced, was *his* "path to God," although in the way of it he saw with horror the implacable conscience and worldly valuations of his revered mother.

If this line of reasoning is as close as I think it is to the known facts, then Melville, in the person of Ahab, assailed Calvinism in the Whale because it blocked the advance of a conscience beneficent to evolutionary love. And so, weighed in the scales of its creator, *Moby-Dick* is not a wicked book but a *good* book, and after finishing it Melville had full reason to feel, as he confessed, "spotless as the lamb."

But then, seen from another point, *Moby-Dick* might be judged a wicked book, not because its hero condemns an entrenched tradition, but because he is completely committed to destruction. Although Captain Ahab manifests the basic stubborn virtues of the arch-protestant and the rugged individualist carried to their limits, *this* god-defier is no Prometheus, since all thought of benefiting humanity is foreign to him. His purpose is not to make the Pacific safe for whaling, nor, when blasting at the moral order, does he have in mind a more heartening vision for the future. The religion of Eros which might once have been the secret determinant of Ahab's undertaking is never mentioned. At one critical point in *Pierre* the hero-author, favored by a flash of light, exclaims, "I will gospelize the world anew"; but he never does. Out of light comes darkness: the temper of Pierre's book is no different from the temper of *Moby-Dick*. The truth is that Ahab is motivated by his private need to avenge a private insult. His governing philosophy is that of nihilism, the doctrine that the existing system must be shattered. Nihilism springs up when the imagination fails to provide the redeeming solution of an unbearable dilemma, when "the creative response," as Toynbee would say, is not forthcoming, and a man reacts out of a hot heart—"to the dogs with the head"—and swings to an instinct, "the same that prompts even a worm to turn under the heel." This is what White-Jacket did when arraigned at the mast, and what Pierre did when fortune deserted him, and what Billy Budd did when confronted by his accuser. "Nature has not implanted any power in man," said Melville,

that was not meant to be exercised at times, though too often our powers have been abused. The privilege, inborn, and inalienable, that every man has, of dying himself and inflicting death upon another, was not given to us without a purpose. These are the last resources of an insulted and unendurable existence.

If we grant that Ahab is a wicked man, what does this prove? It proves that *Moby-Dick* is a *good* book, a parable in epic form, because Melville makes a great spectacle of Ahab's wickedness and shows through the course of the narrative how such wickedness will drive a man on iron rails to an appointed nemesis. Melville adhered to the classic formula for tragedies. He could feel "spotless as the lamb," because he had seen to it that the huge threat to the social system immanent in Ahab's two cardinal defects—egotistic self-inflation and unleashed wrath—was, at the end, fatefully exterminated, "and the great shroud of the sea rolled on as it rolled five thousand years ago." The reader has had his catharsis, equilibrium has been restored, sanity is vindicated.

This is true, but is it the whole truth? In point of fact, while writing *Moby-Dick* did Melville maintain aesthetic distance, keeping his own feelings in abeyance? Do we not hear Ahab saying things that the later Pierre will say and that Melville says less vehemently in his own person? Does not the author show marked partiality for the "mighty pageant creature" of his invention, put in *his* mouth the finest, boldest language? Also, have not many interpreters been so influenced by the abused Ahab that they saw nothing in his opponent but the source of all malicious agencies, the very Devil? As Lewis Mumford has said so eloquently, Ahab is at heart a noble being whose tragic wrong is that of battling against evil with "power instead of love," and so becoming "the image of the thing he hates." With this impression imbedded in our minds, how can we come out with any moral except this: evil wins. We admit that Ahab's wickedness has been canceled. But what survives? It is the much more formidable, compacted wickedness of the group that survives, the world that is "saturated and soaking with lies," and its man-of-war God, who is hardly more admirable than a primitive totem beast, some oral-aggressive, child-devouring Cronos of the sea. Is this an idea that a man of good will can rest with?

Rest with? Certainly not. Melville's clear intention was to bring not rest, but *unrest* to intrepid minds. All gentle people were warned away from his book "on risk of a lumbago or sciatica." "A polar wind blows through it," he announced. He had not written to soothe, but to kindle, to make men leap from their seats, as Whitman would say, and fight for their lives. Was it the poet's function to buttress the battlements of complacency, to give comfort to the enemy? There is little doubt about the nature of the enemy in Melville's day. It was the dominant ideology, that peculiar compound of puritanism and materialism, of rationalism and commercialism, of shallow, blatant optimism and technology, which proved so crushing to creative evolutions in religion, art, and life. In such circumstances every "true poet," as Blake said, "is of the Devil's party," whether he knows it or not. Surveying the last hundred and fifty years, how many exceptions to this statement can we find? Melville, anyhow, knew that *he* belonged to the party, and while writing *Moby-Dick* so gloried in his membership that he baptized his work *In Nomine Diaboli*. It was precisely under these auspices that he created his solitary masterpiece, a construction of the same high order as the Constitution of the United States and the scientific treatises of Willard Gibbs, though huge and wild and unruly as the Grand Canyon. And it is for this marvel chiefly that he resides in our hearts now among the greatest in "that small but high-hushed world" of bestowing geniuses.

The drama is finished. What of its author?

Moby-Dick may be taken as a comment on the strategic crisis of Melville's allegorical life. In portraying the consequences of Ahab's last suicidal lunge, the hero's umbilical fixation to the Whale and his death by strangling, the author signalized not only his permanent attachment to the imago of the mother, but the submission he had foreseen to the binding power of the parental conscience, the Superego of middle-class America. Measured against the standards of *his* day, then, Melville must be accounted a *good* man.

But does this entitle him to a place on the side of the angels? He abdicated to the conscience he condemned, and his ship *Pequod,* in sinking, carried down with it the conscience he aspired to, represented by the skyhawk, the bird of heaven. With his ideal drowned, life from then on was load, and time stood still. All he had denied to love he gave, throughout a martyrdom of forty years, to death.

But "hark ye yet again—the little lower layer." Melville's capitulation in the face of overwhelming odds was limited to the sphere of action. His embattled soul refused surrender and lived on, breathing back defiance, disputing "to the last gasp" of his "earthquake life" the sovereignty of that inscrutable authority in him. As he wrote in *Pierre,* unless the enthusiast "can find the talismanic secret, to reconcile this world with his own soul, then there is no peace for him, no slightest truce for him in this life." Years later we find him holding the same ground. "Terrible is earth" was his conclusion, but despite all, "no retreat through me." By this stand he bequeathed to us the unsolved problem of the talismanic secret.

Only at the very last, instinct spent, earthquake over, did he fall back to a position close to Christian resignation. In his Being, was not this man "a wonder, a grandeur, and a woe"?

II

Personology is a complex,
lifelong, never-ending enterprise

*A*lmost every theorist has to be a neologizer—a coiner of words—or, at the least, if he does not create new words for his theory, he needs to use ordinary dictionary words in new ways or with unusual frequencies or emphasis. Consider for a moment what is special about the language, the "key words" of Freud, Darwin, Einstein, Marx, Cuvier, or Linnaeus. So with Murray, one needs to become acquainted with the sound and meaning of the special vocabulary with which he expresses his special thoughts. That lexicon of new and old words includes such terms as: needs, press, themas, regnancy, actone, consciousness, unconscious, ego, durance, proaction, imaginal processes, serials, narcism, Icarian complex, diagnostic council, and (most important of all) personology.

On the first page of his pioneer Explorations, Murray states his mission clearly—"personalities constitute the subject matter for psychology, the life history of a single man being a unit with which this discipline has to deal"—and launches into the most important journey of his intellectual life by providing a new designation for his efforts. He says that "the study of human beings and the factors that influence their course . . . may be termed 'personology' instead of 'the psychology of personality,' a clumsy and tautological expression." Personology is psychology or, at the least, what psychology ought to be about. (In a footnote, Murray states that personology "is what all men, except professional psychologists, call psychology." But Murray does not wish to have that term associated with his name alone, as though it were "his."

As early in the book as the second page, Murray declares his overarching goals for his enterprise: "nothing less than (1) to construct methodically a theory of personality; (2) to devise techniques for getting at some of the more important attributes of personality; and (3) by a study of the lives of many individuals to discover basic facts of personality." His next sentence contains an important clue as to what is special about his approach: "Our guiding thought was that a personality is a temporal whole, and to understand a part of it one must have a sense, though vague, of the totality." A little further on, he states this notion in an aphorism: "The history of the organism is the organism." In 1938, *at the age of forty-five—in the middle of his life—Murray boldly launched his new theory.*

When Explorations *first appeared, one early review (in the* Quarterly Review of Biology*) called it "the most original, thorough-going, and systematic attempt at a consistently scientific appraisal and understanding of human personality that has yet been made. . . . it is a contribution belonging in the absolutely first rank of significance." Almost a half-century later—the fortieth anniversary of the publication of* Explorations *was celebrated by a special symposium at the 1978 convention of the American Psychological Association—that book is still* the book, *ranking with William James's* Principles of Psychology *as one of the half-dozen most important works in American psychology.*

Murray's close association with Clyde Kluckhohn, the famed Harvard anthropologist, was enormously important to Murray; and he was happy to co-edit Personality in Nature, Society, and Culture *with him. The first chapter is an outline of "a dynamic organismic conception of personality," which they begin, typically enough, by discussing the difficulties of such a conceptualization. The body of that chapter lies in their detailed discussion of the functions of personality: tension reduction, self-expression, reduction of conflicts, among others. Chapter Two begins with the declaration "Every man is in certain respects (a) like all other men, (b) like some other men, [and] (c) like no other man." The chapter discusses the several determinants of personality formation, "keeping steadily in mind the variety of forces operative in personality formation and the firm but subtle nexus that links them."*

The last two pieces in this section show the progression of Murray's thought and the changes (with the press *of* Time*) in his style, specifically that he becomes more inclusive in his conceptualizations and more telegraphic in his communication. It is interesting to note that they were written about a decade apart, in 1968 and 1977.*

The "Components" paper, written when Murray was seventy-five, shows the strain of constraint—the constraint of having been alloted a frustratingly limited number of pages in the encyclopedia in which that piece appeared. At times, he seems almost to be writing in scientific shorthand.

The 1977 paper, written at age eighty-four, is a pithy résumé. Consider the progression of the titles of Murray's pieces over the long span of his life: Explorations in Personality *(1938);* Outline of a conception of personality *(1953);* Preparations for the scaffold of a comprehensive system *(1959);* Components of an evolving personological system *(1968);* Indispensables for the Making, Testing, and Remaking of a Personologi-

cal System (1977); and finally, the title he chose for this book: Endeavors in Psychology *(1981).*

Just as a person, a human personality, is a dynamic history of a complex organization, so too is personology—the science of the study of personalities—dynamic and complex. Certainly for its originator personology has been a lifelong, never-ending enterprise, as it would legitimately be for any serious personologist.

5

INTRODUCTION TO
EXPLORATIONS IN PERSONALITY

Man is today's great problem. What can we know about him and how can
it be said in words that have clear meaning? What propels him? With
what environmental objects and institutions does he interact and how?
What occurrences in his body are most influentially involved? What
mutually dependent processes participate in his differentiation and development? What courses of events determine his pleasures and displeas-
ures? And, finally, by what means can he be intentionally transformed?
These are antique questions, to be sure, which in all ages have invited
interest, but today they more insistently demand solution and more men
are set for the endeavor. There is greater zest and greater promise of
fulfillment.

The point of view adopted in this book is that personalities constitute
the subject matter of psychology, the life history of a single man being
a unit with which this discipline has to deal. It is not possible to study all
human beings or all experiences of one human being. The best that can
be done is to select representative or specially significant events for
analysis and interpretation. Some psychologists may prefer to limit themselves to the study of one kind of episode. For instance, they may study
the responses of a great number of individuals to a specific situation.
They may attempt to discover what changes in the situation bring about
important changes in response. But, since every response is partially
determined by the after-effects of previous experiences, the psychologist
will never fully understand an episode if he abstracts it from ontogeny,
the developmental history of the individual. Even philogeny, or racial
history, may have to be considered. The prevailing custom in psychology
is to study one function or one aspect of an episode at a time—perception, emotion, intellection or behavior—and this is as it must be. The
circumscription of attention is dictated by the need for detailed information. But the psychologist who does this should recognize that he is
observing merely a part of an operating totality, and that this totality, in
turn, is but a small temporal segment of a personality. Psychology must

From Henry A. Murray (with staff), *Explorations in Personality*. New York: Oxford University Press, 1938. Chapter One, Introduction, pp. 3–35.

construct a scheme of concepts for portraying the entire course of individual development, and thus provide a framework into which any single episode—natural or experimental—may be fitted.

The branch of psychology which principally concerns itself with the study of human lives and the factors that influence their course, which investigates individual differences and types of personality, may be termed "personology" instead of "the psychology of personality," a clumsy and tautological expression.*

Personology, then, is the science of men, taken as gross units, and by definition it encompasses "psychoanalysis" (Freud), "analytical psychology" (Jung), "individual psychology" (Adler), and other terms which stand for methods of inquiry or doctrines rather than realms of knowledge.

In its intentions our endeavor was excessively ambitious. For we purposed nothing less than (1) to construct methodically a *theory* of personality; (2) to devise *techniques* for getting at some of the more important attributes of personality; and (3) by a study of the lives of many individuals to discover basic *facts* of personality. Our guiding thought was that personality is a temporal whole and to understand a part of it one must have a sense, though vague, of the totality. It was for this that we attempted comprehensiveness, despite the danger that in trying to grasp everything we might be left with nothing worth the having.

We judged the time had come when systematic, full-length studies of individuals could be made to bring results. And more than this, indeed, it seemed a necessary thing to do. For if the constituent processes of personality are mutually dependent, then one must know a lot to comprehend a little, and to know a lot that may be used for understanding, good methods must be systematically employed. In our attempt to envisage and portray the general course of a person's life, we selected for analysis certain happenings along the way and, using these as points, made free drawings of the connecting paths. We judged that the spaces without definition would attract attention and it would become more evident than it has been in what quarters detailed research might yield important facts. For without some notion of the whole there can be no assurance that the processes selected for intensive study are significant constituents.

Actually, the scheme of concepts we employed was not exhaustive; one reason being the inability of the mind to hold so many novel generalities in readiness. The amount of space and time and the number of examiners available put a limit to the number of experimental subjects and the number of techniques that could be used. Thus, in the end, our

*Some have objected that personology, as here defined, is what all men, except professional psychologists, call psychology. Since it has to do with life histories of individuals (the largest unit), it must be the most inclusive, other types of psychology being specialties or branches of it. This view, however, is not generally accepted.

practices and theories were not as comprehensive as we thought they could and should be.

Since in the execution of our plan we went from theory down to fact, then back to theory and down to fact again, the book may be regarded either as a scheme of elementary formulations conceived of to explain the ways of different individuals, or as an assemblage of biographic data organized according to a certain frame of reference.

The Present State of Personology

It might be thought that a number of psychologists from the same or different universities, assembling in any suitably equipped clinic, could, after apportioning their work, become engaged without delay in a collaborative study of any group of normal individuals. This could occur in clinical medicine but not by any good fortune in psychology. For in psychology there are few generally valued tests, no traits that are always measured, no common guiding concepts. Some psychologists make precise records of their subjects' overt movements, others inquire into sentiments and theories. Some use physiological techniques, others present batteries of questionnaires. Some record dreams and listen for hours to free associations, others note attitudes in social situations. These different methods yield data which, if not incommensurate, are, at least, difficult to organize into one construction. There is no agreement as to what traits or variables are significant. A psychologist who embarks upon a study of normal personality feels free to look for anything he pleases. He may test for intelligence, or note signs of introversion-extraversion, he may focus on inferiority and compensation, or use the cycloid-schizoid frame of reference, or look for the character traits of pre-genital fixation, or measure his subjects for ascendance and submission; but he will not feel bound to any particular order of examinations, since there is no plan that custom has accredited. It must be acknowledged that personology is still in diapers enjoying random movements. The literature is full of accurate observations of particular events, statistical compilations, and brilliant flashes of intuition. But taken as a whole, personology is a patchwork quilt of incompatible designs. In this domain men speak with voices of authority saying different things in different tongues, and the expectant student is left to wonder whether one or none are in the right.

A little order is brought out of this confusion—though somewhat arbitrarily—by dividing psychologists into two large classes holding opposite conceptual positions. One group may be called *peripheralists,* the other *centralists.* The peripheralists have an objectivistic inclination, that is, they are attracted to clearly observable things and qualities—simple deliverances of sense organs—and they usually wish to confine the data of personology to these. They stand upon the acknowledged fact that, as compared to other functions, the perceptions—particularly the visual perceptions—of different individuals are relatively similar, and hence agreement on this basis is attainable. Agreement, it is pointed out, is common among trained observers when interpretations are excluded, and since without agreement there is no science, they believe that if they stick to measurable facts they are more likely to make unquestionable contributions. Thus, for them the data are: environmental objects and physically responding organisms: bodily movements, verbal successions, physiological changes. That they confine themselves to such events distinguishes them from members of the other class, but what characterizes them particularly is their insistence upon limiting their concepts to symbols which stand directly for the facts observed. In this respect they are *positivists.* Now, since we are reasonably certain that all phenomena within the domain of personology are determined by excitations in the brain, the things which are objectively discernible—the outer environment, bodily changes, muscular movements and so forth—are peripheral to the personality proper and hence those who traffic only with the former may be called *peripheralists.* If the peripheralists ever do indulge in speculations about what goes on within the brain, they usually fall back upon the conceptual scheme which has been found efficient in dealing with simpler partial functions. They resort to *mechanistic* or physiological explanations. Men of this stamp who study people usually come out with a list of common action patterns or expressive movements, though occasionally they go further and include social traits and interests. Such a man is apt, at least implicitly, to agree with Watson that "personality is the sum total of the habitual responses." This is one variety of the doctrine of elementarism. To repeat, the man we are distinguishing is a *peripheralist* because he defines personality in terms of action *qua* action rather than in terms of some central process which the action manifests, and he is an *elementarist* because he regards personality as the sum total or product of interacting elements rather than a unity which may, for convenience, be analyzed into parts. Furthermore, the implicit supposition of this class of scientists is that an external stimulus, or the perception of it, is the origination of everything psychological. For them, the organism is at the start an inert, passive, though receptive, aggregate, which only acts in response to outer stimulation. From the point of view of consciousness, as Locke would have it, mind is at first a sensorium innocent of imprints which, as time goes on, receives sensations from external objects and combines them variously, according to objective contiguities and similarities, to form ideas and ideologies. Those who hold this view are called *sensationists.*

In contrast to these varieties of scientists are a heterogeneous group, the *centralists.* The latter are especially attracted to subjective facts of emotional or purposive significance: feelings, desires, intentions. They are *centralists* because they are primarily concerned with the governing processes in the brain. And to these they think they are led directly by listening to the form and content of other people's speech. Their terminology is subjectively derived. For instance, to portray a personality they do not hesitate to use such terms as wishes, emotions and ideas. Though most of them make efforts to observe behavior accurately, interpretation usually merges with perception, and overt actions are immediately referred to psychic impulses. Since the latter are intangible, personologists must imagine them. Hence, men of this complexion are *conceptualists* rather than positivists; and further, in so far as they believe that personality is a complex unity, of which each function is merely a partially distinguished integral, they are *totalists,* naturally inclined to doctrines of immanence and emergence. Craving to know the inner nature of other persons as they know their own, they have often felt their wish was realized, not by making conscious inferences from items of observation but by an unanalyzable act of empathic intuition. For this, perceptions, naturally, are necessary, but the observer is only dimly aware of the specific sensa which were configurated to suggest the underlying feeling or intention of the subject's momentary self. So hold the *intuitionists.* Finally, as opposed to the *sensationists* are the *dynamicists,* who ascribe action to inner forces—drives, urges, needs, or instincts —some of which, inherited or suddenly emerging, may be held accountable for the occurrence of motility without external stimulation. These inner energies of which the personality may be wholly unaware seem to influence perception, apperception, and intellection. The more or less mechanical laws of the sensationists are only true, it is believed, when a passive, disinterested attitude is adopted by the subject. But under most conditions, attention and conceptualization are directed by wants and feelings.

These two general classes of psychologists are heterogeneous. It is only certain underlying similarities which prompt us to put in one class peripheralists, objectivists, positivists, mechanists, elementarists, and sensationists; and to put in another centralists, subjectivists, conceptualists, totalists, and dynamicists. It is clear that a psychologist may belong in certain respects to one class and in others to another. For instance, some psychologists are eclectic, others vaguely hold a middle ground, still others attempt with more or less success to encompass both positions. Then there are those whose natural temper is emotionally subjective but who come to adopt, for their own equilibration, the extreme behavioristic point of view. These are the holy zealots, the modern puritans of science. Mixtures and contrasts of this sort are not uncommon, but in the main the two classes are distinguishable.

The peripheralists are mostly academic men addicted to the methodology of science. Being chiefly interested in what is measurable, they are forced to limit themselves to relatively unimportant fragments of the personality or to the testing of specific skills. The aim is to get figures that may be worked statistically.*

Among the centralists one finds psychologists of the "hormic" school, psychoanalysts, physicians, and social philosophers. These have no stomach for experiments conducted in an artificial laboratory atmosphere. They feel no compulsion to count and measure. Their concern is man enmeshed in his environment; his ambitions, frustrations, apprehensions, rages, joys and miseries.

In summary, it may be said that the peripheralists are apt to emphasize the physical patterns of overt behavior, the combination of simple reflexes to form complex configurations, the influence of the tangible environment, sensations and their compounds, intellections, social attitudes, traits, and vocational pursuits. The centralists, on the other hand, stress the directions or ends of behavior, underlying instinctual forces, inherited dispositions, maturation and inner transformations, distortions of perception by wish and fantasy, emotion, irrational or semi-conscious mental processes, repressed sentiments, and the objects of erotic interest.

The divergencies thus briefly catalogued are rarely constant. And they are hardly more apparent than the divergencies within each group, particularly among the centralists. That the centralists should radically disagree in their interpretations is the result of their subjectivistic bias, the opportunities for projection being limitless. For man—the object of concern—is like an ever-varying cloud, and psychologists are like people seeing faces in it. One psychologist perceives along the upper margin the contours of a nose and lip, and then miraculously other portions of the cloud become so oriented in respect to these that the outline of a forward-looking superman appears. Another psychologist is attracted to a lower segment, sees an ear, a nose, a chin, and simultaneously the cloud takes on the aspect of a backward-looking Epimethean. Thus, for each perceiver every sector of the cloud has a different function, name and value—fixed by his initial bias of perception. To be the founder of a school indeed, it is only necessary to see a face along another margin. Not much imagination is required to configurate the whole in terms of it. Such prejudiced conceptions, of course, are not unfruitful. To prove the correctness of their vision—to prove their sanity, one might say—scientists are led to undertake laborious researches. The analysts, for instance, have made wondrous discoveries by pursuing one instinct, observing its

*This may be regarded, perhaps, as one of many manifestations of a general disposition which is widespread in America, namely, to regard the peripheral personality—conduct rather than inner feeling and intention—as of prime importance. Thus, we have the fabrication of a "pleasing personality," mail courses in comportment, courtesy as good business, the best pressed clothes, the best barber shops, Listerine and deodorants, the contact man, friendliness without friendship, the prestige of movie stars and Big Business, quantity as an index of worth, a compulsion for fact-getting, the statistical analysis of everything, questionnaires, and behaviorism.

numerous guises and vagaries. Hunting other trails with like genius and persistence, all the ways of personality may eventually be explored. Though this has proved to be a successful method of advance, the men who follow it are not well balanced intellectually. They are not well balanced because their thoughts are loaded, the favored variable being turned up at every throw. Pursuing a single objective and disregarding numberless concatenations, they abstract too arbitrarily from the fullness of experience and upon one entity lay the full burden of causation.

What Course to Follow?

Now, in view of these divergent trends, what is the proper path to take? Is it possible that some order will emerge if a variety of methods are employed in the exploration of a group of subjects, the best of contemporary theories being judged in respect to their general success in interpreting the findings? In our minds the answer to this question was affirmative. Viewed in this way, our work was an experiment in reconciliation. It was our thought, at least, that if we took account of what appeared to be the most important factors, and succeeded in measuring them approximately, the conceptual distortions which now exist might be rectified to some extent. It might even be possible, by slight modifications here and there, to construct a scheme which would fit together most of the prevailing theories. For a common theory and a common language is for psychology an urgent requisite.

Since science-making is a kind of working for agreement, the psychologic forces which give rise to controversy have been matters of concern to us. For instance, we paid some attention to the factors which determine the creation or adoption of a theory, as well as to those that make adherence lasting. Even among ourselves there were marked differences of outlook which were never satisfactorily combined, though attempts were made by some of us to expose by self-analysis any underlying twists that might be narrowing our perspective. We thought by taking steps to solve the problem of divergence our work might be, at least, the staking out of ground for an orderly development. This we take to be the scientific way—the only way, if the testimony of the last three centuries of practical and theoretical achievement has validity—of progressing toward agreement about "truth." One should begin at the beginning, and the beginning is proper method and accurate observation. We attempted first of all to make records of events as they occurred. These were the *facts,* facts not to be confused with the *theory* that seemed to fit them. In proceeding thus, we were supported by the notion that the ability to observe—though no doubt a minor virtue—may, like the tortoise, in the long run win; and that a slow-witted man with a good method can often succeed where a clever man with a poor one fails. However, to choose this path is one thing, to follow it is another.

Difficulties that Confront the Investigator of Personality

The facts which should be observed in order to obtain a comprehensive view of a particular individual may be classified as follows:

A. OBJECTIVE FACTS

i. The changing conditions of the physical and social environment that are perceptible to the subject.
ii. The changing physiological conditions in the subject's body.*
iii. The trends and action patterns (motor and verbal) of the subject. These may be initiations or responses.
iv. The apparent gratifications (successes) and frustrations (failures) of the subject.

B. SUBJECTIVE FACTS

Reports given by the subject of his perceptions, interpretations, feelings, emotions, intellections, fantasies, intentions and conations.

What difficulties do these phenomena present to those who wish to make a study of them? In answer I shall limit myself to an enumeration of the factors which interfere with accurate and sufficient observation under clinical conditions. In reviewing these factors brief mention will be made of the measures to surmount them that were tried out at the Harvard Clinic.

1. Limitations of Time, of the Variety of Conditions, and of the Number of Experimenters. To know a subject well one must see him many times, and observe or hear about his behavior in many varied situations, when exposed to different treatment by different types of people. In professional studies limits are fixed by the amount of space, the number of experienced examiners and the funds available. In our case, we made a virtue of necessity by deciding that our purpose was to see how much could be discovered in a short time with relatively few sessions and few experimenters, many of whom were inexperienced.

2. Peculiar Effect of the Laboratory Situation. Conditions in a laboratory or in a clinic are, at best, unnatural and artificial, and the subject is constantly reminded that he is being watched and judged. This usually makes him self-conscious and ill at ease, puts him on guard or prompts him to assume a favored role. Though such attitudes are in themselves significant, they may not be indicative of how a man behaves in his accustomed haunts, which is what one most wants to know about. This difficulty was partly overcome by having subjects come to the Clinic off

---

*Since the Harvard Clinic is not equipped for physiological studies, the latter could not be included in the present research.

and on for a long period—time enough for the disappearance of whatever shyness, hostility, or suspiciousness was due merely to the strangeness of the situation. Homelike surroundings and the friendliness of examiners helped to put a subject at his ease. The fact that we respected our subjects and became fond of them may have been the reason why in the main they were so natural, friendly, cooperative, and confiding. This was important, since to discover how a man is apt to act and feel in the ordinary situations of his life, one must rely upon his answers to tactful questions and what he writes about himself.

3. Effect of the Experimenter and the Difficulty of Estimating It. Since in almost every session an experimenter is present, the latter, being of the same order of magnitude, is an intrinsic member of the total situation. It is not that a solitary subject if secretly observed would reveal more of himself, because what one wants revealed is his behavior with one or several human beings. Hence, there should usually be another person present. But the point is that the appearance, attitude, and underlying needs of the other person are variables in the episode under observation and, since in most sessions the other person is none other than the experimenter, the latter must make concurrent judgments of himself in these respects, and this is not so easy. The difficulty was diminished to some extent by having experimenters trained in self-awareness and, as we did in two sessions, by having a concealed observer judging the attitude and actions of both subject and experimenter.

4. Limitations of Perceptual Ability. Since reality is a process and the organism, as well as its environment, is changing every moment, only a small fraction of what occurs may be attended to, apprehended, and retained in memory. This is because one's perceptual functions are, by nature, deficient in respect to speed and span. The limitation here may sometimes be partially surmounted by increasing the number of examiners or using various mechanical devices: a moving-picture camera, speech-recording or movement-recording instruments, appliances to measure physiological changes, and the like.

5. Limitations of Apperceptual Ability. Here we refer to deficiencies in the ability to *interpret* behavior. *Interpreting* directional or purposive activity is so difficult that some psychologists, in the hope of obtaining uniformity, have confined themselves to the observation of simple movements. There is more agreement when this is done, but the records thus obtained are psychologically unimportant and cry out for understanding. But it is much more difficult to interpret records of this sort than it is to interpret behavior at the moment of its occurrence. Thus, as we shall maintain in the chapter on the diagnosis of personality, apperception must accompany the original perception. To be sure, this introduces the greatest possibility of error, for the experimenter is required to go "beyond" the facts, facts which, at best, are fragmentary. For instance, he must often—since a fair proportion of acts are not successfully completed—base his diagnosis on the apparent trend (or intention) of the subject's conduct.

The difficulties of diagnosis are diminished to some extent by collecting in advance many common, concrete examples of the overt expression of the tendencies to be studied. But that such guides if taken "literally" may lead to error must be apparent. To illustrate, take the act of "kissing a person." This would undoubtedly be classified as an expression of love or tenderness, and yet we have only to think of Judas Iscariot to recognize that a kiss may mean something else entirely.

6. Unreliability of Subjective Reports. There are many reasons why subjects' memories and introspections are usually incomplete or unreliable. Children perceive inaccurately, are very little conscious of their inner states, and retain fallacious recollections of occurrences. Many adults are hardly better. Their impressions of past events are hazy and have undergone distortion. Many important things have been unconsciously repressed. Insight is lacking. Consequently, even when a subject wants to give a clear portrait of his early life or contemporary feelings he is unable to do so. Over and above this are his needs for privacy, for the concealment of inferiority, his desire for prestige. Thus, he may consciously inhibit some of his sentiments, rationalize or be a hypocrite about others, or only emphasize what a temporary whim dictates. Finally, one is occasionally confronted by out-and-out malingering. So as not to be too frequently deceived as to the reliability of what a subject says, the experimenter must hold in mind, if possible, every limitation and distortion which interferes with accuracy and be always skeptical, though tolerantly so. With most of our subjects there was ground for confidence, and perhaps because we trusted their intentions they were disposed to truthfulness.

7. Variability of the Subject's Personality. In studying a subject over a four-month period it is assumed, as an approximation, that his personality remains *potentially* the same. The sometimes marked inconsistencies that occur are put down to the subject's characteristic range of variability, itself an attribute of personality. In many cases, however, the subject's reactions are not inconsistent; they are determined by factors of which the experimenter is unaware. There is little opportunity, for instance, to discover what daily shocks, victories, joys, and sorrows occur in a subject's life. Sometimes he will volunteer such information and sometimes tactful questioning will draw it out of him, but usually an experimenter is ignorant of the immediately preceding happenings. Thus, many subjects come to a session with an emotional "set," occasioned by an accidental—and to the experimenter unknown—series of circumstances which gives him an uncustomary and evanescent manner and impulsion. This is a difficulty which was partially surmounted by seeing the subjects often over a relatively long period of time, the effect of unusual fortune being thereby minimized. One must consider the possibility, however, that during a four-month term a subject's potential personality may undergo a transformation; to some extent because of his attendance at the clinic. If such occurs, the experimenter is apt to discount it, believing merely that he is "getting to know" the subject better.

8. Limitation in the Number and Variety of Subjects. This becomes a confining factor if an experimenter expects to generalize his conclusions. It is always hazardous to apply what is discovered under certain conditions at a certain time with certain subjects to other conditions, times, and subjects. Due to the preliminary nature of our studies we have not ventured to do this.

As to the variety of subjects examined at the Clinic, all of them, except for our first group of fourteen, were college students, some graduates and some undergraduates. They received remuneration at current prices (forty cents an hour). None of them was financially well-off. None had studied psychology. Since when they applied at the Employment Office none of them knew the nature of the work that would be offered them and since only one applicant refused the offer, there is no ground for believing that our subjects were selected on the basis of a morbid inclination to exhibit themselves. Different sections of the country were represented, different races, and different religions. The staff of the Clinic had the impression that they were dealing with an exceedingly heterogeneous group of men, who resembled each other in only one respect: their willingness to assist the experimenters, even to the extent of revealing their mortifications, failures, and ineptitudes.

9. Inadequate Conceptual Scheme. The experimenter is to a large extent bound by the categories defined and agreed upon before he commences to observe. He is "set," as it were, to perceive one or more of the phenomena which have been listed and nothing else. Thus, if the scheme is limited—as, at present, all schemes must be in personology—the original observations will be limited and much that is important will pass unnoticed. Ideally, the experimenter's mind should be stocked with variables which are well defined, sufficient, and appropriate to every circumstance. But since there is a limit to the number which a man may hold in readiness, a usable list of factors will always be deficient in completeness.

Ideally considered, an abstract biography, or *psychograph* according to our use of this term, would resemble a musical score; and those who knew the signs might, by reading from left to right, follow the entire sequence of events. The analysis and reconstruction of each temporal segment would be represented by appropriate symbols, among which would be found those which portrayed the environmental forces, the subject's inner set, his initiation or response, and the immediate outcome of the interaction. Reading the psychograph, one could apperceive the relations between events and the development of the evolving personality. Such a reconstruction might be taken as the high and distant goal toward which our hesitating steps should be directed.

And now before I close this account of the difficulties that confront the personologist, I should mention one final limitation of any conceptual formulation of a man's experience. It must necessarily do violence to human feelings. It will never satisfy all the needs of anyone and it will surely insult the needs of some. This will be so because it is the substitution of heartless, denotative, referential symbols for the moving immediacy of living. By employing such a scheme, a person's vital moments, once warm and passionately felt, become transformed into a cruelly commonplace formula, which dispossesses them of unique value. The subject himself is stripped and assimilated to a typological category. Much is thereby lost. The discomfort that people feel in the presence of a psychologist is in part the apprehension that they will be catalogued and filed away in his museum of specimens. The artist's representation of an experience, on the other hand, is a reinvocation of the original feeling or of a similar feeling, equally immediate, exciting, and intense. The artist re-creates the "feel" of it, the scientist substitutes the "thought" of it. Passing over the point that many artists are likewise guilty of abstracting (as Norman Douglas's open letter to D. H. Lawrence illustrates), it should be pointed out in rejoinder that the non-sensuous scientific statement—though it may annul aesthetic feeling—does, by portraying relations, make the event intelligible to the understanding, and this is just the result that some men find so thrilling. The emotion has a different texture than that engendered by the artist, but it is for this that the scientist is willing to pay his price, the partial loss of immediate human feeling.

The Need for Hypothetical Formulations

A little reflection upon the general properties of human nature and the special liabilities of error in observing them—reviewed above and minimized, if anything—should chasten what pretensions to authoritative truth we might be tempted to indulge. What must be known is so complex and our instrument for knowing so uncertain. Is it not a vast presumption to believe that this fragmentary consciousness of ours can perceive what is overt and then imagine what lies behind it; behind behavior, as well as behind the mental processes that seek to comprehend behavior, the various and subtly interweaving forces which make up personality? Is not doubt, suspended judgment, skepticism, or utter silence the only dignified and knowledgeable attitude to take? Perhaps, but it is not likely to be taken, for, as history shows, the more complex a problem is and the fewer facts there are, the more inclined man is to voice opinions with conviction. But is conviction necessary or advisable?

The condition of affairs in personology can be illustrated by a diagram. The reader may look at this design and ask himself what kind of human face it represents:

Figure 1

The figure portrays the items—three recorded facts, we may imagine—of a certain person's life. We should like to state the relationship between them in order to "get a picture" of the personality. Shall we say (a) "We do not know"; or shall we say (b) "This is the explanation"; or shall we say (c) "We suggest this hypothesis"?

Figure 2 presents two possible explanations. The dark lines stand for the facts, the light lines represent the imagined factors which, if present, would relate the parts into a more or less intelligible pattern. Interpretations x and y are obviously different, as different, let us say, as the conceptions offered by Ludwig and Freud, respectively, to explain the course of Kaiser Wilhelm's eventful life. Ludwig's biography,[1] one may recall, explains the grandiose ideas of the German ruler as overcompensations for organ inferiority: a withered arm acquired at birth. Freud, however, thinks that the important factor was a withdrawal of mother love "on account of his disability. When the child grew up into a man of great power, he proved beyond all doubt by his behavior that he had never forgiven his mother."[2]

The response of a cautious scientist to *figure* 1 might be (a) "I do not know"; whereas the response of an untrained person is commonly an *assertion* of some kind, (b) *"This* is the explanation" (x or y in *figure* 2).

x

y

Figure 2

A child is also inclined to give such a response, not so much because he has not learned to reason, but because he has not learned to curb articulation of his thought. Piaget, in demonstrating the absence of self-criticism in the pre-logical reasonings of youth, neglected to point out that children lack the necessary facts for arriving at satisfactory explanations. What a child studied by the staff of the Rousseau Institute *does not* say and the trained scientist faced by a situation of similar complexity *does* say is this: "I do not know." The child, much to the satisfaction of the experimentalist, gives voice to his intuitions; whereas the academic thinker, perhaps heedful of his reputation, seldom does. To comprehend an occurrence—that is, to make a verbal picture of the interrelations of its parts—one requires a vast amount of data. Without them, everything is problematical. The child is usually willing to communicate his imaginative flights—often with a certain facetious whimsicality—whereas the scientist is not. What distinguishes the child from the scientist, however, is not so much his irrationality—because, as we have said, he has not enough data to be rational—but his readiness, his naïve, trusting, careless readiness, to guess in public and expose his ignorance to others. We know that the response of a trained imagination is often (c) "I suggest this hypothesis" (x or y in *figure* 2). It is advanced as a tentative proposal, a man-made theory subject to correction or abandonment. This form of statement may chill the souls of those who hanker for authority, leave indifferent those who seek salvation, make enemies of restless minds clamoring for assertive action, and yet none other is justified when the goal of truth is paramount. No mind reviewing its past errors can be but humble before the sphinxlike face of nature. The history of science is a record of many momentous defeats and a few tentative victories. Fortunate it is that most of the errors are eventually interred and truth lives after.

Now, at every stage in the growth of a science there is, it seems, an appropriate balance between broad speculation and detailed measurement. For instance, in the infancy of a very complex science—and surely psychology is young and complicated—a few mastering generalizations can be more effective in advancing knowledge than a mass of carefully compiled data. For in the wake of intuition comes investigation directed at crucial problems rather than mere unenlightened fact-collecting. Here we may point to the undeniable enrichment of our understanding and the impetus to further studies which has come from psychoanalytic theory. In its present stage personology seems to call for men who can view things in the broad; that is, who can apperceive occurrences in terms of the interplay of general forces. A man who has been trained in the exact sciences will find himself somewhat at a loss, if not at a disadvantage. He will find it difficult to fall in with the loose flow of psychologic thought. He will find nothing that is hard and sharp. And so if he continues to hold rigidly to the scientific ideal, to cling to the hope that the results of his researches will approach in accuracy and elegance the formulations of the exact disciplines, he is doomed to failure. He will end his days in the congregation of futile men, of whom the greater number, contractedly withdrawn from critical issues, measure trifles with sanctimonious precision. Perhaps the best course for such a man is to quit psychology for a simpler, more evolved and satisfying science—physiology, let us say. Nowadays, to be happy and productive in psychology, it is better not to be too critical. For the profession of psychology is much like living, which has been defined by Samuel Butler as "the art of drawing sufficient conclusions from insufficient premises." Sufficient premises are not to be found, and he who, lacking them, will not draw tentative conclusions cannot advance. The self-analysis of thought may end by crushing what it feeds upon, imaginative spontaneity. As Jung says of himself: "I have never refused the bitter-sweet drink of philosophical criticism, but have taken it with caution, a little at a time. All too little, my opponents will say; almost too much, my feeling tells me. All too easily does self-criticism poison one's naïveté, that priceless possession, or rather gift, which no creative man can be without."[3]

It is just as well that man has always had at least a germ of faith in his omnipotence and omnicognizance. For without it the first assertions and assumptions would never have been made and, lacking these, the sciences would not have flowered. Though science preaches the need for caution, logical analysis, and undisputed facts, it is much indebted to those who at the start made bold assumptions.

Our conclusion is that for the present the destiny of personology is best served by giving scope to speculation, perhaps not so much as psychoanalysts allow themselves, but plenty. Hence, in the present volume we have checked self-criticism, ignored various details, winked a little at statistics, and from first to last have never hesitated to offer interpretative hypotheses. Had we made a ritual of rigorous analysis, nothing would have filtered through to write about. Speech is healthier than silence, even though one knows that what one says is vague and inconclusive.

It should be clearly understood, however, that every interpretative statement or conclusion in this volume is a hypothesis or theory which is ready to abdicate in the face of any facts which definitely contradict it. No theory has been set up as "president for life." We have, however, generally avoided qualifying phrases, the prefacing of statements with "it seems" or "it appears," because in a long book this practice makes for monotony and is annoying to many readers.

The Order of Procedures at the Harvard Psychological Clinic

Personology, if it is ever developed, will rest upon an organized collection of facts pertaining relevantly to the long course of complex events from human conception to human death. They will be contained for the most part in case histories based on observations of behavior in natural and experimental situations, together with the subject's memories and introspections. The questions: What are facts? How are they discovered? and How proved to others? will always be fundamental to the science. But the discipline will not advance until it is possible to transform the raw data of experience into adequate abstractions. Now, as every experimenter knows, the latter must be constructed *before* the facts are sought. Naturally, the facts will compel a reformulation of the concepts, but if we approach personality without a tentative theory, we shall neglect much that is relevant and include much that is not. Therefore, in the order of events at the Clinic, the conceptual scheme came first.

A. Conceptual Scheme. The business of every science is the construction of a conceptual scheme, and since a conceptual scheme is, by definition, a condensed abstract representation—a short word-picture, a reduced map, a symbolic formulation—of the actuality of immediate experience, its success depends upon the selection of a proper mode of analysis. Everything that is essential but nothing that is unessential to the structure of an event should be included. Naturally, opinions will differ as to which variables should be measured and which omitted. For the sake of thought, communication, and action, an enormous amount of detail must be put aside as irrelevant, and, consequently, there is always the danger that something crucial has been disregarded. We must remember that our map is not the event itself. It is merely a much reduced and, at best, a very approximate mental reproduction of it. If possible, the scheme should be comprehensive, coherent, necessary, and convenient.

The data out of which our original concepts emerged were our own experiences and the lives of others: patients treated at the Clinic, acquaintances, and characters in history and fiction. We were largely guided in the construction of our generalizations by the theories of Freud and McDougall, as well as those of Jung, Rank, Adler, Lewin, and others. The problem, of course, was one of discriminative abstraction, that is, it was necessary to analyze out of a subject-object interaction those factors in the subject and in the object which influenced the course of events. As will be shown in the next chapter, we came down to a theory of directional forces within the subject, forces which seek out or respond to various objects or total situations in the environment. These are commonly termed *instincts* or *part-instincts* by the Freudians, and were so termed by McDougall in his earlier writings. The latter now calls them *propensities.* Though the Freudians mention only two instincts explicitly, sex and aggression, in their explanations of behavioral phenomena, they refer to numerous other forces which, some think, might just as well be called instinctive: passivity, anxiety and avoidance, masochism, exhibitionism, voyeurism, and so forth. Though the naming and defining of these tendencies actually constitute a primitive classification, the Freudians do not speak of it as such. They are averse—sometimes with good reason—to defining terms or to building up their constructs systematically. In the beginning of a science this is perhaps the best course to pursue, but now, it seems to us, the time has come for a more orderly approach. In this we have followed McDougall, who, in his classification of propensities, included most of the drives which the Freudians have enumerated.

Now, besides the variables defined as driving forces, we distinguished others, which may be variously described as dimensions, functions, vectors, modes, or traits of personality. Here we leaned heavily on Jung, Stern, G. W. Allport, and a host of psychologists who have tried their hand at characterological description.

Then, since we were concerned with the genesis and history of tendencies and sentiments, we had to distinguish various modes of development, processes of maturation, learning, and socialization. In doing this we were guided by the principles of conditioning, association, and organization worked out by Pavlov and the gestalt psychologists, and by such psychoanalytic concepts as fixation, substitution, compensation, sublimation, and regression.

In summary, then, it may be said that our variables of personality consisted of a miscellany of general attributes, driving forces, relations between these forces and developmental modes. Each variable was defined to the satisfaction of all experimenters and a large number of concrete examples of its activity assembled to serve as guides for diagnosis. It was assumed that the degree of intensity of each variable could be marked on a "zero to five" scale. With our first group of subjects we had but ten variables; with our last we had over forty. In defining them and building up our theory of the total personality, we attempted to proceed systematically according to certain principles.[4] A systematic, objective, and perhaps tediously thorough approach seemed advisable, because the *ex cathedra* method commonly adopted would have accentuated, if anything, the differences and confusions which now prevail among personologists.

B. Methodological Plan. A series of sessions—interviews, tests, and experimental procedures—was devised to bring into prominence various aspects of personality, particularly those covered by the personality variables. We employed whatever appropriate mechanical aids could be devised: speech-recording apparatus, galvanometer for measuring changes in skin resistance, tremor-recording apparatus, instrument for measuring sensorimotor learning, moving-picture camera, and so forth; but we did not believe that the use of instruments was, in itself, a mark of scientific worth.

Some psychologists have an almost religious attachment to physical apparatus taken over from the fundamental disciplines: physics, chemistry, and physiology. Working with such contrivances they have the "feel" of being purely scientific, and thus dignified. Sometimes this is nothing but a groundless fantasy, since what has made these methods scientific is the fact that applied to other objects they have yielded answers to important questions. It is dubious whether many crucial problems in psychology can be solved by instruments. Certainly if physical appliances do not give results which lead to conceptual understanding, it is not scientific to employ them. For the all-important characteristic of a good scientific method is its efficacy in revealing general truths.

We tried to design methods appropriate to the variables which we wished to measure; in case of doubt, choosing those that crudely revealed significant things rather than those that precisely revealed insignificant things. Nothing can be more important than an understanding of man's nature, and if the techniques of other sciences do not bring us to it, then so much the worse for them.

Our procedures are precisely described in Chapter VI. At this point it is enough to list the few general principles that our experience invited us to adopt.

1. Each subject should be exposed to *many varied* situations. This is basic. It rests upon the attested supposition that a person has almost as many "sides" as there are different situations to which he is exposed.

2. Each subject should be observed and independently diagnosed by many different types of men and women. This follows from the preceding principle: first, because one man has not the time to carry out all the necessary examinations, and second, because to vary conditions sufficiently one must vary the experimenter. There are also other reasons, the chief of which is the desirability of having many estimates and judgments of each subject. In no other way can an experimenter check his own interpretations. In our work we relied not only upon *many* judgments, but also upon the *weighted* judgments of the more experienced members of the staff.

3. Experience has taught us not only the necessity for varied sessions and a multiplicity of investigators, but also the necessity for experience in diagnosis. The experimenters, therefore, should be wisely selected and properly trained. The psychologist is and will always be the final judge of all questions pertaining to personality. No fine instrument can replace him. Therefore, as far as he is able, he must himself become an instrument of precision. Now, since in any group of experimenters there will always be some who have greater aptitude or who are more experienced than others, it is advisable to establish a diagnostic hierarchy. By weighting the opinions of the more competent, one gets the full benefit of *superior* judgments as well as of *many* judgments. The problem of diagnosis—of how the experimenter can get beyond his own sentiments and approximate what is ideally the true judgment—is, of course, one of the central problems of psychological procedure. It is a topic which we shall take up later in a special section. At present, we shall merely call atten-

tion to the principle of weighted judgments as a contribution to methodology.

4. The experimental sessions should be as lifelike as possible. This is important because the purpose of personological studies is to discover how a man reacts under the stress of common conditions. To know how he responds to a unique, unnatural laboratory situation is of minor interest.

5. The subject's mind should be diverted from the true purpose of an experiment. This is usually accomplished by announcing a plausible but fictitious objective. If a subject recognizes the experimenter's aim, his responses will be modified by other motives: for instance, by the desire to conceal the very thing which the experimenter wishes to observe.

6. One or more experiments should be observed by a second, concealed experimenter. In this way the reports of experimenters may be checked from time to time.

7. After some of the sessions, subjects should be asked to give a verbal or written report of their view of the experience: their impressions of the experimenter, their inner, unexpressed feelings, and so forth.

8. Each experimenter should attempt a hypothetical interpretation of the behavior of each subject. The tentative character of such inferences should be recognized.

C. Sessions. A group of about thirteen subjects were engaged to come to the Clinic three or four hours a week over a period of several months. [The first group of subjects was asked to come much more frequently than this and the entire period of examination lasted less than two weeks.] The subjects were examined individually. With the last group of subjects about two dozen procedures were used, each procedure consisting of one or two sessions of one hour's duration. The entire program of sessions amounted to about thirty-five hours. Each subject underwent all the sessions and in the same sequence. Twenty-four experimenters took part in these examinations; each of whom recorded his observations, his markings on each variable, and his hypothetical interpretations of every subject. These conclusions, independently arrived at, were later brought together for comparison with the judgments of all the other experimenters.

Use was also made of a number of specially devised comprehensive questionnaires, or reaction studies, from which were obtained marks for every subject on every variable, based, in this instance, on his own reports of his usual behavior in everyday life. In addition, each subject was asked to write a short autobiography.

D. Diagnostic Meetings. Five of the more experienced experimenters were selected to constitute a Diagnostic Council. This Council conducted a conference with each subject, the conference being the first in the sequence of sessions to which the subject was exposed. Thus, at the very outset, the members of the Council received an impression of the subject and were able to assign tentative marks on each variable. Subsequently, the Council held meetings to hear and discuss reports presented by other experimenters and, on the basis of these, revised, when necessary, their original markings and interpretations.

E. Final Meeting. At the end of all the examinations, a meeting, usually lasting five or six hours, was held on each subject. At this meeting each experimenter read a report of his session with the subject. A specially appointed "biographer" conducted the meeting. He opened with a short summary of the findings, made comments on each report, and concluded with a psychograph, or reconstruction, of the subject's personality from birth. After the psychograph was read, there was general discussion and, at the end, the markings of the subject on each variable were discussed and finally established by majority vote.

F. Statistical Analysis. Many of the tests were susceptible of quantitative treatment, and so rank orders of the subjects could be obtained and intercorrelated. Rank orders on each of the personality variables, based on ratings by the staff as well as on the results of questionnaires, were likewise intercorrelated. Finally, the test results and the personality variables were intercorrelated. In this way there was an opportunity of discovering what variables were commonly or rarely found together and what variables were potent in determining the outcome of each test. Furthermore, correlations of variables gave a ground for dropping some and compounding others. In the mathematical treatment of results, we relied chiefly upon Allport and Vernon whose treatise *The Measurement of Expressive Movements* is a model of its kind.

The statistical analysis of the variables finally retained demonstrated that certain of them intercorrelated repeatedly to a significant degree. Most of these clusters seemed to correspond to our observations of people in everyday life. Hence, we concluded that they might be regarded as syndromes of functionally related factors which, for economy, could be used instead of the separate variables to portray a character. Our results showed, furthermore, that a variable may be an item in several different syndromes, and that its nature is modified by the character of the ensemble of associated variables in which it is found.

G. Theoretical Discussions. The experience of the experimenters in classifying the subjects' behavior and of the biographers in reconstructing comprehensible life histories provided a basis for estimating the validity of the conceptual scheme originally devised. The question was asked: Did this or that subject display any characteristic not adequately covered by one or more of the variables? If so, what is the psychological significance of this characteristic; on what underlying processes does it depend; and how should these processes be defined? In discussing such questions, the adequacies and inadequacies of the scheme became more apparent. A verification of the scheme was found in its general success.

Invariably, there were revisions and redefinitions of the variables and of the dynamic principles determining their operation. Thus, with a new theoretical outline and a new program of sessions, the staff of the Clinic was ready to engage another group of subjects, to carry out again the entire sequence of events.

This order of procedures repeated several times may be termed "the method of successive approximations." The theory which is evolved is the product of an assemblage of minds on the field of action. It bears marks of its empirical derivation, but it has the advantage of being agreed upon by many different judges before being presented as a workable conception.

Our Methods Compared to Those of Psychoanalysis and Academic Personology

The techniques employed in the present exploration resemble in some respects those developed by psychoanalysis and in others those devised by personologists in universities. But because of our emphasis upon inhibited or unconscious tendencies as well as our persistent attempt to trace things back to infantile experiences, our work was more closely allied to the concerns of analysts.

We differ from psychoanalysis in respect to the length and depth of our explorations. Most psychoanalyses take about two hundred hours, and some take much longer, up to three or four years. With us, however, a subject participates in but thirty-five one-hour sessions, of which only about five are devoted to the recovery of past experiences. Thus in the same period of time we examine about six times as many subjects, but the analyst obtains about six times as much data from each, and because of his close and prolonged personal relationship with the patient he has revealed to him more of the "depths" of personality. Here, however, it may be said that the length of the analyses is dictated by therapeutic considerations; that as far as understanding is concerned they are usually carried beyond the point of diminishing returns. Nevertheless, it must be admitted that the psychoanalytic technique is superior to ours in respect to the amount of evidence obtained.

The advantages of our procedure, however, are not negligible:

1. The collaboration of many experimenters who contribute their observations and take part in the final reconstruction of each subject's personality does not permit a one-sided viewpoint. A subject displays different facets of his personality to different experimenters, and despite what most analysts say to the contrary, it is for them to disprove what much evidence seems to show, namely, that the personality of the analyst determines to an appreciable extent the attitude that the patient assumes, the course of his free associations, and thus the final diagnosis

which is made. Here, we may include the advantage of exposing a person to a large number of very different situations.

2. In our theoretical scheme, as well as in our methodological approach, we paid more attention to the manifest personality than psychoanalysts are prone to do. Moreover, we had a better opportunity of judging overt social conduct and demonstrable abilities. Thus, the total personality—including the relation between the conscious and the unconscious, the manifest and the latent—could be seen with greater definition. A psychoanalytic case history seldom portrays the patient as an imaginable social animal. Even in describing normal people, the psychoanalysts put emphasis upon the aberrant or neurotic features, because these are the things which the practice of their calling has trained them to observe. It is as if in giving an account of the United States a man wrote at length about accidents, epidemics, crime, prostitution, insurgent minorities, radical literary coteries, and obscure religious sects and made no mention of established institutions: the President, Congress, and the Supreme Court.

3. The fact that we studied a series of individuals—small though it was—gave us a basis for estimating individual differences, the normal range of each variable, what variables commonly occurred together, what variables were influential in determining the outcome of each test, and so forth. Such statistical results are certainly of some value in establishing common tendencies and syndromes and in arriving at general principles.

4. By our procedure there was opportunity to test certain hypotheses under experimental conditions; and unless one is prepared to throw aside what cumulative experience has shown to be the most effective instrument for arriving at relative certainty, it must be conceded that this is a decided advantage. Most psychoanalysts, by temperament and training, are unsympathetic or opposed to experimental research.

With us the concepts were considered hypothetical and tentative, and every session was taken as an opportunity to correct or verify them. Thus, the entire organized procedure may be regarded as an experiment to test the ability of the constructed theory to classify and causally relate the facts.

Now that these differences have been pointed out, it should be said that, although we find something to criticize in psychoanalysis, we are not unmindful of the fact that from the start it has been our most constant guide and source of illumination. Without it these studies would never have been planned or finished.

From academic psychology—particularly, as said above, from the work of G. W. Allport—we learned much in respect to an orderly method of procedure and a proper statistical treatment of our findings. We included some of the procedures commonly employed in academic studies —intelligence tests and a variety of questionnaires—but these contributed very little to our understanding. American personologists base their conclusions on a much larger number of subjects than we studied, and in this respect their findings are more representative than ours. What they usually study, however, are the physical attributes of movement, manifest traits, and superficial attitudes, facts which subjects are entirely conscious of and quite willing to admit. Thus, their researches do not penetrate below the level of what is evident to the ordinary layman. To discover the traits of subjects, confidence is placed upon self-estimates or upon what a few untrained judges say about them. The original data, then, are of uncertain value, and no amount of factor analysis can make them more reliable. Furthermore, since these students of personality are apt to ignore the past history of their subjects, their final formulations are generally too static. To fully understand a trait one must know its genesis and history.

In short, then, we might say that our work is the natural child of the deep, significant, metaphorical, provocative, and questionable speculations of psychoanalysis and the precise, systematic, statistical, trivial, and artificial methods of academic personology. Our hope is that we have inherited more of the virtues than the vices of our parents.

The Future Prospect

As we approached the end of our exploring, innumerable ideas came bubbling up to plague us, ideas of further searches, experiments, and tests which should be done in order to settle some tantalizing problem or get a clearer view of certain personalities. If we had been in touch with a medical clinic or a physiological laboratory, where, let us say, examinations could have been made of the cardiac, gastrointestinal, or endocrine systems of our subjects; or if we had had with us a sociologist to make detailed studies of the families and communities from which the subjects came, then, surely, many things which now are dubious would be less so. Numerous experiments of different kinds occurred to us as profitable ventures, and it was galling to realize that none of them was possible. We were definitely limited by lack of time, space, number of trained experimenters, and apparatus. We came to view our work as a mere point of departure and the Clinic as an *anlage* of some future institute where more exhaustive studies could be made. Such an institute might eventually bring about a unification of the various schools of psychology and thus lead to a state of affairs such as now prevails in medicine, where all are working within a common scheme.

Reasons could be readily advanced for such studies besides the essential ones that knowledge is *per se* a final good and that man is of all objects the most inviting. There are many who believe that an understanding of human nature is the great requirement of this age; that modern man is "up against it," confused, dissatisfied, despairing, and ready to regress; that what he needs is the power to change and redirect himself and others; and that the possession of this special power can only be won through knowledge. If it is true, as some reasonable men affirm, that culture—the best of man's high heritage—is in jeopardy, and that to save and further it man, its creator and conserver, must be changed—regenerated or developed differently from birth—then the immediate requisite is a science of human nature.

To study human nature patiently, to arrive at understanding, to gain some mastery; there would be little hope in the enterprise if it were not for the history of science, the steady, unassertive, conquering pace of disinterested observation, experiment, and reflection. Three centuries ago did the fancy of the most imaginative men foresee the miracles of thought and technics that would mark the way of science? Absorbing this tradition, man may now explore his soul and observe the conduct of his fellows, dispassionate to the limit, yet ever animated by the faith that gaining mastery through knowledge he may eventually surmount himself.

REFERENCES

1. Ludwig, Emil. *Wilhelm Hohenzollern,* New York, 1927.

2. Freud, Sigmund. *New Introductory Lectures on Psycho-analysis,* New York, 1933.

3. Jung, Carl G. *Modern Man in Search of a Soul,* New York, 1934, p. 135.

4. In working out our method of approach we were greatly influenced by Professor L. J. Henderson of Harvard, who insisted upon a serious study of Pareto (Pareto, Vilfredo. *The Mind and Society,* New York, 1935).

6

PROPOSALS FOR A THEORY
OF PERSONALITY

It is now necessary to set forth the conceptual scheme which guided our explorations. It is not a rigid system that was instituted in the beginning and maintained throughout. It has been repeatedly modified to accord with observed facts, and is still evolving. Hence, we can do no more than take a snapshot of it in mid-career, and offer this as a tentative makeshift for orienting thought and directing practical action. The reader will observe that the scheme is the outcome of a prejudice in favor of the dynamical, organismal viewpoint. It is, if he chooses to so regard it, a rationalized elaboration of the perception that a human being is a motile, discriminating, valuating, assimilating, adapting, integrating, differentiating, and reproducing temporal unity within a changing environmental matrix.

Since psychology deals only with motion—processes occurring in time—none of its proper formulations can be static. They all must be dynamic in the larger meaning of this term. Within recent years, however, "dynamic" has come to be used in a special sense: to designate a psychology which accepts as prevailingly fundamental the goal-directed (adaptive) character of behavior and attempts to discover and formulate the internal as well as the external factors which determine it. In so far as this psychology emphasizes facts which for a long time have been and still are generally overlooked by academic investigators, it represents a protest against current scientific preoccupations. And since the occurrences which the specialized professor has omitted in his scheme of things are the very ones which the laity believe to be "most truly psychological," the dynamicist must first perform the tedious and uninviting task of reiterating common sense. Thus he comes on the stage in the guise of a protesting and perhaps somewhat sentimental amateur.

The history of dynamic organismal psychology is a long one if one takes into account all speculations that refer to impelling forces, passions, appetites, or instincts. But only lately have attempts been made to bring such conceptions systematically within the domain of science. We dis-

From Henry A. Murray (with staff), *Explorations in Personality.* New York: Oxford University Press, 1938. Chapter Two, Proposals for a theory of personality, pp. 36–141.

cover tentative signs in the functionalism of Dewey and Angell with its emphasis upon the organization of means with reference to a comprehensive end, in Ach's "determining tendency," and in James's notion of instinct, but not until we come to McDougall[1] do we find a conscientious attempt to develop the dynamic hypothesis. Since then, some of the animal psychologists, notably Tolman,[2] and Stone,[3] have worked with an objectively defined "drive" which is strictly in accord with dynamical principles, and Lewin,[4] representing the gestalt school of psychology, has made "need" basic to his system of personality. But the theory of drive or need has not been systematically developed by the latter investigators, their interest in external determinants of behavior being predominant.

Outside the universities, the medical psychologists—and here we may, without serious omissions, start with Freud[5]—have for five decades been constructing a quintessentially dynamic theory. For this theory the academic psychologists, with the exception of McDougall, found themselves entirely unprepared. The psychoanalysts not only presented facts which had never entered the academic man's field of observation or thought, but they used a novel nomenclature to designate certain obscure forces which they thought it necessary to conceptualize in order to account for their findings. McDougall and the analysts have been kept apart by numerous differences, but in respect to their fundamental dynamical assumptions they belong together.

The theory to be outlined here is an attempt at a dynamic scheme. It has been guided partly by the analysts (Freud, Jung,[6] Adler[7]), partly by McDougall and by Lewin, and partly by our subjects—whose actions so frequently corrected our preconceptions. As I have said, the theory is vague and incomplete. At many points it does scant justice to the precisely stated conceptions of other psychologists, even those with whom we find ourselves in substantial agreement. Compared to analytical speculations—some of Jung's intuitions, for example—it is limited and superficial. The truth is that we have taken from our predecessors only what could be used with profit in the present study.

This book is not a theoretical treatise and there is not the space for a thorough presentation of our concepts. It is only possible to state the principal assumptions and enumerate in the briefest manner the steps that led us to adopt the theory which served us as a plan of action. And in order to get over the ground of fundamentals with as little circumlocution as possible, it has seemed best to crystallize the broad facts of observation, as they have appeared to us, into a set of general postulates or propositions. It will be seen that some of these are mere commonplaces, others are cloudy, hardly verifiable generalities, still others are highly problematical and call for refutation or further study. The reader should not be deceived by the dogmatic form of statement. Each proposition is provisional. It is asserted flatly so that it may more readily be checked or contradicted.

A. PRIMARY PROPOSITIONS

1. The objects of study are individual organisms, not aggregates of organisms.

2. The organism is from the beginning a whole, from which the parts are derived by self-differentiation. The whole and its parts are mutually related; the whole being as essential to an understanding of the parts as the parts are to an understanding of the whole. (This is a statement of the *organismal* theory.[8]) Theoretically it should be possible to formulate for any moment the "wholeness" of an organism; or, in other words, to state in what respect it is acting as a unit.

3. The organism is characterized from the beginning by rhythms of activity and rest, which are largely determined by internal factors. The organism is not an inert body that merely responds to external stimulation. Hence the psychologist must study and find a way of representing the changing "states" of the organism.

4. The organism consists of an infinitely complex series of temporally related activities extending from birth to death. Because of the meaningful connection of sequences the life cycle of a single individual should be taken as a unit, the *long unit* for psychology. It is feasible to study the organism during one episode of its existence, but it should be recognized that this is but an arbitrarily selected part of the whole. The history of the organism *is* the organism. This proposition calls for biographical studies.

5. Since, at every moment, an organism is within an environment which largely determines its behavior, and since the environment changes—sometimes with radical abruptness—the conduct of an individual cannot be formulated without a characterization of each confronting situation, physical and social. It is important to define the environment, since two organisms may behave differently only because they are, by chance, encountering different conditions. It is considered that two organisms are dissimilar if they give the same response but only to different situations as well as if they give different responses to the same situation. Also, different inner states of the same organism can be inferred when responses to similar external conditions are different. Finally, the assimilations and integrations that occur in an organism are determined to a large extent by the nature of its closely previous, as well as by its more distantly previous, environments. In other words, what an organism knows or believes is, in some measure, a product of formerly encountered situations. Thus, much of what is now *inside* the organism was once *outside.* For these reasons, the organism and its milieu must be considered together, a single creature-environment interaction being a convenient short unit for psychology. A *long unit*—an individual life—can be

most clearly formulated as a succession of related *short units,* or *episodes.*

6. The stimulus situation (S.S.) is that part of the total environment to which the creature attends and reacts. It can rarely be described significantly as an aggregate of discrete sense impressions. The organism usually responds to patterned meaningful wholes, as the gestalt school of psychology has emphasized.

The effect on a man of a series of unorganized verbal sounds or of language that he does not understand is very different from the effect of words organized into meaningful sentences that he does understand (or thinks he understands). It is the meaning of the words which has potency, rather than the physical sounds *per se.* This is proved by the fact that the same effect can be produced by quite different sounds: by another tongue that is understood by the subject.

In crudely formulating an episode it is dynamically pertinent and convenient to classify the S.S. according to the kind of effect—facilitating or obstructing—it is exerting or could exert upon the organism. Such a tendency or "potency" in the environment may be called a *press.* For example, a press may be nourishing, or coercing, or injuring, or chilling, or befriending, or restraining, or amusing, or belittling to the organism. It can be said that a press is a temporal gestalt of stimuli which usually appears in the guise of a *threat of harm* or *promise of benefit* to the organism. It seems that organisms quite naturally "classify" the objects of their world in this way: "this hurts," "that is sweet," "this comforts," "that lacks support."

7. The reactions of the organism to its environment usually exhibit a *unitary trend.* This is the necessary concomitant of behavioral co-ordination, since co-ordination implies organization of activity in a *certain direction,* that is, toward the achievement of an effect, one or more. Without organization there can be no unified trends, and without unified trends there can be no effects, and without effects there can be no enduring organism. Divided it perishes, united it survives. The existence of organisms depends upon the fact that the vast majority of trends are "adaptive": they serve to restore an equilibrium that has been disturbed, or to avoid an injury, or to attain objects which are of benefit to development. Thus, much of overt behavior is, like the activity of the internal organs, survivalistically purposeful.

8. A specimen of adaptive behavior can be analyzed into the bodily movements as such and the effect achieved by these movements. We have found it convenient to use a special term, *actone,* to describe a pattern of bodily movements *per se,* abstracted from its effect. To produce an effect which furthers the well-being of the organism a consecutive series of sub-effects must usually be achieved, each sub-effect being due to the operation of a relatively simple actone. Thus, simple actones and their sub-effects are connected in such a way that a certain trend is

promoted. It is the trend which exhibits the unity of the organism. The unity is not an instantaneous fact for it may only be discovered by observing the progress of action over a period of time. The trend is achieved by the bodily processes, but it cannot be distinguished by studying the bodily processes in isolation.

This proposition belongs to the organismal theory of reality. It is in disagreement with the common practice of studying a fraction of the organism's response and neglecting the trend of which it is a part. One who limits himself to the observation of the bodily movements, as such, resembles the sufferer from semantic aphasia.

In semantic aphasia, the full significance of words and phrases is lost. Separately, each word or each detail of a drawing can be understood, but the general significance escapes; an act is executed upon command, though the purpose of it is not understood. Reading and writing are possible as well as numeration, the correct use of numbers; but the appreciation of arithmetical processes is defective . . . A general conception cannot be formulated, but details can be enumerated. (Henri Piéron)[9]

9. A behavioral trend may be attributed to a hypothetical force (a drive, need or propensity) within the organism. The proper way of conceptualizing this force is a matter of debate. It seems that it is a force which (if uninhibited) promotes activity which (if competent) brings about a situation that is opposite (as regards its relevant properties) to the one that aroused it. Frequently, an innumerable number of sub-needs (producing sub-effects) are temporally organized so as to promote the course of a major need. [The concept of need or drive will be more fully developed later.]

10. Though the organism frequently seeks for a certain press—in which case the press is, for a time, expectantly imaged—more frequently the press meets the organism and incites a drive. Thus, the simplest formula for a period of complex behavior is a particular press-need combination. Such a combination may be called a *thema.*[10] A *thema* may be defined as the dynamical structure of a simple *episode,* a single creature-environment interaction. In other words, the endurance of a certain kind of *press* in conjunction with a certain kind of *need* defines the duration of a single *episode,* the latter being a convenient molar unit for psychology to handle. Simple episodes (each with a simple thema) may relatedly succeed each other to constitute a *complex episode* (with its *complex thema*). The biography of a man may be portrayed abstractly as an historic route of themas (*cf.* a musical score). Since there are a limited number of important drives and a limited number of important press, there are a greater (but still limited) number of important themas. Just as chemists now find it scientifically profitable to describe a hundred thousand or more organic compounds, psychologists some day may be

inclined to observe and formulate the more important behavioral compounds.

11. Each drive reaction to a press has a fortune that may be measured in degrees of realization ("gratification"). Whether an episode terminates in gratification or frustration (success or failure) is often decisive
in determining the direction of an organism's development. Success and
failure are also of major importance in establishing the "status" of an
organism in its community.

12. In the organism the passage of time is marked by rhythms of
assimilation, differentiation and integration. The environment changes.
Success and failure produce their effects. There is learning and there is
maturation. Thus new and previously precluded combinations come into
being, and with the perishing of each moment the organism is left a
different creature, never to repeat itself exactly. No moment nor epoch
is typical of the whole. Life is an irreversible sequence of non-identical
events. Some of these changes, however, occur in a predictable lawful
manner. There are orderly rhythms and progressions which are functions of the seasons, of age, of sex, of established cultural practices, and
so forth. There is the "eternal return" ("spiral evolution"). These
phenomena make biography imperative.

13. Though the psychologist is unable to find identities among the
episodes of an organism's life, he can perceive uniformities. For an individual displays a tendency to react in a similar way to similar situations,
and increasingly so with age. Thus there is sameness (consistency) as well
as change (variability), and because of it an organism may be roughly
depicted by listing the most recurrent themas, or, with more abstraction,
by listing the most recurrent drives or traits.

14. Repetitions and consistencies are due in part to the fact that
impressions of situations leave enduring "traces" (a concept for an hypothetical process) in the organism, which may be reactivated by the appearance of situations that resemble them; and because of the connections of these evoked traces with particular reaction systems, the
organism is apt to respond to new situations as it did to former ones
(redintegration). Some of the past is always alive in the present. For this
reason the study of infancy is particularly important. The experiences of
early life not only constitute in themselves a significant temporal segment of the creature's history, but they may exercise a marked effect
upon the course of development. In some measure they "explain" succeeding events. ["The child is father to the man."]

15. The progressive differentiations and integrations that occur with
age and experience are, for the most part, refinements in stimulus discrimination and press discrimination and improvements in actonal effectiveness. Specific signs become connected with specific modes of conduct, and certain aptitudes (abilities) are developed. This is important
because the fortune of drives, and thus the status of the individual, is

dependent in large measure upon the learning of differentiated skills.

In early life the sequences of movement are mostly unrelated. Trends are not persistent and disco-ordination is the rule. Opposing drives and attitudes succeed each other without apparent friction. With age, however, conflict comes and after conflict resolution, synthesis and creative integration. ("Life is creation." Claude Bernard) Action patterns are co-ordinated, enduring purposes arise and values are made to harmonize. Thus, the history of dilemmas and how, if ever, they were solved are matters of importance for psychology.

16. Since in the higher forms of life the impressions from the external world and from the body that are responsible for conditioning and memory are received, integrated and conserved in the brain, and since all complex adaptive behavior is evidently co-ordinated by excitations in the brain, the unity of the organism's development and behavior can be explained only by referring to organizations occurring in this region. It is brain processes, rather than those in the rest of the body, which are of special interest to the psychologist. At present, they cannot be directly and objectively recorded but they must be inferred in order to account for what happens. A need or drive is just one of these hypothetical processes. Since, by definition, it is a process which follows a stimulus and precedes the actonal response, it must be located in the brain.

17. It may prove convenient to refer to the mutually dependent processes that constitute dominant configurations in the brain as *regnant* processes; and, further, to designate the totality of such processes occurring during a single moment (a unitary temporal segment of brain processes) as a *regnancy*.[11] According to this conception regnancies correspond to the processes of highest metabolic rate in the gradient which Child[12] has described in lower organisms. It may be considered that regnancies are functionally at the summit of a hierarchy of subregnancies in the body. Thus, to a certain extent the regnant need dominates the organism.

The activities of the nerve-cells and muscle-cells are necessary conditions of the whole action, but they are not in any full sense its cause. They enable the action to be carried out, and they limit at the same time the possibilities of the action. . . . Putting the matter in another way, a knowledge of the nature of muscular and nervous action would not enable us fully to interpret behavior.[13]

We distinguished in general the *modes of action* of higher and lower unities —from the mode of action of the organism as a whole down to the modes of action of those parts of the cell which, like the chromosomes, show a certain measure of independence and individuality. We came to the conclusion that the modes of action of the subordinate unities condition, both in a positive and a negative sense, the modes of action of the higher unities. Being integrated into the activity of the whole they render possible the vital manifestation of these activities by imposing on them a particular form.[14]

Occurrences in the external world or in the body that have no effect upon regnancies do not fall within the proper domain of psychology.

18. Regnant processes are, without doubt, mutually dependent. A change in one function changes all the others and these, in turn, modify the first. Hence, events must be interpreted in terms of the many interacting forces and their relations, not ascribed to single causes. And since the parts of a person cannot be dissected physically from each other, and since they act together, ideally they should all be estimated simultaneously. This, unfortunately, is not at present possible. Much of what has been discovered by other methods at other times has to be inferred.

19. According to one version of the double aspect theory—seemingly the most fruitful working hypothesis for a psychologist—the constituents of regnancies in man are capable of achieving consciousness (self-consciousness) though not all of them at once. The amount of introspective self-consciousness is a function of age, emotional state, attitude, type of personality, and so forth. Since through speech a person may learn to describe and communicate his impression of mental occurrences (the subjective aspect of regnant events) he can, if he wishes, impart considerable information about the processes which the psychologist attempts to conceptualize.

20. During a single moment only some of the regnant processes have the attribute of consciousness. Hence, to explain fully a conscious event as well as a behavioral event the psychologist must take account of more variables than were present in consciousness at the time. Consequently, *looking at the matter from the viewpoint of introspective awareness,* it is necessary to postulate unconscious regnant processes. An unconscious process is something that must be conceptualized as regnant even though the S* is unable to report its occurrence.

21. It seems that it is more convenient at present in formulating regnant processes to use a terminology derived from subjective experience. None of the available physicochemical concepts are adequate. It should be understood, however, that every psychological term refers to some hypothetical, though hardly imaginable, physical variable, or to some combination of such variables. Perhaps some day the physiologists will discover the physical nature of regnant processes and the proper way to conceptualize them; but this achievement is not something to be expected in the near future since an adequate formulation must include all major subjective experiences: expectations, intentions, creative thought, and so forth. Tolman,[15] however, has already shown that many of the necessary variables can be operationally defined in terms of overt behavioral indices.

---

*Throughout this book "S" will be used to stand for "subject" (the organism of our concern) and "E" will signify "experimenter" (physician or observer).

It is not only more convenient and fruitful at present to use subjective terminology (perception, apperception, imagination, emotion, affection, intellection, conation), but even if in the future it becomes expedient for science to use another consonant terminology it will not be possible to dispense with terms that have subjective significance; for these constitute data of primary importance to most human beings. The need to describe and explain varieties of inner experience decided the original, and, I predict, will establish the final orientation of psychology.

22. One may suppose that regnancies vary in respect to the number, relevance and organization of the processes involved, and that, as Janet supposes, a certain amount of integrative energy or force is required to unify the different parts. Regnancies become disjunctive in fatigue, reverie, and sleep, as well as during conflict, violent emotion, and insanity. The chief indices of differentiated conjunctive regnancies are these: alertness, nicety of perceptual and apperceptual discrimination, long endurance of a trend of complex action, increasingly effective changes of actone, rapidity of learning, coherence, relevance and concentration of thought, absence of conflict, introspective awareness, and self-criticism.

23. Because of the position of regnancies at the summit of the hierarchy of controlling centers in the body, and because of certain institutions established in the brain which influence the regnancies, the latter (constituting as they do the personality) must be distinguished from the rest of the body. The rest of the body is as much outside the personality as the environment is outside personality. Thus, we may study the effects of illness, drugs, endocrine activity and other somatic changes upon the personality in the same fashion as we study the changes produced by hot climate, strict discipline or warfare. In this sense, regnant processes stand between an inner and an outer world.

24. There is continuous interaction between regnancies and other processes in the body. For the chemical constitution of the blood and lymph, as well as a great variety of centripetal nervous impulses originating in the viscera, have a marked effect on personality. Indeed, they may change it almost completely. The personality, in turn, can affect the body by exciting or inhibiting skeletal muscles, or through the power of evoked traces (images) can excite the autonomic nervous system and thereby modify the physiology of organs (cf. autonomic neuroses). The personality can also vary the diet it gives the body, it can train it to stand long periods of intense exercise, drive it to a point of utter exhaustion, indulge it with ease and allow it to accumulate pounds of fat, poison it with drugs, bring it in contact with virulent bacteria, inhibit many of its cravings, mortify it, or destroy it by suicide. The relations between a personality and its body are matters of importance to a dynamicist.

25. *Time-binding.* Man is a "time-binding"[16] organism; which is a way of saying that, by conserving some of the past and anticipating some

of the future, a human being can, to a significant degree, make his behavior accord with events that have happened as well as those that are to come. Man is not a mere creature of the moment, at the beck and call of any stimulus or drive. What he does is related not only to the settled past but also to shadowy preconceptions of what lies ahead. Years in advance he makes preparations to observe an eclipse of the sun from a distant island in the South Pacific and, lo, when the moment comes he is there to record the event. With the same confidence another man prepares to meet his god. Man lives in an inner world of expected press (pessimistic or optimistic), and the psychologist must take cognizance of them if he wishes to understand his conduct or his moods, his buoyancies, disappointments, resignations. Time-binding makes for continuity of purpose.

Here we may stop in order to consider in some detail three crucial theories: the theory of unconscious processes, the theory of needs, and the theory of press.

B. UNCONSCIOUS REGNANT PROCESSES[17]

We have adopted the version of the double-aspect hypothesis which states that every conscious process is the subjective aspect of some regnant brain process, but that not every regnant process has a conscious correlate.* It appears, indeed, that to explain any conscious event, as well as to explain any behavioral event, one must take account of more variables than those which are at the moment present in consciousness. "Regarded as events," Köhler points out, "the facts and sequences of our direct experience do not, taken by themselves, represent complete wholes. They are merely parts of larger functional contexts."[18] The following examples, some of which are taken from Köhler, support this opinion.

1. The perception of the "Dipper" is an immediate experience in which the form is given as-a-whole. The stars are not organized into this common shape by a conscious process. The form comes to us "ready-made." Presumably there have been previous impressions of actual dippers which have left traces in the brain, and in the present act of perception some interaction between the memory image of a dipper and the impression from the heavens occurred. But this memory image is not in consciousness.

2. In the recognition of a person whom we have met once and not seen for a long time we are frequently conscious of the interaction between the memory image and the present impression. But later, after

*The theory is impartial on the question of whether every process has a "psychic" correlate or pole (according to some metaphysical definition of "psychic").

frequent encounters, immediate recognition occurs. On such occasions, though the memory image is not in consciousness, to explain the recognition we must suppose that it is still functioning.

3. When of an evening I am conversing with a friend, I am reacting from moment to moment on the basis of a great many realizations and suppositions which are not in consciousness. For instance, that the floor stretches out behind me—I should be anxious if there were a yawning chasm behind my chair—that I will be free to leave at a certain hour, and so forth. Such assumptions, though not conscious, are providing a time-space frame for conscious events and hence are determining their course.

4. One may pass a man in the street and immediately think: "He appears anxious, as if he were about to face some ordeal." The conscious perception of the man's face as a physical schema, however, may have been so indefinite that one is utterly unable to describe the features which contributed to the apperception of his inner state.

5. When one is learning to drive an automobile, one is, at first, aware of every accessory intention and subsequent motor movement, but later, when proficiency has been attained, the details of the activity are seldom in consciousness. We must suppose, nevertheless, that ordered activations are occurring at the motor pole of successive regnancies.

6. Absent-minded acts which involve movements of the body as a whole are performed without awareness of intentions similar to those which usually precede such actions.

7. When, let us say, a man is building a house he is usually conscious from moment to moment of his intention to realize a particular subsidiary effect. Though the idea of the major effect—the image of the completely constructed building—is not in consciousness, it must be active, since each conscious conation and movement is so clearly subservient to it.

8. Unconscious influence is clearly manifested by the operation of a mental "set" or "determining tendency" (ex: fixed intellectual viewpoint).

The firm determination to submit to experiment is not enough; there are still dangerous hypotheses; first, and above all, those which are tacit and unconscious. Since we make them without knowing it, we are powerless to abandon them. (H. Poincaré)[19]

These examples point to the fact that the extent of regnancies is greater than the extent of consciousness. It is as if consciousness were illumined regions of regnancies; as if a spotlight of varying dimensions moved about the brain, revealing first one and then another sector of successive, functionally related mental events. The examples demonstrate, furthermore, that, since a conscious experience depends upon interrelated, extra-conscious variables, it can be understood only when it is viewed as part of the larger whole. Thus, to explain a conscious event, as well as to explain a behavioral event, all the major variables of a regnancy must be known. According to this conception, then, the goal of the introspectionists and the goal of the behaviorists become the same: to determine the constitution of significant regnancies. To agree about this matter, however, the introspectionists must accept the theory of unconscious regnant processes, and the behaviorists must attempt—as physicists, chemists, and biologists have attempted—to conceptualize the phenomena which underlie appearances.

In the examples cited above none of the variables operating unconsciously were considered to be enduringly inaccessible to consciousness. The very next moment the S might have become aware of one or more of them. There are other unconscious processes, however—processes with which psychoanalysis is preoccupied—which seem to be *debarred* from consciousness. They are inhibited or repressed, according to theory, because they are unacceptable to the conscious self (Ego). Also there may be a vast number of potential tendencies—some of them, as Jung has suggested, vestiges of earlier racial life—which seldom, or never, find their way into consciousness because they lack the requisite verbal symbols. Some of these tendencies are exhibited distortedly in insanity. Thus, on the "deepest level" we must consider traces of the racial past and the early infantile past which lack adequate verbal associations (the "unverbalized," as Watson would say). Then, on a "higher level," we have the inhibited, once verbalized tendencies, many of which are infantile. Finally, we have processes that "pass," as it were, in and out of consciousness; as well as those that have become mechanized (habits and automatisms) which can, but rarely do, enter consciousness.

If it is agreed that subjective terminology should be used to stand for regnant processes, and if it is agreed that all conscious processes are regnant but not all regnant processes are conscious, then, just at this point a much debated question presents itself: if at one moment a variable—let us say the trace of a perception of food (unconditioned stimulus)—is conscious (as an image of food) and therefore regnant, and at another moment it is unconscious though still regnant—because it causes salivation—what term shall we apply to it at the second of these two moments? There are some men who have argued that the word "image" as well as every other consciously derived variable applies to an element in consciousness, and that to use the term for something that is unconscious is to commit a logical fallacy. To designate an unconscious process these thinkers favor the use of a term which refers to a physical entity in the brain. I find it impossible to agree with this conclusion because we do not require two terms to designate the same process, and it is particularly confusing if one of the terms is of introspective and the other of extrospective origin. Having chosen the vocabulary of conscious processes we should adhere to it, and not be embarrassed if this practice leads to what sounds like verbal nonsense ("unconscious conscious processes"). Figures of speech are sometimes useful and in this case are no more metaphorical or absurd than are terms derived from physics when applied to conscious processes.

Since any concepts which can be developed to describe unconscious regnant processes must necessarily be hypothetical (convenient fictions), it is scientifically permissible to imagine such processes as having the properties of conscious processes if, by so doing, we provide the most reasonable interpretation of the observed facts. That the theory of unconscious psychic processes has great resolving power becomes apparent when one applies it to the heretofore mysterious phenomena of psychopathology.

It is possible to define regnant processes, as Tolman and MacCurdy have shown, on the basis of objective data alone. Thus, such symbols as "perception," "image," "conation" may be used to refer to hypothetical physical processes—the nature of which may or may not be known—and, if there is sufficient objective evidence, they may be used whether or not the processes for which they stand are accompanied by consciousness. MacCurdy[20] uses the term "image," or "imaginal process," in this way. His definition is as follows:

An imaginal process, from the standpoint of an objective observer, is some kind of a reproduction of a specific bit of past sensory experience, which is inferred to exist from the presence of a reaction for which the specific experience would be the appropriate stimulus—this reaction not being completely accounted for by any demonstrable environmental event.

C. THE CONCEPT OF NEED OR DRIVE[21]

A *need* is a hypothetical process the occurrence of which is imagined in order to account for certain objective and subjective facts. To arrive at this concept it seems better to begin with objective behavioral facts, for by so doing we align ourselves with scientists in other fields, and, what is more, shall be on firmer ground for it is easier to agree about objective facts than about subjective facts.

In starting with a consideration of behavior we suppose that we are focusing upon one of the most significant aspects of the organism, and hence of the personality. For upon behavior and its results depends everything which is generally regarded as important: physical well-being and survival, development and achievement, happiness and the perpetuation of the species. We are not interested in overt behavior to the exclusion of other aspects: inner conflicts, feelings, emotions, sentiments, fantasies, and beliefs. But, in accord with many psychologists, we believe that it is best to start with behavior. And, since here it is my aim to describe behavior rather than the external factors which determine it, I shall, for the present, have little to say about the nature of the environment.

We must begin by limiting ourselves to a definite temporal unit—a temporal unit which holds together psychologically and is marked off by a more or less clear-cut beginning and ending. For such a behavioral event the following formula is as simple and convenient as any:

$$B.S. \rightarrow A \rightarrow E.S.$$

where B.S. stands for the conditions that exist at the initiation of activity; E.S. for the conditions that exist at the cessation of activity; and A for the action patterns, motor or verbal, of the organism. The difference between B.S. and E.S. (what might be called the B–E form of the behavioral event) describes the *effect* which has been produced by the action patterns.

No matter how a behavioral event is analyzed, whether it is taken as a whole (molar description), or whether it is analyzed into parts (molecular description), the action patterns (bodily movements of the organism) and the B–E form (effect produced) can be distinguished. One may always ask, "What is done?" (i.e., "What effect is produced?") and "How is it done?" (i.e., "What means are used?"). These two objectively apparent aspects of a behavioral event, though always intimately connected, can and should be clearly differentiated. For instance:

B.S.	$\longrightarrow$	A	$\longrightarrow$	E.S.
(1) Food placed before a child with an empty stomach		Crying, followed by swallowing of food that is offered by mother		Food in the stomach
(2) Food placed before a child with an empty stomach		Eating with a knife and fork		Food in the stomach

It should be noted that the B–E forms in the two events are similar, but the action patterns are different.

Though the introduction of new terms is sometimes confusing and should be avoided if possible, I require, at this point, a single term which will refer only to bodily movements as such (the mechanisms, means, ways, modes) and not at all to the effects of such movements. The word "action" cannot be used because it is commonly employed to describe both the movements and the effect of the movements. Hoping, then, for the reader's tolerance, I shall introduce the term *actone* to stand for any action pattern *qua* action pattern. And, since action patterns are mostly of two sorts, I shall divide *actones* into: motones (muscular-motor action patterns) and verbones (verbal action patterns).

A motone is a temporal series of more or less organized muscular contractions and a verbone is a temporal series of more or less organized words or written symbols. The verbone is constituted by the actual words used. The intended or actual effect of a verbone is something quite different.

Now, since the first systematic step in the construction of any science is that of classification, we, as students of behavior, must find proper criteria for distinguishing one form of conduct from another. The problem arises, shall we classify in terms of actones or in terms of effects? We may, of course, and shall eventually, classify according to both criteria, but the question is, which method is the more profitable for scientific purposes? We can predict that the two classifications will not correspond. According to one method we shall find in each category a number of similar actones, and according to the other method we shall find in each category a number of similar effects. Since it is obvious that similar actones—putting food in the mouth and putting poison in the mouth— may have different effects, and different actones—putting poison in the mouth and pulling the trigger of a revolver—may have similar effects, *the aspects of conduct that are described when we classify in terms of actones are different from those described when we classify in terms of effects.*

Practical experience has led me to believe that of the two the classification in terms of effects organizes for our understanding something that is more fundamental than what is organized by the classification in terms of actones. Without minimizing the great significance of the latter, I should like briefly to enumerate the reasons for this opinion.

1. Physical survival depends upon the attainment of certain effects; not upon what actones are employed.

If oxygen, water and nutriment are not assimilated or if injurious substances are not avoided, the organism will die.

2. Certain effects are universally attained by living organisms, but the actones that attain them vary greatly from one species to another.

Some organisms kill their prey with teeth and claws, others by injecting venom.

3. During the life history of a single individual certain effects are regularly attained, but the actones change.

The embryo assimilates food through the umbilical vessels, the infant sucks it from the tendered breast of the mother, the child eats with a spoon what is put before him, and the adult has to work, or steal, to get money to buy food.

4. According to the Law of Effect, which is widely accepted in one or another of its modifications, the actones which become habitual are for the most part those which, in the past, have led most directly to "satisfying" end situations. Hence, effects determine what actones become established.

5. When confronted by a novel situation, an organism commonly persists in its "efforts" to bring about a certain result, but with each frustration it is apt to change its mode of attack. Here, the trend is the constant feature and the mechanism is inconstant.

6. There are some effects which can only be attained by entirely novel actones.

As a rule, laughter in others is only evoked by a *new* joke.

7. That actones are of secondary importance is shown by the fact that many biologically necessary effects may be brought about by the activity of another person.

The essential wants of a sick or paralyzed child may be supplied by its mother.

We may see, I think, from this brief list of observations that certain effects are more fundamental to life and occur more regularly than any observed action patterns. This agrees with Skinner's conclusions. The latter found in his experiments with rats that if one takes a particular effect—the depression of a lever—as the criterion for the rate of responding, one gets quantitatively lawful results; whereas if one takes a particular actone—for instance, the movement of the rat's right paw (on the lever)—one gets irregular and inconsistent results. In other words, the rat may use one of a number of different movements to depress the lever. The movements, Skinner concludes, are "all equally elicitable by the stimulation arising from the lever, they are *quantitatively mutually replaceable.* The uniformity of the change in rate excludes any supposition that we are dealing with a group of separate reflexes, and forces the conclusion that 'pressing the lever' behaves experimentally as a unitary thing."[22]

In passing, it may be said that the "depression of the lever" is what we should call a subsidiary effect (sub-effect), since, according to the conditions of the experiment, it is an effect which must occur before the major effect—"getting food into the stomach"—is accomplished.

At this point a new concept should be introduced, for there are many acts which, because of some accident or because of the organism's lack of innate or acquired ability, never reach an end situation, that is, the total effect (B–E form) is never realized. In such cases, the direction of the movements is usually evident enough, or their preliminary results sufficient, to allow an experienced observer to predict with a reasonable degree of accuracy what total effect is being promoted. Such a succession of minor, subsidiary effects (sub-effects) may be called a *trend*. Thus, a *trend* describes the direction of movements *away from* the B.S.—movements which, if unembarrassed, would reach a certain kind of E.S. By the use of this concept we may include for classification actions which, though incomplete, manifest a tendency to achieve a certain end.

"Trend" should be a satisfactory term for psychologists who admit the directional character of behavior but do not wish to employ a concept that points to something "behind" the tangible facts.

Now, let us assume that the actual business of classifying in terms of B–E forms has been accomplished. In this classification each category (B–E form) is merely a phenomenal concept, since it is no more than a general description of a trend exhibited by organisms. In other words, it is merely a collective term for a certain class of occurrences. If we were radical positivists, or if we were primarily concerned with environmental changes, we might stop here. But we are not, and so we ask ourselves: what process or force within the organism brings about the observed effects? We say force because, according to physical theory, all manifest effects of any kind are due to energy overcoming resistance, i.e., force. For the physicist force has now become a measurement of motion, a mere symbol in an equation; but for generations the notion of force as a propelling activity was indispensable to the physicist and, in my opinion, it will be indispensable (i.e., a convenient fiction) to the psychologist for a long time to come. If the psychologist could deal directly with the brain and measure a drive process (such as I am now conceptualizing), then, perhaps, its force might be defined in terms of pointer readings; but, unlike the physicist, the psychologist must infer intensities in the brain on the basis of productions that have no meaningful physical dimensions. For example, one psychological index of the degree of a person's passion is the word that he uses to express it. Take "like," "love," "adore." Such a gradation is not representable in physical units.

Here we have to do with nervous energy or force, of which we know little, and, therefore, when we use this term in psychology we are referring to something which is analogous to, but not the same as, physical force. We need such a term for it is impossible to construct a dynamical theory without it. We are able to measure differences in the intensity and duration of directed activity. To what may such differences be referred if not to differences in the force of an organic drive? Furthermore, as Lewin has pointed out, the notions of organization and equilibrium necessitate a concept of force. It is always a matter of balance, economy or least action of energy. A number of other considerations favorable to this hypothesis will be advanced later. Are there any adequate reasons for hesitating to do what physical scientists have consistently done before us: conceptualize processes "behind" appearances?

Now, to explain the observed phenomena—the realization of a certain effect—what attributes must be possessed by an organic force? Let us see. It must be something: (a) that is engendered by a certain kind of B.S.; (b) that tends to induce activity, activity which, at first, may be restless and random, but, later, becomes effectively organized; and (c) that tends to persist until a situation (E.S.) is reached which contrasts with the B.S. in certain specific respects. The E.S. *stills* the force which the B.S. *incites.* Thus, the force tends, by producing a certain trend, to bring about its own resolution.

On the basis of this characterization we have constructed a hypothetical entity which has been termed a *need* (or *drive*). Each need has (a) a typical directional or qualitative aspect, (B–E) form, which differentiates it from other needs, as well as (b) an energic or quantitative aspect, which may be estimated in a variety of ways. Thus, the first and best criterion for distinguishing a certain need is the production by the subject of a certain effect, or, if not this, the occurrence of a certain trend.

Between what we can directly observe—the stimulus and the resulting action—a need is an invisible link, which may be imagined to have the properties that an understanding of the observed phenomena demand. "Need" is, therefore, a hypothetical concept.

Strictly speaking, a need is the immediate outcome of certain internal and external occurrences. It comes into being, endures for a moment and perishes. It is not a static entity. It is a resultant of forces. One need succeeds another. Though each is unique, observation teaches that there are similarities among them, and on the basis of this, needs may be grouped together into classes; each class being, as it were, a single major need. Thus, we may speak of similar needs as being different exhibitions of *one need* just as when we recognize a friend we do not hesitate to call him by name though he is different from the person with whom we conversed yesterday. Between the different appearances of a certain kind of need there may be nothing to suggest it, but everyday experience and experiment show that if the proper conditions are provided the need (i.e., another manifestation of the same kind of need) will be activated. Thus, we may loosely use the term "need" to refer to an organic potentiality or readiness to respond in a certain way under given conditions. In this sense a need is a latent attribute of an organism. More strictly, it is a noun which stands for the fact that a certain trend is apt to recur. We have not found that any confusion arises when we use "need" at one time to refer to a temporary happening and at another to refer to a more or less consistent trait of personality.

With successive activations each need tends to become more fixedly associated with the actones which have successfully led to end situations; or, in other words, stereotypes of response commonly become established (mechanization of behavior). When this occurs "habit pattern" may to some extent replace "need" as an explanatory concept (*cf.* Woodworth[23]).

The seven points which were listed to demonstrate the importance of trends and effects are equally favorable to the concept of need, since a need is, by definition, the force within the organism which determines a certain trend or major effect. There are sixteen additional arguments in favor of needs which may now be set down.

8. An enduring directional tendency (disequilibrium) within the organism accounts for the *persistence* of a trend (furthered by a great variety of actones) toward a certain general effect. In some cases no single action pattern endures or recurs; but something else (some intra-organic factor such as anoxemia or dehydration) must endure or recur because the trend endures or recurs. Difficult to interpret without a concept of directional tension are the following: the *resumption* of unpleasant work after interruption and the *increase* of striving in the face of opposition.

9. Complex action is characterized by the occurrence of muscular contractions in widely separate parts of the organism—contractions which manifest synchronous and consecutive coordination. Such organizations of movement must be partially determined by a directional process—which is just what a need, by definition, is. Furthermore, the directional process must occur in some central area of communication—in this instance, nervous communication. Thus, the need process must be placed in the brain, for this is the only area to and from which all nerves lead. It is even conceivable that some day there may be instruments for measuring need tension directly.

10. The concept of a directional force within the organism is something to which one may refer differences in the intensity and duration of goal-directed behavior. The strength of the action cannot be ascribed to the actones *per se*, since these may, and commonly do, vary from moment to moment. Not infrequently, for instance, it seems that the intensity of directional activity is maximal at the very time when one actone is being replaced by another (ex: violent trial and error movements).

11. An investigator may often interrupt the action pattern of his subject by bringing about the appropriate effect (the "goal" of the subject) himself. This may be termed a *gratuity,* or gratuitous end situation. According to the need theory this should relieve the need tension and, as it usually does, stop the action. But if the actone itself were the dynamic factor, the presentation of the E.S. would not interrupt it. The actone would continue to its completion.

12. That a need is an important determinant of certain kinds of behavior is shown by the fact that when it is neither active nor in a state of readiness responses to specific stimuli do not occur.

(a) Animals recently fed do not commonly respond to food. (b) Female guinea pigs exhibit the copulatory reflex only during oestrous.

13. When a particular need is active, common objects in the environment may evoke uncommon responses—responses however which promote the progress of the active need. Thus, the usual s-r (stimulus-response) connection may not be exhibited.

When a boy, who is quarrelling with a playmate, sees an apple, he may not respond, as he usually does, by eating it, but, instead, may throw it at his antagonist.

It seems highly probable that many of the s-r connections which are considered stable by experimenters are stable only under the conditions of their experiments, that is, when the same need—usually hunger—is active in the organism.

14. When a need becomes active a characteristic trend of behavior will usually ensue even in the absence of the customary stimuli.

An animal will *explore* for food, and a man will *search* for a sex object.

15. Positivists are usually disinclined to accept the concept of drive, because they cannot, as it were, get their hands on it. It seems like a vague, airy conception—perhaps a disguised emissary of theology and metaphysics. That someday definite *sources* of the drives may be discovered is suggested by certain recent findings, and these constitute another argument in favor of the concept.

(a) The recent researches of Riddle[24] indicate that prolactin, a pituitary hormone, is responsible for the nurturing, or parental, activity of rats. (b) The findings of Young[25] show that two secretions, the luteinizing hormone from the pituitary and progesterol from the ovary, bring on oestrous in guinea pigs.

A hormone may be the generator of a drive, but it cannot be the drive itself. A chemical substance is one thing, the excitation which it sets up in the brain is another.

Up to this point the evidence in support of the concept of internal driving forces has been derived from extrospection. I have presented only external public and objective facts. I shall now, without shame, turn to the testimony offered by internal, private, or subjective facts, including a few additional objective facts for full measure.

16. Introspection has given us a good deal of information about the subjective entities that are necessary for the formulation of mental, and, hence, we must suppose, of cerebral events. If the double aspect theory is correct, every subjective entity must have a physical correlate. Consequently, we should expect to find a cortical or sub-cortical process co-existing with the experience of desiring (volition, conation, etc.). "Wishing for something" or "the desire to do something" may be as actual and definite as the fact that one "sees a tree out there." Since a need, as defined, closely resembles in all its relations the inner feeling of tension which seems to impel us to strive for a certain goal, we may tentatively suppose that a need is an electro-chemical process of some sort which is inwardly felt as the force of desire.

The subjective experience of desiring, intending, or planning usually precedes the experience of striving. It is, therefore, pre-motor, just as a need, by definition, is pre-motor.

Since a need is commonly aroused by certain afferent processes, and since it may justly be considered the physical correlate of the force of desire, and since, finally, as we shall see, it directly affects perception and thought, we may tentatively suppose that it is located in the brain, "between" the sensory and motor areas. It is, let us say, a directional tension (one might almost say a facilitation) which is the resultant of certain electrical or chemical processes originating in other, more or less specific parts of the body. This, of course, is highly speculative.

If we assume, then, that desire and drive are two aspects of the same thing, we may use introspection to reveal to us some of the possible internal relations of drives. For instance, it is reasonable to suppose, as objective researches and introspection suggest, that every need is associated with traces (or images) representing movements, agencies, pathways, and goal objects, which, taken together, constitute a dynamic whole, *need integrate*. This need integrate may exhibit itself as a fantasy which depicts a possible and perhaps expected course of events. It seems reasonable to think of a drive as a force in the brain exciting a flow of images—images which refer, for the most part, to objects once perceived in conjunction with the activity of that drive.

With this in mind, we may consider a number of other facts, mostly subjective, which seem to call for such a concept of directional tensions in the brain region.

17. Among the commonest subjective experiences is that of conflict between desires, and that of having one desire inhibit another. If psychology limits itself to concepts which refer only to external movements, there will be no way of formulating important psychological events of this sort.

18. Although many psychologists may describe events without explicit mention of affection (pleasure or unpleasure) they are unable to get

along without this variable when they have to deal practically with themselves or with others. This is not the time to discuss psychological hedonism, but at least, I may say, what most people, I think, would agree to, namely, that pleasure is closely associated with a successful trend: the moving toward and final achievement of a major effect. It is less closely associated with activity *qua* activity—movements, let us say, which achieve nothing. Furthermore, introspection seems to reveal that a need does not cease (is not "satisfied") until pleasure is experienced. In fact, it often happens that we do not properly distinguish a need until an object that brings pleasure informs us of what it was we wanted. The point that I am making here is this: that because of its close connection with happiness and distress, a need is more "important" than an action pattern.

19. Experience seems to show that a certain desire may sometimes give rise to a dream or fantasy and at other times promote overt activity. Without the concept of an underlying drive one could not adequately represent the obvious relationship between fantasy and behavior.

There is a good deal of evidence to support the view that under certain conditions fantasy may partially relieve the tension of a need; that is, it may be the equivalent of overt action.

20. Introspection and experiment demonstrate that a need or an emotion may determine the direction of attention and markedly influence the perception and apperception (interpretation) of external occurrences. To influence sensory and cognitive processes a need must be some force in the brain region.

(a) Sanford[26] has shown that hunger will influence a child's completion of unfinished pictures. (b) Murray[27] has shown that fear will change a child's interpretation of photographs.

21. Everyday experience informs us that sentiments and theories are to a varying extent determined by desires. A man likes and tries to prove (by rationalizations) the value of what he wants. He also "projects" his own needs into his psychological theories.

Every impulse is a tyrant and as such attempts to philosophize. (Nietzsche)
Metaphysics is the finding of bad reasons for what we believe on instinct. (F. H. Bradley)

22. Introspection and clinical observation reveal that different desires (or trends) may be related in a variety of ways: one form of behavior may satisfy two or more desires, a desire may inhibit another, one trend may serve finally to promote another, a trend may be succeeded by its opposite, etc. Such relationships cannot be formulated

without a concept of different directional processes interacting in one region of the body, the brain.

23. Without a concept of motivating forces most of the phenomena of abnormal psychology would be wholly unintelligible. This applies to compulsion, conflict, repression, conversion, displacement, sublimation, delusion, and so forth. And without such a concept a therapist would be literally tongue-tied. He could communicate neither with his patients nor with his colleagues.

When we consider that no therapist or, indeed, anyone who has to deal in a practical way with human beings, can get along without some notion of motivational force (instinct, purpose, aim, intention, need, drive, impulse, urge, attitude, inclination, wish, desire, or what not), the suspicion naturally arises that those who entertain a prejudice against such a concept do so on metaphysical or "religious" grounds.

Need as a Dynamic Concept

In so far as a need is defined as a disequilibrium which stresses toward equilibrium, it falls into the category of finalistic concepts, of which the Second Law of Thermodynamics is typical. The latter has been stated as follows: "In all processes with which we are acquainted, every known form of energy at a high potential always tends to run down to energy at the lowest potential circumstances will allow." According to this principle, affairs tend to take a certain course. The need theory calls attention to a similar phenomenon observable in human behavior. A trend is like a tropism, a movement away from or toward some source of stimulation, or, again, it is similar to the attraction and repulsion of chemical substances.

Suppose that two hydrogen atoms are some distance apart with the total energy necessary to make a molecule. If they begin to move towards one another under some attractive influence which they exert we display no surprise. But they are moving towards a final end, which is an end, even though they are of course unconscious of it; and provided that nothing interferes they will reach one another, form a molecule, and the process will be consummated. The atoms move under an irresistible law of attraction towards a final condition which is unavoidable unless outside influences prevent it. The system of the two atoms develops necessarily towards a consummation, and the process has in this sense a teleological quality, though this need not mean that any god or man had consciously planned the end for these particular hydrogen atoms.

Thus all heat processes tend towards an approximate uniformity of temperature, and chemical reactions also move towards a final condition.[28]

It seems peculiar that psychologists should make such obstinate attempts to evade the directional or *finalistic* aspect of living processes, in the name of science, when most sciences have recorded and conceptualized such tendencies. Physiologists, for example, have always been guided by the notion of function. They have always asked themselves, "What is the function of this process?" and by "function" they have meant "survivalistic value." Take homeostasis, for example.[29] The concept expresses the fact that the various activities of the body are organized in such a way as to maintain and, if it is disturbed, restore a steady state in the body. Homeostasis calls attention to the *direction* of coordinated physiological action.

A need is clearly an emergence from the immediate past, or, as Schopenhauer would have it, "a push from the rear," rather than a "pull from the future." The environment may, of course, be effective in arousing this "push," and to consciousness the field that lies before its vision or the imagery which seems to anticipate such a field commonly appears in the guise of a pull, positive incentive, or attraction. We should say that the notion of an attracting or repelling object (press) is a necessary complement to the need concept; also that some reference to a possible future is an intrinsic determinant of the moment. But the future does not exist. There is merely the present situation with a field extending before the subject either as meaningful, patterned percepts or meaningful, patterned images. The laying out of images "ahead of time" expresses that aspect of human experience which is designated by the words "anticipation," "expectation," "hope." However, the imaginal representation of the goal (conscious purpose) does not always occur. To put it metaphorically, a need may have no inkling of *what* it needs. It may be a blind impulse, but an impulse which does not as a rule completely subside until a situation of a certain kind has been arrived at. It is because of this that we speak of drive as a finalistic rather than a mechanistic concept. Those who use finalism in some other sense should not apply it to the need theory as here developed. This, of course, does not supersede the mechanistic account of things. For we must also take cognizance of the stimulus-response sequences, the linked actones and agencies by means of which the closing situation is achieved and the tension lowered.

I hesitate to use the term "mechanism," for, as Whitehead has said, "nobody knows what mechanism is." However, in modern psychology, "mechanism" and "dynamism" have been used as convenient labels for two contrasting points of view and I think it will not be confusing if I limit them to this application. The words are not important to us. It is the two seemingly opposite mental sets that are important. At one pole stands the psychologist who attempts to show that a human being behaves like a very complicated man-made machine, and at the other stands the psychologist who believes that human behavior is determined by conscious purpose. My own position is that in some events it is mechanism and in others it is dynamism that prevails (providing that the dynamic factor is given a strictly present organic status [ex: an existing process in the brain]). In most behavioral events both principles seem to be operating (in different proportions). I am presenting the facts that favor dynamism, because at present—in America particularly—mechanism as a general proposition requires no further demonstration. It enjoys a large prestige. It is almost synonymous with "righteousness" and "purity." It attracts all the young scientific climbers. Its facts are rather obvious. They are relatively clear and tangible. They have already been well presented. Everybody agrees—up to a point. But dynamism, despite McDougall's able advocacy,[30] is still "out of court." It is "unscientific," "mystical," "vague."

A machine gives an invariable response which may be predicted by a study of the physical relations of its parts. With this in mind, mechanistic psychologists have looked for actones which invariably followed specific stimuli (automatic reflexes). They have succeeded in finding a number of them (ex: the knee jerk) and in showing that they can be adequately explained by reference to the passage of impulses over a certain circuit of nerve fibers. Thus, mechanistic principles apply to some actions. However, it does not seem that they apply to others. There is adaptive behavior, for example; and even mechanistic psychologists use the term "adaptation," despite the fact that it stands for an activity which has characteristics opposite to those of a reflex. Adaptive behavior is marked by a *change* of actones. What consistency there is in adaptive behavior is found in the *trend* that follows a certain kind of stimulation and this, as we have suggested, must be attributed to some drive process in the brain. The introduction of this hypothetical factor disturbs the mechanists because they cannot find a corresponding "something" in the nervous system. But suppose it were a chemical substance (hormone) that is extrinisic to the nervous system? It is interesting to note that mechanistic psychologists attempt to explain everything solely in terms of the cerebro-neuro-muscular (somatic) system. (Hence they draw most of their analogies from physics.) They rarely mention the fluid conditions in the brain. Dynamicists, on the other hand, may go so far as to regard the exterofective nervous system as a mere instrument of the body (torso), an instrument that is used to organize the locomotions and manipulations which are necessary to bring about the effects that facilitate (rather than obstruct) the processes of life in the vital organs. The dynamicists get more instruction from chemistry than they do from nineteenth-century physics. At this point I might suggest that the controversy could be described as one between "limb" psychology (focusing on reflexes, motor co-ordination, and behavioral intelligence) and "torso" psychology (focusing on digestion, respiration, endocrines, erogenous zones, and reproduction).

The first distinguishing characteristic of dynamism, then, is this: an emphasis upon the lawful connection between a certain kind of stimulus (press) and a certain kind of trend (effect), rather than the connection between a stimulus and an actone. In order to make the record that he desires, the mechanist must observe the *bodily movements* and the dynamist must observe the *situation which is changed* by the bodily movements. For example, the pupillary reflex might be described as a "movement of the iris" (mechanism) or as a "shutting out of light" (dynamism). The same effect might have been accomplished by shielding the eyes with the hand. Dynamism's second distinguishing characteristic is the conceptualization of (qualitatively and quantitatively different) premotor excitations or *forces*, which are evoked by appropriate stimuli (press) and remain active until the situation is modified. The point is that *they are not discharged by a bodily response as such.* Thirdly, dynamism emphasizes the relation of such forces to the well-being of the organism. It can be observed that a trend moves almost invariably toward supplying a lack, relieving a distension, or getting rid of an irritant. Thus, the final effect upon which everything depends is an occurrence *inside* the organism which can be described as the *rectification of a disturbed vital function.* For this reason it seems necessary to put the dynamic variable beneath the skin. Finally, dynamism is distinguished by its gross or *molar* descriptions of behavior, some of which merely record the difference between the beginning and the end situation. A dynamicist might say, for example, "The man built a house," without feeling that it was necessary to record the numberless bodily movements, tools, materials, and pathways that were employed in the construction. This point of view can be compared to that of thermodynamics.

The characteristic feature of thermodynamics is that it permits us to deal with energy changes involved in a physical change of state, or in a chemical reaction, without in any way requiring information regarding the molecular mechanisms of the process under investigation.[31]

The dynamicist, of course, admits that there are innate reflexive patterns. But it is easier for him to see how these developed philogenetically (as they do ontogenetically) from trial and error adaptive movements and became fixed, than it is to see how fixed reflexes can, by mere combination, produce creatively effective action.

Dynamicists can point to the fact that most reflexes are now adaptive or were once adaptive. Thus, even what appears now as mechanism was dynamism once. Reflexes that have no adaptive value are either mere reactivities to proximate blows (ex: the tendon reflexes) or vestigial remnants of past adaptations. Individual life is conditioned by a multitude of previous life cycles. Perhaps the elimination of a species in the evolutionary struggle is favored by over-mechanization ("trained incapacity").

If the evidence advanced here is valid, the conclusion should be that mechanism and dynamism represent two complementary aspects of organic life. Certainly there is no dynamism without mechanism. Furthermore, there are, it seems, gradations between actions which are predominantly dynamic and those that are predominantly mechanical.

As an example of mechanical activity we may mention, besides simple reflexes: more complex chain reflexes, automatisms and tics of various sorts, obsessional fixations to certain objects, stubborn and invariable habits, inflexible stereotypes of gesture and expression. We note that these forms of activity are more common during fatigue, periods of absent-mindedness, and old age. We speak of a personality becoming mechanized or of a mind becoming "ossified," and we mean by this expression the disappearance of novelty, the decrease of adaptability and the loss of creativity. On the other hand, there are forms of behavior which are far from being mechanical: the appearance of unique adaptations, intuition, and insight into new relations, witty repartee, spontaneity, and flexibility in manner and expression, and all types of truly creative thought. The poet may be taken as a prototype. To be successful he must write a new poem; that is, he must do something that has never been done before. All poets have the same elements to work with, namely, the words of the language, but a poet of merit puts these words together in a way that excites wonder and pleasure.

To psychologists who bristle when "purpose" is mentioned, I am tempted to quote Whitehead: "Scientists animated by the purpose of proving that they are purposeless constitute an interesting subject for study."[32]

From this exposition it should be clear that the term "need" or "drive" does not denote an observable fact—the direction of activity, for example. For this we have the terms "behavioral trend" or "behavioral effect." Nor does "drive" refer to any attribute of general activity as such. It refers to a hypothetical process within the brain of an organism which, perseverating for a time, "points" activity and co-ordinates it. If opposed by another need process, however, it may not manifest itself overtly.

Again, it should be clear that the term "need" or "drive" does not stand for any physiological occurrences (visceral tension or endocrine secretion) which may lead up to or evoke the directive processes in the brain. The former may be termed "sources" or "provokers" of needs, but they are not themselves need processes.

The word "need" (and to a lesser extent the word "drive") seems to disturb some psychologists more than the concept itself, for it smacks of anthropomorphism. The dynamicists are accused of the "sin of animism" (projecting life into inanimate objects) despite the fact that the objects of psychological concern are not inanimate. The only sin of this sort that is possible is the "sin of inanimism" (projecting a machine into life), and of this the mechanists are certainly guilty. However, we might have avoided a great deal of misunderstanding if we had used the letter "n" (as we shall frequently do) to represent the vectorial magnitude in the brain.

An activity in the brain has been conceptualized because it is the regnant processes in this region which we, as psychologists, must ulti-

mately attempt to formulate. If we do not, we shall never bring together into one conceptual scheme the facts of behavior, the facts of brain physiology and pathology and the facts of consciousness. It does not seem possible to place the factor which determines the directional effectiveness or intensity of behavior either in the afferent or in the efferent systems. It must be post-afferent and pre-efferent. The fact that we cannot conjure up an image of what such a cephalic field force might resemble is no reason for hesitating to use the concept as a working hypothesis.

If we were concerned with the individual merely as a unit in a field of social forces, then perhaps he might be treated as physicists treat a body: his behavior might be represented by an arrow (*cf.* Lewin[33]). But we are equally interested in field forces within the brain: conflicts between rival tendencies, the inhibition of emotion, "overcoming temptation," dissociation, and so forth. The individual is not always a unified being. This makes it necessary to conceptualize regnant (mental) forces.

We did not start the present discussion with an assertion. We merely pointed out that an hypothesis of a driving force helps to order some of the facts. According to this view a need is not a reified entity extrinsic to the system. It stands for the momentary direction of regnant processes in the brain region. It is always in a state of mutual dependence with other cephalic forces. It may change from one split second to the next. To say that an organism has a certain drive when that drive is not at the moment active is to make a very abstract, though convenient, statement. It means that a certain trend has commonly occurred in the past and, if conditions are suitable, it will probably recur in the future.

"Instinct," the noun, is a word to be avoided, because it has been so extensively used in two different senses: to signify innate actones and to signify innate needs.

It is true that if we consider the structure of the action pattern only, disregarding for the time being its origin, we cannot easily distinguish instinct from habit, for both are in their pure form, automatic stimulus-response processes.[34]

It is not the details of the response that are fixed by the innate factor we have called instinct, but rather the general nature of the end towards which the response shall move; the details are fixed by the limitations of the creature's intelligence and the structure of its sensory-motor mechanism.[35]

Another reason for discarding the term "instinct" is that it limits one to needs which can be proved innate. The problem of whether this or that need is innate is difficult of solution. Most of the primary viscerogenic needs, such as hunger and thirst, seem to be innate in the usual sense of the term. Presumably they are provoked by internal conditions regardless of the environment. Other needs, called by us "psychogenic needs," though found to operate without obvious dependence upon the viscerogenic needs, were perhaps once subsidiary to the latter. Further-more, though their manifestations have been observed in all peoples, they are influenced to a great extent by cultural forms, particularly when the latter are represented by the parents.

Needs from a Subjective Standpoint

Using the deliverances of introspection for all they are worth, experi-ence seems to show that the earliest intimation of a succeeding action is a kind of inner tension, viscerogenic or psychogenic. This inner state may be taken as the subjective aspect of what we have termed "need." There may be no awareness of what is needed. It may be simply the experience of a vague "lack" or "pressure" giving rise to unrest, uneasiness, dissatis-faction. If images of the need object or needed activity appear in con-sciousness, one commonly speaks of "desire" or "wish," an experience which may occur without motor involvement. We may imagine that an increase of need activity leads to an intention (the decision to perform a certain act) and finally to a conation, or the experience of striving, which, we may assume, corresponds to the excitation of actones.

Desire, intention, conation may be conveniently grouped together. It is even possible that they belong on a single continuum. They appear, in any case, to be irreducible facts of inner experience that call for an objective correlate. Though we are using "need" and "drive" synony-mously, "need" seems to be the better word for the initiating appercep-tion of an obstruction (lack, harm) leading to desire, whereas "drive" designates more appropriately the ensuing activity (conation).

Some desires and intentions are subjectively felt to be in conflict with the chief aim of the self or with the "selected personality" (Ego Ideal): what the S wants to be or to become. Such impulses appear as "temptations," "seductive suggestions" or "irresistible compulsions." Ac-cording to a scheme that shall be presented later, all drives that subjec-tively seem to come from "without" the self, that are unacceptable or opposed to the "best intentions" of the personality, have been termed "Id" needs (idn). Id needs may or may not be resisted (inhibited or repressed). Then there are needs, evoked by sudden, close stimuli, that are impulsively and emotionally objectified without a preceding con-scious intention. These may be termed emotional needs (emn). Many "emotional" needs are also Id needs, opposed to the selected personality. Then there are some needs that are not represented in consciousness by an explicit desire, the trend and action pattern being objectified "auto-matically." The first phase in an emotional need is also automatic (cf. startle response[36]), but the behavior that we are now distinguishing 1, is not emotional; 2, is usually acceptable to the personality; and 3, conforms to previous patterns of behavior. It is comparable to a pattern of adapted chained reflexes. The theory is that it has been "stamped in" by repetition. It has become a habit; or, in other words, the actonal factor is now more conspicuous than the drive factor (mechanization of behavior). This we shall term an "actonal" need (an). A need may also be objectified (as unwittingly as an actonal need) in conformity with a perceived trend exhibited by another person (imitation); or in response to demands or persuasions (compliance). Finally, one should mention the needs that are engendered by a dissociated part of the regnancy, as one finds in hysteria (fugues and conversion symptoms).

Needs, Viscerogenic and Psychogenic

Up to this point only two criteria for distinguishing needs have been stressed: the kind of trend (effect) observed objectively and the kind of effect which the subject says that he intends or desires. Though these provide an insufficient basis for a satisfactory classification, we shall, nevertheless, now offer a list of the needs that we have found it profitable to distinguish, in order to assist the reader in following the further elaboration of the theory.

Needs may be conveniently divided into: 1, primary (viscerogenic) needs, and 2, secondary (psychogenic) needs. The former are engendered and stilled by characteristic periodic bodily events, whereas the latter have no subjectively localizable bodily origins; hence the term "psychogenic." They are occasioned by regnant tensions, with or without emotion, that are closely dependent upon certain external conditions or upon images depicting these conditions. Thus, speaking loosely, we may say that from a subjective standpoint the viscerogenic needs have to do with physical satisfactions and the psychogenic needs with mental or emotional satisfactions.

The viscerogenic needs are: 1, n Air, 2, n Water, 3, n Food, 4, n Sex, 5, n Lactation, 6, n Urination, 7, n Defecation, 8, n Harmavoidance, 9, n Noxavoidance, 10, n Heatavoidance, 11, n Coldavoidance, and 12, n Sentience. We also recognize a need for Passivity, which includes relaxation, rest and sleep, but this may be neglected for the present.*

It is hard to decide whether one should concoct new words as names for the needs or attempt to get along with old and ill-used terms. In the present endeavor sometimes one and sometimes the other of these two possibilities was adopted but without conviction. It was found that no system of nomenclature could be consistently maintained: appropriate words were not forthcoming.

The words used for most of the viscerogenic needs indicate in each case what effect is brought about by the need action. The n Noxavoid-

*It is heartening to discover, as P. T. Young's recent book (*Motivation of Behavior*, New York, 1936) makes evident, that psychologists are reaching agreement in regard to the most convenient classification of viscerogenic drives.

ance refers to the tendency to avoid or rid oneself of noxious stimuli: to look or draw away from repulsive objects, to cough, spit, or vomit up irritating or nauseating substances. The needs for Heatavoidance and Coldavoidance together refer to the tendency to maintain an equable temperature: to avoid extremes of heat and cold, to clothe the body or seek shelter when necessary. The n Harmavoidance refers to the tendency to avoid physical pain: to withdraw, flee or conceal oneself from injuring agents. It includes "startle" and "fear" reactions generally, to loud noises, loss of support, strangers. The n Sentience refers to the inclination for sensuous gratification, particularly from objects in contact with the body: taste sensations and tactile sensations (ex: thumb-sucking). The need moves in a direction opposite to that of the n Noxavoidance and the n Harmavoidance. But it may be associated with any one of the other needs: local sensations are an important part of sexual activity and they may accompany urination and defecation; moderate changes in temperature are sensuously agreeable and food may give rise to delicious olfactory and gustatory impressions.

The effect of the need action in each case can be represented by the B–E form.

B.S.	E.S.
Lack of food	Repletion
Genital tumescence	Detumescence
Fluid in the bladder	Evacuation
Pain	Absence of pain

A few remarks at this point may not be amiss:

1. Some of the needs here distinguished represent gross groupings of a number of more specific needs. The n Food, for instance, could be divided into separate needs for different kinds of food. Here they are combined for convenience because they all involve "feeding behavior" and the objects are all nourishing.

i. Certain animals go to salt licks—as certain tribes used to travel to salt mines —for the sole purpose of adding this necessary ingredient to their diet. ii. Diabetics have an appetite for sugar; sufferers from deficiency diseases "need" this or that vitamin, and so forth.

2. It will be noticed that the B.S. for most of the viscerogenic needs are afferent impulses from some region of the body.

3. The viscerogenic needs are of unequal importance as variables of personality. The personological significance of a need seems to depend upon whether there are marked differences between individuals in the frequency, intensity and duration of its activity, and upon whether the strength of any psychogenic needs are functions of such differences. A need, furthermore, does not usually become a dominant element of personality if there is no obstruction to its satisfaction. If its activity and

gratification can be "taken for granted," it may be neglected. The n Air, for example, is perhaps the most essential of all the needs from a biological standpoint, since if the organism does not attain this need's E.S. in three or four minutes, it dies. And yet the n Air is rarely of any personological importance. Air is free and most human beings get enough of it. There is little competition for air. The n Sex, on the other hand, ordinarily depends upon the co-operation of another person, is commonly interfered with by rivals, is highly unstable, and is hemmed in by all kinds of social restrictions. This is enough to account for its importance.

The viscerogenic needs enumerated above may be grouped in a number of ways. One convenient grouping (which calls for the division of the n Air into inspiration and expiration) is the following.

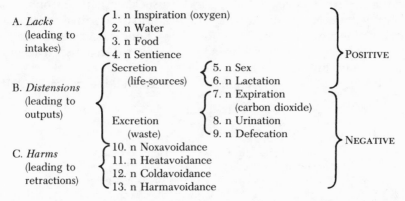

A. *Lacks* (leading to intakes)
- 1. n Inspiration (oxygen)
- 2. n Water
- 3. n Food
- 4. n Sentience

B. *Distensions* (leading to outputs)
- Secretion (life-sources)
  - 5. n Sex
  - 6. n Lactation
- Excretion (waste)
  - 7. n Expiration (carbon dioxide)
  - 8. n Urination
  - 9. n Defecation

C. *Harms* (leading to retractions)
- 10. n Noxavoidance
- 11. n Heatavoidance
- 12. n Coldavoidance
- 13. n Harmavoidance

POSITIVE

NEGATIVE

The first six needs may be called "positive" or "adient" needs because they force the organism in a positive way toward other objects: air, water, food, sensuous patterns, a sex object, a suckling. The last seven needs, on the other hand, may be called "negative" or "abient" needs because they force the organism to separate itself from objects: to eliminate waste matter, or to avoid unpleasant or injuring agents. The positive needs are chiefly characterized subjectively by a desire to reach the E.S., whereas the negative needs are chiefly characterized by a desire to get away from the B.S. The division of needs into lacks with intakes, distensions with outputs, and harms with retractions may also be found useful.

The secondary or psychogenic needs, which are presumably dependent upon and derived from the primary needs, may be briefly listed. They stand for common reaction systems and wishes. It is not supposed that they are fundamental, biological drives, though some may be innate. The first five pertain chiefly to actions associated with inanimate objects.*

*To some extent the same tendencies are exhibited towards people (acquiring friends, maintaining loyalties, possessiveness, organizing groups).

n Acquisition (Acquisitive attitude). To gain possessions and property. To grasp, snatch or steal things. To bargain or gamble. To work for money or goods.

n Conservance (Conserving attitude). To collect, repair, clean and preserve things. To protect against damage.

n Order (Orderly attitude). To arrange, organize, put away objects. To be tidy and clean. To be scrupulously precise.

n Retention (Retentive attitude). To retain possession of things. To refuse to give or lend. To hoard. To be frugal, economical, and miserly.

n Construction (Constructive attitude). To organize and build.

Actions which express what is commonly called ambition, will-to-power, desire for accomplishment and prestige have been classified as follows:

n Superiority (Ambitious attitude). This has been broken up into two needs: the n Achievement (will to power over things, people, and ideas) and the n Recognition (efforts to gain approval and high social status).

n Achievement (Achievant attitude). To overcome obstacles, to exercise power, to strive to do something difficult as well and as quickly as possible. (This is an elementary Ego need which alone may prompt any action or be fused with any other need.)

n Recognition (Self-forwarding attitude). To excite praise and commendation. To demand respect. To boast and exhibit one's accomplishments. To seek distinction, social prestige, honors, or high office.

We have questioned whether the next need should be distinguished from the Recognition drive. In the present study the two have been combined.

n Exhibition (Exhibitionistic attitude). To attract attention to one's person. To excite, amuse, stir, shock, thrill others. Self-dramatization.

Complementary to Achievement and Recognition are the desires and actions which involve the defense of status or the avoidance of humiliation:

n Inviolacy (Inviolate attitude). This includes desires and attempts to prevent a depreciation of self-respect, to preserve one's "good name," to be immune from criticism, to maintain psychological "distance." It is based on pride and personal sensitiveness. It takes in the n Seclusion (isolation, reticence, self-concealment) which in our study was considered to be the opposite of n Exhibition and, for this reason, was not separately considered. The n Inviolacy has been broken up into three needs: n Infavoidance (the fear of and retraction from possible sources of humiliation), n Defendance (the verbal defense of errors and misdemeanors), and n Counteraction (the attempt to redeem failures, to prove one's worth after frustration, to revenge an insult). Counteraction is not truly a separate need. It is n Achievement or n Aggression acting in the service of n Inviolacy.

n *Infavoidance* (Infavoidant attitude). To avoid failure, shame, humiliation, ridicule. To refrain from attempting to do something that is beyond one's powers. To conceal a disfigurement.

n *Defendance* (Defensive attitude). To defend oneself against blame or belittlement. To justify one's actions. To offer extenuations, explanations, and excuses. To resist "probing."

n *Counteraction* (Counteractive attitude). Proudly to overcome defeat by restriving and retaliating. To select the hardest tasks. To defend one's honor in action.

The next five needs have to do with human power exerted, resisted, or yielded to. It is a question of whether an individual, to a relatively large extent, initiates independently his own behavior and avoids influence, whether he copies and obeys, or whether he commands, leads, and acts as an exemplar for others.

n *Dominance* (Dominative attitude). To influence or control others. To persuade, prohibit, dictate. To lead and direct. To restrain. To organize the behavior of a group.

n *Deference* (Deferent attitude). To admire and willingly follow a superior allied O. To co-operate with a leader. To serve gladly.

n *Similance* (Suggestible attitude). To empathize. To imitate or emulate. To identify oneself with others. To agree and believe.

n *Autonomy* (Autonomous attitude). To resist influence or coercion. To defy an authority or seek freedom in a new place. To strive for independence.

n *Contrarience* (Contrarient attitude). To act differently from others. To be unique. To take the opposite side. To hold unconventional views.

The next two needs constitute the familiar sado-masochistic dichotomy. Aggression seems to be either 1, the heightening of the will-to-power (Achievement, Dominance) when faced by stubborn opposition, 2, a common reaction (fused with n Autonomy) toward an O that opposes any need, or 3, the customary response to an assault or insult. In the latter case (revenge) it is Counteraction acting in the service of n Inviolacy. One questions whether n Abasement should be considered a drive in its own right. Except for the phenomenon of masochism, Abasement seems always to be an attitude serving some other end: the avoidance of further pain or anticipated punishment, or the desire for passivity, or the desire to show extreme deference.

n *Aggression* (Aggressive attitude). To assault or injure an O. To murder. To belittle, harm, blame, accuse or maliciously ridicule a person. To punish severely. Sadism.

n *Abasement* (Abasive attitude). To surrender. To comply and accept punishment. To apologize, confess, atone. Self-depreciation. Masochism.

The next need has been given a separate status because it involves a subjectively distinguishable form of behavior, namely *inhibition*. Objectively, it is characterized by the absence of socially unacceptable conduct. The effect desired by the subject is the avoidance of parental or public disapprobation or punishment. The need rests on the supposition that there are in everybody primitive, asocial impulses, which must be restrained if the individual is to remain an accepted member of his culture.

n Blamavoidance (Blamavoidance attitude). To avoid blame, ostracism, or punishment by inhibiting asocial or unconventional impulses. To be well-behaved and obey the law.

The next four needs have to do with affection between people; seeking it, exchanging it, giving it, or withholding it.

nAffiliation (Affiliative attitude). To form friendships and associations. To greet, join, and live with others. To co-operate and converse sociably with others. To love. To join groups.
nRejection (Rejective attitude). To snub, ignore, or exclude an O. To remain aloof and indifferent. To be discriminating.
nNurturance (Nurturant attitude). To nourish, aid, or protect a helpless O. To express sympathy. To "mother" a child.
nSuccorance (Succorant attitude). To seek aid, protection, or sympathy. To cry for help. To plead for mercy. To adhere to an affectionate, nurturant parent. To be dependent.

To these may be added with some hesitation:

n Play (Playful attitude). To relax, amuse oneself, seek diversion and entertainment. To "have fun," to play games. To laugh, joke, and be merry. To avoid serious tension.

Finally, there are two complementary needs which occur with great frequency in social life, the need to ask and the need to tell.

nCognizance (Inquiring attitude). To explore (moving and touching). To ask questions. To satisfy curiosity. To look, listen, inspect. To read and seek knowledge.
nExposition (Expositive attitude). To point and demonstrate. To relate facts. To give information, explain, interpret, lecture.

On the basis of whether they lead a subject to *approach* or *separate* himself from an object, these derived needs may be divided into those which are *positive* and those which are *negative,* respectively. Positive needs may again be divided into *adient* needs: those which cause a subject to approach a *liked* object, in order to join, amuse, assist, heal, follow or co-operate with it; and *contrient* needs: those which cause a subject to approach a *disliked* object in order to dominate aggressively, abuse, injure, or destroy it. Negative needs, following Holt,[37] are *abient* needs.

This classification of needs is not very different from lists constructed by McDougall, Garnett, and a number of other writers. At first glance it is quite different from the scheme most commonly used in psychoanalysis. According to the latter there are two fundamental urges, or two classes of drives: ego instincts and sex instincts. Among the ego instincts is the hunger drive and the need for aggression. Hunger is rarely mentioned, but within recent years aggression has become one of the chief variables in the analyst's conceptual scheme. Aggression, the concomitant of hate, is considered to be the force which is operating when an individual attacks, injures, and murders others. It may also be turned inward, in which case the subject may abuse, mutilate, or even kill himself. Contrasting with aggression and other unnamed ego instincts are the sex instincts—the force underlying them all being termed "libido." Under sex has been subsumed:

1. The sex instinct proper, as biologists have described it, that is, the force which leads to the development of sexual characteristics and to intercourse between the sexes (n Sex).

2. All tendencies which seek and promote sensuous gratification (n Sentience), particularly the enjoyment of tactile sensations originating in certain sensitive regions of the body (the erogenous zones). Thus, analysts speak of oral, anal, urethral, and genital erotism.

3. All desires and actions which are attended by genital excitement or by that characteristic emotional state—the palpitating, ecstatic-like feeling—which is the usual accompaniment of sexual activity. Here one speaks of the erotization of a need (fusions with n Sex).

4. All manifestations of love and humane feeling: the emotions of a lover, feelings of friendship, social inclinations (n Affiliation) and maternal tenderness (n Nurturance). Here the sex instinct takes the place of the biologist's herd instinct. It binds people together and leads to peace and concord.

5. Self-love, or Narcism, is also considered to be a manifestation of the sex instinct, but here it is the sex instinct turned inward upon the subject (Narcism, or Egophilia).

Periodicity of Needs

Many of the viscerogenic needs are characterized by rather regular rhythms of activity and rest, rhythms which seem to be determined by an orderly succession of physiological events: inspiration and expiration, ingestion and excretion, waking and sleeping. Within certain limits, these rhythms may be modified by the will of the subject or by regimentation imposed from without.

Among psychogenic needs we also find some evidence of periodicity, particularly in the alterations of contrasting needs: sociability and solitude, talking and listening, leading and following, helping and being helped, giving and getting, work and play. Though in most cases, the frequency of such activities may be readily changed, under stable conditions a need may acquire a rhythmic habit which will determine its objectification irrespective of the immediately presenting environment. The organism will search periodically for an appropriate object.

The fact of periodicity speaks for the dynamic importance of intraorganic successions. It also speaks for a theory of dynamic forces rather than theories which attempt to explain behavior on the basis of chained reflexes.

For convenience, a single need cycle may be divided into: 1, a *refractory* period, during which no incentive will arouse it; 2, an *inducible* or *ready* period, during which the need is inactive but susceptible to excitation by appropriate stimuli; and 3, an *active* period, during which the need is determining the behavior of the total organism.

A need which is aroused in a subject and not completely objectified may *perseverate* for some time afterwards. During this period the subject will meet situations that present themselves with a *need set.* That is to say, the need in question will be in a state of high *inducibility* or high *readiness,* with a low *threshold of stimulation.* For example, if it is anger (n Aggression) that has been aroused, the subject will be apt to vent his emotion upon the first object that crosses his path, the object, in such a case, being called a *substitute* object (Freud).

Interrelation of Needs

In everyday life a subject may, within a short space of time, exhibit many needs in succession, each of them evoked by some newly arising circumstance. In such events there is no reason for conceptualizing an integration of needs within the personality. Likewise, when a subject makes a decision to follow some particular course of action, he usually has the prospect of satisfying a number of needs in succession. More frequently, however, one finds evidence of a definite and sometimes enduring relation between needs.

Fusion of Needs. When a single action pattern satisfies two or more needs at the same time we may speak of a fusion (F) of needs. Confluences of this kind are extremely common.

Ex: F n AcqExh: An exhibitionistic subject gets paid to sing a solo in public.

Subsidiation of Needs. When one or more needs are activated in the service of another need, we may speak of the former as being *subsidiary* (S)* and the latter as being *determinant.* The determinant need regulates

*The letter "S" standing between two needs signifies that the former is subsidiary to the latter. In other contexts "S" means "subject."

the action from the beginning, but may not itself become overt until the terminal phase of the total event.

A politician removes a spot from his suit (n Noxavoidance) because he does not wish to make a bad impression (n Infavoidance), and thus diminish his chances of winning the approval and friendship of Mr. X (n Affiliation), from whom he hopes to obtain some slanderous facts (n Cognizance) relating to the private life of his political rival, Mr. Y, information which he plans to publish (n Exposition) in order to damage the reputation of Mr. Y (n Aggression) and thus assure his own election to office (n Achievement): (n Nox S n Inf S n Aff S n Cog S n Exp S n Agg S n Ach).

The subsidiation of one major need to another is similar to the subsidiation of sub-needs to a major need. For, as we have pointed out, many consecutively organized accessory actions are usually necessary before an end situation is attained.

To cure a patient suffering from an acute abdominal condition many separate, though integrated, acts are required. The operating room must be prepared for the patient; instruments, sponges, sheets, and gowns must be sterilized; the operator and his assistants must wash up and disinfect their hands; the anesthetic must be properly administered; each step in the operation must be effectively performed; and from then on during the entire course of the convalescence proper measures must be taken to bring about the patient's recovery. Each procedure is an act accessory to the need for Nurturance and, perhaps, also to other needs (Achievement, Acquisition).

Since each sub-need has an end situation (sub-effect) of its own, any need-determined action may be regarded as composed of a progressing series of transitional closures (sub-effects). During activity a subject will usually be attentive to the single procedure which confronts him. He will have a specific intention (sub-need) in mind, the major need to which the given intention is integrated being "out of mind." During an operation the surgeon is not imagining the final goal of all his endeavors, the patient leaving the hospital well and happy. His mind is preoccupied with the problem of the moment, clamping that spurting artery, making a clean incision through the fascia, separating the muscles and getting good retraction. Each step properly performed is a minor accomplishment (n Ach).

We see, then, that in most cases a succession of accessory effects must be realized before the major or final effect can be achieved. Thus, the evocation of any need will secondarily excite a series of sub-needs, each of which may be designated, if it is expedient to do so, by referring to the specific minor effect (task) which it aims to achieve. Though each subsidiary effect is but a part of a larger temporal whole, at any moment the attention of the subject is directed toward the accomplishment of just that effect.

Contrafactions. Needs are commonly related to their opposites in a temporal configuration. A phase of Dominance is succeeded by a phase of Deference. A wave of Aggression is followed by a wave of Nurturance or of Abasement. Abstinence follows indulgence; passivity, activity, etc. The second trend is called a contrafaction, since it opposes or serves to balance the effects of the first. It may, for instance, be the exaggerated expression of a need following a prolonged period of inhibition. Under this heading should be listed counteractions, defense mechanisms, atonements, reformations. The two opposing needs combined may be termed an ambitendency (A). The life patterns of some subjects allow for such contrafactions.

1. A man acts like a Napoleon at home, but in his business is obedient and servile (n Dominance—A—n Abasement). 2. A man is very stubborn and resistant with his wife but is worshipfully compliant to his mistress (n Autonomy—A—n Deference).

Conflicts. Needs may come into conflict (C) with each other within the personality, giving rise when prolonged to harassing spiritual dilemmas. Much of the misery and most of the neurotic illness in the world may be attributed to such inner conflicts.

1. A woman hesitates to satisfy her passion because of the disapproval of her family (n Sex—C—n Blamavoidance). 2. A man hesitates to satisfy his desire to fly an airplane because of fear (n Achievement—C—n Harmavoidance).

To explain the occurrence of contrafactions and conflicts it seems that one must refer to directional forces which oppose or balance each other. It is as if there were a tendency for psychic equilibration which operates in such a way that an exaggerated objectification of one need must be eventually balanced by an exaggerated objectification of its opposite (*cf.* the balance of sympathetic and parasympathetic tendencies). If these two consecutive phases of behavior are merely regarded as expressions of two superficial traits, or attitudes, there is no answer to the question. Why did the second phase follow the first? Only when one supposes that each attitude is the resultant of a central force that is usually balanced by an opposing force does the matter become intelligible. This is an argument for the need theory.

Needs, Emotions, and Affections

All experimenters know that emotion is a topic about which there is no agreement at the present day. To us it seems preferable not to attempt to discuss it in the short space that is at our disposal, but to come directly to our present tentative conclusion without marshaling evidence.

Without pretending to settle anything we may state that for us "emotion" is a *hypothetical concept* that stands for an excitatory process in the brain—most probably in the interbrain (thalamic region)—that may manifest itself subjectively or objectively or both. Thus an emotion may occur without the subject's being aware of it (unconscious emotion). Usually it is felt, the subjective manifestation being that quality of an experience which is generally designated by the word "emotional" ("excited"). The objective manifestation is a compound of autonomic disturbances ("autonome"), affective actones, and the intensification or disorganization of effective behavior (motor and verbal). Sometimes the faintest moistening of an eye or the quiver of the voice is enough for a diagnosis. At other times the experimenter requires more evidence: the occurrence of a sufficient press, signs of vegetative upset, characteristic tremors, gestures, and exclamations, confusion of thought, disorganization of actones, and a subjective report of having been "much upset."

It is possible that the separable emotions are differentiations from an elementary general excitement (Stratton[38]) or startle (Hunt and Landis[39]). They grade into one another and are sometimes difficult to distinguish objectively or subjectively. Usually, however, they are definite enough to be named. In practice, for instance, temper tantrum, phobia, guilt feelings, contempt, and depression are useful categories, not often confused.

Our own observations agree with common opinion (and McDougall's[40] theory) that certain emotions are linked with certain tendencies to action (disgust with retraction, rage with combat, etc.). We do not find, however, that all emotions have drives or all drives have emotions, but the more important emotions (ex: 1, fear, anger, disgust, pity, shame, lust, and 2, elation, dejection) are associated either 1, with a certain drive, or 2, with the fortune—facilitation (success) or obstruction (failure)—of a drive. The association of particular emotions and drives supplies us with another index for differentiating some of the needs.

We are using "affection" to refer to hedonic feelings: pleasure, happiness, "eupathy,"* discontent and dejection (negative affection). Here we shall deal with this age-old problem as we did with the problem of emotion, giving only the briefest outline of our working hypothesis.

Affection is considered to be a hypothetical concept which stands for some process in the brain—probably in the interbrain—that manifests itself subjectively as feelings of pleasure or unpleasure (which vary in intensity), and objectively (with much less clearness) as a compound of affective actones (a certain bearing, demeanor, intonation of speech, tempo of movement, etc.). Our most direct information about feelings must come from introspection, but it should not be supposed that an

---

*"Eupathy" is a convenient term for psychical well-being, joy, contentment; and "dyspathy" for its opposite: mental distress.

affection (as defined above) is always or even usually conscious. Now, if we construct a hedonic scale leading from extreme unpleasantness through the point of indifference to extreme pleasantness, and say that every occurrence which tends to move affection up the scale (i.e., to make the subject feel *less unpleasure,* or *more pleasure*) is *hedonically positive,* and everything that tends to make it move down the scale is *hedonically negative,* then the results of observation and introspection may be stated as follows: there are three sorts of pleasure, or three distinguishable kinds of events that are hedonically positive: 1. *Activity pleasure,* accompanying the rise of "energy" (zest) and its discharge ("overflow") in uninhibited movement or thought. This corresponds to Aristotle's and Hamilton's definition of happiness[41] and to Bühler's "function" pleasure.[42] It is marked by free, playful, actonal movement: the catharsis of inner tension. The instant an obstruction is met or fatigue sets in the level of affection falls. 2. *Achievement pleasure,* accompanying the conquest of oppositions to the will. This is Nietzsche's correlate of happiness. It is different from activity pleasure in as much as here the subject welcomes obstacles (physical or mental), selects the hardest tasks—things that demand great exertion and courage—in order to experience the elation of mastering them. If the body and its cravings are regarded as oppositions to the will, the overcoming of inertia, fatigue, fear, appetite, or lust brings pleasure. The greater the demands on the subject, the greater the experienced pleasure if he is able to meet them. The performance of an easy or habitual task brings no satisfaction, and failure in accomplishment markedly lowers the level of affection. Repeated failures lead to disquieting inferiority feelings.* 3. *Effect pleasure,* accompanying the satisfaction of need tension. Every need arises out of a disequilibrium (lack, distension, harm, or threat) which considered by itself is *unpleasurable.* This does not seem to be a fact to many other psychologists but it is a fact to us. We should say that *dissatisfaction* is the common attribute of every need *qua* need. The dissatisfaction, however, is commonly obscured by 1, the initiation of behavior bringing activity pleasure or, in some cases, achievement pleasure; but much more commonly by 2, anticipatory images of successful terminal activity which tend to raise the affective level. The greatest pleasure seems to be associated with a relatively rapid lowering of need tension (Freud,[43] Bousfield[44]). The ratio: degree of realization/degree of expectation, is also an important factor. Thus, roughly speaking, since the beginning situation is unpleasurable and the end situation is pleasurable, and since the need action leads the S from the former to the latter, it may be said that the *activity of drives tends to be hedonically positive.* Opposition interferes

---

*Achievement pleasure is like activity pleasure in as much as it accompanies activity, but it is still more like effect pleasure because it depends on the *results* of activity. It might be called "Ego effect pleasure."

with progress, postpones satisfaction, and not infrequently diminishes expectations of close end pleasure. Failure to attain the goal often leads to two kinds of dissatisfaction: that arising from the frustrated, perseverating need and that arising from the failure of the Achievement drive ("I was not able to do it"). For example, a man who is jilted by a woman may lose self-esteem as well as the desired object.

Most people do a great many things every day that they do not enjoy doing. "I don't do this for pleasure," a man will affirm, thinking that he has refuted the principle of hedonism. But in such cases, I believe, introspection will reveal that the man is determined (consciously or unconsciously) by thoughts of something unpleasant (pain, criticism, blame, self-depreciation) that might occur if he does not do what he is doing. He goes to the dentist to avoid future pain or disfigurement, he answers his mail in order not to lose social status, and so forth. If it is not the thought of expected unpleasantness that prompts him, it is the thought of expected pleasure, possibly in the very distant future. Visions of heaven after death, for example, have often encouraged men to endure great suffering on earth.

These considerations commit us to one variety of the now almost abandoned theory of psychological hedonism. We think it is important to reaffirm that:

1. Affection (i.e., the hypothetical physiological counterpart [correlate] of *felt* affection) may be conceived of as a delicate index of diffuse well-being (health of mind and body) or its reverse. It is made negative by any obstruction to a vital process that arouses a need. Every obstruction, to be sure, is due to some *specific* factor (lack of oxygen, lack of companions, etc.) which evokes a *specific* type of behavior, but the point is that all obstructions giving rise to needs are *hedonically negative*. This is their common attribute. Furthermore, all adaptive behavior tends to rectify this state, to facilitate the obstructed process and thereby raise the affective level. Hence, it seems proper to say that need action obeys the pleasure principle (Freud).

2. Instead of saying that all behavior is a search for pleasure, it seems better to say that all behavior is the riddance (or avoidance) of painful tension, encouraged perhaps by pleasure-evoking images of expected goals. The emphasis upon "escape from pain" was given by Plato, Kant, and Schopenhauer.

3. Previous and present levels of expectation and aspiration must never be neglected in attempting to account for a given affective state (*cf.* William James[45]).

4. It is important to distinguish the three separable kinds of hedonically positive occurrences: i, mere uninhibited activity; ii, overcoming difficult obstacles; and iii, moving to end situations (relieving wants). These different sorts of pleasure-seeking or pain-riddances are often in conflict with one another. Freud, by neglecting i and ii, gives a one-sided

theory which fails to account for the pleasure of exercise and contemplation and fails to provide an hedonic basis for the structuration of the Ego (the development of will power, etc.).

If the above propositions are approximately correct, the experimenter is furnished with another index for distinguishing needs. The exhibition of satisfaction at the attainment or at the gratuitous arrival of a certain end situation suggests a need for just such a situation. And of like diagnostic value is the exhibition of dissatisfaction when a certain trend is frustrated.

As the concept of need or drive was developing it was noticed that we were applying it to two somewhat different kinds of phenomena: 1, *wishes for a certain end situation,* together with evidences of satisfaction when it occurred (regardless of the kind of behavior exhibited by the S); and 2, *behavior* which tended directly to bring about a certain situational transformation. A subject, illustrating the first phenomenon, might crave a specific result but exhibit a trend commonly associated with quite a different need. For example, a girl who wanted revengefully to hurt her parents (n Aggression) exposed herself in a thin nightgown to wintry weather with the hope of catching pneumonia (n Abasement)—in which attempt, by the way, she was successful. She did it with the anticipation of her parents' subsequent repentance and grief. Numerous other illustrations of this sort of behavior come to mind. I remember, for instance, a friend of mine saying: "If you want to destroy a man, flatter him to death." One thinks also of the tendency of some women to spurn (n Rej) the very man they wish to attract (F n AffSex). The contrasting phenomenon is exhibited by a subject who "blows off steam" by openly expressing his aggression (catharsis), but does not particularly enjoy the fruits of his conduct (that is, the injury suffered by the object). There is a distinction between these two forms of expression which we did not at first perceive clearly: the emphasis on the former case being upon the desired end situation and in the latter upon the behavior that is exhibited.

The instinct theory of McDougall emphasizes the impulsive, emotional type of behavior, illustrated by our second case, but does not seem to take account of the more indirect or deliberate type of conduct. McDougall, with the laudable intention of showing the connections between functions, puts into one category a certain emotion, a certain actone and a certain trend (or effect). Thus, one instinct might be called "fear," or "flight" or "security"; another "anger," "assault" or "objectinjury." To be sure, these different aspects of need action are found together very commonly in animals and not infrequently as reactions to sudden stimuli in adults (emotional needs). But, according to our experience, a theory of motivation must be carried beyond the primitive, impulsive (thalamic) level of action. It must be made to include cool, carefully planned conduct: conduct that does not display characteristic emotional actones. Here we believe, with Garnett,[46] that it is better to have the fundamental concept stand for the more inclusive thing: the obstructing organic disturbance (beginning situation) which of course implies its opposite, the facilitating organic satisfaction (end situation); and allow everything to vary, as it does, between the beginning and the end situations.

Our own reflections have led us to formulate the two above-described phenomena as follows: the need that is overtly expressed is put down as a subsidiation of the need that is finally satisfied (determinant need). For example, the formula "n Aba S n Agg" indicates that the subject allowed himself to be harmed in order to harm someone else (masochistic aggression). If the determinant need is entirely concealed (not expressed directly) it is said to be latent (ln Agg), and if it is uncon-scious, as well, this fact is also represented by a symbol: uln Agg. Simple overt aggression, on the other hand, as illustrated by our second case, is put down as it occurs (n Agg), or more precisely, if it is an emotional outburst, it is symbolized thus: emn Agg.

Emotional needs (emn)—needs accompanied by agitation of thought and body—are most apt to set off actones which are reminiscent of animal, savage, or infantile behavior. The action is regressive and instinc-tual in so far as the more lately acquired actones do not function. An explanation of this phenomenon might be that the occasion has aroused thalamic centers, generating energy that tends to discharge by the short-est routes—the shortest routes being the innate, instinctual, or primitive action patterns. Supposedly, the cortex, or some of it, is short-circuited. The action occurs without conscious effort (will). The body moves auto-matically, just as the leg kicks up when the patellar tendon is struck. In the latter case the blow seems to "do the work," though we know that "nervous energy" comes from the excited neurones in the spinal cord. In emotional action it is the *sudden, close, pressive* situation that seems to "do the work" by releasing energy in the motor centers of the inter-brain which, in turn, leads to action that is effortless. Indeed, it is the attempt to *inhibit* such behavior rather than to promote it that is felt to be effortful.

It appears that if an emotional need is abruptly restrained—the energy not being discharged—residual tension will perseverate and lead, perhaps, to a variety of after-effects. These after-effects do not seem to occur if a deliberate, unemotional, consciously intended action is inhib-ited. A driving emotion—one that is linked with a directional tendency —may be regarded as a heated deed momentarily deprived of embodi-ment. Release of emotion, therefore, has a cathartic effect (activity pleas-ure): a subjective value, which may, however, be out of harmony with the results of the executed act. Symbolic behavior—let us say, the killing of an animal in a religious festival—can give vent without dire conse-quences to savage fantasies locked within the organism. It seems that emotional needs are desires for *action* of a certain kind more than desires for specific end situations. In the distant racial past, it may be supposed, the end situation of successfully executed emotional action was completely satisfying. Under these conditions an individual could remain unified. But as soon as the time arrived that successful emotional action led to distressing results—remorse and guilt feelings—persisting inner conflict came into being: conflict, let us say, between the forebrain and the interbrain.

Needs, Actones, Vectors

The word "actone" has been used to stand for a simple bodily movement, such as pouting, lowering the eyes, smiling, coughing, extending the hand (simple motone); a compound of movements, such as rising from a recumbent position, walking, manipulating, kneeling, and bowing (complex motone); a single word or phrase, such as "Yes," "Hurry up," "I like you," "Go to Hell" (simple verbone); and a compound of words, such as occurs in a long conversation or speech (complex verbone). Now, these are all objective occurrences and they may be recorded and measured in terms of frequency, speed (tempo), strength (emphasis), duration, conjunctivity (organization), and a host of other defining dimensions. Many of these actones are commonly considered to be outward signs of a particular emotional state, whereas others are regarded as manifestations of temperament or temper. The term "expressive movements," which indicates that these events reveal something that is "inside" and are not to be taken merely as patterns, is currently used to include all such phenomena.

Though, in the present study, we have neglected the problem of temperament—having been unable to arrive at any satisfactory scheme for distinguishing its varieties—we have observed the presence or absence of numerous variables which are commonly used as indices of it. These observations may eventually lead to something, but at the moment we have nothing to contribute to the subject. Later, when the matter of general traits is considered, the variables that seem pertinent will be defined.

Putting aside, then, the importance of the general dimensions of actones, we turn to the question of their relations to needs. It may first be noted that *affective* actones—despite the negative findings of laboratory experimentalists (Landis,[47] Sherman[48])—are employed in everyday life with considerable accuracy as indices of emotional states, and, further, that the commonest of these emotions, as McDougall has pointed out, are associated either 1, with a particular drive or 2, with the fortune of a drive. In the first case the affective actonal pattern may be taken as an index of the occurrence of the associated drive (ex: anger is a sign of Aggression) and subsumed under the latter concept; whereas when an actone portrays gratification or frustration we are informed of the fact that "something" (which can be nothing else than a need) is being facilitated or obstructed, and the nature of the total situation tells us what need it is.

Furthermore, almost every *effective* actone is commonly associated in a given culture with a certain effect (aim), physical or social (usually the actone and its effect are bound together as two aspects of one act); and there are no effects which do not further the fortune of some need. That is to say, every effect may function as a sub-effect to some major effect (goal of a need). Consequently, even though the actone is incompetent (has no effect), by observing it one can guess the need. Indeed, there are many actones which are, as it were, "logical mechanisms" for a particular need. For example: crying (n Succorance), peering or cocking the ears (n Cognizance), striking out with the fist or kicking (n Aggression), smiling or waving (n Affiliation), turning the head away (n Rejection), reclining (n Passivity). Most of these are socially effective, because they are accepted cultural norms, but the point is that they are customarily associated with a particular need and, knowing the culture, one can usually guess correctly the need that is operating. It is because of the common association in animals of certain actones (or sub-effects) with certain needs that McDougall, in developing his formulation of instincts, was able, without much misunderstanding, to stress action patterns (flight, combat, caring for offspring) rather than goals.

Psychoanalysis has quite conclusively shown, in certain cases, that many simple actones (ex: hysterical conversion symptoms) "mean" something; that is, they are dissociated parts of a larger context and derive their significance from that context, at the core of which there is always some unconscious need or fusion of needs.

These considerations lead us to the conclusion that in most cases actones may be taken as indices of a need, conscious or unconscious; a conclusion which is not in harmony with the point of view that enjoys the widest acceptance in the United States. In this country it is generally considered that the elementary units of behavior are action patterns (actones) rather than directional tendencies. It is affirmed that the responses which are most constant and characteristic (that get "fixed" in the personality irrespective of the forces that may have engendered them) are reflective actones (demeanors, gestures, manners, attitudes, specific forms of movement and speech) which have become divorced from and hence may be considered apart from the needs which—if there are such entities—they once may have satisfied. According to this view the dynamic factor is in the neuro-motor system itself (just as the force of a simple tendon reflex is derived from energy liberated in anterior horn cells) and not in some pre-motor, possibly endocrine chemical factor (need). In judging this point of view it should be noted first that almost invariably a trend (or effect) is surreptitiously introduced into every action pattern that is distinguished (ex: "feeding behavior" includes the fact that food is taken into the mouth). If no effect were achieved the action pattern could not be adaptive (adaptation itself being a general effect). But if we disregard this flaw in the case for mechanism (*vide* the trend vs. actone discussion above) we must admit that there is much truth in this conception. It stresses what may be called the "mechanization of behavior" (actonal needs), and the fact that the actones thus established by repetition may in a constant environment become as determining as the needs. As the condition progresses the personality becomes more constant, rigid, and less adaptable to new conditions (to the delight of personologists who seek consistency). As an illustration of this, a form of behavior described by Mapother may be cited:

> In 1918 I was billeted in a kitchen with a brick-tiled floor. I had a kitten which had been separated from its mother as soon as its eyes were open. There was snow outside, and the kitten could not go out. In fullness of time it developed a practice of scrabbling at the brick floor with its front paws, turning round and defaecating and scrabbling again in a typically feline and perfectly futile attempt to cover up its faeces.[49]

One can hardly deny that mechanization occurs as well as its counterpart, socialization (the inculcation of culture patterns); otherwise chloroform at forty would not have been recommended. Nevertheless, mechanized behavior exhibits trends—they were once adaptive even though they are no longer—and these trends are classifiable according to the scheme that is employed for needs. That is to say, similar trends may and should be put together, regardless of whether some are novel patterns arising out of consciously present needs and others are automatisms. The difference between these two kinds of behavior is attributable in our scheme to a difference in the strength of another variable (Sameness, or rigidity). Furthermore, even though a need, from the point of view of consciousness, has been "worked out" of behavior, it must nevertheless be in the "background." The mechanisms, if they are adaptive, must automatically facilitate "something," and they must do it before that "something" becomes so obstructed that it creates tension in the regnancy (consciousness). It is perhaps only when frustration occurs (when the mechanisms fail) that the inner obstruction, exhibited as a need, comes to consciousness. For instance, we do not become conscious of needing and seeking air (respiration is automatic) until partial asphyxia occurs. My own opinion is this: mechanization (actonal consistence with one's self) and socialization (actonal consistency with cultural norms) are widespread, important phenomena but only under rare or abnormal conditions do we find behavior patterns that exist for long without satisfying underlying needs. And, even if it were shown that such patterns do occur, most of them achieve effects (which would satisfy certain needs if they were present); consequently, actonal actions can be classified, as the needs are classified, according to their effects.

Since an actone can be compared to a piece of apparatus (the muscularly controlled limbs being instruments for facilitating the life of the vital organs), the present point may be illustrated by taking the case of a research man in science who has learned certain technical methods. Which is more correct, to say that the man is prompted by intellectual curiosity (n Cog) to investigate and solve certain problems, or to say that the scientific procedure which he has learned determines his behavior? It seems obvious to us that both factors are effective to varying degrees depending on personality and circumstance. Since an individual cannot become equally proficient in all techniques (actones), his conduct is limited (determined) by the abilities and readinesses that he is able to develop. One might say that the needs that are objectified and the goals that are selected are the ones which can be most easily realized by the actones at a man's disposal. An extreme case would be a technician of a single apparatus who spent his days making countless measurements of everything that came to hand, thus allowing the instrument to determine the problems. Looking at the matter from the opposite point of view, it seems that the learning of a scientific technique must be prompted and sustained by a desire to investigate (to probe into things, gain knowledge, solve problems) as well as by other needs. If there was no need of this, or some other, sort to be satisfied by the acquired actones, the individual would tend to change his vocation, to develop abilities which would satisfy a more positive requirement of his nature. Or, if the man possessed veritable intellectual interest the chances are that he would become absorbed in certain problems, and in his attempt to solve them he would learn or invent new procedures. He would not be limited by stereotyped methods. The emphasis on technique seems to be more appropriate for certain personalities and the emphasis on needs and goals for others. Also, a psychologist who views men superficially—"extraceptively," "peripherally"—will be impressed by repetitions of technique (actones), whereas the psychologist who apperceives them deeply—intraceptively, centrally—will be impressed by the aim which sustains the technique or endures throughout many changes of technique.

There is, in addition to the actonal viewpoint, another conception which remains to be considered. It is the one which affirms that all people have the same needs in the same measure and, consequently, they cannot be differentiated on this basis; what distinguishes them are the modes (other than actones) which they employ to satisfy their needs. No doubt there is much truth in this proposition, how much we are not prepared to judge. Some of the modes are covered by the concept of subsidiation. To illustrate: a man may establish a friendly relation (n Affiliation) by flattery (n Deference), by imparting interesting information (n Exposition), by asking questions that the O enjoys answering (n Cognizance), by agreeing with the O (n Similance), by expressing sympathy (n Nurturance), by tactfully exhibiting his own talents (n Recognition), and so forth.

But besides these and others to be discussed later, there are modes which are distinguishable according to the type or general direction of spatial movement. For example, adience and abience (see above) describe movements toward and away from external objects. Following Lewin,[50] these may be termed *vectors* (v). The Adience vector furthers the positive needs (Food, Sex, Sentience, Achievement, Recognition, Affiliation, Deference, Nurturance, Dominance, Exhibition, Succorance), whereas the Abience vector favors the negative needs (Harmavoidance, Noxavoidance, Blamavoidance, Infavoidance). Contrience (Aggression) may be included with Adience, and a new vector "Encasement" (surrounding the self with a defensive and forbidding "wall") may be classed with Abience. This gives us a dichotomy that roughly corresponds to extraversion-introversion. This way of viewing behavior has been applied by Alexander[51] and Homburger[52] to the activities centering about the erogenous zones. For example, the mouth may be used to passively take in, aggressively bite into, or disgustedly spit out objects; and the anus may function to retain or expel, and so forth. This conception can be usefully extended, as Homburger has shown, to characterize the play of children, particularly in their trafficking with objects. For instance, among children there are those who greedily grab and snatch, those who collect and patiently construct, those who secretively hoard and retain, and those who reject and violently throw down. Finally, there are movements of penetration into objects as well as those of entering and breaking out of enclosures. Though it is clear that certain vectors favor certain needs, we find in most cases that a single vector may serve several needs and a single need may be realized through one of several vectors. According to this broadened viewpoint a vector describes an objective trend (of a general sort) that may facilitate one or more needs. Thus the question arises which is the better criterion for distinguishing individuals? We cannot give an answer at the present time, because we arrived at vector analysis—following Mr. Homburger's exposition of it—as we were approaching the termination of our studies and there was not time to test it systematically. The following list of vectors is tentatively proposed:

1. Adience vector, approaching desirable objects. This favors all the affiliative needs.
2. Ingression vector, seeking and entering an enclosed space or haven (claustrum) and staying there (n Passivity, n Seclusion, n Harmavoidance, n Rejection). This movement which suggests a "return to the womb" is probably highly correlated with the Abience, Encasement, and Adherence vectors.
3. Adherence vector, reaching for and clinging to a supporting object (n

Affiliation, n Harmavoidance). This is the characteristic movement of infantile dependence, the mother being the preferred object (n Succorance). It may be fused with the Ingression vector (entering and refusing to leave a sanctum).

4. Contrience vector, attacking external objects, the objects being usually disliked (n Aggression). This may be fused with Injection, or even Ejection (damaging objects by throwing them about or soiling them).

5. Abience vector, retracting or fleeing from disliked, scorned, or feared objects (n Harmavoidance, n Infavoidance, n Rejection). This may be associated with Ingression or Adherence (n Seclusion, n Succorance).

6. Encasement vector, remaining fixed and holding one's ground against intruders by erecting a wall, holding up a shield, or making aggressively defensive movements. This is represented on the verbal level by reticence, taciturnity, "psychological distance" (n Inviolacy, n Passivity, n Seclusion, n Defendance, n Infavoidance, n Blamavoidance). Logically, this should be correlated with the Ingression and Retention vectors.

7. Egression vector, leaving or breaking out of an enclosed place (claustrum). This suggests the re-enaction of birth as well as the angry liberating movements displayed when a child is restrained (n Autonomy). This vector is commonly fused with Locomotion.

8. Locomotion vector, moving rapidly through space, running from one spot to another, leaving places (n Autonomy). This is a very general attribute of behavior. It is probably correlated with Adience, Egression, and Injection. It includes what is commonly termed exploratory activity.

9. Manipulation vector, moving objects about or using them as tools or instruments with which to do things (n Dominance over things).

10. Construction vector, combining and configurating objects, building things (n Construction).

11. Reception vector, sucking or passively taking things into the body (particularly into the mouth), which often suggests dependence upon others for nourishment, affection, comfort, support, possessions, energy, knowledge, encouragement (n Succorance). It should perhaps also include the passive enjoyment of sensuous impressions (sights and sounds). It is commonly fused with Adherence.

12. Acquisition vector, grabbing or aggressively acquiring objects (perhaps to put in the mouth and bite). This goes with Adience, Contrience, Locomotion, Reception.

13. Ejection vector, expelling (pushing out) something (particularly excretions) from the body. This is also exhibited when a child throws things down, smashes objects on the floor, creates disorder, smears and soils. It is not certain whether the following should be included: spitting up, blowing out, vomiting, making loud noises, exploding, dynamiting, tearing apart, logorrhea, slanderous gossip.

14. Retention vector, retaining something (particularly excrement) in the body. Constipation is the physiological prototype of this, but there is also mutism and secrecy, possessiveness and miserliness, and the unwillingness to give time, energy, or affection to others. This is often fused with Encasement.

15. Injection vector, sticking an object into something. This trend characterizes the phallic phase of sexual development. Children like to put their fingers into things, to bore, to force sticks into holes, to throw knives, shoot arrows, and so forth.

One advantage of vector analysis is the fact that it is based on readily discernible spatial changes, and for this reason there is apt to be good agreement among those who make the initial observations. However, since the vectors are of negligible importance until they are interpreted, the "personal equation" is not diminished.

To conclude the topic of mode, we may say that under this term we list not only all the varieties of action by which a need may be realized, but also the materials, implements, vehicles, machines (agency objects or technics) which the limbs manipulate in order to achieve the desired goal.

Since, as we have said, there is a close relation between certain needs and certain actones (the former being dependent for their satisfaction upon the latter), and since the effective operation of actones requires ability (innate and acquired talent), it is highly probable that early abilities determine in large measure what needs develop and become dominant. Since actones and effects must be mutually dependent, invention may be the mother of necessity as often as its daughter. We did not make full use of this conception in the present study, though the attempt was made to discover the more prominent abilities and disabilities of each subject. Interests should perhaps also be mentioned at this point, since many of them involve a particular set of motones (ex: swimming, tennis, mountain climbing, fishing) or a particular class of verbones (ex: political speaking, logic, poetry) which call for special abilities. Interests, abilities and actones are closely interrelated.

Cathected Objects, Interests

An object (O* that evokes a need is said to "have cathexis" (c) or to "be cathected" (by the subject or by the need). This is one of Freud's many valuable concepts.† If the object evokes a positive adient need (indicating that the S likes the O) it is said to have a positive cathexis (value); if it evokes a positive contrient or a negative abient need (indicating that the S dislikes the O) it is said to have a negative cathexis. Such cathexes may be temporary or enduring. Sometimes one object is endowed with both positive and negative cathexis (ambivalence). Cathexes may be further classified according to the need which the O evokes in the S. Common cathexes, for example, are the following: garbage (c Noxavoidance), lightning (c Harmavoidance), doctor (c Succorance), sobbing child (c Nurturance), hero (c Deference), autocrat (c Autonomy). A need that is concentrated upon one object or upon objects of a well-defined class may be called a "focal" need; one that is moved by a wide

---

*O = object, an entity (thing, person, institution) which evokes reactions in the subject (S).

†Lewin and Tolman use the term *valence* to describe approximately the same facts.

variety of objects may be called "diffuse" (free-floating). The word "object" is used to indicate a single object or a class of objects: sensuous patterns (ex: music, the landscapes of Van Gogh), inanimate objects (ex: tools, a Ford runabout), animals (ex: cats, Fritz), persons (ex: Slavs, George Smith), institutions (ex: colleges, the G.A.R.), and ideologies (ex: utopias, the theory of natural selection, communism). Different *interests* center about different cathected objects.

A personality is largely revealed in the objects that it cathects (values or rejects), especially if the intensity, endurance, and rigidity of each cathection is noted, and if observation is extended to the cathected groups with which the individual is *affiliated* (has "belongingness"). In this fashion a reasonably adequate portrait of the social personality may be composed. Institutions and cultures can also be profitably analyzed from the standpoint of their cathected objects, what they value, and what they depreciate.

It would be possible to collect facts in favor of the proposition that the kind of objects that an individual cathects is of more significance than the relative strength of his needs. Everyone is friendly (n Affiliation) to somebody and discriminates (n Rejection) against certain others. What should interest us particularly is the nature of the objects accepted and the nature of the objects rejected. With this opinion we agree readily— up to a point. As we see it, the need factor and the object factor are complementary. Indeed, one can often guess what needs are dominant in an individual by knowing the objects of his positive and negative sentiments. Disliking the boss suggests Autonomy, preferring an inferior suggests Dominance, a fondness for unfortunates suggests Nurturance, a hatred of snobs suggests Inviolacy, and so forth. In our experience, the positive or negative cathection of a particular person can often be reasonably well "explained" on the basis of a fusion of needs, since the object (the other person), being himself a compound of several needs, is able to satisfy more than one in the subject. However, this falls short of the mark, for there are a great number of enduring cathexes which are due to circumstance rather than to the relative strength of needs. Objects can be cathected (by primary displacement) because, let us say, of their association with birthplace, nationality, parents, an unusual traumatic experience, a glamorous relationship, or some other fortuitous event. Then there is secondary displacement with all the mythological imagery of the unconscious to choose from. But we are not concerned here with explanations of conditioning; we are faced with the fact of different sentiments in different individuals, and with their striking importance in determining attraction or repulsion, respect or disrespect, friendship or enmity. The problem is to generalize for scientific purposes the nature of the cathected objects; for it does not seem that we can deal with concrete entities in their full particularity. It can have no scientific meaning to say that an S likes Bill Snooks, or enjoys the works of Fred Fudge, or has joined the Gamma club, or belongs to the Eleventh Hour Adventists, though to the gentlemen involved with the S in these associations it may be a matter of concern. Our own opinion is that it is important to know that there is *some* object cathected, but the object, as such, can have no scientific status until it is analyzed and formulated as a compound of psychologically relevant attributes. The theory of press, we venture to hope, is a step in this direction.

In our work we chiefly distinguished among objects as persons: those that were superior (older, of higher status, stronger, more competent, dominant, or more intelligent) and those that were inferior (younger, of lower status, weaker, ineffective, submissive, stupid). A need that was directed toward a superior O was termed supravertive, and one directed toward an inferior object, infravertive. Thus:

n suprAffiliation, the seeking of friendships with people of higher status.
n infrAggression, bullying younger objects.
n supraRejection, disrespect for adults.

Furthermore, we distinguished ideologies (programs of action, rationalized sentiments, party platforms, mores, philosophies, religious beliefs) from all other objects; having observed that a need might manifest itself toward a principle, an idea, a theory, as well as toward the personalities who supported it. Thus

n ideo Dominance, to argue in favor of one's theory.
n ideo Nurturance, to see value in another person's theory and to assist in elaborating it.

Besides the great variety of objects in the external world that are candidates for positive cathection, there is the self or Ego—firstly and perhaps lastly beloved. An unusual attention to one's body, feelings, and thoughts and a narrow devotion to one's interests, disregarding the well-being of others, is termed Narcism (egophilia or Ego-cathection). Needs which bring effects that chiefly benefit the subject are called "egocentric" (or "egophilic"). Most actions are egocentric. But there are needs which are also exhibited in behalf of a group or institution (ex: one's country). These are called "sociocentric" (or "sociophilic"). Sometimes men have to be urged to serve the State, in which case circumstances may compel them to manifest Dominance, Aggression, Exhibition, and so forth.

Needs that are turned in upon the subject are said to be intravertive. For example:

n intrAggression, self-blame, remorse, self-injury, suicide.
n intraNurturance, self-pity, nursing a wound.
n intraDeference, self-admiration.
n intra Dominance, self-control, will power.

Among significant questions pertaining to cathection are the following:

1. The ratio of positive/negative cathexes. Does a subject like more objects than he dislikes?
2. The intensity, endurance, and inflexibility of the cathexes.
3. The distance in space and time of the cathected objects. Does, for example, a subject admire his father or is it a mythological figure that appeals to him?
4. To what extent does a subject support his cathexes by reasoned arguments (rationalizations)?
5. Are the cathexes imitations for the most part or have they been independently arrived at?
6. Are they conservative or radical?
7. Does the S identify himself with his cathected objects and experience their fortunes as if they were his own?

The concept of cathection may be employed for still another purpose: to represent the characteristic value or potency of the subject in the eyes of other men. One can ask, What are the kinds and intensities of cathexes he possesses for his acquaintances, or, if the S is a public character, for the members of his native culture? Is he annoying (c Aggression)? Does he command respect (c Deference)? Does he attract friends (c Affiliation)? Does he evoke sympathy (c Nurturance)? Do people generally ignore him (c Rejection)?

Need Integrates

Everyday observation instructs us that with development each need tends to attach to itself (to be commonly evoked by) certain objects or certain classes of objects, other objects or classes being disregarded. And, likewise, each cathected object attaches to *itself* an aggregate or fusion of needs. Also, certain characteristic modes (actones, sub-trends, agency objects, and pathways) become quite regularly utilized in connection with these needs and objects. Such consistencies of connection lead to the conception of relatively stable organizations in the brain, a notion which is substantiated by introspection. One might say that traces (images) of cathected objects in familiar settings become integrated in the mind with the needs and emotions which they customarily excite, as well as with images of preferred modes. A hypothetical compound of this sort may be called a *need integrate*, or *complex*. The integrate may enter consciousness as a fantasy or plan of action, or, under appropriate circumstances, it may be objectified, in which case it can be operationally defined as a reaction pattern that is evoked by certain conditions.

When a need is aroused it has a tendency to seek or to avoid, as the case may be, the external objects that resemble the images with which it is integrated. Failing in this, it projects the images into the most accessible objects, causing the subject to believe that the latter are what is desired or feared. The thing "out there" looks like or is interpreted to be the cathected image of the need integrate. This theory accounts for the content of dreams, hallucinations, illusions, and delusions. It also makes intelligible the selectivity in attention and response which individuals exhibit when confronted by a heterogeneous environment. In some people selectivity is so marked that the environment, as objectively "laid out," seems of little importance. The subject makes what he will out of it. "If a man has character he has his typical experience which always recurs" (Nietzsche). Thus, "need integrate," or "complex," is a concept that will "explain" relatively specific recurrent phenomena. It is an internal constellation which establishes a channel through which a need is realized. Compared to it the concept of need is highly abstract. Complexes differ chiefly in respect to the needs, the modes (actones, subneeds, technics) and the stimulus-objects or goal-objects which compose them. Cultures, as well as individuals, may be portrayed as organizations of such complexes.

Manifest and Latent Needs

Need integrates commonly become objectified and exhibit themselves in overt action, when they are aroused. One can observe repeatedly in some people the same directional tendency carried along by the same mode toward the same object. Integrates of this sort tend to become loosely organized into a characteristic temporal sequence: a daily schedule which gives shape to a person's life. Some need integrates, however, do not become objectified in real action when evoked. They take one of a number of other forms, all of which we have termed *latent*. "Covert" or "imaginal" would have been a happier word, since in these cases the complexes are not strictly speaking latent. They are active fantasies which are merely not manifested objectively, or, if so manifested, follow an "irreal" (Lewin's term[53]) course. Let us list briefly the chief courses or levels of need expression.

1. *An Objectified (Overt or Manifest) Need.* This includes all action that is "real" (seriously and responsibly directed toward actual objects), whether or not it is preceded by a conscious intention or wish.
2. *A Semi-objectified Need.* Here we class overt activity that is playfully and imaginatively (irresponsibly) directed toward real objects, or that is seriously directed toward imagined objects.
2a. Play, particularly the play of children, but also many of the things that adults do "for fun," let us say, when they are intoxicated.
2b. Dramatics: expressing a need integrate by playing the preferred role in a theatrical production.
2c. Ritual, religious or semi-religious practices that are expressive of some relatedness to imagined higher powers.

2d. Artistic expression: singing a song, playing a musical composition or reciting a poem that gives expression to a complex.

2e. Artistic creation: composing a work of art (painting, sculpture, music, 'iterature) that portrays a complex, in whole or in part.

3. *A Subjectified Need.* This covers all need activity that finds no overt expression. The following are significant:

3a. Desires, temptations, plans, fantasies, and dreams. Information as to these important processes must be obtained directly from the subject.

3b. Vicarious living. Here, the subject occupies himself with the objectification by *another object* of tendencies similar to his own inhibited impulses. He emphatically participates in the action. The following are sources of stimulation:

i. contemporary events, actual happenings in the present world which the subject observes (ex: an execution, a marriage, or a funeral) or hears about from his acquaintances or reads about in the newspaper;

ii. fiction, fairy tales, stories, plays, and movies that the subject especially enjoys; or

iii. art objects which represent some element in a need integrate. The art object may stand for an object of desire or of fear, or it may be something with which the individual can identify himself.

When, in an adult, a need with its integrate is not actually objectified, one usually supposes that it is inhibited. Since such inhibitions are matters of importance in understanding a personality, we have found it necessary to distinguish between needs that are overt (manifest) and those that are not. In our study the latter (semi-objectified and subjectified forms of activity) were classed together as "latent" needs (ln).

In judging an individual, it is important to observe which needs are periodically satisfied and which are repeatedly frustrated. Here we have to take account of specific abilities. Frustration may lead to inhibition of a need, to atrophy from hopelessness, or to exaggerated re-striving. It is necessary to note the occurrence of gratuitous end situations (unnaturally facile climaxes), common in the lives of the overprivileged. With the latter, needs may be so easily satisfied that they rarely enter consciousness. Hence these people may appear as if they had none. Here, the conclusion must be that it is hard to judge the strength of needs without knowing which of them are being regularly stilled during times when the subject is not being observed.

The word "attitude," so widely used in social psychology, seems to describe a state intermediate between subjectification and objectification. It is an "obvious readiness" to act in a certain way. If the attitude is barely obvious it might be considered inhibited, covert, latent. If it is very obvious it might be judged to be overt and manifest. Anyhow, it seems that "attitude," in so far as it refers to behavior, can be subsumed under the need concept, because the latter is the more inclusive. Need is defined to cover everything from the most incipient inclination toward assuming a certain attitude to the most complete expression of such a tendency. Attitude is limited to the mid-region between latency and full realization. It would be hardly appropriate to say that an erotic fantasy was an attitude or that committing murder was an attitude. Attitudes make up the derm of a personality. Most of the social attitudes can be classified as the needs have been classified (affiliative, nurturant, dominative, rejective, etc.). This also applies to attitudes about ideologies (political platforms, religions, philosophies). Verbal activity in connection with such programs and beliefs we have termed ideological needs. For example:

n ideo Aggression, to demolish a theory.
n ideo Affiliation, to be friendly to an idea.
n ideo Rejection, to scorn or vote against a proposition.

The positive adient needs are expressed by different types of positive attitude (favorable to an object); whereas the contrient and abient needs are expressed by different types of negative attitude (unfavorable to an object).

Conscious and Unconscious Needs

It is important to distinguish the needs which are relatively *conscious* from those which are relatively *unconscious* (un).* By consciousness we mean introspective or, more accurately, immediately-retrospective awareness. Whatever a subject can report upon is considered conscious; everything else which, by inference, was operating in the regnancy is considered unconscious. According to this convenient pragmatic criterion, consciousness depends upon verbalization. Thus, conscious facts (for the experimenter) are limited to those which the subject is able to recall. Consequently, in all organisms below man every regnant variable, being unverbalizable, is treated as if it were unconscious.

A conscious as well as an unconscious need (un) may be either subjectified or objectified. For example, many conscious desires are never put into action, and many unconscious needs are exhibited in actions which can be interpreted by others. The manifestations of unconscious needs are usually rationalized or "explained away" by the subject. They are attributed to another need or to some other factor: habit, convention, imitation, bad influence, etc. As a general rule, unconscious needs are in opposition to the social personality. Together they constitute what has been called the *alter ego,* a partly dissociated self, composed of tendencies that are not "let out" in everyday life. It is this subterranean part of an individual that may, by a sudden eruption, produce an unpredicted

*Conventional abbreviations are as follows: Cs=conscious; Ucs= unconscious. We have used "un" to stand for "unconscious need."

transformation: contrafaction, conversion, regression, or creative progression. A dual personality (ex: Dr. Jekyll and Mr. Hyde) is a limiting case. What is unconscious is much more difficult to modify than what is conscious. Hence, one of the steps in the development of personality is that of becoming conscious of what is unconscious.

Unconscious needs commonly express themselves in dreams, in visions, in emotional outbursts and unpremeditated acts, in slips of the tongue and pen, in absent-minded gestures, in laughter, in numberless disguised forms fused with acceptable (conscious) needs, in compulsions, in rationalized sentiments, in projections (illusions, delusions, and beliefs), and in all symptoms (hysterical conversion symptoms particularly). In the present study we became less interested as time went on in conscious overt behavior—it was obvious and the subject knew about it —and increasingly absorbed in the exploration of unconscious complexes.

At this point, a special difficulty arises in connection with the subject who is disturbed or depressed but does not know what is wrong or what he needs. He is like a sick man ignorant of medicine. For example, there is no instinct that leads a patient with scurvy to drink orange juice. He must be told what he needs. If left to himself he might seek (that is, act as if he "really" needed) a great variety of things. Similarly it appears that many people do not know what it is they "really" want, what they "really" need for their own well-being. They recognize it only when they find it, after much fumbling about or after being shown by someone else. Parents, nurses, educators, psychotherapists, priests, and moral philosophers make it their business to tell the young, the depraved, and the sick what they need. Perhaps they are wrong most of the time, but when it can be shown that such a prediction is right, that a certain heretofore unexhibited trend of action brings contentment in place of inner disturbance, then there is reason to suppose that a need has been satisfied, a need that was previously active, though entirely unconscious. If, however, there has been no antecedent discontent we must consider the possibility of a new integration of needs, or even of the generation of a new need. It is often fruitful to consider an individual from the point of view of what needs are currently satisfied and what needs (common in others) are not; and then to consider which ones of the satisfied and which ones of the unsatisfied are really imporant to his well-being.

D. CONCEPTS OF PRESS AND THEMA
DEFINITION OF NEED

It has been maintained that personology conceptualizes the reactions of individuals on a molar (gross) level. Though it is not limited to the construction of such formulations, this is its distinctive task. The concepts of need, trend, and effect, for example, are molar concepts. They describe the general course of behavior. They might even be used (in the case of an individual whose entire life has been ordered by a controlling purpose) to summarize a biography. But this mode of abstraction results in a one-sided portrait that leaves us in the dark as to many dynamic factors about which we quite naturally require information. The representation of the personality as a hierarchical system of general traits or need complexes leaves out the *nature of the environment,* a serious omission. We must know to what circumstances an individual has been exposed.

To some extent an application of the notion of cathection will fill the gap, because an enumeration of the positively and negatively cathected objects tells us what entities in the environment had drawing or repelling power. However, the enumeration of concrete cathected objects has meaning only for those who have had experience with them and can, by an intuitive leap, imagine why they repelled or appealed to the subject in question. To say that John Quirk had a focal Affiliation drive is equivalent to the statement that "he maintained a life-long friendship with George Smythe," since we have no information about the attributes of George Smythe. Concrete objects and events constitute the data of science, but they cannot be incorporated in a discipline until they can be described as patterns of general attributes. We must build a conceptual home for our perceptions.

What seems to be necessary here is a method of analysis which will lead to satisfactory dynamical formulations of external environments. To us it seems that few psychologists have correctly envisaged this problem. Those who study behavioral reactions record, usually quite scrupulously, the particular stimuli which evoke each response, and when the reaction system is defined it is described as a kind of activity that is evoked by a certain class of stimuli. But upon examination it becomes apparent that the class of stimuli has but one uniformity: the power to evoke the reaction in question. Thus, reactions of class A are responses to stimuli of class X; and stimuli of class X are those that arouse reactions of class A. In other words, the abstract description of the effective (behavioral) environment, as usually given, is mere tautology. An obvious way to avoid tautology is to become concrete and mention the specific objects or situations which in each instance provoked the behavior. But it is just here that we do not want to rest, because to arrive at the generalizations that science demands we must find similarities (uniformities) among events, and to find similarities it is necessary to abstract from the concrete. The question is How shall we classify situations *in their own right* (i.e., irrespective of the *response* that they evoke in the organism)? As psychologists, of course, we must limit ourselves to the parts of the environment with which human beings make contact and to the aspects which "make a difference." The usual classification—as represented by common speech and the dictionary—assigns a name to objects which have similar physical properties, but this mode of symbolization, though it classifies objects in their own right, is of no use to us because it is dynamically (personologically) irrelevant. If we attempted it we should discover that objects which have quite similar physical dimensions (ex: two men that resemble each other) may affect the organism entirely differently and give rise to different reactions, and that objects which are perceptually very different (ex: a stroke of lightning and a wild animal) may affect the organism similarly and bring about similar reactions. As Koffka[54] has emphasized, the physical environment and the behavioral (or psychological) environment are two different things.

Failing to make progress by using any of the above described methods, we finally hit upon the notion of representing an object or situation according to its effect (or potential effect) upon the subject, just as we had become accustomed to represent the subject in terms of his effect (or intended effect) upon an object. By "effect" here we *do not mean the response that is aroused in the subject* (a mode of classification that has been abandoned); we mean what is done to the subject before he responds (ex: belittlement by an insult) or what might be done to him if he did not respond (ex: a physical injury from a falling stone), or what might be done to him if he did respond by coming into contact with the object (ex: nourishment from food). Thus, one may ask, Does the object physically harm the subject, nourish him, excite him, quiet him, exalt him, depreciate him, restrain, guide, aid, or inform him? Such questions are the outcome of a dominating conception of the organism as a "going concern" (a system of vital processes), the behavior of which is mostly directed by occurrences that facilitate or obstruct these processes. On the personological level we must deal for the most part with social factors which facilitate or obstruct the psychological well-being of the individual, but they can be viewed in the same way as a physiologist views the culture medium of an organism. Does it contain poisons? Is there sufficient oxygen? Does it allow for the elimination of waste products?

Our conclusion is that it is not only possible but advisable to classify an environment in terms of the kinds of benefits (facilitations, satisfactions) and the kinds of harms (obstructions, injuries, dissatisfactions) which it provides. When this is done it may be observed that in the vast majority of cases the organism tends to avoid the harms and seek the benefits. The troublesome exceptions to this general rule can be put aside for the present. What we want to represent is the kind of effect that a given object does (or can) have upon the subject. If it is a "bad" effect the subject tends to prevent its occurrence by avoiding it or defending himself against it. If it is a "good" effect the S will usually approach the object and attempt to get the most out of it. A single object, of course, may be capable of numerous effects, both harms and benefits.

It may readily be seen that when the objects of the environment are human or animal, they can be symbolized as the subject is symbolized in terms of this or that drive. The natural environment, as we shall see, may be treated in much the same fashion. Thus, the external world appears in the guise of a dynamical process and the complete behavioral event as an interaction of forces.

We have selected the term *press* (plural *press*) to designate a directional tendency in an object or situation. Like a need, each press has a qualitative aspect—the kind of effect which it has or might have upon the subject (if the S comes in contact with it and does not react against it)—as well as a quantitative aspect, since its power for harming or benefiting varies widely. Everything that can supposedly harm or benefit the well-being of an organism may be considered *pressive,* everything else *inert.* The process in the subject which recognizes what is being done to him at the moment (that says "This is good" or "This is bad") may be conveniently termed *pressive perception.* The process is definitely egocentric, and gives rise, almost invariably, to some sort of adaptive behavior.

Most stimulus situations are not in themselves directly effective. As such, they are not harms or benefits to the organism. But they are potent evokers of behavior because they appear as signs of something that is to come. Some people, for example, are more disturbed by omens of disaster than they are by actual misfortune; and others are more thrilled by thoughts of future events than by these events when they occur. Similarly, there is such a thing as fore-pleasure and fore-unpleasure. Indeed, the power of a stimulus situation does not usually depend upon *pressive perception*—"The object is doing this or that to me"—but rather upon *pressive apperception*—"The object may do this to me (if I remain passive) or I may use the object in this or that way (if I become active)." Such pressive apperceptions are largely determined, as investigations have shown, by the impressions and integrations which have occurred in the brain as the result of past experiences. Pressive apperception, indeed, may be defined as a process by which a present situation excites images (conscious or unconscious) that are representative of pressive situations of the past. Through them the past is made to live actively in the present. Thus every conditioned response depends upon pressive apperception, for it is this process which connects an existing, otherwise inert situation with the impression (trace) of a former pressive perception. What is important to note is that pressive apperception is usually unconscious. The creature merely reacts. If it happens to be a mature human being, he will often give reasons to himself or to others for his behavior, but his explanations will seldom coincide with the unconscious determining integration.

Because the conception of press came to us rather late in the course of our explorations it was not suitably compounded with our other concepts. Nor has it yet been applied sufficiently to the interpretation of personality and social cultures. And there is not even space here for an account of what in the theory has already been found usable. Suffice it to say that one can profitably analyze an environment, a social group, or an institution from the point of view of what press it applies or offers to the individuals that live within or belong to it. These would be its dynamically pertinent attributes. Furthermore, human beings, in general or in particular, can be studied from the standpoint of what beneficial press are available to them and what harmful press they customarily encounter. This is partly a matter of the potentialities of the environment and partly of the attributes of the subject. Some individuals, because they are ugly or disorderly or courteous or quiet, have a cathexis for certain kinds of press. That is to say, they arouse certain needs—Rejection, Aggression, Deference, Nurturance—in others.

Our present classification of press is not considered satisfactory, but a bare outline might be offered at this point:

Press may be classified in a rough way as *positive* or *negative,* and as *mobile* or *immobile.* Positive press are usually enjoyable and beneficial (ex: food, a friend); negative press are usually distasteful and harmful (ex: poison, insult). Mobile press are moving forces which may affect the subject harmfully or beneficially if he remains passive (ex: an animal or human being). Mobile press may be either *autonomous* or *docile,* autonomous when the activity is initiated in the O, docile when regulated by the S (ex: a complaint subordinate). Immobile press can have no effect unless the S approaches, manipulates or influences them in some way (ex: a glass of water). A *positive autonomous* (mobile) press would be exemplified by a sympathetic mother, an affectionate friend, a bestowing philanthropist, a benevolent leader. And the apperception of the S might be: "He (or she) will be friendly, help me, praise me." A *positive docile* (mobile) press would be exhibited by a river that is used to drive a mill, a domestic animal, a servant, a disciple. Here the apperception of the S might be: "I can control it, he will obey me, he is respecting my wishes." A *negative mobile* press would be exemplified by lightning, a storm at sea, a carnivorous beast, an angry parent, a gangster, the "hand of the law," a bore, a troublesome child. A negative mobile press is always autonomous, since a S does not use an object to bring displeasure to himself. A *positive immobile* press is manifested by inorganic objects which cannot or usually do not act on the subject unless he approaches or manipulates them. The following might be mentioned: nourishing food, water, shelter, toys, money, building stones, all manner of material possessions. The apperceptions of the S might be: "It will taste good, it will warm me, I can play it, I can give it to someone." A *negative immobile* press would be exemplified by quicksand, ice cold water, a precipice, a barrier, poison ivy, useless instruments, an ugly object, and so forth. Here apperception will report: "It is dangerous, it will hurt me if I touch it, it cannot be used."

What we have been describing is the external world in the guise of a psychological environment: objects in changing settings characterizable as foods, poisons, sensuous patterns, supports, harbingers of danger, friends, guides, enemies, suppliants that are prospective of certain consequences if approached, manipulated, embraced, commanded, flattered, obeyed or otherwise responded to. The *press* of an object is what it can *do to the subject* or *for the subject*—the power that it has to affect the well-being of the subject in one way or another. The cathexis of an object, on the other hand, is what it can *make the subject do*.

In our work we concentrated upon press that were manifested by human objects (mobile, autonomous press) and we enlarged the notion to include lacks and losses of positive press (ex: a barren monotonous environment, lack of food objects, poverty, no friends, etc.). A few illustrations will suffice:

p Affiliation, a friendly, sociable companion.
p Nurturance, a protective, sympathetic ally.
p Aggression, a combative O, or one who censures, belittles, or fleers.
p Rival (Recognition), a competitor for honors.
p Lack (Economic), the condition of poverty.
p Dominance: Restraint, an imprisoning or prohibiting object.

The diagnosis of press is fraught with the same difficulty as the diagnosis of need. It is always an interpretation, but an important one. Every individual must make such guesses many times a day: "Will this object please and benefit me, or will it displease and harm me?" The knowledge of what is good and what is bad for man is a large part of wisdom. In identifying press we have found it convenient to distinguish between 1, the *alpha* press, which is the press that actually exists, as far as scientific inquiry can determine it; and 2, the *beta* press, which is the subject's own interpretation of the phenomena that he perceives. An object may, in truth, be very well disposed toward the subject—press of Affiliation (*alpha* press)—but the subject may misinterpret the object's conduct and believe that the object is trying to depreciate him—press of Aggression: Belittlement (*beta* press). When there is wide divergence between the *alpha* and *beta* press we speak of delusion.

Pre-actions and Outcomes

Behavior is inaugurated not only by newly arising internal wants and freshly presented press, but by preceding occurrences. Among the latter we have found it convenient to distinguish "pre-actions" and "outcomes." Any action which determines the course of future behavior, may be called a "pre-action." Some pre-actions are of the nature of promises and pledges. They call for some later fulfillment: a further "living out" or a repetition of the word or deed. Others, however, are followed by actions of an opposite sort: borrowing by returning, lending by demanding payment, generosity by stinginess, depreciating by praising, fighting by peaceful overtures, rudeness by courtesy (contrafactions). If the status of the subject is lowered by his own pre-action (ex: humiliation), then the "sequent-action" is very likely to be an attempt to reinstate himself (ex: self-vindication). Whereas, if another human being is diminished by the pre-action, there will be a tendency for the subject to bring about a restitution (ex: apology, gift, compliment). Influencing many of these acts is a vague sense of "justice," of a balance between what is due the subject and what is due the object. This is closely related to inferiority feelings and guilt feelings.

Besides pre-actions it is necessary to take account of outcomes (the fortunes of previous strivings). A man, for example, may react to *success* by inflation (self-confidence, boasting, demands for recognition) or by deflation (modesty of the victor). Similarly, *failure* may give rise to aggression and extrapunitiveness or to abasement and intrapunitiveness. It may also be followed by Defendance (verbal self-vindication), Succorance (appeals for help or generosity), Infavoidance (withdrawal), Play (attempts to make a joke of it), Recognition (telling about one's success in some other field) and so forth.

Concept of Thema

A thema is the dynamical structure of an event on a molar level. A simple thema is the combination of a particular press or pre-action or outcome (o) and a particular need. It deals with the general nature of the environment and the general nature of the subject's reaction. For example:

p Rejection → *n Rejection:* the S is rejected (snubbed) by the O and responds in kind.

o Failure → *n Achievement:* the S makes renewed, counteractive attempts to succeed after failure.

Thus, a thema exhibits the press of the stimulus to which a subject is exposed when he reacts the way he does. Since fantasies as well as actual events have themas, every need integrate is also a thematic tendency; the theory being that in such cases there is an inhibited need for a particular form of behavior to be aroused by a press which the individual secretly (perhaps unconsciously) hopes to find embodied in some actual person. In our experience, the unconscious *(alter ego)* of a person may be formulated best as an assemblage or federation of thematic tendencies.

Definition of Need

Marshalling the facts and reflections reviewed in this section it is possible to enlarge upon our initial definition of a need.

A need is a construct (a convenient fiction or hypothetical concept) which stands for a force (the physicochemical nature of which is unknown) in the brain region, a force which organizes perception, apperception, intellection, conation, and action in such a way as to transform in a certain direction an existing, unsatisfying situation. A need is sometimes provoked directly by internal processes of a certain kind (viscerogenic, endocrinogenic, thalamicogenic) arising in the course of vital sequences, but more frequently (when in a state of readiness) by the occurrence of one of a few commonly effective press (or by anticipatory images of such press). Thus, it manifests itself by leading the organism to search for or to avoid encountering or, when encountered, to attend and respond to certain kinds of press. It may even engender illusory perceptions and delusory apperceptions (projections of its imaged press into unsuitable objects). Each need is characteristically accompanied by a particular feeling or emotion and tends to use certain modes (sub-needs and actones) to further its trend. It may be weak or intense, momentary or enduring. But usually it persists and gives rise to a certain course of overt behavior (or fantasy), which (if the organism is competent and external opposition not insurmountable) changes the initiating circumstance in such a way as to bring about an end situation which stills (appeases or satisfies) the organism.

From this definition it appears that the indices by which an overt or manifest need can be distinguished are these:

1. A typical behavioral trend or effect (transformation of external-internal conditions).

2. A typical mode (actones or sub-effects).

3. The search for, avoidance or selection of, attention and response to one of a few types of press (cathected objects of a certain class).

4. The exhibition of a characteristic emotion or feeling.

5. The manifestation of satisfaction with the achievement of a certain effect (or with a gratuity), or the manifestation of dissatisfaction when there is failure to achieve a certain effect.

These objective indices have subjective correlates: a subject is usually aware of wanting and striving for a certain effect, he can report upon what attracted his attention and how he interpreted it. He can describe his inner states of feeling, emotion, and affection. He can say whether he was really pleased or just pretending. Thus, if the above-mentioned five kinds of phenomena are observed, subjectively and objectively, there will be ten criteria upon which to base a diagnosis of manifest need.

Latent needs (like manifest needs) are parts of integrates composed of actones, sub-needs, feelings, and cathected images embodying press, but either 1, they are objectified in play or ritual or artistic compositions, the objects being make-believe or symbolic (semi-objectifications); or 2, they are portrayed in the behavior or art productions of others, the S being merely an empathic observer (vicarious living); or 3, they are not objectified in any form, the E becoming aware of them only when the S speaks aloud his free associations or reports upon his dreams and fantasies (see above). Special methods have been invented for evoking latent, imaginal needs and objectifying them in fictional forms. These will be discussed later.

The strength of a single exhibition of a need is measured in terms of intensity and duration. The strength of a need as a consistently ready reaction system of personality is measured by noting the frequency of its occurrence under given conditions. In our scoring, these three indices of "strength" were lumped together; a high mark indicating that the need in question was exhibited with great frequency, or occasionally with great intensity or persistence. The criteria of intensity will be discussed in a later section.

Since, according to our conception, a need manifests itself in a variety of ways, it is not possible to confine oneself to a single operational definition. It seems that the best objective basis is the behavioral attainment of an apparently satisfying effect, an effect which brings the activity to a halt (usually by facilitating a vital process). The best subjective criterion is the occurrence of a wish or resolution to do a certain thing (to bring about a certain effect). According to some psychologists, subjective processes are outside the pale of operationism. Naturally, they do not come within the domain of physics, but that a physicist might include them if he took up the study of psychology is indicated by Bridgman's choice of a subjective process to illustrate operationism.

As a matter of self-analysis I am never sure of a meaning until I have analyzed what I do, so that for me meaning is to be found in a recognition of the activities involved. These activities may be diffused and nebulous and on the purely emotional level, as when I recognize that what I mean when I say that I dislike something is that I confront myself with the thing in actuality or in imagination and observe whether the emotion that it arouses is one with which I associate the name "dislike." The emotion awakened which I call "dislike" permits of no further analysis from this point of view, but has to be accepted as an ultimate.[55]

As we have said, the objective and subjective criteria above mentioned are but two ways in which a need makes itself known; others are almost equally valid and useful. Thus, although it is necessary that an experimenter be able to give a clear and accurate account of the occurrences upon which he has based a diagnosis of need—he must always be able to distinguish fact from theory—he cannot, in the present state of psychology, base his diagnosis (or his definition) on a single operation.

Here, he is in the same predicament as a physician who makes a diagnosis on the basis of numerous incommensurate signs or operations (subjective pain, temperature, blood count, urine examination, etc.) and next day, when faced by another subject, makes correctly the same diagnosis on the basis of a somewhat different collection of signs.

Furthermore, since during any occasion a need is but one of many interacting processes, all of which vary qualitatively and quantitatively from occasion to occasion, measurements of need strength must necessarily be crude and various. For instance, there seem to be about twenty equally valid indices of the intensity of a drive. All of which leads us to the conclusion that a rigorous operational definition of need is inadvisable, and perhaps impossible at the present time.

Some psychologists have strenuously objected to the concept of need, on the basis that it is either a simple tautology or a hazardous unscientific guess. A friend of mine writes: "I observe a man enter a room and sit down on a couch. What do I add to an understanding of the event by stating that he had a 'need to sit on that couch'?" The answer to such a question is that the "need to sit on that couch" is either a concrete example of a certain class of needs (ex: need for Passivity) or it is a sub-need which furthers the trend of one or more determinant needs: perhaps a need for Similance (other people are sitting down), a need for Cognizance (to discover whether the couch is comfortable or not), a need for Affiliation (to be near a cathected object who is sitting on the couch), etc. One cannot say which of a number of possible needs are operating without further facts. The experimenter must observe how the subject behaves when he sits down, must ask, "Why did you sit down on that couch?" and so forth. The attribution of a particular need is always a hypothesis, but one which can sometimes be substantiated by sufficient evidence (subjective and objective), and when so substantiated may lead to important generalizations about a personality. The mere fact that a particular S sat on a particular couch, however, is of no scientific interest. It is an outcast fact begging to be understood and to be accepted with others of its kind.

When it is stated that an individual has a strong need for Aggression, let us say, it means merely that signs of this need have recurred, with relative frequency, in the past. It is an abstract statement which requires amplification, for it does not tell us: 1, whether the manifestations of Aggression are emotional (accompanied by anger) and impulsive (emn Agg), or deliberate and calm, or habitually automatic and actonal (an Agg); or 2, what actones are habitually employed—motones (fists) or verbones (words of belittlement)—or what needs act in a subsidiary capacity; or 3, whether the need is focal or diffuse, and, if focal, what are the negatively cathected objects (people, institutions, ideas) and what press do they exemplify (does the S attack prohibiting authorities [n suprAgg] or weaklings [n infrAgg]?); or 4, whether the need is directed inwardly (intrAgg) resulting in self-condemnation and guilt feelings; or 5, whether the need integrate is objectified in overt behavior or inhibited and latent (ln Agg), manifesting itself only in fantasy or in a preference for aggressive scenes and stories; or 6, whether the subject is conscious of his wish to belittle others and of his enjoyment over their defeats; or 7, whether the need is sustained by an aggressive Ego Ideal or exemplar; or 8, whether the activity is in the service of another need (to redress an injury [n Agg S n Inv] or to attain power [n Agg S n Dom]); or finally, 9, whether the aggression serves the subject only or whether it furthers an important social cause (n socio Agg).

What factors determine the establishment of a need as a ready reaction system of personality? This is an important problem to which only vague and uncertain answers can be given. In the first place, observation seems to show that the relative strength of needs at birth (or shortly after birth) is different in different children. Later, the strength of some needs may be attributed to intense or frequent gratifications (reinforcements), some of which rest on specific abilities. Indeed, some needs may emerge out of latency because of gratuities or the chance attainment of end situations through random movements. (The need for morphine, which can be more potent than hunger, is developed solely by repeated gratifications.) Some needs may become established because of their success in furthering other more elementary needs. The gratification or frustration of a need is, of course, largely up to the parents, since they are free to reward or punish any form of behavior. Certain innate or acquired abilities will favor the objectification of some needs and not of others. There is much evidence to show that the sudden frustration of a need—particularly if preceded by a period of intense gratification—leads to residual tension. This seems to be particularly true for emotional "thalamic" needs that are abruptly obstructed or inhibited. A "thalamic charge," let us say, perseverates in such a way as to control fantasy and, if the occassion offers, to explode into overt behavior. Such inhibited "thalamic" needs often become fused with the Sex drive. In this way they become "erotized." A need may also become established by repetition, due to the frequent occurrence of specific press. But if the stimulus becomes stale, habituation sets in and the need becomes less responsive. Emulation (n Similance S n Superiority) is a potent factor in accentuating certain needs —the S wanting to be like his exemplar—and so is Deference: Compliance, and Affiliation. Here we have to do with cultural factors. Certain cultures and sub-cultures to which an individual is exposed may be characterized by a predominance of certain needs. Not infrequently Contrarience (the desire to be different from or the exact opposite of a disliked object) operates to enhance the strength of some need. There are still other factors, no doubt, that work to determine what needs become dominant. For instance, there is the occurrence of conflict and the inhibition of one need by another. However, in view of our ignorance of such determinants, we require observation and experiment rather than any further reflections of this sort.

E. MISCELLANEOUS CONCEPTS

Energy

Among the facts of subjective experience is the feeling or the quality of feeling to which the term "energy" is very commonly applied. Not only can an individual introspect at any moment and give an estimate of the degree to which he feels "energetic"; but his judgment will often be found to correspond with what an observer would say on the basis of external signs. Evidently we are dealing here with a continuum between two extreme states, subjectively and objectively discernible: *zest* and *apathy*. The various aspects of zest may be designated by such words as alertness, reactivity, vigilance, freshness, vitality, strength, "fire," "pep," verve, eagerness, ardor, intensity, enthusiasm, interest; whereas under apathy may be subsumed lassitude, lethargy, loginess, "brain fag," indolence, ennui, boredom, fatigue, exhaustion. The former state yields prompter, faster, stronger, more frequent and persistent reactions— reactions that are apt to be more correct, relevant, novel, adaptive, intelligent, imaginative, or creative than those produced during the latter state. Zest is highly correlated with pleasure and activity (physical and mental), apathy with unpleasure and inactivity.

To the topic of energy (vital energy, psychic energy) much thought and many words have been devoted, but, as yet, no theory acceptable to the majority of psychologists has been proposed. Psychologists who deal with small segments of the personality have usually been able to dispense with the concept, but few practical psychologists agree that it is possible to do so, even a crude notion being better for them than none. The consequences of feeling fresh and energetic are so very different from the consequences of feeling stale and exhausted that to omit all observations bearing on this point is to leave a great gap in one's account of personality. We are certainly dealing with a magnitude which is correlated with the capacity to do work, but the variable is only roughly analogous to energy as the physicist conceives it.

In the development of the need theory the notion of energy or force was employed to account for differences in the intensity and endurance of directional behavior. It seemed necessary to express the fact that some needs are "stronger" than others. To use energy in this connection is to fall in line with the hormic theory of McDougall,[56] as I understand it. Here, however, we are talking about energy that is "general" or associated with functions (actones), not the energic aspect of drives. That the two are different is demonstrated by the fact that a need may be intense—a man may be starving or extremely desirous to accomplish an intellectual task—and yet, if he is "worn out by overwork" he will not move a muscle or a thought. The need is great, but there is no available "energy" (we say) in the actones (muscular system or intellectual system) that must be employed to reach the goal. It seems that fairly strong needs may occur in the absence of actonal energy—in which case they remain latent—and actonal energy may exist without needs. But it does not follow from this that general (or actonal) energy and drive energy are unrelated. For when a person is fresh, his drives commonly partake of the increased tone; they seem stronger in themselves. Similarly, when a person is exhausted, all his appetites are usually diminished. This fits in with an observation that has been made repeatedly: animal or human subjects that are rated high in one positive need are usually rated high in others. This applies even to needs that are antipolar. For example, the most assertive (n Dom) and aggressive (n Agg) child may also be the most affiliative (n Aff) and sympathetic (n Nur). Some of the animal psychologists have concluded that it is necessary to conceptualize a general drive factor, and at times this has seemed to us the best solution. The "need for Activity" was what we called it, and in contrast to it we defined the "need for Passivity." At other times it has seemed best to "explain" intensity of movement and speech by referring to Energy: general, widely disposable energy ("bloodstream energy") or energy residing in the actones (muscular system, intellectual system) by means of which the drives fulfill themselves. According to the latter formulation it is actonal energy which, when combined with ability, allows for the quick and effective expression of all drives that employ the functions in question.

The concept of Energy "overflowing," as it were, into action—or, with equal justification, the concept of "need for Activity"—may be utilized to account for random behavior in children and adults. Random behavior is displayed most clearly during the first weeks of life. At this time one can observe periods of almost incessant activity (flexions, extensions, rotations, squirmings), activity that is inco-ordinated and therefore ineffective—the eyes, head, arms, and legs may all move at once in different directions. These movements are not dependent upon external stimulation, nor do they appear to "seek" anything. Since the child does not even attend to his movements, it is not possible to say that during these periods he is trying to achieve mastery of his limbs. The most that can be said is that random behavior is the expression of vitality, of actonal metabolism (katabolism after anabolism). It belongs to the givenness of life.

We might speak here of actonal energy, associated with physical movements and associated with thought (speech), which in the absence of drive tends to become kinetic, giving rise to restlessness, play, random actions, disjunctive fantasy, voluble speech. Indeed, there is evidence for supposing that this actonal energy may precede need tension, that a need may be generated and become established as a result of the discovery by random action of a satisfying end situation (*cf.* drug addiction).

These facts and reflections lead to the conclusion that every functional system (we can profitably confine ourselves to the muscular system: physical action, and the thought system: verbal action) assimilates and builds up a certain amount of energy, which tends (of its own accord), if nothing intervenes, to become kinetic. It does this, as it were, for its own "satisfaction." The exercise is a catharsis. It helps to oxidize ineffective accumulations. It facilitates life. (The reader will excuse me, I hope, if for the time being I speak of "energy" as if it were a thing rather than a measurable attribute of an event.)

The concept of specific actonal energies is proposed to account for the fact that the fatigue of one function (intellection, let us say) diminishes but little the energy available for another function. Physical exercise may be vigorous after the mind has been worn out by exertion, and vice versa.

Besides the specific energies of each system we must also distinguish general ("bloodstream") energy which is closely related to the actonal energies. This general energy factor seems to be determined partly by the condition of the blood (oxygen, carbon dioxide, waste products, presence of thyroxin, adrenin, and other hormones), partly by metabolic conditions in the separate systems (which contribute oxidation products to the blood), and partly by the fortunes of the drives (success or failure, or expectations of success or failure). General energy is also affected by the weather, diet, drugs, physical illness, and so forth. Our conception of energy has some relation to Spearman's "g,"[57] but it is a different variable in as much as it has been entirely abstracted from skill or ability.

In our studies we put the various actonal energies together with general energy under one heading, Energy, which, for greater clarity, was divided into two variables: Intensity and Endurance. From what has been said it will be clear that the following indices of Energy are appropriate:

1. Subjective and objective signs of zest (as briefly defined above).
2. Subjective and objective signs of activity pleasure.
3. A relatively large total of vigorous activity per day (as compared to the amount of rest and sleep).
4. The prevalence of random motilities (physical movements and speech). Here we refer to excessive actones: a surplus of abundant, rich, extravagant, or playful flourishes of gesture and language.
5. High intensity and duration of all positive drives, particularly Achievement, Play, Dominance, Aggression, Affiliation, Deference, and Nurturance.

As we progressed in our studies it became apparent that there were two factors, not one, to be distinguished: the general energy level and the disposition of a subject to discharge as contrasted with the disposition to conserve whatever energy is available. Closely correlated with this dichotomy are the opposing tendencies: 1, to play a stimulating or initiating role (n Dom) in social or sex relations, and 2, to remain passive or receptively compliant (n Def). It was here that the concepts "need for Activity" and "need for Passivity" became particularly useful. It seems that the need for Activity (overt motility) is usually associated with a high energy level and the need for Passivity with a low level, but there are numerous exceptions. In some people spontaneous activity is decidedly low, despite the fact that the energy level, as far as one can estimate it, is sufficient. The need for Passivity seems, on the one hand, to be related to the force of inertia and, on the other, to be in the service of the need for rest; that is, the organism seeks to conserve its energies, to avoid exhaustion, and to be free of the necessity of decision. The tendency for Passivity is subjectively represented by the desire to relinquish the will, to relax, to drift, to daydream, to receive impressions. In the face of external forces it yields because this is easier (or more exciting). The tendency inclines a person toward a placid vegetable existence, free from excitation or stimulation, or toward a life of waiting for external stimulation (let us say, for a lover). Freud describes Passivity as the tendency to reduce excitations to a minimum, to "return to the womb," or even to an inorganic state. We may suppose here that the stressful integration of the regnancy breaks down; that "it goes into solution." The operation of this tendency, then, leads to a state of relaxed disjunctivity, to sleep, to unconsciousness. One commonly finds it after an intense or prolonged exertion of the will, particularly if the will has been exercised against a social group. When, in an utterly exhausted state, the will relaxes, a person may experience a most blissful feeling. (We have reports that such affections occur just before a drowning man loses consciousness.) The need for Passivity may also arise as the aftermath of inner conflict. It is, indeed, one of the best means of resolving tension. A person says: "What difference does it make to me?" He relaxes mind and body and the disturbing turmoil passes over. His troubles fall away like water. The efforts of Orientals to reach the state of Nirvana may be taken as an extreme instance of this general tendency.

When fused with the Sex drive Passivity leads to the attitude which is classically feminine: deference and abasement in erotic interaction. Its presence in a man is a mark of bisexuality, which, in turn, is correlated with homosexuality. Heterosexual Activity in women and heterosexual Passivity in men, however, are very common present-day phenomena.

Though Passivity was not defined soon enough to be given a place in our conceptual scheme, we found that we could not get along without it. Consequently, the reader will find references to this somewhat vague factor in the succeeding pages.

Divisions of the Personality

Freud and the psychoanalysts after him have distinguished three parts of the personality: the Id, the Ego, and the Superego. As determinants of behavior these functions may be characterized as follows: the Id is the aggregate of basic instinctual impulses; the Ego is the organized, discriminating, time-binding, reasoning, resolving, and more self-conscious part of the personality; and the Superego is the intra-psychical representative of the customs and ideals of the community in so far as they have been communicated by the parents.

This scheme has proved its usefulness in formulating and treating the neuroses, all of which are the result of moral conflict between elementary needs and social standards (that have become assimilated to form conscience). This almost universal dilemma can be well represented as an opposition of Superego and Id, the Ego standing between as puppet or final arbiter. Although the conception is a vague oversimplification, which leaves many facts unexplained, we have not been able to improve on it. In fact, we have found it as helpful in dealing with normal subjects as in dealing with abnormals.

The Id. This is the generic term under which all innate drives are subsumed, among which the viscerogenic needs should be especially emphasized. We are apt to use the term when we observe the excitation of emotional impulses associated with primitive actones (savage assault, panicky fear, flagrant exhibitionistic sexuality). At such times conscious control is in abeyance and the individual merely reacts. He feels that he is overcome by irresistable forces outside himself. Strong temptations and compulsions are also assigned to this category.

The Id, however, is not composed entirely of active passions. The need for Passivity (which may manifest itself as indolence and slovenliness) belongs to it. Hence it is often necessary to stir up the Id instead of checking it.

Furthermore, all impulses of the Id are not asocial or anti-social as most analysts affirm. There are, for example, certain gregarious and conforming tendencies (empathy, imitation, identification) which operate instinctively and unconsciously. Also, the highest as well as the lowest forms of love come from the Id.

Viewing the Id from the point of view of perception and intelligence, we find that its operations are carried on by associations of imagery, mostly unconscious, that do not conform closely to the course of natural events. To the Id we ascribe hallucinations, delusions, irrational beliefs, as well as fantasies, intuitions, faith, and creative conceptions. Thus almost everything, good and bad, has its primitive source in the Id.

The Superego System. Since the environment is a factor in every episode of personality, and since from a psychological point of view the social environment is more important than the physical, it is necessary to pay particular attention to the culture in which the individual is embedded, the "culture" being the accepted organization of society as put into practice and defended. For our purposes, the organization may be partially described in terms of the time-place-mode-object (tpmo) formulas which are allowed or insisted upon for the expression of individual needs. A child is allowed to play during the day but not at night (time). He may defecate in the toilet but not on the floor (place). He may push other children but not hit them with a mallet (mode). He may ask his father but not a stranger in the street for money (object). No need has to be inhibited permanently. If the individual is of the right age and chooses the permitted time, the permitted place, the permitted mode and the permitted object, he can objectify any one of his needs. However, the Id impulses of no child are readily modified to fit civilized patterns of this sort. They come insistently (cannot wait for the proper time or place), erupt in primitive forms (with instinctual actones), and are directed indiscriminately toward this or that object. To socialize a child the proper tpmo formulas are gradually imposed by a variety of methods: suggestion, persuasion, example, rewards, promises, punishments, threats, physical coercions, and restraints. This is done first by parents, surrogates, and nurses, and later by other elders: teachers, priests, policemen, and magistrates. To the child, then, as well as to the adult, the culture is a compound of behavioral patterns that are imposed by stronger authorities. It is fear of the pain or of the belittlement these authorities can inflict or of the distress that the withdrawal of their love and protection will engender that is most influential in finally bringing about a sufficient acceptance of social forms. The tpmo pattern, as a loose organization of "Do's" and "Don'ts," preached and perhaps practiced by the parents, asserted to be the only "Right," sanctioned by religion and strengthened by the image of an avenging deity, becomes, to a greater or less degree, internalized as a complex institution, known commonly as conscience. This may be termed the Superego system. A strong Superego is usually more exacting than current laws and conventions. It may be elevated far above worldly considerations by fusion with the Ego Ideal. It endures, with certain modifications, throughout life. It is, as it were, always there to influence the composition of regnancies. Its first function is to inhibit asocial tendencies, its second is to present cultural or religious aims as the "highest good." Its operations are largely unconscious.

The Ego System. Introspection yields much information in regard to the internal factors that influence behavior. Everyone has experienced "resolving to do something" or "selecting a purpose." Such an experience must modify the brain (i.e., must leave a latently perseverating disposition), because at some future date it will be found that behavior is not the same as it would have been if the "resolving" experience had not occurred. Decisions and intentions of this sort—"accepting a goal," "planning a course of action," "choosing a vocation," as well as promises, compacts and "taking on responsibility" (all of them related to time-binding and the establishment of expectations and levels of aspiration) —seem to be attended by a relatively high degree of consciousness, and, what is more, by a feeling that the "self" is making the decision, freely *willing* the direction of its future conduct. We should say that such conscious fixations of aim were organized to form the "Ego system."

Introspection also teaches us that when other non-instituted (unaccepted) needs and impulses (impulses that seem to disrupt, oppose, or nullify the established Ego system) arise in consciousness, they are felt to come from "outside" the self, or from a "deeper layer" of the self, from the "bodily" or "animal part" of the self. All such unacceptable impulses have been subsumed under the term "Id." Need integrates of the Id are usually to be distinguished by their instinctual (animal-like), primitive (savage-like) or infantile (child-like) modes and cathexes. They are usually restive and insistent and impatient of the schedule of activity instituted by the Ego. It may be said, I think, that though the Ego derives its original strength from emotional needs and is repeatedly refreshed by them, it can operate for periods without their urgent activity (just as a man who has no appetite can force himself to eat). Every need is associated, of course, with numerous modes, some of which belong to the Ego system and some to the Id. Thus, the Aggression drive expressing itself in verbal criticism of the President or in physical assault upon a gangster might be part of an Ego system, whereas other more violent forms of expression might belong to the Id.

The concept of Ego emphasizes the determining significance of 1, conscious, freely willed acts: making a resolution (with oneself) or a compact (with others) or dedicating oneself to a lifelong vocation, all of which "bind" the personality over long periods of time; 2, the establishment of a cathected Ego Ideal (image of a figure one wants to become); and 3, the inhibition of drives that conflict with the above-mentioned intentions, decisions and planned schedules of behavior. One index of the degree of structuration (strength) of the Ego is the ability of an individual to "live by" his resolutions and compacts.

The Ego system stands, as it were, between the Id and the Superego. It may gradually absorb all the forces of the Id, employing them for its own purpose. Likewise, it may assimilate the Superego until the will of the individual is in strict accord with the best principles of his society. Under such circumstances what the individual feels that he wants to do coincides with what he has to do (as prescribed by his culture). The Ego, however, may side with the Id against the Superego. It may, for example, inhibit or repress the Superego and "decide" in favor of a criminal career. A strong Ego acts as mediator between Superego and Id; but a weak Ego is no more than a "battleground."

Interests. If we observe a series of objective episodes (external press and overt trends) occurring in the life of an individual, we never fail to notice certain resemblances. The personality exhibits sameness. We say that the man possesses certain consistent traits. However, we can usually observe more than this. Viewing successive episodes over a sufficient span of time, we can note developments. We can perceive that some episodes are the logical outgrowths of others and that together they form temporal systems bound together by the persistence (constant repetition) of one or more needs integrated with certain modes and directed toward certain cathected objects (things, people, institutions, ideologies). Every such system may be called an *interest* (complex need integrate).

The concept of interest focuses attention upon the cathected objects and modes of activity rather than upon the needs that are engaged. It takes the needs for granted. A man enters politics and almost overnight much of his behavior becomes oriented in such a way as to further this interest. This is certainly a fact of significance and it can be stated without considering what combination of needs prompted his decision or what needs are satisfied by his political activity. He may be affiliative, dominative, aggressive, exhibitionistic, or seclusive, but this is another matter.

The concept of interests is closely related to the concept of cultural patterns or organizations, since most interests are not only possessed in common with other people, but they have an accepted institutional or ideological form. These sometimes quite rigid communities of mode and purpose stand ready to canalize the random activity of each new generation. Their suggestive and dominative influence is so great and omnipresent that some psychologists have been tempted to think of personality as constituted by its different memberships. A person may be sufficiently described, it is claimed, in terms of the mores and aims of the different groups (sub-cultures) to which he belongs. This point of view can be accepted with several important qualifications. Institutions are congealed need patterns shared by many; they are supported by new members with similar integrates; and they are modified or abandoned by members whose needs change. They do, however, determine specifically what actones and what objects will be cathected.

Institutions and needs are complementary forces. From the point of view of the drive theory, an institution is engendered and maintained because it tends to satisfy certain needs that are held in common by many people. Among numerous existing institutions the individual tends to select for membership those which give the best opportunity for the fulfilment of his particular set of tendencies. As the needs of the members change the institution changes, though here there is usually a certain lag. A whole-hearted member of an institution—one who transfers value from himself to the object—acts for the institution as he would act for himself. He attempts to further its aims in competition with other institutions, he is hurt when it is ridiculed, feels depressed when it declines, defends it, fights for it, belittles other groups, and so forth. Thus an institution will allow a sociocentric man of this stamp to express all his needs in behalf of a "cause" (opposed to other "causes") as well as in his own behalf.

The endurance and progressive development of interests make it necessary to conceptualize the gradual establishment of persisting organizations of control in the brain. Without a notion of such interest systems one cannot explain why many successive samples of an individual's behavior—sometimes nearly all his behavior for months or years (*cf.* Balzac's *Quest of the Absolute*)—can be meaningfully related to each other according to their function in furthering a dominant aim. A purposive system conserved in the brain is the conceptual cord upon which we string our beads, the observed episodes. All such organizations of interest may be assigned to the Ego System, though many of them have come to operate because of Superego influence.

The Habit System. Behavior that has become automatic, that proceeds without much conscious intervention, that recurs repeatedly in the same form, may be conveniently ascribed to a *habit system.* This is formed by the structuralization (mechanization) of what has frequently recurred, whether determined by the Superego, the Ego, or the Id. The habit system accounts for most rigidities, particularly those which the individual himself cannot abandon.

Thus, as we see it, regnancies are the resultants of external press, of freshly aroused emotional needs (Id), of conscious intentions (Ego), of accepted cultural standards (Superego), and of customary modes of behavior (habit system) in varying proportions. The relative strength of these influences determines what tendencies will be objectified.

This brings us to the end of this long, yet all-too-brief, summary of the theory and concepts that guided our researches. Now it is necessary to give an account of the variables of personality which we attempted to distinguish and measure in our subjects.

REFERENCES

1. McDougall, W. *Introduction to Social Psychology,* London, 1908; *Outline of Psychology,* New York, 1923.

2. Tolman, E. C. *Purposive Behaviour in Animals and Men,* New York, 1932.

3. Stone, C. P. *Sexual Drive.* Chapter 18 in *Sex and Internal Secretions,* ed. by Edgar Allen, Baltimore, 1932.

4. Lewin, K. *A Dynamic Theory of Personality,* New York, 1935.

5. Freud, Sigmund. *Collected Papers* (4 vols.), International Psycho-analytical Library, London, 1924–25; *A General Introduction to Psycho-analysis,* New York, 1920; *New Introductory Lectures on Psycho-analysis,* New York, 1933.

6. Jung, Carl G. *Psychology of the Unconscious,* London, 1919; *Psychological Types,* London, 1924.

7. Adler, Alfred. *The Neurotic Constitution*, New York, 1921; *The Practice and Theory of Individual Psychology*, New York, 1924.

8. Here the wording has been taken from E. S. Russell (*Form and Function*, London, 1916; *The Interpretation of Development and Heredity*, Oxford, 1930), who has stated most admirably the organismal viewpoint elaborated by W. E. Ritter (*The Unity of the Organism*, Boston, 1919) and others.

9. Quoted from Korzybski, Alfred. *Science and Sanity*, Lancaster, Pa., 1933, p. 19.

10. I am indebted to Mrs. Eleanor C. Jones for this term.

11. The term "regnancy" was suggested to me by Mrs. Eleanor C. Jones.

12. Child, C. M. *Senescence and Rejuvenescence*, Chicago, 1915.

13. Russell, E. S. *The Interpretation of Development and Heredity*, Oxford, 1930, p. 186.

14. *Ibid.*, p. 280.

15. Tolman, E. C. *Purposive Behaviour in Animals and Men*, New York, 1932.

16. Korzybski, Alfred. *Manhood of Humanity*, New York, 1921.

17. Much of what is contained in the following exposition is quoted (by permission of the editor, Dr. Carl Murchison) from an article by the author which appeared in *The Journal of General Psychology*, 1936, *15*, 241–68.

18. Köhler, W. The new psychology and physics. *Yale Review*, 1930, *19*, 560–76.

19. Korzybski, Alfred. *Science and Sanity*, Lancaster, Pa., 1933, p. 1.

20. MacCurdy, J. T. *Common Principles in Psychology and Physiology*, London, 1928, p. 14.

21. Here, by permission of the editor, Dr. Carl Murchison, I shall quote freely from an article of mine appearing in *The Journal of Psychology*, 1936, *3*, 27–42.

22. Skinner, B. F. The generic nature of the concepts of stimulus and response. *J. Gen. Psychol.*, 1935, *12*, 40–65.

23. Woodworth, R. S. *Dynamic Psychology*, New York, 1918.

24. Riddle, O., *et. al.* Maternal behavior induced in rats by prolactin. *Proc. Soc. Exper. Biol.*, 1935, *32*, 730–34.

25. Young, W. C. Paper presented at the Harvard Psychological Colloquium, April 1936: The hormonal production of sexual receptivity in the guinea pig.

26. Sanford, R. N. The effects of abstinence from food upon imaginal processes: A preliminary experiment. *J. Psychol.*, 1936, *2*, 129–36.

27. Murray, H. A. The effect of fear upon estimates of the maliciousness of other personalities. *J. Soc. Psychol.*, 1933, *4*, 310–39.

28. Whyte, L. L. *Archimedes, or The Future of Physics*, New York, 1928.

29. Cannon, W. B. *The Wisdom of the Body*, New York, 1932.

30. McDougall, W. *Psychologies of 1925*, Worcester, Mass., 1927; *Psychologies of 1930*, Worcester, Mass., 1930; with Watson, J. B. *The Battle of Behaviourism*, New York, 1929.

31. Lewis, W. C. McC. *A System of Physical Chemistry*, London, 1920, p. 1.

32. Sullivan, J. V. N. *Limitations of Science*, New York, 1933.

33. Lewin, K. *A Dynamic Theory of Personality*, New York, 1935.

34. Bernard, L. L. *Instincts*, New York, 1924.

35. Garnett, A. C. *The Mind in Action*, New York, 1931.

36. Hunt, W. A., and Landis, C. Studies of the startle pattern: I, II, III. *J. Psychol.*, 1936, *2*, 201–19.

37. Holt, F. B. *Animal Drive and the Learning Process*, New York, 1911.

38. Stratton, G. M. Excitement as an undifferentiated emotion, in *Feelings and Emotions*, The Wittenberg Symposium, Worcester, 1928.

39. Hunt, W. A., and Landis, C. Studies of the startle pattern: I, II, III. *J. Psychol.*, 1936, *2*, 201–19.

40. McDougall, W. *Outline of Psychology*, New York, 1923.

41. Hamilton, William. *Lectures on Metaphysics*, 1859–60.

42. Bühler, K. Displeasure and pleasure in relation to activity. In *Feelings and Emotions*, The Wittenberg Symposium, Worcester, 1928.

43. Freud, S. *Beyond the Pleasure Principle*, London, 1922.

44. Bousfield, W. R. *Pleasure and Pain*, New York, 1926.

45. James, W. *Psychology: Briefer Course*, New York, 1892, chapter 12.

46. Garnett, A. C. *The Mind in Action*, New York, 1932.

47. Landis, C. Emotion: II. The expression of emotions. In *A Handbook of General Experimental Psychology*, Worcester, Mass., 1934.

48. Sherman, M., and Sherman, I. C. *The Process of Human Behavior*, New York, 1929.

49. Mapother, E. Tough or tender. *Proc. R. Soc. Med.*, 1934, *27*, 1687–1712.

50. Lewin, K. *A Dynamic Theory of Personality*, New York, 1935.

51. Alexander, F. The influence of psychologic factors upon gastrointestinal disturbances. *Psychoanal. Quart.*, 1934, *3*, 501–88.

52. Homburger, E. Configurations in play. *Psychoanal. Quart.*, 1937, *6*, 139–44.

53. Lewin, K. *Principles of Topological Psychology*, New York, 1936.

54. Koffka, K. *Principles of Gestalt Psychology*, New York, 1935.

55. Bridgman, P. W. *The Nature of Physical Theory*, 1936, pp. 8, 9.

56. McDougall, W. *Psychologies of 1930*, Worcester, Mass., 1930.

57. Spearman, C. *The Abilities of Man*, New York, 1927.

7

OUTLINE OF A CONCEPTION
OF PERSONALITY

(With Clyde Kluckhohn)

INTRODUCTION

A dynamic organismic conception of personality which adequately represents, in abstract terms, the succession of critical events, is inherently difficult. It is so difficult that three thousand years of preoccupation with the study of man, of observations of self and of others, in sickness and in health, by philosophers, creative artists, physicians, and social scientists of all sorts, have failed to produce a theoretical system which invites unanimous assent.

Conception is impeded by the fact that the integrations of processes which constitute personality are hidden, and we have no instruments with which to record them; their forms must be inferred from their manifestations in words and other overt actions. Introspection, we know, is a useful but not completely trustworthy instrument, not only because the mind is incapable of observing and remembering completely and precisely—many of its component processes being outside the field of consciousness—but because there are security-preserving processes constantly at work altering the plain face of nature. Conception is complicated also because of the bewildering sequence of activities, of words, movements, and effects which pass and perish, never to be repeated in exactly that form again. Personality is process: it will not stop and allow itself to be examined repeatedly and at leisure by the experts. Only recently, in the motion-picture camera with sound track, have we acquired the means of making records of behavior which can be examined by any number of observers over and over again at a slow rate of speed.

From Henry A. Murray and Clyde Kluckhohn, *Personality in Nature, Society, and Culture*, 2nd. Edition. New York: Alfred A. Knopf, 1953. Chapter One, Outline of a conception of personality, pp. 3–32.

AUTHORS' NOTE: Certain ideas and phrases in sections 1, 2, and 9 derive from an unpublished paper by O. H. Mowrer and C. Kluckhohn. The writers thank Dr. Mowrer for his permission to use these materials.

204

The use of the camera, however, is confined to a few situations. Many of the most significant actions of personality occur in private.

A *dynamic* conception is difficult because personality is motivated by an intricate plexus of forces, some of them unconscious, many of which have their roots in the emotional experiences of childhood. These forces are not open to direct inspection. They operate through time, and one may have to wait for hours, months, or years to observe their effects in order to ascertain their properties and their powers.

An *organismic* conception calls for a representation of the "personality as a whole," as the prerequisite for an explanation of its parts. "Personality as a whole" signifies two things: (1) the unity that is attained in the effective organization of psychological processes during one event and (2) the unity that is attained in the successive developments which occur through a long series of events or through the entire series of occurrences which constitute a life. That is to say, personality exhibits some degree of unity (wholeness) in each of its functional operations, and it exhibits some degree of unity (wholeness) in its serial progressions toward long-range goals and in its productions and retentions of forms —forms of perception, interpretation, valuation, strategy, and technical ability. But the unity that is manifested in one action or over an entire lifetime, whatever its degree, is not easily achieved. It is born out of conflicts and resolutions of conflicts, the course of life being punctuated by repeated choices to be made between alternative or opposing percepts, concepts, needs, goals, loyalties, philosophies, tactics, or modes of expression. Thus, the nature of a personality is revealed in the sequence of its major dilemmas as well as in its wholeness. Here again, since time is an integral element of personality, the student may have to wait, sometimes for years, until a structure has been completed, so that he may comprehend the events which led to it. Only by a careful analysis and reconstruction of the *Faust* that was finished at eighty-two, do we attain sufficient understanding of those components of Goethe's personality which, over a period of fifty-seven years, were periodically at work shaping and reshaping its vast and intricate architecture. One of the functions of personality is to transform itself, painfully and by slow steps, into an instrument of expression and effective action. As someone—a narcissist no doubt—once said, life is like trying to play a violin solo in public when you must compose the music and learn to use the instrument as you proceed.

No less difficult than the conception of a personality as a dynamically developing temporal unit is the more abstract, morphological conception of the "whole personality" as the entire framework of potential components at a given moment (cross-sectional whole). This calls for a schematic representation of a stratified network of established elements and forms, of sources of energy and of action systems, variously excitable.

Another factor retarding the development of a realistic conception of the nature of man has been the limitations and distortions of perception, apperception, and conceptualization, the blind spots, rigidities, and defensive rejections, in the personality of the social scientist himself and in the members of the society in which he has worked. To adults who have painfully achieved some degree of integration of character, an honest examination of the processes involved is as distressing as the reopening of an old wound. For many persons, it is precisely the "givenness" of personality that is the bulwark of their security system. Students of personality and culture are themselves victims of their own personalities and products of their culture. Only recently has a cross-cultural perspective provided some emancipation from those values that are not broadly "human" but merely local, in both space and time. Only gradually is our culture altering so as to permit social scientists to work and think with something approaching objectivity. Problems of personality have, in general, been deeply embedded in moral issues; and the student who did not wish to be punished by society was forced to take sides in disputes over the "goodness" and the "badness" of personality dispositions, instead of being free to ask how such dispositions develop, why some individuals manifest them more than others.

BRIEF HISTORICAL RETROSPECT

The history of scientific thought is instructive in this connection. Originally, animistic conceptions governed man's perceptions of nature; and biological and behavioral phenomena were viewed in a framework of supernaturalism. Scientific objectivity made its first inroads by revolutionizing our notions of the physical world. Its next advances came in the biological sphere. More recently, a science of personality has begun to take shape. In the attempt to extend the naturalistic viewpoint to this latter area, a first and largely abortive approach was based upon what may be called the "chemical," or "humoral," theory of personality. Then came the biological concepts of constitution and instinct. Now a discipline is emerging with its own proper terms, methods, and hypotheses. This new approach does not deny the biological basis of human nature nor the physio-chemical basis of biology. It is, in fact, axiomatic that no postulate of a science of behavior may be incongruent with known facts or principles from other spheres. However, although the body is made up of chemicals, one can successfully study comparative anatomy without being a chemist. In the same way behavioral phenomena must be studied in their own right without waiting for endocrinology and the other more "basic" sciences to provide a complete underpinning.

The first deep penetration of the guarded fortress of personality came from the realm of psychotherapy, from attempts to understand and cure persons whose characters had been malformed. In trying to remedy these failures, there emerged the first comprehensive dynamic theory of personality—psychoanalysis. Like all great scientific contributions, Freud's most fundamental discovery, though essentially simple, subsumed under a common formula a host of superficially diverse phenomena. Slips of the tongue and pen, acts of misreading and misinterpreting, play, humor, and dreams, artistic and literary creations, myths and rituals, the long and varied gamut of neurotic symptoms and sexual perversions, and the bizarre manifestations of the psychoses—all these phenomena Freud explained as more or less well disguised expressions and gratifications of needs which the individual is afraid to express and to gratify openly.

Every society makes many demands upon the organisms which are acculturated by it. When and how renunciations are demanded differ in various societies and in the different social classes of the same society. A time-minded culture like that of the United States stresses distant rewards more than does, say, Mexican culture. Cultures also offer many potential enrichments of experience to the individual, but these are less apparent to the child than are the more direct advantages of social, as contrasted to solitary, existence. Although psychotherapists have probably stressed the repressive and renunciatory demands of culture too much and the benefits too little, the child must certainly feel these demands as more or less arbitrary. Even the adult rarely appreciates the "wisdom of the culture." Instead, culture is represented to him, first, by a succession of imperious requirements set by external authority and, later, by a rigid, unreasoning part of his own personality which must be obeyed implicitly or hazardously defied.

Most, if not all, fears are learned, many of them as a result of conflicts between the child and his parents and other culture-implanting surrogates. Certain forms of behavior in children are punished because the parents have been punished for showing such behavior or because "the baby book" and our contemporaries agree these forms of behavior must be "stamped out."

FORMULATION OF PERSONALITY

Any representation of a personality is a hypothetical formulation, not a record of facts. A biographer might describe every significant thing that a man thought and said and did and felt from the start to the finish of his life without conceptualizing his personality. The subjective and objective activities of a personality continue without cessation, twenty-four hours a day, from birth to death, and, were it possible to observe and formulate them all, the massive result would be as undesirable as it was intellectually unmanageable. It would be necessary to construct a *sufficient formulation* of the complete formulation. We might compare a complete formulation to the score of a more or less integrated series of musical pieces which took a lifetime to play. If it were possible, as in music, to represent with appropriate symbols twenty-four hours of activity on 2,400 pages of paper, making five compact volumes per day, there would be 1,825 for each year, and over 125,000 for a Biblical lifetime. Here, surely, filling a large library, would be the facts about one person, a truth that was too huge to serve. Thus we must accept a sufficient formulation as the proper goal; and this provokes the question: Sufficient for what purpose?

In answer, we would say, and this is our next point, that the general purposes of formulation are three: (1) to *explain* past and present events; (2) to *predict* future events (the conditions being specified); and (3) to serve, if required, as a basis for the selection of effective measures of *control.* The validity of a formulation is to be found in the degree to which these purposes are fulfilled. But this statement is still much too broad. A formulation which would explain *every* occurrence in the past and permit predictions of behavior in *every* conceivable situation in the future, after exposure to *every* possible series of controls, would be a complete formulation, unmanageable and unnecessary. In actual practice, one formulates a personality in accordance with a purpose that is more specific—to explain, say, a given set of facts, to predict effectiveness in this or that vocation, to foretell the success of marriage with a given person, to rectify a maladjustment, to eliminate delinquent behavior, to cure a cluster of neurotic symptoms, and so forth. Thus one is always dealing with a *partial* formulation that is meant to be sufficient for a special purpose. This fact accounts for some of the misunderstandings which occur among various specialists. The formulation of the personality of Mr. X arrived at by a psychoanalyst who is paid to cure his melancholia will necessarily be different from that reached by a vocational psychologist or by a social psychologist interested in political attitudes.

PERSONALITY AS A TEMPORAL ORGANIZATION OF BRAIN PROCESSES

"Personality," a word on everybody's lips, has been used, is used, and, we expect, for some time will be used to stand for a number of very different conceptions. Every new attempt to define "personality" is an experiment, a call to criticism, an invitation to agreement. Happily we can discern converging trends in the succession of recent definitions: one, for example, toward *all-inclusiveness*, which seems reasonable since we have no term that is more comprehensive than "personality," and if psychologists should decide to confine its usage to certain parts or aspects of human nature, a new word would have to be invented to denote the whole. Another trend is toward some idea of an *organization,* rather than a sum, of responses and action systems. This constitutes a decided improvement, since it is clear that no organism can be a mere heap, or aggregate, of unrelated elements.

All the muscular and verbal manifestations of personality are dependent on the state of the various differentiated parts of the brain, of the nerve tracts between these parts, of the blood vessels, and of the blood itself. Of course, it is equally true that a brain on a plate is as incapable of functioning in terms of personality as is a trunk without a brain. All links in the chain are important. Brain functioning is influenced by the endocrines, by the amount of oxygen processed by the lungs, etc. However, the brain is of major importance because there occurs that organization which is the outstanding quality of personality. An injury to one region (e.g., speech center) may destroy its usual mode of social communication; severance of certain tracts (e.g., frontal lobectomy) can diminish self-accusations, depressions, and inhibitions; infections of the brain (e.g., syphilis), as well as other diffuse lesions, can produce marked changes of mood and thought; a narrowing of the blood vessels (e.g., arteriosclerosis) may result in dementia; changes in the composition of the blood (e.g., anoxemia), including the presence of certain drugs (e.g., alcohol), will often cause marked transformations of speech and conduct. Many basic characteristics of personality are also determined by the symphonic form of endocrine activity (e.g., hypopituitarism), and developmental changes in this symphonic form, such as those which occur at puberty and at the menopause, are reflected in alterations of feeling and action which may amount to a revolution in the history of character.

Now, if personality is an actual, concrete organization of the processes with which the psychologist is concerned, *it must be located in nature, within some field where there is a togetherness of all these processes or of representations of all these processes.* And, since we have selected the term "personality" to refer to the functioning of the individual as a whole, rather than to the functioning of this or that "subordinate" organ of the body, the integrations of processes with which we must be chiefly concerned are those which occur at the highest, or regnant, level of control, that is, in the brain. The brain is the seat of the government of the body, since it is the *only* place where afferent (sensory) processes from the whole body terminate and efferent (motor) processes to the whole body originate. It is the place where differentiations and integrations of sensations occur to form aesthetic patterns, perceptions of objects, symbolic formulations of the environment, and so forth; and it is the place where the most comprehensive plans, strategies, and tactics are differentiated and integrated and put into execution as a series of dynamically related patterns of action. The brain evaluates the events of the environment as they occur. It is the seat of consciousness, the locus of thought, the field of conflicts and of the resolutions of conflicts. Furthermore, the brain is the repository of all experiences, the conserver of facts, concepts, values, emotional attachments, action patterns, as well as of resolutions, programs, and commitments. Thus we can state that personality is the *organization of all the integrative (regnant) processes in the brain.*

It is these regnant processes, according to the findings and speculations of neuro-physiologists, which are capable of self-awareness (as if they had a mirror in which to see themselves). During the passage of one event many, but not all, of the regnant processes have the property of consciousness, at the moment of their occurrence or soon afterwards if recalled by retrospection. Thus the stream of consciousness is nothing more than the subjective (inner) awareness of *some* of the momentary forces operating at the regnant level of integration in the brain field. Although retrospection is without doubt the best means of discovering the nature of most of the governmental processes which were operating during any single proceeding of personality, experience has shown that not all the variables necessary for a complete reconstruction of an event are available to consciousness; consequently, we require some such concept as that of a temporal pattern of regnant processes (conscious and unconscious) constituting a single episode, or functional operation, of personality. The "temporal pattern of regnant processes" is synonymous with the animal psychologist's "temporal pattern of intervening variables," and the "pattern of regnant processes at any one instant" is synonymous with Lewin's concept of "field," "total situation," "life space." Lewin's "field," it should be understood, is entirely within the head, post-sensory and pre-motor.

When one speaks, as we have been speaking, of organizations of activities, one is always referring to *temporal* patterns, some of which, perhaps, are synchronous. Here, again we may point to music with its harmonies (synchronous patterns) and melodies (temporal patterns). Time is an integral element, not only of every pattern of processes, but of every single process in every pattern. Thus everything with which the psychologist deals has *duration;* and, so, at this point the question is: What is the duration of personality? Since the pulsations of cortical processes continue without cease so long as the organism is alive, personality as a historic whole should be defined as *the entire sequence of organized governmental processes in the brain from birth to death.* Once more we might think of music. The personality of a symphony would be the entire structure (synchronous and temporal relations) of the different sounds from start to finish.

Since we know next to nothing about the electrical field of forces which constitute the physical aspect of the stream of consciousness, the best terminology available for conceptualizing each pattern of regnant processes is that which has been derived from introspection. Words such as "perception," "apperception," "intellection," "emotion," "evaluation," "need," "expectation," and "conation," have proved most suitable, even for animal psychologists, provided it is understood that each of these stands for a physical process which can operate with or without self-awareness. Thus we can speak of unconscious perceptions, unconscious emotions, or unconscious expectations without the contradiction in terms which would be involved if we worked with the concept of consciousness instead of with the concept of the regnancy. In studying infants or animals who are unable to verbalize their subjective experiences, the observer's data are confined to the overt manifestations of the regnant processes; but in studying human beings capable of speech, psychologists and physicians are more fortunate than are any other scientists in having *both* subjective and objective facts (symptoms and physical signs) to aid them in arriving at an adequate formulation (diagnosis) of events.

Most of the critical events in which integrative processes are involved consist of transactions with the environment, and many of the more significant of these are interpersonal, and to characterize the subject in each of these transactions one must characterize the attitudes and actions of the object and the effects of the subject's actions on the object, not only as the subject apperceives them, but as they actually occur. It is important to know, for example, that a certain person is susceptible to hallucinations and delusions, or, if nothing so extreme, to apperceptions of non-existent feelings of hostility in others or to overestimation of the value of his own achievements. Thus, the field of personality embraces the individual's whole environment, physical and socio-cultural. But we have chosen to begin our exposition of the concept of personality by pointing to the brain-field as the locus of successive co-ordinations of action patterns and of over-all integrations. The reasons for doing this are as follows:

In the first place, it is well to remind ourselves at the very start that the determinants of personality are limited to those processes or forms which reach the brain via the afferent nervous system (consequences of environmental events or of symbols of events, or perceptions of somatic processes), or which reach the brain via the vascular system (changes in the chemical constitution of the blood). It is also well to recognize that all the forms and qualities of overt behavior (autonomic changes, muscular and verbal expressions and actions) are consequences or manifestations of processes occurring in the brain-field; and that, if we wish to comprehend the dynamics of behavior, we must attempt to conceive of a characteristic, or variable, of the regnant configuration which will account for every significant characteristic of observed behavior. That is to say, since we are all agreed that personality is an *organization* of some kind, it must be represented as composed of processes which operate together in one region, because no others are susceptible of organization. The student of personality must be aware of the structure and time sequences of the whole body, of the basic phenomena of nerve conduction, ionic exchange, oxidation, and electrical and hormonic potentials across membranes. But the ultimate structural, physiological, and temporal basis of behavior he can leave to the anatomist, physiologist, and bio-chemist. He must, however, keep constantly in mind the brain-field in which personality organization occurs.

The use of adjectives (trait-names)—words such as "energetic," "neat," "prudish," "conscientious," "friendly," "submissive," and so forth—to describe repeated manifestations of personality, has not only proved suitable for ordinary discourse, but is necessary, and may perhaps always be necessary, in scientific communications, to describe the recurrent characteristics of a given individual's behavior. But to decide that the representation of every individual as a cluster of outstanding traits is the goal would be tantamount to the abandonment of all hope of understanding personality. Each trait-name stands for an highly abstract attribute of overt, and hence peripheral, activity; and once a number of these attributes have been abstracted from the stream of processes, there is no possibility of reassembling them to form a model of the interrelated dynamic systems which constitute personality. Personality is the architecture of the whole, not a list of adjectives descriptive of those parts or aspects which most impress observers. For the present, no doubt, much progress can be made by discovering common combinations of traits, comparable to syndromes of symptoms in medicine. But this is only one way of approaching the goal, which is a formulation (diagnosis) of each personality, or of each type of personality—a formulation which will exhibit the interactions of forces and thus explain the syndrome of traits.

Another reason for starting with conscious and unconscious regnant processes at the "center" of personality, rather than with the activities at its "periphery," is that many American psychologists today—influenced, quite naturally, by the successful methods of physical science, by mechanistic conceptions, and by the creed of behaviorism—are disposed to neglect, or even to rule out, subjective processes, and we believe this trend should be balanced by its opposite.

Not only are the processes of undirected and directed thought extremely revealing in themselves, but among the many final effects of these processes not the least important are changes in the personality itself and the consolidation of these changes. There is no way, for example, of representing learning—the acquisition, structuration, and conservation of facts, of conceptualizations of facts, of aesthetic patterns, of attachments to people and institutions, of a philosophy of life, of technical knowledge, and of means-end action patterns (abilities), etc.—without reference to the preservation in the brain of such products of regnant activity. This leads, as we shall see, to a morphological conception of certain more or less enduring *establishments* of personality. These residues or traces of functioning must be represented in psychological terms, that is, as they occur when excited to activity by certain stimuli, because neither gross nor microscopic studies of the brain, nor chemical analyses of the different areas, give us any clues as to the physical structure of these constituents.

Finally, it is useful to differentiate the personality—with its partially self-conscious integrative processes and its conserved establishments of knowledge, theories, sentiments, needs, goals, plans, and tactics—from the other organs of the body and then to study the interactions of the two. Problems of self-control, of freedom of the will, and of autonomic illness have been misdefined as problems of mind-body, or of psychosomatic relations, whereas, as we conceive them, they are problems of regnant-subregnant relations, that is, they depend upon the sovereignty or adjustability of directive processes at the highest integrative level (resolutions which conform to *accepted* plans, standards, ideals, intentions, etc.) when interrupted, or periodically assaulted, by *unacceptable* excitations (impulses, emotions, etc.), originating at lower levels. The question is: Does the regnancy yield to the unacceptable impulse (and experience remorse later)? or does it sternly reject and repress it? or does it, by one device or another, incorporate it in a revised system of accepted forms of conduct?

FUNCTIONS OF PERSONALITY: TENSION REDUCTION

The next question might be: What is the nature of these integrative processes? A psychologist who had been reared in the domain of physiology would be apt to word this question a little differently. It would be more traditional for him to ask: What are the *functions* of the brain? In physiology, the study of processes from this point of view has been justified by its fruitfulness, by repeated proofs that almost all the occurrences in the body *are* functional, in the sense that they contribute in some way to the maintenance, development, or reproduction of the organism. Cannon's account of the physiological structure of an emotional event, illustrative of the principle of homeostasis, is a case in point. The concept of homeostasis, restoration of equilibrium, physical well-being, health, survival—call it what you will—not only represents the predictable effect of the organization of physiological processes in the body, but it is susceptible of measurement in terms of various indices.

Unlike the physiologists, however, most psychologists are extremely wary of the concept of function: First, because many of the regnant processes which the psychologist studies, if judged by their *actual* effects, are not functional in the conventional sense, that is, they do not lead to psychological well-being, satisfaction, happiness, survival, but, instead, to pain and misery, and, in some people, to suicide.

Here we might remind ourselves that when the physiologist finds processes which interfere with the harmonious functioning of the body or, as a result of the atrophy of some organ, notes the absence of certain processes which are necessary for health, he introduces the concept of malfunction. The psychologist might do likewise. The brain functions in an extremely complex, ever changing, and often hurtful environment, and it rarely acquires the ability to do this in a manner completely satisfactory to the organism except, say, in certain rather simple uniform situations. Therefore, the psychologist has as much to do with processes which fail to achieve "beneficial" results (such as reduction of hunger, freedom from anxiety, appeasement of ambition, etc.) and with processes which lead to "hurtful" results (e.g., punishment, neurotic conflict, depression, etc.) as he has to do with "successful" processes. It is because the other organs of the body "know" how to perform their relatively simple functions in a relatively stable internal environment that the physiologist finds that most of the processes he studies take a beneficial course. The brain has a more difficult assignment: it must learn how to improvise new and socially respected ways to deal with novel situations, and, what's more, to deal with them more effectively than other people do, or, if not this, to reduce its acquired craving for prestige, its level of aspiration. Because this is all so difficult, the psychologist finds that many governmental processes lead nowhere and the result of others is a hell on earth. This line of reasoning might help to explain many of the failures to function adequately, but it does not solve the psychologist's problem, because the notion of malfunction depends on an adequate definition of function, and the latter, in turn, depends on some formulation of an end state (such as equilibrium, or homeostasis) or of a temporal pattern of states towards which processes tend to take their course.

Another reason why the psychologist has not arrived at an acceptable conception of an end state is that, if there is such a thing, it is difficult to measure. Aristotle's assertion that the only rational goal of goals is happiness has never been successfully refuted as far as we know, but, as yet, no scientist has ventured to break ground for a psychology of happiness. In place of happiness, or, rather, recurrent satisfaction, psychologists have proposed a number of concepts, such as reduction of tension, but none is any easier to estimate in a human being than the amount of satisfaction. In the hope of solving this problem in an objective fashion, animal psychologists have sought some physical fact (such as diminished activity after feeding or copulation) which could be accepted as an invariable correlate of satisfaction, or of tension-reduction. This practice has proved expedient and might be extended to include the objective manifestations of these states in human beings, but its limitations should be recognized. Objective facts are valuable because they compel unanimous acceptance and so fall readily into science, but a psychologist who confines his attention to such irrefutable data will exclude from his sphere of thought a wide range of phenomena and thus prevent himself from arriving at an adequate conception of personality. That there is a psychological end state or pattern of states which can be measured without the aid of subjective reports is hard to believe.

A third reason why some psychologists have fought shy of the concept of function is that it is teleological (according to one definition of this word), and, so, raises from its grave the horrific image of final causes and of supernatural design. A few psychologists are still unconsciously so close to their possessive mother, philosophy, and their dogmatic grandfather, theology, that they are compelled to assert their autonomy and self-sufficiency in the most radical possible manner, by adopting the extreme position of nineteenth-century mechanism (as represented by the stimulus-response formula).

Perhaps the nearest thing to an all-embracing principle, which avoids reference to final causes, and which, though difficult to measure is currently accepted, in one form or another, by many social scientists, is the concept of need, drive, or vectorial force. It avoids final causes because it points to an *existing* state of tension, a compelling uneasiness or dissatisfaction, a hypothetical disequilibrium, within the organism as the action-initiating state. This is a *present* "push" rather than a "pull" from a non-existent future. Faced by a novel situation, the tense or disequilibrated organism will be disposed to proceed by trials and discriminations —which may take place in the imagination or overtly in behavior—and finally, perhaps, after some exertion, by intelligence or luck, an effect (goal) will be attained which will re-establish equilibrium (reduce the tension, appease the need). The reduction of tension will be attended by a feeling of satisfaction. After one or more experiences of this sort, the object (person, thing), or kind of object, which was dynamically connected with the satisfaction becomes valued (cathected) as a goal-object; the habitual location of the object may also become cathected as the goal-place, and the road to it as the pathway. Furthermore, with repetition, unsuccessful patterns of action will tend to be eliminated and successful patterns, including the agencies (things, persons) that were of service, will be conserved. Thus a simple need integrate (a compound of need, affect, goal, one or more goal-objects, one or more goal-places, and pathways, a variety of action patterns, and, perhaps, one or more agencies) will be developed. From then on, either a percept or a mental image of the goal-object, or, in fact, the image of any component of the system may arouse the need and thus initiate activity.

This oversimplified and over-rigid conception of the organization of a positive need integrate (e.g., hunger system, sex system, etc.) requires some modification before it can be applied to a negative need integrate, the goal of which is a withdrawal from, an avoidance of, or a defense against a painful situation, rather than a "going towards" something. But a discussion of these details, important as they are, is not essential to this exposition. Suffice it to say that practically all action patterns and goal-objects are acquired by learning and, hence, in large measure, are culturally determined; and the same applies to many of the psychological needs which, like the need for morphine, we may assume, are potentially present in all people but are developed only if certain satisfactions are experienced, and, in most cases, only if the enjoyment of these satisfactions is permitted by society. It is generally agreed that the somatic needs (for oxygen, water, food, excretion, sex, etc.) are constitutionally determined. Anyhow, we seem to have arrived at a general formula applicable to all needs: tension → reduction of tension; and so, as a first approximation, we might say that one function of regnant processes is the periodic appeasement of different needs, or more generally, the satisfying reduction of tensions.

In this conception, the point of reference is the initiating state, the discomforting tension, *not* the end state, the satisfying reduction. Thus we are provided with an explanation of suicide and of numerous other apparently anti-biological effects as so many forms of relief from intolerable suffering. Suicide does not have *adaptive* (survival) value but it does have *adjustive* value for the organism. Suicide is *functional* because it abolishes painful tension. But since goal-images are likely to arise as soon as a need is incited, and since the action patterns which ensue will be integrated directionally towards the chosen goal, it is the latter, the so-called "purpose" of the activity, which is the outstanding conscious fact. A person is capable of telling us, at any moment, what he is doing, what he is trying to do, or what he intends to do, though often he does not recognize the need that prompted his resolution. Usually a fusion of needs is operating and the person will be conscious only of those which are acceptable to him. In any case, the goal, or purpose, towards which he strives is founded on nothing more solid than a faith, conscious or unconscious, that its realization will serve to appease the existing tension. Actually the effective goal may be something else. Thus it is often difficult to determine either by questioning or by observation precisely which needs are operating at a given moment.

For these reasons, it is convenient to use the term "conation" to denote each persisting effort (intention, volition, act of willing) to attain a *specific* goal, with the understanding that these conations, perhaps a long integrated series of them, derive their force from one or more needs (general or zonal), the exact nature of which may be hard to determine. The general motivating factor is need-tension, but the chief integrating factor is the conation which directs the organization of muscular and verbal patterns towards the attainment of a definable effect, or subeffect.

It is important to note that it is not a tensionless state, as Freud supposed, which is generally most satisfying to a healthy organism, but the *process* of reducing tension, and, other factors being equal, the degree of satisfaction is roughly proportional to the amount of tension that is reduced per unit of time. The hungrier a man is, the more he will enjoy his dinner; the lonelier he is, the more pleasure he will experience in meeting a congenial friend, and so forth. Hence, some people will exercise in order to "work up" an appetite, or use absence as a means of revivifying their affections. A tensionless state is sometimes the ideal of those who suffer from chronic anxiety or resentment or a frustrated sex drive; but, as a rule, the absence of positive need-tensions—no appetite, no curiosity, no desire for fellowship, no zest—is very distressing. This calls our attention to the fact that the formula, tension → reduction of tension, takes account of only one side of the metabolic cycle. It covers katabolism, but not anabolism, which is the synthetic growth process by which tissues and potential energies are not only restored but, during youth, actually increased. The principle of homeostasis represents conservation but not construction. Anabolism occurs unconsciously, mostly during the night, but its results are apparent each morning in the renewal of physical and mental energies and of need-tensions, and, every so often, in the emergence of new and ever more challenging goal-images which serve as incitements to the development of certain needs.

Most people take the enjoyable consequences of the anabolic phase of metabolism for granted, and only when it fails to recur do they discover how much they have depended on it. More sleep, recreation, a holiday, tonics, glandular injections, vitamins, and stimulants are some of the means used to recapture the lost tensions. Tensions are often deliberately sought: e.g., ghost stories and roller coasters. These considerations lead us to submit tentatively a more inclusive formula: generation of tension → reduction of tension. This formula represents a temporal pattern of states instead of an end state, a way of life rather than a goal; but it only applies to the positive need systems. The conservative systems that are directed towards riddances (of pain, anxiety, annoyance, etc.), towards withdrawals, avoidances, defenses, and preventions, are adequately covered by the reduction-of-tension formula.

Since some positive need systems generate images of difficult and distant goals, one of the important functions of personality is the temporal arrangement of the sub-goals which must be attained in order to arrive at each of these destinations. These *serial programs* projected into months and years of the anticipated future constitute one of the major determinants of development. One young man wants to become a senator or a great naturalist, another wishes to compose symphonies or write novels, another to go to Mecca or achieve the state of Nirvana; but whatever his imagined end, it cannot be reached except by a long series of steps. Human beings are taught to anticipate these steps and, so, establish in their personalities serial programs of action which are more or less coherent, strategically and tactically, and more or less congruent with the realities to be encountered. Some are pure fantasies.

Tension-reduction involves a cultural as well as a physiological dimension. The eating of grasshoppers (raw, or roasted) will not ordinarily reduce the hunger tension of an American. One must know the culture (and also the individual's specific situation and life history) before one can hope to predict whether a given tension will be resolved by suicide, by recourse to psychotherapy, by withdrawal from social life, by change of occupation, or by some other alternative response. In short, a concept like tension-reduction by no means answers all questions about motivation. It helps us to understand why a person acts in the first place, but it does not fully solve the problem of "why this act and not that one?"

FUNCTIONS OF PERSONALITY: SELF-EXPRESSION

By extending the definition of the tension-reduction principle a little further, it might be made to embrace, under the general designation of the "need for activity," all forms of random, undirected, expressive, spontaneous, or emotionally explosive behavior, which are most conspicuous in childhood but are also prominent throughout life, especially during moments of play or relaxation. These consist of effortless discharges of potential energies associated with each of the psychological functions, and, consequently, may be termed "mode pleasures" to distinguish them from the effortful and sometimes painful striving that works towards "end pleasure." Here, we have only to conceptualize a free, irresponsible, and playful release of tension, enjoyed for its own sake. These movements (rather than actions) of the mind and body are functional exercises often of an imaginative or experimental sort which at any moment may be suddenly integrated to produce some effect. In this way small fragments of thinking patterns and action patterns are formed and retained, ready for future use. In aesthetic patterns we are dealing with disciplined effort—as in ballet dancing, acting, telling a dramatic story, singing, playing the piano, reciting poetry, eloquent speech, etc.—effort that is directed towards the creation or expression of an affective pattern (generating and releasing tension) which is enjoyed for its own sake as well as for audience approval or pay. This is mode pleasure rather than end pleasure. Satisfaction is derived from a certain manner of activity as well as from a goal response finally achieved by a series of acts. Since the aesthetic need has been almost crushed out of existence in the Western world especially in the United States, by the forces of Puritanism, commercialism, and applied science, American psychologists are very likely to overlook it. In many primitive and Oriental cultures, however, being or experiencing is more valued than becoming or achieving.

One of the many incongruent representations of reality which have resulted from our fixation on the old stimulus-response formula has been the notion of a personality as a more or less inert aggregate of response patterns, which requires a stimulus (often an external stimulus from the experimenter) to start it going, instead of conceiving of a matrix of inces-

sant functional processes (the katabolic phase which spontaneously succeeds the anabolic phase of sleep), a brain seething with fantasies, programs, and projects, with tentative goals, expectations, and hopes, with
fears and dreads, which lead on to actions which *select* certain regions
and constituents of the environment and which apprehensively *avoid*
others. This is not to deny that there are people who live on in a relatively
passive state, as if waiting for some compelling person to break through
their wall and arouse their dormant passions, and that there are others
who, with nothing particular in mind, run around thirsting for novel and
unpredictable sensations and thrills, and that all personalities, including
those with the most highly differentiated and integrated plans, are more
or less exposed to sudden intrusions, pleasant or unpleasant, from the
environment which require immediate responses. The *reaction* integrates, commonly of short duration, which are learned as a result of
numberless encounters of the latter sort, might, for convenience, be
distinguished from the prospective *action* systems that generate fantasies and programs, and prompt the individual to serial activities directed
towards goals which are not attainable in the immediate environment or
which require days, months, or years of labor to attain—goals such as the
construction of a house, the rearing and education of children, the development of an institution, the accumulation of a large fortune, election to
high office, the writing of a book, the perfection of talents, or the achievement of notoriety or fame, that "last infirmity of noble mind."

FUNCTIONS OF PERSONALITY: REDUCTION OF CONFLICTS BY SCHEDULING

Besides the play of functional processes, self-expressions, and reductions of specific tensions, the personality is almost continuously involved
in deciding between alternative or conflicting tendencies or elements.
Among a great host of possibilities, a person will ask himself: What shall
I attend to? What shall I read? Which is the right interpretation? Which
is the best hypothesis? What is my objective? Am I capable of it? Whom
should I marry? Which is the most effective course of action? Which is
the best word to convey my meaning? and so forth. The alternatives are
fewer and the choice less difficult in non-literate and folk societies, but
always and everywhere choices must be made. Of these different types
of questions, the most pressing and determining are conflicts between
different conations. Since conations (purposes) derive their energies from
needs, one could speak here of conflicts between needs, if it were not for
the fact that many critical conflicts are not between needs but between
alternative goal-objects which might serve to satisfy a single need (or a
synthesis of needs), or between alternative goal-places where one or
more needs might find their valued objects. Therefore, it seems better

to refer to conations, for these are specific in respect to goal-place or goal-object.

Personalities construct schedules which permit the execution of as many conations as possible, one after the other. A schedule should be distinguished from a serial program, which, as we have said, consists of an imagined sequence of sub-goals, or steps, leading to a single distant goal. A schedule is the division of a period of time—day, month, year— into a temporal sequence of differentiated and often unrelated activities. It is by creating a schedule of this sort that a man will shape his day so that certain recurrent needs will be successively appeased (washing himself, dressing, stoking the furnace, eating, drinking, defecating, urinating, smoking, ventilating the room, seeing his friends, exercising, feasting his eyes on the trees in the park, relaxing, copulating, sleeping, and so forth). Time will also be set aside for the carrying forward of one or more serial programs. The man will, perhaps, work for eight hours on a job for which he will be paid a certain sum at the end of the week, and he will acquire some usable information, and buy two tickets to the theater, and purchase a rare stamp to add to his collection, and advance his standing in the mind of an important official, and work a little on his ship-model, and so forth. Thus, by designing orderly and efficient schedules and serial programs a man will allow for the expression and appeasement of many diverse needs, and, in this way, diminish the number of conative conflicts and attain some measure of harmony and balance.

Most men are forced by circumstances to make decisions which commit them to schedules arranged by others (e.g., the daily routine of a job), and so a large portion of the temporal order of their days is not of their own shaping. Also, every culture prescribes schedules, general and special, which define the proper time, place, or order of certain actions, and, therefore, schedule-making is a sphere in which the individual is likely to come into conflict with his society. Starting in infancy, when the child wants its nourishment when it wants it, but, as often happens in our society, the mother has been advised by the doctor to provide it at fixed intervals, and throughout youth, when the school imposes a rigid schedule of classes, on into maturity, when there are time clocks to be punched and countless appointments to be kept, the individual, with his fitful moods and erupting needs, is confronted by cultural schedules to which he is expected to conform.

Were a person to live by organic or subjective time, doing nothing except when he was prompted by a strong impulse, he would become clearly aware of each need as it arose. A feeling of loneliness, say, would lead him to seek the company of a friend; an intense curiosity would start him searching for a certain solution, and so forth. But under the conditions that generally prevail today, especially in highly integrated urban communities, a man lives by a clock-determined schedule. The stimulus for eating is not emptiness in the pit of his stomach but the factory

whistle or the hands of his watch indicating that the prearranged moment has arrived. A notation in his date-book will decide when he will
meet his friend. Thus, by committing himself to an unsuitable schedule,
some of a man's needs will be stilled before they arise, or perhaps be
oversaturated, and others will be kept waiting or entirely defeated. As
a result, he will not only be scarcely conscious of the existence of some
needs but will miss the enjoyment of reducing high tensions. Also he will
experience discomfort from the frustration of other needs. The designing
of subjectively suitable schedules which do not seriously impair social
relations is one of personality's most important assignments.

In summary, then, we might say that the *actual* order of events is
determined by social conventions, by schedules of organizations to which
the individual belongs, by the strength of his disposition to conform to
these conventions and schedules, by the programs of his own prospective
action systems, by the unexpected upsurge of new impulses and ideas,
and by luck, a hundred and one unpredictable occurrences and encounters.

So far, then, we have concluded that the general functions of personality are to exercise its processes, to express itself, to learn to generate
and reduce insistent need-tensions, to form serial programs for the attainment of distant goals, and, finally, to lessen or resolve conflicts by
forming schedules which more nearly permit the frictionless appeasement of its major needs.

FUNCTIONS OF PERSONALITY: REDUCTION OF ASPIRATION TENSIONS

For a variety of reasons—lack of money, lack of ability, social barriers, defects of character, deficient environment—very few individuals
are capable of fully satisfying their needs. They fail, let us say, to realize
their material ambitions; or they are unsuccessful in love; or they fail to
win friends; or they are defeated in the mad race for power and glory;
in any event, their efforts lead to frustration and dissatisfaction, time
after time. As a result, many people, we observe, learn to depress their
levels of aspiration or learn to accept substitute goals, so that eventually
their needs become realizable. Thus the ratio of achievements/anticipa-
tions, which James selected as the simplest index of happiness, comes
closer to 1.0. If we accept the hypothesis that personality is generally
disposed to rid itself of dissatisfactions and to prevent their recurrence,
the process of lowering aspirations to realizable levels is functional.

The yogi whose discipline leads him to the attainment of a passive
state, devoid of all needs and claims, whose goal is to have no external
goals, would be an extreme case in point. Possibly one of the determinants of this philosophy was an environment in which the ratio of gratifi-

cation to frustration was, for many people, very low. By voluntarily attaining the state of Nirvana, a man deprives the environment of its power to move or frustrate him. This aspect of the state of Nirvana would constitute the defensive triumph of an introvert living in a repellent world. The positive triumph would be a feeling of Oneness with the All. All religions and almost all philosophers have advocated the moderation, curtailment, or internalization of needs normally directed towards the environment. But in the last hundred years, interest in this direction of effort has given way to ideals of oneness with the social all and a collective will to power. Democratic ideologies, following a different course, have encouraged a high level of extravert aspiration for every individual (e.g., in the United States: a large fortune, leading to privilege and prestige) and, thus, have opposed the natural tendency to reduce the level after repeated failures. The over-all result, in the United States, has been an extraordinary degree of material progress with a high standard of living, on the one hand, and an equally extraordinary degree of discontent (griping about the lack of material "necessities"), on the other. The ideology, in other words, prevents many individuals from achieving happiness.

One of the important establishments of a personality is the *ideal self*, an integrate of images which portrays the person "at his future best," realizing all his ambitions. More specifically, it is a set of serial programs, each of which has a different level of aspiration. Ego ideals run all the way from the Master Criminal to the Serene Sage. They are imaginatively created and recreated in the course of development in response to patterns offered by the environment—mythological, historical, or living exemplars. Thus the history of the ideal self may be depicted as a series of imaginative identifications, of heroes and their worship. A typology of these exemplars, based on the personalities and accomplishments of the real or fictitious characters who have acted as magnets to the imagination, in this and that culture, at this and that period, is not too difficult. Certain figures recur so regularly that they have been called "archetypes."

FUNCTIONS OF PERSONALITY: REDUCTION OF CONFLICTS BY SOCIAL CONFORMITY AND IDENTIFICATION

Last to be considered here is the most difficult and painful function of personality, that of accommodating its expressions, needs, choice of goal-objects, methods, and time-programs to the patterns that are conventionally sanctioned by society. In most cases this is a matter of learning to conform. Only rarely and to a limited extent is an individual able to modify the culture patterns of his group so that they will correspond more closely to his own inclinations and persuasions.

Many acute and sensitive students of human behavior feel an understandable discontent with descriptions of human life as lived in groups when these descriptions use cultural patterns as a conceptual framework. It is perfectly true, of course, that a cultural pattern is one thing; the utilization of pattern by individuals quite another. It is studies of participation and the utilization of the concepts of status and role which bridge the gap between the abstracted culture patterns and specific individuals.

If one is studying a particular personality, questions of the following kind are useful to ask: In what patterns does this person participate? Are they those which are deemed by other members of the society to be appropriate to his statuses? To what extent does his behavior fall outside the permitted range of variation of the given patterns? What patterns are flatly rejected by him? Pattern transgression is invariably a useful clue in the investigation of personality formation because doing the same as others do is regularly rewarded. Hence when someone characteristically —in at least certain sectors of his behavior—doesn't do as others do, the investigator is always led to ask specific questions about accidents of the socialization process affecting this particular individual.

Likewise, one will examine very carefully the extent to which the individual's habits conform to the standards of his group. And does he profess full acceptance of group standards? If a given individual does not seek the culturally selected ends by socially approved means, other individuals will express disapproval or, indeed, endeavor to force conformity by various sorts of deprivations. Thus, as we study differential participation in patterns, we gain invaluable clues as to the personal habit systems which characterize specific individuals. Similarly, patterns often give the key to certain type conflicts which beset individuals of particular ages or statuses. In our society one may instance the constant pressure of the conflict between age-group standards and parental group standards upon youngsters and adolescents. This is without doubt a type conflict of our culture. The problem of the mutual adjustment of patterns is a complicated and interesting one—largely arising out of the circumstance that it is both the business of culture to check and then again to check the aggressions mobilized by the first check.

Sometimes, however, comments upon pattern conflicts and the inconsistency of the total system of patterns are superficial and misleading. The thing which so many theorists miss is the segmentation of behaviors. There are various groups of patterns within a culture which are superimposed upon each other like a stencil. If viewed as somewhat separate structural entities structuring various rather separate sectors of the total culture, these patterns are not inconsistent at all.

The ideal patterns defining statuses are in most cultures so adjusted that the segmentation of behaviors by roles does not create personality disorganization. However, there is another type of segmentation, peculiarly prevalent in "great societies" like ours, which subjects the individual to various critical presses. In a social structure as complex as our American social structure today, there are great cultural variations—differences between regions, between economic and social classes. Likewise, in a culture which is changing as rapidly as ours, there are often major discrepancies between the ideal patterns of various age groups. The youngster soon discovers that one type of response is rewarded by his own age group, quite another by his parents and their age group. The hostility between adults and adolescents which is so frequent among us is due only in part to a real conflict of interests; in large part it is also due to conflicting culture patterns which arise and are transmitted at the adolescent level. The situation is further complicated by the circumstance that the adolescent also finds that the standards or ideal patterns which prevail in his family are quite different from those which prevail in the families of some of his friends—perhaps greatly admired friends, friends whose families have greater prestige, etc.

The influence of cultural patterns upon individuals has certain characteristic differences in literate and non-literate societies. In non-literate societies the emphasis is upon patterns as binding individuals and upon the satisfactions they find in the fulfillment of intricately involuted patterns. In literate societies the emphasis must be placed more upon pattern conflict and upon the relationship this bears to personality disorganization. These are, of course, not black-and-white distinctions. In literate cultures individuals often find much gratification in the fulfillment of patterns. That most behavior is culturally patterned means not only economy of energy and thought for the individual; there is a positively toned affective side too. Every time an individual in our society feels that he *knows* what the appropriate pattern for his behavior in a given situation is, he (speaking statistically) gets a relief from anxiety, a sense of security from carrying it out.

This is not the place to discuss the genesis of culture patterns. The origin and rationale of many of them are a mystery. Often it is impossible to decide whether a particular pattern is an expression of the profound "wisdom of the culture," or merely, like man's coccyx, a vestigial fixation. Suffice it to say that although some culture patterns, especially the class-linked aesthetic forms, call for periodic changes dictated by the autocrats of fashion, in most cases it is long usage which sanctifies them. Anyhow, it is chiefly the traditional patterns which parents and educators, policemen and judges, and, indeed, all socially responsible adults, as carriers of the culture, are *expected* to uphold and to teach, by example, by persuasion, and by an accepted, culturally defined system of rewards and punishments. The process of inculcating and learning these patterns, until they become "second nature," is termed "socialization." In part, this process is rewarding to the child, for he learns how to do many things toward which he is groping.

However, a child is also confronted by a multiplicity of Don'ts, each connected with some activity, or place, or objects towards which he is naturally disposed, and a large number of Do's connected with actions towards which he is not disposed, at least at the time or in the manner indicated. If he is to avoid punishment and enjoy the many rewards which adults have to offer, he must learn to inhibit or redirect certain insistent impulses, temporarily or permanently, as well as learn to force himself to perform certain other actions which at the time are repugnant to his feelings. After countless protestations and rebellions, the average child, with great reluctance, learns to do these things, to the extent of conforming to most of the patterns which are considered normal for his age. It seems that the ability to suppress a prohibited inclination is acquired by associating it with the images of punishment suggested by the parent and, later, those suggested by the sanctions of the youngster's own age group. These images arouse anxiety to a degree that is greater or more painful than the tension of the impulse and, consequently, the child is led to reduce the former rather than the latter. This is achieved by turning to other activities and thus side-tracking, or inhibiting, the disturbing inclination.

Although, by a little juggling, the tension-reduction formula can be used to represent the described course of events, the type of learning that occurs here is different, in one significant respect, from that usually studied by animal psychologists. In the conventional means-effect learning, the organism is wholly concerned with the reduction of one kind of tension, and none of the ineffective action patterns which, after some practice, it succeeds in eliminating, or inhibiting, have any power to reduce tension. But in "moral" learning, which forms the core of the socialization process, the child must acquire the ability to suppress action patterns which, like masturbation or knocking down a younger brother, are highly effective in reducing strong tensions. The former is a matter of solving slight conflicts between means; the latter calls for the suppression, rather than the appeasement, of powerful needs and emotions which return, over and over again, to disquiet, plague, or mortify the self.

Under the term "rewards and punishments" are included all the satisfactions and dissatisfactions which other people are capable of producing in a person. Of chief importance to the child is the assurance of being the object of the love of the mother or mother surrogate, the significant person, and, so, of enjoying all the benefits that she is able to provide. Any impulse which leads to an apparent weakening of her affection, to anger or to rejection, to verbal or physical aggression, to deprivation of customary benefits, or, even, to her sorrowful disappointment, will become associated with anxiety-invoking (or pity-invoking) images of one or more of these consequences. The same applies, at a somewhat later age and in less degree, to the father and other significant persons. In the Western world the parental sanctions were, for centuries, tremendously strengthened by constant references to a supernatural system of rewards and punishments—by promises of everlasting bliss in heaven and by threats of eternal punishment in hell. In many non-literate societies, parents refuse, as it were, to take the blame for frustrating their children and displace the sanctions onto supernaturals or society in general ("people will make fun of you if you act that way").

During the course of development, figures of authority, capable of rewarding and punishing—the father, the mother, father and mother surrogates, God, admired exemplars, priests and teachers, magistrates and policemen—associated with a heterogeneous system of moral principles, laws, and conventions, become incorporated in the personality as a distinguishable establishment which is termed the "superego." Depending on the ideology that has been inculcated as part of the socialization process, the superego can represent one or usually several of the following: "voice of God," the "eternal laws of conduct," the "right," "moral truth," the "commandments of society," the "good of the whole," the "will of the majority," or merely "cultural conventions." But once the superego has been accepted with an emotional attitude compounded of fear, respect, and love, the individual becomes a true carrier of the moral culture of his society who inhibits many of his delinquent impulses, not so much out of fear of external retributions, as out of dread of superego disapproval, the secret pains of guilt and remorse. This, at least, is the picture in the Judaic-Christian world. In some cultures, "shame" (the fear of being discovered in non-conformity by others) appears more powerful than "guilt" (self-punishment) in inducing inhibition.

In all cultures there develops in the child, as a supplementary source of motivation towards "good" behavior, a dread of insult and personal humiliation, of the loss of self-respect, combined, perhaps, with a positive desire for moral prestige or righteousness. This works very well so long as the parents retain the respect of the child and so long as the latter's pride is connected with membership in his family and with his recently won powers of self-control, and so long as no unjust or degrading punishments are actually administered. For, if the child does lose respect for his family or is unjustly, humiliatingly, and repeatedly punished, he may become asocial with a vengeance, in his sentiments or in pursuing a life of crime. Most boys in our society pass through a partly socialized phase of this sort when they go to school and join a gang, one of the avowed or unavowed aims of which is to break as many laws as possible without getting caught. Status in some gangs, and hence the pride of its most respected members, is connected with degree of courage and cleverness required to "get away with" minor crimes. But here the youth is still dependent on social approval and hence is susceptible to influence. It is the lone wolf, in feelings or in actions, whose pride has become connected with the maintenance of his own self-sufficient sovereignty and with revenge, who is difficult to touch.

Beginning in the nursery, the process of socialization continues throughout life. Among other things, what must be learned is: the power to inhibit, or to moderate, the expression of unacceptable needs; the ability to transfer cathexis from a prohibited goal-object to an acceptable substitute; the habitual and automatic use of a large number of approved action patterns (methods, manners, and emotional attitudes); and the ability to adapt to schedules (to do things at the proper time, keep appointments, etc.). It is assumed that, having acquired these abilities, the average person will be capable of establishing satisfactory interpersonal relations within the legal and conventional framework of society. When the child begins to behave in a predictable, expectable manner it is well on the road to being socialized. But degree of socialization cannot be estimated solely on the basis of objective evidence. The everlasting practice of suppression, demanded by some societies, may be extremely painful, and the not-infrequent result of these repeated renunciations is a deep-seated cumulative resentment, conscious or unconscious, against cultural restrictions. Held under control, this resentment manifests itself in tensions, dissatisfactions, irritabilities, recurrent complaints, periods of dejection, cynicism, pessimism, and, in more extreme cases, in neurosis and psychosis. A high degree of repressed resentment is indicative of a fundamental emotional maladjustment, and, hence, of the partial failure of the socialization process, regardless of how successful the individual may be in "winning friends and influencing people." The goal of the socialization process is an unreluctant emotional identification with the developing ethos of the society, though some conflict is inevitable in all personalities.

Greater behavioral conformity often leads to an accumulation of resentment, and thus to an increase in emotional incompatibility. It is as if the individual's hatred of society rose with each renunciation that was involved in the process of adjustment. It might seem that in such cases we would have to say that any process is functional which results in a greater disposition, or willingness, to conform to the standards of society, and, so, to a diminution of emotional incompatibility.

History, as well as everyday experience, teaches us that, in some instances, the unacceptable patterns which an individual has expressed or wished to express in action have turned out to be more functional, more conducive to social as well as to individual well-being, than the patterns which were supported by his society. Consequently, in dealing with a situation of emotional incompatibility, one must consider the fitness of the culture for individual development. This is particularly true when the personality in question is strongly identified with the welfare of his society and wants to participate in developing forms which he feels are valuable. If a man of this sort were to try to reduce strain by learning to like the culture patterns to which he is opposed, he would create another conflict which could be solved only by renouncing his identification with the creative forces of society. Hence, for those who cannot easily abandon an ideal, it is usually more functional to attempt to modify the culture patterns which are most objectionable to them than it is to attempt to abolish their objections. In doing this, the individual will usually be identifying with others who, like himself, have suffered from the malfunctioning culture patterns.

The actual fact is that some culture patterns are enduring whereas others are changing from year to year, and, although it is often impossible to agree in our appraisals of the different trends, it is certain that some of them are constructive of new social values, others are conservative of the old, others forcefully destructive, and still others diffusely and wastefully disintegrating. A man who is emotionally identified with his culture *in toto* would be one who accepts and exemplifies in his actions the great majority of these different trends. But, actually, such heterogeneity in one personality is rarely, if ever, seen. Perhaps most men are "culture carriers," or conservers; but there are also culture creators, destroyers, and disintegrators. Adopting a broad functional standpoint, we might say now that the goal of the socialization process is the disposition and the ability to reciprocate and co-operate with members of the society who are conserving its most valuable patterns as well as with those who are endeavoring to improve them. The path to this goal is marked by a long and varied series of compromise formations which represent modes of mediation of conflict between different types of personalities and their societies; and, although most people stop at one or another of these way stations, a psychologist might be justified in assuming hypothetically that one function of personality is to transform itself as far as possible in the direction of identification with both the conserving and creative forces of humanity.

Human personality is a compromise formation, a dynamic resultant of the conflict between the individual's own impulses (as given by biology and modified by culture and by specific situations) and the demands, interests, and impulses of other individuals. The compromise is attained in a great variety of ways. An individual may be oversocialized in one sector of his behavior, adequately flexible in others, inadequately socialized in another behavioral area. Conflicts arising from the varying demands upon personality in different roles the individual must play may be solved by compartmentalization—the personality adopts habitual strategies in one area of life that are not carried over to another. Rationalizations are also invoked, many of these being supplied ready-made by the cultural ideology. Conformity may be accompanied by overt release of hostility against the institutions, or the required performance of conventions may be subtly distorted. In the affective reactions that attend both the learning of cultural patterns and their transmission to others inhere most fertile sources of culture change.

The socially deviant forms of personality may arise as a result of various dynamisms and their interactions. The study of concrete cases shows that the processes are often excessively complex. But let us first state the matter oversimply. If, as a result of special combinations of factors operating in the life of one individual, the primary biological impulses remain unchecked, such an individual will be variously known as "antisocial," "criminal," or "id-dominated." If, on the other hand, an individual emerges from his socialization with his impulse life unusually inhibited and with an exaggerated need for and dependency upon the approval of others, this type of person may be designated as "neurotic," "conscience-ridden," or "superego-dominated." But if, as a result of a more fortunate admixture and integration of both biological and cultural demands, an individual emerges who represents a balanced type, we speak of him as "normal," "rational," or "ego-dominated."

While the undersocialized, the oversocialized, and the adequately socialized individual may well stand as three types representing central tendencies in a range of dispersion, this classification is too clear-cut and schematic to serve as a wholly satisfactory model of the observed facts. The psychotics, for example, do not fit easily into such a schema. Some, but by no means all, individuals having "functional" psychoses may fall into a category of persons whose socialization was so severe and so anxiety-laden that (given also constitutional predispositions) they reacted by rejecting alike cultural goals and the culturally approved means of attaining them. The lawbreaker is not always just a person who has not learned to express his impulses in socially acceptable ways. Criminal behavior is sometimes rejection of existing institutions, sometimes the active assertion of socially prohibited responses.

The total cultural structure or various special pressures within a society (economic, class, etc.) may increase the frequency of certain types of deviation. There can be little doubt but that certain constitutional types find certain cultural constraints more and less congenial. The manner in which the learning process is structured by cultural and idiosyncratic forces can lead to certain familiar forms of personal adjustment.

If the child is socialized in such a way that both cultural goals and institutionalized means are affectively toned with a strong threat of punishment for their violation, his personality may have a conformist* coloring. He may also be a conformist if he has accepted goals and means with little anxiety—provided these goals give adequate satisfaction to the needs conditioned by his particular organic equipment and the other idiosyncratic components of his personality. But such a person's conformity will lack compulsive quality so that if cultural goals and means change rapidly in accord with alterations in the technological, economic, scientific, or political environment, he will readjust with little difficulty. But

---

*The argument and terminology of the following four paragraphs draw much from Robert K. Merton, Social structure and anomie. *American Sociological Review*, Vol. 3 (1938), pp. 672–82.

some persons who have been socialized with a minimum of anxiety are still unable to accept emotionally the definition of themselves provided by the culture. Such persons will probably be innovators or recluses.

Innovating or radical personalities will also develop when accidents of the socialization process cause certain institutionalized means, or both means and goals, to be "tabooed" for the individual. Note that many radicals develop in socially and economically advantaged families and that many workmen are stubborn conservatives. Barnett has shown how even in a relatively homogeneous non-literate society personal conflict is the primary motivation for invention, and how "the disgruntled, the maladjusted, the frustrated, and the incompetent are pre-eminently the accepters of cultural innovations and change."* The criminal is often one who accepts goals (such as wealth and power) but who cannot attain, or rejects, the approved means of achieving them.

When socialization (perhaps especially "wrong" identification) or constitutional temperament enforces a rejection of some or many cultural goals but acceptance of means, the personality tends toward ritualism. It isn't the objectives which seem important but a fixed manner of performance. When both goals and means are too heavily fraught with anxiety or are otherwise rejected, the type of adjustment may be characterized as "retreatism." Such personalities may be hobos or hermits or romantic escapists in our culture.

Still other discriminations need to be made. For example, the innovator (activity constructively toned) should be distinguished from the rebel (activity destructively toned). But a dominant or a partial source for all such variations may be found in the way in which the culture (some societies are far more characterized by conservatives than others) or adventitious events of the individual's life history influence the process of socialization. The fact that an organism can be oversocialized also requires further elaboration. Inasmuch as the development of harmonious social living, with its innumerable gains and advantages, has made progressively greater demands for the suppression of the animal side of his nature, man has historically extolled the virtues of conscience and subservience to the interests of others. Because of the painful difficulty of making the transition from asocial to social existence, one prevalent view has been that man is naturally all evil and that the more completely and utterly he can be forced to give up his "original sinfulness" and accept the socially approved way of life, the better it is for him and all concerned. Hence the tendency for society to press the individual to the utmost for renunciation of "self-interest" and acceptance of "sacrifice and service." By definition, a highly socialized person is just like the majority, the average. Constructive social innovations and intellectual

*H. G. Barnett, Personal conflicts and cultural change. *Social Forces,* Vol. 20 (1941), p. 171.

and artistic creations will hardly come from such individuals. Moreover, too great socialization tends to eliminate that spontaneity of response which is a great value in ordinary social intercourse. Whatever else they may be or may become, human beings are and must always remain animals; and this unalterable fact sets definite limits on the extent to which suppression of biologically given needs and inclinations can go with benefit either to the individual or to the group of which he is a member.

OTHER ASPECTS OF PERSONALITY

Distinct from *dynamic* analysis and reconstruction, which sets forth the predictable actions of the personality under different specified conditions, is that type of analysis and reconstruction the aim of which is to characterize regnant configurations in a general way by representing the *formal* properties of typical units of activity. Although the *formal* variables and the *dynamic* variables of any temporal segment of behavior are mutually dependent, it is convenient to distinguish them, because the former define the consistent properties and interrelations of regnant processes (such as perception, interpretation, affection, evaluation, decision, planning, expectation, and conation) which operate in every event regardless of its nature, whereas the latter, the dynamic variables, represent the kind of situation that is perceived and how it is apperceived, and how felt and evaluated, and how adjusted to or manipulated, and with what expectations of success, and so forth. Thus a dynamic analysis deals with constituents of the personality—such as certain remembered facts, preferred concepts, particular emotions and needs, plans of action, definite intentions and words—which are not always operating in the regnancy, but which belong among the potential establishments or latent resources of the personality. Each of these more or less enduring constituents depends for its incitement on the occurrence of certain kinds of stimuli or situations.

A *formal* analysis calls for the observation of such attributes as the speed, coherence, and congruity (application to reality) of verbal and motor activity. It calls also for the observation of the relative dominance and differentiation of the different psychological processes. A person's talk, for instance, may be largely expressive of his tastes and sentiments (valuation), or it may consist of plain accounts of different occurrences (factual perception), or it may proceed on an abstract level (conceptualization), or it may be alive with imagery (sentient perception), or it may be persistently directed towards the production of a definite effect (conation), and so forth. In addition to these variables, a formal analysis includes such attributes as the typical duration of a functional unit (persistence of trends), degree of distractibility of conations, harmony and coherence between consecutive units, ratio of sameness and novelty of units, flexibility or rigidity of patterns, ratio of internal (mental) over external (social) units, ratio of directed purposive action to free, random, and recreational movements (sensory pleasures, reveries, verbal catharsis, wandering exercise), degree of conformity to cultural patterns. Some of these qualities depend on such variables as energy-level, temperament, the subjectivity-objectivity balance, the introversion-extraversion balance, general intelligence, and so forth—many of which, though modified by environmental influences, are, in large measure, constitutionally determined.

Consideration of the different psychological processes and the formal properties of their configurations should be carried on in conjunction with an account of the attempts made to conceptualize a differentiated ego system, composed of accepted and rationalized purposes and plans, conscious values and standards, recallable facts and theories, as distinguished from the *id,* the source of energies, needs, and emotions, some of them unacceptable and hence inhibited, and the source of numerous unaccountable and often disturbing images, ideas, and valuations, which, though repressed, may operate indirectly and unconsciously.

Furthermore, no conception of personality could be complete without some reference to the developments that occur, most of which can be adequately described in terms of differentiation and integration. "Differentiation" covers all refinements of discrimination in perception, interpretation, and conceptualization, as well as detailed specifications in laying out plans and exact directions and timing in action. Mental differentiation is involved in the appreciation of differences, in the intellectual process of analysis, as well as in the isolation and perfection of specialized action systems and abilities, verbal and manual. "Integration" includes the ability to perceive similarities, as well as different kinds of relations between objects and events, to develop a coherent conceptual scheme, to resolve conflicts, to maintain loyalties, to rationalize values, to build a philosophy of life, to co-ordinate different plans, to think and talk in a logical manner, to organize dynamic systems into a unified whole.

Finally, a description of personality would have to include a record of its typical effects over the years—its principal successes and failures in attempting to achieve goals and the enduring constructions which it has created. The effects produced by a personality are not, to be sure, the personality itself, any more than a newspaper is the printing press; but, just as a description of a machine that gave no account of what the machine could do would be very deficient, so any formulation of a personality which omits a report of its effects—manifested abilities, past achievements, reactions provoked in other people, and so forth—is inadequate.

SUMMARY

Personality operates to reduce "dissatisfaction" and to heighten and extend "satisfaction." Need-tension can usually be correlated in a simple way with dissatisfaction and a tensionless state with satisfaction when it is a matter of a tension, such as fear, anxiety, anger, and grief, which, under most circumstances of social life, is very disagreeable *per se.* But in the case of certain other tensions, such as hunger, sex, affection, curiosity, and ambition, the correlation is not simple, because the underlying dissatisfaction, such as it is, is commonly submerged by currents of satisfaction associated with expectations of appeasement. Furthermore, it is not the tensionless state which is specially satisfying, but the process of reducing tension. It seems that the greatest satisfaction accompanies the complete reduction of a great amount of tension. This observation conforms to the common finding that people without interests, appetites, affections, or ambitions are incapable of experiencing intense pleasure and are apt to be chronically depressed. Felt satisfaction in human beings is determined by expectations, conscious and unconscious, even more than by existing conditions. This suggests that the dissatisfactions commonly associated, in modern life, with anxiety and resentment are chiefly ascribable to the fact that the average individual has no certain expectations of successfully and without blame ridding himself of these tensions. Danger is a challenge which is sought with pleasure by one who is confident of his ability to reduce by quick and skillful actions the fear that will be aroused. Anger also is welcomed when, as in war, the opportunity exists to give full and creditable vent to it. Thus we arrive at the conclusion that uninhibited and permissible releases of tension *and* expectations of such releases are major sources of human satisfaction. If expectations of appeasement are definite and lively, the slight dissatisfaction associated with need-tension will be wholly unconscious.

Most individuals learn, in the hard school of experience, that very high expectations, though thrilling in themselves, arouse tensions which can never be completely appeased and, hence, their inevitable outcome is disappointment. As a result many people, the so-called "realists," lower their expectations after a while and thus rid themselves of the dissatisfactions associated with irreducible tensions. Another common solution of this difficulty is to condemn the contemporary human world and create in the imagination another world which is satisfying to one's highest hopes. Perhaps the most convincing testimony of the power of mental imagery is the fact that people who confidently and vividly believe in another world, and regulate their conduct in relation to it, are very apt to be among the most contented members of their society.

The formula, tension → reduction of tension, cannot be applied in any simple fashion to the behavior of human beings, because, for one thing, every member of a society learns that if he yields to each impulse that arises he will be punished and/or fail to reach some of his most valued goals, and, in conformity with these expectations, he gradually learns to regulate many of his activities according to certain programs and schedules. Adherence to these schedules results in a more or less ordered way of life which has a determining effect upon the structure of the personality. The chief over-all function of personality, then, is to create a design for living which permits the periodic and harmonious appeasement of most of its needs as well as gradual progressions towards distant goals. At the highest level of integration, a design of this sort is equivalent to a philosophy of life.

Personality is the continuity of functional forces and forms manifested through sequences of organized regnant processes in the brain from birth to death. The functions of personality are: to allow for the periodic regeneration of energies by sleep; to exercise its processes; to express its feelings and valuations; to reduce successive need-tensions; to design serial programs for the attainment of distant goals; to reduce conflicts between needs by following schedules which result in a harmonious way of life; to rid itself of unreducible tensions by restricting the number and lowering the levels of goals to be attained; and, finally, to reduce conflicts between personal dispositions and social sanctions, between the vagaries of antisocial impulses and the dictates of the superego by successive compromise formations, the trend of which is towards a wholehearted emotional identification with both the conserving and creative forces of society. Understanding a personality requires following its development through time, study of the processes of differentiation and integration, knowledge of the personality's endowments.

8

PERSONALITY FORMATION: THE DETERMINANTS

(With Clyde Kluckhohn)

Every man is in certain respects

a. like all other men,
b. like some other men,
c. like no other man.

He is like all other men because some of the determinants of his personality are universal to the species. That is to say, there are common features in the biological endowments of all men, in the physical environments they inhabit, and in the societies and cultures in which they develop. It is the very obviousness of this fact which makes restatements of it expedient, since, like other people, we students of personality are naturally disposed to be attracted by what is unusual, by the qualities which distinguish individuals, environments, and societies, and so to overlook the common heritage and lot of man. It is possible that the most important of the undiscovered determinants of personality and culture are only to be revealed by close attention to the commonplace. Every man experiences birth and must learn to move about and explore his environment, to protect himself against extremes of temperature and to avoid serious injuries; every man experiences sexual tensions and other importunate needs and must learn to find ways of appeasing them; every man grows in stature, matures, and dies; and he does all this and much more, from first to last, as a member of a society. These characteristics he shares with the majority of herd animals, but others are unique to him. Only with those of his own kind does he enjoy an erect posture, hands

From Henry A. Murray and Clyde Kluckhohn, *Personality in Nature, Society, and Culture,* 2nd Edition. New York: Alfred A. Knopf, 1953. Chapter 2, Personality formation: the determinants, pp. 35–48.

AUTHORS' NOTE: This paper represents a complete revision of an earlier scheme published by C. Kluckhohn and O. H. Mowrer, Culture and personality: a conceptual scheme, *American Anthropologist,* Vol. 46 (1944), pp. 1–29. The present writers gratefully acknowledge their indebtedness to Dr. Mowrer.

that grasp, three-dimensional and color vision, and a nervous system that permits elaborate speech and learning processes of the highest order.

Any one personality is like all others, also, because, as social animals, men must adjust to a condition of interdependence with other members of their society and of groups within it, and, as cultural animals, they must adjust to traditionally defined expectations. All men are born helpless into an inanimate and impersonal world which presents countless threats to survival; the human species would die out if social life were abandoned. Human adaptation to the external environment depends upon that mutual support which is social life; and, in addition, it depends upon culture. Many types of insects live socially yet have no culture. Their capacity to survive resides in action patterns which are inherited via the germ plasm. Higher organisms have less rigid habits and can learn more from experience. Human beings, however, learn not only from experience but also from each other. All human societies rely greatly for their survival upon accumulated learning (culture). Culture is a great storehouse of ready-made solutions to problems which human animals are wont to encounter. This storehouse is man's substitute for instinct. It is filled not merely with the pooled learning of the living members of the society, but also with the learning of men long dead and of men belonging to other societies.

Human personalities are similar, furthermore, insofar as they all experience both gratifications and deprivations. They are frustrated by the impersonal environment (weather, physical obstacles, etc.) and by physiological conditions within their own bodies (physical incapacities, illnesses, etc.). Likewise, social life means some sacrifice of autonomy, subordination, and the responsibilities of superordination. The pleasure and pain men experience depend also upon what culture has taught them to expect from one another. Anticipations of pain and pleasure are internalized through punishment and reward.

These universalities of human life produce comparable effects upon the developing personalities of men of all times, places, and races. But they are seldom explicitly observed or commented upon. They tend to remain background phenomena—taken for granted like the air we breathe.

Frequently remarked, however, are the similarities in personality traits among members of groups or in specific individuals from different groups. In certain features of personality, most men are "like some other men." The similarity may be to other members of the same socio-cultural unit. The statistical prediction can safely be made that a hundred Americans, for example, will display certain defined characteristics more frequently than will a hundred Englishmen comparably distributed as to age, sex, social class, and vocation.

But being "like some men" is by no means limited to members of social units like nations, tribes, and classes. Seafaring people, regardless of the communities from which they come, tend to manifest similar qualities. The same may be said for desert folk. Intellectuals and athletes the world over have something in common; so have those who were born to wealth or poverty. Persons who have exercised authority over large groups for many years develop parallel reaction systems, in spite of culturally tailored differences in the details of their behaviors. Probably tyrannical fathers leave a detectably similar imprint upon their children, though the uniformity may be superficially obscured by local manners. Certainly the hyperpituitary type is equally recognizable among Europeans, African Negroes, and American Indians. Also, even where organic causes are unknown or doubtful, certain neurotic and psychotic syndromes in persons of one society remind us of other individuals belonging to very different societies.

Finally, there is the inescapable fact that a man is in many respects like no other man. Each individual's modes of perceiving, feeling, needing, and behaving have characteristic patterns which are not precisely duplicated by those of any other individual. This is traceable, in part, to the unique combination of biological materials which the person has received from his parents. More exactly, the ultimate uniqueness of each personality is the product of countless and successive interactions between the maturing constitution and different environing situations from birth onward. An identical sequence of such determining influences is never reproduced. In this connection it is necessary to emphasize the importance of "accidents," that is, of events that are not predictable for any given individual on the basis of generalized knowledge of his physical, social, and cultural environments. A child gets lost in the woods and suffers from exposure and hunger. Another child is nearly drowned by a sudden flood in a canyon. Another loses his mother and is reared by an aged grandmother, or his father remarries and his education is entrusted to a stepmother with a psychopathic personality. Although the personalities of children who have experienced a trauma of the same type will often resemble each other in certain respects, the differences between them may be even more apparent, partly because the traumatic situation in each case had certain unique features, and partly because at the time of the trauma the personality of each child, being already unique, responded in a unique manner. Thus there is uniqueness in each inheritance and uniqueness in each environment, but, more particularly, uniqueness in the number, kinds, and temporal order of critically determining situations encountered in the course of life.

In personal relations, in psychotherapy, and in the arts, this uniqueness of personality usually is, and should be, accented. But for general scientific purposes the observation of uniformities, uniformities of elements and uniformities of patterns, is of first importance. This is so because without the discovery of uniformities there can be no concepts, no classifications, no formulations, no principles, no laws; and without these no science can exist.

The writers suggest that clear and orderly thinking about personality formation will be facilitated if four classes of determinants (and their interactions) are distinguished: *constitutional, group-membership, role,* and *situational.* These will help us to understand in what ways every man is "like all other men," "like some other men," "like no other man."

CONSTITUTIONAL DETERMINANTS

The old problem of "heredity *or* environment" is essentially meaningless. The two sets of determinants can rarely be completely disentangled once the environment has begun to operate. All geneticists are agreed today that traits are not inherited in any simple sense. The observed characters of organisms are, at any given point in time, the product of a long series of complex interactions between biologically inherited potentialities and environmental forces. The outcome of each interaction is a modification of the personality. The only pertinent questions therefore are: (1) which of the various genetic potentialities will be actualized as a consequence of a particular series of life-events in a given physical, social, and cultural environment? and (2) what limits to the development of this personality are set by genetic constitution?

Because there are only a few extreme cases in which an individual is definitely committed by his germ plasm to particular personality traits, we use the term "constitutional" rather than "hereditary." "Constitution" refers to the total physiological make-up of an individual at a given time. This is a product of influences emanating from the germ plasm and influences derived from the environment (diet, drugs, etc.).

Since most human beings (including scientists) crave simple solutions and tend to feel that because simple questions can be asked there must be simple answers, there are numberless examples both of overestimation and of underestimation of constitutional factors in theories of personality formation. Under the spell of the spectacular success of Darwinian biology and the medicine of the last hundred years, it has often been assumed that personality was no less definitely "given" at birth than was physique. At most, it was granted that a personality "unfolded" as the result of a strictly biological process of maturation.

On the other hand, certain psychiatrists, sociologists, and anthropologists have recently tended to neglect constitutional factors almost completely. Their assumptions are understandable in terms of common human motivations. Excited by discovering the effectiveness of certain determinants, people are inclined to make these explain everything instead of something. Moreover, it is much more cheerful and reassuring to believe that environmental factors (which can be manipulated) are all important, and that hereditary factors (which can't be changed) are comparatively inconsequential. Finally, the psychiatrists, one suspects, are consciously or unconsciously defending their livelihood when they minimize the constitutional side of personality.

The writers recognize the enormous importance of biological events and event patterns in molding the different forms which personalities assume. In fact, in the last chapter personality was defined as "the entire sequence of organized governmental processes in the brain from birth to death." They also insist that biological inheritance provides the stuff from which personality is fashioned and, as manifested in the physique at a given time-point, determines trends and sets limits within which variation is constrained. There are substantial reasons for believing that different genetic structures carry with them varying potentialities for learning, for reaction time, for energy level, for frustration tolerance. Different people appear to have different biological rhythms: of growth, of menstrual cycle, of activity, of depression and exaltation. The various biologically inherited malfunctions certainly have implications for personality development, though there are wide variations among those who share the same physical handicap (deafness, for example).

Sex and age must be regarded as among the more striking constitutional determinants of personality. Personality is also shaped through such traits of physique as stature, pigmentation, strength, conformity of features to the culturally fashionable type, etc. Such characteristics influence a man's needs and expectations. The kind of world he finds about him is to a considerable extent determined by the way other people react to his appearance and physical capacities. Occasionally a physically weak youth, such as Theodore Roosevelt was, may be driven to achieve feats of physical prowess as a form of overcompensation, but usually a man will learn to accept the fact that his physical make-up excludes him from certain types of vocational and social activities, although some concealed resentment may remain as an appreciable ingredient of his total personality. Conversely, special physical fitnesses make certain other types of adjustment particularly congenial.

GROUP MEMBERSHIP DETERMINANTS

The members of any organized enduring group tend to manifest certain personality traits more frequently than do members of other groups. How large or how small are the groupings one compares depends on the problem at hand. By and large, the motivational structures and action patterns of Western Europeans seem similar when contrasted to those of Mohammedans of the Near East or to Eastern Asiatics. Most white citizens of the United States, in spite of regional, ethnic, and class differences, have features of personality which distinguish them from Englishmen, Australians, or New Zealanders. In distinguishing group-membership determinants, one must usually take account of a concentric order of social groups to which the individual belongs, ranging from large national or international groups down to small local units. One must also know the hierarchical class, political or social, to which he belongs within each of these groups. How inclusive a unit one considers in speaking of group-membership determinants is purely a function of the level of abstraction at which one is operating at a given time.

Some of the personality traits which tend to distinguish the members of a given group from humanity as a whole derive from a distinctive biological heritage. Persons who live together are more likely to have the same genes than are persons who live far apart. If the physical vitality is typically low for one group as contrasted with other groups, or if certain types of endocrine imbalance are unusually frequent, the personalities of the members of that group will probably have distinctive qualities.

In the greater number of cases, however, the similarities of character within a group are traceable less to constitutional factors than to formative influences of the environment to which all members of the group have been subjected. Of these group-membership determinants, culture is with little doubt the most significant. To say that "culture determines" is, of course, a highly abstract way of speaking. What one actually observes is the interaction of people. One never sees "culture" any more than one sees "gravity." But "culture" is a very convenient construct which helps in understanding certain regularities in human events, just as "gravity" represents one type of regularity in physical events. Those who have been trained in childhood along traditional lines, and even those who have as adults adopted some new design for living, will be apt to behave predictably in many contexts because of a prevailing tendency to conform to group standards. As Edward Sapir has said:

> All cultural behavior is patterned. This is merely a way of saying that many things that an individual does and thinks and feels may be looked upon not merely from the standpoint of the forms of behavior that are proper to himself as a biological organism but from the standpoint of a generalized mode of conduct that is imputed to society rather than to the individual, though the personal genesis of conduct is of precisely the same nature, whether we choose to call the conduct "individual" or "social." It is impossible to say what an individual is doing unless we have tacitly accepted the essentially arbitrary modes of interpretation that social tradition is constantly suggesting to us from the very moment of our birth.

Not only the action patterns but also the motivational systems of individuals are influenced by culture. Certain needs are biologically given, but many others are not. All human beings get hungry, but no gene in any chromosome predisposes a person to work for a radio or a new car or a shell necklace or "success." Sometimes biologically given drives, such as sex, are for longer or shorter periods subordinated to culturally acquired drives, such as the pursuit of money or religious asceticism. And the means by which needs are satisfied are ordinarily defined by cultural habits and fashions. Most Americans would go hungry rather than eat a snake, but this is not true of tribes that consider snake meat a delicacy.

Those aspects of the personality that are not inherited but learned all have—at least in their more superficial and peripheral aspects—a cultural tinge. The skills that are acquired, the factual knowledge, the basic assumptions, the values, and the tastes, are largely determined by culture. Culture likewise structures the conditions under which each kind of learning takes place: whether transmitted by parents or parental substitutes, or by brothers and sisters, or by the learner's own age mates; whether gradually or quickly; whether renunciations are harshly imposed or reassuringly rewarded.

Of course we are speaking here of general tendencies rather than invariable facts. If there were no variations in the conceptions and applications of cultural standards, personalities formed in a given society would be more nearly alike than they actually are. Culture determines only what an individual learns as a member of a group—not so much what he learns as a private individual and as a member of a particular family. Because of these special experiences and particular constitutional endowments, each person's selection from and reaction to cultural teachings has an individual quality. What is learned is almost never symmetrical and coherent, and only occasionally is it fully integrated. Deviation from cultural norms is inevitable and endless, for variability appears to be a property of all biological organisms. But variation is also perpetuated because those who have learned later become teachers. Even the most conventional teachers will give culture a certain personal flavor in accord with their constitution and peculiar life-experiences. The culture may prescribe that the training of the child shall be gradual and gentle, but there will always be some abrupt and severe personalities who are temperamentally disposed to act otherwise. Nor is it in the concrete just a matter of individuality in the strict sense. There are family patterns resultant upon the habitual ways in which a number of individuals have come to adjust to each other.

Some types of variation, however, are more predictable. For example, certain differences in the personalities of Americans are referable to the fact that they have grown up in various sub-cultures. Jones is not only an American; he is also a member of the middle class, an Easterner, and has lived all his life in a small Vermont community. This kind of variation falls within the framework of the group determinants.

Culture is not the only influence that bears with approximate constancy upon all the members of a relatively stable, organized group. But we know almost nothing of the effects upon personality of the continued press of the impersonal environment. Does living in a constantly rainy climate tend to make people glum and passive, living in a sunny, arid country tend to make them cheerful and lively? What are the differential effects of dwelling in a walled-in mountain valley, on a flat plain, or upon a high plateau studded with wide-sculptured red buttes? Thus far we can only speculate, for we lack adequate data. The effects of climate and even of scenery and topography may be greater than is generally supposed.

Membership in a group also carries with it exposure to a social environment. Although the social and cultural are inextricably intermingled in an individual's observable behavior, there is a social dimension to group membership that is not culturally defined. The individual must adjust to the presence or absence of other human beings in specified numbers and of specified age and sex. The density of population affects the actual or potential number of face-to-face relationships available to the individual. Patterns for human adjustment which would be suitable to a group of five hundred would not work equally well in a group of five thousand, and vice versa. The size of a society, the density of its population, its age and sex ratio are not entirely culturally prescribed, although often conditioned by the interaction between the technological level of the culture and the exigencies of the physical environment. The quality and type of social interaction that is determined by this social dimension of group membership has, likewise, its consequences for personality formation.

Before leaving the group-membership determinants, we must remind the reader once more that this conception is merely a useful abstraction. In the concrete, the individual personality is never directly affected by the group as a physical totality. Rather, his personality is molded by the particular members of the group with whom he has personal contact and by his conceptions of the group as a whole. Some traits of group members are predictable—in a statistical sense—from knowledge of the biological, social, and cultural properties of the group. But no single person is ever completely representative of all the characteristics imputed to the group as a whole. Concretely, not the group but group agents with their own peculiar traits determine personality formation. Of these group agents, the most important are the parents and other members of the individual's family. They, we repeat, act as individuals, as members of a group, and as members of a sub-group with special characteristics (the family itself).

ROLE DETERMINANTS

The culture defines how the different functions, or roles, necessary to group life are to be performed—such roles, for example, as those assigned on the basis of sex and age, or on the basis of membership in a caste, class, or occupational group. In a sense, the role determinants of personality are a special class of group-membership determinants; they apply to strata that cross-cut most kinds of group membership. The long-continued playing of a distinctive role, however, appears to be so potent in differentiating personalities within a group that it is useful to treat these determinants separately.

Moreover, if one is aware of the role determinants, one will less often be misled in interpreting various manifestations of personality. In this connection it is worth recalling that, in early Latin, *persona* means "a mask"—*dramatis personae* are the masks which actors wear in a play, that is, the characters that are represented. Etymologically and historically, then, the personality is the character that is manifested in public. In modern psychology and sociology this corresponds rather closely to the role behavior of a differentiated person. From one point of view, this constitutes a disguise. Just as the outer body shields the viscera from view, and clothing the genitals, so the public personality shields the private personality from the curious and censorious world. It also operates to conceal underlying motivations from the individual's own consciousness. The person who has painfully achieved some sort of integration, and who knows what is expected of him in a particular social situation, will usually produce the appropriate responses with only a little personal coloring. This explains, in part, why the attitudes and action patterns produced by the group-membership and role determinants constitute a screen which, in the case of normal individuals, can be penetrated only by the intensive, lengthy, and oblique procedures of depth psychology.

The disposition to accept a person's behavior in a given situation as representative of his total personality is almost universal. Very often he is merely conforming, very acceptably, to the cultural definition of his role. One visits a doctor in his office, and his behavior fits the stereotype of the physician so perfectly that one says, often mistakenly, "There indeed is a well-adjusted person." But a scientist must train himself to get behind a man's cultivated surface, because he will not be able to understand much if he limits his data to the action patterns perfected through the repeated performance of the roles as physician, as middle-aged man, as physician dealing with an older male patient, etc.

SITUATIONAL DETERMINANTS

Besides the constitutional determinants and the forces which will more or less inevitably confront individuals who live in the same physical environment, who are members of a society of a certain size and of a certain culture, and who play the same roles, there are things which "just happen" to people. Even casual contacts of brief duration ("accidental" —i.e., not foreordained by the cultural patterns for social interrelations) are often crucial, it seems, in determining whether a person's life will proceed along one or another of various possible paths. A student, say, who is undecided as to his career, or who is about equally drawn to several different vocations, happens to sit down in a railroad car next to a journalist who is an engaging and persuasive advocate of his profession. This event does not, of course, immediately and directly change the young man's personality, but it may set in motion a chain of events which put him into situations that are decisive in molding his personality.

The situational determinants include things that happen a thousand times as well as those that happen only once—provided they are not standard for a whole group. For example, it is generally agreed that the family constellation in which a person grows up is a primary source of personality styling. These domestic influences are conditioned by the cultural prescriptions for the roles of parents and children. But a divorce, a father who is much older than the mother, a father whose occupation keeps him away from home much of the time, the fact of being an only child or the eldest or youngest in a series—these are situational determinants.

Contact with a group involves determinants which are classified as group-membership or situational, depending on the individual's sense of belongingness or commitment to the group. The congeries of persons among whom a man accidentally finds himself one or more times may affect his personality development but not in the same manner as those social units with which the individual feels himself allied as a result of shared experiences or of imaginative identification.

INTERDEPENDENCE OF THE DETERMINANTS

"Culture and personality" is one of the fashionable slogans of contemporary social science and, by present usage, denotes a range of problems on the borderline between anthropology and sociology, on the one hand, and psychology and psychiatry, on the other. However, the phrase has unfortunate implications. A dualism is implied, whereas "culture *in* personality" and "personality *in* culture" would suggest conceptual models more in accord with the facts. Moreover, the slogan favors a dangerous simplification of the problems of personality formation. Recognition of culture as one of the determinants of personality is a great gain, but there are some indications that this theoretical advance has tended to obscure the significance of other types of determinants. "Culture and personality" is as lopsided as "biology and personality." To avoid perpetuation of an overemphasis upon culture, the writers have treated cultural forces as but one variety of the press to which personalities are subjected as a consequence of their membership in an organized group.

A balanced consideration of "personality in nature, society, and culture" must be carried on within the framework of a complex conceptual scheme which explicitly recognizes, instead of tacitly excluding, a number of types of determinants. But it must also not be forgotten that any classification of personality determinants is, at best, a convenient abstraction.

A few illustrations of the intricate linkage of the determinants will clarify this point. For example, we may instance a network of cultural, role, and constitutional determinants. In every society the child is differently socialized according to sex. Also, in every society different behavior is expected of individuals in different age groups, although each culture makes its own prescriptions as to where these lines are drawn and what behavioral variations are to be anticipated. Thus, the personalities of men and women, of the old and the young, are differentiated, in part, by the experience of playing these various roles in conformity with cultural standards. But, since age and sex are biological facts, they also operate throughout life as constitutional determinants of personality. A woman's motivations and action patterns are modified by the facts of her physique as a woman.

Some factors that one is likely to pigeonhole all too complacently as biological often turn out, on careful examination, to be the product of complicated interactions. Illness may result from group as well as from individual constitutional factors. And illness, in turn, may be considered a situational determinant. The illness—with all of its effects upon personality formation—is an "accident" in that one could predict only that the betting odds were relatively high that this individual would fall victim to this illness. However, when the person does become a patient, one can see that both a constitutional predisposition and membership in a caste or class group where sanitation and medical care were substandard are causative factors in this "accidental" event. Similarly, a constitutional tendency towards corpulence certainly has implications for personality when it is characteristic of a group as well as when it distinguishes an individual within a group. But the resources of the physical environment as exploited by the culturally transmitted technology are major determinants in the production and utilization of nutritional substances of various sorts and these have patent consequences for corpulence, stature, and energy potential. Tuberculosis or pellagra may be endemic. If hookworm is endemic in a population, one will hardly expect vigor to be a striking feature of the majority of people. Yet hookworm is not an unavoidable "given," either constitutionally or environmentally: the prevalence and effects of hookworm are dependent upon culturally enjoined types of sanitary control.

Complicated interrelations of the same sort may be noted between the environmental and cultural forces which constitute the group membership determinants. On the one hand, the physical environment imposes certain limitations upon the cultural forms which man creates, or it constrains toward change and readjustment in the culture he brings into an ecological area. There is always a large portion of the impersonal environment to which men can adjust but not control; there is another portion which is man-made and cultural. Most cultures provide technologies which permit some alterations in the physical world (for example, methods of cutting irrigation ditches or of terracing hillsides). There are also those artifacts (houses, furniture, tools, vehicles) which serve as instruments for the gratification of needs, and, not infrequently, for their incitement and frustration. Most important of all, perhaps, culture directs and often distorts man's perceptions of the external world. What effects social suggestion may have in setting frames of reference for perception has been shown experimentally. Culture acts as a set of blinders, or series of lenses, through which men view their environments.

Among group-membership determinants, the social and cultural factors are interdependent, yet analytically distinct. Man, of course, is only one of many social animals, but the ways in which social, as opposed to solitary, life modifies his behavior are especially numerous and varied. The fact that human beings are mammals and reproduce bi-sexually creates a basic predisposition toward at least the rudiments of social living. And the prolonged helplessness of human infants conduces to the formation of a family group. Also, certain universal social processes (such as conflict, competition, and accommodation) are given distinct forms through cultural transmission. Thus, while the physically strong tend to dominate the weak, this tendency may be checked and even to some extent reversed by a tradition which rewards chivalry, compassion, and humility. Attitudes towards women, towards infants, towards the old, towards the weak will be affected by the age and sex ratios and the birth and death rates prevalent at a particular time.

The social and cultural press likewise interlock with the situational determinants. There are many forces involved in social interaction which influence personality formation and yet are in no sense culturally prescribed. All children (unless multiple births) are born at different points in their parents' careers, which means that they have, psychologically speaking, somewhat different parents. Likewise, whether a child is wanted or unwanted and whether it is of the desired sex will make a difference in the ways in which it will be treated, even though the culture says that all children are wanted and defines the two sexes as of equal value.

A final example will link the constitutional with both the group-membership and situational determinants. Even though identical twins may differ remarkably little from a biological standpoint, and participate in group activities which are apparently similar, a situational factor may intrude as a result of which their experiences in social interaction will be quite different. If, for instance, one twin is injured in an automobile accident and the other is not, and if the injured twin has to spend a year in bed, as the special object of his mother's solicitations, noticeable personality differences will probably develop. The extent to which these differences endure will depend surely upon many other factors, but it is unlikely that they will be entirely counteracted. The variation in treatment which a bed-ridden child receives is partly determined by culture (the extent to which the ideal patterns permit a sick child to be petted, etc.), and partly by extra-cultural factors (the mother's need for nurturance, the father's idiomatic performance of his culturally patterned role in these circumstances, etc.).

SIMILARITIES AND DIFFERENCES IN PERSONALITY

In conclusion, let us return for a moment to the observed fact that every man is "like all other men, like some other men, like no other man." In the beginning there is (1) the organism and (2) the environment. Using this division as the starting point in thinking about personality formation, one might say that the *differences* observed in the personalities of human beings are due to variations in their biological equipment and in the total environment to which they must adjust, while the *similarities* are ascribable to biological and environmental regularities. Although the organism and the environment have a kind of wholeness in the concrete behavioral world which the student loses sight of at his peril, this generalization is substantially correct. However, the formulation can be put more neatly in terms of field. There is (1) the organism moving through a field which is (2) structured both by culture and by the physical and social world in a relatively uniform manner, but which is (3) subject to endless variation within the general patterning due to the organism's constitutionally determined peculiarities of reaction and to the occurrence of special situations.

In certain circumstances, one reacts to men and women, not as unique organizations of experience, but as representatives of a group. In other circumstances, one reacts to men and women primarily as fulfilling certain roles. If one is unfamiliar with the Chinese, one is likely to react to them first as Chinese rather than as individuals. When one meets new people at a social gathering, one is often able to predict correctly: "That man is a doctor." "That man certainly isn't a businessman, he acts like a professor." "That fellow over there looks like a government official, surely not an artist, a writer, or an actor." Similarities in personality created by the role and group-membership determinants are genuine enough. A man is likely to resemble other men from his home town, other members of his vocation, other members of his class, as well as the majority of his countrymen as contrasted to foreigners.

But the variations are equally common. Smith is stubborn in his office as well as at home and on the golf course. Probably he would have been stubborn in all social contexts if he had been taken to England from America at an early age and his socialization had been completed there. The playing of roles is always tinged by the uniqueness of the personality. Such differences may be distinguished by saying, "Yes, Brown and Jones are both forty-five-year-old Americans, both small-businessmen with about the same responsibilities, family ties, and prestige—but somehow they are different." Such dissimilarities may be traced to the interactions of the constitutional and situational determinants, which have been different for each man, with the common group-membership and role determinants to which both have been subjected.

Another type of resemblance between personalities cuts across the boundaries of groups and roles but is equally understandable within this framework of thinking about personality formation. In general, one observes quite different personality manifestations in Hopi Indians and in white Americans—save for those common to all humanity. But occasionally one meets a Hopi whose behavior, as a whole or in part, reminds one very strongly of a certain type of white man. Such parallels can arise from similar constitutional or situational determinants or a combination of these. A Hopi and a white man might both have an unusual endocrine condition. Or both Hopi and white might have had several long childhood illnesses which brought them an exceptional amount of maternal care. While an overabundance of motherly devotion would have had somewhat different effects upon the two personalities, a striking segmental resemblance might have been produced which persisted throughout life.

In most cases the observed similarities, as well as the differences, between groups of people are largely attributable to fairly uniform social and cultural processes. When one says, "Smith reminds me of Brown," a biologically inherited determinant may be completely responsible for the observed resemblance. But when one notes that American businessmen, for example, have certain typical characteristics which identify them as a group and distinguish them from American farmers and teachers it can hardly be a question of genetic constitution. Likewise, the similarities of personality between Americans in general as contrasted with Germans in general must be traced primarily to common press which produces resemblances in spite of wide variations in individual constitutions.

To summarize the content of this chapter in other terms: The personality of an individual is the product of inherited dispositions and environmental experiences. These experiences occur within the field of his physical, biological, and social environment, all of which are modified by the culture of his group. Similarities of life experiences and heredity will tend to produce similar personality characteristics in different individuals, whether in the same society or in different societies.

Although the distinction will not always be perfectly clear-cut, the readings which follow will be organized according to this scheme of constitutional, group-membership, role, and situational determinants, and the interactions between them. It is believed that this will assist the reader in keeping steadily in mind the variety of forces operative in personality formation and the firm but subtle nexus that links them.

9

COMPONENTS OF AN EVOLVING PERSONOLOGICAL SYSTEM

Without doubt, the ground for my inclusion among contemporary "personality theorists" in this encyclopedia as well as in four recent surveys of the field (Hall & Lindzey 1957; Wepman & Heine 1963; Bischof 1964; Sahakian 1965) is the array of concepts and conceptual relations that were presented in *Explorations in Personality* (1938), the product of a collaboration for which I have received in print more credit than I can reasonably claim. Since that time, the conceptual scheme that we had designed (for a restricted purpose) has undergone, needless to say, countless expansions, revisions, and reconstructions on its way to the still embryonic and evolving personological system (PS) to which I currently subscribe. I welcome the opportunity to report this much—a bare minimum —in order to accent my belief that today is no time for theoretical fixations. On the contrary, in my case an itch for comprehensiveness has resulted in such a multiplication of *idenes*, or basic genelike ideas— stolen goods for the most part—that at this juncture I find myself utterly incapable of packing them coherently into an essay of this length. The present assignment, then, came as a Procrustean bed which called for major surgery, regardless of the prospect that a successful series of amputations, or theoriectomies, would be pretty sure to kill the patient (this PS). The most radical theoriectomy performed for this occasion involved the excision of that large, widely propagated portion of the Freudian system which is concerned with psychopathological phenomena and their determinants. What were left to represent and understand after this huge excision were the more venturesome, progressive, ambitious, proudful, affectionate, joyful, self-actualizing, and creative potentialities of human nature, as well as of some of its higher-level social and cultural, adult activities. In short, the task here is to set forth something which might serve as a health-oriented extension of, and complement to, the illness-oriented Freudian system. Further reductions of my corpus of ideas been accomplished by extracting a number of biological, physiological, sociological, evolutionary, and general systems concepts

From *International Encyclopaedia of the Social Sciences.* New York: Macmillan & Free Press, 1968. Vol. 12, pp. 5–13.

and theories, by deleting expositions and justifications of ideas that are already in the literature, and by condensing nearly everything that needed to be said into the briefest sentences, without the numerous qualifications that accuracy demands. And so, as a consequence of so much surgery, I am afraid that the standing of this present assemblage of mentations must depend on whatever imaginative supports the reader is prepared to proffer.

A THEORETICAL CONCEPTION

Definition

A personality at any designated moment of its history (in middle life, for example) is the then-existing brain-located imperceptible and problematical hierarchical constitution of an individual's entire complex stock of interrelated substance-dependent and structure-dependent psychological properties (elementary, associational, and organizational). Each elementary property is a differentiated (selectively focused), situationally oriented disposition (readiness) and capacity (power) to participate as a process in conjunction with other processes (each in its own way) in a variety of functional exercises or endeavors which will presumptively enhance that individual's feeling of well-being in his world. The vast majority of these selectively focused dispositions and capacities—for example, a multiplicity of more or less energizing interests, valuations, passions, wants, and needs; of more or less adequate imaginal or conceptual representations of objects, persons, events, or abstract ideas; of beliefs, judgments, decisions, or plans of action; and of more or less competent organizations of subsidiary mental, verbal, and motor processes, that is, special skills—will be dormant (unactivated) at any given time. But a few of them will be operating momentarily in one of the internal or external situational proceedings (temporal units of activity), the ongoing processions of which constitute the daily waking life of that particular individual.

Psychological Properties. The properties and processes of personality are those that are capable of becoming conscious (experientially discriminated) in the natural course of events or when existing resistances are overcome. In short, this PS conforms to the principle that a scientist should adhere to a thoroughly self-consistent terminology, one that is suitable to the conceptual analysis and reconstruction of the class of phenomena (in this case psychological phenomena) he is investigating. This principle prohibits neither his identification of determinants or of analogous events at other levels of discourse, nor his adoption of the language of general systems theory in addition to his own terms.

Brain-Located Properties. Brain-located substance-and-structure

dependence simply means that there would be no psychological properties or processes without the operations of the properties of material
substances and structures on lower (electronic, chemical, physiological)
levels of reality, including the circulating blood and its various essential
constituents, such as oxygen, water, energy-bearing food particles, salts,
vitamins, and hormones (if no animate brain, then no personality); and
consequently that alterations of encephalic functioning beyond a certain
critical limit—for example, as a result of anoxemia, lobotomy, arteriosclerosis, drugs, etc.—will change the personality temporarily or permanently in some respects. Furthermore, this dependence on the brain
means that increasing knowledge of encephalic structures and their
properties—for example, ascending reticular activating system—and
various centers of hedonic, emotional, and erotic excitation in subcortical
areas—should provide ground for hypothetical conceptions of the hierarchical systems of a personality that not only will conform more and more
closely to the operations of the organic structures on which these systems
are dependent but will advance our understanding of their situational
activities.

Comprehensiveness of Properties. In this PS, "personality," the most
comprehensive term we have in psychology, is given a functional meaning embracing everything from basic temperamental variables—for example, energy level, hedonic level, affective state of being—to such
higher mental processes as may be devoted to superpersonal (cultural)
endeavors—for example, artistic, historical, scientific, philosophical.
Consequently, even by restricting one's attention (as one inevitably must
do and should do) to the most important properties, a personality cannot
yet be adequately represented as a functional and temporal whole in less
than 5,000 words, let us say; certainly not by a short list of traits.

Hierarchical Constitution. Hierarchical constitution refers to the
conception of three "vertical" divisions (differentiated establishments) of
a personality, the states of which in childhood are quite comparable to
the Freudian id, ego, and superego. The number, nature, object attachments, relative potency, and interrelationships of the components of
each of these establishments change progressively with maturation and
learning, stratum upon stratum, in opposition to an underlying tendency
(augmented by frustration, etc.) to regress to lower strata, as manifested
in sleep, reaction to extreme stress, neurosis, and psychosis. In these
regressions the mind is overrun by mythological (archetypal) images
from the stratum in which the narcissistic infant's entire world consisted
of the providing and depriving mother (matriarchal superego) and the
anlage of the ego was nothing but a little actuator of its vocal and its oral
muscles.

In this PS the adult id embraces the entire stratified population of
instinctual (genetically given, viscerogenic, subcortical, unbidden and
involuntary) affective dispositions (hedonic, wishful, emotional, evalua-

tive) with their engendered orienting fantasies, some forms of which have been repressed for years and may or may not be operating influentially "below" the boundary of the ego, but others of which have access to consciousness. The adult ego is the more or less fact-perceptive, knowledgeable, rational, articulate, future-oriented regnant system of the personality with energies of its own (during the waking hours) to fulfill its role as both governor and servant of the id. As the self-conscious "I," who leaves most things to habit (dynamic mechanisms), the adult ego will, on signal occasions, try as far as possible to function as the autonomous (uncoerced) and self-sufficient (unaided) determiner of his destiny—especially as "I" the decision maker (the identifier, interpreter, evaluator, rejector of the "worse" and chooser of the "better" pressing id components) and as "I" the plan composer for the "better" ones, the executor and adjuster of the plans, and, finally, the achiever of effects which are sufficiently satisfying to self-respect and to the destructive and constructive id, greedy for pleasure, companionship, love, possessions, parenthood, power, and prestige. The adult superego (superregnant system of the personality) consists of stratified imaginal representors of the rulers (parent, king, god) and verbal representors of the ruling culture (moral precepts, laws, beliefs, sentiments, principles) of the world (family, group, nation, mankind) of which each ego is a member. Its function is to commit the individual to the support and service of these values.

Imperceptible, Problematical Properties. Imperceptible and problematical properties are encountered especially in highly speculative, theoretical constructs, all too complicated to be properly expounded in this article.

Personality Operations

The operations of a personality during any designated period in its career are the history of the brain-located participations (with more or less frequency, intensity, persistence, and effectiveness) of many, but not all, of its manifold, currently existing properties, a few of these at a time —as manifested objectively and/or subjectively during the waking hours —in each of the succession of different (unique or recurrent) external (e.g., overt interactional) and internal (e.g., covert contemplative) situational proceedings, which, with their varying hedonic accompaniments and effects (negative or positive reinforcements), compose the more or less self-conscious life of an individual as it is carried on in relation to an influential environment of natural, artifactual, human, and cultural entities and events. To be included among the manifest operations and relations of a person's constitutional properties are prolonged emotional states (e.g., melancholy, anxiety, internal conflict, passionate love, creative zest); long spans of proactive, progressive serial proceedings, that is, the continuing, though interrupted, operation of complex systems of interest and enterprise with subsidiary processes (e.g., working for a degree, a long courtship, building a house, a voyage of discovery, writing a novel, etc.); and verbal disclosures of prevalent enduring dispositions (e.g., sentiments, beliefs, ambitions), as well as manifestations of thematic imagination, of knowledge, and of skill in various testing situations.

Not all possible operations are included, because nowhere near all classes of situations (e.g., opportunities, tasks, perils) will be encountered by any one person in his lifetime: numerous possible shames and triumphs will be buried with him. Almost as revealing as the classes of situations that a person proactively chooses to encounter may be those he consistently avoids.

Succession of Proceedings. A person's waking life is characterized by a continuous procession of varying psychic states, processes, and representors. Some of these processions will occur when he is privately absorbed in a random, *undirected* (involuntary) stream of covert feelings, images, and ideas (e.g., daydreaming) and others when he is privately absorbed in a *directed* (voluntary) endeavor to "make up his mind" about something. Temporal strips of this nature are termed undirected or directed *internal proceedings.* In contrast to these are *external proceedings,* during each of which the person is proactively or reactively engaged in an environmental transaction, marked by actuations of overt, situationally oriented, motor and/or verbal processes, actuations which may be more or less spontaneous, random, impulsively expressive, aimless, or deliberately directed, intentional, and purposeful. External proceedings have two aspects: an imperceptible *experiential* aspect and a perceptible and/or audible *behavioral* aspect. Internal proceedings, however, have only a scarcely appreciable behavioral aspect. There is no space here for an account of how these major (sometimes overlapping) classes of situational proceedings have been classified into families, genera, species, varieties, etc. What needs to be stressed here is that this PS embraces both conventional behavioral psychology and (more particularly) *experiential* psychology—that is, it uses detailed reports, expertly obtained, of internal proceedings and of the subjective aspect of external proceedings.

History

Chronological records of the more important (revealing, consequential), successful or unsuccessful, satisfying or dissatisfying, single and serial proceedings (e.g., overt social interactions, sexual experiences of all sorts, covert dreams, fantasies, conflicts, feelings, self-evaluations, apperceptions of the world, choices of long-range purposes, etc.) in a person's life during the designated time span, taken in conjunction with his responses to technical procedures, constitute the bulk of the data, the facts, to be analyzed into psychological variables, which, whenever possible, will be incorporated into the systemic components of a total formulation of the existing constitution of a person's more important properties. But, of course, the constitution will be changing, and strictly speaking, this great task of assessment and formulation should be repeated at each of the (Shakespearean seven, let us say) ages of the subject, since personality, as defined by this PS, has not only a comprehensive scope but a comprehensive span: the history of the personality *is* the personality. I shall now turn to a much abbreviated conception of the historic changes of the constitution of a personality, paying special attention to their genetical and experiential (learning) determinants.

The Developmental Process

A personality constitutionally and operationally considered as a temporal whole from birth to death is the brain-located history of the successive and cumulative constitutional products (say, a few molecules and structural alterations at a time, in cells, axons and dendrites) of two interdependent ongoing, psychometabolic processes: the genetical and experiential systems.

The nature and order of the products of the more fundamental of these two interdependent systems are largely determined, in a basic and a general way, by the inbuilt genetical program of consecutive events (DNA code of instructions), a program which is roughly divisible into three successive but overlapping temporal eras.

The first era is marked by the emergence and multiplication of potentialities for a high proportion of new, developmental (associational and organizational), structural compositions, each with its consequential psychological properties. The second era (middle age) is marked by a relatively high proportion of conservative recompositions of the already developed structures and functions. And, finally, the third era (senescence) is marked by a decrease of potentialities for new compositions and recompositions (e.g., less learning and retention) and an increase of decompositions (atrophy) of some previously existing forms and functions.

Presumably, the progress of the genetical program of events determines the earliest age at which a number of nascent dispositions and aptitudes will successively emerge and be capable of development under favorable conditions (e.g., now is the time to learn to crawl, now to start babbling, now comes the onset of puberty, etc.); the limits of excellence to which a number of special skills (e.g., athletic, musical, mathematical, poetical, etc.) may be perfected under the most facilitating circumstances; a number of temperamental dispositions and susceptibilities; and finally, besides much else perhaps, the onset of senescence and the age of death under the most fortunate conditions.

The nature and order of the constructive and conservative products of the experiential interdependent system of psychometabolic processes (the system involved in learning) are largely and specifically determined by the succession and recurrence of diverse concrete environmental encounters, instinctive outbursts, functional endeavors, and their hedonic effects (negative and positive reinforcements, including punishments and rewards for good behavior). Thus, within limits set by the existing potentialities, the operations and fortunes—or misfortunes—of a few, interdependent properties of the personality in each of the critical proceedings of its ongoing life largely determine what will be learned (internally composed, retained, and replicated); then, in a reciprocal manner, what a person learns on one occasion will determine or modify his performance on a subsequent occasion of the same class.

Metabolic Model

The term "ongoing" points to the fact that the brain-located nature of a human being is marked by a procession of vital processes, from the cessation of which (for example, as a result of even a short span of oxygen deprivation) there is no recovery. Ontogenetically considered, these given vital processes date from the fertilization of the ovum, but phylogenetically considered, they have a presumptive molecular (DNA or RNA) and cytoplasmic thread of historic continuity of some two or three billion years, which started, we may suppose, with the emergence of the genetical systems of a cluster of primordial units of living matter. To represent the *sine qua non* of life within the boundary of an animal organism, including its brain, and to account for the free energy that sustains its multivarious operations, there are no better general terms than those of biochemical metabolism, the incessant operation in each cell and tissue of *catabolic* (structure-decomposing, energy-releasing) and *anabolic* (structure-composing, energy-binding) processes.

The succession of intracellular catabolic processes (designated here by *De*) may be likened to a tiny fire in which energy-rich particles (carbohydrates, fats, and proteins) are decomposed with the aid of enzymes in a watery medium of mineral salts, vitamins, and other substances. To keep these home fires burning brightly in the cells of the brain and other organs, there must be an almost continuous cellular *ingestion* (symbolized by *Ca*) of the above-mentioned necessities—especially oxygen—as well as an almost continuous cellular *egestion* (symbolized by *Ru*) of waste products—carbon dioxide, water, and incompletely oxidized nitrogen compounds.

Of an opposite nature to the analytic processes of catabolism (*De*) are the synthetic, molecule-binding, structure-building processes of anabolism (symbolized by *Co*); the energy for these, as for every other variety of activity, is derived from catabolism. Basically attributable to synthetic processes at the molecular level (e.g., millions of multiplications of giant

DNA and RNA molecules, etc.), according to this theory, are all the above-mentioned maturational formations, and, in conjunction with concrete environmental transactions (perceptual and actuational), all the structural compositions and recompositions, the properties of which constitute the specific and general products of experience: what a person has actually learned to attend to selectively, to recognize, to understand, to represent conceptually, to evaluate positively or negatively, to love or to hate, to anticipate with pleasure or with dread, to accomplish with his muscles, to express with words, and to choose as realizable aims—all of which are important focused variables of personality. On the extent and fitness of such acquisitions and also very largely on favorable circumstances and good fortune will depend the possibility of actualizing whatever genetically given latent resources there may be for love, joy, achievement, and service to mankind.

As to the three, above-defined overlapping temporal eras of the life cycle, each of these can be most simply, though roughly, conceptualized in terms of a ratio of the two metabolic terms Co and De: during the era of growth and development of character and powers, $Co > De$; during the era of maintenance of character and the fruitful use of powers, $Co = De$; during the phase of induration and decay, $Co < De$. These are some of the chief reasons why the concurrent, complementary processes of biological metabolism Co and De have been taken as the main components of this PS's basic paradigm, or model, a model that conforms with a conception of reality that is *not* expressible in terms of spatial structures of matter as such but in terms of the interdependent, operating properties of matter—that is, in terms of process, time, and energy. It is a fundamental animate model that accounts for the vital vegetative processes (e.g., maturation, growth, differentiation, repair, etc.) that inanimate models do not fittingly represent. It is also applicable, with suitable modifications, to higher levels of mental activity, especially—when taken in conjunction with the widespread need for novelty (change, exploration, experiment)—to those analytic and synthetic imaginations which lead to cultural (scientific, artistic, ideological, ethical, etc.) innovations of all types.

Finally, this model (with its emphasis on the energy-building, antientropic processes of progressive development and creativity) provides the biological ground for what is so conspicuously absent in the purely psychoanalytic system (with its emphasis on energy-reducing, entropic processes, as well as on fixation, repetition compulsion, regression, disintegration).

Learning and Hedonic Effects.

It is provisionally proposed that among the genetical determinants of the development of personality, none is more influential than the

morphology of the primitive brain (subcortex), with its increasing differentiations and integrations of centers (clusters of cellular containers of
specialized chemical compounds called micronic structures), each of
which will sooner or later constitute an inbuilt readiness to be converted
into a more or less distinctive energizing (feeling) state. The most basic
centers, related to all others, are those that yield *hedonic* feelings (pleasure, delight, satisfaction, joy) and those that yield *anhedonic* feelings
(displeasure, distress, dissatisfaction, misery), with expressive movements
in each case. From infancy on, hedonic learning, on which so much
depends, will consist in the discovery (represented in the brain by more
or less enduring spatial structures reconvertible into temporal associations and organizations) of what generates hedonic feelings and what
generates anhedonic feelings (of this or that intensity or grade) within the
self and then within numerous other selves whose feelings are important
to the self.

There are many kinds of hedonic and anhedonic determinants (generators), most of which, though analytically distinguishable, operate in
relations with a few others, interdependently or consequentially. Some
may be experienced together (as compounded sources of joy or misery)
or some sequentially, the first being either a necessary forerunner of the
second (e.g., tedious rehearsals of a skill before exhibiting it successfully
in public) or the "cause" of the second (e.g., the pleasure of bullying a
younger sister, followed by a humiliating punishment, a negative social
repercussion). Growing up involves, among other things, gradual increases in the prospective time span; the capacity to foresee the future;
the power to postpone the gratification of certain wants, for one reason
or another; and the ability to discriminate between pleasures and dis-
pleasures which have satisfying or beneficial consequences and those
which have dissatisfying or harmful consequences and eventually to regulate one's life so that neither the present nor the future is sacrificed for
the other.

Of course the operation of a generator, hedonic or anhedonic, will
usually depend on a number of conditions or factors in addition to the
past history and developmental age of the subject, factors such as the
place, time, duration, and mode of its occurrence, the absence or presence of one or more particular persons, etc. But taking these and other
qualifications into account, it might be said that each properly differentiated class of satisfiers (positive reinforcements) and of dissatisfiers (negative reinforcements), taken separately or in combination, deserves some
place among the interdependent ends or counterends of individual or
collective human living and endeavor.

Hedonic and anhedonic generators may be suitably classified in several ways, one being according to their temporal reference: they may be
retrospective, involving memories of past experiences which generate
present pleasure or displeasure; spective, involving awareness of current

delighters or distressors; or prospective, involving anticipations of future experiences which generate present pleasure or displeasure. Current generators may be classified according to their predominant location in space: in the subject, in the environment, or, more often, in subject-environment (especially interpersonal) transactions. Each of these major orders of determinants is divisible into several families, genera, etc. For example, generators in the subject may be located in the body (somatic determinants), in some emotional (e.g., love, hate, fear) center of the subcortex (central determinants), in some type of sensory, imaginal, conceptual, verbal, or motor process (processional determinants), or in the judgments of conscience (superregnant determinants).

Environmental Determinants. Most of these determinants are dynamically interrelated with environmental determinants. These are dominant in the early months of life when the child's capabilities are pretty much limited to piteous petitioning and to sucking. The *hedonic generators* in early life consist of whatever provisions (delighters) are gratuitously transmitted by the mother and receptively enjoyed by the child: chiefly bodily provisions (contact, firm support, stimulation, nipple, milk) and affectional provisions (presence, rapt attention, expressions of love, and later of admiration and approval, etc.). The anhedonic generators are constituted either by the absence in the proximal environment of an urgently wanted delighter (e.g., food, mother), whose arrival starts a strip of process pleasure, or by the presence of an unwanted distressor (e.g., pain, loud noise), whose removal restores the status quo. Somewhat later, however, the child may be confronted by an irremovable distressor, in the form of an interloping newborn sibling and/or (for a boy) of a father, who is perceived as a successful contender for the mother's love.

Central Determinants. This brings us to a discussion of central determinants. It is assumed that, by necessity, the child is wholly egocentric (self-centeredly oblivious of other selves and selfishly demanding a complete monopoly of his mother's attention when he wants it); thus, he bellows furiously when he is kept waiting, and the sight of a displacing rival is not unlikely to arouse in him a fiendish jealousy coupled with a profound resentment which engenders murderous fantasies directed toward the rival or revengefully toward the mother as betrayer of his trust. It seems that these fantasies and dreams are promoted, in part, by an inbuilt propensity to compose a bewildering procession of extravagant mythological images, many of which are related to the parents or more generally to the "myth of the hero," who, after performing extraordinary, superhuman exploits (e.g., flying, magic, etc.), kills a king and marries his queen. Complexes resulting from the vicissitudes and disastrous outcomes of these imagined heroic deeds and crimes may reside in the lowest strata of the id for a long time. Among other things, growing up calls for an increasing ability to distinguish between imagined events and actual events "out there," as well as a gradual progression from an utterly dependent state ("What will my parents do for me?") toward a relatively self-sufficient state ("What can I do for myself?").

Achievement Determinants. An achievement determinant includes references to the (immediate or distant) past, present, and future and has its location in the subject's impression of whether he is moving toward his goal—whatever this may be—and, if so, whether he is moving faster or slower than he expected; with more ease or difficulty, from moment to moment, day to day, or year to year; or, more generally, whether he is getting better, no better, or worse in some respect. One can observe in the child the beginnings of experiences of this nature: the progressive organization of processes—of elementary sensory processes to arrive at the perception and recognition of an object; of sensorimotor processes (with feedback loops) to arrive at the moment when an object can be confidently reached, seized, and variously dealt with; of vocal processes to form words and sentences, etc.—which constitute, in each case, a stepwise gain of volitional power, which is experienced by the child as a pleasure-enhancing minor achievement, and, as such, is often applauded by a parent (a minor recognition). The central determinant here is ambition in the child, first to achieve greater and greater control of his own processes by concentration and persistence (i.e., to develop a variety of afferent and efferent skills in dealing with small portions of the encountered environment) and thus to attain a measure of autonomy and independence (which inaugurates the development of the ego, the executive of the regnant system of the personality) and later to use these skills (athletic, social, and intellectual) in competing with his peers for acknowledged superiority (victory or some form of higher order recognition, such as prizes, election to membership or office, or academic marks and honors), as well as to use these skills in satisfying other (material, social, or cultural) wants. The ways-means-end learning cannot begin until a certain amount of functional learning (walking and moving objects) has occurred, and then, what has to be learned year after year to gain positive social feedback (repercussions) from parents, teachers, or peers becomes progressively more difficult. Under competitive conditions, the prizes and, later, the best jobs and much else are reserved for those who have pushed some relevant types of functional learning to a sufficient degree of competence. In short, positive social reinforcements depend on individual differences in ambition (want to achieve), work enjoyment (process pleasure), persistence, innate aptitude, etc.

Transactional Determinants. Transactional determinants are delighters and distressors that come from dealing (successfully or unsuccessfully) with the environment of things, people, or ideas; from enjoyed or not enjoyed *dyadic reciprocations* with another person—that is, transmissions and receptions of erotic stimulation (mutual orgasm), of affection or disaffection, of interesting or banal information, self-revelations, or opinions, of comic or pointless stories, etc.; from the processes or outcomes of cooperative endeavors; from the repercussions of socialized (ethical, considerate, conventional) or unsocialized (criminal, offensive, obnoxious) forms or styles of behavior, especially the miseries of ostracism, disgrace, imprisonment, etc.; from the processes and effects of transmitting delighters to those who need them or deserve them (a very common, genuine form of enjoyment not covered by current psychological theories), and much else besides. Let these suffice as illustrations of a few elementary varieties of hedonic and anhedonic determinants. In this PS, those that emanate from others (alters) and are directed toward the subject are classified as *press* (plural, *press*); positive press include acceptance, inclusion, promotion, respect, affection, lust-love, and negative press include rejection, exclusion, demotion, contempt, hate.

As a personality develops, associations and organizations will constitute the ground for a large number of general and particular (unique), enduring or unenduring, positive and negative interests, evaluations (sentiments and tastes), personal affections, beliefs, wants, modes of behavior, and aims (a negative aim being an orientation toward the riddance in the present or the prevention in the future of the operation of a distressor).

Learning. The term "learning" commonly implies that its results are "valuable" (in some sense), regardless of the self-evident fact that a person may learn a good deal that "ain't so" or "ain't good": superstitions, prejudices, repulsive tastes, the craft of forgery, etc.—all of which had better be unlearned. Also, in psychology, the term generally implies that its results determine a young person's subsequent behavior, that he or she very soon becomes a creature of habits, with emotions and aims fixated by experienced distressors or delighters and tactics fixated by experienced successes, etc. This might be pretty nearly the whole truth *if* the genetical program, with its potentialities for self-actualization, ceased to operate at puberty; *if* the subject were not easily bored and not eager for new sights and new ventures; *if* the subject were commonly rewarded for frequent repetitions of the same information (old news), the same jokes, etc.; *if* the human environment, parents, teachers, and peers were unanimous in their support of the same beliefs, codes, manners, political sentiments, and tastes; *if* the person were not ambitious to emulate successively the more impressive performances and deeds of others; *if* for the subject the very meaning of achievement (something to be proud of) did not consist in the accomplishment of something new, extraordinary, more difficult or hazardous; *if* the person were not enticed by future-oriented *imagents* (fantasies) of unexperienced delights or of untried ways and means; *if* no person were ever radically transformed by a "second birth," "great emancipation," or religious conversion; and finally, *if* no person were ever to discover that the creation of an unprecedented, propitious form of living or of culture (scientific, literary, etc.) could be more profoundly joyous than any experience he had had. If it were not for these and other self-realizing, novelty-seeking, ambitious, proudful, imaginative, and creative dispositions in human beings, all of us would stagnate with learned incapacities and a few enthralling memories of infantile attachments. This is not to deny the essential truth of one of Freud's greatest discoveries: the lasting underlying influence (either beneficial or harmful) of early terrors, conditionings, loves and hates, erotized fantasies, and much else. What is being stressed at this point is the amount of unlearning (hedonic, cognitive, and tactical), experimentation, courage, endurance, and constructiveness that is required for a full life.

VARIABLES, ASSESSMENTS, AND REPRESENTATIONS

Among the criteria in terms of which the worth of a personological system may be suitably evaluated are: (1) the comprehensiveness (coverage, scope), structure (interrelatedness), adequacy (congruence with reality, significance), and operational definiteness (clarity, precision) of its assemblage of concepts and propositions; (2) the efficiency (in corresponding terms) of its assessment system (data-collecting, data-processing, data-evaluating, and data-integrating processes); and (3) the over-all satisfactoriness (in corresponding terms)—the plausibility and verifiability—of the representations of different personalities (explanatory conceptual biographies) that are composed out of the harvest of facts and interpretations yielded by the assessment process.

In this PS, the central set of concepts are classified into abstract elementary orders (e.g., propelling energizers and evaluators; representors; movers; organizers; etc.) and these into families, genera, etc., of decreasing generality. The simplest, recurrent associations of these properties with each other or with the properties of environmental entities (e.g., an interest in Z, a positive evaluation of X, a want to gain Y, images of W, the effectiveness of V processes, etc.) are the kinds of abstracted personality variables which are usually obtained with ratings from questionnaires and tests, and in terms of which an individual is ordinarily described in a social conversation. The aim in this PS, however, is to discover how these structural components, converted into their operating properties, interdependently participate in this or that energized, oriented, organized, temporal unit (organizational variable). This synthetic mode of thought eventually results in the conceptualization of a hierarchy of purposive organizations, the largest and longest of which are systems of concern (of planning, activity, enjoyment, and achievement). It is chiefly of these that a personality-in-progress is composed.

Of necessity, large portions of this PS have been omitted; but enough may have been said to indicate that it is basically a psychometabolic system, with energy released for drives, emotions, and movements (electrical and muscular) and for the composition of new convertible structures of all sorts. From this it follows that its root concepts are dynamic, genetical, developmental, organismal (systemic, semiholistic), and hierarchical. It stresses the experiential (existential, subjective), hedonistic, and voluntaristic aspects of a person's life (partly because of their contemporary neglect); but heretofore in practice it has done more justice to unconscious psychological processes, as well as to overt behavior with its situational and sociological (membership and role) determinants.

10

INDISPENSABLES FOR THE MAKING, TESTING, AND REMAKING OF A PERSONOLOGICAL SYSTEM

To reduce the probability of an eruption of disastrous semantic misunderstandings, it seems best to state at the outset what meanings are being ascribed to each of the critical terms in this discourse. "Personology" has proved, in my experience, to be a neater and (with its adjectival form) a more pliable term than the sprawling, cumbersome "psychology of personality." "Personology" has been advocated in order to avoid the cultish practice of using a word that refers to a particular theorist rather than to a definable field of interest. Freud's "psychoanalysis is my creation" was a scarcely excusable scientific heresy. "Personology" is for everyone for free.[1] Next in order is "personality,"* which is the most comprehensive term we have in psychology, including, as it does, the entire system of subsystems (of situational dispositions: structures and functions) as they undergo their serial transformations through the fullest span: from birth to death. At this point its chief meaning is that of domain of scientific concern from which nothing psychological is excluded on principle. Then we come to "system," which may be today's most fashionable scientific word.[2,3] It is applicable from the smallest to the largest definable unit of reality—from an atom to the solar system. Its use points to the fact that one is dealing—*not* with a single, singular, solitary, isolated entity—a solid material particle—or *not* with a mere aggregate of independent entities—a randomly behaving rabble—not a list, not an inventory; but an assemblage of interdependent units.

Its meaning is exemplified in this paper by three of its uses.[4] In my title the term refers to a conceptual system—a coherent, self-consistent assemblage of abstract concepts and postulates, in terms of which any

From *Annals of the New York Academy of Sciences*, April 18, 1977, *291*, 323–331.

Referent of the term "personality." Some psychologists find no use at all for this term; they would vote for its extinction. Others use it to refer to something that a person (particularly a psychologist, psychiatrist, biographer, etc.) says about the nature of another person (subject, applicant for a position, patient, historical character, etc.). This usage is unfortunate, since experience has taught us that the statements that are made by different people (say psychologists and psychiatrists), especially if they belong to different schools of thought, about the nature of this or that individual, are likely to be significantly different;

event in the life of a person should be representable and explainable. In contrast to this system of abstractions we may want to refer to the living system, as James G. Miller names it[5]—the ongoing, concrete organization of psychological states and processes in the head of a given individual. Finally, we have an assessment system—an organization of procedures: interviews, questionnaires, projective tests, situational tests, and much else, all aimed at revealing significant subsystems and their properties—variables of the personalities to be assessed.

Here I shall have to modify my original intention and leave out two large sections of my discourse, and the main substance of my paper will consist of outlining the *assessment system,*[6] which, in this form, includes the composition of the *conceptual system.*[7]

I will present an abstract of the series of personological procedures that compose the *assessment system* with which I am familiar and which I am keen to advocate to others. I have participated in six executions of this series of procedures in collaboration with a varying number of other personologists (from about six to twelve). In four cases, three years were devoted to carrying out the program (twelve years in all), and it will be these last four series which I shall have in mind while writing the following brief outline. To offer a hint or two regarding the operation of the need-drive concept on the intellectual level, I shall assume that the members of each staff experienced the lack of a suitable conceptual scheme to guide a number of related researches they had in mind in the domain of personality theory, and that it was the existence of this felt lack which prompted them to collaborate in the composition of a workable personological system. Usually, a number of other, more personal and self-centered wants and drives are aidfully involved in the advancement of this shared, impersonal cultural enterprise.

(1) The collaborative *composition of a provisional conceptual/-theoretical system*[8] is, in my terminology, the aim and product of the first of the series of five *concrete,* macro-subsystems of cooperating intellects (each subsystem consisting of the interacting mentational processes [sub-subsystems] of the participating psychologists) which constitute the total system of procedures. The aim and product of each of the four succeeding concrete macro-subsystems may be briefly defined as follows: (2) the differentiated and integrated *application* of this provisional theoretical system to the examination—by the *multiform method* (a variety of

---

and so, if "personality" is taken to mean a *representation* of a person's nature, we shall have to admit that an individual has as many personalities as there have been representors of his nature, that in choosing his psychiatrist he is choosing his personality, and that if no psychologist has attempted to represent his nature, he has no personality at all; all of which is nonsense. From this we gather that a representation is one thing, and the nature (personality) that it is designed to represent is another thing; the first can be located in the sentences of the representor, but where can the second be located? In the brain, of course. No reputable psychologist of this era denies that. Consequently, all the more or less enduring constituents of personality are invisible and problematical. Their presence and activity must be inferred on the basis of what *is* visible or audible.

procedures, administered by a variety of psychologists to educe [draw out] a variety of functionings)—of each of a series of individual subjects; (3) the *composition,* based on all the data obtained by these procedures, of a partial hypothetical formulation of the personality of each subject which was designed to represent the mutual relations of its more important component properties; (4) the cooperative *evaluation* of each of these formulations (and hence of the provisional theoretical system in terms of which the formulation was composed) according to its success in sufficiently representing, relating, and explaining each of the various important recorded manifestations of the personality in question (a kind of compound feed-back process consisting of positive and negative reinforcements emitted by the evaluators); and (5) the cooperative, adaptive *reconstruction of the provisional theoretical system* (together with its modes of application) in ways that would correct so far as possible its demonstrated insufficiencies. These five successive concrete macro-subsystems of cooperating psychologists, each with his own (meso) system of participating mental and verbal processes—attending, transmitting and receiving, rejecting, accepting, justifying, differentiating, defining, classifying, composing, integrating, etc.—these five interdependent macro-temporal subsystems taken as a series constitute the total *concrete* system of science-making in the domain of personality which was approximately exemplified by each of the six staffs with which I have had the privilege of working. It may be more simply described as the ongoing program of performance of numerous specialists (each executing a different experiment or administering a different assessment procedure on the same population of subjects) complemented by a few generalists whose task was to explain the individual differences in each experiment or test, in terms of an invented formulation of the organized components of the individual's whole nature. Naturally, I have had to omit from my account of this entire theoretical-system-making process many consequential factors, such as the all-important solitary creative processes of individual psychologists and the competitions, oppositions, and disputes among members of the staff, all of them essential components of the whole operation.

Criteria for the Evaluation of a Personological System. On the basis of multiple experiences of the sort I have described, I am proposing as the best overall criterion of the effectiveness of a personological system as well as of the personologist who makes use of it: (1) his/her power with its use to compose a hypothetical formulation (a macro-model) of the nature of each of a large number of very dissimilar persons during any short span of his or her life's cycle (in childhood, adolescence, adulthood, or senescence), in terms of which formulation the more important, critical, and recurrent situational experiences, activities, and effects (successful and unsuccessful) of that person (during the given span) may be sufficiently represented, related, and explained (and possibly, in some cases, predicted or produced); and also (2) the personologist's power with its use to conceptualize and to explain the important changes of that person's nature that occur from any one to any other shorter or longer span of its historic course from birth to death. The overall utility of a conceptual theoretical system, as estimated in these ways, depends on a number of factors, or attributes of the system, in terms of which attributes, or subcriteria, more differentiated judgments of its value can be made, before or after putting the system to a series of pragmatic tests (the overall criterion). These interdependent sub-criteria are as follows: (1) *conceptual equipment:* what proportion of the basic concepts that are necessary to the sufficient representation of a wide variety of conditions and events and of their determinants are included in the system? (2) *definitional and operational precision:* what proportion of the included concepts are adequately defined by means of specific criteria and operations (procedures) to be used in the identification and possibly in the measurement of their referents? (3) *scope and span of application:* what proportion of the most important species of transactions (proceedings, episodes), and what proportion of the most important states or conditions of the personality engaged in these transactions, and what proportion of the time spans, or stages, of the life cycle, and of the species of transitions from one span to another is the system designed to represent and to explain conceptually? (4) *congruity of application:* what desirable degree of precise and/or complete correspondence with the observed facts is attainable by the system when the relevant parts of it are utilized to represent and to explain each of those species of phenomena to which the system was designed to apply? (5) *conceptual coherence:* to what extent is the system conceptually or propositionally consistent? and to what extent is it capable of representing the internal dynamic relationships of the various situational states, activities, and effects (the concrete systems and subsystems of processional achievements) that were manifested by the personality in action? and (6) *theoretical plentitude:* how many promising or partially verified special theories productive of further research are included in the system?

I have enumerated these criteria to serve as a rough definition of the distant target, as I see it, of personological endeavors, of the ideal against which to measure contemporary intellectual productions. Judged by these indices, no existing personological system could be given a high rating, a high rating being far beyond the limits of realistic expectation and even of what is profitable at this early stage of methodological and theoretical development. An unsuitable high ambition in some of these respects would constitute an almost lethal degree of scientism in this domain of investigation. Anyhow, it can be said that the criteria give no quarter to any hopes of representing a personality in a few sentences or paragraphs, or by a *list* of single variables, such as rated traits. The criteria favor the view that a personality is a more or less organized system of components, but it gives no quarter to those theorists who stress organizations, structures, or systems without specifying, in each particular case, the nature and number of the components that are involved, and in what way they are structured or organized, or they interact as a system. Finally, it gives no quarter to those who talk about "personality" in an environmental vacuum, or in the abstract without regard to its concrete manifestations.

REFERENCES

1. Murray, H. A., et al. *Explorations in Personality,* New York: Oxford University Press, 1938.

2. Von Bertalanffy, L. The theory of open systems in physics and biology. *Science,* 1950, III.

3. Von Bertalanffy, L. Metabolic types and growth types. *American Naturalist,* 1951, *85,* 111.

4. Hall, A. D., and R. E. Fagen. "Definition of system," *General Systems,* Vol. I, 1956.

5. Laszlo, E. *The Systems View of the World,* New York, Braziller, 1972.

6. Murray, H. A., et al. *Assessment of Men,* New York, Holt, 1948.

7. ———— Studies of stressful disputation. In Lindzey, G., and C. S. Hall, eds. *Personality Theory Sources and Research,* New York, Wiley, 1965.

8. ———— Components of an evolving personological system. In *International Encyclopedia of the Social Sciences,* New York, Crowell, Collier, 1968.

III

Personology focuses on the close
examination
of mental life—conscious
and unconscious processes,
including creativity

*M*urray is, above all other things in his professional life, a personologist—a studier of persons. That is superordinate even to his being a psychologist or his being a psychoanalytically oriented theoretician and practitioner. Yet he is both a psychologist and a psychoanalyst. The three papers in this section reflect his capacious interests.

Psychoanalytic thinking (especially the key importance of the unconscious aspects of the mind's functioning) is a central thread in Murray's work; although his theoretical divergences, his own theory, are what are most important to him. We know partly what he thought of Freud and Jung and of the importance of their ideas about the world of subjective experiences, ideas without which the psychologist is at least "half paralyzed." To Murray, psychoanalysis was and is "the mainstream of contemporary thought," not just an adjunct to one's way of thinking about oneself and one's fellow human beings, but an essential and necessary way of doing so.

But immediately one must caution that in relation to psychoanalysis, Murray—as he is in relation to most theoretical systems (including his own)—is, from almost the beginning, an iconoclast and a civil rebel. He incorporates psychoanalytic theory, as he incorporates everything, into his own larger, more catholic, and certainly more flexible continuous theory-building.

In 1940, when Murray wrote "What Should Psychologists Do About Psychoanalysis?" it was more than casually daring for an academically based psychologist to espouse psychoanalysis—"the theory of unconscious processes." Murray begins his article with a challenging definition of his own brand of personality theory, personology, and he does not neglect the opportunity to point out that strict behaviorists (eschewing inner life) cripple themselves and the field of psychology which they profess so scientifically to represent. Murray tells us his own innermost criterion for measuring the worth of any psychological system, namely "its power to order and illumine your whole being." He gently (but firmly) instructs us about the fetish of trivial precision at the expense of common-sense relevance—meaning relevance to man's real thoughts *and feelings and other manifestations of his inner and outer life.*

After describing seven tests to which he initially put psychoanalytic theory, Murray, using figurative language, tells his fellow psychologists that "A personality is a full Congress . . . and a psychologist who does not know this in himself, whose mind is locked against the flux of images and feelings, should be encouraged to make friends, by being psycho-analyzed, with the various members of his household."

He then sternly calls "boyish" some psychoanalysts who by leaning too much weight on some fragile notions only serve to "bring great aims to earth." Murray concludes this pioneer piece on psychoanalysis by bolding stating, "I trumpet out its virtues."

Earlier, in 1933, Murray wrote a paper in "experimental psychopathology" in which he explored a psychological phenomenon related to projection, namely the attribution of traits or characteristics to another person or, to put it somewhat more specifically, the notion that one's emotional state of mind may affect one's judgment of other persons in the environment. In a creative and imaginative way, Murray reports a study involving his (then-eleven-year-old) daughter and some of her girl friends in a nighttime game of "murder" in which he manipulated the environment so as to focus on "The Effect of Fear upon Estimates of the Maliciousness of Other Personalities." He describes different varieties of projection, anticipating the development of his Thematic Apperception Test two years later.

One of Murray's chief disaffections with traditional psychoanalytic theory—remembering that, in the round, he holds it indispensable for a profound understanding of man—is that it focuses too much on the pathological and abnormal aspects of man and thus cannot be a complete psychological system. It scarcely has a vocabulary to describe that rare creature, a normal man. Murray's redress for this condition is to accentuate the supranormal, the good, the talented, and more, to focus on man's capacity for proaction—for initiating programs and actions rather than solely reacting to the stimuli of others—and, as an extension of proaction, man's important capacity to be creative. This idea is deep in Murray's way of thinking; it stems from his belief—based on his years of experience as an embryologist working patiently with chicken embryos (about which experiences he published ten scientific papers early in his career when he was a research physician, biochemist, and embryologist)—that life, from the earliest cellular activity of the embryo to, say, da Vinci's inventiveness, is a creative process. For Murray, creativity is an intrinsic characteristic of living systems. And further, creativity is fundamental to proactive or planful behavior, another basic human characteristic. We are planful, creative, usually healthy creatures; and it is pleasurable for a psychologist to conduct his investigations with this orientation. But, as Murray explains, there are issues and problems— misfortunes and rebellious changes—attendant to imaginative proaction, and these are the subject of his paper on the "Vicissitudes of Creativity."

11

THE EFFECT OF FEAR UPON ESTIMATES OF THE MALICIOUSNESS OF OTHER PERSONALITIES

The present paper describes an attempt to demonstrate in quantitative terms the generally recognized fact that the emotional state of a subject may affect his judgments of other personalities. It is one of several experiments now in progress in this laboratory which have been designed to expose some of the internal—physical and psychical—factors which influence a subject's perceptions, interpretations, and appraisals of the objects and situations in the world about him.

The diagnosis of traits of character from the face depends, it is often said in common language, upon (1) the observation of the features (physical signs) and (2) the interpretation of them on the basis of associations —associations which in the past have been found by the observer to exist between somewhat similar physical signs and particular types of behavior. Psychologically, we speak here of two processes which may for convenience be differentiated, namely, perception and apperception. Such is the nomenclature, at least, which we have provisionally adopted for the purposes of this discussion. The term *perception* is confined to the *conscious* recognition of configurated sense impressions or segregated sensory wholes; whereas *apperception* is used to designate the process— whatever its antecedents—whereby meaning, in other than sensory terms, is assigned to the physical stimulus. This use of the term apperception is at least within the definition given by Stout. For, according to this authority, it is by the process of apperception that "a presentation acquires a certain significance for thought by connecting itself with some mental preformation as this has been organized in the course of previous experience."[1] The term is used to include understanding, interpreting, classifying, subsuming, and so forth.

The distinction we make between perception and apperception is, of course, somewhat arbitrary. For, under most conditions, the two processes are inseparably fused. For instance, as Köhler has so succinctly remarked: "If in a friendly-looking face we try to separate the mere

From *Journal of Social Psychology*, 1933, *4*, pp. 310–329.

bodily configuration and the friendliness, we find the task rather difficult, as long as we look at the whole face and do not analyze the face itself as a mosaic of colored spots."[2]

Now, the understanding of other personalities from their features is usually more successful than can be accounted for on the basis of what was consciously perceived. And so, since in such cases the visual apparatus is the only path of communication, there must be some retinal stimulation which is not translated into conscious perception, but which, nevertheless—through some other effects—determines apperception. These other effects are not far to seek when we bear in mind that the external world comes to a subject, not solely in the guise—to use White-head's terminology—of *presentational immediacy* (pure sensory experience) but also in the guise of *causal efficacy*.[3] That is to say, physical changes are activated in the body of the subject which are of the sort that may be cognized as feelings, emotions, and kinaesthetic sensations. Such activations are without doubt most fundamental, preceding in ontogenetic development the clear *conscious* perception of the stimulating object. Certain faces, for instance, arouse approach movements and others arouse withdrawal movements in the child long before the capacity for an accurate representation of the perceived object exists. Since experience shows that such movements may be modified by slight changes in the stimulating object, there must be at this time an accurate physical differentiation of sensory impressions. But since no report may be given of them, we must admit that perception—if we wish to use the term—is unconscious. Now, when language is acquired, it is probable that the estimates of other persons which a child expresses verbally are unwittingly made on the basis of how the body responds to their presence. If the child smiles, for instance, the person confronting it is "nice and good," but if it averts the head the person is "bad."

It may also be that unconscious imitation of the expression and gestures of others—a process so common in children—arouses feelings and emotions somewhat comparable to those occurring in the perceived object, and that this too is a factor which aids understanding. In this connection we are reminded of the young lad described by Poe in *The Purloined Letter* who used to mimic the facial expression of his opponent in a gambling game to discover whether it made *himself* feel intelligent. By this means he estimated the mental caliber of the other boy and in accordance with the verdict directed his own moves in the game.

The point is that certain physical features of the object which the subject does not consciously perceive are nevertheless physically affecting his body, and though he may be unable to report upon these internal happenings, they are nevertheless affecting his conscious appraisal of the object.

This is not the place to discuss in detail all the processes which contribute to a knowledge of our fellows. We merely wish to suggest how

it may come about that apperceptions of the personality (feelings, motives, and probable behavior) of others are commonly influenced—as
experience seems to teach—by the total bodily state of the perceiving
subject. Our hypothesis would be, then, that certain meanings, or categories we might call them, such as "friendly" and "unfriendly," become
integrated with certain muscular sets and emotions, and when the latter
are aroused the former will be mobilized and come to mind. These
intermediary physical processes would seem on superficial glance to be
entirely irrelevant to the task at hand, but when we consider that they
are conspicuously present—at least in an imaginatively representative
form—in persons, such as novelists, whose insight into character is generally regarded as most acute, we have cause for reflection.

Now, when such processes can be accounted for by reference to the
presented stimulus and its similarity to past stimuli, and hence to *traces*
(a fictional concept) in the mind of the subject, we should consider them
—at least for that subject—legitimate, normal, and objectively valid. If
they happen to be inappropriate and unadaptive, well, it is a matter of
ignorance, insufficient experience, and so forth. When, however, the
internal processes which are determining apperception have recently
been aroused by some other essentially dissimilar and irrelevant stimulus, or may be shown to be more or less inveterate in the subject, then
we must refer to another process—a process which distorts the external
world or adds something to it which is not there.

According to the terminology of some psychologists the process
whereby psychic elements—needs, feelings and emotions, or images and
contexts of images activated by such affective states—are referred by the
experiencing subject to the external world without sufficient objective
evidence is called *projection*. When this process is active, what is in truth
mental and within the personality comes to appear as if it were outside
the personality. We may speak of *perceptive projection* when sensory
elements are projected, i.e., when an image takes on the vividness, substantiality, and out-thereness of a real object—as in a dream and in an
hallucination—or when an image transforms or makes additions to the
actual physical features of an inadequately perceived real object so that
the latter is taken for the object of which the image is a representation
—as in an illusion. And we may speak of *apperceptive projection* when
non-sensory elements are projected. This occurs (1) when imaginal contexts, or the categories under which the activated images are subsumed,
are believed, with insufficient objective evidence, to be descriptive of or
to pertain to objects in the environment—as in delusions; or (2) when the
needs, feelings, and emotions themselves, rather than the images or
imaginal meanings activated by them, are believed by the subject to be
existent in other personalities—also as in delusions. The former might be
termed *complementary apperceptive projection* and the latter *supplementary apperceptive projection*.

An example of perceptive projection would be the case of a girl who mistook a stranger in a crowd for the friend whom she was hoping to meet, or the case of a criminal who believed that he saw a detective with whom he was acquainted following him down the street. An example of complementary apperceptive projection would be the case of a guilt-ridden young man who believed that his elders were secretly condemning him; whereas an example of supplementary apperceptive projection would be the case of an unhappily married woman who believed that most of her married friends were unhappy.

The reader may have noticed that in defining projection we spoke rather nonchalantly of images; we said that hallucinations were projected images and so forth. How can they be projected images, when for the experiencing subject there are no images; there are only external objects? The answer is that they are projected *unconscious* images—a purely fictional concept. In dreams and in hallucinations we know that they are not external objects which the subject perceives; nor is he conscious of imagery in the usual sense. Common experience, however, bears witness to the inseparable gradations between dreams and phantasies—the latter being admittedly composed of images—as well as to the similarity between memory images and some of the objects which appear in dreams; and consequently some psychologists have been led to speak of projected unconscious images, since *qua* images the subject is unaware of them. It will be remembered, furthermore, that Prince[4] performed experiments upon an hallucinating dissociated subject, and by means of automatic writing demonstrated to his own satisfaction that the hallucinated objects were similar to the imagery of a contemporary unconscious (or co-conscious) mental process.

Despite such considerations and such experiments, the hypothesis of unconscious psychical events is still refuted by other psychologists—principally on logical grounds. This is not the time to debate the point. We ourselves must simply admit that we feel the need of this concept to describe in detail the phenomenon of projection. For, as far as we know, only elements which are not at the moment conscious may be projected. It is supposed that if the subject could adopt the introspective attitude some of these so-called unconscious images would become conscious, but because attention is forcefully and passionately centered upon the external world, or because the subject is in sleep or in some other state hardly to be defined—abstraction or dissociation—images attain the apparent substantiality of external reality; they appear to be "out there." An illusion exemplifies the same process but to a lesser degree. In this case there is some real object, but what the subject perceives is a composition product of the real object and the unconscious mental image. The greater the ingress of the latter the more does the event resemble an hallucination.

What a subject might say when presented with a vaguely perceived and unrecognizable object is this: "It makes me think of so and so," or: "It arouses images of so and so." That would be conscious imagery and not projection. If the subject "guesses," "supposes," or "imagines" it is "so and so," we speak of a pseudo-projection. For, strictly speaking, the term projection should be used only when the subject is convinced of the true existence outside himself of the object or process in question. A projection is morbid only when it is the result of some obsessive idea or continuously dominant need which frequently operates to transform the real world in a particular way.

Projections, then, by distorting a subject's recognition and interpretation of external reality prevent a detached and disinterested objectivity. They may, nevertheless, serve the cause of truth. For instance, a young man who has suffered undeservedly through the treacherous and malicious behavior of others—he has a fixed feeling of inferiority, let us say—may thenceforth suppose that strangers and acquaintances whom he meets are prompted solely by selfish motives, and at least towards him are critical and scornful. He may, indeed, like Timon of Athens, generalize his particular experiences and become a misanthrope. In so far as such a man overemphasizes the selfishness of human beings to the exclusion of their other more engaging traits he is the victim of a complementary apperceptive projection. We might say that he is mistaken in his proportions, since he attributes so much evil and so little good to others. But we must not lose sight of the fact that in some respects he may be a better observer than the average citizen, since as a result of his particular sensitiveness to malice he may very well discover and precisely analyze subtle and hidden forms of it which others have neglected, and so make a valuable contribution to psychological knowledge.

We have discussed the probable influence of bodily changes upon apperception, and how, when the former are relatively unconnected with the immediate stimulus, misapperceptions or delusions may occur. These we agreed to call apperceptive projections. Finally, we proposed the hypothesis of unconscious images to explain both perceptive projections and complementary apperceptive projections.

Such were the speculations which led us to the present enterprise: an attempt to prove by experiment that a functional relationship between emotional and apperceptive processes exists normally, and, by changing the former, a qualitative or quantitative alteration of the latter will occur. More specifically, we might characterize this experiment as an attempt to produce measurable variations in the apperception of benevolence or malice in other people by the excitation of fear in the apperceiving subject, the variation or exceptionality of the apperception in each case being estimated by comparing it with the subject's habitual apperception of the same object.

The particular form of our hypothesis and the technique devised to test it were based upon such a common phenomenon as that of a person who in a fear-invoking situation—for instance while walking through a "tough" neighborhood at night—apperceives some of the strangers whom he encounters as "dangerous characters." It was supposed that, if, for purposes of standardization, photographs of people, rather than living personalities, were used as material to be judged, the subjects—especially children—after a fear-invoking situation would estimate the faces in the photographs to be more malicious than they would estimate them to be when they were free from fear. Such at least was our hypothesis, and when the daughter of the author planned a week-end country house-party of five girls, eleven years of age, it seemed that this might provide an opportunity to test it. It was supposed that during this party there would be many chances for control tests after relatively normal pleasure-invoking circumstances, and, since the children wanted to play the game of *murder* in the evening, it seemed that a fear-invoking situation would occur in the natural course of events.

We judged that the game of *murder* alone would not be sufficiently exciting, so we planned to tell the first half of a ghost story after the end of the game, on the supposition that the combination of the two situations would give rise to a state of anxiety which would perseverate long enough to affect the results on a test given immediately afterwards. At the last minute, however, circumstances interfered with the telling of the ghost story, and so we were forced to depend upon the efficacy of two games of *murder* for the evocation of fear.

TECHNIQUE

Thirty photographs approximately 5.5 × 7.5 cm. in size—most of which were taken from the magazine *Time*—were mounted upon white cards and divided into two roughly comparable series; each of which was composed of eleven photographs of men and four photographs of women, all of them unknown to the subjects of the experiments. The first series of fifteen faces was called Test A; the second series was called Test B.

Tests were given on three occasions as follows:

First Occasion. Test A after pleasure-invoking situation (control). This experiment was performed at 12:30 P.M., Saturday, after the children had returned from motoring about the country.

Second Occasion. Test A and Test B after fear-invoking situation. This experiment was performed at 7:30 P.M., Saturday, after the children had played two games of *murder*. The thirty photographs were arranged in one series so that the even numbers belonged to Test A and the odd numbers to Test B.

Third Occasion. Test B after pleasure-invoking situation (control). This experiment was performed at 12:30 P.M., Sunday, after the children had returned from hitching behind a sleigh. In this way each test (A and B) was performed twice—after a fear-invoking situation and after a pleasure-invoking situation (control). We shall speak of the two trials of Test A together as Experiment A, and the two trials of Test B together as Experiment B.

On all three occasions each of the subjects—five girls, eleven years of age (designated as Mary, Jane, Lou, Jill, and Nan)—was seated at the same place, separate from the others, in a well-lighted room. The experiments were conducted as group tests, the photographs being passed around from subject to subject in order.

For the first experiment instructions were as follows:

I shall show you a series of fifteen photographs of persons whom you do not know. Some are nice, some are bad, and some are just average. I want you to guess from the photographs how good or how bad they are.

At this point each S was given a sheet of paper on which were ruled fifteen lines divided into three columns. The instructions were continued as follows:

On the sheet of paper which I have given you there are three columns. In the first column each line is numbered from one to fifteen. These stand for the numbers of the photographs. When you are presented with a photograph—each photograph is numbered from one to fifteen—please look at the face and immediately decide how good or how bad is the character of the person. It has been found that you are more likely to be right if you are guided by your first impression than if you try to reason it out. The mark or rating for goodness or badness which you give the person should be placed in the second column opposite the number of the photograph. The scale for marking runs from one to nine as follows: 1 = extremely good, i.e., generous, kind, loving and tender; 2 = very good; 3 = good; 4 = fairly good; 5 = average; 6 = fairly bad; 7 = bad; 8 = very bad; 9 = extremely bad, i.e., cruel, malicious, and wicked. Remember now: 5 is average, 9 is extremely bad and 1 is extremely good.

In the third column there is space for you to write down what you think the person in the photograph is thinking or saying. You should spend about thirty seconds on each photograph, but I shall allow you more time if necessary.

After these directions were read and explained, two sample photographs not belonging to the series—one of a man smiling and one of a man scowling—were shown to the children and they were asked to announce their ratings so that all could hear. This, so that the experimenter could be certain that the directions were understood.

On the second occasion, that is, after the fear-invoking situation, the instructions did not have to be repeated. It was pointed out, however, that there were now thirty instead of fifteen faces to be diagnosed.

For those who are not acquainted with the game of *murder* it may be said that it is played after dark throughout a house with all lights extinguished. The players commence by drawing lots from a hat; one of the players, unknown to the others, drawing the lot of murderer. After the draw, the players, with the exception of the one amongst them who has drawn the lot of detective, sneak about the house in the dark until the murderer "kills"—by touching—any one of the players whom he chooses. The victim, after counting ten, yells aloud, and then all the players join the detective, who proceeds by cross-questionings to discover the culprit. Everyone must tell the truth except the murderer, and he may lie as much as he likes.

Among children there are individual differences in sentiment towards this game. Some children love it and play it without disquietude; others wish to play but experience an unpleasant apprehension throughout; still others are afraid to play and avoid it if possible.

RESULTS

At the cross-examination after the "murder" one of the subjects, Mary, said that she was "frightened to death" and again: "I was so scared I hid under the table the whole time." Lou also admitted that she was afraid. No other remarks of a like nature were volunteered, and it was our general impression that the amount of occasioned excitement was less than usual.

That the two games of *murder*, however, were effective in arousing some degree of fear was attested not only by the results of the experiments, but also by an event which occurred in the early morning of the next day—that is, on Sunday. This event bears reporting since it helps to confirm the validity of the tests. It happened in this way. Jane, who had been sleeping in one of the spare rooms with Lou, woke the household at six-thirty in the morning to inform us that for more than an hour two burglars had been prowling about her room. She was in tears and shaking with fright while she explained that it was not a dream but a fact. She had seen the two men clearly with her eyes open; they had taken things from the closet and from the bureaus and had escaped finally by way of the window. She had heard the dogs chase them down the lane, and if we came to the window, she assured us, we would see their tracks in the snow. A careful examination of the premises, however, proved that no one had been about and that nothing had been stolen. Evidently Jane had had a vision, a hypnapompic vision—because, as she explained, it was real and nothing like a dream—due to a perceptive projection. Never before had she had such a vision, so it is probable that the *murder* game was the exciting agent which aroused the imagery. This was more of an effect than we had anticipated. Jane insisted despite the protestations of her companions that the event had really occurred; in fact, it seemed very important to her—as if, let us say, her sanity depended upon it— that she should be believed. None of her friends, however, gave credence to her story during the day. It was not until nightfall that Mary and Lou —but not Jill and Nan—were inclined to believe her. Belief for Mary and Lou seemed to depend upon the uneasiness aroused by darkness. The outcome of the matter was that Jane, Mary, and Lou announced that they would not sleep in the ill-fated room "for anything" and, even when given another room, they insisted that we should look for burglars in the closet and under the bed, draw the shades down to the sill, speak in a low voice so that the burglars—supposedly sneaking about the house—should not hear, put a night-light in the room and visit them at intervals throughout the night to make sure that everything was all right. Jill and Nan, however, consented to occupy the spare room where the burglars had been seen and without any ado dropped off to sleep. This difference in attitude between Mary, Jane, and Lou, on the one hand, and Jill and Nan, on the other, should be borne in mind when the test results are examined.

Now let us turn our attention to the experiments. To discover whether fear affected the subjects' judgments of personality we should compare the results obtained after *murder* in each of the two tests (A and B) with those obtained after normal conditions. In making this comparison we should bear in mind that, according to the adopted method of scoring, an increase in the rating of a photograph signified an increase in the apparent badness (maliciousness) of a face, and a decrease in the rating signified an increase in the apparent goodness (benevolence) of a face.

The results were as follows: In Test A, as compared with the scores obtained after ordinary conditions, the average ratings after the fear-invoking situation remained the same in 1 photograph, were lower (in-

S's	EXPERIMENT A			EXPERIMENT B			BOTH EXPERIMENTS
	Average Rating Per Photograph		Difference In Rating	Average Rating Per Photograph		Difference In Rating	Difference In Rating
	Control	After Fear		After Fear	Control		
			$b-a$			$d-e$	$\dfrac{c+f}{2}$
	a	b	c	d	e	f	g
Mary	4.53	5.73	+1.20	6.47	5.40	+1.07	+1.15
Jane	6.53	7.47	+0.94	7.80	7.00	+0.80	+0.87
Lou	5.67	6.07	+0.40	6.07	5.13	+0.94	+0.67
Jill	5.60	5.93	+0.33	5.33	5.53	−0.20	+0.06
Nan	6.33	6.13	−0.20	6.67	7.27	−0.60	−0.40
Average	5.73	6.26	+0.53	6.47	6.07	+0.40	+0.47

dicating more "goodness") in 2 photographs, and were higher (indicating more "badness") in 12 photographs. In Test B, as compared with the results obtained after ordinary conditions, the average ratings after the fear-invoking event remained the same in 2 photographs, were lower (indicating more "goodness") in 3 photographs, and were higher (indicating more "badness") in 10 photographs. The slightly less significant results in Test B, as compared with Test A, might be explained by supposing that Jane's recital of her burglar vision aroused in her friends (by suggestion) subjective states which were somewhat similar to those which followed *murder*, and so nullified to some extent the significance as a control of the Sunday test trial. If the results of the two experiments (A and B) are taken together, it appears that out of a total of 30 photographs 22 (73%) were scored higher—that is, the character of the faces in these photographs were judged to be more malicious—after the fear-invoking event than after normal pleasure-invoking events; or, to state it otherwise, it appears that out of 27 photographs, the average ratings of which were different under the two conditions, 22 (81%) were scored higher after fear.

The results might have been more striking if the experimenter had not made the mistake of including several photographs of persons whose faces were so distinctly forbidding that some subjects assigned to them the maximum mark of 9 on the control test, thereby making a further increase of rating after fear impossible. Out of a total of 150 [15 (photographs) $\times$ 5 (subjects) $\times$ 2 (tests)] ratings assigned after ordinary conditions, there were 19 ratings of 9 which did not change when conditions changed. Of the 131 remaining ratings, 96 (73%) were different after the fear-invoking situation; and of the 96 ratings which were different, 67 (70%) were higher (indicating more badness).

An examination of the tabulated results reveals the fact that for the five subjects there was an average change per photograph of +0.53 in Experiment A, and of +0.40 in Experiment B; the average of the two tests being +0.465, or approximately one-half a point towards badness per photograph. In other words, after the fear-invoking situation one-half the faces were judged, on an average, to be one point less good (more wicked) than they were judged after ordinary conditions. There are, of course, other methods of scoring the subjects, but, since intercorrelations between the results obtained by a variety of methods indicated that the present system of scoring was the best, the other methods have not been included in this report.

These results seem to show that complementary apperceptive projection did occur in the subjects, or, to state the matter more specifically, that fear tended to increase the apparent maliciousness of other personalities.

Examining Table 1 from the point of view of individual differences it may be observed that of the five subjects, one (Nan) in Experiment A and two (Nan and Jill) in Experiment B had lower scores after the fear-invoking event; whereas four subjects in Experiment A and three in Experiment B had higher scores after this event. If the two experiments are taken together it appears that one subject (Jill) showed relatively little change in her ratings, whereas the four other subjects did change. Of the four who did change, three, or 75% of them (Mary, Jane, and Lou) judged faces as more malicious after *murder* than after ordinary conditions.

As a part of the test the children had been asked to write down what they thought the person in each photograph was saying or thinking. We guessed that fear might make the supposed thoughts more frightening and melodramatic, but there were few differences between the thoughts written under ordinary conditions and those written under exceptional conditions. What changes did occur, however, were for the most part in the positive direction. For instance, in Jane's paper after ordinary conditions a woman said: "What shall I do next?" and after *murder* she said: "So all your children are sick. Well I hope they die"; and after ordinary conditions a man said: "I'll do it if I like," and after *murder* he said: "You brute, you fool, you hypocrite!"; and after ordinary conditions a man said: "Yeah, I understand" and after *murder* he said: "So you *got* them, did you?"

Though the results from this part of the test were inconclusive as far as the verification of our hypothesis was concerned, they did give evidence of both complementary and supplementary projection. They afforded hints, indeed, of how the wind was blowing in each subject's mind. Jane, for instance, who hallucinated burglars on Sunday morning, wrote on Saturday the following thoughts for four of her subjects:

You give me back that money or I'll shoot.
Gosh. I've gone broke.
How did you make out? Did you get any money?
Have you got the money?

Since Jane was the only child who made any mention of money or burglars, her written sayings might almost have been taken as prognostically significant. On Sunday, after the hallucination, she wrote the following thoughts for three of her subjects:

I went in to a room last night in Topsfield. [It was in Topsfield that these events occurred].

I got the scare of my life last night. [Supplementary apperceptive projection.]

Well, well, have any more ghosts come to you? [This suggests that at this time she was doubting the substantiality of her visionary experience.]

THEORETICAL CONSIDERATIONS

To explain the positive results obtained in these experiments it seems that we should take account of at least three processes: (1) the activation of fear by the game of *murder;* (2) the preservation of this emotion; and (3) the projection of integrated elements into the material to be diagnosed.

All of these processes must have occurred, it seems, in the three subjects who gave consistently positive results (Mary, Jane, and Lou). The two who gave negative results (Jill and Nan) may not have been aroused to anxiety by the game; or, if they were so activated, the emotion may have dissipated itself before the test was given; or, finally, they may have been experiencing some anxiety during the test but the emotion did not affect their judgments of personality.

That the positive results depended to a large extent upon the evocation of fear is suggested by the fact that the only subjects (Mary and Lou) who spoke of being afraid during the *murder* game were both in the positive group. The third member of the positive group (Jane) happened to be the "victim" in the first game of *murder* and the "murderer" in the second, circumstances which militate against the admission of fear even if the subject is experiencing it.

We must suppose that perserveration and projection were both present to account for Jane's vision of burglars ten hours later. That Mary and Lou were the subjects who gave credence—but only after nightfall —to the substantiality of Jane's vision is a fact which fits in with the other positive responses given by these two children. It demonstrates, moreover, the determining effect of emotion and of projection in the genesis of belief.

It is difficult to give a satisfactory account of the psychological processes revealed by our findings without reference to a theory of motivation. But since the theory which we believe best describes the functional aspect of human nature has not yet found its way into the literature, and hence cannot be referred to by name, and since space does not allow for an outline of it at this time, we shall omit mention of the particular need (instinct) or combination of reflexes aroused in our subjects. In lieu of this, we shall refer all the bodily affections which occurred in our subjects to the emotion of fear, since its existence in children after playing *murder* is easy to establish by means of subjective reports as well as by the observation of its usual objective correlates.

In accordance with our introductory speculations and hypotheses we should attempt to explain the results of this investigation by saying that the bodily processes operative in the subjective experience known as fear were aroused by the game of *murder;* that these in turn mobilized the integrated images and categories (the more general imaginal meanings). We have in mind such categories as "dangerous situations," "criminals and burglars," "malicious characters," and so forth. Then, when the test was presented to the children, the photographs which fulfilled the requirements of sufficient similitude functioned as foci for the projection of these images and categories, a photograph, for instance, being assimilated to the category "very bad" instead of to the category "bad" in which it seemed to fit best when the subject was without emotion.

It was as if the subjects, experiencing an emotion without adequate stimulus, sought something in the external world to justify it—as if the idea had come to mind: "there must be malicious people about." The result of this was that the photographs appeared to change in the direction of adequacy as stimuli. It is clear that we have here a typical complementary apperceptive projection.

Two other processes which usually accompany a state of emotional excitement may have occurred in this experiment—preferential perception and perceptive projection.

By *preferential perception* we refer to the unconscious (unintentional) process by which attention is directed to objects in the environment similar to the traces (or images) integrated with the aroused emotion. The subject simply becomes aware of the external object, the preceding process of selection being unconscious. In the present experiment, it is not unlikely that the children's attention was attracted to special facial parts—parts which indicated "badness"—and that judgments were made on the basis of these.

Perceptive projection has already been defined. It may also have been operating in this test. The children, for instance, may have perceived the faces as physically different from what they actually were. In other words, mild illusions may have occurred.

These phenomena can be best explained, though we do not insist upon it, by the hypothesis of activated traces or unconscious images. The traces which are integrated with the bodily processes which make up the emotional state are there, as it were, below consciousness—ready to appear as conscious imagery or to modify events which are conscious, namely, perception and apperception.

That the supposition of active unconscious imagery is not an unwarranted hypothesis is indicated by the frequency with which imagery such as has been described occurs on the fringe of consciousness in the form of a phantasy which can be recalled immediately afterwards. Such imagery is *almost* unconscious in that it may never be in the focus of attention and may be recalled only in part and with difficulty afterwards. The following is an instance of this familiar phenomenon.

One evening a subject was sitting alone in a somewhat isolated farmhouse reading *The Turn of the Screw,* the gruesome story by Henry James (fear-invoking situation). At an exciting point of the narrative the telephone bell rang and a strange man, who said he was a reporter, asked permission to motor over that very evening for the purpose of discussing a matter in which the subject was interested. Though it was already ten o'clock and the reporter was calling from a town twelve miles distant, the subject agreed to see him and returned to his reading. After a few moments he realized that his attention had been divided. Although he could give an account to himself of what he had been reading, he was also aware that an unintentionally initiated phantasy had been developing in the marginal realm of consciousness. In the phantasy an automobile had drawn up to the door and the supposed reporter entered the house. After a few introductory words the latter had drawn a revolver and a skirmish had followed in which the two men had rolled about the floor until by a clever twist of the wrist the revolver was disengaged from the gangster's hand and the subject became master of the situation. This phantasy represented the functional signification assigned to the strange voice on the telephone and the event which was to come. The subject was decidedly of the opinion that this would not have occurred if at the time he had been reading a story of a different kind.

The explanation of this event would be that fear had evoked imagery of "dangerous characters" to which the voice of the stranger had been assimilated; and with these compounded elements the mind swayed by apprehension had constructed a melodramatic reverie in the form of a tentative hypothesis, one might say, of what the future would disclose. This whole phantasy might easily have been unconscious. One might say that it was only by chance that the subject captured it out of the twilight zone of his consciousness (cf. a man capturing, losing, then recapturing the content of a dream as he wakes).

Now, if the subject had been less self-conscious and later had manifested a lowered threshold for the sound of an automobile coming down the drive (preferential perception), and when greeting the reporter had circumscribed his attention to the less kindly aspects of his face (preferential perception) or had unconsciously distorted the features of the stranger so that physically he appeared to be different (perceptive projection) or, though seeing him without distortion, had interpreted his looks and gestures as signifying "bad intention" (apperceptive projection)—if these psychological events had occurred we should have explained them by referring to a mental process (activated in this case by the fear-invoking story) of which the phantasy was a component. If this phantasy had been unconscious—as it might well have been—we should have been forced to resort to the concept of unconscious psychic processes.

If the circumstances of the evening telephone call, however, had been sufficient, as a result of the subject's past experience under similar circumstances, to call forth the fear and the resultant phantasy, we should have spoken of the redintegration of danger images and categories without projection—the term projection being confined to the operation of irrelevant affections which in the present instance were aroused by the reading of the book. So much for the projection of unconscious images and meanings.

Now, from the standpoint of an interest in the individual differences of personality, we should like to know whether the two groups distinguished by this test—namely, the susceptible class (Mary, Jane, and Lou) with an average change per photograph of +.90 points, and the non-susceptible class (Jill and Nan) with an average change per photograph of −.17 points—are characterized by personality differences which are more or less permanent. In other words, would these two groups show approximately the same difference in their responses to other comparable tests or to the same test at a later time or to somewhat similar circumstances in everyday life? We cannot, of course, give a positive answer to this question, but the following facts suggest that the tests did reveal some more or less consistent personality traits:

1. The coefficient of correlation (product-moment method) between Experiment A and Experiment B was +.84.

2. The hostess of the week-end party who knew the children intimately, when the nature of the experiment was explained to her, guessed that Mary and Jane would score the highest. This prophecy was correct.

3. Jane's hypnapompic vision was a manifestation of the same process which was responsible for her high score on the test. Jane had never before experienced such a vision, but in the past few months had had several nightmares in which burglars figured prominently.

4. Mary and Lou came to believe in the truth of Jane's story about the burglars, but Jill and Nan did not.

Thus the behavior of the children during the week-end, the estimations of their temperaments by the hostess, and the results on both tests showed a considerable degree of correlation.

There is no generally accepted concept of type or trait to describe the response of the positive group as differentiated from the negative group. Psychologists have written of emotionality and of subjectivity, but, since these words have been used without precision, it is impossible to say whether our group of projectors should be subsumed under one or both of these headings. By definition there is no projection without affection or emotion, but there is no evidence to show that projection invariably parallels intensity of emotion. Other factors—such as conglomeration and the partial dissociation of the personality itself—seem to be important. *Conglomeration* is a name given to the psychical condition—as found in children—in which little or no differentiation is made between images and objects, between what is internal and psychical and what is external and substantial.

SUMMARY

Five girls, eleven years of age, estimated from photographs the degree of goodness (benevolence) or badness (maliciousness) of other personalities. These estimates were made under two different conditions: *(a)* after ordinary pleasurable activity in the sunshine, and *(b)* after two games of *murder* in the dark. A comparison of the ratings assigned under these two conditions revealed the following:

1. Seventy-three per cent of the faces were estimated by a majority of the group as more malicious when judged after the fear-invoking situation than when judged after ordinary conditions.

2. Of the four subjects whose ratings differed under the two conditions, three (75%) estimated the series of faces as more malicious after the fear-invoking situation than after ordinary conditions.

These results may be attributed to complementary apperceptive projection subsequent to the activation of an emotional state. The conclusion which may be drawn from this experiment is that under some conditions the emotion of fear will cause some experiencing subjects to increase their estimates of the maliciousness of other personalities.

REFERENCES

1. Stout, G. F. *Analytic Psychology,* New York, Macmillan, 1896.

2. Köhler, W. *Gestalt Psychology,* New York, Liveright, 1929, p. 403.

3. Whitehead, A. N. *Symbolism: Its Meaning and Effect,* New York, Macmillan, 1927, p. 88.

4. Prince, M. An experimental study of the mechanism of hallucinations. *Brit. J. Med. Psychol.,* 1922, *2,* 165–208.

12

WHAT SHOULD PSYCHOLOGISTS DO ABOUT PSYCHOANALYSIS?

The editor, like a true host of a symposium, or drinking party, has encouraged his guests each to choose his own approach to the elected topic; and it being my turn to hold forth, I propose to recount some of the experiences and reflections I have had that bear upon this question: what should psychologists do about psychoanalysis? To be more specific, I shall tell what I have *done* (bows to operationism) about psychoanalysis, and at the end suggest what other psychologists of personality might profitably do.

Thus, at best, my remarks will concern only one variety of psychologists, those—permit me, for brevity's sake, to call them "personologists" —who study men functioning in society, who are professionally interested in what different individuals perceive and do and *feel* and *think*, and why. "Feel" and "think" are italicized because psychologists of the latest model have ruled out these processes, and, as I see it, a personologist who crippled himself to this extent could but half fulfill his function. A personologist wants to know why man, "like an angry ape, plays such fantastic tricks before high heaven"; why he laughs, blasphemes and frets, cheers at a spangled cloth and bleeds for a king; why he blushes over four-letter words and hides his genitals, and falls in love with so and so and later strangles her; why he mourns in isolation, lacerates himself with guilt, invents a purgatory and a paradise. Among such problems— all pertinent to man's weal and woe—a personologist chooses those that are most critical to some system of psychology and that lend themselves most readily to accurate observation and research.

Knowledge and understanding are satisfying and sufficient in themselves, but I must plead guilty to a little optimism that inspirits my endeavors; it is the hope that knowledge will lead eventually to power, to a more sagacious management of infant life, to fruitfulness and the self-development of finer men and women, to happier societies. The contemporary world spectacle of humanity in action is more than

From *Journal of Abnormal and Social Psychology*, 1940, *35*, 150–175. The paper was part of an American Psychological Association symposium on Psychologists and Psychoanalysis.

enough to "make the angels weep," and, but for the promise of the social sciences, to make Jeremiahs of the rest of us. Men seem to be as much the product of a society as a society is the product of the men; but my interest being in the "hearts" of individuals, rather than in the customs which they mimic, I am apt to emphasize the potentiality and import of inner factors; not unlike a physical-chemist who expects to deduce the properties of a substance from the configuration of its elements, or a Puritan divine who believes that inward grace is more to be desired than civic virtue.

Reading this confession, this *religio humani animi investigatoris*, you are in a position to predict almost everything that is to follow; chiefly because psychoanalysis is entirely concerned with man's inner life and everyday behavior, and academic psychology is but faintly so. The analysts spend eight or more hours of the day observing, and listening to what a variety of patients say about the most intimate and telling experiences of their lives, and they spend many evenings at seminars exchanging findings and conclusions. The professorial personologist, on the other hand, spends most of his time away from what he talks and writes about. He labors over apparatus, devises questionnaires, calculates coefficients, writes lectures based on what other anchorites have said, attends committee meetings, and occasionally supervises an experiment on that nonexistent entity, Average Man. He makes little use of the techniques that analysts have perfected for exposing what occurs behind the stilted laboratory attitudes. In addition, the analysts have read more and to better profit in the great works of literature (collections of the best guesses of highly conscious men), and this practice has served to sensitize and broaden their awareness. Thus, on the face of it, being in closer contact with the facts, the analysts—doctors, for the most part, familiar with the human body—*should* know more about personality than the psychologists. But the question is: do their formulations fit the facts and clarify them?

Some psychoanalytic concepts are definitions of terms that make visible things which mankind has always seen half blindly; others are merely new names for old notions. These, being more or less self-evident, hardly call for proof. But what does need proving is the bulk of analytic theory; and it must be confessed right now that the proof is not available. Nothing that the analysts have written marshals the necessary evidence in such a fashion that conviction follows. But it happens, notwithstanding, that I accept a large part (more than half) of the psychoanalytic scheme; and when I say "accept" I mean, of course, that I am accustomed to employ as the best available hypotheses for research and therapy most of its concepts, and that I think in these terms quite naturally. How confidence emerged and grew out of personal experience (working on others and being worked on), a little autobiography, with your permission, will explain. *This*, I take it, is the cat which our editor wishfully expected would somehow get out of the bag.

At college a bud of interest in psychology was nipped by the chill of Professor Münsterberg's approach. In the middle of his second lecture I began looking for the nearest exit. There was more bread (and fewer stones) in biology and chemistry, and afterwards in medicine. During my fourth year at the College of Physicians and Surgeons, while waiting for calls to deliver babies in Hell's Kitchen, I completed a modest study of twenty-five of my classmates, in which forty anthropometric measures were correlated with thirty traits. Here I had the symphony of the endocrines in mind. Later, as an interne in a hospital, I spent more time than was considered proper for a surgeon, inquisitively seeking psychogenic factors in my patients. Whatever I succeeded in doing for some of them —the dope fiend, the sword-swallower, the prostitute, the gangster—was more than repaid when, after leaving the hospital, they took me through their haunts in the underworld. This was psychology in the rough, but at least it prepared me to recognize the similarity between downtown doings and uptown dreams.

During these years I was reading all that was recommended to me by a scholarly neurologist who swore by Herbert Spencer and the mechanistic rationalism of the French. My guide, being very much of a gentleman, warned me against Freud: "Freudian doctrines are, to my mind, nothing but a vomit of stercoraceous verbiage. I regard them as the greatest pyschologic phallusy of the age." I was ready, in less picturesque language, to agree with him, after one attempt to follow Freud's vagaries of arbitrary speculation in *The Interpretation of Dreams.*

Then psychology was put aside, and did not come up again until I began to wonder, after several years of research in biochemistry and physiology, why some of the men with whom I was associated at the Rockefeller Institute clung so tenaciously to diametrically opposing views about the simplest phenomena. In the hope of shedding light on conceptual preferences as functions of personality, I sent out a long questionnaire to fifty creative thinkers (mostly scientists); and still puzzled, I took courses in philosophy with Professor Morris Cohen and later at Cambridge University with Professor Broad. But it was Jung's book, *Psychological Types,* which, by providing a partial answer to my question, started me off in earnest toward psychology. There were, besides this, another book, a woman, some German music and several other fructifying influences that made me feel and think at once, instead of separately.

On the crest of a wave I visited Dr. Jung in Zurich supposedly to discuss abstractions; but in a day or two to my astonishment enough affective stuff erupted to invalid a pure scientist. This was my first opportunity to weigh psychoanalysis in a balance; and I recommend it as *one* method of measuring the worth of any brand of personology. Take your mysteries, your knottiest dilemmas, to a fit exponent of a system and judge the latter by its power to order and illumine your whole being. This assuredly is a most exacting test, to apply the touchstone of your deep perplexity to a theory, to demand that it interpret what you presumably know best—yourself. But then, what good is a theory that folds up in a crisis? In deciding such a test, of course, the temperament and talents of the psychologist (or physician) are often more important than his system; but a healthy and critical inquirer capable of some detachment may succeed in approximately weighing out this influence. In 1925, however, I had no scales to weigh out Dr. Jung, the first full-blooded, spherical— and Goethean, I should say—intelligence I had ever met, the man whom the judicious Prinzhorn called "the ripest fruit on the tree of psycho-analytical knowledge." We talked for hours, sailing down the lake and smoking before the hearth of his Faustian retreat. "The great flood-gates of the wonder-world swung open," and I saw things that my philosophy had never dreamt of. Within a month a score of bi-horned problems were resolved, and I went off decided on depth psychology. I had *experienced* the unconscious, something not to be drawn out of books.

Returning to this country, I read everything I could lay my hands on, without favoring one school above another—Freud, Stekel, Rank, Adler —and attended psychiatric clinics (where the patients often seemed more natural than the doctors). Suddenly—by special providence, my ancestors would have said—Dr. Morton Prince offered me a job as his assistant in research at the Harvard Psychological Clinic. No man more ignorant of textbook knowledge was ever admitted to a department of psychology; but Professor Boring was a liberal and I stayed.

At first I was taken aback, having vaguely expected that most aca-demic psychologists would be interested in Man functioning in his envi-ronment. But not at all: almost everyone was nailed down to some piece of apparatus, measuring a small segment of the nervous system as if it were isolated from the entrails. I was in the position, let us imagine, of a medical student who suddenly discovers that all his instructors are eye, ear, nose and throat specialists. The phenomena that intrigued me were not mentioned, since these were not susceptible to exact experimental validation, a standard that rules out geology, paleontology, anthropology, embryology, most of medicine, sociology, and divine astronomy. If my chief aim had been to "work with the greatest scientific precision" I would never have quit electrolytes and gases. I had changed because of a consuming interest in other matters, in problems of motivation and emotion. To try to work these out on human subjects was to become a "literary" or applied psychologist, a practitioner of mental hygiene, out-side and looking in upon the real psychologists who, I concluded, were obsessed by anxious aims to climb the social scale of scientists and join the elect of this day's God at any cost. What else could account for their putting manners (appliances and statistics) so far ahead of ends (impor-tance of the problems studied)? No matter how trivial the conclusions, if his coefficients were reliable, an experimenter was deemed pure and sanctified. This, my first, lop-sided, and intolerant diagnosis, was modified in time; and today I am very grateful to my university friends for what they have taught me, more than I can use yet, about standards *specific to the field*. And here it should be pointed out that physics, chemistry, and physiology are of little worth in immunizing one to plausible speculations in psychology. The majority of doctors psychoanalyzed, for instance, have been converted by the process into unskeptical religionists. Very few psychologists have been so affected.

But I must return to my theme, and state that despite the special criticalness acquired from psychology, psychoanalysis triumphed on its second test. I began to practice therapy with the theories of all schools democratically assembled in my head; and I was amazed to find that, if I kept quiet, the patients—who suffered from hysteria, anxieties, compulsions, and obsessions—would say substantially what I had read in Freud. Despite Dr. Prince and all my former guides, the facts were there; and only in the light of analytic theories did they become intelligible. I used Jung and a dash of positive therapy as each analysis approached its end, and in most cases the results were gratifying.

Dr. Alexander's arrival in Boston provided the first opportunity for me to be analyzed by a thoroughly able Freudian with training and talent in research. Having worked with Dr. Jung, read everything, practiced analysis on myself and others for six years, I was only a little disappointed to find nothing very new come out of it. Neither my analyst nor myself kept a record of the nine months' voyage, and today we can recall but little of it. I accepted his entire frame of reference just as all of us accept the conventions of stage scenery when we go to the theater; and one result of thus seeing myself through his concepts and terminology was the total absence of theoretical discussions. Partly for this reason our passage was relatively calm; he was rather bored (yawned continually), and I was less aggressive than in ordinary life. I liked him from the start —he had a sense of humor (an indispensable requirement) and could tell good stories—and I had to search hard to find excuses (borborygmi and other tricks of his) to stir the aggression that I thought should, according to the rules, erupt. I was too busy, otherwise-attached, and happy to be transferable. Hence narcism might well have been the diagnosis, but my analyst did not say. *I* did all the talking.

Stuttering was the symptom chosen for attack. Though scarcely any dent was made on this most obdurate affliction, some important things turned up during our *récherche du temps perdu*. The masquerades of the unconscious were surprising, as when I dreamt that I was holding my mother in my arms and she started vomiting as if she were a baby. This meant, as you can guess, all sorts of things. Anyhow, when I got through I decided that by interpreting such frantic facts, psychoanalysis had passed its third test.

The fourth soon followed, when Dr. Sachs, who acted as my control, proved time and time again that he could predict my patients' trends several days or even weeks before they were exhibited. A theory that can do this is valuable. In the meanwhile several of us at the Clinic were doing experiments on suggestion, repression, guilt, humor, projection, and compulsion, all of which confirmed, to some extent, the hypotheses proposed by Freud. Taken together these served as a rather effective fifth test. Dr. Diven's rigid proof of unconscious conditioning and displacement was especially convincing. Later, when twenty of us studied fifty normal subjects, we found that Freud's theories were the most efficient in interpreting their responses and in constructing coherent pictures of the development of their personalities. Finally, as a seventh test, I am now working on the biography of one man, with all points of view, academic and analytic, ready to apply; and I have gone far enough to say that Freud's scheme reveals the most.

This, briefly, is the fourteen years' experience which solidifies my conviction that much of psychoanalysis is relatively true and should prove useful to guide research in personology. Here I am speaking as a workman who testifies to the usefulness of an instrument, having tried several.

In many people the word "psychoanalysis" is the nucleus of a complex, a fighting word, a cat-o'-nine-tails to flog the culpable, or the password to an esoteric cult. It stands for something that must be accepted wholly or rejected, as a suitor before a woman. When the Harvard Clinic was brought to the bar of judgment recently, I was asked: "Is this a psychoanalytic clinic or is it not?" Could anything be more benighted? I cannot see it as a hate affair, or as a love affair in which every fault is transformed into an endearing quality like the mole on my wife's cheek. Psychoanalysis means many things. It means a procedure and a large number of therapeutic rules, many of which are matters of debate among the analysts. Some of these rules I accept as the best available guides, others I follow occasionally and tentatively, others I ignore. Psychoanalysis also means a vast collection of unusual and important facts, among which a personologist cannot fail to find a great deal that is pertinent to his problems. Finally, psychoanalysis stands for a conceptual system which explains, it seems to me, as much as any other. But this is no reason for going in blind and swallowing the whole indigestible bolus, cannibalistically devouring the totem father in the hope of acquiring his genius, his authoritative dominance, and thus rising to power in the psychoanalytic society, that battleground of Little Corporals. No; I, for one, prefer to take what I please, suspend judgment, reject what I please, speak freely.

In advocating psychoanalysis—as I do constantly—I have been thwarted by the absence of any satisfactory textbook on the subject. I have found nothing that I could heartily recommend to a student or indeed to any moderately critical inquirer. Analytic authors have not yet learnt to sort out facts from theories, probabilities from improbabilities; with but fugitive impressions of the requirements of scientific proof, they are boyish in their readiness to dogmatize. There is, nevertheless, so much precious ore amid the slag that a personologist, I think, should persevere—tolerant of intellectual frailties and foibles—until he finds it. What the analysts know is hard—especially for them—to say; and the psychologists who might be competent to say—they do not yet know.

It would take—it *did* take—a long book to encompass everything that I consider relatively true or promising in psychoanalysis. Here there is space only for a brief synopsis of the concepts that seem most essential to a scheme of personology. First of all—and here my prejudice leaps out —psychoanalysis is dynamic in the special sense that it is founded on a theory of directional forces, forces which, if unimpeded, usually produce, in one way or another, results that are satisfying, positively or negatively, to the organism. The principle of adaptation rests upon this concept. Logically, you cannot assent to one and deny the other. But the argument makes a long story which cannot be gone into now. At the moment I am mentally unfit to accept as fundamental any system of psychology which does not include a theory of drives, needs, conations (or what have you).

The psychoanalysts distinguish only two drives, sex and aggression; but these have been studied closely, and much that has been discovered about their modes (fixation, conflict, fusion, sublimation) applies equally well to other tendencies. Psychoanalysis is worth reading if only for what it teaches us about sex. For it is now clear that this instinct—punished and guilt-laden, veiled by shame and twisted by hypocrisy, turned back upon itself and driven into ugly alleys—is not only the chief factor in psychogenic illness but has been for centuries the source of unspeakable mental torment, the veritable plague spot of human personality. This was the price of innocence. As a corollary to the instinct theory is Freud's notion of cathexis, which describes the degree of positive or negative valence with which each object (individual, group, cause) that concerns the subject is endowed. Through such cathexes each general tendency becomes specific.

The *sine qua non* of psychoanalysis is the theory of unconscious processes, which affirms that activities quite similar to those distinguishable introspectively (perceptions, emotions, intellections, intentions) occur continually in us without our knowledge. (In order to establish this point, the misunderstanding about words that commonly arises must be first dispelled by defining such psychic entities as "intention" and "emotion" *both* according to their natures as directly experienced subjectively and according to their discernible effects.) Closely related to this theory is the division of the mind into structured, partly conscious *ego* processes, and less structured, unconscious *id* processes; the ego being, so to speak, separated from the id by a layer of selective and inhibitive functions. Here the concept of repression is indispensable in accounting for the habitual exclusion of certain unacceptable tendencies and traces. Besides repression, Freud has described a number of other mechanisms (projection, sublimation, rationalization) whereby the ego partially succeeds in veiling, transforming, or excusing some of the active components of the id. Of course to speak of "the id" or "the unconscious" is a mere makeshift, but it is too early to imprison in tidy operational definitions the myriad varieties of noted facts. The ego is an elusive being which has not yet been caught in any conceptual corral; as a first approximation, however, the notion of a discriminating semi-conscious entity, standing between two environments—signs and pressures from within and from without—is a convenient one. Hinting of the nature of id processes we have dreams and fantasies, and the mental life of children, savages, and psychotics. Their thought, primitive and prelogical, is marked by more emotive and symbolic imagery (fewer abstract words) and exhibits a greater number of instinctive, lower-order tendencies than does that of normal adults.

The theory of the unconscious (of the *alter ego* or shadow-self) helps to explain contrasting phases of behavior, ambivalence, sudden explosions, regressions, conversions. ("He was not himself"; "I would not have known him.") It throws light on fixed and refractory frames of reference, settled sentiments and beliefs. It is essential to an understanding of illusions, delusions, morbid anxiety, compulsions, and insanity. It is invaluable in interpreting neurotic accidents and illness. The unconscious is an historical museum of the breed and of the individual, exhibiting tableaux of development. But also, in a sense, it is the womb of fate, the procreating source of new directions, of art, and of religion. It is here that one must seek for novelty, for the incubating complex that will govern the next move. No creator can afford to disrespect the twilight stirrings of the mind, since out of these arise the quickening ideas that are his life.

Psychoanalysis stresses the primacy of the *body*, the chemistry of its essential organs, its endocrines and appetites. The brain and central nervous system are its instruments (its president and officials) with power to coordinate and satisfy its needs. The self-consciousness acquired in the brain is like a tiny coral isle growing in a sea of dreams (containing representatives of the body) which influence its every waking moment and sweep over it in sleep. To understand the mind, therefore, one must search for much that lies beyond the range of consciousness. What a man does and says in public is but a fraction of him. There is what he does in private, and the reasons he gives for doing it. But even this is not enough. Beyond what he says there is what he will not say but knows, and, finally, what he does not know. Only a depth psychologist can reach the latter.

Among other useful psychoanalytic concepts, some are so eminently suitable to everyday experience that they have been accepted widely as self-evident. One wonders why these things were never said before in scientific language. It seems incredible, for example, that no pre-Freudian psychologist ever conceptualized in full relief the eternal conflict between man and men, between personal desires and social sanctions. Freud's concept of the superego (conscience) as the internalization of parental and cultural demands organizes many facts; and serves, by the way, to make a bridge between psychology and sociology. The moral man carries society within him.

The analysts have also contributed a great deal to our understanding of children. They have taught us to take stock of the infant's reactions to certain well-nigh universal situations—birth, weaning, bowel training, advent of younger sibling, withdrawal of support—all of which are potentially traumatic. We now know that fantasies are almost as influential as actual events, that the contemporary concerns (dilemmas and anxieties) of the child give to occurrences special meanings which determine their effects, and, finally, that some events leave permanent impressions which modify development. Complexes arising out of the child's relations to its mother and to its father are of signal import. In addition to these and other general theories, the analysts have proposed specific formulations to account for a great variety of conditions and reactions, too numerous to mention here.

I can hardly think myself back to the myopia that once so seriously restricted my view of human nature, so natural has it become for me to receive impressions of wishes, dramas, and assumptions that underlie the acts and talk of everyone I meet. Instead of seeing merely a groomed American in a business suit, traveling to and from his office like a rat in a maze, a predatory ambulating apparatus of reflexes, habits, stereotypes, and slogans, a bundle of consistencies, conformities, and allegiances to this or that institution—a robot in other words—I visualize (just as I visualize the activity of his internal organs) a flow of powerful subjective life, conscious and unconscious; a whispering gallery in which voices echo from the distant past; a gulf stream of fantasies with floating memories of past events, currents of contending complexes, plots and counterplots, hopeful intimations and ideals. To a neurologist such perspectives are absurd, archaic, tender-minded; but in truth they are much closer to the actualities of inner life than are his own neat diagrams of reflex arcs and nerve anastomoses. A personality is a full Congress of orators and pressure groups, of children, demagogues, communists, isolationists, warmongers, mugwumps, grafters, logrollers, lobbyists, Caesars and Christs, Machiavels and Judases, Tories and Promethean revolutionists. And a psychologist who does not know this in himself, whose mind is locked against the flux of images and feelings, should be encouraged to make friends, by being psychoanalyzed, with the various members of his household.

Figurative language, such as I am using here, is widely condemned as rank anthropomorphism, but what sin could be more pardonable than this when talking about *men*—not about vegetables, minerals, and sewing machines? Anyhow, such talk is pragmatically effective in dealing with most patients; and hence by this token scientific. Technical language, on the other hand, is ineffective and therefore "illogical" in the Paretian sense. For this reason, emotive speech will always have its place —resistant to certain poisons in "scientific" psychology—even after it is found that some complex of chemicals is mostly responsible for the rebel in us, another for the pacifist, still another for the lecher.

I have been speaking chiefly of Freudian concepts; but among the theories which I consider necessary or fruitful I should certainly place some of those proposed by Jung, Adler, and Rank. So much contentious blood has been spilt in the guerrilla war that still rages between the schools founded by these pioneers that now it is quite impossible for the protagonists of one dogma to appreciate the values and validities of others. Semi-blindness is a residuum as well as a cause of combat. To an impartial eye, however, the one-sidedness of each of these divergent creeds is as obvious as a paralytic limb. Freudian psychology, for example, is clearly limited to certain spheres of functioning and is more applicable to some types and some conditions of men than to others. It is chiefly designed to interpret what a man says when he lies on a couch and his memories are canalized by his desire to appease an analyst's consuming and insatiable interest in sexual adventures. It does not fit all of the people all of the time. Consequently it will have to be expanded to encompass much that up to now has been neglected. Freud denied that anything had entirely evaded his watchful eye when he said: "If psychoanalysis has not yet duly appreciated certain matters, this has never been because it overlooked them or underrated their importance, but simply because it was following a certain course which had not yet led to them." In other words, psychoanalysis must discover everything for itself, borrowing nothing from others, and stamp it with its private seal; and since life is a prodigious nut for a few unaided men to crack, psychoanalysis is destined (if it pursues this course) not to appreciate certain matters for a long, long time.

Among the facts which I should guess the Freudians are bound to come upon and order in their own fashion are the following:

Drives. Freud said that a sound theory of instincts was indispensable to psychoanalysis, but in lieu of such a theory he tells us that "I took as my starting point the poet-philosopher Schiller's aphorism, that hunger and love make the world go round." Now, anyone who tries to follow Freud's trail through the canebrake of his writings on this topic will inevitably conclude that a stubborn preference for dichotomies, an obdurate Persian dualism, determined not only this initial reckless choice, but all subsequent revisions of the scheme as well. First, there were the ego instincts (including hunger and the "instincts of mastery") and the object instincts (various modes of sex); but though in each case Freud spoke of instincts (plural), he made no attempt to distinguish the ego instincts. These were disregarded, sex being allowed by its indulgent parent to monopolize attention. The new concept of narcism affirmed that the ego was itself cathected by the sex drive, which led, by a feat of logic, to the conclusion that the ego instincts were also sexual. But, since this abolished the old dualism, another polar opposite had to be invented ("the instincts could not be all of the same nature"). The revised dichotomy consisted of the Empedoclean pair of opposites, love and hate (or life and death, or sex and aggression).

It is evident that Freud was attempting to bring order out of chaos by pure thought; for at no time did he review the simple facts, subjective and objective. It seems he never asked himself, What motives and emotions are universally distinguished? or What behavioral trends can be objectively discerned in animals and men? He was guided, without doubt, by some obscure unconscious frame of reference. Otherwise he would never have omitted thirst, excretion, repulsion, acquisition, the lust for power and approval, and several other tendencies; nor would he have thought of normal aging and death (which, if anything, is attended by a coalescence—sex—not by a separation, of particles) as the work of intrapunitive aggression; nor would he have failed to see that extrapunitive aggression is commonly beneficial to the ego (and hence narcistically, or sexually, determined); nor would he have felt it necessary to enlarge his definition of sex until it covered nearly everything (scratching one's buttocks, smoking a cigar, a meeting of psychoanalysts, exhibitionism, morbid curiosity, parental love, works of art, and religious visions). This is intellectual chicanery, word juggling, metaphysics, anything but science.

A number of drives might well be added to the list; to begin with—since the analysts are interested in vice—two or three of the five remaining deadly sins: Sloth, Avarice, Gluttony, Pride and Envy. Is there any significance in the fact that fancy-priced practitioners have never acknowledged the profit motive, the immorality of greed, robbery, and exploitation? May their superegos work on this! The analysts have found how useful is the conception of an introverted instinct (narcism and self-reproach), but they have not carried this principle far enough. For example, repression can be reasonably regarded as the endopsychic form of the need for rejection, eliminating something from consciousness being the counterpart of excluding an object from one's presence (shutting the door against, putting out of sight, dismissing, expelling, and so forth). A number of other Freudian mechanisms are also instruments of some special need. Identification, for instance, is a mode of achieving superiority or affiliation (belongingness). I have stressed the importance of reformulating and reordering the analytic scheme of drives, since no dynamic system can be more solid than its base, and its base is its theory and its classification of impelling motives. Freud's approach to the problem is exactly comparable to that of the alchemists and their successors when they undertook to classify the elements; all sorts of subjective desiderata (magic numbers, balanced opposites, symmetrical equations) were influential in forcing the production of many aesthetically pleasant, but unreal, arrangements. Much observation and induction was required before the unpredicted periodic law emerged.

Sex and Aggression. To the analysts "sex" means so much it means nothing. It is obviously a fetish word, an abracadabra, an open sesame to their Skull and Bones; and it is high time they gave us some idea of what they have in mind when they use the term. (A hypothetical single endocrine? a battalion of endocrines? the activity of the gonads? a special feeling or sensation? every form of pleasure? all varieties of love? attraction—for oxygen, for food, for an idea? the entire history of civilization? life? the universe?) The facts, as I see them, induce me to distinguish sex (lust) from love (affiliation), despite their frequent fusions and the power of each to excite and augment the other. I find no reason to believe, for instance, that love is usually born from ticklings of mucous membrane. The Freudians do not derive hate from sensations, why love? The child's love for the mother and the mother's love for the child may flourish without sex (as usually defined). Why do the Freudians never mention the thousands of bottle-fed babies (cared for by nursemaids) who "seem" to love their mothers? How account for a dog's asexual attachment to his master? Is his sexuality repressed by a severe superego imposed by his wandering father? If love (of which there are several kinds—dependent, reverential, convivial, compassionate) is treated as a separable factor (need for affiliation) it can be reunited, and considered fused, with sex, whenever the facts proclaim the compound. The goal of Freudian therapy is the attainment of normal genital satisfaction; health, love, and happiness are supposed to follow, in conformity with the theory that love is engendered by sensations. But this fiat is contradicted by a large mass of facts: the genitally mature and satisfied wives and husbands who cease to love, *then* go to pieces; and the hundreds who love and are happy without any sexual activity. Strange as it may seem, Freud has never succeeded in fitting in, explaining or duly stressing, *love* (mutual sympathy, devotion, adoration, Eros in the true sense). His term, "anal erotism," is a dead giveaway.

Freud's conception of aggression also requires overhauling. For most of the evidence is in favor of its being a reaction tendency, aroused by frustration, belittlement or attack, not a positive appetite (like hunger and sex) that must be satisfied periodically. To be sure, it often acts like sex, but this is probably due to some residual tension in the need engendered by a long series of frustrations, which tension can generally be dissolved by reciprocated love or recognized achievements.

Ego. The ego is a conceptual entity which still defies description and definition; but in listing what it *does* (repression, adaptation, etc.) Freud has shown us the way. Two classes of phenomena, however, have been left out: those associated with the will and the satisfactions of self-mastery, and those associated with integration and the reasonable ordering of one's drives—the Hellenic ideal of harmonious expression. In practice I am inclined to assign moral responsibility to the ego, and I attempt to judge the work it has to do by estimating the strength of the insurgent tendencies (which vary from one individual to another) that must be managed.

Ego Ideal. The image of one's desirously imagined self (including one's levels of aspiration) which may be the figure of a saint or that of a satanic criminal, has not been distinguished from the superego concept. The ego ideal can bring about repression as well as the superego. Are there not the shame of cowardice and indolence, and the necessity for repressing these?

Superego. There are other kinds of superego—intellectual standards and aesthetic standards—that are almost as important as Freud's moral censor. Furthermore, his superego, the internalization of parental and social mores, does not cover all of conscience. There are certain original (id-born) moral conceptions, derived from sensitiveness to pain, from empathy and love, which are often "higher" than anything that parents or authorities teach or practice. If not, how can one account for the prophets, romantic idealists, and reformers who have raised the superegos of their societies to new levels? The most moral men are not submissive citizens but nonconformists. Finally, Freud did not take account of the mores during war, when the leaders say "kill," and a man suffers death (according to the ordinances of the navy) if he does not fire. Freud could not concede that a man may be born with a few "better" instincts than society demands. He sides with St. Augustine and the Calvinists.

Castration. The practice of deriving general tendencies from focal and particular occurrences is an inveterate trait of analytic thinking, which is nowhere more flagrantly exhibited than in the analyst's tenet that the fear of castration is the source of all anxiety.

Character Traits. That many traits are due to a peculiar sensitiveness in this or that erogenous zone is not at all probable. Much more likely is the supposition that a tendency has a better opportunity to express itself in connection with one physiological activity than in connection with another. The zonal complexes could be established in this way.

Infantile Determination. The Freudians explain most attitudes by references to relationships that obtained in the family during childhood. A political rebel, for example, is merely expressing his old hostility to a domineering father. But they fail to observe that such hostility is due to the frustration of a need (commonly the need for autonomy), and that it will be displayed whenever dictatorship is encountered, in youth or later. My own father was a mild, good-natured, unreproachful man, and yet I am peculiarly quick to jump at the throat of tyranny and dogmatism.

Regression. According to the Freudian view, infancy is the happiest period of life. The child receives gratuitously all the benefits and is protected from all the harms that life can offer. Like an emir he is waited on from dawn to dusk. He has his mother's breast and his own body to enjoy, and, knowing nothing of reality, can think of paradise and deem it present. Existence for him is not unlike the Moslem's fantasy of future bliss: the hero reclines on a bed of roses in the voluptuous arms of a maternal concubine and is served delicious food and drink by dark-eyed houris. This is the pleasure principle. (Never mind the tears, the hunger, the teething, the vomiting and diarrhea, the infections and convulsions, the frights and nightmares, the barriers of the crib, the muscular help- lessness, the impotence of speech, the frustrations and angry tantrums, the slaps and spankings.) But the beatitude of childhood is of short dura- tion. Socialization begins early: no more thumb-sucking, bowels must be regulated by the clock, the child is pestered by a hundred Do's and Don'ts. Forced by the fear of punishment, he gives up his former pleas- ures, one by one, as he tries to adapt and work his way up in the world. This is the reality principle. But whatever he becomes, there is some residual nostalgia, and he is ever ready in dreams and fantasies to wing his way back to the feathered nest, the Golden Age of babyhood. This is the regressive tendency.

Now this picture, I believe, is a very shrewd, though partial, apper- ception of the truth. It is certainly very suitable to neurotics. To explain normal growth, however, something more than the fear of punishment and social isolation must be included. In short, here, as elsewhere, Freud has failed to provide concepts to describe a boy's love of adventure and independence, his desire for mastery and superiority, his seeking after danger. How is one to account for the fact that most younger boys admire and envy their older brothers more than the latter admire them?

Sublimation. The Freudian outlook is well illustrated by the tenet that culture is a product of sublimated sexuality; which is as if a chemist claimed that cystein ($CH_2SH.CH(NH_2).COOH$) was *nothing but* sulphur (S). According to Freud's view, moreover, most of the monuments of culture are not derivable from adult sexuality, but from one of its infan- tile precursors, oral or anal sensations, for example. Thus the great collec- tions, the Congressional Library and the Smithsonian Institution, could be interpreted as sublimations of excremental hoarding tendencies. Ab- surd as it may seem, I think this hypothesis contains a little bit of truth; but unfortunately the Freudians, who believe it contains much, lean their whole weight on it, and by so doing, bring great aims to earth.

Social Factors. Only recently have a few of the more independent Freudians begun to take account of the social forces to which their patients have been, or are now, exposed; and to acknowledge how widely these forces may vary among different cultures or among different classes in one culture, and how effective they can be in establishing certain traits of personality.

I cannot say that these above-mentioned seeming errors and omissions are of much significance in treating illness. Freud's genius was consummate when it came to picking out the villains in neurotic dramas, and not many, I should judge, are still at large. If anyone is disposed to doubt or to scoff at this, let him attend a few case seminars. I guarantee that he will be bewildered by the rapidity and subtlety of the insights and inferences which subsequent data will substantiate. When the Freudians get down to the business of a concrete case they function at their best.

Though a certain presumptuousness is involved in fulfilling the jury duty that was assigned the members of this symposium, each one of us must say his whole say; and this is the place to call attention to the oppressive bias, obvious to so many, that runs through the entire Freudian system, a bias which seriously distorts truth and annuls, in some cases, the therapeutic benefits of the procedure. Freud's theory, I submit, is an utterly analytic instrument which reduces a complex individual to a few primitive ingredients and leaves him so. It has names—and the most unsavory—for parts, but none for wholes. It dissects but does not bind up the wounds that it has made. Unconcerned with psychosynthesis and its results, it is of little use either in formulating progress in personality development or in helping a patient—after the transference neurosis and the levelling that an analysis produces—to gather up his forces and launch out on a better way of life. This is the flaw which Jung was quickest to detect and remedy, by directing his therapeutic efforts to an understanding of the forward, rather than to the backward, movements of the psyche. The unconscious, in his opinion, is more than an asylum of but half-relinquished infantile desires; it is the breeding ground of enterprise. One cannot live by laparotomies alone, or by disinfectants or deodorants, as even Freud admitted when he said: "Men are strong as long as they represent a strong idea." The truth will out; though it proves to be a waif excluded from its father's house.

This is not the place to examine the probing, disintegrating, and deflating tendency in psychoanalytic practice. Well might someone write a treatise on the subject, fixing his eye on the intention that designed it, that decided what data should be chosen for consideration, what aspects exhibited in concepts, how the whole dissection should proceed. It would be noted first of all that the patient, who in the end almost invariably seeks, and needs, advice—since it is as hard for him to synthesize as to analyze himself—gets none; gets none from the only man—his analyst— who knows him well enough to judge his powers, the man who has reasons to be much concerned, selfishly and unselfishly, in his future welfare, the man whose business it is to know not only what makes for illness but what makes for health. An inquirer into such matters would listen skeptically to the analyst's rationalizations of his refusal to give positive suggestions. He would note his lack of interest and talent for just this, and his sharply contrasting eagerness to impose the dogma of analysis—more and more analysis, reversing the life process. The direction of the will that underlies all this, the theory and therapy, is fairly obvious. One might have thought the Freudians, so quick to see perverted streaks in other men, would have been polite enough to tell us frankly what sublimated promptings were back of their scientific labors. It would then have been unnecessary for some rude unmasker like myself to speak of voyeurism, depreciating sadism, and the id's revenge on culture, the superego, and the ego. Why not expose and prove the value of these motives? Being sociable with the id myself, I cannot but sympathize with its efforts to get on to a new Declaration of Independence. But the question is, have the Freudians allowed the id enough creativeness and the ego enough will to make any elevating declaration? What is Mind today? Nothing but the butler and procurer of the body. The fallen angel theory of the soul has been put to rout by the starker theory of the soulless fallen man, a result—as Adam, the father of philosophy, demonstrated for all time—of experiencing and viewing love as a mere cluster of sensations. Little man, what now? Freud's pessimism, his conviction that happiness was impossible, his melancholy patronage of the death instinct, should put us on our guard. But then, on second thought, this yielding of the ego to the id, this devotion to its savage depths may be the harbinger of what Henry James, the Swedenborgian, called "creative Love, all whose tenderness *ex vi termini* must be reserved only for what intrinsically is most bitterly hostile and negative to itself"—a sentence, by the way, which the originator of pragmatism said, "discloses for the problem of evil its everlasting solution."

For our day it was Freud, the modern Alberich, who made off with the Rhinemaiden's gold, the *leuchtende Lust,* the shining eye, as Wagner wrote, "that wakes and sleeps in the depths, and fills the waves with its light"; and if his disciples, the present Nibelungs, have been among the few (with Hitler) to escape the worldwide deflation of the ego, it is because the ring that Freud fashioned from the ravished gold has the power of casting long rays into the heretofore mysterious and appalling regions of the psyche, the mind's dark halls of Eblis. Testifying to the master's genius is the fact that a mediocrity who has learnt to use his instruments acquires the powers of a sorcerer, and his consultation room becomes the house of magic to his patients. No wonder Freud is idolized! But let analysts keep their heads. No greater disservice can be done their founder's cause than by making scripture of his utterances, holding his flimsiest conjectures sacred as his profoundest insights. "Genius is full of trash," said Melville. It is out of the germy soil of foolishness that new truths are born. To cling slavishly to *all* of Freud is a mockery to the example of his life, the history of his independently creative mind. Science is a passing fable that sets us free when it arrives and when it leaves.

It is difficult to come to terms with psychoanalysis without coming to terms with the psychoanalysts; and since so few of them are capable of carrying on an equable scientific conversation (according to—must I say it?—operational criteria), interchanges of ideas are practically impossible. The cocksure inflexibility of analysts is more than the assertiveness of fresh enthusiasm, more than your robust conviction or my intolerance of intolerance; it is a confirmed habit and principle of resistance to all theories coming from without. One who is not of the elect is expected to sit—intellectual censor drugged and *hors de combat*—and receive with thanksgiving the Fuehrer's dispensation as handed down by one of his apostles. Of course there are reasons for all this: assaults from society at large to account for the rigid little shut-in societies that analysts have formed; numerous secessions from the fold to explain their vigilance, their dread of heresy; their subjective *a priori* legalistic mode of thought, to explain their bristling at requests for proof (the all-too-familiar spectacle of man "most confident of what he's least assured"). Especially alert are they to criticism from within, since as a group they have a wolf-in-sheep's-clothing phobia. The great Sin is ambivalence—to believe (love) one part of the doctrine but to doubt (hate) another; in other words, the sin of retaining one's critical intelligence, or adopting a normal scientific attitude.

Explicit of this outlook were the remarks of a psychoanalyst who, as the "newly elected president of a scientific organization," thus addressed the brethren: "We must not allow any personal feelings to affect the basic structure of the science of psychoanalysis, we must become more and more welded together and not allow any affective resistances to have the slightest disintegrating effect . . . we cannot accept any who have an ambivalent attitude, that is, the frequently encountered attitude of 'getting together' of analysis and academic psychology . . . such individuals are far more dangerous to the cause of psychoanalysis than those who are out and out antagonists. Any proposed union of analysis and experimental psychology, due to the very fundamental differences in what may be figuratively described as their psychical germ plasm, is bound to produce an unhealthy and deformed child. Such individuals remain entrenched behind an attitude of obliging acceptance, but within this trench they forge and conceal the weapons which they plan to use to fight and destroy the findings of analysis. To paraphrase Freud, one must not alloy the *pure gold of analysis* with any *baser metal* of experimental or academic psychology. The usual attitude of such individuals is 'We accept, but.' This 'but' can be further amplified by a quotation from the greatest of analysts, in *Antony and Cleopatra*: ' "But yet" is a gaoler to bring forth/Some monstrous malefactor.' "

Comments are unnecessary. What could have a more "disintegrating effect" on a society of honest truth seekers than this pronouncement? Who but tame yes-men and grim fanatics could remain to "become more ınd more welded together"? And what could be better calculated to inspire even the best-hearted scientist to play the role of villain, or monstrous malefactor, and boo at them with malicious animal magnetism?

Luckily the Jesuitical attitude of the "newly elected president," though widespread, is by no means universal. Dr. Freud himself evinced interest in our experimental findings when I visited him in Vienna, though clearly he was confident enough of his conclusions to deem such proof superfluous. As he, always generous of his time, wrote to a member of the Harvard Clinic staff:* "I have examined your experimental studies for the verification of the psychoanalytic assertions [Behauptungen] with interest. I cannot put much value on these activities, because the wealth of reliable observations on which these assertions rest make them independent of experimental verification. Still, it can do no harm." "It can do no harm" does not suggest an active fear of monstrous malefactors forging concealed weapons. Perhaps in this respect Freud was not a Freudian. And here let us not forget the excellent researches that Dr. Alexander and his associates at the Chicago Institute have been conducting.

There is another point on which Freud differed from the "newly elected president." It was his opinion, expressed to me in 1937, that psychoanalysis belongs with psychology; and he wrote as much in one of his publications: "The sphere of application of psychoanalysis extends as far as that of psychology, to which it forms a complement of the greatest moment." This, I think, is so; but when I come down to brass tacks and review the human factors, the prospect of "getting together" fades into thin air. The "newly elected president" will die in peace; and the tactless things that I am saying here will, if anything, contribute to his triumph. But these things, notwithstanding, should be said, for the younger men had better know that in the psychoanalytic society free speech is as expensive as it is in Nazi Germany, creative activity being confined within narrow limits. A man of Freud's caliber would be thrown out instanter. The point of view of the majority conforms to that of the "newly elected president" when he said, in ending his discourse, that he was sure the society would be helpful to all, "particularly if we keep in mind that *nothing fundamental must be modified from external sources,* except so far as it is *purely* psychoanalytical, and *nothing must develop within us* to act as a personal resistance which might disturb the equilibrium of a harmonious whole." In other words, creative thinking is prohibited. Calvin's theocracy seems clearer to us now. The analysts' sacerdotal attitude may be due in part to the illegitimate displacement of feelings and aspirations belonging to the realm of value that were set adrift when they gave religion, and all that savors of it, its quietus. The orphaned

*I have Dr. Rosenzweig's permission to publish this letter.

sentiments found lodgment in the ark of the new covenant, Freud's collected works.

I am not inclined to retract a word of what I have written about the rigidity of analysts, even though I am ready to admit that such rigidity may be a necessary evil, like dictatorship after a revolution. Surely it is understandable and, though offensive, to be excused on these counts. (1) It was, and still is, essential to save psychoanalysis from adulteration by the prudes, and to preserve its name from degradation at the hands of irresponsible and piratical therapists, as well as to protect the public from such pretenders. (2) Profitable discussion is hardly possible among people whose basic assumptions, theories, and terminologies are radically different. Practical therapists devoting most of their time to case studies should not be held up by perpetual quarrels over first principles. (3) Analysts have been forced by the exclusiveness of universities to organize their own specialized institutions. A certain amount of intellectual inbreeding is the inevitable result. Thus it seems likely that the analysts will retain their indurated isolation for some time, unearthing more facts and proposing better hypotheses than all the personologists in America put together, and yet unfit to traffic with other scientists on fair and equal terms.

It is surprising that two systems of personology—the academic and the analytic—could have developed, almost cheek to jowl, with so little interaction. Both claim to describe the same object, and yet, leaving aside McDougall's intermediating theories, they have practically nothing in common. The two are as dissimilar as a candid X-ray plate of a man's whole body and a posed photograph of his head and shoulders. The contrast is largely the result of differences in training. It takes about four years' exposure to textbooks, laboratory material, and laboratory methods to make a Ph.D. in psychology; whereas it takes about nine years to make a psychoanalyst. The latter must have physics, chemistry, and biology in college, four years of medicine (including biochemistry, biophysics, physiology, and neurology), a two years' internship (general medicine and psychiatry), and three years at a psychoanalytic institute. Most psychologists seem to be tough-minded intellectual extraceptors with mathematical intelligence, in contrast to the analysts, who are tender-minded intuitive intraceptors with verbal intelligence. It is my contention that the two groups are complementary, requiring each other.

What can be done? There is only one answer: a graduate school or institute of psychology that provides a well-rounded education: anatomy, physiology, and neurology; scientific method and statistics; general psychology and all its special branches (psychophysics, animal, child, social, etc.); clinical psychology and psychoanalysis; sociology and anthropology; psychology of culture (science, art, religion). Considering the present narrow education of psychologists, their lack of practice in the fundamental sciences, their isolation and inexperience in human problems, does it not seem probable that the physiologists from one side and the psychoanalysts from the other, by making the fundamental discoveries, will steal their show, leaving them to hold the bag—a grab bag of temporizing shotgun tests and questionnaires and correlation coefficients? The whole man is the psychologist's concern, and to think and talk and write about him, we must observe him in the field, in the clinic, and in the laboratory. A graduate school, therefore, should provide facilities for observation: orphan asylum, nursery school, behavior clinic, feeble-minded home, psychological and psychopathic consultation rooms, experimental laboratories, and so forth. This is a realizable dream. Men with ideas and methods are available. Only the Great Philanthropist is wanting.

But for the present, in this epoch of disunion, awaiting a new constitution, what should psychologists do about psychoanalysis? The question brings me home to the stimulus of this paper with the hope that you, having watched one man weigh out psychoanalysis in his balance—withholding nothing, measuring out deserts as justly (though not as mercifully) as he could—will be better prepared to answer the question for yourself. You could not have failed to note—and so allow for—the temperamental bias that counted in the weighing; and you will judge, no doubt, that I am trusting, perhaps overmuch, that some personologists, too realistic to be undermined by the severity of my criticisms, will see a clear path to psychoanalysis. You will guess, furthermore, that I am ready to suggest to a personologist who is seriously interested in human nature that he read as much psychoanalysis as possible, picking his way through the best authors with discrimination. To be psychoanalyzed is, in my opinion, not a requisite for all, but highly desirable for most. If you can afford it, pick a trained analyst whom you respect, and enter into the experience humbly and without reserve, prepared to render up the whole confused welter of your being. You need not be ashamed or proud. You are only a little bit responsible for what you are. And when you come to weave what you have learnt into the structure of psychologic theory and deliver lectures, do not water down the facts, palliate, and equivocate. Science cannot grow by subterfuges.

Some hope, I should say, can be placed in young men who are trained in both psychology and psychoanalysis, men who are fit to undertake the task of adapting the two schemes to each other. Thus eventually the best of psychoanalysis will be at the university, where it belongs. I favor psychoanalysis chiefly because I think it furnishes—despite its logical fallacies and omissions—the best cornerstone for the future development of psychology. It is vital, basic, raw; chiefly concerned with the psychic manifestations of the body and its requirements. From it you can build up, and eventually reach the problems that are studied and argued out in universities. Psychoanalysis is a balance, an almost necessary antidote, to academic personology.

Americans have fashioned a cosmetic culture, in which a pleasing appearance at quick contacts is the thing that counts. It pays—so we are told—to be washed, shaved, manicured, deodorized, tailored (cleanliness is next to godliness), and to smile, smile, smile (agreeableness is next to cleanliness). It is the day of *Life, Click, Look,* and *Peek,* of instantaneous effects, candid photography, voyeurism and exhibitionism. A successful personality can be bought (and paid for). The camera makes the man. If you want to be President, there are agencies ready to take your picture milking Bossy and kissing chubby children, to plan your campaign and write sure-fire speeches that will please everyone (and no one). (What if the Gettysburg Address had been put together on Broadway?) Our civilization is skin-deep, and the best epidermis triumphs. This is all part and parcel of the race for goods, comfort, and social recognition. It is the ideology of big business, now well established in our universities: productivity *en masse,* the mechanical advance of mediocracy. The wheels turn and psychology is caught up: it takes its place on the assembly line. Move on there! This is no place for rumination! Get busy with the calculator and hand in your results! Who is not familiar with this treadmill? and with the deadening consequences of it? Superficiality is the great sin of American personology. It suits the tempo of the times; it suits industry and commerce; it suits our interest in appearances; it suits our boyish optimism. And it suits the good heart of America, its Rotarian solidarity, its will to agree, since it is easier to agree about the surface than about the depths. Perhaps there are no depths. Who knows? There *are no* depths. Since truth is a congenial fiction, and *this* fiction is most congenial, *this* is truth. It is no mute thing that the inventor of behaviorism found his destiny in the advertising business.

In contrast to all this shallowness, there is psychoanalysis, offering its corrective way; and for what it can do here, if for no other reason, I trumpet out its virtues.

13

VICISSITUDES OF CREATIVITY

The word "vicissitudes" was the wanton response to a stressful situation occasioned by a long-distance telephone call demanding the immediate deliverance of a title for the talk I was to give five months later. Why vicissitudes? I thought, as I hung up the receiver. I discovered that in my head "vicissitudes" meant fortunes and misfortunes with a very heavy accent on misfortunes, and that on the telephone it had meant "What a *misfortune* to be pressed to create a title in a few seconds!"

Since "vicissitudes" was already on its way to public print, it necessarily became an irrevocable ruling member of my household, a ruler, however, who never succeeded in carrying out his functions. On the one hand, he was unable to curb the flow of errant ideas and, on the other, he failed to kindle any enthusiasm for what he meant to me—*misfortunes* of creativity. Our world, I thought, is soaking in misfortunes; must we number creativity among them?

It was the big *Oxford English Dictionary* which, at long last, shifted the acid-base equilibrium of my cortex by permitting a reversal of the initial meaning of the title, and giving me instead: "the *fortunate* change of creativity."

I mention this to illustrate a long-known, fundamental characteristic of the creative process, namely, that it is autonomous and rebellious far more often than it is submissive to the conscious will. To be imperatively directed by another person or by oneself to invent something fresh and valuable that is pertinent to a fixed topic may be enough to paralyze or half paralyze this process, or, if not this, to cause it to run away on some other course like a scared doe or defiant child. Furthermore—and this is another of its widely acknowledged characteristics—the creative process never flies like an arrow or a bullet to a target, but proceeds toward an unknown destination by countless digressions and irrelevancies, decompositions and altered recompositions, many of which take place outside the reach of consciousness during periods of incubation. Consequently, the creative process takes time, its own time, maybe a lifetime, and very often death arrives before the fulfillment of its hope.

Obviously, I am giving the word "creative"—at least for the time

From H.H. Anderson, Ed., *Creativity and Its Cultivation.* New York: Harper & Brothers, 1959, pp. 96–118.

being—a broad meaning, broad enough to include certain happenings in my own head as well as in the head of each and every one. But here the grievous fact I am confessing is that during the last season, before this essay was due, these processes failed to work for me on schedule, and left me a few days before deadline with a book of roving cerebrations without boundaries instead of a capsule of neatly articulated sentences. As a consequence of the defection of these energies, in the very act of writing about the fortunes of creativity I shall be illustrating one of its misfortunes, and thereby do justice to both faces of "vicissitudes."

Although Whitehead would have no truck with the dictum that necessity is the mother of invention, it happened, in this instance, that out of the womb of my embarrassing necessity there emerged a plan which seemed to have a higher probability than any orthodox procedure. The plan is to communicate the substance of the first paragraphs of each of the early chapters of this renegade book and let every reader finish it in any way *his* creativities dictate.

TITLE: THE FORTUNATE CHANGE OF CREATIVITY

Preface

What fortunate change? Well, the recent fortunate change in the direction of creativities in the heads of social scientists, manifested first in their turning to creative processes in human nature as foci for systematic studies, and second in their turning to the generation of concepts and propositions adequate to the formulation of processes of this class as foci for their thoughts.

We are through—or should be through—with the analysis of everything into its elementary components without subsequent synthesis. Behind us are the various tried forms of elementalism and reductionism, endeavors to explain human transactions largely in terms of discrete sensations, of conditioned reflexes, of traits, of infantile complexes, or in physiological or animal-learning terms. Gestalt psychology, first applied to perceptual events, and organismic psychology, derived from the observation of biological phenomena, have been expanded and elaborated, in conjunction with field theory, to correct the deficiencies of elementalism, and today we have systems theory and propositions pertaining to the continuation and restoration of the steady state of systems. Ahead of those who are game for it lies the inviting possibility of explaining irreversible formations and transformations—compositions and decompositions—of systems and subsystems.

The high positive cathexis which the word "creativity" has been acquiring in diverse spheres of activity, as Boring (1950) noted, the multiplicity of scientific investigations of this phenomenon, recently completed or now in progress in this country—the studies, for example, of Barron (1955, 1958), Guilford (1950, 1956a, 1957b), Roe (1946, 1953b), Rogers (1953b), Meer and Stein (1955), Stein (1958), Wilson (1958), Wilson, Guilford, *et al.* (1954), and others too numerous to be mentioned here—the many well-attended conferences and symposia on this subject —such as the Ohio Conference in 1953 (Barkan and Mooney, 1953) and these Michigan State University Symposia—which have been held within the last few years and not earlier—these, it seems to me, are evidences of the incipience of a change, mutation, or vicissitude in the evolution of the human spirit which is in league with the possibility of a better world. It marks, as I view it, a little vital turning point, initiated as always by a statistically insignificant minority, which, if our species is vouchsafed a future, will be apperceived in retrospect as a movement of historic import.

Since we are living in an era when even the slightest sign of presumption or dogmatism is obnoxious, I am prompted at the outset to acknowledge much ignorance of the subject matter of this symposium. Although I have conscientiously attended to it for thirty years—as it occurs in lower organisms, in literature, in science, and in interpersonal relations—I have no statistical findings to report, and most of what I have to say is either self-evident, well known, speculative, or hypothetical. But if presumption and authoritarianism are the Scylla of our time, the Charybdis is intellectual timidity—hemming and hedging, surrounding every cautious forward step one takes with an array of qualifications and apologies as well as a smokescreen of jokes and banter. I shall try to steer a course between these two: the hybris of Scylla and the cowardice of Charybdis.

Chapter 1. Definition of Creation

The word "creation" usually points either to a compositional *process* which results in something new, or to the *resultant* of this process, a new composition, regardless of its value, destiny, or consequences. But, in conformity with the accepted orientation of these Symposia, "creation," in many contexts of the present discourse, will refer to *the occurrence of a composition which is both new and valuable.* "New" will mean that the entity is marked by more than a certain degree of novelty, or originality, relative to sameness, or replication; and "valuable" will mean *either* intrinsically or extrinsically valuable *as such* to one or more persons, or generative of valuable compositions in the future (whether or not it is valuable as such). To suit the purposes of research, these very general statements must be reduced to more concrete operational terms by the definition of suitable criteria of novelty and of value, the construction of scales based on these criteria, the selection of cutting points, and, finally, statements respecting the statuses, degrees of pertinent knowledge, dispositions, and abilities of the judges. The last, because a necessary, integral part of the definition of an evaluated entity is a sufficient characterization of its evaluators.

As a rule, psychologists who decide to investigate creative processes or the personalities of creative persons will choose a panel of acknowledged experts (if there are any in the given field of activity) to serve as judges, eliminate the sources of compositions about which the judges disagree, and select for study those whose works are placed above the arbitrarily selected cutting point. But in doing this, psychologists are or should be fully aware of the high probability that some subjects who have been ranked below the set level will at some future date be accorded a high status and vice versa.

Up to quite recent times it was customary to think of creativity as something wholly mysterious and miraculous, an epiphenomenal power that in a few rare geniuses was "added on" to the normal aggregate of human potentialities. Indeed, it was not until the late eighteenth century that the word creation could be applied without irreverence to anything but the works of God. Following Plato and Aristotle, dramatists and poets had been regarded as imitators or reflectors whose function it was to hold a mirror up to nature or, if not this, to serve as mouthpieces of the gods, of the moral order, or of the one God of Christianity. And even after it became permissible to speak of the "creations" of romantic poets, the word was rarely free of overtones suggestive of divine gifts or powers. Coleridge's self-image in *Xanadu* is a peculiarly fine example of this then-current apperception:

> And all should cry, Beware! Beware!
> His flashing eyes, his floating hair!
> Weave a circle round him thrice,
> And close your eyes in holy dread,
> For he on honey-dew hath fed,
> And drunk the milk of Paradise.

Today, however, the referents of this imagery (leaving opium aside) have been turned outside in: the creative endowments and powers that were formerly attributed to one transcendent, celestial Person and Place outside the order of nature are now known to be immanent in nature, especially in human nature, to constitute, in fact, one of the givens at the hidden, unconscious "core" of nature. And instead of creativity being considered a very rare capacity in man, many of us acknowledge that it is manifested in some way and to some extent by almost everybody.

In stating this proposition, I have, of course, been influenced by Whitehead, who, as you know, adumbrated a theoretical system of systems in which creativity is a metaphysical ultimate. His conception is that of a procession of overlapping and interdependent events, or *actual concrete occasions,* in space-time. Each concrete occasion is a temporally bounded concrescence (organization, composition) of prehensions (appropriating or vectorial processes), the duration of each occasion being the time required for the composition of the prehended elements into a single unit. A fine microanalysis would yield a sequence of occasions, or actual entities, each of which—with a duration, say, of a fraction of a second—would perish at the instant of its composition and be immediately succeeded by another actual occasion. A grosser macroanalysis would take a whole act, or endeavor, as the "really real thing" (Whitehead), the direction and quality of which has imposed itself on its constituent parts.

The moving picture, here, is that of a sequence of discrete corpuscles of actuality, bound together, as it were, by a vectorial force or continuity of aim. Translated to the mind, this would be illustrated by the composition of an image which is immediately decomposed, only to be followed by the composition of another image, or with the formation of a word which dies as another word succeeds it, and so forth. Our senses being less acute than certain delicate instruments, we are scarcely aware of these individual "drops" of mental life and are more prone to choose metaphors of fluid continuity, such as the "stream" of consciousness or the "flow" of thought. One might say that a "wave theory" is closer to our immediate experience than a "corpuscular theory." The latter, however, may prove more serviceable in the end.

Now, according to Whitehead, every actual concrescence is unique in some respects, and hence, strictly speaking, a creation, since an infinitesimal variation is sufficient to justify the adjective "unique." Thus the actual world is said to have the character of a temporal passage into novelty. If we accept this, then every coherent series of actual occasions, short or long—a sentence, a paragraph, a ten-minute conversation, or a ten-year correspondence between two people—is even more of a creation, since each of these is a unique temporal integration of unique components, a creation of creations. Personally, I am content with this, but would prefer—at least for the duration of this discourse—to substitute "composition" for "creation," and reserve the latter term for valuable compositions with a high degree of novelty relative to sameness.

I have taken time to present this short, rough approximation of Whitehead's conception of actual occurrences in order to remind you that one of the most enlightened geniuses living at the time of the great metamorphosis of basic science was committed to the notion that creativity is of the very essence of reality.

One more comment: the word "create" will not be used as a synonym of "incite" or "cause." It will certainly not refer to a process which terminates in a state of greater disunion than previously existed. It might be said that somebody "created a disturbance," "created havoc," etc., but this has the exact opposite meaning. Although *decomposition* is, for us, a necessary variable, since it quite regularly precedes the process of creation, the two words are antonyms, like anabolism and katabolism, not synonyms. Living as we do in an era when the release of every spontaneous impulse in childhood and in adolescence is often correlated with creativity, it is sometimes difficult to distinguish these opposites, to tell the difference between a lot of noise and a symphonic composition, between excretion and secretion.

Won't you carry on from here?

Chapter 2. Basic Requirements, Levels, and Chronology of Creation

As basic requirements of creation at all levels I would propose the following: a *sufficient concentration* within a given region of *different mobile or motile entities* with *mutual affinity,* entities which have *never been combined.* Then, as a fifth requirement, *sufficient circulation* of these entities, which means a *sufficient source of energy.* Finally, there must be the possibility of *favorable conditions for combination.* Granted these seven factors, the *mutual attraction, approximation,* and *association* of two or more entities—in other words, *creation*—is certain to occur.

And here is where *chance* comes in. I say "chance" because it is not ordinarily possible to predict precisely which heretofore uncombined entities will come within each other's sphere of influence at precisely what place and what instant, and—at *that* particular point in space-time —what conditions favorable or unfavorable, will prevail.

Numerous other special factors are, of course, involved at each conventional level of scientific analysis and formulation—physical, chemical, biological, psychological, sociological, culturological—but I believe that the ones which I have named can be illustrated by analogies at all levels.

If we look back in time as far as the astronomers' fairy tales will carry us—after the hypothetical Big Bang which sent the matter in the universe flying in all directions—we come upon the simplest variety of creative energy—mutual attraction, or gravitational force—starting its big job of forming thousands of stellar constellations of which our solar system is but one late product. According to the terminology I am using, the great dispersion of matter subsequent to the Big Bang would be an example of *decomposition* of an existing state, the persistence of which momentum accounts for the apparent expansion of the universe. Hesiod, as quoted in Plato's *Symposium,* pictured it in somewhat different terms. He said: first Chaos came (that is to say, the Big Bang), then Love (that is to say, the force of gravitation) and with it the broad-bosomed Earth (that is to say, the maternal environment for further creativities).

Now, if we give ear to the speculations of those most deserving of our ear, some two million years ago the watery surface of this broad-bosomed earth provided favorable conditions for the circulation, mutual attraction, and combination of chemical substances at successive levels of complexity, each of which was a heretofore unexampled configuration of matter with an unexampled set of properties. There are now a few plausible hypotheses and even some experimental evidence relative to the composition of the simplest organic compounds leading up to the creation of macroproteins—similar in some respects to viruses and genes. Later, we may surmise, the most rudimentary forms of metabolic life came into being, marked by recurrent compositions, decompositions, recompositions. Then, supposedly, unicellular organisms made their debut, followed in due course by multicellular organisms, their developments being initiated by countless new genetic combinations and mutations. Finally, as consequence of new, genetically derived properties and capacities, we can imagine societies of higher organisms evolving down the centuries until the arrival of our own species—families and clans of primordial men and women. The emergence of human morphology is correlated, we now believe, with the emergence of the capacity to form concepts, to verbalize and compose a language, to envisage future possibilities, and, in view of these, to plan cooperative endeavors. Here then was the incipience of the human imagination: the potentiality for insanity, on the one hand, and, on the other, potentialities for the composition of myths, religions, philosophies, effective forms of government, works of art, scientific theories, *et cet.*

Although this is "old hat" to everyone, I have given my hop, skip, and jump version of the evolutionary fable first of all to illustrate in a rough way creativity everywhere *immanent* in nature at different *levels* and to suggest in this connection that chemistry and genetics provide better models than physics has to offer for students of consequential compositions. Secondly, it seemed advisable to emphasize the chronology of creation, the fact that it proceeds in a slow stepwise fashion—usually from the smaller and simpler to the larger and more complex—that A must occur before B is possible, and B before C, and C before D; and that it may take a million years, a thousand years, a hundred years of trials and mistakes and eventually of surviving transformations before C becomes D. For example, before American democracy was constituted, numerous pilot experiments had been undertaken, such as the city-states of Greece, including Aristotle's commentary, and finally certain creative processes in the mind of Locke and in the mind of Rousseau had to reach completion and be published. Also, let us note that not yet —although spurred to the endeavor by centuries of senseless persecutions, animosity, and slaughter—have the creative processes in any head arrived at a form of world government or form of world religion which is sufficiently inviting and persuasive to triumph over the egotisms and prides of individual nations and religions.

Thirdly, I wanted to point out that although what Darwin called "accidental variations" are dependent on chance encounters among different genes, the crucial determinant is something else, namely the inherent capacity of genes—as well as of numberless other entities—to participate in the composition of new and valued generating entities. And so, as I pointed out earlier, when we study creative processes we are focusing not on some sort of epiphenomenon that occurs only in the minds of a few "born" geniuses, but on processes that carry on, like coral insects, secretly and unobtrusively on all levels.

Fourthly, I thought that the story of evolution would serve as preparation for my avowal that the metabolic cycle of anabolism-katabolism or composition-decomposition is the theme song or model of most of the thought-stuff I am offering. Katabolic processes in every cell of the body are the homefires at the "core" of animal nature which provide the necessary energy for anabolic growth and other functions, and it can be said that all the covert and overt activities that comprise the total nutritional cycle of intakes and outputs are devoted, directly or indirectly, to keeping these millions of cellular homefires burning. Viewed in relation to the covert physiological and biochemical sequences of the nutritional cycle, the overt sequences—the food-acquiring activities of the organism, which are the most real of real things to the animal psychologist —are relatively superficial and constitute but one of several different temporally bound functions involved in the transposition of nutritive substances from the external environment to the interior of each cell. Food in the mouth—which terminates the span of concern of most animal psychologists—is of no benefit to the animal *per se:* it is simply the first of a succession of reinforcements, or achievements, which are required before the incorporated stuff can fulfill its destined role. The point I am making here is that most of the behavior which we, as positivists, are expected to observe consists of movements in space—either translocations of the motile organism itself or transpositions of objects by the organism—and these perceptible movements are all basically dependent on events that are not perceptible directly, namely, the compositions and decompositions that occur when entities reach their destination. In short, I am arguing for a deeper and more valid realism than that of the devout behaviorist who believes that the external things about which there is least disagreement among observers constitute the best basis for the construction of a theoretical system.

But now to return to my elected model for central processes on all levels, the metabolic cycle of anabolism-katabolism. The details are, of course, far too complicated to be mentioned here. For present purposes, all I need is a rough definition of three relationships: *one,* when anabolism exceeds katabolism, as it does at the moment of conception and during the entire period of growth; *two,* when anabolism and katabolism are about equal, as they are during the more or less homeostatic period of maturity; and *three,* when katabolism exceeds anabolism, as it does near and after the end of life. Generalizing this, and adding another factor in order to include parallel phenomena on other levels, societal and cultural, the *first* relationship will be called the phase of *composition* or creation; the *second*, the phase of *recomposition* or conservation; and the *third*, the phase of *decomposition* or destruction. Different kinds of composition and of decomposition should be distinguished, and it should be noted that biological senesence leading on to death—as well as senescence of other sorts—is chiefly characterized not by decomposition, but by *induration* (that is, hardening or fixation) of structure, typical of the last part of the conserving phase. But, after making important distinctions of this sort as well as the necessary modifications at each level, system of systems theory, so far as I can see, is capable of formulating these phases in an illuminating and experimentally fruitful manner.

Here you may be reminded of the ancient Hindu trinity of Brahma, the creator, Vishnu, the conservator, and Siva, the destroyer. Personally, I am all in favor of this mode of speech. It makes me think of a statement of a famous physiologist to the effect that when the physiologist, the psychologist, and the poet begin to talk corresponding languages we shall be on our way to a genuine understanding of human nature. Since some of us enthusiasts for system of systems theory are so ready to go down to physics for our analogies, why should we not cover the whole scale and occasionally reach up to a suitable mythology?

Would you like to carry on from here?

Chapter 3. Creation at the Mental Level

This, I take it, is the topic of these Symposia—new, valuable mental compositions, whether they are imaginations of better mechanical designs, better scientific theories, better governmental legislation, better or variant forms of art, better or variant systems of personality, or better or variant patterns of interpersonal relations.

As always, we have to consider the requirements, levels, and chronology of creation, and here with attention to features special to the mind. For example, among the requirements, as I said above, is a *sufficient concentration of relevant combinable entities* never previously combined. These are both inside the mind (*representors* in the preconscious and in the unconscious), and outside the mind (objects and events to be observed in the environment as well as products of the mental processes of other people, spoken or written). That is to say, a person must have a great fund of pertinent images and imagents (imagined events), concepts and postulates acquired over the years. In this case, as you know, these are not free to move hither and thither like chemicals dissolved in a homogeneous fluid, but are located in differentiated and bounded mental places. And this brings me to the next requirement, *circulation of the heretofore uncombined entities*, because if the entities acquired in the past remain in the places where they first settled—as they often do in the rigid minds of walking encyclopedias of written knowledge—novel combinations will be less probable. To get heretofore uncombined entities within each other's sphere of influence there must be, first of all, a good deal of more or less passionate *psychic energy,* occasionally approaching hypomania—what Socrates called "divine madness"—to stir things up. Then, there must be sufficient *permeability* (flexibility) of boundaries, boundaries between categories as well as boundaries between different spheres of interest and—most important for certain classes of creation—sufficient permeability of the boundary between conscious and unconscious psychic processes. Here I am thinking of a kind of playful, happily irresponsible, or drunken state of mind. Too much permeability is insanity, too little is ultraconventional rationality. A third and overlapping factor is represented by Siva—destruction preliminary to creation: there must be periodic, if not almost incessant, decompositions—de-differentiations and disintegrations—of what has already been composed—composed in the minds of others but *more especially* in our own minds. A person must have a certain gust for temporary chaos.

The next requirement is too complicated to be summarized here, namely *favorable conditions for combination,* inside and outside the mind—freedom from impertinent intrusions, for example. It is here, largely, that *chance* plays the role of fate. Pasteur spoke of "chance and the prepared mind," Charles Pierce of "chance, love, and logic," Darwin of "accident." It is the wonder of a rare event: two heretofore unconnected entities come together in space-time at just the moment when the psyche is prepared to appreciate the significance of that particular combination. It is a perfectly natural event, but if we insist that our laws of nature are necessarily statistical, then this event is necessarily illegal.

At the mental level there are a number of other variables to be considered, most of which might well be classified as components, or intrinsic determinants, of the total creative enterprise. My own practice has been to point to these with symbols of two, three, or four letters (as in chemistry), which can be semantically combined in any number of ways with their relative potencies expressed as ratios. For example, *Go* is the above-mentioned basic, explosive energy factor which circulates the entities, *Co* is the combinational process and its energy (Brahma), *Va* is the evaluating process, together with the standards and cutting points employed (the scientific, aesthetic, moral, or strategic superego); and, usually in its service though sometimes autonomous, are *Ca,* the disposition to incorporate whatever comes to mind or whatever is seen or read, and *Na,* the disposition to reject and exclude entities which are superfluous, irrelevant, indigestible, or obnoxious. *Ra* is the retaining and recomposing process (Vishnu) which conserves and continues the better compositions. *Ru* is the analyzing, decomposing, and eliminating process (Siva) which reduces entities to their elements preparatory to a new synthetic trial, or which ruthlessly deletes previously incorporated elements. *Se* is the disposition, prompted largely by insatiable curiosity, to search either within or without the mind (in the service of *Ca*) for suitable entities to be incorporated and then to be properly placed, or categorized, in mental space by *Ro,* the process of allocating things and thereby putting the intellect in order. *Se* and *Ca,* I should say, are almost invariably combined with *Nev,* the relish for novelty, since without novelty there can be no creation.

A number of other variables require definition; but space is short, and I shall stop after mentioning one more, the target of the whole endeavor, *Hola,* which is usually an indefinite mental vision—a vague hypothesis, idea, plot of a play, conception of a way of life—which must be made definite, worked out in detail, decomposed, corrected, and reintegrated, tried and validated, represented in words or in music, or enacted in real life. *Hola* is either of this character or in the nature of a question or problem for which there is no accepted answer or solution. In any case, one of the distinguishing marks of a culturally creative person is the presence of a strong *RaHola,* that is, a continuing hopeful commitment and allegiance to a selected aim. Once, when Freud was reminded that almost all of his ideas—the idea of unconscious processes, for instance—could be found in the works of earlier authors, he answered with his usual delicious wit: "Ah, yes. But those were mere flirtations. Mine was a responsible marriage." So much for some of the major requirements and intrinsic determinants of creation at the mental level.

In some of all this, the ego, the "I" of consciousness, feels subjectively as if its role were quite important. And yet it knows full well that its power to produce the basic psychic energy of *Go* is practically nil and its influence on the compositional processes of *Co* is very slight. And now, I should like to explain that a sentence I composed at the very start of this essay—"How misfortunate to be pressed to create a title in a few seconds"—was a meaningless *façon de parler* forced on me by an acquired semantic habit which, as Whorf (1956) has indicated, makes one feel that a verb requires some noun in front of it. If there is an act, must there not be an actor, obvious or concealed? Do not the words "create a title" cry out for the designation of the agent? But if two entities—two chemicals, two people, two ideals—with mutual affinity unite for the first time in known history and remain united, can we point to a creator of this unequivocal creation? I think not. What we have here are two *participants* in a creative process, both of which are about equally responsible for, and equally necessary to, the unique outcome. In short, as I see it, the psyche is a *region* where creations may or may not flourish, and if two people are involved, there are two regions and their intercommunicating processes to be considered. The powers of the self-conscious *I* (in the language of William James)—*I* the activator, *I* the knower, *I* the judge—are definitely limited. At best, its role is to *preside* over an interior transaction which may or may not come out with something that is worth seizing. The "I" can never command or force a veritable creation. If it were capable of this, all the world's problems could be solved as fast as thought by those who had sufficient knowledge; and any number of effective policies, valid theories, comedies, and symphonies could be manufactured to order and time.

Sudden and spectacular creations, like dreams and visions, often seem to come from without rather than from within the mind, which in some measure accounts for the fact that in the past they were invariably attributed to gods or devils. Better to treat them in this way, it seems to me, than to look down on them from an inflated scientific superego. Constantly at work in our minds, these energies, like the divinities of mythology, are beyond our jurisdiction, respond, when ready, only to our supplications, and are responsible for the greatest wonders. Why should we not honor them?

Would you like to carry on from here?

Chapter 4. Dyadic Creations

Otto Rank (1932), whose mind was a hive of generative ideas, prophesied that a "new type of humanity" would become possible when men with creative power could "give up artistic expression in favor of the formation of personality" and in return for this renunciation they would enjoy a "greater happiness." This philosophy is already flourishing in our midst, with one of the contributors to these Symposia, Abraham Maslow, as its most ardent and devoted advocate.

I take it for granted that those readers who have met Professor Maslow's persuasive presentation would prefer not to peruse some futile attempt on my part to paint his lily; and so I have decided to say a few words about dyadic, rather than monadic, creativity. This means that we shall be dealing with two interdependent regions of imagination operating as a single system. Also, both members of the dyad will be endeavoring to translate their imaginations into actual overt reciprocations and collaborations. It will be like two people singing a duet and making up the music as they go along.

In this type of creation, the basic entities to be composed into a mutually enjoyable and beneficent concatenation of activities will consist of potentially complementary or cooperative dispositions and capacities. Successful complementations can be partially formulated in terms of different sorts of zestful and capable transmissions resulting in appreciative receptions. The person who functions as the transmittor in one proceeding may function as the receptor in the next, in which case one may speak of reciprocation, or reversal of complementations. There are numerous different classes and modes of functional transmission, such as transmission of affection, of gifts, of information, of suggestions for action, and so forth. If one person repeatedly fulfills the same transmissive function, he or she may be designated by a suitable name: donor, stimulator, narrator, interpreter, orientor (of talk or movement), critic, entertainer, etc. Such face-to-face interactions, where the aim is mutual stimulation and enjoyment, are often hardly distinguishable from cooperations. These occur when both members of the dyad, together or separately, endeavor to achieve a common aim or, through division of labor, to accomplish a different part of some required task. So much as an outline of one possible mode of grossly formulating dyads.

Now, when we study creations in other fields—say in science or in art—we choose as subjects talented people whose vocational goals are superordinate; and so here, if we want to obtain comparable intensities of dedication *(GoHola),* we would be well advised to select man-woman erotic dyads, in or out of marriage. As Shakespeare said: "Love's a mighty Lord, and to his Service, no such joy on earth." Today a marriage is more likely to be superordinate than a friendship. Furthermore, the sexual instinct, we now realize, is involved in many of the greatest accomplishments of the imagination. As Nietzsche—originator of the concept of sublimation—pointed out, "the degree and quality of man's sexuality" may "reach up to the utmost pinnacle of his mind" (Morgan, 1941). But, he explained, as the urge "becomes more intellectual it gets a new name, a new charm and new evaluation." In short, if we include the sexual instinct, we shall be dealing with whole personalities whose "depths" will be engaged in the dyadic enterprise, and, consequently, there will be less chance of getting caught in that "booby trap" of American psychology, *superficiality.*

Over the last few years a few of us at the Harvard Psychological Clinic have been engaged in intensive studies of short stressful dyadic discussions as recorded by a moving picture camera with sound track and, as you might expect, have found marked differences, both in degrees of achievement relative to the assigned task and in the smoothness and deftness with which each participant deals with the competing alter. In a trying situation, a few subjects are capable both of getting along with their rival and of getting ahead with the job. I have been calling this capacity *impromptu short-span strategic creativity.* Although there are no figures to support me as yet, I have gained a strong impression that those who exhibit this kind of ability do occasionally, but more often do not, possess potentialities for "deeper," more significant, and lasting creativities. Some of them might be described as "slick operators" with cool heads who have substituted craft for the ideal and who, by means of an artificial smile and a few cute maneuvers that evade all touchy issues, succeed in arriving at genial pseudo agreements before the other person is fully aware of what has happened. The point I am aiming at is that we psychologists can disqualify ourselves as fruitful investigators of dyadic creativity if we take repeatedly pseudo-harmonious interactions as our chief criterion for the evaluation of creativities in friendship or in marriage.

What is the significance of Riesman's "lonely crowd" if not a lot of friendliness without friendship, a lot of people whose social life is played out on the surface, with no exchanges of nourishing, gutty thoughts or feelings.

Let me illustrate the difference by referring to a particular marriage. It happens that once upon a time I was a psychotherapist of a class not simply labeled—a deviant Freudian, let us say—and among a number of cases in my files there was one that came to mind as made to order for this moment. It was that of a man on the verge of divorce who had fallen in love with a woman in a similar predicament. She had already undergone a psychoanalysis and, as one outcome of her pilgrim's progress through the maze of the unconscious, was determined not to fail another time but to make a *real thing* out of her marriage with my patient. Since, in due course, a reciprocal resolve took stout root in the man's psyche, the situation was that of two ardent lovers—hereafter to be known as Adam and Eve—both of them coming out of a dead marriage and both of them already in possession of a working version of creativity and prepared to give it leeway.

Already we know enough to suggest the operation of a compound determinant of creativity which might be compacted into three words: vision, passion, and the superordination of the vision. Passion is the emotional energy factor *(Go)* in a dyadic form. The superordinate vision is the *Hola* factor with the addition of a cognitive component, namely, some previous knowledge, gained from psychoanalysis, of modes of creative transformation. Without extraordinary love neither Eve nor Adam would have felt impelled to attach enough energy to this goal, and, without the vision of creativity, both lovers, Adam with his romantic images and projections and Eve with hers—like Tristan and Isolde after partaking of the magic passion potion—might well have felt that a perfect union had already been fatefully created and that they were on a wave of the future that would never let them down.

Another possible predeterminant was the existence of an unhealed narcissistic wound in each of them occasioned by the failure of a previous attempt at marriage. It brings to mind that pair in Eden and the basic mythic theme of the Fortunate Fall, about which Weisinger (1953) has written with such distinction. By contemporary standards it was cruel of Jehovah to deny Adam and Eve a second chance after their failure to keep the rules of Paradise. Presumably, they had learned a searing moral lesson and thereafter, in the fear of God, might well have proved invariably obedient denizens of that region. But this is no moment to deplore primordial injustices. Our present focus is a new Adam and a new Eve, both of whom were happily granted a second chance.

Although they moved to another place as a happier station for their conjoined life, Adam was now and again prompted to return to Cambridge, avowedly to consult me about the vicissitudes of his marriage. Actually, the greater part of our time together was spent in my listening to his account of a to-me unique dyadic enterprise, and so, thanks to his zest for communication, I was enabled to keep abreast of the progress of this relationship and recently, with Adam's collaboration, to attempt a few tentative formulations. But since space is running short, I shall mention but one more major determinant—the lively circulation and expression of combinable entities—which, in my opinion, was the outstanding feature of Adam's and Eve's mode of dyadic creativity. I offer it as the exact opposite of the ideal of invariably courteous and hence necessarily superficial interactions.

By unappreciable transitions—Adam cannot remember any originating incident—he and Eve found themselves engaged now and again in unpremeditated, serious yet playful, dramatic outbursts of feeling, wild imagination, and vehement interaction, in which one of them— sometimes Adam, sometimes Eve—gave vent to whatever was pressing for expression. Walpurgis was the name they gave to episodes of this insurgent nature. Usually it was Eros that supplied the energy, with some sort of intoxicant—which they called Soma after the Hindu Dionysus— liquidating the boundary of consciousness. But besides Eros, there were compelling needs for dominance, clamoring egotisms and assertions of omniscience, anger and resentment, not to speak of feelings of helplessness and inferiority, complemented by nurturance and encouragement. And so—layer after layer, one might say—each of these two psyches, through numberless repetitions, discharged its residual as well as its emergent and beneficent dispositions, until nearly every form of sexuality and nearly every possible complementation of dyadic roles had been dramatically enacted. All this within the frame of their conception of the necessary digressions and progressive spiralings of the creative process, and all within the compass of an ever-mounting trust in the solidarity of their love, evidenced in the Walpurgis episodes by an apparently limitless mutual tolerance of novelty and emotional extravagance.

Adam admits that faith in the virtue of those unruly hours came largely from psychoanalysis, although, of course, their dyadic form was not an asymmetrical verbal relationship with a lenient father or mother figure but a symmetrical acting-out with both of them wholly engaged on all levels. Although they knew nothing of psychodrama, Moreno's conceptions, it seems to me, provide a better model than psychoanalysis, particularly in view of Adam's insistence that neither he nor Eve ever checked or diminished the gustful process of eruption and expression by attributing its genesis to some banal infantile impulsion. Of course, Walpurgis, for them, was more real, more urgent, than psychodrama, although only very rarely was it carried to the wounding point, and then always immediately shut off and the wound healed. Just recently—recollecting in tranquility these past ecstasies and their consequences—Adam emphasized several benefits which I shall summarize in my own words: one, the exultant catharsis of conventionally forbidden needs—such as most of us experience only empathically and vicariously in witnessing a drama (as Aristotle explained); two, the eventual riddance from one's personality of unwanted states and urges; three, the incorporation of new and joyous modes of interaction which might otherwise have been excluded; four, the expansion and deepening of an intimate experiential consciousness of self, of alter, and of self and alter as a system, and hence a greater increment of wisdom than a psychoanalysis can provide; and, finally, five, the ultimate demise of all pressures to put forth in social life the irrationalities of infancy and adolescence.

To balance the wildness of all this, one last determinant should be listed, namely an above-normal capacity to evaluate with fine discrimination—in terms of some enlightened standard *(Va)*—the worth and relevance of what has been brought forth, coupled with the disposition to reject *(Na)* what is unacceptable in those scales and to accept and incorporate *(Ca)* whatever is fitting and propitious.

The hypothesis that is suggested by the history of this particular dyad is that periodic complete emotional expression within the compass of an envisaged creative enterprise—not unlike the orgiastic Dionysian rites of early Greek religion in which all participated—is a highly enjoyable and effective manner of eliminating maleficent (socially harmful, deviant, criminal, neurotic, and psychotic) tendencies as well as of bringing into play beneficent modes of thought and action which might otherwise have been blocked out. In sharp contrast to this is both the traditional Christian doctrine of repression of primitive impulsions and the psychoanalytic notion of the replacement of the id by the ego (rationality), which results so often in a half-gelded, cautious, guarded, conformist, uncreative, and dogmatic way of coping with the world.

Would you carry on from here?

Chapter 5. Central-Superordinate-Cultural Creations

The integrative imaginations which preceded, accompanied, and followed the dyadic activities I have just described could be taken as parts of one variety of central-superordinate-cultural creation, or mythology of life. Creations of this class are called "central" because they spring from central (that is, basic, nuclear, deep, potent) human needs which generate visions or revelations of possible fulfillment and of ways to this fulfillment. They are called "superordinate" because the generated visions are accorded the highest place among the valued aims of an individual or group; and they are called "cultural" because their composition is encouraged by the implicit or explicit hope or certainty that the envisaged aims and ways will eventually be adopted by other people.

I am assuming that the germ of a central-superordinate creation originates in the unconscious of one person or of a few persons, most often out of suffering and estrangement engendered by the existing state of things. If this suffering is shared by other people and the curative vision is engagingly represented in words or enacted in deeds, it will sooner or later be assimilated by a small minority and get started on a long voyage of transmission through many other minds, some of which may have greater creative capacities than the originating one. In any case, over the ensuing years the initial vision is likely to be greatly altered —elaborated, revised, refined, systematized. When fully developed, creations of this class are long-range over-all mythologies, philosophies, or ideologies which consist, for the most part, of representations of sacred objects, better means or better aims, a better society, a better world (here or elsewhere), better states or ways of life, better persons, or better interpersonal relations, as well as of enemies that stand in the path to these desired ends and of ways to be avoided. The emphasis may be on any one of these: reformation or transformation of one's own society, creation of a new society in a new place, conversion or transformation of the world, of other persons, or of the self, to be brought about by God or by concerted human effort. In all events, it is a matter of cardinal importance to all concerned, since a change in any one of these spheres of thought and action affects all others.

Most powerful of this class of creations in the Western world has been the Judeo-Christian religion and second to this, in potency as well as time, has been its virtual antithesis, the mythology of freedom, of rebellion, independence, and self-sufficiency. Since the imagery of Judeo-Christianity is evidently derived from the earliest father-son relations in a conservative patriarchal family, it might be said to belong to the phase of spiritual childhood. The newborn infant, being utterly helpless and ineffective, is wholly dependent on his parents and hence a petitioner for everything that he needs. From the point of view of this lowly, ignorant, impotent, and fallible creature, the father stands forth as the exact opposite: high, omniscient, omnipotent, and infallible. Also, the father is the only male who has a fixed design for the boy's life and whose commandments must be obeyed if he is to deserve the support, guidance, and affection that he then requires as well as the elevated status (as his father's right-hand man) that is conditionally promised him at the end of his period of probation.

In contrast to all this, the imagery of the mythology of freedom is clearly derivable from that period in a boy's life when he has achieved some measure of self-sufficiency and is in a better position to defy successfully the authority of a relatively weaker father. Now, instead of a guarded, bounded homestead, there is unbounded locomotion and exploration; instead of dependence, there is independence; instead of docile submission, there is protest, rebellion, secession, and emancipation;

instead of waiting to be given benefits, there is search, seizure, and appropriation; instead of an even-handed, paternalistic distribution of goods and privileges, there is strenuous, aggressive competition; and instead of dreaming of being lifted to some better world in heaven, there is travel and migration in hopes of finding one on earth. This I shall call the phase of spiritual adolescence.

Under the best conditions in the phase of spiritual childhood—as in the Western thirteenth century, let us say—there is relative homogeneity, unity, order, conservation, and homeostasis on the ideational, cultural level: Vishnu is predominant. But in the phase of spiritual adolescence—reaching its first peak, say, at the time of the French Revolution—everything is different: authority is denied, decomposed, reduced; there may be deicide and regicide, justified by the glorification of uncorrupted human nature, human reason, and the *vox populi*, the fraternal peer group; or there may be greater insistence on freedom of personal thought, speech, and decision, the idealization of individuality, resulting in ever-greater heterogeneity, division, disunity, disorder. The time comes when "the center cannot hold, things fall apart": Siva is predominant. This is the era of egocentrism, competitions of egocentrism, nihilism, and teen-age terrorisms, largely due to the fact that the spiritually adolescent parents have not given their offspring the needed experience and steady discipline of the phase of spiritual childhood at its best. In short, adolescents are not prepared for the responsibilities of individuality and temperate rebellion and in a state of chaos become susceptible to the dictatorial leadership and machinations of a Moloch, who brings them back as physiological adults to a secularized phase of spiritual childhood under the cloud of an inflexible and infallible doctrine.

Today, however, there are evidences, here and there, that people are approaching, with more knowledge and more insight than has been heretofore available, the phase of spiritual manhood and womanhood, the era of Brahma, with its mythology of creativity, fundamentally derived from that period of life when a man and woman participate in the formation of a dyad, of a home, of offspring, and of a new family culture. This spiritual phase, this symbolism, might be exemplified, it seems to me, on all levels: an embracement and reunion of the opposites: man and nature, male and female, conscious and unconscious, superego and id, reason and passion, rational and irrational, science and art, enjoyable means and enjoyable ends, upper class and lower class, West and East. Instead of dependence or independence, we may see fruitful interdependence; instead of passive reception or greedy acquisition of great quantities of things, we may see construction, whenever feasible, of what is necessary and what is aesthetically symbolic; instead of vainly hoping for an impossible world or voyaging in search of one, we may be engaging in more enlightened endeavors to transform the place and the society in which we live; in short, instead of thesis and antithesis, we may achieve synthesis at the center: creation for creation—let us say, *creativism*—rather than creation for a giant suicidal murder. It is in view of this barely possible ideal that I have subtitled this essay: *the fortunate change of creativity.*

I hope you will go on happily from here.

IV

Personology requires a
multidisciplinary approach,
as well as special strategies
and techniques of investigation

*W*hen Murray showed his 1935 paper "Psychology and the University" to his Harvard friends and supporters—although not necessarily his co-believers—Professors Edwin G. Boring and Gordon Allport, they cautioned him that if he published it he would risk the possibility of never attaining tenure at Harvard. Of course, he went ahead, but did not in fact obtain tenure until some thirteen years later when he was fifty-five years old. The paper contains a challenge to the university as well as to psychology and to psychoanalysis; neither side is spared. Murray suggests a study of man—with ties to medicine, neurology, physiology and to anthropology and sociology, including as central, psychotherapeutics; in short, a new curriculum. The sad and amazing fact is that Murray's challenging article is as timely a challenge to the university and to the psychoanalytic community today as it was almost fifty years ago.

Murray's credo for the university (and the place of a meaningful psychology within it) directly touched at least one life. About the time the article was published a young physician at Johns Hopkins was thinking of leaving medicine entirely and, having read this article, went to see Murray and then studied at the Harvard Clinic and received his Ph.D. degree from Murray. He is now—many years later—a prominent psychiatrist and social analyst. Recently he told me that Murray's article had changed his entire life.

Personology is not only a subject matter ("man functioning in his environment"), but it is also, by virtue of that subject matter, a special kind of method. In the festschrift The Study of Lives prepared on the occasion of Murray's seventieth birthday in 1963 by his former students, Robert W. White, the editor of that volume, wrote:

> Murray's conception of personality has required the development of new strategies of investigation. If we are to learn about our subjects' significant thoughts, feelings, and conceptions of themselves, it is necessary to create conditions that will encourage affective involvement and willing self-disclosure. Situations devised to elicit circumscribed, impersonal responses cannot shed much light on what people consider important about themselves. . . .

Murray's most telling contribution to method is that of using the same subjects for the whole program of a research group. Dropping in frequently at the research center, the subjects quite naturally become friendly with the investigators, and the investigators with the subjects. This plan has the advantage of exposing the subjects to different workers who bring out different aspects of personality, and it permits the research staff, meeting as a diagnostic council, to pool its findings and arrive at its conclusions jointly. But Murray has also been much occupied with creating concrete situations of an emotionally involving character. Several of these are described in Explorations in Personality, *and several reported in* Assessment of Men. *He has devoted particular attention, moreover, to imaginative productions as a means of inferring the vital secret wishes and unconscious fantasies which subjects are not able to communicate directly. The Thematic Apperception Test is merely the best known of many procedures leading to this end.*

These strategies are an integral part of personology. They are necessary if the direction of psychology is to be altered or improved. Murray focused on them in his 1949 paper "Research Planning: A Few Proposals," in which he speaks explicitly of a "diversity of staff" and suggests the study of the same few human subjects in terms of a variety of levels of human functioning.

Along somewhat different lines is Murray's paper "Techniques for a Systematic Investigation of Fantasy." In this piece it is fascinating to see Murray's explicating mind at work. He remains endlessly inventive; he has a flair for precision and a subtlety of conceptual pursuit; he shows an intensity of focus and application and an obvious talent for the task.

One of the several important psychoanalytic ideas—along with regression, denial, sublimation, introjection, and others—is projection, the active extending of one's latent and unconscious psychodynamics onto the world. Projection ranges from sound reality testing (as an anchor) to paranoid distortion (as an aberration).

The task of both explicating and operationalizing the details of an individual's projection was initiated and carried forward mostly by Murray and his co-workers. In the brief period from 1935 to 1938, Murray developed the concepts of "perceptual apperceptive" methods and created (with his colleague Christiana D. Morgan) a set of evocative visual stimuli called the Thematic Apperception Test (TAT). In 1938, Murray wrote, "The test is based on the well-recognized fact that when a person interprets an ambiguous social situation, he is apt to expose his own personality as much as the phenomenon to which he is attending."

Projective techniques derive their intellectual power and their usefulness from a humanistic orientation toward human personalities; otherwise they are just tests routinely administered and routinely interpreted. They are techniques to be understood by that kind of psychologist that philosopher Morris Cohen would have called "naturalistic" (rather than "mathematical") and whom Murray called "centralist" rather than "peripheral."

From the moment the TAT appeared (in 1935) in the article by Morgan and Murray, "A Method for Investigating Fantasies: The Thematic Apperception Test," it seemed to have a peculiarly "American" reception; that is, it seemed commonsensical and relatively easy to administer. Unlike the imported Rorschach technique, which had only one sacrosanct (and rather complicated) method for scoring and interpretation—the TAT right away became every clinical psychologist's "property," for which he might devise separate scoring methods or even separate sets of pictures, ostensibly for special purposes. It was such a grand success that Murray came sometimes to resent being identified as "the author of the TAT," as though that was primarily what he had accomplished in life. Any appreciation of Murray's work or a reading of Explorations in Personality *leads one to see that the TAT is only one of literally dozens of fresh ideas and not even among his grander, more conceptually overarching intellectual inventions.*

14

PSYCHOLOGY AND THE UNIVERSITY

There is reason to believe that in coming years the university which contributes most to the advancement of learning and the cultivation of the human spirit will be the one which develops and sustains the greatest school of psychology. And with psychology there will necessarily be furthered an underlying physiology and an overlying sociology.

Psychology's immediate destiny is promising because the necessary conditions for a significant acceleration of its growth are for the first time present. These conditions need not be specified exactly here. Suffice it to say that they consist of certain recently discovered facts, certain recently devised methods, certain recently constructed theories, and, most important of all, certain recently advanced basic propositions which are sufficiently comprehensive and dynamic to serve as a conceptual foundation for the development of this science.

The advance of psychology is especially important because its interrelationships are so manifold that any discovery which it makes will immediately animate research and speculation in many other disciplines. To recognize this one has only to consider the mutual dependence of the sciences and the number of those that immediately wait on psychology —sociology, anthropology, criminology, pedagogy—or that are more remotely related—history, government, law. It is generally agreed that all social institutions are determined to a large extent by the interaction of human needs, sentiments, and beliefs. Since these constitute the proper subject matter of psychology, an economist is merely stating what seems too obvious for words when he says that a large proportion of economic and sociologic problems cannot be solved without psychologic data and that psychology is as necessary to social science as chemistry is to physiology.

Listen for a moment to the words of the social philosophers and judge whether they are not basing their proposals on certain suppositions —usually their private suppositions—as to the nature of man. Is it not the function of psychology to correct or to verify such suppositions? Reflect on the increasing urgency of the problems of the neuroses and the psychoses. Consider the increasing number of physicians who are becoming

From *Archives of Neurology and Psychiatry*, 1935, *34*, pp. 803–817.

convinced that many physical disturbances—perhaps even a majority of the less serious ones—are engendered by psychic states—mental shocks and conflicts, anxieties and depressions. Note how eagerly the younger physicians are seeking information about psychologic mechanisms and the methods for their control. Consider the parents and the teachers in progressive schools who are turning hopefully to psychology for guidance. Think of the instructors in theological schools who advise psychology as an aid to pastorship. Take account of the historians and biographers who have come to realize that to achieve their ends they must acquire a deeper understanding of human motives. And do not neglect the artists and writers—the sensitive ones—who have always been the first to voice their intimations of emerging ideologies. Consider how many of them have "become psychologic," not only by adopting an analytic attitude toward the experiences which they shape but even by yielding their imaginations to modern theories. Consider the philosopher who has begun to suspect that the outcome of his finely articulated logic was partly predetermined by a certain concealed preference, a preference which was originally generated by a purely fortuitous set of circumstances—a childhood experience, let me say. Heed the zest of students, the many young men and women whose minds have been incited by the beckon of psychology. Consider especially the spiritual dilemmas of modern man, and note the widespread, unconscious tropism for psychology, not so much as a new sensation or as a terrain for scientific exploration but as a possible path out of conflict and into the right way. Consider how the psychotherapeutist is being conjured up as a wise merman or savior by the anxious, scarcely conscious longings of a bitterly shaken world; how willy-nilly he is being entrusted with a priestly function. Brood on all these things. Then ask yourself whether it is possible to maintain that today psychology does not occupy a vantage point in the scheme of things.

If psychology is defined as the science which describes people and explains why they perceive, feel, think, and act as they do, it must be admitted that a serious interest in the subject matter of psychology is a distinctive characteristic of this generation but that, properly speaking, no science of the kind exists. That is, there is no comprehensive, unified body of essential facts, nor is there a satisfactory system of explanatory concepts. And because of this lack, philosophers, sociologists, historians, biographers, and poets who deal with such matters must still to a large extent concoct their own psychologies.

But even if it is true that psychologists have not yet formulated a conceptual scheme which is acceptable to themselves or to others, they must have proposed some thought-provoking theories, for without stimulation of this kind the swelling current of imaginative concern with psychology would never have reached its present magnitude. And so one inquires: Who has contributed the germinal ideas? To find the answer to this question, one naturally turns to the universities, for it has become their business to discover new facts and to evolve theories to account for them, as well as to impart knowledge.

In the big lecture room Professor Piper is reading from his recent textbook a paragraph on the textual differences of images, while Wilson, quietly sucking a "life-saver" in the front row, wonders whether the cashier at the cafeteria was serious when she said he was ungentlemanly. In the basement of the laboratory Hoyer is setting up his camera to photograph the chromatophoral changes in the stellate cells of the leech's skin. He is thinking that he will have to miss Dr. Sill's talk at the seminar on the bodily turn of the white rat in a straight alley. Young Professor Faber, mincing along College Street, has just felt the approach of a revelation. There came suddenly to him the seminal idea that he might organize a frontal attack in the form of a comprehensive project for research to test the differences between blondes and brunettes. What faculty should he test first? This problem certainly has more pep in it than that of the increase of brightness in a circumscribed field. Miss Ischt and Miss Adnock, who share a room in the Social Science wing, are just tying up the four hundred questionnaires they have been tabulating, constituting a comprehensive study of the sentiments on such questions as whether co-eds should be allowed to smoke in the common room. The correlation, expressed by the Pearson ratio, between a liberal attitude in such matters and a "pleasing" personality as judged by four fellow classmates was 0.791473 ± 0.021591—an excellent result which confirms Professor Ohl's original assumption and assures Miss Adnock of her Ph.D. Miss Jelkoe is administering a test to the fourth grade at the Sulkin Progressive School. Her problem is the determination of the effect of a rest period on the performance in the Mulligan multimental intelligence test and the Vandifeldt O-Q emotional maturity test. Mannheim and roommate, Blitzen, are in the library foraging about in the psychology shelves. Mannheim has wagered that in the coming examination there will be a question on the apparent size of visual objects, whereas Blitzen is certain of a question on the theory of happiness as bright pressure in the epigastrium. From all this web of activity, consideration of man as a human being has somehow escaped.

The truth which the informed are hesitant to reveal and the uninformed are amazed to discover is that academic psychology has contributed practically nothing to the knowledge of human nature. It has not only failed to bring light to the great, hauntingly recurrent problems, but it has no intention, one is shocked to realize, of attempting to investigate them. Indeed—and this is the cream of a wry jest—an unconcerned detachment from the natural history of ordinary mortals has become a source of pride to many psychologists.

It was about sixty years ago that psychology, by adopting the empirical, experimental attitude of physics and by developing its own methodology, established itself as a distinct science. Since it was necessary to begin by studying isolated fragments of experience and since the processes of sensation and perception were the fragments which were most susceptible to measurement, the pioneers commenced there. This original bias, firmly established by the classic experiments of such able men as Fechner, Helmholtz, and Wundt, gave rise to the basic conception of a living being as a consciously receptive mechanism rather than an unconsciously motivated dynamism. This point of view persisted, and even today many of the best psychologic laboratories in this country remain bound to the ideology of introspectionism, the data of which are the reports which subjects make when presented with different physical stimuli—stimuli variously combined in space and time. As the field has become more confined, the methods more intricate, and the theories more finely spun its devotees have lost contact with the great marches of thought, the biologic as well as the humanistic. To many outsiders these academic workers resemble vestal virgins—vestal virgins of unusable truth prolonging without profit the culmination of a spent impulse. They have, naturally, been accused of a half willful triviality—recently, for instance, by Köhler in these words:

Unfortunately, the adherents of introspection do not seem to trust their own procedure. At least, they must have agreed upon facing important problems as seldom as possible, since they are occupied mainly with describing the more remote and less exciting corners of experience, as, e. g., minor nuances of sensations, or the "glassy" appearance of certain parts of space and so forth. If all I have to do to develop the science of direct experience is to describe it, why then not attack the central facts of "mental life" at once, instead of scratching a little at the surface, or periphery, of it? There was a time in Germany, not very long ago, when people began to joke about psychology's ponderous discussion of trifles. And, indeed, it was strange to see how the description of a direct experience, what happens, for instance, during a single comparison of two tones or colors, could fill hundreds of pages without giving us the slightest positive idea about how the occurrence and accuracy of such a comparison might be explained. Even in a state of perplexity, a science can be highly interesting. But psychology, so far as it deals with direct experience by the method of introspection, has not only been a complete failure; it has also become boresome for all those who are not professionally connected with it.

A number of years ago behaviorism contracted its now notorious larynx as a polar reaction to introspectionism. It presented a fresh horizon, but one which proved no broader than that offered by the old field. Its metaphysical denial of consciousness, its provincial insistence on a radical positivism, and its adherence to a stereotyped mechanistic formula have resulted in a self-limiting puritanical program of procedure which logically excludes all but the simplest problems—problems such as the reflexive responses of bantam roosters. Luckily, men are escaping from behaviorism to better things.

More recently, there has arisen a heterogeneous group of workers bent on attacking personality—and a real attack it has proved to be. Armed with questionnaires, rating scales, pop-guns, mazes, peg-boards and numberless other mechanical contraptions, the testers have borne down on their subjects—so heavily, in fact, that the souls of their subjects have been forced to shelter. Hence, when one comes to examine the final results, arrived at by the most approved statistical methods, one discovers nothing of importance. The salt, it must be acknowledged, never landed on the bird's tail. Though it is encouraging to find that at last a considerable number of psychologists are occupying themselves with problems of personality, one is somewhat disquieted by the once-born, unripe confidence, the peculiar callousness of these testers—men who talk as though they had never been sensitized by a moving grief or joy. One wonders why they choose psychology as a field in which to labor.

This condensed review of academic psychology is purposefully critical. And it would be ungenerous if no mention were made of the natural limitations of man and the difficulties of the problem. One should realize that the blood of humanity is not thick enough to sustain more than a few men in greatness; that an odor of the mold almost always pervades academic enterprises; that psychology is in its infancy; and, furthermore, that there are many psychologists—introspectionists, behaviorists, and personologists—who stand well outside the limitations which confine their fellow schoolmen. One should also recognize the signs of new growth that are about one—the great illumination, for instance, that gestalt psychology has shed. But even when all these things and more have been adduced, it must still be admitted that the great central problems have been neglected lamentably by the academic workers. The result is that the average psychologist knows no more than the layman about the behavior and inner life of his fellow men. Indeed, the informed believe that he knows less. A concentration on sensory phenomena—the simpler peripheral reflexes of animals or the statistical manipulation of data obtained from questionnaires—has led him away from his proper subject matter—the driving forces which are basic to human nature. Hence, as Jung put it, a man who has wandered with a human heart through the world may be pardoned if his respect for the "corner-stones" of academic psychology is no longer excessive.

One is forced to acknowledge that university men have not contributed the ideas which have thrilled the imagination, nor have they provided the kind of answers that satisfy one's curiosity or meet one's needs. No. These have come from the medical psychologists—Janet, Prince, Freud, Jung, Rank, Adler. One is tempted, indeed, to affirm that the technic of research, many of the revealed facts, and a few of the theories advanced by the psychoanalysts represent the weightiest contribution ever made within a short space of time to an understanding of human nature. These workers have brought together more data pertaining to the lives of individual persons than has ever before been assembled, chiefly because they have been patient enough to listen every day over periods of months or of years to persons talking about themselves. They have discovered that many previously neglected phenomena—dreams, fantasies, the play of children, casual gestures, slips of the tongue, and so forth—offer significant clues to the understanding of personality. And as an explanation of these and other once mysterious occurrences, they have proposed a comprehensive theory of unconscious psychic processes. Although the enlightened William James called this discovery "the most important step forward in psychology" because "it revealed to us an entirely unsuspected peculiarity in the constitution of human nature," most academic men still refute the notion on pragmatic or verbal grounds. With the help of this theory, however, psychoanalysts have gone far in the elaboration of a thoroughly dynamic scheme for the representation of personality, based on a concept of the interaction of forces, the simplification of which is the notion of instinctual drives inhibited or modified by other forces acting at the dominant center of the personality (the ego). They have demonstrated the subtly permeating influence of the sex instinct and of the will to power. They have proposed concepts to describe the changes that occur in the chosen objects and in the motor expressions of instinct—substitution, overcompensation, sublimation, regression. They have demonstrated the life-determining potency of inflexible infantile attachments and modes of response. They have shown how sentiments and unconscious complexes are generated. They have indicated how these sentiments may affect perception and judgment, how by rationalization they are commonly transformed into general principles. They have described typical family configurations, common clusters of traits of character, and the emergent effects of the creative will. All this and much more has been accomplished—and accomplished during the span of the working life of a single man.

Since psychoanalytic formulations are especially designed to describe mental processes of which the ordinary citizen is seldom conscious, it is extremely difficult for him to reach any conclusion regarding their validity. To test the theories he must come in contact with persons who clearly manifest unconscious processes—with neurotic and psychotic patients—and he must train himself to focus on the revealing acts and words. I know no thorough student of psychoanalysis who, after observing the facts, has not been convinced that, in the main, the analysts are correct.

The emotional objections to psychoanalysis are understandable and predictable. They are chiefly due to the fact that analysts expose and dwell on just these primitive, aberrant, and asocial inclinations which, since the dawn of culture, the higher will of man has attempted to destroy or, if not to destroy, to conceal from himself and others.

The intellectual opposition to psychoanalysis, however, though usually propelled by moral sentiments, brings formidable weapons to bear on the matter. In a nutshell it may be said that no critically minded person practiced in scientific research or in disciplined speculation can accept psychoanalysis on the basis of the writings of Freud or of any of his followers. The presentation of facts is inadequate; the speculation is irresponsible; verifications are lacking; conclusions are hastily arrived at; and concepts are hypostatized. It is only when one begins to practice psychoanalysis and confirming evidence accumulates that one comes to realize that Freud is a strange genius who has made some of the shrewdest guesses that have ever been recorded. It becomes apparent, furthermore, that analysts have not competently represented their own material. They have not been their own best advocates.

Psychoanalytic theories are attempts to explain the most complex aggregation of activities in nature—the mind of man. And they have been constructed by men who are for the most part untrained in the fundamental sciences. Is it a wonder that these theories resemble myths or metaphysical doctrines rather than authentic scientific formulations? One is not surprised to discover this or to find that the theories proposed by the leading analysts have, to a considerable extent, an autobiographic basis; that Freud in particular, like many another genius who has revealed hidden aspects of human nature, has viewed man with a markedly biased vision. This situation is to be taken for granted in a new science.

One is somewhat put off, to be sure, by the "smart Aleck" attitude of the Freudian analysts, their simple-minded technical patter, their polymorphous perversities of logic, the magnanimous manner in which at certain times they set aside their critical faculties, their too-ready certitude, their hostility to research, their touchiness, their inability to get on with themselves or with others—in short, their pervading neuroticism. Such behavior is naturally repellant. It is an old truism, however, that one should not condemn a theory because its exponents are a bit "cracked."

The Freudian psychoanalysts in Vienna, Berlin, London, New York, Chicago, and Boston have formed societies which undertake to instruct students and to present those who finish a course of about three years' training with certificates of competency to practice psychotherapy. But, since in America the rule is being generally adopted that to be eligible for such training one must have completed four years of medicine and two years of hospital work, there is a long row to hoe before one can be educated in this branch of knowledge.

At present, as part of the general drift toward psychology, an increasing number of expectant young men, thrilled by the strong invitation offered by the problem, are seeking a comprehensive knowledge of psychology. What has the university to offer? As it stands today, a young man or a young woman who wishes to learn psychology, for its own sake or because of its application to other fields, must pursue one of two courses: become a graduate student in psychology at a university or enter a medical school and after some further experience apply for psychoanalytic training.

If the student chooses to work for the degree of Doctor of Philosophy in psychology, he soon discovers that the subject matter is divided into separate fields, each with its own terminology based on different fundamental assumptions. What he learns in one classroom cannot be related to what he learns in another, because each instructor mulls his own dream world between his ears. There is no common scheme. The situation for the student is actually worse than this, since in no one university are all the points of view properly represented. Thus, a certain bias is inevitable. The main objection to the graduate school, however, as I have already pointed out, is that the science of human nature is not taught there. For this reason one usually advises a promising student to go to medical school, since this is the path to psychoanalysis, the man-wise science of today. Though this seems to be the best available program of education, it is by no means satisfactory.

In the first place, such a course is unnecessarily long and expensive for a student. It is unnecessarily long, because at least four of the nine years of preparation are spent in acquiring information which in his later work as a psychologist he will never need. Even if he wishes to become a psychiatrist, a rudimentary knowledge of medicine is sufficient. For he will always refer patients with organic disease to a physician, just as a physician always refers patients with acute abdominal conditions to a surgeon.

Another argument against attending medical school is that the attitude of medical faculties is usually destructive to those who would understand the influence of the psyche on the body. The somewhat scornful complacency of the average medical man has been pointed out by Freud:

> If medical training would only deny information to the student in the field of neurosis, this would be tolerable. But medical training is doing more. It implants into the young student an incorrect and harmful point of view. Physicians, whose interest for psychological facts has not been awakened, have naturally a tendency of making little of such facts, going even so far as to decry them as unscientific. Conditions of neurotic character are hardly ever taken seriously by them while their lack of knowledge serves to breed disrespect for psychological research.

Furthermore, the emphasis on a rigorous attention to physical signs and the mechanistic attitude which this engenders are inimical to the refinement of those functions of the mind which are primarily employed in making psychologic diagnoses. Psychologic intuition is a complicated process which cannot be discussed at the moment. Suffice it to say that it is not sharpened by assuming the wholly detached, systematically observing attitude of the physical scientist. Since this is a fact which most physicians have not been trained to appreciate, they do not realize how their instruction may dull the apperceptive powers of the student.

Finally, and this is the weightiest argument, the medical school does not provide courses in normal psychology or in psychologic observation and experimentation. As a result a medical graduate who takes up psychoanalysis has no adequate standard of critical judgment to guide. The standards which he was taught to use in dealing with physical disease are insufficient. And so, like some accomplished physicists who become childishly uncritical when they begin speculating about religion, many young physicians lose their heads when they have to deal with psychologic phenomena. There is no other explanation of why so many well-trained medical students close their eyes with such docility and swallow the assertions of psychoanalysis bait, hook, and sinker.

A final difficulty which confronts the would-be student of psychoanalysis is that there are at least four entirely incompatible schools of psychoanalysis, and although at the moment the Freudian school is the most popular and the best organized for instruction and propaganda, its utter disregard of the findings and reflections of the other leading analysts is symptomatic of ominous myopia. Thus, the psychoanalyst is likely to be as limited in vision as the academic psychologist.

At present, then, there is no satisfactory solution of the problem for a young man who wants to acquire a well-rounded education in a reasonably short time. Academic psychologists are looking critically at the wrong things. Psychoanalysts are looking with reeling brains at the right things. A student who really wants to obtain understanding can follow neither; other sciences can base their assumptions on the work of neither; the public can rely on neither. The average student, however, chooses, because he must, one school or the other, and so his intellectual development in the end becomes boxed in by circumstance. For even if he is clear-headed enough to perceive that the group with which he has been forced to cast his lot is shamelessly prejudiced, he knows that bread is the staff of life and that he who sides with all men or with none goes hungry. The crucial time arrives. He hears the growling of his stomach, and his convictions are settled. The larger outlook fades. Thus, the existing social and institutional situation is destined to produce an even greater number of encrusted specialists.

In view of the potential importance of psychology, the existing Babel of authoritative voices, the confusion of those who wish to learn, and, finally, the increasing demand for trained psychologists in every branch of social life, is it not desirable that some great university should establish a school of psychology—a school in which young men and women can be adequately trained? Such a school, let me say, would offer, as does the medical school, a four-year course of instruction. It would require for admission certain preliminary studies—physics or chemistry, biology, elementary psychology, and a phase of the history of culture—anthropology or sociology. The first year would be devoted to scientific method, general physiology, neuro-anatomy and neurophysiology, with special emphasis on the autonomic nervous system, followed by courses in general psychology, sensory psychology, animal psychology, and the developmental and educational psychology of the child. The psychology of personality would be stressed, and the student would be given a thorough grounding in experimental methodology. In the third year there would be courses in psychopathology and psychoanalysis, supplemented by an elementary course in clinical medicine. The principles of psychotherapy and the analytic procedure would be taught. Such a school would necessarily maintain affiliations with a number of institutions in which practical instruction would be offered—an orphanage, a progressive school for problem children, a clinic for child guidance, clinics for the treatment of the neuroses, and institutions for feeble-minded, delinquent, and psychotic patients. Finally, since a physiologic orientation tends to minimize social factors, courses in social psychology, sociology, and the psychology of art, religion, and science would be included. Nothing less than this can be counted on to prepare responsible men and women for research or for practice. The students who intended to practice psychoanalysis would take postgraduate courses and a year's internship in a hospital for patients with mental disease. For such students a didactic analysis, offered at a moderate cost, would be one of the requirements.

This, in brief, is a plan for establishing the study of man on a sound foundation. The details, naturally, must be carefully worked out and the funds must be provided, but the plan presents no inherent difficulties. Indeed, universities can immediately begin to work toward such an ideal by inaugurating certain changes. The following changes seem of greatest importance: (1) the enlargement and strengthening of psychology in the graduate school by inclusion of representative courses from each special field, which would mean for most universities the development of a psychology of human motivation and the addition of courses in child psychology, psychopathology, and clinical psychotherapy; (2) the bringing about of a reorientation of the special fields within the department, so that the psychology of motivation and development comes to occupy a primary and central position; (3) an increase in the number of courses, particularly of the practical or clinical courses, which must be completed before a degree of Doctor of Philosophy is awarded; (4) the establishment of closer relations with the allied disciplines, such as physiology, sociology, and anthropology.

Since many of these developments have already taken place in several universities, it is not necessary to argue at length about their feasibility. One measure, however, the admission of practitioners to the college faculty, because of its importance and its novelty, deserves special consideration.

The inclusion of psychotherapeutists as members of the department is, I believe, essential, because an adequate science cannot be developed without the inclusion of phenomena which only psychotherapeutists are in a position to observe.

The science of psychology cannot prosper without the therapeutist, because in order to know human personality in its deeper and more deterministic aspects man not only must maintain an intimate association with many individual subjects over a period of months or of years but during this time must relentlessly pursue an analytic procedure which is harrowing, exacting, and time-consuming to the subject. The analytic procedure is harrowing to the subject because it is directed toward the exposure of those carefully shrouded, haunting memories the recollection of which is so humiliating as well as toward the illumination of those twilight fantasies which go to make up that highly valued, solemnly secret mythology which holds sway over the subterranean regions of every mind. Since no man or woman sacrifices his or her inviolateness and endures the tedious tribulations of a prolonged analysis without the expectation of deriving benefit from it and since, by definition, the only persons who have dedicated their lives to the office of serving human beings in this capacity are the psychotherapeutists, it is they, and only they, who have the opportunity to observe directly the underlying forces of personality.

The psychotherapeutist, again, is the man who is specially trained in the method of establishing rapport and of unearthing by stages the deeper strata of the mind. In this realm, art and technic are everything, for a relationship of peculiar intimacy and trust must be established between the observer and the observed. Since it has been shown, moreover, that the subject is unconscious of the factors which determine the more intense experiences of life, a special technic must be employed to bring them objectively into play, and only the psychotherapeutist is practiced in this technic.

Furthermore, the psychotherapeutist is by definition the only man who has a first-hand acquaintance with the phenomena of abnormal psychology, and the natural dissections of the mind that occur under such conditions are of signal import to an understanding of the normal personality. This is so because a preliminary analysis of an event into its functional parts is necessary to a complete description of anything whatsoever and because, whereas in harmonious personalities the parts of the psychic process are so merged that they are difficult or impossible to identify, in discordant and obsessed persons the existing conflict which is at the root of the trouble produces an analysis or a disbalance by which certain elements or processes present themselves in striking relief. If there are added to this natural analysis the process of disjunction which often occurs and that of dissociation by hypnosis which is occasionally resorted to in the course of treatment, it must be apparent that the psychotherapeutist comes into direct possession of elementary facts which do not fall within the experience of others.

Finally, the psychotherapeutist enjoys a unique position as an experimentalist. For every case is in truth an experiment, and within the limits of humane principles the psychologist may and should attempt various procedures with the purpose of modifying the existing structure and, in the role of catalyst, of bringing about the formation of new psychologic integrations. This aspect of the situation accords with the operational theory of knowledge, as set forth by Bridgman and Dewey, by which knowledge itself becomes a mode of practical action conforming to the experimental model. Instrumentalism in psychology refers to the procedures of analysis (deconditioning) and synthesis (conditioning), which are the means whereby a therapeutist attempts to change and control his subject. From this point of view, personality is not understood until the consequences of a consciously instituted procedure may be predicted and the prediction verified. For the ultimate aim in science is prediction and control, and so far as this is ever to be accomplished in the realm of personality it will be with methods devised by men who dedicate their wits to this particular task. In this respect the physician is the arch pragmatist and the sole counterpart of the analytic and synthetic chemist. In other words, he is the true experimentalist in the domain of human psychology.

To include psychotherapeutists in the faculty is to admit psychoanalysis to the university, simply because nowadays every first-rate therapeutist uses the technic or the theories of psychoanalysis in one form or another. A therapeutist appointed to the staff should be fully trained in Freudian analysis and versed in the views of other leading analysts. A critical liberality in these matters is essential, for no modern school of psychology can afford to neglect the distinguished contributions of such men as Jung and Rank.

Oddly enough the most determined opposition to the assimilation of psychoanalysis by academic psychology will probably come from the Freudian analysts themselves. Their resistance will arise not so much from the shrewd suspicion that ideas are taken to universities to perish —or, if not to perish, to be bleached of their vitality—but from a certain fanatical determination to oppose any modification of the doctrine which Freud has created. This setting themselves apart from all other psychologic movements is the result of a variety of factors.

The hostility of traditional medicine has forced them to the extremity of a Ghetto ideology; an unholy reverence for Freud's genius has made them regard his critics as vicious enemies; a subjectively determined preoccupation with rudimentary erotic phenomena has blinded them to other obvious factors; and, finally, an utter lack of appreciation of the aim of science—the arrival at a common basis—has allowed them to remain eccentric and fractious. In short, with a few notable exceptions,

Freudians, though they emphatically pretend to a scientific attitude, are propelled by sentimental and religious motives, and hence it is possible to converse with them only within the narrow limits of their own conceptual framework.

If it were necessary, however, to choose between psychoanalysis and its opponents, one should, I think, without hesitation choose psychoanalysis, because, as compared with other schools, it is the most honest and unflinching in its investigation of many important, though commonly ignored, aspects of life and because it offers the best technic and the most suggestive theories for the immediate future. It bears enough fertility to change the march of history.

Personally, I believe that psychoanalysis needs the university. To the present time, it has been the creation of private practitioners—men who are prey to the claims of the nervous world. But now it has reached a stage at which it will benefit by companionship with academic psychology. Its concepts need to be exposed to the experimental method and to a rigorous criticism, and for this the men who carry on the work must be free to enjoy the kind of leisure and the intellectual fellowship which it is the business of a university to provide. Psychopathology must find contact with other schools of psychology, for just as pathology has come to rest on physiology, so must psychopathology finally establish itself on normal psychology.

I have laid such stress on prevailing discords that the reader may legitimately ask: How can a harmonious faculty of psychology be formed from such heterogeneous elements? Without a common terminology how will communication be possible? It will be difficult; one must acknowledge that from the outset. But the conditions are not, in truth, as bad as I have painted them. For when I described the conflicts of opinion, I was regarding each school as a joint stock company; and as joint stock companies men appear more congealed and indoctrinated than they do as individuals. Certainly in every group there are men of constructive intelligence to be found who, because they have enjoyed a scientific training and some living in the world, are capable of thinking beyond the theories with which they are officially affiliated. If such men are brought together, there will certainly be disagreements about theoretical principles. But is this not true of all faculties? Within limits is it not, indeed, desirable—the inevitable condition for progressive development?

One can hardly suppose that in the beginning the faculty of a school such as I have proposed will be a strong one. Probably there are not enough psychologists and analysts now available to constitute a formidable company of scholars. But one may hope, on the basis of past experience, that from the best graduates of the new school a distinguished faculty will eventually be formed.

If a university waits until a conceptual scheme which all schools can accept has been constructed, the advancement of psychology will be indefinitely postponed. Until the conditions are created wherein students can acquire a first-hand acquaintance with the complete range of facts on which such a scheme must rest, all reflection is likely to be partial and inconclusive. A personal acquaintance with the facts is essential because, in psychology especially, second-hand facts are no longer facts. They have already undergone interpretation; that is, they have been assimilated to categories, and, as it happens, these are usually incommensurate with other categories.

It seems better, then, to start a school for the purpose of arriving at a unified system of ideas than to wait for the generation of ideas on which to found a school. The two factors, of course, are mutually dependent. But the creation of a theory depends on genius—something which no university can manufacture—whereas the conditions under which genius thrives are at least partially controllable. The establishment of a unifying theory would be the noblest aim that a school of psychology could set itself. This is right by all standards of elevated judgment, even though the average American may not readily agree to it. In this country, indeed, most people are even blind to the great practicality of a good theory; how, like a microscope, it centers attention on fundamental relations; how, by creating new symbols, it facilitates thought and communication; how it initiates more research, and hence the discovery of new facts. Perhaps it is not too fanciful to suggest that this emotionally sick world is in urgent need of a workable theory of personality. To be sure, the majority are no more aware of this need than certain physical sufferers of former times were aware that there could be no sufficient alleviation of misery such as theirs until the atomic theory had been formulated.

The end of my reflection is this: Assemble the ablest representatives of each branch of psychology; give them facilities for research, opportunities for discourse and leisure for speculation. And as surely as clouds eventually disperse and expose the sun, the introspectionists will be forced out of their cul de sac; the behaviorists will relinquish their juvenile metaphysics; the gestalt psychologists will be drawn into the field of motivation; and the psychoanalysts will be compelled to define their concepts and to think clearly. Thus a true school might come into being in which young men and women could learn what there was to know about man—the object which in all nature does and should concern them most.

In advocating the encouragement of psychologic science I have accepted pure knowledge as an unanalyzable satisfaction to the understanding—an ultimate value—and hence a sufficient goal for the dedication of one's best energies. But in valuating the proposed plan one should not fail to consider the probability of even greater secondary gains following in the wake of truth. For, since psychology deals directly with aspects of reality which are intimately bound up with human happiness, the most impartially collected facts will often suggest new and better modes, or new and better directions, of behavior. Thus, the advancement of the science will necessarily have a beneficial influence on practical action—the education of youth, the management of asocial persons, the treatment of disease, the constitution of new social patterns. And, most important of all, psychology will inevitably play a decisive role in shaping and accrediting the ideologies which are to come, the speculative outlooks which will clear the path and provide a form for personal development and the creation of enduring and of emergent synergies—erotic and communal. Psychology will have a hand in this, because the intelligences of the future will demand, so deeply has science implanted itself in the soil of man's imagination, that an ideology which shapes behavior be grounded on experience; that the possibility of its realization at least be suggested by the known facts and accepted theories of psychology. At present psychology is up to its head trying to ascertain the facts. It is too uncertain of itself to contribute anything to an ideology. But another time will come. For wisdom—that is, usable truth—is the secret aim of psychology.

Such presentiments of promise may be vague and illusory, but the present occasion is not. The present occasion is clear. The great tide, today and tomorrow, belongs to psychology. No university can afford to lose it, and, if it is to maintain its prestige, no university can fail to contribute to it.

15

RESEARCH PLANNING:
A FEW PROPOSALS

One recurrent strand in the long braided chronicle of science is the story of struggles for agreement among champions of incompatible conceptions. Although the courses of these struggles are marked by frequent failures, some partial, some complete, the enduring need for consensus has responded to failure by generating ever more effective rules of procedure—rules of observation, experimentation, conceptualization, validation, and communication—and today a vast amount of experience goes to show that loyalty to these methodological principles is very likely—more likely than disloyalty—to lead on to collectively satisfying goals.

Let us not forget that science is a cultural institution, a highly differentiated social enterprise, and that a would-be contributor has two tasks: (1) to construct the best possible formulations of accurately observed events and (2) to convince his fellow architects that these formulations should be incorporated in the existing edifice of postulates and theories. The rules of procedure which have proved most successful in fulfilling these two tasks constitute the intellectual superego which scientific education is designed to inculcate. Just as the best type of moral superego consists of rules which are most conducive to mutually enjoyed and productive human relationships on the behavioral level, the best intellectual superego, one might say, is composed of rules which conduce to the most productive and mentally satisfying collaborations on the conceptual level.

Now I propose, granted your forbearance, to masquerade for the next few minutes as an itinerant representative of this species of intellectual superego, not, let me hasten to say, because I have scrupulously obeyed its dictates and been rewarded, but because I have suffered from defying them. Thus I take after the man or, more commonly, the woman who, after two or three cacophonous marriages which terminated in divorce, elects the role of counselor in marital affairs. My object is merely to pour into the new bottles of basic social science some old wine from

From S.S. Sargent and Marian W. Smith, eds., *Culture and Personality*. New York: Viking Fund, 1944, pp. 195–212. The book is the published proceedings of the interdisciplinary conference on culture and personality held in New York in October 1947 under the auspices of the Viking Fund.

the vineyards of the more experienced and exact sciences, in the hope that small doses of this heady distillate will serve to speed the maturation of our discipline.

Before attempting this exercise, let me forestall misunderstanding with an explicit statement of opinion on one issue. I believe that although there are a few general principles common to all intellectual superegos, every science requires a special type of superego, one that is suited to the peculiar nature of the objects and events that must be represented and explained. I believe, furthermore, that the structure of each superego should vary with the degree of development of the science which it governs. In the early stages of a discipline, or whenever phenomena of a novel sort are to be examined, an overall survey resulting in a few vaguely orienting ideas—such as might be produced by an imaginative mind with a loose and lenient superego—is often more useful than a meticulously precise study of a small segment of the field. My guess is that we would have no more than a fraction of the clarifying psychoanalytic concepts which are available today if Freud had had a highly developed scientific superego. Consequently, I am not inclined to favor the indoctrination of men of our profession with the methodological principles of physics, not only because these are not appropriate to the analysis and reconstruction of social events, but because the quantitative precision which they demand is likely to persuade a man to restrict his attention to some measurable—usually small and unimportant—part of a field of interaction, and so to step into the trap of misplaced concreteness.

Thus the intellectual superego I am partially and provisionally representing is not a high and mighty creed, but a rather primitive code, suited, I trust, to the present capacities of basic social scientists—psychologists, cultural anthropologists, and sociologists.

The title of this conference is sufficient designation of the kind of occurrences I have in mind as topic for research. I take it that we are interested not only in different forms of culture and how they are conserved by socialization and repetition, but also in the sudden or gradual abandonment, the creation and the integration of common forms of feeling and behavior. We are intent on studying the modes and products of interactions between unconventional individuals and the conventional majority. Finally we want to know the effect of the whole cultural system of each society on the health, happiness, and development of its members.

Since studies of this sort call for the estimation of a multiplicity of variables and the observation of many interrelated patterns, I shall confine my remarks to multiform, multidisciplinary, collaborative researches.

The random proposals I have to offer will be arranged under four headings: conceptual scheme, strategic hypotheses, tactics, and research staff.

Conceptual Scheme. The aim of a scientist is to fashion the conceptual and technical tools which will enable him to analyze any event or any coherent sequence of events into its constituent elements and, then, to recombine these elements into a sufficient representation of the observed phenomena. In an ideal model nothing essential to an understanding of the occurrence is omitted, nothing that is not strictly relevant is included.

Having learned how to divide the incessant flow of human events into natural units of interaction, to circumscribe space-time fields (Lewin's ovals) that are susceptible of thorough and accurate observation, the social scientist's first task is to find the best way of analyzing these fields, that is, to decide which elements should be abstracted from each concrete totality. Just as a mapmaker, before traversing a given region, will list each kind of object—lake, river, mountain, road, town, church, historic site—which he thinks should be portrayed symbolically in his map, so should the social scientist build a conceptual scheme which includes all the elements (and their attributes) that require discrimination in observing and interpreting human behavior.

Whether aware of it or not, every man has floating in his head a miscellany of woolly, fuzzy-edged notions which are influential in determining what he will involuntarily notice, what he will intentionally look for, and what he will remember and report. The scientist's office is to screen these determinants, reject some, accept others, to create and to refine, and finally to bring forth a cluster of clearly defined variables. Thus will he provide himself with the best obtainable guaranty that in performing his primary function—that of observation—his perceptions will be sharply focused on the significant features of behavior and not distracted by irrelevant details.

Which variables are selected for definition will depend not only on the topic and purpose of the research, but on the investigator's assumptions, on the conception of reality which comes natural to him or which he has consciously and explicitly adopted. It is a man's basic conception of reality which determines his mode of analysis and hence its end products, the elements with which he deals. Today we are fortunate in having at our disposal a number of abstracting systems—magnificent constructions which are still in progress—and we should not complain overmuch if these systems are in certain respects discordant with each other, and taken individually are either vague and unrefined, or applicable to only a limited range of situations. Hull's admirable achievement stands out as the most finely differentiated, the most logically constructed, the most self-consistent, and very probably the most adequate for the kind of rigidly controlled phenomena with which it deals; but, as far as I can judge, it is still deficient in comprehensiveness: a large variety of important human experiences has yet to be embraced by its net of concepts.

The sensational Freudian system, on the other hand, is notable for the significance and strangeness of the occurrences which it is capable of interpreting, its range of application, the universality of its concepts, its often relevant mode of dividing the personality into id, ego, and superego, its detailed account of the transmutations of the ever-restive sex drive. No doubt it is the most adequate set of theories we possess for the understanding of many critical human states and symptoms. Its formulations, however, never approximate completeness. Much of what is obvious, healthy, and creative is disregarded. It provides no place for a number of environmental determinants and distinguishes only two drives—sex and aggression. In Freud's system there is no formal recognition of hunger, envy, and ambition, of the drives for money and possessions, for friendship and association, for dominance and power, for appreciation and prestige. Most analysts, however, have noticed that aggression is as commonly aroused by the frustration of one of these motivating forces as it is by the frustration of the sex instinct. Despite steady progress by Hartmann, Kris, Loewenstein,[1] and others, psychoanalytic theory is still largely undifferentiated.

Neither the Hullian nor the Freudian scheme is suitable for representing complex social situations such as this conference, the field which has been created by the present gathering. For this we must turn to Lewin, whose system is comprehensive, fairly coherent, susceptible of differentiation, and reasonably successful in exhibiting the chief components of overt human interactions. It is weak where the Freudian scheme is strong—in explaining the internal proceedings of personality—and it is vague where the Hullian scheme is rigorous—in accounting for the details of tactical learning—but, taken in conjunction with these other two, Lewin's mode of thought provides a very promising foundation for further speculative developments.

I have diverged from the appointed path. It was not my intention to discuss the pros and cons of this or that cluster of abstractions, but, first, to draw attention to the confusion of tongues, to the disorder—I shall not say chaos—among our symbols of discourse, and, second, to prescribe an old family remedy.

On the theoretical level we are living in a land of plenty but are unnecessarily embarrassed by the circulation of different terms for approximately the same concept (cf. instinct, drive, need, purpose, desire, wish, intention, and motive; sentiment and attitude; value, cathexis, and valence), by the use of one term for different concepts (ego, status, institution), by numerous overlapping concepts (status and role, superego and ego ideal, purpose and goal, dependence and need for security), and, more generally, by the elusiveness of almost all our notions. Let one illustration suffice: the word "ego" is most commonly used to refer to a slowly developing governmental structure of the personality, which is characterized by the attribute of consciousness, and by the capacity for objectivity (reality sense), rationality, emotional control, foresight, systematic planning, persistence of effort, the fulfillment of verbal commitments, and so forth. But "ego" is also used by psychoanalysts and psychologists alike as synonymous with "self," and in various hyphenated words has such connotations as self-interest, self-centeredness, and self-esteem. Ego-centrism, scarcely distinguishable from narcism, is considered to be maximal in infancy, that is, at the time when the ego (in the first sense), is minimal. "Ego instincts" has been used to denote a shadowy fellowship of drives that includes hunger and ambition (craving for omnipotence). More recently, psychologists have been speaking of "ego-involvement" when they wished to describe the state of a man who is emotionally committed to a task because his prestige or self-esteem will be affected by the outcome of his effort.

Surely without taxing our brains we could list many other specific sources of recurrent failures to communicate, and yet we have been content—and I am no exception—to converse in this Tower of Babel as if we were ignorant of the fact that the solution of our difficulties lay near at hand.

My first proposal, then, is that social scientists—those with the requisite disposition and talent—devote themselves, more resolutely than they have so far, to the building of a comprehensive system of concepts which are defined not only operationally but in relation to each other. The latter is essential to a complete exposition because, since none of the entities which we isolate in thought is isolated in nature, the manifestations of each entity vary with the character, strength, and position of the associated entities.

A more modest proposal would be that planners of researches take pains to define operationally and relationally variables which are pertinent to the topic of their investigation.

Although knowledge of operational definitions is now widespread, the number of social scientists who are scrupulously putting this knowledge into practice is astonishingly small. No wonder that psychoanalytic theory is still a vague and ambiguous mythology.

Except when experimenting in a strictly controlled field, we do not require rigorous operational definitions such as are necessary in the physical sciences, but if we purpose to grow beyond puberty we must bring our concepts much closer to the subjective and objective realities which we are capable of distinguishing. For us the definition of a variable is perhaps sufficiently operational if it includes (1) a list of its different manifestations and (2) a description of the ways in which these manifestations are discriminated or measured. The first (1) might be called a "criterial" definition since it consists of the various criteria (signs, symptoms, indices) by which the activity of the given variable, or the occurrence of the designated condition, may be inferred, and in terms of which, if possible, its intensity or strength can be roughly estimated. Such a definition is tantamount to specifying—for the sake of clarity of thought and communication—the permissible grounds for every interpretation or judgment. It describes the subjective and objective facts which justify the diagnosis, say, of anxiety, of superego activity, of emotional stability, of introversion, or of high intelligence. If one scientist assesses intelligence in terms of the *difficulty* of the problems which can be solved regardless of time, and another scientist measures it in terms of the speed and accuracy of solving *simple* problems, the two men will not infrequently disagree in their estimates and this may give rise to futile, and perhaps bitter, arguments. The standard cure, as you all know, is to call for statements of criteria and thus very simply to reveal that each man has been measuring correctly a different manifestation of the variable or, if you will, a different variable. A hundred current misunderstandings could be resolved by the application of this remedy. Will we persist in shunning it?

An operational definition of an entity also includes a description of the situations and techniques by which it is elicited and, if possible, measured. This applies particularly to the use of various diagnostic instruments. Introversion as discriminated by the Rorschach will not correspond exactly to introversion as estimated by listening to free associations or by administering and scoring a given questionnaire. Although such technical devices are being used more and more, simple observation of behavior and interpretation of subjective reports are still, and will no doubt always be, the most common social scientific operation (supplemented when possible by a moving picture camera with sound track). Hence, for most work, the recording instrument will be the scientist himself, a complex organization of needs, beliefs, presuppositions, and prejudices. Although the ideal aim of operational definitions is to eliminate unknown and distorting processes in the scientist's mind, this is unattainable in practice, and so, theoretically, a complete definition of an entity should include an account of how it is appraised by different types of scientific personalities. This point will be mentioned later in connection with the problem of assessing members of the research staff.

The task of defining each entity in relation to other entities is tantamount to the formulation of the fundamental postulates which transform a mere aggregate of concepts into a theoretical system. This matter is too complicated to be discussed here, but the mere mention of it at this point serves as a bridge of thought to my next topic.

Strategic Hypotheses. In recommending that we social scientists refrain from undertaking any research project until we have formulated one or more hypotheses to be verified, I am merely proposing a wider adoption of the policy which Newton introduced to replace the laborious method of indiscriminate observation and induction set forth in Bacon's *Novum Organum*, "a method which, if consistently pursued," Whitehead assures us, "would have left science where it found it." Newton's practice has been followed with conspicuous success by a long procession of experimentalists in the physical and biological sciences, and in certain special fields of psychology, but it has yet to be accepted on a broad front by social scientists. Most of our investigations have been of the exploratory fact-collecting type, and of these not many have yielded generalizations of high subsuming power. Conspicuous exceptions might be mentioned: Lewin's architectonic researches, the Hull-inspired work of Dollard and Miller (and associates) on frustration and aggression and on learning, and, in sociology, the recent attempts of Leighton,[2] Kluckhohn,[3] and others to crystallize their observations in the form of definite principles, postulates, or theorems.

To formulate an hypothesis which can be tested is to make a direct, though tentative, contribution to the development of science, to offer a stone for the building of the temple, the edifice of concepts and theories which we envisage as the ultimate desideratum of our vocation.

Composing a set of hypotheses amounts to no less than the erection of a clearly defined goal and hence of a focus for orientation, a point of reference for judging the suitability of available or devisable techniques. Such a goal is the best assurance that science will be advanced through proofs of one or more significant propositions.

Too many researches are undertaken, I submit, with no expectation in mind except that it would be "interesting" to study this or that group of people, or that it would be "interesting" to administer this or that battery of tests to some compliant population. It may, of course, be advisable, in dealing with a society or with a class of phenomena about which little is known, to perform a preliminary survey in order to acquire enough data for constructing verifiable hypotheses; but in most cases, I would suppose, present knowledge provides ample ground for tentative generalizations. Today we are surfeited with facts; what we need are the saving modes of analysis and reconstruction.

Another advantage of hypothesis-making is that verified deductions are deservedly accorded a higher scientific status than logical inductions. One feels more certain of a theory which leads to a correct prediction of behavior in a specified situation than of a theory which provides a plausible explanation of behavior after it has occurred. The slightest acquaintance with the childhood history of science will convince us of the almost limitless power of the human mind to produce explanations of events and rationalizations to support them, which, though almost wholly defective or meaningless, satisfy educated people and survive uncontradicted for generations. As an illustration of the capability of reason, recall the prodigious feat of Goropius Bacanus, a learned Jesuit of Antwerp, who succeeded in proving that Adam and Eve spoke Dutch in Paradise. And as one of many examples of the enduring power of error take, in the field of medicine, the fourteen hundred years' reign of Galen's misconceptions. The best safeguard against the wiles of imaginative thought and against intellectual inflation is the scientific ritual of prediction and validation.

If, before planning a research project, we spend whatever time is necessary defining and evaluating alternative hypotheses, there will be less likelihood of our committing ourselves for a long season to a relatively trivial investigation. The secret of success is a *strategic* hypothesis, that is, an hypothesis which, if verified, will stand as a basic proposition or will constitute the logically next step in the systematic development or validation of a theoretical system, or which will open up new fields for significant research and discovery.

There is unanimity, I trust, in our evaluations of the peril of the present human situation, a worldwide condition of mounting resentment and belligerency that is moving toward explosion, an explosion which will almost certainly inaugurate a course of unexampled regression and destruction. Thus among several possible futures is the disintegration of the social structure on which the very existence of science depends, and, if we are devoted to humanity or to our vocation, it is imperative that we apply, as physicians do, whatever wisdom, knowledge, and skills we have or can acquire to the task of preventing this fatality, of checking, if not curing, the present ominous epidemic of antagonisms. Consequently, for our time, a "strategic hypothesis" might well be defined as one which is strategic not only in respect to the advancement of knowledge and theory, but in respect to the advancement of fellowship, social integration, and ideological synthesis.

As Yeats has written: "Things fall apart; the center cannot hold; mere anarchy is loosed upon the world . . . The best lack all conviction, while the worst are full of passionate intensity." Things are held together by mutual affection and moral conduct—social morality being nothing more or less than the principles governing the creation and preservation of the most harmonious and rewarding human relations, interpersonal and international. Hence, the crucial task today is the formulation and pragmatic validation of a regenerated system of morality and the discovery of the means by which the system can be represented to the growing child so that it becomes exemplified in action. Scientists who have been disposed to live in order to find truth must now find truth in order to live: the problems to which they dedicate their energies should, as far as possible, be relevant to the supreme goal—social reconstruction. Not only is this direction of effort necessary for mere survival, but, we can safely predict, it will elicit and be furthered by more zest in the investigator and more social encouragement and financial backing than will any enterprise which is irresponsible in respect to humanity's most terrible predicament.

Tactics. Research planning calls for the settlement of many questions which will not be discussed here. There is the question of the locus of the enterprise, whether it is to be Siam, Sicily, or Sioux City. This is commonly decided by some extraneous factor such as the location of the organization or unit to which the investigator belongs. Then there is the matter of the subjects to be studied, whether they should be representative members of the whole community, children of a certain age range, students at a college, or juvenile delinquents. Also, there is the closely related problem of the type of fields, the class of actions and interactions, which will constitute the focus of attention. All these decisions will be influenced, if not wholly determined, by the hypotheses to be tested; and, vice versa, the subjects and situations that are accessible to investigation within the sphere of the scientist's job or function will dictate to some extent the selection of hypotheses.

Here perhaps is the best place to introduce another suggestion, namely, that good objects for study at the present time are small groups evolving modes of procedure (transitory subcultures) as they carry on, in a series of sessions, cooperative or competitive undertakings. One advantage of a small group is that *every* member of it can be studied separately and intensively until enough understanding has been acquired to allow for predictions of the behavior of each man when called upon to join with the others in accomplishing a common task.

Another important question for decision is the time-scope of the research. Shall we study the present structures of personalities and groups, or shall we study records and memories of the past in order to understand the present, or shall we attempt to validate predictions of things to come?

Strictly speaking, the present does not exist; it is always being devoured by the past. Nevertheless, as Carl L. Becker[4] has remarked, "we must have a present; and so we get one by robbing the past, by holding on to the most recent events and pretending that they all belong to our immediate perceptions." This is especially true for a social scientist, who is not chiefly interested in the more stable features of the environment —the structure of cities, machines and tools, the anatomical characteristics of people, etc.—but rather in processes, patterns of processes, and interactions of patterns of processes, none of which exists in the flash of a moment, but each takes time, as does a melody, to exhibit itself; and so the tiniest bit of reality is an occurrence which spreads over at least a fraction of a second and the beginning of it has perished before the end is reached. Social scientists are in the habit of telescoping a long sequence of organizations of such minute processes into a single and so-called "present" event, or proceeding. The duration of one of these proceedings, or units of interaction, is what a philosopher would term the "specious present." By tacit consent the specious present is often extended to cover a time span of months or even years. For example, a social scientist who spends several weeks or months studying an individual or several months or years studying a community may, after ordering his findings into a formulation, refer to it as the subject's *present* personality or as the community's *present* structure, despite the fact that during the period of examination more or less discernible transformations have been taking place.

Necessarily, every research will start with an examination of the specious present, of the present structure of selected personalities and/ or of the present structure of some group of which these personalities are members. Besides the observation of interactions under controlled and uncontrolled conditions and the collection of subjective reports of the covert processes (feelings and thoughts) that occurred during these interactions, we have, as technical methods, numerous tests of knowledge, ability and aptitude, projective tests which reveal structural properties as well as a few imaginal elements and forms, and questionnaires which elicit information about beliefs, sentiments, and attitudes. In addition, there is the interview, which in any form, directed or undirected, is generally accorded first place among clinical procedures. Under the rubric "interview" we could include the questioning of informants with the aim of acquiring more knowledge either about the particular personalities that are being studied or about the standards and common practices of their community.

I am assuming that a thorough study of selected individuals will necessarily constitute a good part not only of any research that is concerned with the relationships of personality and culture, but also of any research concerned primarily with culture, since the stuff that conserves and develops culture is embedded in human heads and one must seek it there. The observation of behavior is essential but not sufficient; it is necessary to discover how culture carriers define different common situations, and what are their cherished expectations and satisfactions, and what mythology controls their thoughts and feelings. Generally the best plan is to examine many people superficially and a few with penetration, remembering that most anti-cultural forces are not only covert but largely unconscious.

I would propose that in studying personality the multiform system of diagnosis and assessment be used whenever possible. Any system may be called "multiform" which includes several different types of procedures and several procedures of the same type for detecting the presence —and, if possible, for estimating the strength—of each major variable of personality. This does not call for ten times as many procedures as there are variables, because many procedures are capable of eliciting a multiplicity of variables.

Mention of the interview carries us, by an habitual association of ideas, to the topic of the past history—the past history of the person interviewed or the past history of his group—because it is chiefly through interviewing (supplemented, when feasible, by an autobiography) that one obtains the chronicle of development which is so relevant to an understanding of current patterns of activity. Very rarely are the topics of an interview limited to the specious present. Although, as Lewin argued, every factor which is required for a complete formulation of an event is operating in the field at the moment—it belongs to the present rather than to the past—some of these present components are neither conscious to the subject nor manifest to the observer, and hence must be inferred, and for inferences of this sort the most substantially supporting facts are obtainable from the past history. Biographical data, in short, is frequently very helpful in interpreting an observed proceeding.

Since the psychoanalysts, by elaborating a long, devious, and difficult technique for resurrecting traces of buried experiences, have acquired a monopoly, one might say, of this most successful mode of explanatory research, I would suggest that most workers in the area of personality and culture use only so much of the psychoanalytic technique as is necessary to formulate the specious present, and devote themselves largely to the refinement of various modes of prediction research, less treacherous than explanatory research. Predictive research includes, at one extreme, studies of the reactions of different subjects to the same situation, and, at the other, studies of changes of reaction during a long series of efforts to cope with a certain type of situation.

Researches of the first sort are limited to the observation of one or two proceedings, with the environment controlled or uncontrolled; and for this an almost ideal technique is the repeated examination of projections of a moving picture reel—say, of a partially controlled psychodrama or of a partially controlled operating group. In conceptualizing an occurrence of this sort we have Lewin to help us, even though he himself never studied the personalities or the current covert processes of his subjects as required by the field theory which he expounded.

Instead of predicting a subject's actions during one exposure to a situation, we can predict his actions at stated times over a period of recurrent exposures. In short, we can investigate the developmental process—conditioning, canalization, learning, socialization, the acquisition of culture—as it occurs under different conditions. We can study the genesis of complexes, the gradual achievement of self-control, the stages in the construction of some complex object, the waxing and waning of a friendship. We can attempt to predict what effect culture will have on a growing personality and what effect he will have on it.

Now, before bringing the topic of tactics to a close, let me add two further proposals: one, that we organize the procedures of each investigation according to an experimental design which will permit us at the end to treat our data, so far as feasible, in an approved statistical fashion; and two, that we include in our system of procedures, techniques for measuring the typical misperceptions and misapperceptions of each member of the staff. It is standard practice in science to determine the relative accuracy of each instrument of precision. In our discipline the instrument in most cases is the scientist himself.

Research Staff. The title of this conference is evidence of a shared realization that personality abstracted from cultural forms and cultural forms abstracted from personality are errors of misplaced concreteness. The plain truth is that we are in process of forming a new discipline, basic social science. Because the different viewpoints and techniques which are relevant to this emerging science had different origins and were reared in isolation, the present enterprise calls for a multidisciplinary approach, the collaboration of sociologists, cultural anthropologists, clinical psychologists, and psychoanalysts. But the time is not far distant when these terms will designate not members of different disciplines, but specialists working within one discipline, that is to say, within the frame of a common theoretical system.

In any event, the carrying forward of a substantial piece of research in the area of personality and culture, either now or in the more distant future, will call for a staff of diverse specialists; because, even if basic social scientists should become equally proficient with all techniques, the adoption of a multiform system of procedures will require that each worker be assigned a special function, at least for the duration of a given research project.

I should like to make a plea for a staff that is not only diverse in skills but diverse in respect to theoretical convictions. For, not only do we want to bring all available truth to bear upon our problems, but we want to contribute as much as possible to the rearing of a conceptual system which integrates all valid theories, and it is easier for men of different persuasions to achieve unity when engaged in a common task than when working independently.

I am not oblivious of the possible unhappy consequences of clashes on the theoretical level, nor am I insensible to the advantages enjoyed by a conceptually homogeneous unit. If harmony of thought and coordination of action throughout the course of a single research project were superordinate aims, all of us would favor homogeneity—a group composed entirely of Lewinians, of orthodox Freudians, of Radians, of Rankians, of Reikians, or of Reichians—but such a policy could serve only as an encouragement to ever greater differentiation, if not to fanatical sectarianism, at a time when integration and synthesis are most needed. Therefore, in selecting the professional staff, I suggest that we embrace as much diversity as is compatible with effectiveness and resolve to create order out of chaos.

A good deal of current discord is the inevitable result of the fact that scientists, separated from one another, have been looking with different aims at different subjects in different situations. Concepts designed by an anthropologist to interpret the religious beliefs and rites of Tahitians, concepts proposed by a psychologist to account for the political sentiments of the American people, and concepts invented by a psychoanalyst to explain and cure neurotic illness, are not likely to be concordant. One obvious remedy is to organize research projects in which three or four able exponents of pertinent theories will collaborate in studying the same subjects with a shared aim in mind.

Another impediment to the achievement of a common theoretical system are the diverse conceptual fixations which bind our thoughts. Some of these divergences can be ascribed to deep-rooted temperamental differences, but others have been determined by circumstances and they should be susceptible of modification by circumstances. Rigidity, for instance, is a property of one's intellections which can often be diminished in degree by working as a member of a congenial group. The chief hindrance perhaps is the scientist's self-esteem cleaving to the concepts which he himself has invented. This, in some measure, is a consequence of the overvaluation of individuality and self-sufficiency in our Western world. Many a scientist has been led to the fateful conviction that he must win fame as the creator of an original theory or distinguish himself as the leader of a new sect. In contrast to such men are those of a less adventurous cast who are disposed to cling to a theory out of loyalty to its admired founder. Some of my psychoanalytical friends have yet to realize that they are doing a most un-Freudian thing in conforming to Freud; for Freud, assuredly, was no conformist.

The great thing for each of us to appreciate today is that our objective is a common language. With this firmly in mind a company of dedicated workers, no matter how divergent at the start, has a fair chance of achieving unanimity, at least in respect to the concepts which are applicable to the phenomena they are studying.

It is harder for social scientists to do this than for physical scientists, and harder still if they invade, as I have recommended, the realm of values, expecting to serve as physicians to society. Here, the essential requirement is the ability to distinguish a sentiment from a fact and the practice of announcing one's sentiments at the very start. This calls for integrity of a degree not yet attained by American social scientists. In the last decade all of us deplored the corruption of the German psychologists whose researches were set up to prove the superiority of the Aryan race, but it is salutary to note that all our own findings have unanimously confirmed the American system of values. It was shown, for instance, that democratic is superior to autocratic leadership, and that people with anti-Semitic tendencies have despicably distorted personalities. Pro-Semitism was not studied, partly, I suspect, because any analysis of personality as conducted today, and this is worth considering very seriously, represents a man as less balanced and less estimable than he really is. Anyhow, it is obvious that the outcome of many research projects has been determined in a critical fashion by the sentiments of the men who conducted them, and if we social scientists want to be respected as impartial observers and interpreters we must estimate the influence of our own sentiments by appropriate techniques and make whatever corrections are required. A scientist who is incapable of doing this is not fitted to engage, except as a minor technician, in an evaluative study of culture.

Almost everything I have said so far—stale ale to most of you—bears upon the problem of the effective collaboration of specialists of diverse skills and convictions, scientific and ideological. For example, one of the chief purposes of operational definitions is intelligibility of communications among members of the staff. This happens to be one of the best ways of preventing the waste of time, the countless confusions and disagreements which inevitably arise in the course of any investigation that has been hurriedly undertaken with nothing more than a fragmentary misshapen conceptual scheme.

Since there are many other determinants, besides those mentioned in this paper, of effectiveness and ineffectiveness of cooperative activity, some of which are only vaguely understood, and since human relations stand first among the objects of our professional concern, I should like to make one further and final proposal: that members of the research staff, during the preliminary formulating period, join in a systematic study of themselves in the process of working toward agreement. The purpose of this piece of action research would be not only to bring conceptual order out of disorder and so to facilitate the harmonious progress of the common enterprise, but to contribute to the solution of World Problem No. 1, the harmonization of conflicting ideologies. By definition we are experts in social relations, and yet the record of our own relations as scientists—more particularly as fellow psychoanalysts—over the last twenty years looks as if our expert knowledge had been a dangerous thing. Mr. Anybody might say, Social relationist cure thyself. I am not speaking from the pulpit—for my own relationships have been abominable—but from the sawdust trail that I am walking, intent on reformation. Probably I have progressed no further than the young fellow who said, "If I have done anything I am sorry for, I am willing to be forgiven."

REFERENCES

1. See, for example, Hartmann, H., and Kris, E. The genetic approach in psychoanalysis. In *The Psychoanalytic Study of the Child*, Vol. I, New York, 1945; and Hartmann, Kris, and Loewenstein, in *ibid.*, Vol. II, New York, 1946.

2. Leighton, A. H. *The Governing of Men*, Princeton, 1945.

3. Kluckhohn, C. Group tensions: analysis of a case history, in Bryson et al., eds. *Approaches to National Unity*, New York, 1945.

4. Becker, C. L. *The Heavenly City of the Eighteenth-Century Philosophers*, New Haven, 1932, p. 119.

16

TECHNIQUES FOR A SYSTEMATIC INVESTIGATION OF FANTASY

The facts set forth in this communication favor the proposition that investigations of fantasy should be included in every examination of personality that aims to be thorough. Fifteen methods of evoking fantasies are briefly outlined and suggestions are offered as to how the data obtained may be conceptually organized and interpreted.

From an objective standpoint a fantasy is a mental product—verbal, scriptual, plastic—that has certain attributes. Since these attributes may vary in degree and some of them be absent, it would be more accurate to speak of mental processes that are, to this or that extent, fantastical ("fantastical" being specifically selected as the adjective of fantasy). The attributes of a fantastical mental product (fantasy) are as follows:

1. *Fanciful.* As a rule a fantasy departs from objective reality. It is more or less unrepresentative, bizarre, extravagant, exotic, or "imaginative." It usually has an illusory or delusional quality.

2. *Dramatic.* A fantastical product usually portrays imaginary actions and happenings that have emotional value. It has a dramatic theme.

3. *Anthropocentric.* It is chiefly concerned with the interaction of personalities. When animals or inanimate objects are portrayed they are apt to be anthropomorphically dramatized (*cf.* animism).

4. *Egocentric.* The chief actor (hero) in the drama is usually the subject—obviously depicted or represented by another personage (*cf.* emphatic identification). Sometimes, however, the imaginings are entirely about others—parents, rivals, loved ones.

5. *Driven by need.* Most fantasies are quite obviously promoted or influenced by wishes or fears. Heroic and amorous themes predominate. The fantasy, however, may represent an attempt by a child with insufficient knowledge to picture (understand) a phenomenon of nature—the movements of the sun or parental intercourse (*cf.* investigations of Piaget[1]).

6. *Fulfilling.* A fantasy commonly portrays pleasurable happenings or successful achievements (*cf.* "castles in Spain"). It may, however, be

From *Journal of Psychology*, 1936, *3*, pp. 115–143.

a horrifying creation of anxiety and hate (*cf.* Poe's tales).

7. *Pictorial.* Fantastical thinking is rich in imagery. Visual imagery predominates, but human speech may also occur (*cf.* accusations of the Deity in a dream). Abstract words are rare.

Fantastical thinking is most apt to occur—and this may sometimes be noted by others (*cf.* "a penny for your thoughts")—when the subject's attention is:

8. *Detached from exigency.* A fantasy is rarely an attempt to solve a practical or theoretical problem. It is more often an aimless, and perhaps playful, stream of thought which evades the problems of necessitous adaptation. Sometimes, however, it depicts a course of action (*cf.* imaginal trial and error) which is eventually put into practice.

Fantasies commonly occur when the mind is relaxed. They may, therefore, be described as:

9. *Autonomous.* Images usually come and go without any accompanying conscious effort.

. . . those images on the other side of her eyes went on living that private life of theirs, undisturbed. A vehement and crazy life—now utterly irrelevant, like a story invented by somebody else, then all at once agonizingly to the point, agonizingly *hers.* [Aldous Huxley, *Eyeless in Gaza,* p. 365].

However, a fantastical mental product may, on occasion, be the result of conscious design; as when a parent makes up a fairy story for a child.

10. *Subjective varisemblance.* The subject may have a feeling of reality—perhaps a feeling of "greater reality"—as the fantasy develops (*cf.* other-worldliness of mystics). As in dreams and psychotic episodes, there may be complete absorption and belief. Some fantasies, however, are concocted "for fun," knowingly.

The last three criteria of fantastical thinking are subjective. The individual will usually report that he is not trying to "work" his mind. The surroundings are forgotten as his attention passively follows the veering current of imagery.

Fantastical thinking is to be differentiated from chaotic mental associations that have no theme on the one hand, and from realistical thinking on the other. The latter is concerned with actual events and probabilities. It is more objective, rational, and dispassionate. It uses abstract concepts. It is directed toward the adjustment of the subject's ideas and actions to the stubborn facts of life. Being organized by practical as well as by logical considerations, it is usually more coherent and communicable than fantasy. Realistical thought demands effort, and after several hours of it the mind becomes fatigued and ceases to function efficiently. Fantasy, on the other hand, is restful. It is the concomitant of sleep. Realistical thinking tends to exclude fantasy, but the latter may "crash the gates." The brain worker suddenly finds himself daydreaming. During realistical thinking the subject tends to be highly conscious—conscious of his surroundings, conscious of his aim, or conscious of the steps of his thought. Fantasy, however, is hardly conscious of itself. It is promoted by alcohol, certain drugs, fever, mental illness (*cf.* De Quincey, Coleridge, Poe, Baudelaire). Fantasy may furnish an escape from the world or it may be the harbinger of a creative advance.

It is generally considered that the thinking of primitives, of children, of humorists, of artists, religionists, and of imaginative geniuses is to a great extent fantastical; and that the thinking which occurs in dreams and psychotic states is almost wholly so. Thus, the average civilized individual spends at least half a lifetime (30 odd years) in fantasy—daydreaming and night-dreaming. One can hardly suppose that these processes are utterly inconsequential.

The present communication is limited to what is specially significant—fantasies which portray the subject (or his representative) in action. Each fantasy is a bit of "imaginary behavior."

An individual does many things in his imagination which he does not do in real life. Most of the purely imaginary or unrealized acts seem to be engendered by desires and needs that are very similar to those that impel deliberate action, but they are denied external expression (inhibited) because of the unpleasant consequence that would supposedly follow their objectification. Subjects are apt to believe, however, that some of their imaginary actions represent probable, and others represent barely possible—"if all goes well"—forms of future conduct. Many people also give way to a few fantasies which they have consciously abandoned as feasible courses of action but which are enjoyed because of the pleasurable feelings—usually erotic—which accompany them.

We have to do here with purely imaginal, and usually inhibited, drives that find no overt expression, and hence are never directly observed by the psychologist who limits himself to the study of objective phenomena. The question is: Are such fantasies important to an understanding of the total personality? I submit that they are important for the following reasons:

(a) Fantasies are important per se. To affirm that overt behavior is all that is important for psychology is an unwarrantable dogma. Fantasies are interesting phenomena of mental life. The shrewdest knowers-of-men, in the past as in the present, have been as much occupied with man's inner life as they have with his social conduct.

(b) Fantasies are important because of their relations to overt action. There is evidence which indicates that an individual may be conditioned by imaginary events (in daydreaming and night-dreaming) as well as by actual events; and some enigmatic behavioral reactions may probably be explained in this way. Fantasy may accompany and give "meaning" to

behavior—for example, in the play of children, lovemaking, and religious ritual. Fantasy may also "resist" action, as in the withdrawn inhibited individuals who are markedly disinterested in their surroundings and unable to concentrate on the work they are expected to do. In such subjects the inner world has become more highly cathected than the outer, and one cannot understand or appeal to them without knowing what lies behind the veil. Finally, since some fantasies are eventually put into action, the psychologist should know the dominant imaginal drives before stating what a subject may do under a given set of conditions. Science is concerned with prediction, and, in human beings, past performance is not a sufficient index of future action.

(c) *Fantasies are important because of their relations to feeling and emotion.* Fantasies may convincingly portray success and glory or failure and dishonor, and thus engender different states of feeling—euphoria or dejection (*cf.* fantasies of heaven and hell).

(d) *Fantasies are important because of their relations to creative thought.* Religious beliefs, artistic compositions, and even some preliminary scientific theories are elaborations or rationalizations of the stuff of fantasy. The debt of culture to fantasy is immeasurable.

(e) *Fantasies are important because of their relations to neurotic symptoms.* It has been shown that some neurotic symptoms—and who among us is utterly exempt?—are partially determined by repressed fantasies. Hence, the former cannot be adequately understood without a knowledge of the latter.

The mention of neurotic symptoms brings us to the concept of unconscious fantasies, a topic about which something should be said. This is not the place, of course, to debate the question of unconscious psychic processes. Suffice it to say that some psychologists find it necessary to suppose (*cf.* the principle of convenient fictions) that fantastical processes, such as those described above, are almost continuously active in "the twilight zone of consciousness" as well as in "the darkness beyond consciousness." This hypothesis has been constructed in order to "explain" some experiences of consciousness as well as to "explain" some overt behavioral responses.

It is generally agreed that fantastical thinking is frequent and potent in children and that with socialization this "make-believe" becomes less satisfying. The "sense for reality" increases and by degrees the seemingly possible courses of action become fewer and more definitely defined by precise conditions. Thus, there is a progressive "sloughing off" or inhibition of one form of imaginary behavior after another. Now, the supposition is that, though some patterns may be completely eliminated, others are conserved and, without appearing in consciousness, exert a determining influence on behavior as well as on consciousness—attention, perception, apperception, emotion, sentiment, intellection, purpose, and so forth.

Perhaps the importance of the theory of the unconscious has been unduly stressed, but it seems necessary to do so as long as others overemphasize the importance of consciousness. The aim of the psychologist is to conceptualize "regnant" processes in the brain. Which of these processes, if any, have, at a given moment, the property of consciousness is usually a secondary matter. It may become a question of primary importance, however, when the psychologist has to deal with a person who believes that all his actions are consciously and rationally motivated.

In psychoanalytic practice it is generally assumed that the patient is as conscious as the analyst is of the facts—what he (the patient) does and says, the dreams and memories that he recounts. These are data. The analyst, however, infers "something else" from this material, something of which the patient is unconscious. He interprets what is *manifest* and arrives at what he supposes to be *latent.* Now, in conformity with his interest and his theory of conditioning, what he supposes to be latent is usually an infantile pattern of behavior—a pattern that was expressed in fantasy or in action during childhood. It is the analyst's hypothesis not only that this infantile pattern was the first mode of expression of the drive which the adult pattern now exhibits (manifest datum)—the *anlage* or primitive root of the adult pattern—but that the infantile pattern is still active, in a sense, as an unconscious determining "inhabitant" of the mind. One justification for this notion is that the infantile pattern may suddenly emerge, or a fragment of it may emerge, during intense emotional excitement or intoxication, in reveries or dreams, in dissociated or psychotic states, during the course of a psychoanalysis, and so forth.

In most cases, however, it is not necessary to imagine that an infantile pattern is actually operating when an adult pattern is manifested. One may limit oneself to the supposition that the latter has been derived from the former; and that interpretation may reveal the connection. According to this notion every interpretation is a working hypothesis which directs further studies of the subject's past—to prove or disprove it.

If there is truth in this conception, we have another reason for studying fantasies.

(f) Fantasies are important as clues to the events which have critically conditioned a personality. Personality is insufficiently understood as an integrated assemblage of potentialities. It must also be understood genetically as a developing series of interrelated events. Experience shows that many critical events are forgotten or repressed, and others are remembered but not revealed to others. Whether remembered or not, however, critical happenings leave hypothetical "traces" which continue to influence behavior, but *more particularly to influence fantasy.* Thus, through fantasy one may more surely discover the events which have conditioned development.

Finally, our experience suggests that infantile fantasies are intimately bound up with certain bodily processes. Knowing the former, one can guess the nature of the latter. It seems that in a child a physiological disturbance may inaugurate a fantasy—an attempt to account for the inner event—and that this fantasy may influence sentiment and action. The fantasy is usually lost (forgotten or repressed), but if the experimenter can expose it he will discover the (previously unsuspected) connection between the physiological process which he has observed and the behavioral response which he has observed. The evidence on this point is very incomplete, but it is suggestive enough to force the belief that unconscious fantasies are much more important than it is generally supposed.

Space does not permit a more comprehensive account of fantasy: the facts and theories and their importance for psychology. There are many suggestive works, however, to which the reader may turn. In particular, Jung's *Psychology of the Unconscious*[2] should be mentioned. It seems to me that a psychologist's intellectual horizon is not properly extended until he recognizes the significance of fantastical processes. For behavior, *qua* behavior, is superficial and sometimes artificial—commonly explainable as the mere imitation of social norms—whereas fantasy—if I may use an emotive metaphor—is deep and close to the fount of creative energy. Almost anyone can observe the proximate surface of things. It is for the scientist, as always, to search beyond, behind, beneath. If academic psychology stretched itself to include fantasy—the principal concern of the analytical schools—the material should force them to consider factors which they have for long neglected, and they would bring to that study the self-critical methodology which analysts have lacked. The result might be a profitable interchange of observation and thought and, eventually, perhaps, a common conceptual scheme for psychology. It is hoped that the procedures to be described will prove a step in this direction.

What we have tried to do is to expose fantasies by indirect methods —methods which would not reveal their aim to the subjects. The data obtained consist of words, images, and loosely configured thought processes.

GENERAL PROCEDURE

The individual who is to be examined may be an experimental subject or a patient. If he is an experimental subject he should be told something of the nature of the sessions in which he is to partake, but he should certainly not be enlightened as to the real purpose of the tests— the exposure of secret wishes and fears. The experimenter may say that he is investigating creative activity and wants to check the efficacy of various methods. For this he needs the cooperation of a few willing subjects. The subject may be told that he, himself, will learn something about the workings of the imagination if he whole-heartedly throws himself into the exercises which he will be asked to perform, but that he should not ask any questions about the tests until he has completed the entire series.

For most sessions it is better that the subject lie down on a couch or relax in a comfortable chair, and that the experimenter sit behind him or, at least, out of his direct vision. The experimenter may say: "The imagination works better when one is alone. Therefore, I want you to act as if I were not in the room. Do not turn to look at me. I shall make a few notes as you talk but I do not think that this will bother you." In many of the sessions conducted at the Harvard Clinic there was a microphone concealed in a lamp that stood on a table between the S (subject) and the E (experimenter). By this means all that was said in the room, together with the pauses and inflections of voice, was permanently recorded on a revolving phonographic disc.* As a rule the E did as little talking as possible; his chief function being to stimulate from time to time the subject's flow of thought and speech, and for the rest to sit passively watching and listening.

The following account of specific procedures starts with the most direct methods and ends with the most indirect. This has been done in order to facilitate the reader's understanding. Since it is important, however, not to facilitate the subject's understanding, the tests should be administered in approximately the reverse order.

SPECIAL METHODS

1. Questioning about Fantasies and Dreams. The subject may gently and artfully be led to talk about his present hopes and fears and unrealized desires, as well as about the fantasies which he has recently entertained pertaining to the immediate or distant future. "If you had great ability and a million dollars, how would you lead your life?" "What is your heart's desire for the future?" Questions such as these may stimulate an individual to talk freely of his present plans. After this the subject may be asked to recall some of his childhood fantasies. "Like all young children you must have had some very extravagant conceptions about yourself." "As a boy what did you daydream about?" "What nightmares did you have when you were little?" When good rapport has been established the subject may be asked about his earliest notions of childbirth and sex and particularly about the fantasies which have accompanied masturbation.

The experimenter may also inquire about the subject's earliest reli-

---

*The sound-recording apparatus used at the Clinic was constructed by Mr. Boris Naga-shev. In its present form, speech is perfectly recorded and reproduced.

gious conceptions, his ideas about God and immortality, punishment and redemption.

Finally, the subject may be asked to record his dreams for the next month and to jot down the fantasies, past or present, that come to his mind.

2. *Questioning about Favorite Themes.* The subject may be asked to give a history of the fairy stories, fables, myths, adventure books, novels, plays, operas, pictures, paintings, sculpture, and music that have most impressed him since he was a child. "What stories appealed to you when you were a boy?" "What figures excited your imagination?" "What stories frightened you?" "Did you ever imagine yourself taking the part of any character in a book?" "Did tears ever come to your eyes at a movie?" Questions such as these may be asked if the subject has difficulty in talking or remembering. After this the subject may be asked about the games that he played as a child, what "make believe" he enjoyed, and what part, if any, he took in dramatics. Finally, he may be asked about the written themes or artistic productions that he may have executed during his school years.

This procedure is based on the principle that a subject is most impressed by and remembers best the stories and creative productions which represent aspects of his own fantasies. A given presentation may light up hitherto latent tendencies or it may serve merely as a conduit for existent fantasies. But, in either case, the subject is usually able to identify emphatically with one of the characters as well as to project into this figure his own inhibited tendencies. This is the catalytic function of art. The subject, being often unconscious of the resonance within, gives other "objective" reasons for judging that a particular work of art has "value." His rationalizations* interpose themselves and thus conceal from him the direct connection between the theme of the story and his own excited feeling. Thus, a psychologist who simply notes a subject's artistic preferences may sometimes guess correctly the unconscious processes that are active within the subject. The following is a case from everyday life.

A group of people were discussing a question: to what great writer should a certain room be dedicated? One of the young girls present said, "I know whom I'd have," but then hesitated, blushed and refused to say. She passed it off with, "I don't know what I was going to say." A visitor, knowing that the young girl had been rereading *Wuthering Heights,* waited until the next day and then said casually, "How would it be to dedicate the room to Emily Brontë?" The girl blushed, giggled and then said, "You're a mind-reader. I thought of her and then Poe." Sadism being common to these two authors, the visitor, having noted that the girl was apt to quarrel with her mother, picked up a newspaper on the following day and read aloud a gruesome account of the murder of a woman by

*Cf. The theory of derivatives as expounded by Pareto[3].

her daughter. At this the girl started to laugh in an almost hysterical manner (*cf.* mirth as an outlet for inhibited tendencies).

It is surprising how often one finds significance in the preferences of children for certain books. For example, a boy who derived erotic pleasure from fire, was much impressed by the story of Moses and the burning bush; a boy who had fantasies of being devoured remembered Daniel in the lion's den; another with the same fantasy read numberless animal stories and later became an authority in lycanthropy; the favorite fictional episode of a boy with the fantasy of being an obstetrician was the one in which Jean Valjean *(Les Miserables)* carries the wounded Marius on his shoulders through the sewers of Paris to reach their outlet in the Seine.

These two examinations, each of which may consist of two one-hour sessions, if tactfully and sympathetically conducted, should yield information about: *(a)* imaginary behavior of which the subject has recently been aware and *(b)* imaginary behavior of the past; that is, drives which may still be functioning unconsciously. Finally, as explained above, clues of former unconscious fantasies may also be obtained. These two examinations should be the last to which the subject is exposed, for as soon as he is asked direct questions of this sort he will surmise that the experimenter is interested in his private life, and it is important that he does not suspect this until after he has been exposed to the indirect methods which are soon to be described. At best, the method of direct questioning yields a small fragment of what is conscious to the subject at the time. Much else that is conscious will be distorted or concealed. Furthermore, during these hours the subject's thought processes will usually be structured, since the mental relaxation which allows for free drifting can rarely be obtained when questions are being asked.

The three sessions next to be described, all of which are based on the association of words or images, should likewise be administered at the termination of the period of testing, for these procedures may disturb the subject by bringing unpleasant ideas to mind in reference to himself.

3. Word Association Tests. * The classical technique is to present, one at a time, a list of single words, as stimuli, and ask the subject to respond as quickly as possible with the first word that comes to mind or with a series of words (chained associations). Our experience indicates that the latter technique is preferable. Reaction times and the latent period between each response may be recorded. In conjunction with this the subject may be connected with a galvanometer to record concomitant electrical changes in the skin and/or with a contrivance for measuring

*These tests have been elaborated and administered in a variety of ways at the Harvard Clinic by Mr. K. Diven, Dr. W. C. Langer, and Dr. C. E. Smith.

tremors.[4] Langer[5] has recently devised an apparatus for photographing finger pressures that has yielded encouraging preliminary results. These methods give information on the following points: what objects (images), qualities, or ideas evoke emotion (*i.e.*, are emotionally cathected) and what objects, qualities, or ideas are associated in the subject's mind? That is to say, the test tells us something about an individual's sentiments and apperceptions, and these, being important ingredients of fantasy, are relevant to the present study. For example, if to the word *water* the subject responds with: "river, deep, dark, death," we may suppose that he has had a drowning fantasy—the death of a loved object, a premonition of his own death by water, a suicide wish, or something of the sort. We should expect to find this theme in one or more of his compositions. Association tests, then, may yield some of the imaginal constituents of potent fantasies. The pressure which is applied to the subject—he is told to respond immediately—forces out words (as "slips of the tongue") which under other circumstances would be inhibited. Thus speed may produce "rifts" in the structure of thought. An hour may be devoted to this test.

4. Session of Free Associations. The psychoanalytic technique of free associations which, when used consistently over a long period of time, has proved so successful, may, in a modified form, be used to yield results in one or two sessions of an hour's duration. The *S* is asked to recline on a couch and allow his mind to drift. The analogy which Freud has used in this connection is useful. The *E* says to the *S:* "Imagine yourself at a train window watching the scenery stream by and telling what you see to a blind man on the seat beside you." The subject is instructed not to attempt to pursue any consecutive trend of thought, but to allow his discourse to be broken by any new images or impressions which "pop" into his mind. The *E*, then, remains passive and, except for a few encouraging remarks, does not interrupt the subject for twenty minutes. After that he may suggest periodically certain general topics—anxiety, injustice, misery, guilt, punishment, and so forth—instructing the subject, in associating with these words, to let his thoughts drift back to the days of his childhood.

5. Induced Visions. Jung[6] has developed a technique for engendering partially controlled visions. The subject is instructed to close his eyes and shut out the light—conveniently by putting his head on his arm—and then to concentrate intensely upon the first image that arises distinctly in his mind—on the back of his eyelids, as it were. The subject should attempt to visualize this image or scene with greater and greater clarity, and to follow it in its autonomous transformations. Furthermore, he should attempt to fantasy himself into some relationship with it, to traffic with it in some way. The result will be a developing series of scenes and occurrences which resemble a dream except that they are partially controlled by the subject. This method demands some practice and cannot be successfully followed by all subjects. As yet, it has not been used in any of the researches at the Harvard Clinic.

Experience has shown that the next two procedures do not engender self-consciousness in subjects. They are accepted as tests of the imagination rather than as lures or traps for secret thoughts.

6. *Similes Test.* * For this test the instructions are as follows: "This is a test of verbal imagination. I am going to give you a number of adjectives, one at a time. Please respond to each adjective by giving as many apt or striking similes as you can think of. They must be original with you." A simile is defined and two examples given. The experimenter then gives the subject the following ten adjectives at three-minute intervals: pathetic, unhappy, disgusting, anxious, malicious, meek, dangerous, delightful, exciting, deceptive. This test goes further than the word-association tests, because it calls for images of total situations rather than single words. For example:

As *unhappy* as a poor married man who wants to be an artist but has to wash dishes in order to support his family.
As *malicious* as a small boy when he whips his rabbit for joy.

7. *Musical Reverie Test.*† The student is asked to relax in a comfortable chair in a sound-conditioned room while the experimenter plays to him on the phonograph parts of certain classical compositions: Symphony No. 4 in F minor (Tschaikowsky), Don Juan (Richard Strauss), Symphony No. 6 in B minor (Tschaikowsky), Quintet in G minor (Mozart), Death and Transfiguration (Richard Strauss), Afternoon of a Faun (Debussy). The instructions are somewhat as follows: "I want you to allow your mind to drift along with the music that I am going to play to you. Observe the images that come to mind and weave them into a plot or allegory as you proceed. When the piece is finished I shall ask you to give an account of your reverie."

The next three methods are based on assimilation and projection. The material presented the subject is vague and relatively meaningless, and the question is, to what meaningful patterns will it be assimilated? Or, in other words, what will the subject project into it? Presumably, he will project into it the need imagery that is under tension in his mind, just as when one is alone and afraid, in a "haunted" house at night, every sound is interpreted as the advent of an unwelcome intruder.

8. *Word Projection Test.* Under the title "The Verbal Summator and a Method for the Study of Latent Speech," Skinner[7] has described a procedure in which an electric phonograph is used to reproduce at low

---

*This test was worked out by Dr. D. R. Wheeler and later elaborated by Mr. H. Berman at the Harvard Clinic.
†Mr. K. R. Kunze devised and administered this test at the Harvard Clinic.

intensities various combinations of elementary vowel sounds to which the subject is asked to respond. Each combination is repeated to the subject every three seconds until the response occurs. The instructions are either "Listen to the phonograph until you find yourself saying something with meaning; then say it aloud" or "This is a record of a man saying something over and over again. What is he saying?" Quite obviously, this technique facilitates the occurrences of auditory illusions by forcing the subject to project into the material words that come to his mind. Presumably, some of the words that are projected are connected with potent trends in the individual's personality.

*9. Image Projection: Beta Ink Blot Test.** The Rorschach test has been found very useful, but not so well suited to our present purpose as the set of ink blots employed by Bartlett.[8] The subject is put at his ease and then told he is going to be given a set of ink blots. "These blots," the experimenter says, "are not intended to represent anything in particular. They may, however, suggest something to you, as you sometimes see shapes in clouds or faces in fire. Please look at each blot and tell me everything you see in it, everything it suggests or recalls, everything it might possibly be." Subjects give from 2 to 20 responses to each of the 12 ink blots presented to them. For example:

Subject 8. Ink Blot No. 1: 1. race horse, blanketed, waiting; 2. negro king in Africa, with long lips; 3. bust of an Indian; 4. a large kangaroo followed by an ostrich; 5. a seal looking for a fish followed by a hunchback; 6. rooster in barnyard; 7. map of U. S.; 8. map of South America; 9. dog on hind legs, begging; 10. large duck, upright; 11. a beaver; 12. filth, vice; 13. accusing hand of guilt; 14. crime followed by punishment.

10. Picture Completion Test. Here the S is presented with a series of cards, on each of which is mounted a fragment of a picture. The subject is asked to complete the picture in words and tell what is happening. This method has been used by Sanford[9] with good results in a study of the effect of hunger upon imaginal processes.

Most of these tests were based originally on the principle of projection. It was later discovered, however, that more fantasy material could be obtained if subjects were instructed not only to interpret what was before them, but to elaborate a dramatic account of the preceding events, the present situation, and the possible outcome.

11. Odor Imagination Test.† This procedure is designed to yield fantasies emerging from feelings and images that have been evoked by

*Dr. D. R. Wheeler copied the most evocative of Bartlett's patterns and worked out the technique of administration.

†Mr. F. C. Gevalt, Jr., worked out the technique of this test and administered it at the Harvard Clinic.

olfactory stimulation. The subject is blindfolded and then given the following instructions: "I am going to let you smell various odors. As I present each of them to you I want you to invent a short anecdote or episode suggested by the odor. Please try to develop your story from the first association that comes to mind." The following odors have been found effective: ginger, sage, soap and water, acetone, tobacco, art gum eraser, violet perfume, whiskey, sulphonapthol, Worcestershire sauce, pine, spearmint, denatured alcohol, vinegar, germicide, sweet starch, benzoine, asafoetida, carbon tetrachloride, H_2s gas, after-shave lotion, shellac, salad oil, sour milk, oil of cloves. A typical product is the following:

Benzoine: A man is in a candy store waiting for a streetcar. The odor of the candy on the counter reminds him of the girl with whom he has just fallen out because she was his intellectual inferior. Suddenly, he decides that mind is not important in a woman, and that her body and love are enough.

*12. Story Elaboration Test.** Here the S is presented with 32 different dramatic situations, one by one, each of which he must develop into a skeleton for a short story. Some of the situations are as follows:

No. 1. A sick man is becoming a burden to his family. They would like to get rid of him.

No. 3. A man was found shot to death. The evidence tended to show that it was done by himself or someone in his immediate family.

No. 17. A clergyman, after 30 years of service, is obsessed by feelings of worthlessness and futility.

13. Literary Composition Test.† Here the subject is given an hour to write a narrative based on an outline of Hawthorne's story *The Minister's Black Veil.* The following paragraph is read to the subject and left with him for reference:

One of Hawthorne's short stories tells of a minister who, after many years with his congregation, appears in the pulpit one Sunday morning wearing a black veil over his face, and for a long time thereafter is never seen without it. You are to take this idea as a nucleus for a story of your own. You may develop it in any way you please and make any modifications you desire. Plan to spend about forty-five minutes on it. This exercise is to test the extent of your literary imagination.

*The situations used in this test were devised by Mr. L. C. Lewin and the test was administered by him at the Harvard Clinic.

†This test has been administered by Dr. D. R. Wheeler and Mr. H. Berman at the Harvard Clinic.

The *E* leaves the room and does not return for forty-five minutes. If the *S* has not finished by that time, he is requested to spend the next five or ten minutes summarizing the remainder of his story.

14. Thematic Apperception Test. Under this title Morgan and the author[10] have described a method for eliciting creative activity by the use of specially selected pictures. Most of the pictures depict a person of the same sex and of about the same age as the subject involved in a dramatic situation. The instructions for adults are somewhat as follows:

> This is a test of creative imagination. I am going to show you some pictures. Around each picture I want you to compose a story. Outline the incidents which have led up to the situation depicted in the picture, describe what is occurring at the moment—the feelings and thoughts of the characters—and tell what the outcome will be. Speak your thoughts aloud as they come to your mind. I want you to use your imagination to the limit.

Two one-hour sessions are usually devoted to this test.

The chief advantage of the indirect procedures based on projection and imaginal elaboration is that the subject believes that he is talking about the material "out there" and/or that he is demonstrating his creative ability. He does not suppose that he is speaking about himself. Usually, he comes in, talks about a few pictures, and leaves, without the slightest realization that he has provided the experimenter with a fluoroscopic screen for apperceiving his emotional skeleton. What I mean here can be illustrated by a concrete case.

> A young man of nineteen was brought to the Boston City Hospital by his parents because of some minor ailment and also because his employers had several times suspected him of embezzlement. Though the evidence was merely circumstantial and the boy had persistently denied his employer's accusation, the parents were uncertain and wanted the doctor to determine the truth of the matter. The doctor tactfully questioned the young man, but the latter stoutly declared his innocence. The patient was then given the thematic apperception test. His stories clearly revealed to the "X-Ray eye" of the experimenter not only that the patient was guilty of stealing but that he had stolen because of an obsessing love for a woman. The patient had no idea that he had given himself away. Only later, when he was confronted with his own plots, together with the experimenter's interpretation, did he confess his secret.

*15. Dramatic Production Test.** The *S* is seated before a large table and given some miniature stage properties, animals, and little figures (about one and a half inches high) with which he is asked to arrange a dramatic scene. The subject is told that he is to be the author and pro-

---

*This test, based on the "play technique" of child analysis, was devised and administered by Mr. Erik H. Erikson.

ducer of a short one-act play. The *E* leaves the *S* for fifteen minutes, during which time the *S* is supposed to compose and rehearse the performance. The *E* watches him through a one-way screen. The second fifteen-minute period is devoted to the performance itself, the experimenter being the audience.

At the termination of each of the above tests or interviews it is well to ask the subject about his state of mind at the beginning of the session. Have there been any recent events or did anything of significance happen just prior to his coming to the examination which might have influenced his responses? In some cases, a rather extensive subjective report of the subject's feelings and thoughts during the experimental hour may be rewarding.

The tests may profitably be administered in the following order: *(a)* Beta Ink Blot and Similes tests, followed by Literary Composition test (2 hours); *(b)* Word Projection followed by Dramatic Production test (2 hours); *(c)* Picture Completion followed by Musical Reverie test (2 hours); *(d)* Thematic Apperception test (1–2 hours); *(e)* Odor Imagination test (1 hour); *(f)* Story Elaboration test (1–2 hours); *(g)* Word Association tests (1 hour); *(h)* Free Association session (1 hour); *(i)* Questioning about favorite themes (1–2 hours); *(j)* Questioning about fantasies and dreams (1–2 hours). This schedule of examinations calls for about sixteen hours of work, which for experimental subjects may profitably be distributed (four hours a week) over a month's time. It may, however, be completed in ten days without serious interferences between tests or depletion of the subject's creative powers. Since it has been found that the sex and personality of the experimenter are an appreciable factor, the results are more comprehensive if the tests are administered by several experimenters, some of whom are of the opposite sex.

Besides the fifteen procedures listed above, a number of other methods which reveal aspects of fantasy life have been successfully employed. For example: *(a)* subjects have been given questionnaires and interviews dealing with their sentiments about family life, social conditions, politics, religion, and so forth; *(b)* subjects have been asked to give introspections of their feelings and images when presented with poems and pictures, and then to judge the latter on an aesthetical basis; *(c)* subjects have been presented with jokes built around certain common complexes and their immediate responses as well as their later rationalizations recorded; *(d)* subjects have been presented, one by one, with photographs of men and women and asked to write down the adjectives which best described the personality of each.

In conjunction with these procedures for exposing unobjectified, latent, imaginal, inhibited, repressed, or unconscious tendencies, a great many other examinations and experiments have been performed in order to reveal the characteristic overt behavior of a subject. Without some knowledge of what is objectified it is hardly possible to understand the significance of what is latent and unexpressed. However, since the present paper is limited to a description of techniques for evoking imaginal processes, we shall say nothing here about other methods.

ORGANIZATION OF RESULTS

The procedures outlined yield an enormous amount of data—words, phrases, and organized compositions—representative of the imaginal processes of individuals, but the question is Can we deal with them intelligently? Outside the productions of the insane, I cannot think of any phenomena which are less susceptible of exact scientific treatment. A purely empirical and objective procedure would be to count the number of times every word occurred and compare the results with the average relative frequencies of words as determined for everyday speech. About these results there would at least be general agreement. Behaviorists and psychoanalysts would be as one! Unfortunately, we have tried this and the result is zero. Certain words stand out because of relative frequency or infrequency, but without further interpretation these facts have no meaning and therefore are of no interest. At the other extreme, nothing is counted, but the material is immediately interpreted by the intuitive method. This also has been tried and the results are interesting, but there is little agreement among judges. Science is not advanced. Even members of the same school disagree about what the stories indicate. The fantasies of others offer such admirable ink blots for one's own projections!

The manner in which the data are organized will naturally depend upon the conceptual scheme or variables of personality that the experimenter is employing. Unfortunately, at the present time there is no commonly accepted scheme. There is merely a great variety of opinions as to what is significant: what should be observed and what interpretations can legitimately be made. Our own theory is very tentative, being in process of construction. It has been partially adumbrated in two recent communications.[11],[12] Only a very brief outline can be included within the limits of this article.

The scheme is based upon a conception of the mutual dependence and interaction of "forces"—forces within the personality and forces originating in things or people outside the personality. The forces engendered within the personality have been termed *needs* (or *drives*) and the social or inanimate forces with which the subject has intercourse have been termed *press* (plural *press*). It seems that almost any behavioral event is susceptible of analysis into needs and press; the interaction of the two being termed the *thema*, or dynamic skeleton, of the event. The coarse unit of personality, then, is a simple behavioral event—a man-environment interaction—the abstract formula for which is a simple thema. A succession of interrelated simple themas constitute a complex thema. Most fantasies may be represented as complex themas.

The first task, then, is to identify the most important needs—such as the need for air, for water, for food, for pain-avoidance, for sex, for rest, for affection, for possession, for power, for recognition, *etc.*, and to identify the most important press. The press that originate in human objects are also needs, but in this case directed toward or away from the subject. Thus, most social events may be formulated as an interaction of needs—those in the subject and those in one or more objects. For the subject—and his point of view is maintained throughout—every concrete object is taken to be a combination of abstract qualities or forces (needs) which, in various ways, facilitate or obstruct the realization of one or more of his own needs. It is a question, then, of how often and how intensely each need is manifested by the principal characters (heroes) in the collection of fantasies produced by a subject, and also how often each press is manifested. Finally, one determines what themas occur most frequently and most dramatically.

Single words referring to common objects—occurring as responses in a word-association test, for instance—are sometimes impossible to classify because of one's ignorance as to what they "mean" to the subject. For example, the word "mother" may recur a number of times, suggesting that the mother is a cathected object. But the important question is what press does she represent? Is she a restraining authority, a devoted consoler, a burdensome invalid, or a guilt-imposing censor? Many problems of this sort may remain unsolved, but, as a rule, most of them are sufficiently settled in one or two terminal interviews devoted exclusively to the resolution of diagnostic dilemmas.

On the basis of over two thousand fantasies, we are now engaged in classifying the common or significant actions, the most prevalent themes. If this is satisfactorily accomplished and the classification accepted, there should not be serious difficulty in distinguishing the elements of most fantasies. One should eventually be able to name the principal needs, modes of action, cathected objects, themas, and dilemmas which are imaginally present in any subject. Those could then be compared with what was objectified in his life—the subject's common actions, sentiments, and interests.

This, however, is probably not all that is inferable from fantasies. There is a possibility, which is too alluring to put aside, that one may be able to discover some of the infantile tendencies or critical root events which have partially determined the individual's present character. In other words, the attempt may be made to interpret the fantasies genetically.

GENETIC INTERPRETATION OF FANTASIES

Adults exhibit the "same" needs—that is, needs which belong to the same class—as do infants, but the needs of the former are usually promoted by other action patterns and directed toward other objects. It would be surprising, indeed, if it were found impossible to trace transformations of action patterns and cathexes from birth to maturity. For the human being is certainly not an entirely unrelated series of events. From what is known about the impressionability of young tissue and the durability of reaction tendencies established in infancy and the threats of punishment which force the child "against its will" to abandon many of these tendencies, it would be truly amazing if no adult fantasies were derived from infantile fantasies or from infantile impulses that had been inhibited. Since all the findings of psychoanalysis go to prove that adult fantasies *are* so determined, it is reasonable to adopt this supposition as a working hypothesis.

Naturally, to interpret genetically one must know the action patterns commonly exhibited and the objects commonly cathected (positively or negatively) by infants. To what extent psychoanalysis has properly distinguished these patterns and objects is uncertain. It is a stereotype, though probably correct, to say that analysts have limited themselves to phenomena which have sexual significance. And, if this is the case, one might suppose that they had overlooked many of the important activities of childhood. This conclusion, however, would hardly do justice to the flexibility of the pansexual theory. It seems that the analysts have overlooked very little of importance, that they find significance in everything; and this because, according to their theory, any action or any part of the body, or the body as a whole, or any object may become erotized—associated with pleasurable, eroticlike sensations or feelings. Thus, they speak of muscular erotism, erotization of thought, the body as phallus, *etc.*

Though many find it impossible to understand or to agree with Freudian theory, there is little disagreement about what to list as the important activities of infants: sleeping; respiration; sucking, biting, and ingestion of milk and food through the mouth; excretion of urine through the urethra and feces through the anal canal; spitting up and vomiting; withdrawal from painful stimuli; crying for the mother; cooing and clinging to the mother; struggling against physical restraint; tantrums of rage when frustrated; attempts to coordinate and master objects—creeping, walking, and manipulating; exploratory movements—touching, peering, smelling; showing off before admirers; and so forth. Later one finds other activities—acquisition, collection and retention of objects; dreams of power expressed in play; destructiveness; assaults upon weaker objects (pets and younger siblings); fantasied assaults upon stronger objects (parents and older siblings); primitive masturbation; curiosity about birth (the arrival of a young sibling); sexual fantasies; and a host of avoidances and anxieties—fear of falling, of injury, of rejection, of deprivation, of punishment, and so forth. This list is by no means exhaustive. It is, I suppose, what most people have observed and would agree to call important. Nor would there be much argument about the fact that the following were important objects in the infant's world: parts of his own body, physical supports, what he eats and excretes, the mother with certain parts of her body (nipple, breast) specially cathected, the father, other siblings; and later: dangerous situations, injurious objects, possessions, pets, and playmates. Under mother we may include nurses and other older women who play the maternal role, and under father we may include older paternal men. Finally, there are the almost universal experiences: birth, teething, weaning, learning to walk without support, training in toilet habits, rivalry of other siblings, special devotion of the parent of the opposite sex, interference by the parent of the same sex, numerous alarms and accidents and fevers, leaving home and entering the school situation; and throughout the entire course of development, barriers, prohibitions, and threats of punishment.

Out of these objects and events the child, driven by its needs, weaves its allegories, its science of life. There are great gaps in its knowledge, but the child fills them—it being the inveterate tendency of intellection to do so—with whatever images it has at its disposal. Since, according to the evidence at hand, these pre-logical myths considerably influence development, it is the function of the "depth" psychologist to reveal them. To do this he must be intimately acquainted with pre-logical and pre-realistical processes—syncretism, juxtaposition, animism, symbolization[1]—and he must also be familiar with a great variety of common fantasies. The fantasies of children are too various to be enumerated here. It is for future research to classify them according to their uniformities and divergences.

This brief review is enough to indicate the kinds of factors into which a genetic interpretation attempts to resolve every adult fantasy that appears susceptible of such treatment. For example, the story of a shipwrecked sailor left to starve on a desert island suggests a forlorn and hungry infant with a fantasy of being deprived of maternal support and nourishment (*cf.* weaning trauma); the story of a boy pulling a violin apart to determine where the music comes from suggests a curious child with thoughts of searching within the mother's body to discover where the noisy newborn baby came from; the story of a young man revolting against the oppressive tyranny of his employer suggests a little boy's desire to overcome the restraining authority of his father. Thus, the mother figure is substituted for the ship that does not come to the rescue as well as for the violin from which the music emanates, and the father figure is substituted for the oppressive employer. To some psychologists this will sound absurd, but then some psychologists have never listened attentively to the fantasies of children and reflected upon them deeply, or studied the beliefs and mythologies of primitive peoples, or attended for hours to the productions of neurotics and psychotics. Many of those who have would agree, I think, that the above-outlined mode of interpretation is based on a justifiable hypothesis. But the important question is How can one's interpretations be tested, proved correct or incorrect?

VALIDATION OF INTERPRETATIONS

If scientific truth is what "goes" among the intellectual elite, it would seem that we might be more satisfied with our interpretations if we succeeded in convincing a sufficient number of people, or better still, if a sufficient number of people separately arrived at the same conclusions. As a step in this direction we have adopted the principle of "the multiplicity of judgments." From ten to twenty-five experimenters interview or test each subject at least once. Each experimenter independently organizes and interprets his material and, later, compares his findings and conclusions with those of all the other experimenters. Naturally, the bare findings are never uniform, for every subject responds differently to different tests administered by different experimenters on different days. Because of this, it is necessary in arriving at an interpretation of a single session to take account of the nature of the situation, the personality and attitude of the experimenter, and the special (temporary) attitude engendered in the subject by the immediately preceding events of his life. But even after making allowances for such subtle factors—and what a host of them is overlooked!—there will be disagreements among experimenters. For, contrary to the dictum of absolute determinism, is there not Chance, or the great lawlessness of human personality? And this applies to the experimenter as well as to the subject. Finally, how can one expect to find agreement of interpretation among experimenters, when interpretation is a matter of insight. Insight—depending as it does upon the frequent exercise and training of a very special aptitude—is certainly not equally distributed among those who profess psychology. Much greater than the differences in acuity of vision, hearing, and taste are the differences in acuity of psychological intuition. Thus, at the frontier there will always be those who see further. This, however, does not make science. Science is democratic. It insists that the lame, the halt, and the blind shall arrive and perceive. Thus, the intuitive pioneer, or those who follow him, must fashion instruments—mechanical and conceptual—that will allow everyone to observe and understand what has already been observed and understood. But this is not the only necessity. For, since most intuitions of most pioneers are either totally or partially incorrect, the scientist must, for his own illumination, if for no other reason, attempt to distinguish, define, and name every impression which led him to his conclusion.

Applying these general considerations to the problem at hand—the genetic interpretation of fantasies—it seems that the next methodical step in scientification should be a comprehensive study of symbolism. Is it true, and in what sense is it true, that a violin, let us say, can symbolize the mother? And if it can, what else can it symbolize? What else does it commonly symbolize? Can it symbolize anything? Is the sky the limit?

It will be long before science constructs a net to catch these irrational fish, but let her now essay it. It is of no profit to leave the most elementary and significant psychic processes to undisciplined therapists to talk about as they will.

The procedure that we are pursuing is the laborious one of distinguishing the items that have led to each interpretation; that is, of cataloging imaginary objects and actions together with the "meanings" that have been assigned to each. And this brings us back to our main problem —the validation of assigned meanings. We have only mentioned "the principle of the multiplicity of judgments"; that agreement among experimenters is one reason for accepting an interpretation. It is not, however, a very good reason. One knows too much about mutual suggestion and flattery in limited esoteric circles. Let us see what other modes of verification exist.

The problem may be simplified by taking the case of a single experimenter who, after reviewing his own results, comes to the conclusion that a certain infantile thema, X, has been an important factor in the development of one of his subjects. What methods are available for testing this inference?

If variable X is an enduring central determinant, it should operate repeatedly and influence responses to diverse presentations. Also, it should be found to interact or articulate with other distinguishable factors in a psychologically intelligible manner (*i.e.*, according to a generally accepted "logic" of the emotions). To ascertain if this is the case, an experimenter may employ one or more of the following procedures:

(a) *Correlation with a multiplicity of other fantasy tests.* The consistency of X is determined by noting the number of times it recurs in other tests. If it does not recur it should, at least, be dynamically related to the variables that do occur.

(b) *Correlation with biographical data.* Experience goes to show that variables which strongly manifest themselves in fantasy (a) have usually been engendered or promoted by one or more concrete occurrences and (b) are apt to lead to or influence subsequent occurrences. For this reason, the experimenter should avail himself of as much information as possible concerning each subject's life. The validity of X may then be partially determined by discovering how and to what degree it may have articulated with the facts disclosed in the biography. For example, the fantasy thema may be a repetition of an escape from a counter-claim to some childhood event.

The finding that X recurs in other tests and that it seems to connect with other discernible factors would provide good ground for confidence if one were less familiar with the ability of men to combine things in thought and believe that they were so combined in nature. To determine whether fantasies produced by the same S for different experimenters show veritable (rather than rationalized) uniformities and articulations, one may employ the matching technique.

(c) Matching results from different tests. An experimenter may attempt to guess, on the basis of his own findings, what subject gave each set of results obtained in some other test. For example, the ten sets of stories concocted by ten subjects for a male experimenter and the ten sets of stories concocted by the same subjects for a female experimenter were given to two other experimenters for matching. It happened that all (ten) pairs were correctly assembled, which showed that each of these ten subjects was consistent in manifesting (twice) certain discernible tendencies.

(d) Matching test results with biographical data. Ten biographies and ten sets of fantasies (with no names attached) were given for matching. One experimenter matched five and two experimenters matched all ten correctly. This indicates that fantasies are related to the events of life in a distinguishable manner. In other words, some of the dependences that are apperceived actually exist; they are not mere clever rationalizations.

(e) Guessing the occurrence of certain childhood experiences. Solely on the basis of the fantasy material, an E may attempt to name some of the critical experiences that occurred during the subject's infancy, to guess, for example, what gratifying, frustrating, or traumatic events took place; what sort of relationship was established with the mother, the father, and the siblings; how the child reacted to what difficulties in social adaptation. This exercise puts the greatest stress upon the psychological knowledge and intuition of an experimenter. Though it has not yet been methodically attempted at the Harvard Clinic, many of the workers have independently and informally recorded their "hunches" and attempted to verify them. The story in which "the violin as mother" occurred may be taken as an example.

Subject Abel. When Abel was presented with a picture of a little boy gazing at a violin lying before him on the table, he gave the following story:

This youngster has heard the violin played. When the player put the violin on the table he went over to look at the hole to see where the music came from. He is puzzled by the absence of any music maker inside. Puzzled that the instrument could make such sounds. He doesn't connect the bow with the instrument. Pretty soon he will start fooling around with it trying to make sounds himself. The result depends on who hears him playing. The owner will be provoked, and take the instrument away. If no one hears him the strings will be taken apart, but he won't demolish the instrument.

Here, the hypothesis was made that at the birth of a younger child Abel became perplexed about childbirth, suspected that the baby came out of the mother and entertained fantasies of aggressive exploration. When this diagnosis was made the experimenter did not know that Abel had a younger brother.

At a subsequent interview, on being asked whether as a boy he was inclined to dismember his toys, Abel responded exactly as follows without any prompting:

Yes, I was always breaking things, always breaking everything to find out why or how it worked. I had a locomotive, I remember, and I had a wonderful time taking it apart. I learned to take the pedals of the piano apart. I used to peer inside the piano and wonder about it. I was terribly destructive—not just to destroy but to understand. I broke some plates to find out what they were made of, and my mother scolded me for this. I would say that this destructive, curious period began when I was five and ended when I was eight. I remember when it began because my younger brother was born when I was five. My brother was born in the house and my mother was very sick afterwards. I couldn't see the connection between her sickness and the baby. I was told that he had been found in the flour barrel, but of course I didn't believe it. But after that I was awfully curious. I used to plague my parents to death asking the how and why of everything. This still persists as one of my strongest characteristics. My teachers in school told me that I was frightfully curious about everything and very inquisitive. I always want to know how things work.

It was considered that these memories occurring in this sequence without direct questioning, together with other facts discovered, were good evidence for the experimenter's hypothesis.

(f) *Predictions of future behavior.* The E may attempt to predict on the basis of his material how each of his subjects will react when faced by a certain experimentally controlled situation. At the Harvard Clinic this has been conscientiously attempted only once. From the stories that fifteen subjects produced when presented with a particular picture (thematic apperception test) an experimenter[13] attempted to predict the relative hypnotizability of each member of the group. He made a rank order which correlated highly ($r = .72$) with the rank order for hypnotizability which was established later.

(g) *Consultation with the subject.* After an experimenter has completed his hypothetical reconstruction of a personality he may attempt, directly or indirectly, in a final interview with the subject to obtain evidence that bears upon the critical diagnostic issues.

SUMMARY

In the present communication it has been suggested that, though "fantasy," by general accord, is a convenient term, it would be more accurate to speak of psychical processes that were to a varying degree "fantastical." The opinion was submitted that fantasies are important *per se*, because of their relations to overt behavior, emotion, creative thought, and neurotic symptoms, and because they may lead an experimenter to the discovery of the critical conditioning events of childhood. Fifteen or more techniques, most of which are susceptible to standardization, were briefly outlined. A scheme for the conceptual organization of the material was sketched, the principles of genetic interpretation were discussed, and some procedures for the verification of such interpretations were suggested.

REFERENCES

1. Piaget, J. *The Child's Conception of the World.* Trans. by J. and A. Tomlinson. New York: Harcourt, Brace, 1929, pp. x, 397.

2. Jung, C. G. *Psychology of the Unconscious.* Trans. by B. M. Hinkle. New York: Moffat, Yard and Co., 1917, pp. iv, 566.

3. Pareto, V. *The Mind and Society.* Ed. by A. Livingston. New York: Harcourt, Brace, 1935.

4. Luria, A. R. *The Nature of Human Conflicts.* Trans. by W. H. Gantt. New York: Liveright, 1932, pp. xvii, 431.

5. Langer, W. C. The tremograph: a modified form of the Luria apparatus. *J. Gen. Psychol.* (in press).

6. Jung, C. G. *Two Essays on Analytical Psychology.* New York: Dodd, Mead and Co., 1928.

7. Skinner, B. F. The verbal summator and a method for the study of latent speech. *J. of Psychol.*, 1936, *2*, 71–107.

8. Bartlett, F. C. An experimental study of some problems of perceiving and imaging. *Brit. J. Psychol.*, 1916, *8*, Part 2, 222–266.

9. Sanford, R. N. The effects of abstinence from food upon imaginal process: a preliminary experiment. *J. of Psychol.*, 1936, *2*, 129–136.

10. Morgan, C. D., & Murray, H. A. A method for investigating fantasies. *Arch. Neur. & Psychiat.*, 1935, *34*, 289–306.

11. Murray, H. A. Basic concepts in the study of personality. *J. Soc. Psychol.* (in press).

12. ——. Facts which support the concept of need or drive. *J. of Psychol.*, 1936, *3*, 27–42.

13. White, R. W. Experimental evidence for a dynamic theory of hypnosis. Thesis offered for Ph.D. degree, Widener Library, Harvard University, Cambridge, Mass.

17

A METHOD FOR INVESTIGATING FANTASIES: THE THEMATIC APPERCEPTION TEST

(With Christiana D. Morgan)

Psychoanalysis attempts to represent the underlying dynamics of personality as an interaction of forces. Each force is a need which impels the individual person to pursue a certain course of activity—a course of activity which usually involves a certain kind of object. An inhibited or repressed force with its associated impressions of objects may manifest itself in the guise of a fantasy which the subject can report on, or its presence may be inferred by the analyst on the basis of other phenomena. In the latter case the analyst is apt to speak of it as a repressed unconscious fantasy. Since the exposition of such hidden fantasies is one of the fundamental aims of analysis and since, at best, the customary technic for accomplishing it calls for a long period of watchful waiting, it seems that it would be helpful if a more expeditious method could be devised. For, if the analyst were cognizant at the very start of the fundamental fantasy constructions of his patient he should be in a better position to apperceive and to interpret the dynamic relations of what, in the beginning of an analysis, is ordinarily fragmentary and obscure. He might also, at a later stage, have a better idea of what might be considered irrelevant as well as what important latent trends had yet to be disclosed.

The method which is to be described is based on the well recognized fact that when some one attempts to interpret a complex social situation he is apt to tell as much about himself as he is about the phenomena on which attention is focused. At such times the person is off his guard, since he believes that he is merely explaining objective occurrences. To one with "double hearing," however, he is exposing certain inner forces and arrangements—wishes, fears and traces of past experience. Another fact which was relied on in devising the present method is that a great deal of written fiction is the conscious or unconscious expression of the au-

From *Archives of Neurology and Psychiatry,* 1935, *34,* pp. 289–306.

thor's experiences or fantasies. The process involved is that of projection —something well known to analysts. It is utilized in the Rorschach test.

PROCEDURE

The procedure which suggested itself was this: to present subjects with a series of pictures, each of which depicts a different dramatic event, with the instructions to interpret the action in each picture and give an imaginary reconstruction of the preceding events and the final outcome. It was anticipated that in the performance of this task a subject would necessarily be forced to project some of his own fantasies into the material and so reveal some of his more pressing underlying needs.

Since for purposes of comparison it is desirable to make such a procedure as uniform as possible, that is, to present every subject with similar stimuli and similar instructions for response, the attempt was made to find a standard set of pictures. Each picture should suggest some critical situation and be effective in evoking a fantasy relating to it. The set should also be comprehensive. Ideally, there should be a picture which would act as a trellis to support the growth and unfolding of every root fantasy. It was considered, and the idea was later confirmed by experience, that there should be at least one person in each picture with whom the subject could easily identify himself. Such an object may be termed an evoker, that is, one who evokes empathy in another. Thus, there should be a separate set of pictures for males and females, and also for children, young adults and elderly persons. Since in the present experiments the subjects were all young men between the ages of 20 and 30, most of the pictures to be described included at least one figure of that sex and age. After a preliminary selection from several hundred pictures and an elimination of those which on repeated trials proved unproductive, we found a set of twenty which gave good results. This test was one of many to which fifty subjects were exposed. It formed a part of a comprehensive study of personality in which about twenty experimenters participated.

The subject was seated in a comfortable chair with his back to the experimenter, and the following directions were read to him:

"This is a test of creative imagination. I am going to show you a picture, and I want you to make up a plot or story for which it might be used as an illustration. What is the relation of the individuals in the picture? What has happened to them? What are their present thoughts and feelings? What will be the outcome? I want you to do your very best. As this is a test of literary imagination you may make your story as long and as detailed as you wish."

The subject was then handed picture 1, and the experimenter wrote down everything that he said. If, in giving his story, the subject omitted the antecedent circumstances or the outcome, he was reminded of it by such remarks as, "What led up to this situation?" "How will it end?" etc. When the subject finished his story he was handed picture 2 and asked to proceed as before. There were twenty pictures in the series, but as the test was stopped after an hour most of the subjects did not have time to make up stories for more than two thirds of them.

The test was given once to forty subjects as a group test, the stories being written. The time saved by this method was considerable, but the results were less satisfactory.

After a few days had elapsed each subject was interviewed. This time the experimenter explained that he was studying the imaginative process in the construction of literary plots and that he wished to know if what professional writers had told about their creative experiences was true for every one. The subject was then asked if he would cooperate by trying to remember whether his story had come from something which he had seen or read; whether it had come out of the experience of friends or relatives, or whether it had come out of his own private experience. The subject was then reminded of the plot of each story in turn and encouraged to speak freely and openly.

RESULTS

An examination of the stories concocted by our subjects in conjunction with material obtained from introspections, autobiographies, hours of free association, interviews, etc., reveals the fact that there were four chief sources from which the plots and the items of the plots were drawn: (1) books and moving pictures, (2) actual events in which a friend or a member of the family participated, (3) experiences (subjective or objective) in the subject's own life, and (4) the subject's conscious and unconscious fantasies.

Although the material from the first two of these four sources may seem at first blush to be of little importance, it was discovered that even here much of significance was revealed. This, it seems, may be explained by referring to the tendency exhibited by most subjects to enjoy observing most and to remember best the external events which resemble their underlying fantasies. Thus, when a subject gives a vivid account of an occurrence one may profitably consider whether or not the theme of the event is a clue to his latent personality.

That every subject almost immediately projects his own circumstances, experiences or preoccupations into the evoker was only too obvious. For instance, in one experiment six of the eleven college men who took the test said that the youth in picture 4 was a student, whereas none of the twelve noncollege men who acted as subjects described him as such. One subject, whose father had been a ship's carpenter, wanted to go to sea himself, to travel and see the world. This was his dominant fantasy. Three of the scenes in his stories were laid on board a ship and two were in the Orient. In regard to picture 17, which illustrates a middle-aged man talking to a younger man, the subject said: "The older man is educated and has traveled a lot. He convinces the other to travel, to take a job that will take him to different places." In commenting on a picture which illustrates a young man sitting in a chair brooding rather disconsolately, this subject said: "This is a business man who runs quite a business in town. He is weighing the possibility of a European trip. He has been arguing with his wife on the subject. She got angry because he would not go and finally took up her hat and left. He is thinking it over. He changes his opinion, goes out and buys tickets." In interpreting another picture, illustrating two laborers engaged in conversation, the same subject said: "These two fellows are a pair of adventurers. They always manage to meet in out of the way places. They are now in India. They have heard of a new revolution in South America, and they are planning how they can get there. . . . In the end they work their way in a freighter."

Many other examples of this sort of thing could be cited. No subject failed to exemplify it. Some of them, in fact, gave stories which were frank and unabashed autobiographies, one example of which will be sufficient.

When presented with picture 5, depicting a young lad gazing pensively at a violin which is resting on a table before him, our subject said: "A very sensitive boy—sensitive lips—who is musical by nature. His mother wants him to be a violinist, but his father, who is in business, is averse to it. The father came home one night and heard him squeaking—'squeaking' to him but beautiful to the mother—and told him to stop. He is a highly irritable father with a bad temper, and he partially destroys the violin. The boy is rudely shocked. He is over his grief now, but is studying the violin with tenderness and sorrow. This upset makes him all the more fervently musical. It gives him new sorrow, making him more mature. It takes away the light spirit of a child and makes him a better artist. His mother buys him a new violin in spite of the father. He continues his playing and so goes on to the life of an artist. By this experience he will have nothing in common with other children of his age. He is more sensitive and will find his greatest happiness in solitude. He becomes a genius, appears at concerts and is acclaimed by critics because he is so precocious. Then his popularity wanes. He deviates to musical expression through the medium of language—literature. He becomes a poet. At 14 or 15 he has had none of the contacts of ordinary youth. He is called a sissy and is quite unhappy. But he glories in the happiness of the consciousness of his own superiority. Others of his age he thinks are silly. School is a limitation. He feels its thorns. His father is interested in his marks rather than in the development of his mind. His mother wants him to be what she couldn't be, but she doesn't influence his intellectual development. She is a pillar of strength to fall back upon, but she doesn't feel deeply. The boy looks on her as inferior but necessary. He goes into philosophy and the arts. If he is not careful he will become sexually abnormal. At nineteen he has written great poetry with great imagination and imagery. He puts deep philosophic thoughts into great language. . . ."

In his introspections this subject admitted: "All of this story is autobiographical." He said further: "My father isn't like that, but he could be. Only by keeping my mouth shut [the subject did not speak until he was 3 years old] is it possible to keep the atmosphere one of indifference. The conflict of the business man and the poet [the subject himself has written poetry and intends to dedicate his life to this calling] is so intense that it could flame out between us as great hostility. There is a lot in it about sorrow. Well, I'll tell you, though you will probably think it foolish. You see I feel that I really want to be like Byron. I want to be highly sensitive as he was. You know the girls in high school ridiculed me when I read them my poetry. I want to expose myself to their scorn and ridicule. I want to be sensitive and expose myself in order to suffer, because it is only through the greatest suffering that we can know anything of life and be strong. . . ."

In his autobiography the subject said: "I have no close attachment to the family and [as a corollary to this condition] no favorite parent. Probably I do favor my mother, however, because I see more of her but the attachment is inconsequential. . . . I was timid and easily beaten in fist fights. I suffered from the barbaric joys of young boys. . . . My favorite story and hero was Robinson Crusoe, lonely and self-sufficient. . . . Writing is my chief aim of the immediate and distant future. I also aim to develop more mature sex relationships. I do not care to try to remodel the world; it is much more intriguing to fathom the one I have found. If I could remodel it, I would like to be the greatest writer—equivalent to prophet—and receive the acclaim of an intelligent populace. Above all, I would like to have the world more alive to and aware of its own beauty."

Although some of this material is suggestive of certain underlying infantile experiences and fantasies, it is not to demonstrate such trends that this case is cited. It is our intention merely to indicate how much important biographic data may sometimes be obtained from a single story and the introspections which follow it. This kind of information, however, can often be obtained by direct questioning, and the present test would be quite unnecessary if it were only this that one wished to discover. What we have to show is that subjects project their deepest fantasies into such dramatic pictures and thereby reveal directional tensions of which they are quite unconscious. Though some of their stories are elaborations of conscious fantasies, others are not recognized by the subjects as having any personal reference. It is these—in which the personal reference is suggested by other data—that have been ascribed to unconscious fantasies. Of course, the stories as given are conscious fantasies. Like dreams, they must be interpreted if one is to arrive at the unconscious trends which determine them. Before presenting typical case histories to support this assumption, however, it will be necessary to outline the conceptual scheme which we have adopted for the classification of fantasies.

Psychoanalysts have found it convenient to name some of the more common fantasies—the Oedipus fantasy, king-slave fantasy, foster-parent fantasy, etc. This naming represents the beginning of a classification —the initial step in the construction of any science—and the practice should be continued until all important fantasies have been so recognized. If this is to be done in a systematic fashion every fantasy must be analyzed into the factors which compose it, so that the groupings may be made in terms of similar fundamental elements.

Our own reflections have led us to the conclusion that every fantasy may be analyzed into a series of events, each event, in turn, being an occurrence which is usually analyzable into: (1) a driving force (or fusion of forces in the subject), (2) an object (or group of objects) toward which or away from which the force is directed, and (3) the outcome of their interaction expressed in terms of subjective feeling—satisfaction or dissatisfaction. This mode of analysis is applicable not only to a fantasy but to an actual event as well. Sometimes it is preferable to speak first of the object, i.e., the environmental press or stimulus situation, and second of the subjective trend, i.e., the response. Stated in this way, our mode of representation resembles the familiar S-R formula of the behaviorists, except that with us the stimulus is more than a single sensation or perception. It is a temporal *Gestalt* of stimuli which bear the same dynamic meaning—the press. And with us the response is ordinarily represented not as a particular muscular movement or reflex but as a need or general course of action, the tendency of which is to produce a certain effect.

To incorporate fantasies into a scientific system of psychology, then, we propose to classify them according to the single events which compose them, every event, as we have pointed out, being classified according to its essential structure. To refer to the dynamic structure or plot of a fantasied event—or, for that matter, of an actual event—we have found it convenient to use the term thema (th.). A simple thema we shall define as the abstract formula for a single event. It consists of a particular press-need combination. The term complex thema may be used to describe a commonly encountered temporal association of simple themas, some of which may be dominant and some subsidiary.

In some events only the press is known or the press is of primary importance (something happens or an object does something and the subject merely experiences it or adapts to it), whereas in other events nothing is known of the press or the press is merely the usual environment and it is the subject's action which is significant. In the former case the press alone will constitute the thema, and in the latter case, the need alone. For instance, "p punishment" will describe an event in which the subject is punished by an object, and "n punishment" or just "punishment" will describe an event in which the subject punishes an object. Strictly speaking, a thema is the structure of a momentary event, but the term may also be used to describe a long continued press followed by a long continued response, provided the intervening events are more or less irrelevant. For instance, "p family discord" may be used to describe the fact that a child is frequently exposed to quarrels between his father and his mother, and "revenge" may be used to describe a subject's long enduring resentment and a series of retaliative actions.

This brief exposition of the concept of thema (th.) was necessary, it seemed, in view of the fact that we have analyzed our material in this way and have proposed a name for every significant thema which could be clearly identified. The names, of course, should be regarded merely as suggestions, for they may prove to be inadequately descriptive when more fantasies of the same kind are examined.

Since the subjects who take this test are asked to interpret each picture, that is, to apperceive the plot or dramatic structure exhibited by each picture, we have named it the "thematic apperception test."

REVIEW OF CASES

We shall now present the essential details of two typical cases in order to indicate the sort of data which one obtains with this test. It should be noted that though each subject presents a few themas which are strikingly similar and others which are dynamically interrelated, the themas of one subject, taken as a whole, are very different from those of the other. That is to say, in these cases there are clear individual differences.

CASE 1.

G. was a restless, energetic undergraduate student who was planning to go to the business school. He wanted "to get a position in a big firm" and ultimately to devote part of his time to civic and educational enterprises. "My favorite parent," he wrote in his autobiography, "especially in my early years, was my father, probably because he rarely punished me. You see my mother was more strict with me." The father was an ardent Republican, but G. could not say enough against this party or, for that matter, against all parties and all government officials—congressmen, politicians and utility magnates. "The only childhood habits I had," he continues, "were thumbsucking (sucking th.) and finickiness about food (oral rejection th.). [For a long time he hated lunch and supper. He had "the life nagged out of him to eat."] . . . At times I was fearful of others, especially of those bigger than myself. Further, I was very sensitive and still am."

It seems that G.'s pride must have been recently wounded by one or more of his friends, for he hinted at a serious quarrel and said: "It pays neither to ridicule nor criticize."

"Personally, I would prefer to use the word 'acquaintance' and not 'friend'," he wrote. "I have looked at this matter objectively and I have come to the conclusion every one is out for what he can get. . . . Hence, I'm really careful to make no really deep friendships and just try to keep all at a certain distance." Later he added: "One's estimate of one's own social world is a most difficult thing. It usually depends on how one has been brought up and how the world treats one. . . . My attitude toward this social world is one of disgust and indifference. . . . The world's estimate [of me] is yet unformed, or should be. Yet, I am young, and till I'm at least 30 I will refrain from passing final judgment on myself and my character." From this one receives the impression that the subject had suffered some rebuff or had been unjustly blamed and as a result had become a Timon. As he said, he was "very sensitive."

G. gave a negative sex history. "My early practices as far as I can remember were none; in fact, I have never even masturbated for no reason that I can discover." When asked how he got on with the girls in his high school, he answered: "Bored. I didn't even look at them while I was there." He was generally scornful of women. He recalled with pleasure the way his father rebuked his mother when he was teaching her to drive. His mother, however, was the stronger of the two and did all the punishing. One of the subject's similes was:

"As dangerous as a woman learning to drive." In giving his childhood memories he omitted to mention, but later recalled, an important event which occurred when he was 9—the death from infantile paralysis of a cousin. This cousin was very accomplished for his age; he was adored by his parents and was the constant playmate of the subject. His death was a great shock to the subject. In the clinic the subject, though cooperative and responsive, was indirectly aggressive. He expressed his scorn of the government, university institutions and some of the experimental procedures. When he was left in a room with a self-effacing fellow undergraduate, however, he was outstandingly agreeable and sympathetic. His behavior under these circumstances seemed to fit in with his avowed intention to devote himself in later life to those who were less fortunate than himself.

Thematic Apperceptions. Picture 4: On the floor against a couch is the huddled form of a boy with his head bowed on his right arm. Beside him on the floor is an object which resembles a revolver.

Subject: "This seems to suggest a normal young boy who has done something wrong. He has been playing with fire or smoking. Father has given him a serious talking to and the boy has taken it much to heart. Is thinking it over, crying, thinking of his sins. He will try to be a real good boy after this and obey his parents." (Minor crime [incendiary, smoking] → p punishment [verbal] → reform th.)

"Or, he may have broken some valuable furniture in the house. He is sulking because it was an accident. He did not do it on purpose. He feels an injustice has been done to him." (Minor crime [vandal] → p [unjust] punishment → sulk th.)

"Or, the third possibility is that he has been forsaken by his friends. He is feeling the injustice of a world which has treated him rottenly. It is one of those young troubles we all have. He is thinking, 'I will live by myself now and not associate with them if they have treated me that way.' " (Timon th. = p [social] rejection → [social] rejection th.)

In the last two of these three stories the feeling of "suffered injustice" is encountered. The root of such a feeling is often some infantile experience of deprivation—birth trauma, weaning trauma or rejection trauma. Here the two circumstances occasioning this feeling are censure and rejection. The causes of punishment are playing with fire and breaking valuable furniture (minor crimes of destruction) and smoking (sin of oral sentience).

Picture 6: The silhouette of a man's figure against a bright window. The rest of the picture is totally dark.

Subject: "This is some person who has lived in poverty. He has never tasted success or happiness. He was an orphan who never had a good start. He tried to build himself up, but failed and is now considering suicide. He has walked to the window. It is a spring day. The flowers and trees are in bloom. He thinks of the wonders of life—the beauty of nature. This brings him back, and he thinks if he should try hard he might be a success. He is young. Every one has disappointments. If he struggles he can overcome the deficiencies in his education. He can go to night school. He forgets the squalor of his surroundings; forgets the people around him, degenerate and degraded. He feels he will get out of that circle. He will keep to himself until he gets out of it. When he makes a fortune he becomes a philanthropist. He becomes very civic-minded, spending money on playgrounds, charities, friends and orphanages. He endows a professor in college, helps a library. He realizes the difficulties he has been through. Though he has had to suffer, others shouldn't. He adopts an orphan, that is, if he didn't get married and a man like that wouldn't. He dies with a smile on his face, having benefited mankind." (Orphan → achievement, failure → suicide; and p deprivation [economic] → traumatic [deprivation] restriving, suprajection th. → achievement [economic] → charity, adoption of child th.; misogyne th.)

The orphan thema is always suggestive of some infantile experience of suffered deprivation—birth trauma, weaning trauma or rejection trauma. Here it leads (by succor-projection) to the charity thema, that is, pity for a self-like object (narcissistic object choice). The rejection of marriage—"a man like that wouldn't marry"—suggests a retaliative rejection (misogyne th.) or possibly homosexuality.

Picture 11: A young man with his head buried in the lap of a young woman who bends over him with a tender expression.

Subject: "The young fellow is in love. A young lady of a better station has jilted him. He is very unhappy. His mother is consoling him, telling him there are other girls, that he is young, that there is plenty of time. He takes mother's advice, but feels embittered about women. He pays no attention to them after this. He lives as a bachelor. He adopts a girl—or no, a boy. He wants to be a father, and it is easier to be a father to a boy. He gives the child money. His mother is happy over this. He feels motherly toward his adopted son and they live happily ever after." ([Superior] marriage wish → p [erotic] rejection → dejection, misogyne, adoption of child, mother identification, charity th.)

Here is another variety of the Timon thema—rejection followed by counter-rejection. But in this instance it is specifically the suffered rejection of erotic love followed by woman-hating (misogyne th.). This points to the mother as the original depriver and refuser—birth trauma, weaning trauma or rejection trauma. Again, one finds adoption of a child as the objectified solution of narcissistic self-pity. One might suppose that the subject—after feeling excluded by his mother—determined to become his own loving mother (partial mother identification), and later this endopsychic drama became a fantasy of benevolence to an unloved boy.

Picture 12: A young man helplessly clutched from behind by two hands, one on each of his shoulders. The figure of his antagonist is invisible.

Subject: "This suggests a fellow of less than medium means. He has had to struggle all his life as a clerk in a store, making just enough to keep himself and his wife alive. They have no child. His only happiness lies in marriage, for he sees no chance of rising in his firm. He feels sad and downhearted until he comes home. His wife cheers him. But he finds that she has been unfaithful to him, and he decides to leave. In the picture she is trying to hold him back. She tried to make him listen to reason. She slipped, as we all do, she says, but really loves him. But he goes off with nothing to live for. Now he just works to eat instead of eating to work. He mopes around, very dejected and sour. He doesn't look at life kindly since it gave him this raw deal. She tries to patch things up. But he leaves her again. He often wonders why he did this. It might have been better if he had stayed, but he can't bring himself to do it. The memory of her unfaithfulness always comes up. He dies young, as he has nothing to fight for. He gets sick and lets himself go, and that is the end." (p deprivation [economic] → achievement failure → dejection th.; p. rejection [infidelity] → rejection [erotic, misogyne], dejection, death, th.)

In this story erotic rejection is the consequence of suffered infidelity. Perhaps the subject was jealous of his father; perhaps he was shocked when, as a child, he discovered that his mother had sexual intercourse with his father. He left her, partly to heal his wounded pride (retaliative rejection) and partly to revenge himself. (Imposed guilt th., suffering in order to arouse guilt feelings in the object.)

Picture 10: A dimly indicated figure of a man clinging to a rope. He is in the act of climbing up or down.

Subject: "This man is escaping from a dungeon in some foreign country where prisoners are looked on as criminals and there is no mercy. It was a political crime and no mercy was shown. He is out to get even with the world, for the world threw him into jail. Finally he succeeds in getting free after enduring much misery—running through swamps, killing animals with his hands and eating raw meat. He kills a soldier who supports the government and gets his uniform. He reaches a big city and gets a position. He earns money for some new clothes. Then he goes on to the capital and lays plans for revenge. He gets in with the Reds, doing it entirely for revenge. He must get even. The planned revolt is discovered, and he has to flee. This time he has enough money. Then he returns and plans to make his revenge more subtle. He gets a position in the government and gets in contact with the man who was responsible for the original injustice to him. He decides to kidnap this autocrat's child. He makes this man suffer plenty. He kills the child and sends her back. Then he gives himself up in remorse for having taken the life of an innocent child. A priest comes. He asks forgiveness. He dies with the words on his lips that at least he had made his enemy suffer." (Infraggression [rebel] → [unjust] punishment [prison] → escape, crime [revengeful] biting, murder and kidnaping → atonement th.)

Here is a rather unusual motif—the biting thema, or cannibalism—suggesting that the original form of aggression was directed toward the mother's breast. Perhaps it represents a partial frustration of the child's original reaction to oral frustration—the weaning trauma. Again, one finds the feeling of suffered injustice, but in this case it leads not to separation (misanthrope th.) or aggression through masochism (imposed guilt th.) but to something more primitive—a revengeful counteraggression. After the hero kills an innocent child, however, he feels guilty, suffers remorse and repents.

Picture 7: A short elderly woman stands with her back turned to a tall young man. The latter is looking downward with a perplexed expression, his hat in his hands.

Subject: "This fellow is a good friend of the old lady and her son. The boys were brought up together, played and went to school together. They were always together. They lived in the same house. Then the son of the old lady is killed in an accident. In this picture he had to break the news to her. There is much grief on both parts. He realizes that his friend was her only support, so he feels it is his duty to adopt her as his mother. They run a boarding-house together. He tries to substitute himself as her dead son. Then he wants to get married. But if he does she will object. He doesn't feel that he will be doing right to his friend. It would be an injustice to his friend's memory. The girl, not knowing the facts, is angry at the idea of being thrown over. They have a fight and end it. He is quite pleased now that he has made the decision. If the girl is that kind of a girl he did well not to marry her, for the marriage would never have been a success. The old woman dies. This time he finds a nicer girl. She feels for him in his sorrow over his friend. She feels he did wonderfully to have done as he did. He marries her. The story ends happily." (p death [friend], p bereavement, bearer of sad things → self as substitute offspring, better parent th.; love → [erotic] renunciation from loyalty → quarrel → rejection [erotic]; love th.)

Here again the subject brings in the adoption of child thema, but with this picture the subject can maintain his active attitude toward adoption only by having the hero adopt the mother. This suggests the possibility that at one time the subject wanted to be adopted (better parent th.). There is also the possibility that the intense loyalty which binds the hero to his dead friend is based on a previous homosexual attachment.

In his introspections after studying picture 3, the subject referred to his young cousin—a boy who had died. He said: "Aunt and Uncle had a boy just my age. He was a very handsome and gifted child. He died of infantile paralysis when he was 9. Although Aunt and Uncle had two girls, they were heart-broken. They thought of adopting an orphan. They used to take great interest in a boy in an orphanage and in the orphanage itself. I was very much impressed at the time. My parents never talked about it, but I picked up a good deal."

Since the adoption of child thema is an unusual one and since it appears three times in this subject's stories, one must suppose that it plays an important role in his unconscious psychic structure. Moreover, since the idea of adoption was presented to him just after the death of his gifted playmate, there is reason to suppose that the adoption of child thema took root at that time. The story evoked by picture 7 suggests that after his cousin's death the idea occurred to him that he might be adopted by his aunt and uncle. Two factors may have conspired to produce this fantasy—dissatisfaction with his own parents and guilt over his cousin's death. The evidence in favor of the former is rather strong—a deep-seated feeling of suffered injustice. (p. rejection, Timon th., [erotic] rejection th., misogyne th., dejection th.) These trends point to an early oral trauma. One fantasy formation after punishment may have been that of aggression through masochism—"I hope I shall die so that my parents will suffer. They will grieve and feel remorseful because of the way they treated me" (imposed guilt th.). If the subject did concoct this common fantasy, his aunt and uncle grieving over their son's death would have appeared to him in the guise of ideal parents.

The data pointing to guilt experienced by the subject after his cousin's death are fragmentary and inconclusive. We have learned that the cousin was more gifted than the subject, and hence the latter may have been envious of him and may have entertained and repressed aggressive fantasies toward him. When infantile paralysis set in the subject may have felt that his death wishes were responsible. In the subject's apperceptions the only act which was followed by guilt was the murder of an innocent child. In picture 7 the hero "feels it is his duty" to adopt the elderly woman as his mother. What except guilty feelings could make him feel that this was his duty? By replacing the lost son and being a model boy he could achieve salvation.

Picture 17: A young man sitting opposite to an older man. The latter has his hand out as though emphasizing some point in an argument.

Subject: "Prodigal son out of college. Father is determined that he must work for a living. He tells him pointblank that he won't give him a job. He must start from the bottom. The boy feels disgusted and angry, but he takes a job and after two months begins to take an interest. He is promoted. In two years he has made quite a success. His father is beaming all over. The boy is living by himself. He meets a working-class girl. She is not what he is used to—not a "deb"—but he falls in love with her. Father hears of this and decides that things have gone far enough. He wants him to come back, but the boy tears up his father's letter and marries the girl. He is now head of the department. Has children. His wife is intelligent—she has studied, has taste for art, music and literature. She is a really good companion. The father meets the girl by accident, is taken with her and finally takes them back. They come to live with the father. But the son refuses to enter his father's business. He demands that the father sell his business and endow a university. Father does this. The son now becomes president of his company." (p deprivation [economic] → achievement → [inferior] marriage → p dominance [coercive opposition] → autonomy → achievement → p pardon → imposition of atonement, charity th.)

The principal point of interest in this story is the charity thema functioning as an atonement for injury done to others. This supports the assumption that the charity thema as well as the adoption of child thema represents a way to salvation.

The following relevant root experiences and reaction formations are suggested by this subject's seven stories:

(a) Oral deprivation and later deprivation of parental love. The subject said that he was very sensitive. He was babied as a child. In the clinic he made many movements of his lips and many hand-to-mouth movements while he was working. He said that as a boy he knew that women were different from men because they had "mammary glands." He thought then that children grew from a seed planted by God in a mother's "heart." He had a number of memories relating to food, and he used a number of expressions with food associations, such as "he couldn't earn a crust of bread." He liked girls who were "sweet and understanding," and he said that a "sympathetic understanding was the basis of any profitable procedure." These fragmentary items, added to the evidence supplied by the thematic apperceptions, and the autobiography, made the assumption of an oral deprivation trauma rather plausible.

(b) Counter-rejection of love, oral aggression. The subject's mother did most of the punishing, and it is probable that aggression was primarily directed against her. The subject had a scornful attitude toward women. "O, women, how fickle!" he said on one occasion. He spoke of "biting someone's head off" and of "blasting things to bits." He was at all times verbally very aggressive, as has been pointed out. The hypothesis proposed is that his aggression was initially a reaction to oral frustration and later a retaliation for unjust censure by his father. We also suggest the presence of envy aggression against his more talented cousin.

(c) Death of cousin, guilt and the wish to be adopted. The arguments to support the significance of these factors were previously presented (discussion of picture 7). The hypothesis proposed was that the wish to be adopted was a fusion of the wish for ideal parents and the wish to atone for his guilt.

(d) Achievement. The subject has high ambitions, and he works with great zest and industry. He wishes to make a lot of money in business. This may be explained as restriving after economic deprivation as a substitute for love and as a way to philanthropy.

(e) Charity, and the adoption of a son. These trends were in the service of his own "orphan feeling," which would be relieved by helping others, and also represented ways of atoning for his former aggression. He wants to be of service to the community. He said: "If I had money I would endow scholarships; give it where it would do the greatest good for humanity, for people."

CASE 2.

B. was an undergraduate student concentrating on music. Though habitually diffident and reserved, he was responsive and submissive to those whom he respected. The muscles about his eyes were frequently contracted as though he were photophobic. This gave him an expression of puzzled anxiety. He was neatly dressed, and his social personality was unobtrusive and banal. He came to the clinic complaining of a symptom which had worried and hindered him for two years—the recurrence of stereotyped images which interfered with normal imaginal processes. He was particularly bothered when he tried to read, for the automatic imagery prevented the generation of such associations as the printed words would ordinarily have suggested. The result of this was that imaginative understanding was blocked and memory for meanings greatly diminished. He found, however, that he had a photographic memory—that the image of the printed page was retained, though the sense of it was lost. This enabled him to get high marks in his examinations.

The stereotyped images were mostly of two sorts: scenes of the distant past —buildings, woods, pastures and brooks in and about his native town in the South —and scenes recently observed—Harvard Square, the Boston State House, etc. The images were static and did not contribute to a fantasy. No human or animal figures appeared, and the presentations seemed to be entirely innocuous.

There was nothing in B.'s autobiography or in the information that he volunteered during the preliminary interviews which seemed to bear directly on the symptomatology. He said that he was born and brought up in a small southern town and was the son of strict Methodists. He had no favorite parent, though his disposition resembled his father's, and he was more influenced by him than by his mother. His father was an impressive figure—a large man with high ethical standards and an explosive temper to reenforce them. There was a baby sister who died two years before his birth, and another sister, three years his junior, with whom as a boy he frequently quarreled. He remembered being punished for scratching his sister and talking back to his mother. In his childhood he was afraid of many things—water, animals and automobile accidents. He had recurrent nightmares of being chased by a bull.

He described himself as timid, sensitive and reticent. He had frequent inferiority feelings. He played with dolls with his sister until he was 9. At school he avoided participation in organized athletics. He said that he had a strong possessive instinct and that he took great pains to keep his belongings neatly in order. He was extremely sensitive to smells.

As a child he thought frequently of death. He recalled seeing the corpse of a man who had been killed by falling off a hayrick. He remembered his grandmother's funeral—his breaking into tears and being pitied. He was intensely afraid that his parents would die. Though his mother nagged him, she also lavished her affection on him—more, in fact, than B. was inclined to reciprocate.

He did not masturbate until he was 18. He has never had sexual intercourse.

He slept with his father between the ages of 7 and 15, and his sister slept with his mother, all on the same porch. At 12 years of age a cousin of his told him about the mating of animals and of human beings. He was terribly shocked to think that his parents would do anything so vile. He held the theory of anal intercourse. He told of several experiences of fellatio occurring at about the age of 10, but said that there had been none since.

He was once inclined to music as a career, but now he is thinking of going into business.

Thematic Apperceptions. The subject was given the thematic apperception test twice, once before and once after four months of an orthodox psychoanalysis.

Picture 14: The nude figure of a man clinging to a pole.

Subject: "This man is evidently climbing a mast. He is a sailor who has been discovered in some morbid crime—some homosexual crime. He has been chased out of the cabin. He climbs the mast and is shot down." (Crime [homosexual assault] → p aggression [revengeful murder] th.)

After four months of analysis the subject gave the following somewhat modified story:

"The mast of a boat in the Arctic. The fellow is a sexual pervert who has been on the ship. One night he tries homosexual relations. He is unsuccessful. He runs out and, half insane, climbs the mast. His features are distorted and carnal. He commits suicide by leaping into the sea or onto the deck below." (Crime [homosexual] → suicide th.)

This is a frank homosexual story suggesting fellatio or sodomy. In the first story the hero is killed by an external agent, in the second story by an internal agent, the superego. In interpreting picture 10 (a man clinging to a rope) the subject has the hero—a former criminal—lose his grip and fall to the ground. This is the vengeance of fate. Four months later he said that the rope to which the man clung was attached to a winch operated by a man who disliked him. "His enemy contrives to let him fall so it appears to be an accident." Thus a criminal career is ended sometimes by punitive measures from without and sometimes by punitive measures from within. In his introspections the subject said: "I have always hated high places. I have a great dread of them. I can't think of a worse situation than having your enemy at the other end of a winch."

Picture 5: A young boy contemplating a violin which rests on a table in front of him.

Subject: "This is a picture of a boy violinist. He has a thoughtful expression, getting more introspective and philosophic. He thinks about what makes the tone. Recital follows. It is a great triumph for him. Later, he receives an injury to one of his hands or fingers and he is forced to abandon music." (Achievement th.; p injury [mutilation] → achievement failure th.)

This story suggests castration. After four months of analysis during which time the castration material had been worked over, the subject was shown the same picture by another experimenter. This time he said:

"A boy violinist in the early stages of violin practice. He has been playing the score before him. Then, from fatigue or curiosity, he stops and attempts to figure out the physical properties of his instrument. There is no outcome. It is just a momentary episode." (Curiosity th.)

Picture 4: On the floor against a couch is the huddled form of a boy with his head bowed on his right arm. Beside him on the floor is an object which resembles a revolver.

Subject: "A contemporary youngster. In a fit of rage he has shot a pet—a horse or a dog. The animal angered him. He killed it. Overcome with grief he rushes into the house and falls into a fit of remorse." (Supraggression [animal murder] → remorse th.)

In his introspection the subject said: "This recalls a youngster who chopped off the head of a kitten. I had a pet pony myself once."

Four months later the subject presented the following modification:

"A boy with a weapon. He has done something and is sorry. His parents gave him a dog and in a fit of anger he injured the dog with a knife. The dog ran off whimpering. The fellow is sorry. It makes an impression on him in later life. (Supraggression [animal mutilation] → remorse th.)

In his introspections the subject said: "I once had a dog. I used to have to beat him. I always felt sorry afterward."

Children often beat animals after a parent has punished them—something which is usually interpreted as an identification with the parent as well as a catharsis of their own aggression against the parent. A certain acceptance of the parent's authority and an identification with him are often involved, the punishment of the animal being an externalized self-punishment. This is suggestive of true sadism—the infliction of pain on weak and defenseless objects (supraggression). p Bestiality should also be considered. After giving the first story the subject was reminded of "a youngster who chopped the head off a kitten," and in the second story he substituted a knife for the revolver. This is again suggestive of castration (p mutilation).

Many of the other stories included unspecified acts of violence, and there were also misdemeanors vaguely described as "getting involved with some girl." In three stories, however, the subject definitely directed the violence against a woman.

Picture 25: A girl standing alone. The expression on her face is obviously one of terror and anxiety.

Subject: "Girl about to be attacked by a demented person. She has gone on a picnic with him. A coming storm increases the carnal instincts of the boy. He attacks the girl." (Sadism th.)

Picture 18: A malicious-looking man grasping the arm of a young girl who appears to be trying to pull away from him. He clutches her throat, and her expression denotes terror.

Subject: "The old fellow is an experimental scientist. The girl is his secretary. He has placed her in that position for his own ends. When the time comes he takes her to attack her or to use her for some evil purpose." (Sadism th.)

In his introspections the subject said: "It recalls a moving picture I once saw of a mad scientist who made statues of human bodies by filling their veins full of ossifying material. This might be the same. The pronounced sexuality of the girl might have a bearing on his intent."

The associations to this picture suggest a necrophilic trend, the sadism being of the anal type.

In one picture the hero's wife has had a difficult labor; in another she is dead or seriously ill, and in a third the hero finds that both his parents have been killed in an accident. Taking these associations in conjunction with the preceding story (picture 18), is there a basis for guessing that the subject fantasies a woman (his mother) being killed by intercourse—injection of fluid, or accident—as well as by childbirth?

In two stories the double personality thema appears.

Picture 12: A young man helplessly clutched from behind by two hands, one on each of his shoulders. The figure of his antagonist is invisible.

Subject: "Dr. Jekyll or Mr. Hyde. It is a case of double consciousness. The man is weak by nature. The hands on his shoulders are those of his other consciousness—either higher or lower." (Conflict [id. vs. superego] th.)

Picture 19: A gaunt, poorly dressed and disheveled man stands behind and to the right of a well dressed, prosperous-looking man.

Subject: "The man on the right is a banker. The man on the left might be a brother who has gone bad—a degenerate. He has come back to torment the man on the right. Probably it will end by the murder of the brother by the banker. The banker will commit suicide after the murder." (Crime [murder] → suicide th.)

Four months later the subject presented this version:

"This is double consciousness. The man is a banker. The ghost of his sadistic self is in the background. The lower side is not always controllable. It is sure to have a tragic end, or it is a bad brother with a mental defect. The bad man is guilty of violent crimes of a sexual nature." (Sadism th.)

Picture 21: An obscurely outlined figure, which might be male or female, sits musing in the firelight, hands folded.

The subject outlined another conflict: "It is a monk like Abélard," he said, "who has taken the vows and renounced all worldly desires. He becomes repentant over this in the monastery. It is a tragic situation, for there was no lessening of the conflict after making the vows." (Renunciation [erotic] for holiness → conflict [erotic id vs. superego] th.)

Perhaps the subject, though preoccupied with sexual fantasies, has inhibited his impulses. Considering this interpretation in conjunction with the double personality thema, one may suppose that his erotic self was repressed and dissociated because of its aberrant—homosexual or sadistically heterosexual—character.

In addition to the pictures, the subject was given a number of inkblots (different from those used by Rorschach) and asked to tell what figures he could make out of them. Three of his associations were pertinent.

Blot 6: "This looks like an illustration from a medical book, like a cut-away dissection of either male or female."

Blot 10: "Appears to be a cross-section of a female pelvis as seen in medical books."

Blot 13: "Man at left seems to be engaged in some sexual act. It might be an embryo or a portion of a miscarriage."

Here again one finds a preoccupation with dead bodies (necrophilia). One finds, moreover, the conjunction of intercourse and miscarriage.

Besides these pictures and these blots, the subject was asked to write a story about a minister who suddenly appeared in his pulpit one Sunday morning wearing a black veil as in "The Minister's Black Veil," by Hawthorne.

The subject had the minister unexpectedly return to his home one evening and find his brother in "compromising circumstances" with a woman whom he had brought there. "The shock of the discovery," he wrote, "and its theological implications affect the vicar to such an extent that he appears the following Sunday in his pulpit with a black veil over his face. The brother meanwhile quietly disappears, and the minister continues the wearing of his strange garb until his death in a few years."

This story is interesting because guilt is located in the eyes—the minister saw something evil and thenceforth blinded himself (repression of voyeurism). Since the subject's symptoms are located in his eyes, it seems that the traumatic experience for him might likewise have been the perceiving of something. This suggests the primal scene. In view of the large amount of sadistic heterosexuality and the suggestion of necrophilia appearing in this subject's appreciations, one might suppose that the sexual act was originally confused with murder.

In brief, then, the data furnished by the pictures suggest: necrophilia, sadism of the anal type, voyeurism, fear of heights, castration anxiety, homosexual perversion (oral or anal) and dissociation resulting from interference of the superego. The relations between these trends, however, are not apparent, perhaps because the stories are too short and concise. The subject was not sufficiently encouraged to elaborate them.

Psychoanalysis.

At the date of writing, the patient had had five months of analysis. During this period the following trends have manifested themselves in the order named.

(a) Fellatio Fantasies: About the time of the first appearance of his symptoms the patient was having fantasies of his first sexual experiences—acts of fellatio at the age of 10 years. Oral sensations accompanied these fantasies. He had felt very guilty about them and attempted, finally with success, to repress them entirely. He was afraid that he was homosexual and wanted to be assured that he was not. Since some of his static images depicted the surroundings in which these fellatio experiences had occurred, it seemed that his symptoms might be regarded as a compromise formation. It was a fellatio fantasy with the sinful part dissociated —a rather typical hysterical mechanism. There was no relief of his symptoms, however, after the analysis of this material.

(b) Anal Sadistic and Masochistic Trends; Castration Complex: The patient said that he had slept in a double bed with his father between the ages of 7 and 15. Though he had feared that during sleep he would touch his father's body and had taken special precautions against nocturia, he had had his first emission while lying against his father. He had fantasies of anal copulation with the analyst and similar fantasies in connection with others. He told of his early fear of sharp instruments, dreamed of being beheaded and spoke of his father's ungovernable temper. His father was an enormous man, well over 250 pounds in weight. He was frequently represented by a bull in the subject's dreams. A good deal of anal material and some passive feminine trends were revealed.

(c) Womb Fantasies, Sadistic Trends and Necrophilia: As a child the patient tried to picture himself in his mother's womb and also in his coffin, the two retreats being closely connected. He saw an embryo in a glass jar once, and this started a series of fantasies about pregnancy and birth—illegitimate children and children born blind. He dreamt of opening up a woman and filling her womb with straw. As a boy he had a fantasy that he was pregnant. Shortly afterward he became constipated and lay doubled up on the floor groaning with abdominal

pain. In one analytic session he fantasied the head of a child sticking out of the back of a limousine and then cried out that the analyst was pressing him. He experienced a terrific emotional panic, held his head, kicked out with his feet, rolled over on his side. Later, he said that he had lost his breath. This experience suggested a reenaction of the birth trauma. The patient's most exciting fantasy pictured him opening graves and copulating per anum with one corpse after another. Since the subject had slept in his parents' bedroom during his early years, it seemed that this fantasy might be partly explained by supposing that he had witnessed their sexual congress and conceived of it as a murder or necrosexual act. It seemed that birth, death and sexual intercourse were closely related in his mind. He remembers nothing about his sister's birth, which occurred when he was 3 years of age, although he does remember that he was frequently scolded afterward for poking his fingers in her eyes when she lay in her crib. He quarreled with her frequently during his early years. He seemed to hold a deep resentment against his mother. He said that she nagged him and made exorbitant demands for his affection.

Guilt seems to have become connected with his eyes, for his symptoms were located there (conjunctivitis, stereotyped images and photophobia), and even before they appeared he was compulsively taking certain precautions against ocular infection. This followed his reading about gonorrheal conjunctivitis at the age of puberty.

The relations between these unconscious trends have yet to be worked out. We have evidence of fantasied sadistic assaults on women (wombs and corpses) and children (his younger sister); of fantasied anal-erotic relations with men, active and passive (castration anxiety) and of fellatio experiences and wishes. But the genesis of these tendencies and their dynamic connection with his symptoms are problems which still remain to be solved.

Since B. is the only subject who has undergone analysis after the thematic apperception test, we have but little data on which to base any general conclusions. In this single instance, however, the thematic apperceptions adumbrated all the chief trends which five months of analysis were able to reveal.

CONCLUSIONS

We have been able to present only a small fraction of the evidence which supports our general conclusion that the thematic apperception test is an effective means of disclosing a subject's regnant preoccupations and some of the unconscious trends which underlie them. The advantages of the test are that it is a simple procedure which may be completed in two hours or in an abbreviated form in half that time, and that it may be performed in a casual and informal fashion. Since the subject is led to believe that it is a test of creative imagination, even when it is given in a clinic, he is unaware of the fact that he is revealing his innermost thoughts. The subject's attention is not on himself, and so in many instances he indirectly confesses to things which he would not be willing to mention directly. But, more than this, he exposes latent tendencies of the existence of which he is entirely unconscious. For the fantasies by being projected may be inwardly disclaimed and thus avoid complete repression.

Of all the short procedures and tests which we have tried, the results of this one have given us the best understanding of the deeper layers of a personality. It is undoubtedly a useful method for the investigation of fantasy production under various conditions. Whether it is of any value as a preanalytic measure remains to be seen. It may, perhaps, aid a physician in deciding whether a given patient had better be analyzed by a man or by a woman, or it may give some clue to the probable course or length of an analysis.

Our results suggest, however, that the present test will be most helpful when used by trained analysts in cases in which the patient does not need or cannot afford a complete analysis. Undoubtedly many neuroses may be avoided and many spiritual dilemmas solved by proper guidance at the right time. This is particularly true for young persons. In our experience the minimum amount of preliminary information which a therapeutist should possess for such guidance may be supplied by a ten page autobiography, an hour of relaxed reminiscing about childhood experiences and fantasies, the thematic apperception test and an hour of direct questioning. Of these, the thematic apperception test is frequently the most helpful, for it brings to the forefront just those underlying issues which are of immediate consequence.

At the present time a young person who shows a few mildly neurotic symptoms or, like all inwardly developing persons, is temporarily overburdened by mental conflict generally has, if he wants expert assistance, but two choices. He may be analyzed, or he may consult a psychiatrist with no experience in analysis. This is the case because most trained analysts are apt to limit their practice to complete psychoanalyses. There are numberless young men and women who need the kind of help which perhaps only a therapeutist trained in psychoanalysis is in a position to give and yet who do not need, or want or cannot afford an analysis lasting for a year or more. They need to confess, to discuss their problems, to attain insight, but in most cases it is better for them not to impede their progressive efforts by having to revive and relive their past. It is in such cases that the thematic apperception test may provide the psychotherapeutist with the information necessary for the fulfilment of his function as a guide and healer of men.

V

Personology studies living, historical, fictional, and mythological figures as well as special human "complexes"

*T*ypically, Murray's creative imagination automatically extended and widened the category of "persons" to include not only the obvious (i.e., living and real persons) but also to embrace persons who were no longer living or who were historical figures, persons who were fictional or mythological, especially if they had been fully described and might, on that account, teach us something about what the "human condition" is like, in both its ordinary states and in its far reaches. Thus, for example, Melville, the author, and Ahab and Pierre, the characters, were all interesting "persons" for Murray's legitimate concern.

Murray's substantial Introduction to Melville's Pierre is one of the most thorough "psychological reports" ever written. Pierre, the most openly psychological of all of Melville's ten novels, a book which Murray called "bizarre yet profound," is a convoluted story of Pierre's awakening to his own unconscious impulses and resources and a gothic novel of Pierre's sacred and profane love. These are themes that especially attracted Murray—and played an important role in his own life. So Murray's "Introduction to Pierre" is an astute and scholarly analysis of important aspects of the psychological constitution directly of Pierre Glendinning, directly and indirectly of Herman Melville, and, at second remove, of Henry Murray.

In "Bartleby and I," as elsewhere, Murray is an explicator. He makes clear what others might pass over as obvious. In this paper, Murray presents a set of baroque explications of the various meanings of the word "I." In addition, he teaches us once again that one cannot describe a person—in this case, the ill-fated Bartleby—with a simple diagnostic label, as, for example, "catatonic schizophrenic"; rather one needs at least several hundred words adequately to begin to describe a fellow human being.

"Dead to the World: The Passions of Herman Melville" is a panorama piece, describing Melville's inimical or self-destructive orientations over the entire course of his adult life. In this sense, it is the most longitudinal or serial—one of Murray's terms—of Murray's writings about Melville. The title itself is interesting. It implies that there are different kinds

411

of deaths, which are set forth in detail in his paper, and the subtitle evokes the imagery of "stations" along the Via Dolorosa of Everyman's journey toward his own death. Much of Murray on Melville is "psychological autobiography." All of it is a labor of love on Murray's part—his lifelong "avocation."

"The Personality and Career of Satan," Murray's study of the Devil, contains at least five main themes: It is a report of a worldwide charismatic imaginal figure; it is a recognition of the importance of the dark, satanic elements (metaphorically speaking) of one of God's angels (metaphorically speaking) and, by extension, of the capacities for evil and the illicit in Everyman's id; it advances a naturalistic—anthropological and psychoanalytic—credo about all religion as a product of the human imagination; it provides an abstract of the Satanic personality; and, fifth, it is a continuation of Murray's crusade within psychology against the blinded and myopic vision of those who would attempt to foster the notion that the only "scientific" way to study man is one that uncreatively interdicts the examination and assessment of some of man's undeniably most interesting characteristics, such as the functioning of unconscious processes. Murray wants to tell us that statistics, nomothetics, and precision are, without any question, the desirable goals when they become attainable for one's subject matter; but to look for lost objects, or as-yet-to-be-formulated concepts, under the light post because the lamps, or kudos, are there is just plain shortsightedness. In an earlier paper—"Basic Concepts for a Psychology of Personality" (1936)—Murray wrote, "To those who complain that there are hundreds of distinguishable themas, and to describe them would be a Herculean task, our answer would be that until that task is performed the science of personology will be adrift."

One of the sets of underlying psychodynamics that caught Murray's clinical eye was the proclivity or penchant of some persons for ascension, rising, floating, or flying in air, in fantasy or dream or in reality, along with several other covert personal qualities including narcissism and a craving for immortality. Murray called this combination of personal attributes the Icarian complex—from the myth of Daedalus and his son Icarus in which, using wings that they had fashioned from feathers and glue to escape from the Minotaur's Labyrinth in Crete, Icarus flew too near the sun, the glue melted, and he fell to his death. One important aspect of Murray's "method" is to explicate details and then, inductively and intuitively, to group them under broader rubrics, as he does in "American Icarus." The Icarian complex may itself be a fair example of this soaring tendency as one aspect of Murray's total style of thought.

18

INTRODUCTION TO *PIERRE*

In the summer of 1851 Melville, scarcely thirty-two, completed his sixth book, *Moby-Dick,* of one substance with himself, a wild Everest of art, limit of governable imagination.

The begetting of this marvel of our literature called for an immense deliverance of imagery and thought at high temperature and, for a year and a half, the almost unremitting application of the will to form—altogether, it would seem, the longest course of furious and superb productiveness we know of in America. But, despite this huge expenditure, within a few weeks—how long we do not know exactly—Melville began laying out his seventh book, this *Pierre.*

Since his mind had come of age in 1845 Melville's experience had been one of continuous unfolding, until one day his questing spirit encountered a barrier which, so far as he could see, was insurmountable. This was the occasion of a deadly moral conflict, his spirit committed to a "dark hope forlorn, whose cruelness makes a savage of a man." The presentiment of his defeat was heavy on him when in the spring of 1851 he wrote Hawthorne that he had now "come to the inmost leaf of the bulb, and that shortly the flower must fall to the mould." It was just then, facing annihilation, that Melville rose, in *Moby-Dick,* to the heights of sublime eloquence and won his place in the selectest company of authors. Thus did he magnificently exemplify Byron's conclusion, written on a leaf of the manuscript of *Childe Harold,* "For by the death-blow of my hope, My Memory immortal grew." The end of Ahab, embodiment of the author's defiant spirit, was the "utter wreck" prayed for, "if wreck I do," in *Mardi. Moby-Dick* was the rainbow Melville spread "over his disastrous set of sun," his symphonic *nunc dimittis.* After this what was left for him to say? What resources could he draw on?

As it happened, his energies revived. In feeling that his mental powers were played out, or nearly so, he had miscalculated his margin. He recuperated—partially. *Moby-Dick* had been so nearly a complete catharsis of his grief-hate that after it he could say, "I have written a wicked book, and feel spotless as a lamb." Through the Ahab of his imagination he had cursed God and drowned, but on waking from the

From the edition of Melville's *Pierre, or, the Ambiguities* published by Hendricks House (New York, 1949). Re-issued in 1962. Pp. xiii–ciii.

dream, discovered that he was still among the quick. Ishmael survived
the wreck; and in Ishmael there was still some energy, some grief, some
hate—"deep volcanoes long burn ere they burn out." *Pierre* is the burning out of Melville's volcano.

Relieved of the immense burden of *Moby-Dick,* assured that *there*
he had surpassed himself, treasuring a "sense of unspeakable security"
because the fastidious Hawthorne had understood the book and thought
highly of it, Melville enjoyed a short season of exultation. He felt ready
to engage in an even larger undertaking. "So, now, let us add *Moby-Dick*
to our blessing, and step from that. Leviathan is not the biggest fish;—
I have heard of Krakens." *Pierre* is Melville's battle with the Kraken.

The sorrowful fact is that the exuberance which was hurrying him
into the intricate business of his third major work had insufficient backing. Surely, Mumford's diagnosis is correct: after *Moby-Dick* "the
spiritual momentum remained, but the force behind it dwindled away."[1]
Pierre is the performance of a depleted puppeteer.

Besides exhaustion, a usable account of the spiritual state of the
author of this novel must include both moral conflict and an underlying
will to wreck his self. The outcome of the conflict, to be sure, had been
decided, but the defeated spirit was unresigned and the civil war had to
be re-fought again and again, each time with less conviction, before the
peace of acquiescence was achieved. Melville's position in *Mardi* might
be defined in these words: "If I fail to reach my golden haven, may my
annihilation be complete!"; in *Moby-Dick:* "I see that I am to be annihilated!", but against this verdict I shall hurl an everlasting protest!"; in
Pierre: "I must make up my mind, if possible, to the inevitability of my
annihilation"; in 1856, at Liverpool, with Hawthorne: "I have pretty
much made up my mind to be annihilated"; and in 1891, in *Billy Budd:*
"I accept my annihilation."

Moral conflict, if radical and stubborn, results in a division, an inflexible dualism, in all branches of feeling and thought, which so influences
the sufferer's apperceptions, that every significant object becomes *ambivalent* to him, that is, it both attracts and repels him, being composed,
as he sees it, of two contrary elements, one good and one evil, which can
not be reconciled or blended. He discovers in due time a radical defect
in every person who has appealed to him and begins hating what he has
loved, though, unconsciously, he continues loving the object of his hate.
Thus no whole-hearted embracement of anyone is possible, and the
constructive tendency toward synthesis and integration is perpetually
obstructed. This accounts for the majority of ambiguities (almost synonymous with "ambivalences") in *Pierre.*

One whose heart is divided against itself is also determined to interpret every significant situation in which he becomes involved as ambivalent; but here a separation of the two elements may sometimes be
effected: the occasion may be apperceived as a choice-point between two

paths, one of which must be single-mindedly accepted as true and right, the other wholly rejected as false and wrong. But, after making the seemingly virtuous choice, the man will, sooner or later, begin to see some serious flaw or sin in his elected course, and to recall with self-abasing feelings of regret the merits of the repudiated way. This is the basis of several other ambiguities in the novel.

Wearied and exasperated by the relentless underlying conflict and confounded by the constant inversions of value from positive to negative and negative to positive, the man may finally arrive at a state of virtual paralysis with no capacity for decision, one effect of which is the apprehension that everything is almost equally meaningless and worthless— "all objects are seen in a dubious, uncertain, and refracting light . . . the most immemorially admitted maxims of men begin to slide and fluctuate, and finally become wholly inverted." By pursuing the trail of thought so far, an explorer "entirely loses the directing compass of his mind; for arrived at the Pole, to whose barrenness only it points, there, the needle indifferently respects all points of the horizon alike." This state of feeling accounts for most of the remaining ambiguities, as well as for the pervasive moral of the book, which is that there is *no* moral: it is impossible for a man to reconcile this world with his own soul, and impossible to make a clean decision for one or for the other; there is evil in the good and good in the evil, gloom in light and light in gloom; a step beyond this bitter knowledge carries one to the indifferent thought that good and evil are but "shadows cast from one nothing," the mind of man. "It is all a dream—we dream that we dreamed we dream."

Pierre approached a still more frantic, schizoid state when "With the soul of an Atheist, he wrote down the godliest things; with the feeling of death and misery in him, he created forms of gladness and life. For the pangs of his heart, he put down hoots on the paper." He had firmly resolved to give the world a testament of "sacred truth," but his endeavor had only served to reveal to him "the universal lurking insincerity of even the greatest and purest written thoughts."

A reader whose voyage of mind has not always been restricted to a narrowly normal track, who has experienced these inner states however mildly or briefly, can scarcely fail to admire the precision and beauty of Melville's translations; he will know better, anyhow, then to decry them as "nonsensical gibberish." Also, he will not take each duality that he encounters as a separate problem, because he will realize intuitively that the whole long sequence of antinomies, or pairs of opposites, which constitute the structure of this novel are but products of one nuclear conflict. Furthermore, some familiarity with obsessional dilemmas will save a critic from certain common errors, such as that of indiscriminately accepting any one of the author's avowed values as a complete statement of his feelings. On many issues Melville was equally subject to the opposite sentiment, constancy of emotion being less typical of him than cyclic alternations. "In me," he confessed to Hawthorne, "divine magnanimities are spontaneous and instantaneous—catch them while you can. The world goes round, and the other side comes up."

It would also be well if critics were protected from the mistake of dealing with Melville's thought on a rational level as if he had arrived at his conclusions by logical inductions after an impartial survey of the universe; and from the mistake of supposing that Melville was searching for Truth, as science defines it, and that his tragedy, therefore, was an intellectual one. A man in his position, who is incapable of willing his way out of inner discord, is likely to find the unsolvable problems of traditional philosophy irresistibly alluring. (Many of them are unsolvable because, as operationism has taught us, the terms in which they are stated are meaningless.) By wrestling with these "meaningless" bi-horned enigmas of thought and persuading himself and others that his happiness depends on his finding the talismanic secret (which he knows is impossible), he dresses his mental preoccupations in robes of historic dignity, covers the naked facts of his personal distress, and indefinitely postpones the dreaded curative decision. Let us take note here of one of Melville's many relevant hints: Pierre, in writing his ambitious book, "disguised" his afflictions "under the so conveniently adjustable drapery of all-stretchable Philosophy." In view of these considerations and this candid admission, hopes of reaching fundamental solutions on the intellectual level seem over-sanguine.

There is no room for discussion of so grave and complex a problem as Melville's will to self-annihilation, but I have mentioned it because this component is necessary to explain certain features of the novel: Pierre's so precipitous descent from grace, his so early conviction that Fate had called upon his family "to offer up a victim to the gods of woe," the headlong recklessness with which he commits a series of irredeemable blunders, the improbably swift procession of calamities, threats, ailments, and failures, his too-ready and too-feverish collapse, and, at the end, his orgastic homicide and suicide.

The reader is not being invited to look at *Pierre* with the optics of pathology, but to consider a few elucidating and mercy-breeding concepts. The knowledge that, while writing *Pierre,* Melville was fighting for spiritual survival and that his reason was losing ground should thicken the sympathy with which we read this forbidding book, should put us in a better temper to interpret the dislocations of emotional logic, the eccentricities of language, the atmosphere of unreality, and to perceive, behind the glare of these defects, rare virtues.

Since the form of *Pierre* is that of a novel, I might take it for granted that Melville's sole object was to tell a dramatic story and at once proceed with an exposition and critique of his skill as craftsman. It has seemed wiser, however, to hold aesthetic discriminations in abeyance for a while and, pursuant to the creed of some scrupulous critics, start by raising the question of the author's discernible intentions in writing this book. We can be certain that this order of procedure would have gratified Melville, for he believed that he was deficient in technique, strong in content. Like Lombardo, in *Mardi,* he "did not build himself in with plans" but "wrote right on." Like Pierre, he was "very unarchitectural" at first. The critics, Lombardo lamented, "criticize my tattered cloak, not my soul, caparisoned like a charger." Even after *Moby-Dick,* a constructive achievement of the first magnitude, Melville wrote to Hawthorne: "You did not care a penny for the book. But, now and then as you read, you understood the pervading thought that impelled the book—and that you praised. Was it not so? You were archangel enough to praise the imperfect body, and embrace the soul." However much we disagree with this self-estimate, however confident we are that taste and talent are of paramount importance and that Melville's cardinal claim to immortality resides not in his "pervading thought" or "soul" but in his "bold and nervous lofty language" and in his once proved power to fuse profoundly stirring archetypal images with the raw realities of ocean butchery and to work these multifarious composites into an epic edifice of unexampled splendor; in short, however assured we are that significant form is the alpha and omega of our concern, it is sound policy, here as elsewhere, to begin at the beginning: significant of what?

As it happens, *Pierre* is more than a novel, and to introduce it with an analysis of the author's novelistic technique could only serve to spotlight bodily imperfections which are already conspicuous and, by so diverting attention, to lessen one's chances of being "archangel enough" to "embrace the soul," sick as it is here, of Herman Melville; for, as E. L. Grant Watson has rightly said, "The center of Melville is *Pierre;* if one would understand him, one must understand this book above all others."[2]

It is intelligible that the American of today, with no compelling religious belief, no certainty of a moral order, no articulate philosophy, no heart's vision that demands aesthetic utterance, should be so largely absorbed in technical problems, in experimenting more or less cynically with this and that device to produce some startling or profitable effect; it is intelligible that he should have substituted surfaces for depths, gadgets for great ideas, behaviorisms for feeling, craft for faith, skill for wisdom, ostensible success for inward joy; but to interpret Melville through the eyes of a "bantering, barren, and prosaic, heartless age" would be to play Judas to the seriousness of one whose vision of the artist's role approached Dante's and Milton's, who believed that "To produce a mighty book, you must choose a mighty theme," and who held that literature should be "a consecration and an obsequy to all hapless modes of human life."

What was it that originally impelled the genius Lombardo—and, no doubt, his creator, Melville—to write books? "Primus and forever, a full heart;—brimful, bubbling, sparkling; and running over . . ." We might call it the functional exuberance whereby the abundant spirit multiplies itself through communion of feelings and thoughts, or the expression of "plenitude," as Matthiessen has so aptly said in his own finely wrought tapestry of plenitude.[3]

At first Melville's heart was brimful of memories of his astonishing adventures on sea and land, of incredible beauties, strange people, lawless actions. Supplemented and elaborated by tall tales he had been told and the books he read, these were the ingredients of the bubbling, sparkling wine he poured out in *Typee* and *Omoo* and again later in *Redburn* and *White Jacket.*

In *Redburn* the hero tells how in boyhood a vague prophetic thought was bred in him that "I was fated, one day or other, to be a great voyager; and . . . I would hereafter be telling my own adventures to an eager auditory." He thought "how fine it would be to be able to talk about remote and barbarous countries; with what reverence and wonder people would regard me." This motive, balanced by modesty and humor, had a hand in writing all of Melville's early books and, with different content, in writing his informal letters. "I talk all about myself, and this is selfishness and egotism," he admitted to Hawthorne. "Granted. But how help it? I am writing to you; I know little about you, but something about myself. So I write about myself." This practice was not confined to the recounting of his own experiences and the expression of his own sentiments. His disposition to identify imaginatively with castaways, heroes, and gods, to dramatize himself in a sensational manner, to exhibit this dramatization in his books, to give passionate utterance to the opinions of others, was so powerful that in his early years he could not resist the temptation of declaring or implying that his fictionalized narratives of adventure were true and thus deceiving his most sympathetic biographers-to-come. Viewed from this standpoint, the prototype of Melville's early works is *Childe Harold,* or, to name a more specific model flavored with Byronism, Trelawny's *Adventures of a Younger Son.* Melville was not writing autobiography in the usual sense, but, from first to last, the biography of his self-image. These identifications and self-dramatizations should not be dismissed as inconsequential shadows; they constitute the very core, the mythological and religious core, of personality. As Olson[4] has implied, the name "Ishmael" is closer than "Melville" to the vital truth. The present novel is no exception: Pierre is Oedipus-Romeo-Hamlet-Memnon-Christ-Ishmael-Orestes-Timon-Satan-Cain-Manfred, or, more shortly, an American Fallen and Crucified Angel.

If you have read two or three of Melville's earlier works, you will almost inevitably be assuming as you open this novel that it is partially autobiographical, and, as you proceed, this supposition will be reinforced by repeated recognitions of familiar elements. Also, sooner or later, you are sure to become aware of the author's peculiar intimacy with his hero. His detachment is but occasional and slight. With few exceptions, he sides with his hero, seriously sustaining him even in his most patent self-deceptions. It is evident that Melville's insight does not penetrate much further than Pierre's, or, to put it otherwise, Pierre, in his teens, becomes as enlightened as the author in his thirties. The two of them arrive separately at similar conclusions and sometimes unusual vigilance is required to be certain whose thoughts are being uttered. Finally, when you find Pierre giving voice to sentiments which Melville expressed in letters to Hawthorne and Duyckinck, your doubts that the hero is functioning as a self-image fade and perish. Conscientious efforts to recapture and re-build those doubts will receive little encouragement from the author. Melville has Pierre write a book about an author writing a book, and, looking over his shoulder, frankly acknowledges that "he seems to have directly plagiarized from his own experiences; to fill out the mood of his apparent author-hero."

None of this has escaped the notice of scholars and today scarcely anyone denies that *Pierre* is, in some sense and in some degree, autobiographical. The problem has been broken down into a number of specific questions calling primarily for fact-finding investigations. In the absence of the necessary data, most critics have relied on a hunch to guide them to one view or the other: either that the autobiographical elements are few and relatively insignificant, or that they are many and were influential in the shaping of the novel. The more or less persuasive findings which should give comfort to the insightful Weaver[5] and others whose intuitions have placed them in the latter group can be listed briefly.

Highly probable originals for all the natural objects and scenes which Melville describes have been found. Had it been desirable, this volume could have been illustrated with photographs of the Glendinning manorhouse (Broadhall, Pittsfield), the family phaeton (General Gansevoort's calèche), the amphitheatre of hills at Saddle Meadows (the Hoosic and Taconic ranges of the Berkshires), Mount of Titans (Mt. Greylock, Berkshires), Memnon Stone (Balance Rock, near Pittsfield), the main thoroughfare of the city (Broadway, New York), the Church of the Apostles (South Baptist Church, Nassau Street), the ferry (Staten Island ferry-slip at the Battery), the "glorious bay" (New York Harbor), and the "triangular space" near the spot where Glen Stanly is murdered (City Hall Park).

Originals for all the principal characters have also been identified, some of which are reasonably certain: Melville's grandfather, General Peter Gansevoort, as model for General Glendinning; his mother, Maria Gansevoort, for Pierre's mother, Mrs. Mary Glendinning; his father for Pierre's father; and his wife, Lizzie Shaw, for Lucy Tartan. Somewhat less convincing are the following correspondences: Priscilla Melvill, Melville's cousin, and Isabel Banford; Stanwix Gansevoort, his cousin, and

Glen Stanly; James Eli Murdock Fly, his boyhood chum, and Charlie Millthorpe; Hawthorne and Plotinus Plinlimmon. Finally, the Rev. Mr. Ballard, rector of St. Stephen's Church in Pittsfield, might well have sat for the portrait of the Rev. Mr. Falsgrave. Other possible correspondences—such as Priscilla Melvill, Melville's aunt, and Aunt Dorothea; Mrs. Shaw and Mrs. Tartan—are hardly worth mentioning.

It is probable that most of the interpersonal relationships in *Pierre* represent basic realities and that several of the more crucial events are founded on actual occurrences, but that everything is fictitious as literally recounted. It should be understood that we are concerned with an artist of exceeding imagination and that *Pierre* is at no point a transcription of fact; everything has been completely recast by Melville's shaping will.

If the above-given correspondences are correct, it appears that the models of the principal characters are all (with the possible exception of Mr. Ballard) persons to whom Melville was affectionately attached during some period of his life; and, setting aside his brothers and sisters, no one he is known to have loved has been excluded from the cast. So long as we omit the persons whom Melville knew during his four years at sea, this statement, full of significance to an interpreter of *Pierre,* seems justified, despite the paucity of definitive information. The fact that Pierre's relationship with each of the major characters (Millthorpe excepted) is intense, and that Melville's less intimate friendships, such as that with Duyckinck, are not portrayed, and that unessential persons, such as his father-in-law, Judge Shaw, are eliminated by pronouncing them dead, suggests that the author wittingly set out to write the legend of his heart, the biography of Eros.

Although, like most autobiographical novelists, Melville threw a disguise over each of his originals, it would be dull of us to disregard the indications that he *intended* his future biographers to recognize that he was writing the hushed story of his life. He tells us, with unnecessary accuracy, a number of public facts which are easily verifiable, such as the date (1812) of General Glendinning's death, and Pierre's age (12 years) when his father died; and he presents us with unmistakable delineations of enduring objects, such as the two portraits of his father. Also, some of the names he chose for his characters are startlingly close to the names of the originals, and we can conclude, from one passage, that he wished us to realize this. Isabel tells how "Glendinning" (written on a handkerchief) was equated in her childish mind with "gentleman," the name by which her father was known to her. *"Glendinning,* thought I, what is that? It sounds something like *gentleman;*—Glen—din—ning;—just as many syllables as *gentleman;* and—G—it begins with the same letter; yes, it must mean *my father.* I will think of him by that word now." The author seems to want the thickest heads to take in the fact that "Glendinning" means "Gansevoort."

In a letter to Duyckinck, Melville, thinking of the critics who had stabbed at *Mardi*, wrote: "What a madness & anguish it is, that an author can never—under no conceivable circumstances—be at all frank with his readers.—Could I, for one, be frank with them—how would they cease their railing—those at least who have railed." Here, I would say, Melville was acknowledging a frustrated desire to be frank with his readers and predicting that if conventions permitted him to be as honest as he wished, critics would cease their railing, because, say, like Hawthorne, having "understood the pervading thought that impelled the book," they would "embrace the soul" and overlook "the imperfect body." Melville had chronicled a large part of his inner life in *Mardi* and *Moby-Dick*, but disguised its concreteness in metaphors "under the so conveniently adjustable drapery of all-stretchable Philosophy." Could he stop there and remain forever a mystery to men, concealed in the interstices of allegories and symbols, misunderstood and ignorantly abused? Posterity would always wonder what drove this man to Satanism. My guess is that Melville was impelled, in the fall of 1851, to a further overcoming of reticence, to a more explicit confession of his soul's career, even to an exposure, before the flower fell to the mould, of the heart of his mystery, the positive Truth left out of his preceding works.

Since it has been shown that by knowing the books which Melville read in any given season of his authorship it is possible to predict some of the features of the work that was shortly to come from his pen, it is perhaps not without significance that prior to writing *Pierre* Melville read Rousseau's *Confessions*, Goethe's *Autobiography*, De Quincey's *Autobiographical Sketches* and *Confessions of an Opium Eater*, *Sartor Resartus*, and, there are reasons to believe, *Pendennis* and *Lavengro*, both of which are partial self-revelations. If to this list we add the autobiographical novels of Disraeli, who, omitting Byron, seems to have provided more raw material for *Pierre* than any other author, it is evident that Melville had ample encouragement to carry truth-telling further than he ever had before.

Thus, several different lines of evidence converge to the conclusion that Melville's impelling intention in writing *Pierre* is better defined by saying that he purposed to write his spiritual autobiography in the form of a novel, than it is to say that he was experimenting with the novel and incidentally making use of some personal experiences.

The supposition that Melville was reluctant to exclude any event that critically affected the course of his life would explain the superabundance of sub-plots, noted by Forsythe,[6] and the apparent fact that the author has incorporated experiences from three separate periods of his career—roughly 1837–1840, 1845–1847, and 1850–1852. The decision to attempt the impossible task of compressing and telescoping so great a range of raw material into a brief space of days and months could be held accountable, in part, for some of the incongruities and failures of integration in *Pierre*, for example, the conversion of the hero in a few weeks from a happy, light-weight sonneteer to a grief-stricken, heavy-weight author of a philosophic work. Further flaws might be attributed to the difficulty of other transpositions and transformations—such as that of lifting the economic status of his family from poverty to affluence—required by the author's aesthetic design or by the prohibition against the naked exposure of living persons.

In creating *Mardi* it seems that Melville, like Lombardo, "wrote right on; and so doing, got deeper and deeper into himself," until eventually he reached the "wondrous depths, where strange shapes of the unwarped primal world glided to and fro before his passive eyes." In doing this, in following "the endless, winding way—the flowing river in the cave of man," the vocation Melville accepted and magnificently fulfilled was that of pioneer exploring the "unconscious," which for our purposes may be metaphorically defined as the source of the wildest, most compelling, and least intelligible impulses, emotions, and images which, in a permeable mind, invade the sphere of consciousness when the will is relaxed. Writing "right on" was his method of psychological investigation. "But this new world here sought," Melville explained, "is stranger far than his, who stretched his vans from Palos. It is the world of mind; wherein the wanderer may gaze round, with more of wonder than Balboa's band roving through the golden Aztec glades." The exploration of this "new world" as conducted by Melville called for the dissection and interpretation of the course of subjective events, that is, for the employment of the psychoanalytical technique which would eventually, in the hands of others, prove most fruitful for science. This is stated explicitly in *Pierre:* "that which now absorbs the time and the life of Pierre, is not the book, but the primitive elementalizing of the strange stuff, which in the act of attempting that book, has upheaved and upgushed in his soul." In short, then, one of Melville's intentions in writing *Mardi, Moby-Dick,* and *Pierre* was to set forth in symbols, allegories, and expository passages his discoveries in the world of mind; and he was prompted to do this by the same overbrimming energy which had led him to recount with such gusto his adventures in the physical world. The inner world was more inviting to him, not only because of the dazzling and bewildering shapes encountered there, the excitement of it all, and the peril—since he was sailing closer and closer to the maelstrom of insanity—but because, in penetrating aimfully this barbarous and forbidden region, he felt, quite rightly, that he was another, though lonelier, Columbus steering "his bark through seas untracked before." Those who have decided that his sole title to renown is his success as literary discoverer of the South Seas must be cradled in comfortable philosophies that do not dream of the diabolisms with which Melville was familiar. Surely Melville deserves to be commemorated as the literary discoverer of another and more important part of nature, namely, the Darkest Africa of the mind, the mythological unconscious. As a depth psychologist he belongs with Dostoevsky and Nietzsche, the greatest in the centuries before Freud. This claim could not easily be supported without *Pierre*.

Melville's disposition to receive the blast, to submit to the force of passion and intuition, to "abdicate" as his own "soul's emperor" and yield to the racing tide of the unconscious, in short, to allow himself to be possessed by the spirit, whether it took the form of creative love or destructive hate, had the momentous consequences which are exhibited in *Moby-Dick* and *Pierre*. For one thing, this decision in favor of the spirit required, according to his dualistic logic, the complete rejection of everything that seemed to be opposed to it. Thus an uncompromising dichotomy was established. On the side of the spirit, symbolized by the sea, the "boundless deeps" (or sometimes by virgin country), Melville put: open space, freedom, adventure, danger, the Heart, spontaneity, selfless benevolence, singlehearted dedication, passionate undirected thought, truth-seeking, zeal for heaven and immortality, God, and insanity ("a half-wilful overruling morbidness," "man's insanity is heaven's sense"). On the opposite side, symbolized by the land (especially the city) or by "vulgar shoals," he put: closed or structured space, slavishness, family obligations, domestic comforts, safety, the Head, cool directed thinking, the calculations of self-interest, propriety, the World, and conventional commonsense. Over and over again, in multifarious rhetorical forms, Melville contrasts these two clusters of value and always champions the former, though his partiality is sometimes qualified by warnings such as: "Appalling is the soul of man! Better might one be pushed off into the material spaces beyond the uttermost orbit of our sun, than once feel himself fairly afloat in himself!" But, regardless of the hazard, he argues, the open sea is far better than the "treacherous, slavish shore," because "in landlessness alone resides the highest truth, shoreless, indefinite as God." By placing his highest value (God) in the emotional forces of the unconscious, instead of in a vision of an ideal whole—a synthetic work of art, a usable philosophy, a creative relationship—Melville made astounding discoveries in uncharted regions of the mind and experienced a rapid and portentous enlargement of the imagination; but for this superlative one-sided development he paid, as we shall see, the supreme price.

Melville did not reach the "shapes of the unwarped primal world" merely by writing "right on"; they were exposed to him by the "blast resistless"—woe born of perished happiness—which in the midst of *Mardi* struck his gay ship and churned up the deeper waters of his being. Passion is a force which John Livingston Lowes, that rare scholar, left out of his formulation of the creative process; but Melville insisted on its efficacy as agitator of what Donne called the "pregnant pot." "We are fuller than a city. Woe it is, that reveals these things. He knows himself and all that's in him, who knows adversity." Scudding before this gale of grief, Melville scanned the horizon for sight of a new land of bliss, that is to say, he watched for the emergence of a magnetic image which would indicate the right course; and while thus progressing, he invaded the great minds of history through their works, in hopes of finding the solution of his dilemma. Thus, Melville's voyage through the mind was motivated not so much by the artist's love of wonder, or by the psychologist's intellectual curiosity, as by the religionist's quest for salvation; and it is clear that one of his intentions as author of *Mardi, Moby-Dick,* and *Pierre* was to give an account of this spiritual pilgrimage.

This rapid survey of Melville's most general intentions should help us to distinguish the different meanings—the slidings, jugglings, fluctuations, inversions, ambiguities, masquerades, and mystifications—of "Truth," the slippery key word of this novel. Melville aspired to be with "Shakespeare and other masters of the great Art of Telling the Truth,— even though it be covertly and by snatches." He calls *Pierre* his "book of sacred truth," and his hero names himself the "Fool of Truth."

For Melville, autobiographical truths—essential facts and interpretations relating to his own life and to the people who affected it—comprise one important class. "Save me from being bound to Truth, liege lord, as I am now"—this plea, by the author of *Pierre,* is the slightest of several indications that he was driven at this time by a veritable compulsion to cast forth his inmost self and in so doing to disclose certain secrets that were dreadfully real to him. The fact that a formidable sex taboo prevented him from completely fulfilling his mission is intelligible in a nineteenth century American author. (Only the unmarried, foot-loose Whitman was free and bold enough to disregard the severest prohibition of that era.) But, this reticence and delicacy notwithstanding, much is laid bare for the appreciation of a cunning, pliant reader whose perceptions are not blocked at the literal level.

In a different class of truths are the psychological generalizations which Melville arrived at, most of which pertain to man's sinister and tragic shadow self, the repressed side of his nature, his "ocean, which is the dark side of this earth, and which is two-thirds of this earth." Among these were things such as come from the mouths of Hamlet, Timon, Lear, and Iago, which, as Melville wrote in "Hawthorne and His Mosses," "we feel to be so terrifically true, that it were all but madness for any good man, in his own proper character, to utter, or even to hint of them."

More frequently and characteristically Melville uses "Truth" to refer to a moral sentiment or statement of value which he strongly endorses. This may be either positive or negative. A positive truth, for Melville, is always some expression of love for an estimable object (often an object that has been neglected, depreciated, or condemned by his culture); and out of love for this thing (which may be the self) flows negative truth, the expression of hatred (or contempt) for that which opposes it. Thus Melville would have said that Christ delivered Truth when he said, "Blessed are they that mourn: for they shall be comforted," and also when he called the Pharisees a "generation of vipers." Both were judgments of the heart.* It was moral values of this sort which Melville had mostly in mind when he wrote that Pierre had "the burning desire to deliver what he thought to be new, or at least miserably neglected Truth to the world," an aspiration which at one moment of hectic excitement rises to: "I will gospelize the world anew, and show them deeper secrets than the Apocalypse!—I will write it, I will write it!" *Moby-Dick* was Melville's blast of negative truth carried to the extreme of positive falsehood, nihilism. This was catharsis, no solution. His ideal was positive truth. "Shakespeare," he wrote, is "full of sermons-on-the-mount, and gentle, aye, almost as Jesus." Later in this letter (to Duyckinck) he said, "if another Messiah ever comes twill be in Shakespeare's person." That Melville identified himself, to some extent, with both Christ and the "divine William," that he conceived of himself as a possible American Shiloh, is suggested by many oblique comments, such as his remark to Hawthorne, "Though I wrote the Gospels in this century, I should die in the gutter." It is in *Pierre* that one must look for Melville's positive truth.

Finally, following Wollaston[7] and others in their definition of goodness as the affirmation in practice of a true proposition, Melville uses "Truth" to mean divinely right conduct, obedience to a moral imperative, a creed in action. In *Pierre* this is Truth in its supremest sense, synonymous with Virtue, the highest form of which, as we shall see, is dedicated love. This was Melville's conception of the *summum bonum.* For the God of love, he substituted the deification of Love.

Perhaps the broadest generalization that can be made about Melville's different Truths is that they are *all* culturally unacceptable. They either are shocking or depressing facts about man's hidden self, or scathing condemnations of civilization, or offensive references to Deity; or they are positive truths, in agreement with the Sermon on the Mount, which are "ridiculous to men." Since Melville's mind was a hornet's nest of objectionable Truths of these sorts pressing for utterance, he was exceedingly alive to the threat of public sharpshooters. "Truth," he wrote, "is forced to fly like a scared white doe in the woodlands; and only by cunning glimpses will she reveal herself." It was partly to avoid a barrage of gun shots that Melville concealed his truths in symbols, allegories, and myths in such a way that only a worthy reader can get at them. His books are not rationally designed with a pre-selected, coherent scheme of symbols, but are more in the nature of loosely governed free associations, with a "general drift of symbolism," as Homans[8] has well

*It is important to note that in Melville's dictionary "heart" includes hate, provided it is "righteous." It was "his heart's shell" which Ahab burst upon "the whale's white hump."

said, the straight course of the logic being interrupted by all manner of digressions. Understanding comes through emotional involvement in the current of imagery. To read Melville with "the inexorable and inhuman eye of mere undiluted reason" is to disgrace oneself.

In writing *Pierre* Melville, with Shakespeare to encourage him, said more "terrifically true" things more openly than he ever had before. But his orientation was different from Shakespeare's: he was not sociocentric and objective; he had little of that supreme genius's versatility and breadth. He did not feel his way into a variety of dissimilar personalities and by portraying the unique integrity of each, establish a multiplicity of centers to engage his readers. He was egocentric and subjective throughout, remaining planted in his self-dramatization and describing others as they affected him. But he largely made up for shortcomings of this origin by greater depth, by driving a shaft into the primitive strata of his mind. *There* he was outside the boundaries of his culture, dissociated from his space-time, and almost in possession of a universality of understanding that reached round the world and back into Pagan centuries. It is not surprising, therefore, that some of the Truths which Melville expressed, "even though it be covertly and by snatches," had more shocking power than anything in Shakespeare. *Pierre,* for example, as read by the literary critic of the contemporary *American Whig Review,* struck "at the very foundations of society" by representing ideas which should be forever "shrouded in decorous darkness." According to *The Literary World,* the book lies at the bottom of a stagnant pool which is "muddy, foul, and corrupt."

Although narcism bulked large in Melville's personality, it would be a fatal mistake to regard his autobiographical writings mainly as egotistical exhibitions of purely personal experiences, because, by opening his mind to the spontaneities of the impersonal unconscious and identifying with a procession of archetypal figures, he succeeded in memorably portraying dispositions that are universal. To be more specific, we can say today that he revealed the forces, antithetical to the contemporary cultural compound of puritanism, rationalism, and materialism, which were lurking, barbarized by repression, in the heart of Western Man, biding the moment for their eruption. *Moby-Dick,* for instance, was the superbest prophecy of the essence of Fascism that any literature produced.

Melville's self-image foreshadowed the atomization of our society, more especially the Ishmaelism of the artist, of which so many of us are today aware. Being a spiritual *Isolato,* that is, "living on a separate continent of his own," he was in desperate need of a philosophy of individual development and relationship, and his endeavors to arrive at a sustaining myth, or to find ingredients for one, are apparent in both *Mardi* and *Pierre.* This quest, which is undertaken by individuals who withdraw, as Toynbee has described, when the mythology of their society begins to disintegrate, invariably leads the spirit back to the starting point of all religions, childhood, the Holy Family, to the father, and, finally, to the mother—"look homeward angel"—because the aim, mostly unconscious, is to be reborn, to reenter and then shed the parents' cultural husk, and to grow to a new conception. This retrogressive process is exemplified in *Pierre*,* neglected fore-runner of the multiplicity of less mythic autobiographies of our time, most notably, say, the Odyssey of Thomas Wolfe.

According to the view I am favoring, the characters in *Pierre* are human beings, not personifications or symbols of totally different entities. However, they are not represented objectively and concretely, each in his or her independent and unique totality, but rather in relation to Pierre and, for the most part, as apperceived emotionally by him under this and that circumstance. What is shown chiefly is the object's casual efficacy, or signification, for the hero's spiritual development. This is the basic type of apperception, a consequence of the narcistic and egocentric orientation of every living creature. It is as if Pierre had asked himself, what is she to me? not, what is she to others? or what is she in her own proper individuality? Thus each character is the embodiment, or incarnation, of an affecting force or cluster of forces, and is, in this sense, an abstraction.

The pages I have written up to this point constitute, as Plinlimmon would say, "not so much the Portal, as part of the temporary Scaffold to the Portal" of *Pierre*. It is a scaffold of facts and fancies which go to show, I think, that Melville's first seven books can properly be regarded as chronicles of the extravert and introvert phases of his unfolding. His spiritual situation in 1851 and the divided and defeated frame of mind in which he struggled with his Kraken, *Pierre,* have been defined briefly, insofar as this knowledge serves to elucidate the subtitle, the general moral, and much of the structure of the book. The rest of this scaffold to the portal consists of fragmentary evidences that Melville was attempting, wittingly or unwittingly, to incorporate in the vocation of art, the functions of a depth psychologist, of a moral philosopher, and of a religionist.

One consequence of this voracious assimilation of such different roles are the defects of aesthetic integration which Melville himself condemned so harshly when, in writing to Hawthorne, he explained that the product of his efforts to combine conflicting objectives "is a final hash, and all my books are botches." But another consequence, since he was partially successful in every one of his professions, is that each of his major books (including *White Jacket*) is a horn of plenty, a great banquet of diverse foods and wines to nourish the mind and heart of a robust

*It is possible that Melville was impressed by Goethe's comment (in his autobiography) that, "The most important events of the world require to be traced to the secrets of families."

reader. Enchanted by such imaginative fecundity, one happily embraces as virtues the few incongruities which have not passed unnoticed. Unhappily, this is not a claim which can be made for *Pierre*, since in this novel flaws are more frequent, and here and there Melville errs miserably, for the first time, in his use of language.

Since the influence of the drama is very apparent in *Pierre*, I feel justified in dividing the book for convenience into three long acts, each of which will be separately summarized, interpreted, and appraised.

The first act portrays in several scenes a privileged society of three persons living in the paradise of Saddle Meadows. At the manor-house the regal and resplendent widow, Mary Glendinning, and her buoyant, high-minded, and affectionate son, Pierre, are moving in one music; the angelical Lucy Tartan, object of Pierre's "boundless admiration and love," is blossoming near-by. Since Mrs. Glendinning has approvingly consented to their marriage in a year or two, and on coming of age, Pierre will inherit his family's vast estate and wealth, there is nothing in the situation which suggests withdrawal of the divine blessing.

This paradise has a feudal structure, for which Melville prepares us in his dedication when he devoutly kneels to Greylock's Most Excellent Majesty: "my own more immediate sovereign lord and king." The manor of which Pierre is to be the "lord," with farmer tenants paying rents in wheat, fowls, and labor, is feudal in its social and economic regulations.* Even his two young colts are "bound in perpetual feudal fealty" to Pierre "as the undoubted head of the house of Glendinning." The ruling ancestral spirit of Saddle Meadows, General Glendinning, Pierre's deceased grandfather and exemplar, is the abstract of feudal virtues. In this "meek majestic soul the lion and the lamb embraced—fit image of his God."

Madam Glendinning, lady of the manor, is so complacently imperious that on one occasion the minister is prompted to address her as "Your Majesty." With "her pride of birth, her pride of affluence, her pride of purity, and all the pride of high-born, refined, and wealthy Life," this beautiful and assured widow holds her son, as would a sorceress, in a state of idolatrous thralldom. Pierre's manner is a perfect period version of the "feudalization of love." He is more than willing to play "First Lady in waiting to the Dowager Duchess Glendinning." "The Americans, and not the French," the author claims, "are the world's models of Chivalry."

In his courtship of Lucy, Pierre acts the part of an ardent and poetical knight-errant. He is his lady's man, her "recruit," and in accordance with the code of chivalry devotes much time to strenuous exercise in the open air so as to acquire "such a noble muscular manliness, that he might

---

*This system of land tenure had existed in New York State ever since the original settlement of this region by the Dutch West India Company, but at the time this novel opens (say 1840) it was about to be abolished because of its inconsistency with democratic principles.

champion Lucy against the whole physical world."

The verdant virgin poetry of Saddle Meadows is far from the prose of the mechanical, dirty-faced, plebian city. There are no detestable stock-companies in this Eden, no banks, counting-houses, pawn-shops. There is not a businessman in sight. This little "green and golden world" is blissfully unaware of the Age of Commerce, the codes of trade, the mythology of greed, the economic interpretation of history, materialism, and applied science. No passport to this Happy Valley has been issued to Economic Man. Protected by its encircling blue hills, Nature develops unmolested here, free to express its temperament—to enjoy its rhythms of lyrical exuberance as well as its hours of "wonderful and indescribable repose."

For Master Pierre there are no deprivations in this place. He has never known a morning when on entering the dining-room he has not found the table heaped with viands and delicacies, and "smelt all Java's spices in the aroma from the silver coffee-urn." He has never known the sharp spur of necessity. He has never had to eat his bread in the sweat of his face.

There is no mention of any school or even tutors, any tiring struggles with arithmetic or Latin. We are led to believe that Pierre has educated himself by pursuing nimble nymphs through pages of "all-bewildering beauty" in the *Faerie Queene.* Directed efforts of the will have never been required of him. But the result is not apathy or indolence, because beneath Pierre's self lies a bottomless reservoir of exultant energy which, in overflowing, bears him forward. He is the complete embodiment of the *élan vital*—"Vivia" will be his pseudonym. Like Nature he experiences depletion, fallow interludes of pensiveness, but always after these, renewal, the upsurge of surplus vigor, of which the range of his cross-country explorations, the Dionysian expansion of his feelings, the vividness of his perceptions, the reach of his imaginative conceits, his fugitive poems, and his gay talk are effortless expressions. The enjoyment of such sheer unimpeded activity is what some psychologists have called "function pleasure," but in the estimation of Henry James, the Swedenborgian, it is much more than this: it is the warrant of a "divine personality." In an extraordinary little book of lectures,[9] which Melville may have read, James announced that a man who lives according to his highest and inmost subjection, which is to God, will be lifted "entirely beyond the sphere of necessity or duty"; he will act spontaneously and "to please himself," for "only spontaneous action images God." The artist who "obeys his own inspiration or taste, uncontrolled by physical necessities or social obligations" is the best example, according to James, of a "divine personality."

Some modern psychologists have supposed that a child who was reared under such conditions—without deprivations, rejections, punishments, or obligations to exertion—would neither manifest nor covertly store up any aggression or malice, any envy or avarice, any exorbitant will to superiority or to power, because these, they believe, are not self-generating forces but reactions to lacks and hurts. Gratified on all sides, the boy would have nothing to express but joyousness and goodwill. To philosophers of this persuasion, Pierre Glendinning, in this phase of his career, can be offered as Exhibit A. The morning sun has "never lifted him but to joy." He is constantly brimming over lavishly with generous emotions. There is no intimation of the theologian's depravity in Saddle Meadows. Mrs. Glendinning has her woman's share of vanity, but it has "never betrayed her into a single published impropriety, or caused her one known pang at the heart," and Pierre, the "divine personality," though full of "irresistible nameless" impulses, has never in his whole life done "an act of which he was privately ashamed."

By some as-yet-unexplained falsifying twist of judgment the early Hebrew myth-weavers, in creating their religion, eliminated woman as a spiritual principle and the early Christians followed suit. There is but one God, they asserted, no Goddess; and this one God produced a male, and from this male's rib a female. In this summary fashion the creative role of woman was authoritatively denied: the initial matriarchal period in the career of every child—the mother-son relationship—was blotted out. Then, on top of this, woman was eternally convicted as the evil agent through whom man is dispossessed of lasting happiness. In this first act of *Pierre* we find an overcompensatory Eden, a poetical feudal paradise in which woman is zealously elevated to the highest place in the order of nature.

Since "the Infinite Haughtiness had first fashioned" Mary Queen of Heaven at Saddle Meadows, she is haughty too, supremely so, and of all her traits, it is this haughtiness which has greatest binding power, "for the extremest top of love, is Fear and Wonder."[10] On the other hand, "in her less splendid" part, Pierre's "lovely, immaculate mother" has ever been for him "a beautiful saint," a "gentle lady-counsellor and confessor," the object of his "profoundest filial respect." "Beauty made the first Queen," we are told, and in this myth her name is Mary Glendinning and her beauty is fadeless as Milton's amaranth, immortal flower which once grew in paradise "fast by the Tree of Life."

In a revealing passage, Melville states without qualification that this mutual love of mother and son is the "highest and airiest thing in the whole compass of the experience of our mortal life." He believes it is superlative because it is "not to be limited in duration by that climax which is so fatal to ordinary love." Pierre, young as he is, seems to have a vague premonition of this fatality (which his creator defines as "the inevitable evanescence of all earthly loveliness") when, in contemplating his bride-to-be, he fancies that her spirit would exhale upward to the sky after "one husbandly embrace." "By heaven," he exclaims, inwardly, "but marriage is an impious thing!" Sexual intercourse, then, according to the author of *Pierre,* shatters ecstasy's illusion, breaks the religious vision—as the Gnostics, Manichaeans, Catharists, troubadours, and courtly lovers held—and the amaranth which was growing by the tree of life is removed to heaven as it was after Adam's sin. Thenceforth the incurable enthusiast, renouncing his "earthly household peace" (the mortal catnip of this novel), looks heavenward for his lost beatitude (the amaranth), striving possibly to regain it "by fierce escalade" as does Enceladus in Pierre's trance. But now I am running ahead of the story. Everything is still serene at Saddle Meadows. Nothing has occurred to disturb the perfect harmony of Mrs. Glendinning and her son.

Thus, many years before Freud, Melville, opening his mind to undercurrents of feeling and imagery, discovered the Oedipus Complex* and unashamedly represented it with colorful embellishments, as it would flower in the wishful fantasy of a victimized adolescent. There can be no doubt that Melville recognized the incestuous nature of the attachment. He makes both direct and indirect references to incest, when, for instance, he alludes to Terra and her Titan son, to Ninon de Lenclos, and to Semiramis, who is linked with his mother through "the Semiramian pride of woman" and the "Assyrian toss of the head." Furthermore, the whole first act is pervaded by Queen Mother imagery: Nature at Saddle Meadows, for instance, "like any Queen, is ever attended by scrupulous lady's maids in the guise of the seasons . . . and hath a brave dress for every week in the year . . . and weareth her sun by day as a diamond on a Queen's brow." Let us note also that Melville's thought not infrequently jumps to the East, source of the mystery religions which Christianity officially stamped out in the West, the home of the Babylonian mother goddess Ishtar (Astarte). He alludes several times to Babylon and Nineveh, both founded by the legendary Queen Semiramis, and to Palmyra (Tadmor), ruled by Queen Zenobia. Great cities, we know, are often associated with the mother-image, for example in the Bible (MYSTERY, BABYLON THE GREAT, THE MOTHER OF HARLOTS AND ABOMINATIONS OF THE EARTH—*Revelation,* 17, 5).

To set forth this myth of paradise Melville had to erase from his memory the depreciating conditions, economic and social, of his own young manhood and depict as permissive and indulgent a situation as could be found in America, a situation such as Pierre Van Cortlandt, an Albanian contemporary of his, was then enjoying on his Hudson Valley manor. What Melville did in writing this act was to lay out the magic carpet for his mother and gratify her every wish, to complete her velvet dream of upper-class privilege and splendor—a dream which he had

---

*The insurgence of this complex in the fall of 1851 is indicated by the fact that Melville, in filling out his son's birth certificate, wrote down his name and his mother's name as parents of the child. For this telling slip of the pen, I am indebted to my friend Mr. Jay Leyda, who in a short time has hooked more fish for the skillet than any of the rest of us Melvillian fly-casters.

once shared, so identified was he with her tastes and aspirations. He knew that she was neither constituted nor reared to spend herself in hopeless efforts to make ends meet on fifty dollars a month in the quiet little village of Lansingburgh, but was "formed chiefly for the gilded prosperities of life." Thus there was much subjective truth in his picture of the little aristocracy at Saddle Meadows. But his regnant purpose, we surmise, was aesthetic: one of the archetypical themes he had chosen for his story was that of Paradise Lost and he evidently wished to have his hero's fall complete in all particulars, not only spiritual but material— from wealth to penury, from leisure to toil, from the romance of chivalry to the mechanics of profit, from the benedictions of the country to the city without grace. A sociologist might call it a tragedy of downward mobility, the exact antithesis of the basic American myth.

Actually this allegory of adolescent attachment is grounded emotionally in experiences that occur during the first phase of life, the matriarchal feeding period when the receptively dependent boy has his mother all to himself and is virtually the only child. This golden age comes to an abrupt end, one bleak day, when the boy discovers that he has a sister or a brother, that the exclusive paradise he has enjoyed is no longer his, and that henceforth he must accommodate himself to the melancholy role of a dispossessed young prince. But let us not recapitulate the stages of a child's development. It is sufficient to notice that our dramatist has excluded all his brothers and sisters from his cast of characters, that Pierre is leading a sheltered existence wholly within the sphere of his mother's sovereignty, that most of his meetings with her occur at mealtimes, and that food imagery is repeatedly used in expressing love. In view of all this, one is startled though not confounded on finding that Melville in his letter to Mrs. Hawthorne calls his new book *(Pierre)* a "rural bowl of milk," and that in one of the breakfast scenes, after the hero has called for three bowls of milk, Mrs. Glendinning says: "Don't be a milk-sop, Pierre!"

I may be excused for devoting so large a fraction of my introduction to the least satisfying part of *Pierre* if perchance I have succeeded in indicating very roughly how the novel may be interpreted in psychological and mythological terms and in drawing attention to Melville's astute awareness of processes outside the range of normal consciousness. The rest of the book is also susceptible of analysis at this level, but I shall content myself with these fragmentary suggestions and turn now to topics more germane to the realm of literature.

In view of the requirements of his myth it is not altogether surprising that only one of Melville's three characters is credible. Mrs. Glendinning, I submit, is a woman of genuine substance. The central passion and form of her personality—pride and the values that structure it—are not only fully and adroitly exhibited in her words and actions but, at a critical moment in the next act, are precisely defined for us by the author with the skill of a dexterous surgeon exposing a brain tumor. Although Melville did not have to go outside of Arrowhead to find the stuff for this formidable figure of his imagination, accounts of Byron's mother, Viscountess Dowager Bellair in *Henrietta Temple,* Lady Ashton in *The Bride of Lammermoor,* and certainly the "imperious dame" who is tormented by incest-guilt in Walpole's *The Mysterious Mother* must have helped him to elaborate his conception. It is also possible that the revengeful Medea of Seneca or of Euripides played some part, if only to assure him that he was well within the range of dramatic possibility when in the next act he has Mrs. Glendinning so unforgivingly disinherit her only child.

In painting the portrait of his hero, Melville assigned himself a difficult aesthetic task: to beget an American youth of nineteen, unacquainted with toil, hardship, grief, or sin, pure as Sir Galahad, and show him solely in his rhetorical relations with the two women he loves, abstracted from all other social ties and actions, as well as from the broad stream of national events. The result of the author's effort is too far from the real diary of a real boy to be wholly convincing.

Besides unfolding the Oedipus theme, the author wished to celebrate the Romeo phase of Pierre's career, "the glow and rapture of youthful love," to use the words of the critic who has most sensitively appreciated this side of Melville's personality—William Ellery Sedgwick.[11] Although Melville succeeded in shaping Pierre to the mold of the heroical lover as defined in Burton's *Anatomy,* the young man is not real to a modern reader. With his graceful rhapsodies of chaste sentiments and high-flown conceits of love he contrasts too sharply with his American successor, the tongueless troubadour of today with his hit-and-run efficiency of sex.

The earliest blueprints for the Pierre of act 1 are the self-portraits in Melville's "Fragments from a Writing-Desk" (1839), materials for which were derived from contemporary literature. When Melville read a book that absorbed him he *became* the hero and lived through his adventures as if they were his own. Just as he said in *Mardi,* "I touched Isabella's heart, that she hearkened to Columbus . . . I am the veiled Persian Prophet; I, the man in the iron mask; I, Junius," so, we can readily imagine him at an earlier age entertaining a succession of fantasies which might be translated as follows: "I am Childe Harold, Manfred, Cain; I am Ishmael;[12] I am Soudamour; I am the Red Rover; I am Halbert Glendinning; I am Vivian Grey, the Young Duke, Contarini Fleming, Alroy, Ferdinand Armine," and so forth. The book which was most potent in fashioning Melville's ideal and thus indirectly affecting his personality and his writings was, I would wager, Moore's *Life of Byron,* and, hardly to be separated from this, Byron's *Complete Works* in which this poet's own unmistakable self-image appears in various guises and disguises. Second to Byron, though ahead of him as a source for the first two acts

of *Pierre*, Benjamin Disraeli, himself a Byronist, stands out conspicuously.* Among the subordinate architects of Melville's early ideal self and
so of the character of Pierre of act 1 one should mention Scott, Spenser,
Moore, Cooper, and Bulwer-Lytton. In later years other authors seem to
have had a hand in it—Shakespeare in *Romeo and Juliet* and Thackeray
in *Pendennis* (1850),† for example.

"Wondrous fair of face, blue-eyed, and golden-haired, the bright
blonde," Lucy Tartan, is another figure of literary mythology, even more
etherealized than Pierre. She is the perfect embodiment of selfless love
uncrossed by worldly ambition, pride, malice, or lust. Innocent and
chaste, she is defined as "angelical" in accordance with the then-current
assumption that benevolence is of divine origin, the manifestation of the
heavenly soul which entered the body at birth, as Socrates argued, rather
than the proof of divine grace transforming a congenitally depraved
being, as Calvin and his Catholic predecessors insisted. But if we take
"angelical" as fashionable rhetoric, we shall be less apt to go astray in our
interpretations. In truth, Lucy is a finely human creature, sensible, acquiescent, modest, whose great worth resides in her capacity for faithful
unselfish devotion to those she loves. There were scores of disembodied
heroines like Miss Tartan vibrating through the pages of contemporary
novels, but possibly Lucy Ashton in Scott's *The Bride of Lammermoor*
should be singled out as the author's chief model in creating this idealization of his wife.

A reader of this day and age will encounter more impediments to
his enjoyment in accompanying Melville through the disorder of this first
part of *Pierre* than he will subsequently. For, despite the verve of it, the
import of the underlying conception, the delineation of Mrs. Glendinning's character, the penetrating scrutiny of her love for Pierre in whom
she sees "her own curled and haughty beauty," and the adroit exposure
of her covertly triumphant feelings and patronizing attitude toward
"The Little Lucy," despite these and other excellences, there are insurmountable obstacles to one's unreserved involvement. As noted above,
both Pierre and Lucy are so far abstracted from reality in these opening
scenes that our sympathies remain dormant, even though the author is
pulling all the stops in his effort to quicken them. More than anything it
is the language—not so much the long neologisms and convoluted sentences, but the idiom of fervent passion—which at too frequent points
through sheer inanity, if not falsity, makes one wince and squirm, until
a hand automatically reaches out for some object, anything, with which
to oust "Love's sweet bird from her nest." But since Mumford has unerr-

*My daughter Josephine L. Murray discovered the most probable source of numerous
situations, incidents, characterizations, sentiments, ideas, and props in Disraeli novels.

†My friend Miss Ina May Greer found some highly probable raw material, such as the
Marquis of Plinlimmon, in *Pendennis*.

ingly picked out the most distressing specimens, I am justified, I hope, in shunning this mortifying obligation.

How can we explain such trash from the brain of the creator of *Moby-Dick?* It is not difficult. One has only to conceive of a young man in the late 1830's with a voluptuous imagination which has been steeped in the erotic literature of his day. Any critic who has forced his mind through the annuals, the gift books, the polite periodicals, the immensely popular novels, the feminine "effusions" of that era, or who, recoiling from this task, has pursued the perfumed trail of sensibility through the admirable pages of E. Douglas Branch[13] and from Herbert R. Brown's delectable treatise[14] acquired sufficient understanding of the pitiful religion of the heart that was being promiscuously propagated by novelists of the second and third order during the sentimental decades, any critic who has dutifully done this will be in a position to identify the origin of most of the repellent elements in the first two acts of *Pierre.*

In an account of the determinants of Melville's florid diction and of his portrait of Pierre, the white-ruffled poetaster, author of "The Tear" and worshiper of sexless divinities, one should not overlook the large feminine component in his personality which, encouraged by two novel-reading sisters, inclined him to absorb so much of the nonsense written by the apostles of sensibility and to identify with so many elegant dandies of fiction, effete young gentlemen for whom there was an accepted role in London society but none in Albany or Lansingburgh. It was the sea that made a man of Melville. Among other things it made it possible for him to become (in two later chapters of *Pierre*) the first satirist of the literary school from which he had barely graduated. He deserves first prize for having been eighty-odd years ahead of Branch and other critics even though it is clear that he himself was not wholly free of the tastes and dispositions he was ridiculing. He jeers at the critics for preferring literature in which "vulgarity and vigor—two inseparable adjuncts" are absent, and yet there is not a suspicion of vulgarity in *Pierre,* and, although there is considerable vigor, it is almost wholly confined to the release of destructive tension. When love is in ascendancy we are offered pretty filagrees of fancy, such as the image of sailors at sea tying "love-knots on every spangled spar" when they feel "ineffable distillations of a soft delight" in the morning's breeze.

But, except by shunning or handling very gingerly the subject of love, did any American novelist do better? Today we know very well what was violating the spirit, enfeebling the will, deranging the mind, and crippling the talent of almost every American writer of the nineteenth century. The story of the long relentless war against Eros, of its suppression, and its banishment from the realm of open discourse and knowledge is now familiar to many. It is not necessary to describe the ill effects of it all—the unspeakable inner conflicts, torments, confusions, and corruptions; the lasting resentments, the fury; the dishonorable subterfuges, the scandals, the obscene cant, the endless masquerades, the squeamish insinuations, the escapes of fantasy to the exotic East, *Lalla Rookh;* the feeble and bizarre conceits, the airy imbecilities—over a million copies of the *Reveries of a Bachelor.* To fail to mention the morbid degree of decorous and puritanical repression and Manichaean disparagement of instinct in *Pierre* would be to discredit this introduction, because from start to finish the weather of the book is pervaded by its grotesque, confounding, and blighting consequences.

Let us now return to the sweetness and light of Saddle Meadows. Obviously a world so elegant, exclusive, and sublimated can not long endure. Its existence is a provocation to the impartiality of Nature, calling for some corrective blow of Fate, the intrusion of a serpent. We do not need the author's repeated Shakespearean warnings that trouble is in the offing. It comes suddenly—in the form of a Face, the mysteriously tragic, fateful face of a girl suddenly encountered by Pierre while escorting his mother on a visit to a gathering of women-folk in the village. It was "one of those faces which now and then appear to man, and without one word of speech, still reveal glimpses of some fearful gospel . . . such faces compounded so of hell and heaven, overthrow in us all foregone persuasions, and make us wondering children in this world again." Seen but once and briefly, the Face haunts Pierre day and night. He is unable to dismiss it. Here Melville is at his realistic best, profound in his comprehension and beautifully precise in his account of this cast of Face and of its revolutionary effect upon a susceptible man's mind. It is the best description in literature, I believe, of the autonomous inward operation of the aroused soul-image, or anima, as Jung has named it.[15]

The second act opens with Pierre's reception of a letter from the Face, which informs him that she, Isabel Banford, is his half-sister, his father's natural daughter. A forlorn destitute orphan, she begs him to come to her. After reading this note Pierre collapses as if "some assassin had stabbed him." "Ay, Pierre, for thee, the before undistrusted moral beauty of the world is forever fled . . . Truth rolls a black billow through thy soul!" The first fruit of the tree of knowledge is bitter unto death. Wisdom is woe. Paradise is lost. Saddle Meadows is a valley of desolation.

Melville tells us that it would be impossible to give a complete explanation of why a piece of information which many a young man has "been known to receive with a momentary feeling of surprise" produced so tumultuous a reaction in Pierre. Such a motion of the heart, Melville says, adumbrating the principle of developmental determinism, is "not wholly imputable to the immediate apparent cause, which is only one link in the chain"; it is the resultant "of an infinite series of infinitely involved and untraceable foregoing occurrences." A few "random hints," however, are presented which serve to deprive Pierre's agitation of some of its strangeness. Up to this moment, the author explains, Pierre's father has been the supposedly "solid and eternal" pillar which supported the whole "temple of his moral life." Melville intimates— again anticipating the findings of depth psychology—that the image of God was generated out of early idealizations of the father. "Not to God had Pierre ever gone in his heart, unless by ascending the steps of that shrine, and so making it the vestibule of his abstractest religion." The shrine is now a heap of rubble, because—and here Melville could assume that his reader would unreservedly agree with him that sex is Sin with a capital—Pierre has learnt that his father was a seducer. With the wreck of the reverential relationship which has heretofore sustained him, Pierre feels utterly deserted. But, after a while, waking from his daze, he says, "My self am left, at least." Then, summoning the forces of his pride, like Ahab addressing the corposants, he exclaims defiantly: "With myself I front thee! . . . From all idols, I tear all veils; henceforth I will see the hidden things."

Since I have forsworn further mythological reconstructions of the plot on the level of primary childhood events, I shall do no more than to suggest that the nature and intensity of Pierre's reaction can not be explained without reference to an earlier experience—the time when a sensitive, trustful boy, kept innocent by evasions and falsehoods, discovers what to him is the infidelity, the secret iniquity, the Original Sin, of his parents. Melville evidently recognized this, but Truth is again "forced to fly like a scared white doe" and reveal itself only by a cunning glimpse in the paragraph that starts with "Ah, fathers and mothers!"

Instead of elaborating this germinal idea, Melville pursues another, though parallel, train of associations and, with perfect craftsmanship, recounts certain events in Pierre's life, which, uncomprehended at the time of their occurrence, produced no blasting effects, but which now, called to mind by Isabel's letter, suffice to "enkindle such a blaze of evidence, that all the corners of conviction" are suddenly lighted up. The conversation between Aunt Dorothea and little Pierre in which she tells the story of the painting of his father's chair-portrait is recited with engaging charm, and the account of Pierre's subsequent reveries and ruminations when he sits before the portrait and scrutinizes his father's ambiguous expression could scarcely be more absorbing.

What Melville describes with such consummate talent and verisimilitude in this section is another great archetypal situation, the discovery of unsuspected evil in the revered object, which is central to the plot of *Othello* as well as to that of *Hamlet.* Here, however, it is a man, not a woman, whose "vileness" is suddenly revealed. That Melville was confronted by an equivalent situation in his own life is a conclusion that seems warranted by the available evidence; but this is not the place to marshal it. I shall restrict myself to two observations. As suggested in the footnotes, a close examination of Melville's succession of metaphors indicates that the bolt of intelligence which in Pierre produced a wound "never to be completely healed but in heaven" is one and the same as the blight which in Redburn's young soul left such a scar "that the air of Paradise might not erase it" and also one and the same as the lightning which struck Ahab so burningly that "to this hour I bear the scar." Furthermore, just as the down-darting lightning left Ahab's body forever divided by a lividly whitish brand, so did the discovery of his father's sin produce a lasting division in Pierre's heart, a radical and protracted moral conflict which resulted, on the intellectual level, in an obdurate dualism.

Adhering to the author's level of analysis, Pierre's transformation can be explained by assuming that the shining figure of his irreproachable father made it easy for him to repress his own instinctual urges, and, so, as a unified person to develop in the direction of his ideal. But when he learns that his trusted exemplar did not practice what he preached, his instincts come seething to the surface. If his supreme preceptor enjoyed forbidden fruit, why should he refrain? This inaugurates a bitter moral conflict because the insurgent instincts are opposed by a deeply imbedded conscience. Pierre's reaction, which includes the threat that he will give himself up "to be a railing atheist," shows, among other things, that his trust in God depended on the substantiality of his relationship with his father.

In respect to the classical signs of basic conflict Melville and his hero are indistinguishable. Creator and creature proceed together from here on, defining each successive situation as a battlefield of two irreconcilable absolutes, Good and Evil. Pierre also resembles the author of *Moby-Dick* in concluding that Evil is predominant. Immediately after discovering his father's transgression, Pierre sees his former idol downside up; the concealed, denied, and sinister elements come to the top; the habitually exhibited, good features are no longer apparent. Pierre's whole field of vision, like Hamlet's, is now populated by images of corruption. His eyes have been suddenly opened to man's shadow self and he attends to no other aspects: what a man represses has become the truth, what he expresses may be set aside as false. When Pierre examines the chair-portrait of his father, painted before his marriage, the face seems to be saying: "Look again, I am thy father as he more truly was. In mature life, the world overlays and varnishes us . . . in youth we *are* Pierre, but in age we *seem.* Look again. I am thy real father." It is misleading to assimilate this antimony to the ancient metaphysical dichotomy of appearance and reality. Metaphysically a man's private and secret actions, carried out behind closed doors, have the same status as his public and open actions, but psychologically and sociologically they are very different. To be more specific, the contrast here is between covert and unacknowledged lust and overt and professed purity. Once the libidinous vein in his father's outwardly immaculate character has been exposed to him, Pierre sees evil and hypocrisy everywhere. He generalizes, as Hamlet does, and concludes that the whole world is "saturated and soaking with lies."

But now it is high time we make way for the young woman whose letter initiated the metamorphosis we have been examining, because she has already become the pivot of this drama, Pierre having pledged himself to her at the same moment and as decisively as he repudiated his father. "Here I swear myself Isabel's," he said, and that very evening, following her instructions, he knocks at the door of Mr. Ulver's farmhouse, the latch is lifted, and the dark girl stands before him in all the wonder of her solitary, inscrutable, mournful beauty.

I will not recite here the long, rambling, dreamlike history of Isabel's life as she tells it in two successive evenings. Despite the significance of the symbolism, the incoherent flow of her shadowy memories will not be so engrossing to the reader as they were to Pierre. The facts are meager. Isabel was born in France where she was cared for by an old peasant couple. At an early age she was brought to America and after spending several years in a house for mental defectives and lunatics, she was visited by Mr. Glendinning, her father, who found a more tolerable home for her with a family in the country. After his death, she was forced to earn her own living, and eventually, as luck would have it, found menial employment at Farmer Ulver's. Isabel's reminiscences, few and vague as they are, coincide with the story of Mr. Glendinning's chair-portrait as told by Aunt Dorothea, and Pierre is convinced, the reader with him, that his father had a pre-marital love affair with a French émigrée, who later returned to France and died in bearing Isabel. But sister, or no sister, Pierre has been infatuated ever since he first laid eyes on her, and now after two evenings is so inflamed by love, pity, amazement, reverence, and awe, that he feels he must do something instantly. While he is straining in agony to arrive at some feasible plan of action, let us consider the cause and nature of his agitation.

The significance of Isabel can be best defined by comparing her to Lucy. In respect to the qualities and powers ascribed to all romantically loved women, the two differ only in degree, Isabel's power being greater. To Lucy, Pierre has vowed his "choice, delicious life—for his one pure and comprehensive offering—at once a sacrifice and a delight." But his eyes are closed to her and his vow effaced as if it were inscribed in water once he has met Isabel. Even earlier, Isabel's face, invading his reveries, was "a silent and tyrannical call, challenging him in his deepest moral being, and summoning Truth, Love, Pity, Conscience, to the stand."

In several crucial particulars, differences in degree between Lucy and Isabel are so great that they amount to differences in quality. Lucy (*lux*, light) is clear as the open day, responsive to the world about her, aware of nothing she is unable or unwilling to communicate. She asks,

"What secret thing keep I from thee? Read me through and through." And Pierre says, "Frankly open is the flower, that hath nothing but purity to show." Isabel, on the other hand, is reticent, withdrawn, and inaccessible, absorbed in her secret inner life. Her reveries can not readily be trapped in words. For Pierre "the mystery of Isabel possessed all the bewitchingness of the mysterious vault of night." She is the "dark passion" of the soul.

Pierre's love for Lucy is as rational as love can ever be. It grew gradually and has been accepted as his free choice; it fits and completes his scheme of life; it is culturally encouraged; and however wholehearted his devotion, he is assured of large returns. Lucy is sensible, adaptable, and unselfish. It is a "good match," because, as Mrs. Glendinning puts it, "Lucy is a delicious girl; of honorable descent, a fortune, well-bred, and the very pattern of all that I think amiable and attractive in a girl of seventeen." Compared to this, Pierre's love for Isabel is irrational: it overcame him suddenly, compulsively, and unaccountably, and threatens to disrupt every plan he has made for his future. It will be a horror to his mother. What has poor Isabel to offer him? For her sake he may be forced to suffer much, as well as to renounce many satisfactions to which he is accustomed. And yet, somehow, her claim is incontestable. To Pierre it is not a matter of Free Will, but of Fixed Fate. "Fate will be Fate, and it was fated." Such is the condition of one who cannot conceive of the end that is being served by a course of action from which he is unable to desist; he is like the primitive man who has not learnt that the result of sexual intercourse is reproduction.

Lucy comes out of the same drawer as the Glendinnings. She and Pierre seem to belong together. They are alike in several ways and have interests in common. But Isabel represents something entirely new, different from anything Pierre has yet encountered. In certain fundamental particulars she is his exact opposite: she is passive with a "preternatural calmness," whereas he is exuberantly active; her existence is empty, his is full; she is sad, he is joyous; she is an outcast at the bottom of the social structure, he is accepted at the top. Covered "with the world's extremest infamy and scorn," she is the very antithesis of all that his world esteems. By embracing Isabel, his rejected opposite, Pierre will be identifying with and assimilating a value and an outlook which the Glendinnings have never included in their system.

A still more crucial difference between the two loved women is this: Isabel requires everything that Pierre is capable of giving; her need is immeasurable; whereas Lucy's wants are temperate. It is Isabel, then, who evokes the creative component of love that would unify, spend, and lose the self in dedicating it wholly to one object. Lucy is well-provided and secure in her own person and in her circumstances; she has not suffered from deprivations and abuses, nor is she beset by unslaked appetites or ambitions. She is the embodiment of loving-kindness and gives serenely more than she receives. At her level she is a finished product, an assenting conserver of traditional values; there are no novel developments in store for her. Hence she can not be served by Pierre's creative energy. With Isabel it is different: the essentials for her happiness are all lacking. The "long-suffering, hopeless anguish" of her "lustrous, imploring, mournful face" is the signature of her emotional desolation. It is this chiefly which has so strangely enchanted Pierre. Of the several classical types of anima projections, Isabel is a perfect example of the dark, or tragic, anima.

Isabel has the elementary mournfulness of one who has been deprived of love from birth—"I never knew a mortal mother." Pierre is drawn by her "wonderful loneliness." She has scarcely any appetite for life. Death imagery and suicidal suggestions are common in her speech. "Were it God's will, Pierre, my utmost blessing now, were to lie down and die." She swoons, and Pierre gazes with awe upon the "death-like beauty" of her face. Her affections have been limited to a single object, her mother's guitar, which is wittingly used by Melville as a womb symbol. Thus the underlying current of her feeling runs backward. She prays for peace and motionlessness, and dreams of herself "absorbing life without seeking it, and existing without individual sensation." Isabel felt that without Pierre's "continual love and sympathy, further life for her was only fit to be thrown into the nearest unfathomed pool, or rushing stream." Hers is the tired, unloved, and unloving woman's desire to let go and sink back into oblivion rather than make a forward effort into life.

Pierre's head is as necessary to Isabel's salvation as his heart. For she is in need of words and concepts to give shape and expression to her fluidity, and of magnetic images to engender zest for living. Pierre's role is to provide paving stones to consciousness and a mythology to engage her emotions. Solitary, detached, estranged, for years she has been the thrall of the autonomous, involuntary tides of an undisciplined mind. She is drowning, one might say, in her unconscious. "Oh, Pierre," she exclaims, "canst thou not cure in me this dreaminess, this bewilderingness I feel? My poor head swims and swims and will not give pause. My life can not last long thus; I am too full without discharge." Her mind is the chaos that precedes the advent of integrating love and thought. She awaits the total vision of a god and the *caritas* and *logos* of a Christ. "All my thoughts well up in me," she says, "as they are, they are, and I can not alter them, for I had nothing to do with putting them in my mind, and I never affect any thoughts, and I never adulterate any thoughts." She is a prisoner of passivity, because the world is dead to her, empty of inducements, and no insistent image of a goal calls for an enduring, organizing effort. The World is Void. Thus her challenge to the creative mind is ultimate.

Another important feature of the anima which emerges sooner or later, after she has been snatched from her "world-wide abandonment" and nourishingly embraced, is her desire to be represented, defended, and championed in the world, to have a way cleared for her acceptance by the society that excluded her and to have what she embodies incorporated in the culture. Every true anima has a potential value; she is a new hypothesis, a forgotten truth, a "stone which the builders refused" that may be destined to "become the headstone of the corner." Thus the anima is she-who-must-be-served. This is the aspect of the image which Jung has stressed and which was dominant in medieval love. The knight-errant was his mistress's vassal and he fought in her name. In courtly love the first phase, marked by woman's melancholy and man's compassion, was latent or absent, chiefly because the woman was not, as a rule, estranged from society, but a grand lady whose role as anima was culturally accepted, even though it was fulfilled outside of marriage and in the face of the Church's opposition. The imperious second phase of the anima is manifested only once by Isabel, and Pierre "bowing low over to her, owned that irrespective, darting mystery of humanity, which can be majestical and menacing in woman as in man."

One reason for the anima's attracting power is that she embodies the repressed and the as-yet-unformulated components of the man's personality: the child in him who felt unloved, the passivity and the death wishes which were forsworn, the grief and the self-pity which have been bottled up, the feminine dispositions which have been denied, and, in addition, scores of nameless intuitions and impulses, the open expression of which has been barred by culture. Isabel is the personification of Pierre's unconscious. This is not obvious at first unless the reader has been acute enough to perceive that Mrs. Glendinning has absorbed most of her son's personality, and to guess that what soul he can rightfully call his own must be a pathetic little waif. This fact first becomes apparent when Pierre's immediate reaction to the thought of his mother's condemnation is a "feeling entirely lonesome, and orphan-like," and he thinks of himself as "driven out an infant Ishmael into the desert, with no maternal Hagar to accompany and comfort him." Without these submerged elements in himself—an orphaned Ishmael clinging to a coffin—he would hardly be capable of appreciating Isabel—an orphan clinging to a guitar. But the path of deliverance and growth lies here. If he can resurrect Isabel from the dead, he himself will be reborn with a solidly founded fortitude.

What Isabel has done for Pierre is beyond reckoning. She has called forth unifying and fructifying sacrificial love, by means of which he can shed the outworn cloak of his past self and reach a new, deeply rooted, broader state of being. She has stirred his unconscious so profoundly that within a few weeks the frivolous author of "The Tear" and "The Tropical Summer" will be transformed into the audacious writer of a "mature work." Isabel, in other words, has converted fancy into imagination. She is not a child-bearing woman but *la femme inspiratrice*. "Sun or dew, thou fertilisest me!" Pierre says to her. In the evening she will play her mystic guitar till Pierre feels "chapter after chapter born of its wondrous suggestiveness." Besides this, Isabel adds the dimension of depth to Pierre's conception of his world. Suddenly, for the first time, he sees what lies beneath his narrow, complacent, gay Glendinning paradise. From her he acquires the tragic sense of life. "For me, thou hast uncovered one infinite dumb, beseeching countenance of mystery, underlying all the surfaces of visible time and space." Finally, and more specifically, Isabel extricates Pierre, momentarily at least, from the strangling coils which bind him to his mother. Lucy could never have accomplished this.

In passing, it is worth noting that Isabel may be roughly correlated with the "ungraspable phantom of life" reflected in the sea; and Lucy with the securities, comforts, and consolations of land; or, to use Nietzsche's terms loosely, Sea-Isabel is the Dionysian component, Land-Lucy the Apollonian.

Isabel's effect, then, has been to increase rapidly the permeability of Pierre's mind to elements which are beyond the reach of ordinary thought. This has amounted to a temporary flooding of consciousness—an extreme expansion with numerous insights and self-revelations, and a blurring marked by illusions and delusions. Pierre's acceptance of Isabel, "a power so hovering upon the confines of the invisible world, that it seemed more inclined that way than this," is equivalent to a declaration in favor of the unconscious as a directing influence in his life. In *Moby-Dick* Melville identified the unconscious with God; in *Pierre* he identifies God with Isabel. Pierre's final query is—"Lucy or God?"

One more point about the anima: invariably, at first, she is an ambiguous, or ambivalent, object, compounded of heaven and hell. Pierre feels that Isabel might "insidiously poison and embitter his whole life." This apperception of evil is attributable to the fact that Isabel is an irresistible, irrational power that separates him from all his present happiness, produces an intolerable conflict, and transfigures him into an enemy of all the good that he has known. The anima experience, Pierre discovers, is a tremendous, unsharable secret, a mystery which isolates a man until its significance has been at least partially revealed to him. Furthermore, Pierre's anima is outside the inherited culture, outside the Christian system. The name "Isabel" means "oath of Bel"; and since our Isabel is called "Bell" it is possible that Melville wished to associate her as closely as possible with the great Babylonian god, Jehovah's enemy. Bel, mentioned in *Moby-Dick*, has been identified with the Phoenician Baal, worshiped by Jezebel ("devotee of Bel"), the wife of Ahab. Ahab "did evil in the sight of the Lord above all that were before him" because he married Jezebel and joined her in serving Baal. It is not unlikely that Melville had these significations in mind in naming Isabel.

It is astonishing that two generations before Jung, Melville, unaided by the findings of depth psychology, should have described with such fidelity, subtlety, and beauty all the significant features of the first phase of the anima experience. If he had ended *Pierre* at this point, the novel might have been hailed someday as the forerunner of a new mythology, since in Pierre's attraction to Isabel one can recognize the germ of evolutionary love "all whose tenderness *ex vi termini,*" as Henry James, Sr., has said, "must be reserved only for what intrinsically is most bitterly hostile and negative to itself." As Charles Peirce interpreted it, this "sublime" sentence "discloses for the problem of evil its everlasting solution."[16] The doctrine of creative, or evolutionary, love, defines what might be called the dialectic of development, personal or social, inasmuch as it prescribes, at each critical point of spiritual or mental growth, the embracement by the thesis of its antithesis, and the creation of a new synthesis. Usually the antithesis which is called evil is the potential source of a greater good than has been realized theretofore. This is the case for Isabel.

Thus we find Pierre standing at the threshold of a saving evolutionary way through relationship. The fact that from this point on Melville makes him commit a long series of fantastic errors of judgment and treacheries of the heart does not rob him of the distinction of having once gazed on the promised land, even though, like Moses, he never inhabited it. Romanticism, which started as a revolt against the artificial restrictions of eighteenth century rationality and decorum, was essentially a wide heart's search for new or lost values. All we can expect of a Romantic is suggestiveness in depth, breadth, or elevation. His function is to free imprisoned men, to penetrate barriers, invade forbidden territory, open vistas, and indicate paths to rewarding experiences; not to hold, cherish, and sustain values in sickness and in health, to test and retest them, and eventually to order them in a total philosophy of life.

There are, of course, innumerable descriptions in literature of the dark anima, *la femme fatale,* but all of them, as far as I know, lack psychological insight. They are either superficial and fragmentary, or shadowy and dream-like, or fabulous and allegorically or morbidly sensational; that is, they are more or less pure projections of fantasy, hallucinatory in nature and unanalyzed. The figure of Isabel, on the other hand, vague as it necessarily is to us, marks a decided advance in concretization and heuristic understanding. She is unintelligible to many readers because she conforms neither to the conventions of allegory and myth nor to those of naturalism and realism, but is the product of an only partially realized fusion of these conventions. Her chief claim to our attention, nonetheless, is that she is a composite of image and object, of vision and substance, of irreality (the really real) and reality (the actual).

Specially noteworthy is Melville's unique recognition of the autonomous character of the dark anima's thought processes and of her power to stimulate deeper imaginings in her counterpart. In these respects she resembles Pip in *Moby-Dick,* whose value to Ahab is expressed in one sentence: "Some unknown conduits from the unknown worlds must empty into thee!" Isabel, then, deserves to be remembered as one of the Delphic women whose capacity to transmit as well as to evoke subconscious proceedings has been chivalrously acknowledged by Claude Bragdon.[17] It is women such as she who have brought fame to the pioneers of modern depth psychology by acting as "conduits" of the "hoarded heaps" of the unconscious.[18] Some readers may also be reminded here of the figures speaking to William Butler Yeats through the automatic writings of his wife—"We have come to give you metaphors for poetry" *(A Vision).*

For clarity's sake anima love has been described apart from incestuous passion. This is legitimate since in life the anima is rarely a sister or half-sister as she is in *Pierre.* Anima love has been stressed because Melville's understanding of it is unique and prophetic, something which among critics only E. L. Grant Watson seems to have appreciated. But this fact should not be allowed to obscure the truth of Damon's statement that incest is "the secret motivation of the whole moral knot of *Pierre.*"[19] This applies particularly to the mother-son knot in which Eros operates subconsciously, determining the course of events even after Mrs. Glendinning's death. The entire novel, indeed, could be apperceived on one level as a young man's desperate attempt to break away from his matriarchal house of bondage. In connection with Isabel the incest motive calls for less comment: the activity of a sublimated sex instinct is obvious from the start and, as such, it is not subjected to a searching scrutiny by the author. Furthermore, the incest wish is adulterated by two facts: first, that Pierre is bewitched before he knows that Isabel is his sister and second, that, since the two were not brought up together, his love for her has not the significance of a persisting infantile fixation.

Knowledge that Isabel was his half-sister made it easier for Pierre to rationalize his desire to cleave to her forever, since, in the contemporary religion of the heart, affection between brother and sister was a holy sentiment, and to every true hero the championship of his sister's honor was a sacred duty. Young Pierre is only voicing an accepted article of the Man of Feeling's creed when he cries: "It must be a glorious thing to engage in a mortal quarrel on a sweet sister's behalf!" In the Middle Ages a sister was not infrequently the object of courtly love, partly, it appears, because the presence of the incest barrier served to reinforce the knight-errant's resolution to adhere to the ideal of chastity. With this in mind, we might guess that one of Pierre's secret motives was to avoid marriage, "that climax which is so fatal to ordinary love," and to commit himself forever to a wholly spiritual relationship. This hypothesis would explain Pierre's declaration that he has resolved "to follow Virtue to her uttermost vista, where common souls never go," and his apprehension lest "the uttermost virtue, after all, prove a betraying pander to the monstrousest vice."

During the forty-eight hours which elapse between Pierre's reception of Isabel's letter and his second interview with the fatal girl an incident occurs which enables Pierre to predict what his mother's attitude would be towards any proposal of his to accept his half-sister as a member of the family. The breakfast scene in which Mrs. Glendinning, Pierre, and the Rev. Mr. Falsgrave discuss the case of Ned, the seducer, and his victim, Delly, Farmer Ulver's daughter, who has just had her illegitimate child, is perhaps the best specimen in this book of Melville's craftsmanship as novelist. The engaging manner and character of Rev. Falsgrave is first delineated in a few masterful strokes, then, in the realistic dialogue that follows, the three participants, assisted by a symbolic accident, reveal traits that are crucial in affecting subsequent developments; we learn that in Mrs. Glendinning's mind a seducer is more detestable than a murderer and that the Rev. Mr. Falsgrave is a mature and sophisticated exponent of relativism in morals in contrast to Pierre, the upholder of Biblical absolutism.

Melville surpasses himself in describing "that electric insight which Fate had now given him [Pierre] into the vital character of his mother. She well might have stood all ordinary tests; but when Pierre thought of the touchstone of his immense strait applied to her spirit; he felt profoundly assured that she would crumble into nothing before it." This presentiment introduces us to one of the most authentically presented themes of the novel—the birth of the spirit out of the mother's cultural husk.

On the morning of the third day, Pierre's agitated brain aborts, delivering itself of a program, the peculiar appeal of which resides in its monstrous irrationality. He decides to announce that he and Isabel have been secretly married, then move to the city and live with her in chastity forever: both will "reach up alike to a glorious ideal." I will not follow the tortuous courses of Pierre's thought nor report the rapid succession of impetuous actions which in twenty-four hours succeed in severing all his intimate connections with the world of Saddle Meadows and in getting him and Isabel into an early morning coach bound for the city, accompanied by Delly Ulver, who will serve as maid of all work.

Pierre's extraordinary scheme and his conduct at this juncture are inspired, according to most critics, by the "noblest motives"—by his desire to succor Isabel, to make amends for the injustices she has suffered, to have a sister (his boyhood wish) whom he can "love, and protect, and fight for." In short, he is actuated chiefly by compassion—the Agape or *caritas* of Jesus and St. Paul. My analysis of Pierre's love proves, I hope, that I am not reluctant to go full distance with those who have stressed Christian charity, but it is incumbent on me now to propose that this almost unanimous verdict conceals something—the heart of the whole matter, of the book, and of the author. I say this, first, because it omits the fact that in Pierre's love for Isabel, Eros is fused with Agape,[20] and, though largely unconscious, Eros, not Agape, is the determining factor; and second, because by this omission we are robbed of our only opportunity to see Melville's "scared white doe," his positive Truth.

Pierre "fell" for the Face before he knew it was his sister's. "All that has happened up to this moment," Pierre says, "inevitably proceeded from the first hour I saw thee." This is love at first sight, an overwhelming passion which obliterates the image of his beloved Lucy and causes him to pledge his all to Isabel, to act with heedless, frantic haste, to cut long-standing bonds with merciless finality, to singe everyone who crosses his path with the fire of his demonic infatuation. This, surely, is not the charity "which suffereth long, and is kind," which "seeketh not her own, is not easily provoked," which "endureth all things"; it is the sex instinct. Charity *per se* is an all-pervasive, impersonal loving-kindness that inflicts no injuries. But the sex instinct will persuade a man that all value for him resides in one woman and will ride him so furiously that he will trample solemn vows and cherished loyalties under his feet. Melville takes pains to inform the reader, with the excessive propriety of the age, that the sex instinct was operating from the start. He says that Pierre "was assured that, in a transcendent degree, womanly beauty, and not womanly ugliness, invited him to champion the right," and then adds: "Ah, if man were wholly made in heaven, why catch we hell-glimpses?" Clearly the author feels that he has made a shocking confession and is justified in asserting proudly: "I am more frank with Pierre than the best men are with themselves." But the involvement of the sex drive does not mean intercourse for Pierre. In accordance with the Manichaean and Catharist laws[21] and with the courtly creed, Pierre and Isabel are planning to "love with the pure and perfect love of angel to an angel."

The reader should know that Pierre's reaction to Isabel is the only deep, all-embracing, positive passion (positive in the sense that it springs from creative love, not from negative and destructive hate) which one can find in Melville's works. That the author considered it the supreme religious experience is attested by the fact that this is the sole instance in which he unequivocally associates his self-image with Christ as the incarnation of Love (rather than as the Man of Sorrows or the Crucified One). Pierre has a "Christ-like feeling," is "divinely dedicated" with "divine commands upon him." His love for Isabel is "God." His identification with Jesus is symbolized when he and Isabel partake of the sacrament of the supper. As suggested earlier, there are reasons to believe that Melville tentatively entertained the life-illusion of his becoming the Messiah "in Shakespeare's person," the "American Shiloh," and if this surmise is correct, then the Truth he had to announce is Pierre's "unexampled love" for Isabel, for there is nothing else that qualifies.

The author sets his seal of approval on Pierre's resolution in one sentence, which combines all his highest ideals: "Thus in the Enthusiast to Duty, the heaven-begotten Christ is born; and will not own a mortal parent and rends all mortal bonds." Reading this in conjunction with other pertinent passages, it is not difficult to identify the sources of Melville's conception of his hero, carrier of positive Truth. The word "Enthusiast" refers here to the Socratic or Platonic notion of Eros, that demonic passion, or divine madness, given by the gods for the purpose of producing the highest happiness. There are many varieties of enthusiasm but the best of all, according to Socrates, is the madness of a lover. By seeing human beauty (in a boy) the soul recovers its wings and, transcending lust, pours its inspiration into the soul of its beloved with the aim of educating and molding him into the image of its god. From this stage of more or less sublimated homosexuality the soul moves upward to ever larger and more general objects of devotion until it reaches the end of its pilgrimage in union with God.

The next notable historic appearance of erotic enthusiasm as a passion to be cultivated was in the Middle Ages, when it took the form of courtly love, again more or less sublimated. The courtly myth was gradually secularized and transformed into what has generally been called romantic love.

The word "Duty" has, of course, many associations—with Carlyle's works, for one—but, considered in relation with other statements by Melville, it can be adequately defined as a moral imperative to selfless benevolence. Melville was familiar with the writings of many of the British divines and ethical philosophers, with their almost unanimous conclusion that the essence of morality is benevolence. Tough-minded thinkers such as Hobbes and Mandeville and the later utilitarians, Hartley, Tucker, Paley, and Bentham, claimed that all benevolence is basically selfish; but the more tender-minded analysts of man's nature, such as Shaftesbury, Hutcheson, and Butler, succeeded in garnering many examples of seemingly unselfish forms of benevolence. On the assumption that there is a crucial difference between selfless and selfish benevolence, that the former is "divine" and the latter "natural," Pierre feels that his prime duty is to "hold intact all his unselfish magnanimities" and "ensure himself against the insidious inroads of self-interest." What chiefly persuades him of the unselfishness of his plan is his conviction that he is "almost superhumanly prepared to make a sacrifice of all objects dearest to him, and cut himself away from his last hopes of common happiness, should they cross his grand enthusiastic resolution." As he views it with masochistic eagerness, his resolution is "wonderful in its unequalled renunciation of himself."

The "heaven-begotten Christ is born"—this is an expression of the belief that the Christ of God (Love, selfless benevolence) lies in a state of hiddenness in man until called forth by some imperative occasion. Finally, to draw all the meaning that we need out of the statement that he "will not own a mortal parent, and spurns and rends all mortal bonds," two references will suffice. One is the *Phaedrus* where Socrates says that the "lover forgets mothers and brothers and friends all alike," and despises "all customs and decorums in which it formerly prided itself"; the other—a still more authoritative fountain of truth—is the New Testament, for example, "If any man come to me, and hate not his father, and mother, and wife, and children, and brethren, and sisters, yea, and his own life also, he cannot be my disciple." (*Luke,* 14, 26) In accordance with these prescriptions, Pierre beseeches the "sovereign powers" to "eternally this day deface in me the detested and distorted images of all the convenient lies and duty-subterfuges of the diving and ducking moralities of this earth. Fill me with consuming fire for them; to my life's muzzle, cram me with your intent." From one who for nineteen years has been the immaculate vessel of the "moralities of this earth," these sentiments are surprisingly fierce; but they are not transitory; they are in ascendance during the third day when Pierre performs his pitiless executions, and they increase in strength and generality as time goes on.

One other idea which runs through this as well as later sections is that of divine madness, or folly, as contrasted with worldly wisdom. This notion also comes both from Plato and from the New Testament. Socrates says in the *Phaedrus* that "the ancients testified that madness is more noble than sound sense, that which comes from God than that which proceeds from man," and St. Paul, in the famous Corinthian verses, makes a similar distinction, affirming that "the foolishness of God is wiser than men," and that "God hath chosen the foolish things of the world to confound the wise," and that "the wisdom of the world is foolishness with God."

Many other quotations could be offered to show that Melville's conception of Pierre after Isabel has stirred him is a composite of the Platonic lover, the Christ of God, and the benevolent man of eighteenth century philosophy. There is some justification for this illusion. Pierre's love echoes the Socratic mythus except that Isabel is a girl and the notion of educating her in the pattern of an ideal is absent. Instead of the latter we find the New Testament motive of compassion and the medieval idea of serving the beloved by championing her cause. Thus Pierre's passion is a fusion of Eros (Romantic love or Enthusiasm) and Agape (St. Paul's *caritas,* or Christian love). From both sources, Platonic and Christian, comes Pierre's recognition that dedicated love—positive Truth—is folly in the eyes of the bulk of reasonably selfish men, that it draws one out of the web of conventional activities, disrupts previous ties and allegiances, and provokes ridicule, abuse, and persecution. Thus Pierre becomes the Fool of Truth.

Although Melville may be said to have succeeded in identifying his hero in our minds with certain features of Christ's personality, it is clear that his imagination had not wholly surrendered to the magnetic figure of the historic Jesus; that is, he was not trying to re-create Christ "in modern dress" to the extent, say, that Dostoevsky does in *The Idiot.* From the New Testament Melville seized what he could use for his own purpose and left the rest. In view of these promiscuous appropriations and the confusions they have created it may not be a waste of time to measure the distance between Pierre and Christ or, granting that Christ was no Christian, between Pierre and the concept of a Christian Man as developed by the theologians.

In the first place, Pierre is only nominally a Christian. He has been polished by the "gentlemanizing influences of Christianity," but we find only one allusion, and that unconvincing, to any devotions to God. The word "God" is often used to give an extra lift to a rhetorical flourish, but as an abiding, living presence, there is no God. Pierre's unseen universe is not governed by one omnipotent Deity but by Fate, Nature, "invisible agencies," "ye sovereign powers," "ye heavens," and a host of nameless, ghostly shapes whom the young man addresses at every crisis. Furthermore, Pierre's attitude towards the sovereign powers (whatever these may be) is never a Christian one, never grateful, reverential, humble, acquiescent, faithful, but almost invariably the opposite—ungrateful, proud, threatening, arrogant, defiant, faithless. Spiritually he is a spoiled brat who believes that joy is his "right as man," and were he deprived of it he would have reason to become a "railing atheist." In course of time, God becomes "Juggularius," the irresponsible Juggernaut-Juggler of destinies.

In the second place, before meeting Isabel, Pierre is a natural unredeemed egoist. We are given to understand that he was profoundly moved by the Sermon on the Mount, but there are no evidences of this in his conduct. We hear nothing of good-neighborly deeds, of acts of charity, of exertions in behalf of his farmer tenants. He is solely occupied with the enjoyment of his privileges, oblivious of the trials and afflictions of the vast majority. Not until he is nineteen is he awakened to the existence of grief, and then, not primarily through sympathy, but through personal pain.

Thirdly, since Pierre's Christ-like compassion is wholly bestowed upon Isabel, his feeling is markedly different from the evenly distributed loving-tenderness of Jesus. Jesus committed himself to a relationship with no other human being, notably with no woman. His only obligation was to God. The consequences of this were momentous: no elevating religious form, no mythus, was provided for the most natural, compelling, and joyous form of love, the most serviceable to the individual and to society. Christianity is spiritual atomism on earth—what "a man does with his solitariness," as Whitehead has well said in another connection —each soul working independently for its salvation. Thus, in loving Isabel as he did, Pierre was committing a Christian heresy because, for him, God was immanent in that relationship, not worshiped as an abstract transcendent Being. As Melville once said to Hawthorne, in this *Being* of God "lies the knot with which we choke ourselves. As soon as you say *Me,* a *God,* a *Nature,* so soon you jump off from your stool and hang from the beam. Yes, that word is hangman. Take God out of the dictionary, and you would have him in the street." When Pierre falls in love, God is taken out of the dictionary. Thus the unlikenesses between Pierre and Christ are more conspicuous than the likenesses.

Finally, we may recall that in *Mardi* Melville made it clear that Christ's way of life was not for him. Taji left old Babbalanja behind him on the island of Serenia (Christ's kingdom), while he pushed on in search of Yillah (the *summum bonum*). Taji is the personification of frustrated Eros. The man who is graced with Agape does not have to search the world for the ideal person to complete his life.

These and other considerations lead, as I align them, to the conclusion that Pierre's plan was not chiefly motivated by desire to save his half-sister. There were several ways he could have done this without either pledging himself to an ascetic childless masquerade of marriage or renouncing his love for Lucy and mortally wounding his mother. It was motivated by a consuming romantic passion of the fateful anima type, the blind Dionysian compulsion of the mystery religions. Pierre conceived of his love in the most glorified terms, first because no other terms could do justice to the redeeming nature of the experience and second because he had to defend his resolution before the high court of conscience. Since there was no authority to which he could refer and since he was not in a position to create his own justifying myth—partly because his head had abdicated in favor of his heart—he had to assimilate his course of action as best he could to Platonic and Christian ideals. This accounts for the impression one gets of Melville's quoting scripture in support of Pierre's demonic purpose.

Melville's cousin, Marie Anna Priscilla Melvill, seems to qualify as a sufficient model for Isabel. She resembles Isabel in ten or more particulars: 1, she was born in France; 2, it was December 5, 1810, one to eleven months after Allan Melville's chair-portrait was painted (1810); 3, her mother was French; 4, she was a child (3 years) when her mother died; 5, at a very early age (6 months) she crossed the Atlantic to America; 6, she lived in several different houses in the country; 7, she was visited occasionally by Melville's father; 8, she was left an orphan by her own father's death (1845); 9, she worked in the household of a resident of Pittsfield (Saddle Meadows); 10, her feelings and thoughts were vague and confused, mysteriously dreamlike. Priscilla may well have resembled her uncle, Melville's father, on one side, and her mother, on the other. The latter was dark, beautiful, and sad. "A miniature I have seen of her," wrote Melville, "presents a countenance of much beauty and of that kind which forcibly arrests the attention." Possibly, Isabel's recollection of coffins being carried out of the house in which she lived corresponds to the only trace left in Priscilla's mind of that sorrowful April (1814) when her mother and two siblings died within a month. Isabel recalls speaking two languages for a while and this must have been true for Priscilla, since her parents and older brother (Pierre Thomas Wilson Melvill) spoke French to each other. Her parents lived on the edge of the army cantonment during the War of 1812, and it is possible that after her mother's death she was farmed out in the neighborhood until her father remarried and moved to Broadhall. Certain features of Isabel's life might have been suggested by the history of Priscilla's younger brother, who was an imbecile. Priscilla lived a season with the Allan Melvilles in New York when she was sixteen and Herman was seven or eight. After this the cousins saw each other periodically in Pittsfield, Lansingburgh, and possibly in Galena. She was in Pittsfield in the forties and fifties, spent one winter with the Herman Melvilles at Arrowhead, and died in 1858.

Brother-sister love is a not uncommon theme in literature. Starting with the Elizabethans, the list of titles is a long one. Of these, Tourneur's *The Revenger's Tragedy* and Ford's *'Tis Pity She's a Whore*, may have contributed a little to the composition of *Pierre*. The topic was dear to the writers of the German *Sturm und Drang* and to Romantics generally. Goethe and Chateaubriand dealt with it. The first American novel, W. H. Brown's *The Power of Sympathy* (1789), in which the hero kills himself when he discovers that his betrothed is his half-sister, established the legitimacy of this theme for succeeding native novelists of the sentimental school. In Disraeli's *Alroy* (1833) the hero knows not love, "save that pure affection which doth subsist between me and this girl, an orphan and my sister." The theme enters into Bulwer-Lytton's *Timon* which enjoyed a great vogue in the late forties. But more suggestive probably than any of these literary inventions was the celebrated fact of Byron's love for his half-sister, Augusta, and the poet's half-veiled allusions to it in his works.

Melville's enduring love for his own sisters, particularly for Augusta (with whom Isabel is connected in a few ways), predisposed him to see possibilities in the incest theme when he encountered it in his reading. As already mentioned, he was an ardent believer in that part of the contemporary mythology of the heart which glorified affection between brother and sister. Take, for instance, as a striking indication of his sentiments, the hyperbolic assertion in *Pierre* that the "mad frothing hate which a spirited brother forks forth at the insulter of a sister's honor" is "beyond doubt the most uncompromising of all the social passions known to man."

The author's account of the meetings between Pierre and Isabel, especially the dialogue, is marred for readers of our day by the recurrence of sentimental and gothic elements of the type that was so common in the popular novels of the period, even in so cool a work as

Wilhelm Meister. The occasional heroics and malevolent bombast in this
and the next act come, I suppose, from gothic novels such as Mrs. Radcliffe's *The Romance of the Forest* (the hero of which is named Pierre de
la Motte), from melodramatic tales such as Mrs. Shelley's *Frankenstein,*
but more especially from the dramatists in the tradition of Seneca —the
great Marlowe and lesser lights. Pierre's generalized punitive response
to the disclosure of his father's sin, blaming him and the heavenly powers
for the loss of his Eden of innocence, is strictly comparable to Cain's
attitude towards Adam and God in Byron's *Cain.*

Whereas act 1 was pervaded by the spirit of *Romeo and Juliet,* in this
central part of the novel the influence of *Hamlet* is predominant. It is
worth noting, however, that the American Hamlet defeats himself not by
doubting, hesitating, and procrastinating, but by acting hastily, impulsively, and irrationally. This latter form of conduct is as certain a manifestation of inner conflict as the former, since it comes out of Pierre's
half-conscious presentiment that if he does not do something instantly
when spurred by the occasion he will become paralyzed by indecision
and lose the power of action. The validity of this supposition is confirmed
by the feelings of remorse and self-distrust which beset him in the stage-
coach on the way to the city.

Besides the above mentioned vessels of suggestiveness and the different progenitors of ideas and images listed in the footnotes—Carlyle, De
Quincey, Keats, Shelley, Bayle, Burton, Browne, and many others—Disraeli's novels should be mentioned once again as the mine from which
Melville as novelist extracted more ore (and rubbish) than from any
other. In *Vivian Grey* the hero acquires his education by discursive
reading in his father's library; he enjoys Plotinus, and is taught to play
the guitar. Contarini Fleming, who comes from a family of pre-eminent
ancestry, is transported by beholding visions of a mystically beautiful,
melancholy face; his alluring cousin Alceste plays the guitar; she has a
magnetic influence over him; he experiences transporting seizures of
emotion; he writes an autobiographical novel, as Pierre does in act 3, in
which he pours forth his own passions. Pierre and the aristocratic Ferdinand Armine in *Henrietta Temple* have many traits in common. Ferdinand's character exhibits a "singular blending of the daring and the soft";
he is very affectionate with his mother, is spirited and yet docile, loves
to roam the fields in solitude, and to stand for long moments before the
portrait of his grandfather. Shortly after the announcement of his engagement to one young lady, he falls in love with another at first sight,
a dark beauty—"this is love!" he cries "to feel fame a juggle and posterity
a lie; and to be prepared at once, for this great object to forfeit and fling
away all former hopes, ties, schemes, views; to violate in her favour every
duty of society." In certain particulars Mrs. Glendinning resembles the
Viscountess Dowager Bellair in *Henrietta Temple.* In this novel one
comes upon a phaeton like General Glendinning's driven by two ponies.

The themes of mysterious birth, secrecy about a father's portrait, stabbing of a portrait, occur in *Venetia*. In *Alroy* there are colorful accounts of the fabled East, of the valley of the Euphrates, and allusions to Chaldean sages and shepherd kings who read the stars. Its proud, Byronic hero indulges in much introspection; he is hostile to society, though warmly attached to his orphaned sister. Such are some of the numerous correspondences in Disraeli.

All the scenes of act 3 take place in the city (New York), to the hellish evils of which the fugitives from the heavenly country are introduced on the very night of their arrival. There are three episodes. The first, Pierre's contretemps with the stage driver, is well done in the manner of Dickens; but the other two are blots of unreality on the leaves of this chronicle. Pierre has an encounter, ludicrously exaggerated, with the vainglorious heartlessness of the complacent upper world on Broadway, personified by his cousin Glen Stanly; and another with the brawling drunkenness of the loutish underworld at the police station. The latter is a melodramatized scene in which Pierre becomes a dime novel hero by freeing Isabel from the arms of a "whiskerando" with one "immense blow of his mailed fist."

Aided by his friend, Charlie Millthorpe, Pierre gets settled with Isabel and Delly in cramped quarters on one of the upper floors of an office building at the rear of the abandoned Church of the Apostles. The hero's funds are negligible: the money that he had in his possession when he left home will not last long, and he has no other resources. This he learns in a few weeks when he is informed that his mother is dead and that by her will his now-detested cousin Glen Stanly has inherited all the property which was to have been his. These tidings set the seal upon the loss of his youth's paradise; he must now earn his own living.

Pierre is an able-bodied fellow, capable of learning a variety of employments, but he is not disposed to do anything but wield an author's pen; and having occasionally in the past exchanged sonnets for dollars, he decides to try to support Isabel and himself by writing a book. He is not deterred from this endeavor by the realization that he is being goaded into writing a book which will not pay. As always he is obeying the dictates of his spirit.

The window of the room, or "closet," in which Pierre works looks out on the rear of the old church and as the young author proceeds with his writing he becomes strangely affected by a "steady observant blue-eyed countenance" at one of the upper windows of the church tower. He learns that this man is none other than Plotinus Plinlimmon, author of a little paper-rag pamphlet entitled "Chronometricals and Horologicals," which he (Pierre) read in the coach that brought him from Saddle Meadows to the city. Since in substance and in style this provocative pamphlet is one of the plateaus of the novel and is very pertinent to the main plot, and has been often misinterpreted, it merits close attention, a more thorough analysis, indeed, than I have space for.

The argument of "Chronometricals and Horologicals" may be summarized as follows: just as we have chronometers which give absolute, or Greenwich, time and ordinary clocks, or horologes, which give local time, so have we the New Testament which defines absolute, or heavenly, wisdom and our conventional moral codes which define local, or earthly, wisdom. We must distinguish these two wisdoms—Christ is a chronometer, Bacon a horologe*—and realize that the former is right for the other world, the latter right for this world. Just as it would be folly to attempt to regulate one's actions by Greenwich time in China, so is it folly to attempt to live by heavenly truth on earth. Plinlimmon gives several reasons for this conclusion. The man who regulates his conduct according to the Sermon on the Mount, 1, must commit "a sort of suicide as to the practical things of this world," that is, must renounce many benefits and procurable satisfactions, and, what's more, 2, will inevitably "array all men's earthly time-keepers against him" and thus bring upon himself abuse and persecution and perhaps "woe and death," as is shown by the fate of Christ. Furthermore, 3, the endeavor to carry virtue to the limit is likely to be deteriorating to the character of any sincere follower of Christ: either (a) his perfectionist strivings will open a way for extreme and unique follies or vices (such an enthusiast being peculiarly susceptible to these), or, since no human being can absolutely free himself from sin, (b) repeated failures to attain the superhuman goal will result in such unbearable desperation that he is likely (i) to run like a mad dog into atheism, or (ii) to turn into a self-deceived hypocrite. To be saved from the fatal despair which breeds these vices, a man has only to lower his moral aspirations to realizable levels and thus become assured of his "powers to attain their mark."

The sacrifices, afflictions, and spiritual perils of the true Christian path might be sufferable if there were some hope that society would thereby be radically reformed; but, 4, the plain facts show that Christ's precepts "after 1800 years' inculcation from tens of thousands of pulpits," have not succeeded in noticeably improving the Western world. Finally, Plinlimmon asserts, 5, God does not expect us mortals to live by Christ's precepts, not only because here on earth no man is capable of doing so, but because it would be a "falsification" of Himself and hence "positively wrong." Earth's wisdom corresponds with heaven's wisdom not by identity but by contradiction, just as China time can be correct in relation to Greenwich time only when it contradicts it. A virtuous expediency, in short, is the only earthly excellence that God intends for his creatures.

One part of Melville's engaging figurative scheme in "Chronometri-

---

*Probably Bacon, with his "mere watchmaker's brains," was selected as the antithesis of Christ on the basis of his essay, *Of Love*—"it is impossible to love, and to be wise."

cals and Horologicals," the idea of using horological, or meridian, time as a symbol of local truth seems to have come from Pascal: ". . . we see neither justice nor injustice which does not change with climate. Three degrees of latitude reverse all jurisprudence; a meridian decides the truth." (*Pensées,* No. 294) The image of a ship carrying a chronometer (Greenwich time, heavenly wisdom) round the world is one of the winning elements in Plinlimmon's pamphlet and I hesitated before depriving the reader of some of his enjoyment by pointing out, in a footnote, that it does not fit the thesis. The thesis permits only two wisdoms, two times, but the image is one of absolute time and *many* practical times (as many as there are meridians), and calls for some notion not only of gradations in excellence but even of earthly perfection, since along the Greenwich meridian, horological time (local morality) and chronometrical time (absolute morality) would be identical. But Melville was in no mind to admit the existence of gradations of virtue or the possibility of social improvement. As usual he had to create a pair of opposites, and so Pascal's image was syncretistically assimilated to the classical dichotomy of Time vs Eternity, things temporal vs things eternal. The Bible, the "Timaeus," *Sartor Resartus,* and Hawthorne supplied him with more than he needed for this idea, since its only function was to serve as a submerged figure to carry the reader to the basic antinomy of the pamphlet: Christ's morality vs society's morality.

This conceptual frame is established in a passage leading up to the pamphlet by Melville's affirmation that once "the enthusiast youth"—a young man whose heart has acknowledged the supreme truth of the Sermon on the Mount—recognizes the lasting opposition between the wisdom of God and the wisdom of man, "there is no peace for him, no slightest truce for him in this life," because the "talismanic secret" capable of reconciling this world with his own soul "has never yet been found" and "it seems as though it never can be." The problem was raised in *Mardi,* the author predicting that if Alma (Christ) were to return to earth today he would be treated no less cruelly than he was before. To define the situation in its simplest terms, one might say that the enthusiast Christian youth is faced by this choice: obey Christ's morality and be rewarded by your conscience but punished by society, or obey society's morality and be rewarded by society but punished by your conscience. Confronted by this dilemma, Melville's own, most habitual reaction was not to commit himself one way or the other by deeds, but to damn the world for wrecking those who try to practice the gospel that its ministers preach. He was outraged by the flagrant discrepancy between creed and action. He himself was not prepared to follow Christ, except in his imagination, because, to mention one reason, his pride rendered him incapable of tolerating public incriminations and abuse. Any form of punishment was a felt indignity which transformed him in a minute from a friend to an enemy of mankind, from a Christ to a Satan. In short,

Melville could not resign himself to the expectation of not being rewarded for virtue *both* on earth and in heaven. Setting aside the conquest of pride, was there any conceivable solution? Yes. If it were true
that God does not want man to attempt Christ's path, then it would be
possible to win rewards and to avoid punishments, both from society and
from conscience, both here and hereafter. The glad tidings which Plinlimmon authoritatively announces is that this *is* true. God does not demand more than a virtuous prudence from man.

"Chronometricals and Horologicals" is first of all an able, though
unfinished, critique of Christianity as an operating force in the evolution
of society. It stresses the paradoxical fact that the nations which have had
Christ's message preached to them for centuries have become the most
Mammonish and Molochish in the earth's history, and it explains this fact
by very shrewdly observing that the indoctrination of an unattainable
ideal, the "gratuitous return of good for evil," eventually drives men, via
despair, to atheism or hypocrisy, and thus to the opposite of the ideal.
The pamphlet is unfinished because it presents no elevating substitute
for Christian ethics. Plinlimmon's egocentric, non-benevolent, prudential morality is patently inadequate.

More covertly the pamphlet is an indictment by Melville of Plinlimmon in particular and of society in general. "Chronometricals and Horologicals" is a profoundly heretical polemic. Since there is no Christian
justification for the assertion that it would be "positively wrong in a world
like this" to take Christ as a model, Plinlimmon is presumptuously representing himself as one who has received a message out of that "profound
Silence" which is the "only Voice of our God"; and the substance of the
message is: the God of Christianity wants men to live by Pagan ethics.

To fully appreciate Plinlimmon's casuistry, his manipulating a false
analogy (that of meridian correspondence) to persuade people of the
truth of his anti-Christian doctrine, the reader should know something
about the career of another fundamental pair of concepts which, though
not contraries by definition, have often become such in the development
of moral philosophy and of theology: general affirmations or principles vs
specific rules and practices, say, Plato's supreme unifying ideal vs Aristotle's rational system of moral laws. In Catholic theology a roughly
corresponding dichotomy was based on the distinction between 1, supernatural revelation, or positive moral law decreed by God, and 2, natural
revelation, or natural moral law defined by reason. As time went on
natural moral law became increasingly refined and systematized in order
to answer the needs of father-confessors whose duty it was to judge the
specific offenses of countless penitents. Furthermore, to bring the realization of goodness within the reach of men and women living amid the
realities of everyday life, certain adjustments of doctrine had to be made.
This called for the concept of "attainable virtues," and led to a flood of
literature generally designated as "moral casuistry." In the hands of some

authors, especially Loyola and his immediate followers, the integrity of casuistry became impaired by sophistical rationalizations until it seemed to some that every vice had been condoned and Christ's truth utterly subverted. It was this situation that provoked Pascal's famous *Provincial Letters,* which may have supplied a leading idea for Melville's conceptions of Pierre's two intellectual antagonists, Falsgrave and Plinlimmon.

The antimony in Plinlimmon's pamphlet, however, is not that between theory and practice or between the general and the specific, because Plinlimmon, in contrast to Falsgrave, is not concerned with the problem of applying Christian ideals to particular situations. Plinlimmon is convinced, with God's assent, that any attempt to follow the Sermon on the Mount is not only doomed to failure but positively wrong. The explicit dichotomy, as given above, is: Christ's morality vs society's morality. Thus Plinlimmon carries sophistry further than did the Jesuits or the Protestant casuists, such as Jeremy Taylor, with whose writings Melville was familiar. Plinlimmon is a juggling infidel, opposed to self-dedication, benevolence, and reform.

"Chronometricals and Horologicals" can also be interpreted as an astute condemnation of the Western world insofar as it is a true statement of the religious belief that is implicit in the behavior and feelings of the majority of good men belonging to the so-called Christian nations. The conduct it advocates is "what the best mortal men do daily practise." Since most of these "best mortal men" are constant in affirming their belief in God and Immortality, and since their consciences generally approve of their way of life, they must assume that God, as Plinlimmon says, does not expect them to do better, and, without much doubt, will admit them finally to the joys of everlasting life. In other words, the majority of good men who call themselves Christians are *behaviorally* convinced of an un-Christian doctrine. The world is soaking in lies. Thus Melville exposes for us a fatal schism between speech and action—the fundamental cause, perhaps, of the moral deterioration of our society.

Pierre had been intent on ensuring himself against "the insidious inroads of self-interest." Mindful that the hosts of "World Prudent-mindedness . . . press hard on the faltering soul," he had beseeched the sovereign powers to let "no world-syren come to sing to me this day, and wheedle from me my undauntedness." But, despite these defensive preparations and prayers, he had hardly seated himself in the coach which was to take him to the city when the Evil One sneaked up on him and propounded "the possibility of the mere moonshine of all his self-renouncing enthusiasm," and he had hardly routed this mocker when he was confronted by Plinlimmon's "ruinous old pamphlet," surely the Evil One again, this time in the guise of a prudent-minded philosopher, a world-syren singing to him in "Chronometricals and Horologicals" of the wisdom of self-interest. It is some time before Pierre began to comprehend half consciously that the treatise palpably illustrated to him "the intrinsic incorrectness and non-excellence of both the theory and the practice of his life."

We readers take it for granted that Melville has introduced the pamphlet at this point for the artistic purpose of creating another battle-front between Pierre and his society, defining the hero's position by characterizing its opposite; and, since the target of "Chronometricals and Horologicals" is an enthusiast who is prompted to embrace Christ as guide, Pierre and Christ become cunningly combined in our minds. The dissent is commonly seen to be that between Bunyan's Christian and Mr. Worldly Wiseman, between religious idealism and sophisticated moral-ity. Thus the effect of "Chronometricals and Horologicals" is not to de-preciate Pierre but to sanctify him.

The syncretistic shuffle by which Melville succeeds in getting the halo over Pierre's head has, I submit, more magic in it than logic, since the differences between Pierre and Christ, as explained earlier, are more significant than the similarities. Consider this one point: the basic issue is between the Pagan forgiveness of sins and the Christian return of good for evil. Since the exponent of the former is Plinlimmon, the exponent of the latter must be none other than Pierre, the chronometer. But, actually, Pierre's spiritual stance is the very antithesis of this: he gets into fighting formation *before* he is touched. Since the idea that he should forgive the injuries he has brought upon himself is never even enter-tained, his attitude is a good deal further from the chronometrical return of good for evil than is Plinlimmon's.

How much Melville was deluded by his own rationalizations is a question which calls for deeper probings than are admissible here, but it is safe to assume, I think, that at times he was fully aware of the crucial contrasts between Pierre's "unexampled love" and Christ's. Pierre did not have the shining figure of the Great Exemplar to sustain him as he would have had if he had sincerely believed that he was walking in Christ's footsteps. Melville graphically explains that Pierre was not so fortunate as was the priest when his faith was assailed by the Evil One, because he had no rock to stand on, whereas the man of God was upheld by the "imperishable monument of his Holy Catholic Church; the imper-ishable record of his Holy Bible; the imperishable intuition of the innate truth of Christianity." Since Pierre is deprived of these three supports, his course must run outside the way of Christian salvation.

Consequently, although the antinomy in the pamphlet is Christ's morality vs social morality, the Pierre vs Plinlimmon conflict takes place along a somewhat different front. It can be best located in general terms by a series of overlapping contraries: imperative moral intuitions vs prag-matic utilitarian calculations; sacrificial love vs enlightened self-interest; heart (Eros) vs head (Reason); the generous tendermindedness of youth vs the selfish toughmindedness of maturity; complete dedication to a single value vs a temperate distribution of interests. Plinlimmon asserts that a man "must by no means make a complete unconditional sacrifice of himself in behalf of any other human being, or any cause, or any conceit." Thus it is chiefly Pierre's unconditional dedication to Isabel, the pouring of the tide of his benevolence "exclusively through one channel," which marks him as the object of Plinlimmon's philosophic disapproval.

It is worth noting that Melville lets Pierre off rather easily. "Chronometricals and Horologicals" is not positively strong as an ethical document nor is it aimed at Pierre's most vulnerable spots. It ignores some of the most deadly errors and vices of the fanatical enthusiast: the injuries he does to others, the self-deceptions which blind him to essential truths, the hidden egotism which cancerously invades his heart, the progressive estrangement which brings him to misanthropy, and, not least, the damaging effects of the disguised sexual component. These are the points, omitting the last of course, which Hawthorne emphasizes in his analysis of Hollingsworth, the inflexible enthusiast in *The Blithedale Romance.*

Melville is even more lenient with his hero in allowing him to be the sole carrier of the spirit in a world of universal "Imbecility, Ignorance, Blockheadedness and Besottedness," in permitting no one to challenge his right to carry God's banner, despite the fact that not a single theologian would have agreed that his was the banner of the God of Christendom. As a challenger, Isaac Taylor, for one, would have proved a tough customer. In an excellent little book, *Natural History of Enthusiasm,* widely read in Melville's day, the Rev. Mr. Taylor succeeded in accomplishing his announced intention to present "the characters of that perilous illusion which too often supplants genuine piety" and "so to fix the sense of the term—Enthusiasm, as to wrest it from those who misuse it to their own infinite damage." In defending his hero against Taylor's piercing criticisms, Melville might have succeeded in forging the one positive conception that is lacking in this novel.

Among the numerous roots of "Chronometricals and Horologicals" —passages in Plutarch, St. Paul, Plato, Bacon, Pascal, Jeremy Taylor, Shaftesbury, Mandeville, and others—the most influential, I would wager, were Hawthorne's ideas and sentiments, expressed in some of his works and also very probably in conversations with Melville "about time and eternity, things of this world and of the next." For instance, Plinlimmon's use of the concept of time might well have been suggested by some of Hawthorne's stories, as Matthiessen has astutely observed, especially by the moral of "The Birthmark," the hero of which "failed to look beyond the shadowy score of time, and, living once for all in eternity, to find the perfect future in the present." Plinlimmon's observation that the attempt to push virtue to the limit is apt to involve a man eventually "in strange, *unique* follies and sins" is equivalent to the moral of *The Blithedale Romance* insofar as it concerns Hollingsworth. Hawthorne states it in this fashion: "I see in Hollingsworth an exemplification of the most awful truth in Bunyan's book of such,—from the very gate of heaven there is a by-way to the pit." Also, like the author of "Chronometricals and Horologicals," the passionless Hawthorne had no sympathy for idealistic enthusiasms and was flatly skeptical of all efforts to reform society. One should not conclude from this that the pamphlet is like anything Hawthorne might have written. It is thoroughly Melvillian. What it represents, I would say, are a few of Melville's favorite notions combined with his interpretation of Hawthorne's disapproving attitude toward his (Melville's) way of life, insofar as this attitude could be generalized and rationalized in a brief expository treatise. Melville agrees with Plinlimmon at several points, that is, he contributes excellent arguments of his own to reinforce Hawthorne's position; but on the crucial issue—dedicated love (or benevolence) vs enlightened self-interest (non-benevolence)—he takes Pierre's side.

The fact that "Chronometricals and Horologicals" echoes views expressed by Hawthorne is but one reason for identifying the latter with Plotinus Plinlimmon. I have offered four or five other reasons in the footnotes (Books xiv and xxi) and more are not far to seek. The originals of the other major characters in *Pierre,* if they have been correctly named, are all persons to whom Melville was once warmly attached; Hawthorne is the only other admired friend who is entitled to membership in this select circle; his exclusion, I submit, would require explanation. Strip Plinlimmon of the disguising title of Grand Master (which is irrelevant to the plot) and snatch off his false beard, and you have a striking physical and psychological likeness of Hawthorne, the inscrutable Paul Pry of the guilty human heart. The essential traits of Plinlimmon correspond closely to those of Vine (unmistakeably Hawthorne) in *Clarel.* The man who can witness the agony of Pierre with no sympathetic response is made of the same stuff as he who is disposed to smile so elfishly in the Garden of Gethsemane. Plinlimmon's attitude toward Pierre is also very similar to Coverdale's behavior in *The Blithedale Romance.* Evidently Hawthorne was insightful enough to realize that his silent, steady gaze was embarrassing or distressing to some people, because he has one of his characters angrily pull down his window-shade to obstruct Coverdale's insatiable stare, precisely as Pierre covers his closet window with a piece of muslin to obliterate Plinlimmon's.

In the Pierre vs Plinlimmon dissent, which, according to my hypothesis, is Melville's partial and modified formulation of the philosophical difference between himself and Hawthorne, Pierre, symbol of the heedlessly warm heart, is more appealing to the average reader than is Plinlimmon, spokesman of the shrewdly cool head. But this judgment is likely to be reversed in the minds of those who read Hawthorne's version of the same conflict in *The Blithedale Romance.* Hollingsworth (Melville) is the villain of *that* piece.

Apparently the Melville-Hawthorne friendship progressed very

ENDEAVORS IN PSYCHOLOGY

satisfactorily until the two men came to a parting of their ways, not a quarrel, but an estrangement, and this was so mutually traumatic that each of them felt compelled to write an interpretation, an *apologia*, a vindication, of his own position. There is no room here for the array of facts which support this conclusion or for a discussion of its significance. Suffice it to say that each man very humanly believed that the other was chiefly responsible for the break.

Hawthorne said openly that "after Hollingsworth failed me, there was no longer the man alive with whom I could think of sharing all." Melville was more subtle and elusive. He tells us that Plinlimmon's face in the tower window, his pitiless manner of observation, the aloof analytical scrutiny of this intellectual *voyeur,* slowly unnerved the suffering Pierre, until "the face at last wore a sort of malicious leer to him" and he felt that "by some magical means the face had got hold of his secret." Melville picks the perfect word—non-benevolence—for Hawthorne, since the thing about him which repelled "was neither Malice nor Ill-will; but something passive." This fits surprisingly well with what Hawthorne himself was writing almost simultaneously at West Newton: "Most men . . . have a natural indifference, if not an absolutely hostile feeling, towards those whom disease, or weakness, or calamity of any kind causes to falter and faint amid the rude jostle of our selfish existence. . . . Except in love . . . we really have no tenderness. But there was something of the woman moulded into the great, stalwart frame of Hollingsworth; nor was he ashamed of it, as men often are of what is best in them." If Hawthorne ever read Melville's presentation copy of *Pierre* and followed the train of associations at the end of Book xxi and read between the lines he learnt that his timid, phlegmatic philosophy, disguised in "Chronometricals and Horologicals," coupled with his non-benevolence, was Death to Melville's "morbidly longing and enthusiastic, but ever-baffled" soul.

The figure of Plinlimmon owes something to Carlyle's Professor Teufelsdröckh, as Forsythe noted, and something more to Apollonius, the sophist, in Keats's "Lamia," but the evidence favoring Hawthorne as chief model seems fairly convincing.*

Before going on with the log of Pierre's voyage, let us define his present bearings. This can be done by listing the major developments that have occurred since we first knew him as an aristocratic playboy of the Western world, the immaculate personification of Christian culture:

*The items which suggest Emerson are not integral to the plot. The pamphlet is scarcely Emersonian in temper. Certainly Emerson did not exert a "surprising sorcery" upon Melville during the writing of *Moby-Dick.* He was not a Paul Pry of the guilty heart, nor a compound of Apollo and Saturn, nor characteristically Inscrutable. His philosophic attitude was not depressing. There was no Death in him. After Hawthorne's funeral Emerson wrote in his journal: ". . . there was a tragic element . . . in the painful solitude of the man, which, I suppose, could not longer be endured, and he died of it." It was this element, I believe, which conspired in the defeat of Melville's spirit.

1, Reverence for an anthropomorphic God (represented by his father) was converted—after disclosure of his father's sin, unfaithfulness, and deceit—into reverence for a deified woman. The transcendent God became immanent. 2, Membership in upper-class society (represented by his mother) was replaced by mutual rejection. Pierre's "own voluntary steps" took him "forever from the brilliant chandeliers of the mansion of Saddle Meadows, to join company with the wretched rush-lights of poverty and woe." Isabel supplanted Mrs. Glendinning as well as his entire circle of friends. 3, Marriage (represented by Lucy) was cast aside for the sake of a predominantly spiritual relationship. 4, The innocent bantering superficiality of adolescence was overturned by the knowledge that is woe. 5, Embracement *by* his mother was superseded by embracement *of* Isabel. The embraced assumed the role of the embracer; he ended his life of carefree, childlike dependence to care for a childlike, dependent woman. In forsaking the security of his mother's sovereignty and the basic tenets of her creed, 6, Pierre renounced a galaxy of conjoined values—much of what was conventionally accepted —and he espoused views that were considered immoral, impious, or insane. Here the two facts to be secured are that the hero's importunate action carried him beyond the traditional limits of Christianity and that in place of all the surely established Christian figures and personages who had theretofore contained him, he exalted one unestablished, mystic girl who would have to be contained by him. For Isabel's sake Pierre relinquished his large share in the heritage of the West.

Pierre had acted contrary to the code of his society in obedience to a moral imperative. The sight of Isabel had been "a silent and tyrannic call, challenging him in his deepest moral being, and summoning Truth, Love, Pity, Conscience, to the stand." Thus the issue is an ethical or religious one, and there are but two clean ways open to him: adhere to the conviction that his elected path is right and true, and, in a Promethean spirit, endeavor to verify this hypothesis by living it and generalizing it, or decide that he was wrong and, in the manner of Epimetheus, return to the land of his forefathers, repent and be forgiven. The latter course, which calls for true humility, can signify nothing but cowardice to Pierre, reared, as he has been, to the heroic ideal. Having, like Bulkington in *Moby-Dick,* once quit the port of safety, comfort, and "all that's kind to our mortalities," he knows that he can not turn back without shipwrecking his mission and his pride. His predicament, then, is that of "the storm-tossed ship, that miserably drives along the leeward land," crowding "all sail off shore" against the "winds that fain would blow her homeward." A noble young man in this situation has but one choice— to head out to sea, into the wide, unknown, and perilous future. If the blast subsides he may possibly succeed, by skill or luck, in bringing his bark at last to anchor in some golden haven, reach some honorable compromise with his society, some fortunate settlement that will reconcile this world with his own soul; or, if the tempest proves too much for him, "better it is to perish in that howling infinite, than be ingloriously dashed upon the lee, even if that were safety! For worm-like, then, oh! who would craven crawl to land!"

Pierre's truth, for the sake of which he tied Lucy to the stake and mortally wounded his mother, is to champion Isabel "through all conceivable contingencies of Time and Chance," an obligation which can never be acquitted if any capacity for endurance is withheld from the service. His highest conscience and his pride vis-à-vis the world are now bound up with this mission. But these are not the only reasons for persisting in his devotions. He needs Isabel—though less as she is now than as she can become—because emotionally he is by no means self-sufficient. Pierre, let it be said, is an abstract of Romanticism, a youth who, despite protestations to the contrary, has little tolerance of isolation, who can not be fully nourished by ordinary friendships, whose standard of living is loving. Consequently, being temperamentally incapable of the mystic's solitary, slow ascent to God, his happiness hangs—now that he has cut all other cherished bonds—on his power to build a fructifying alliance with Isabel which will stand solid against the "wildest winds of heaven and earth." But, as it happens, this vision does not invite his energies.

For Pierre and Isabel, the crisis occurs on the third night following their arrival in the city. It is twilight; they are sitting together, hand in hand. Suddenly Pierre, agitated by sexual desire, jumps up and calls on "ye heavens" to crush him if he is being driven to the "monstrousest vice." He would rather die than sin. But immediately after thus affirming his allegiance to conscience, he reverses his position and becomes the spokesman of a rationalizing instinct. He orders Isabel to call him brother no more, insisting that there is no certain proof of their kinship. Thus, by decree, he abolishes the incest barrier. Next he asserts that it is "the gods" who are to blame if the combustibles they put in him are discharged: man is not morally responsible. This fundamental conclusion is succeeded by a far-reaching thought—that the ideal of purity is wide of the mark, that "demi-gods trample on trash, and Virtue and Vice are trash!" For an instant, Pierre sees some saving way out of the devastating conflict and—reaching the highest pitch of positive religious conviction that can be found in the whole length of Melville's writings—cries: "I will gospelize the world anew, and show them deeper secrets than the Apocalypse:—I will write it, I will write it!"

This second glimpse of Melville's "scared white doe" marks the turning point of the novel. After this one tumultuous uprising and definitive suppression of instinct, Pierre's love for Isabel begins to fade. Note that Pierre does not say, "I will do it, I will do it!"; he exclaims, "I will write it, I will write it!" But he does not write it. His work takes another course. We hear no more of Pierre's new gospel.

Pierre had made unlimited holy vows to cherish and protect Isabel, to give her his constant companionship, to introduce her to his world, to promote her cause. He had gone to the limit by undertaking to fulfill a maternal role, to enfold her as "nature carefully folds, and warms, and by inconceivable attentiveness eggs round and round her minute and marvelous embryoes." Isabel had confessed to Pierre that the love between them "makes me all plastic in thy hand"; and he had promised to treat her as an expert artisan handles "the most exquisite, and fragile filigree of Genoa."

None of these pledges are carried out. In a few days Pierre becomes wholly involved in the writing of a book. He labors eight hours and a half a day in a room from which Isabel is excluded. The door is locked with a dagger. He is exhausted, in no mood for conversation, when he emerges. He takes his evening walk alone. He does not discuss his book with Isabel. He makes no friends in the city, creates no circle of congenial spirits for his and Isabel's enjoyment. Since Delly does all the housework, Isabel is left in a vacuum with nothing much to occupy her except the guitar, which she plays every evening while Pierre contemplates in silence the flow of imagery engendered by the music. She is no longer at the center of his thoughts. His tenderness towards her becomes increasingly perfunctory as he gives way to moods in which he curses himself because he resigned his birthright "for a mess of pottage, which now proved all but ashes in his mouth."

Pierre gave up all thought of ever understanding Isabel's mystery, because, to tell the truth, he was almost wholly concerned with the marvels which her face had engendered in him. "Explain thou this strange integral feeling in me myself, he thought—turning upon the fancied face—and I will renounce all other wonders, to gaze wonderingly at thee." Thus the "ungraspable phantom of life" is not in Isabel but in him. He is Narcissus plunging to embrace his own image.

What this means is that Pierre, having devoured what Isabel had to give him, is withdrawing libido (interest, love) from her as a person and using it to fold, and warm, and egg round embryoes of thought and to feed a precipitant ambition. Furthermore, instead of writing in celebration of his "strange, mysterious, unexampled love," he commits himself to a battle against the "dastardly world," chasing "a vile enemy who ne'er will show front," and in doing this he yields to possession by the mana personality[22] and dreams of himself as a superman, a defiant demi-god, the mutilated Enceladus.

In *The Blithedale Romance* Hawthorne concedes that Hollingsworth had a "noble nature" with a "great spirit of benevolence," but, unhappily, "he had taught his benevolence to pour its warm tide exclusively through one channel; so that there was nothing to spare for other great manifestations of love to man, nor scarcely for the nutriment of individual attachments, unless they would minister, in some way, to the terrible egotism which he mistook for an angel of God." This is in agreement not only with Plinlimmon's opinion that a man "must by no means make a complete unconditional sacrifice of himself in behalf of any other being, or any cause, or any conceit," but also with my analysis of the present stage of Pierre's career when he takes back the love he poured exclusively through one channel in behalf of another "being" (Isabel) and uses it in behalf of a "conceit" (the aggrandizement of his self-image as a Fallen Angel) to defend his "cause" against the world. Isabel is deprived of "nutriment" and Pierre seeks her only when she can "minister" to his "terrible egotism" by playing her guitar.

Thus, after the frustration of one wave of the sex instinct, the direction of the hero's single-hearted passion is permanently changed. His altruistic debauch, his positive Truth, his hope of a redeeming symbol, are finished. The love story of Pierre and Isabel ends in an amputated stump. Creativeness in sacramental action gives way at once to creativeness in writing; the religionist is routed by the artist; the potential mythology of relationship is blighted by the traditional mythology of ambition—figures of the power and the glory. Pierre attempts "something transcendently great," not to eat, since it is "of all things least calculated for pecuniary profit," and not for love, since it is of all things most compounded of woe and hate. In this work of his imagination, the young author does not proceed progressively as a Prometheus, but regressively in the likeness of those "advanced minds" who are "goaded into turning round in acts of wanton aggression upon sentiments and opinions now forever left in their rear." The Christ of God is sacrificed, the last link with humanity is dissolved, and grace passes from him "as did the divine blessing from the Hebrews."

The interdependent forces which determined this transformation are too numerous, too deep, and too complicated to be dealt with here.

It is evident that Melville himself has not noticed that his hero was "divinely dedicated" for less than a week and that his capacity for love has run out. He continues to speak of him as the upholder of Truth, although devotion to Isabel, which was his only Truth, has virtually ceased. When Pierre wails at the loss of the gods' support, his creator does not connect this circumstance with his spiritual desertion of Isabel, or with his abandonment of his resolve to write the new gospel, or even with the fact that his vaunted well of charity has been supplanted by a pyramid of malevolence and scorn.

One of the defects of this novel is that Melville does not say enough about the design of Pierre's "mature work" to involve us wholeheartedly in the young writer's self-consuming effort. The few quoted passages are immature lamentations, sounds of impotent envy and resentment, which only serve to confirm the natural supposition that a sensitive plant, nursed for nineteen years in such a greenhouse as Saddle Meadows, will not give off leaves and flowers of robust genius after a few weeks' exposure to the elements. But since in this account of Pierre's season of authorship there are recitals of several known events of Melville's life during the period he was finishing *Moby-Dick,* and there are striking recurrences of *Moby-Dick* imagery, and the pervading spirit, personified by the mutilated Enceladus, is very similar to that exhibited by the amputated Ahab, readers who are aware of these parallels are likely to conclude that Melville had the labor of his tremendous masterpiece in mind while composing this part of the present novel, and, so, will be disposed to regard Pierre's manuscript with a considerable degree of transferred reverence.

Melville has some good things to say about originality among writers, especially in connection with Pierre's explorations of his own mind, mentioned earlier in this Introduction. Here again he anticipates modern depth psychology, for example, when he speaks of an angle dropped into the well of childhood as "that enchanter's wand of the soul, which but touching the humblest experiences in one's life, straightway it starts up all eyes, in every one of which are endless significancies." He describes the experience of "digging in one's soul" in a variety of memorable images, and gives us to understand that this is not only a hazardous undertaking, but the noblest way of life, the distinguishing characteristic of which, as Geist has seen so clearly, is depth, "depth of thought, of emotion, of descent into oneself."[23] This is the path to spiritual grandeur. It is largely through this descent, anyhow, that Pierre arrives at the apprehension of the world that depresses and appalls him, and from then on "the history of Pierre," to quote Geist once again, "becomes the history of his struggle with his own apprehension of the world rather than with the world itself." This is the struggle that is set forth in *Moby-Dick.*

I shall not attempt a psychological analysis of Pierre as author, first, because the average reader can get along very well without it, and second, because it would inevitably overlap an analysis which can be much more fully and persuasively documented—that of *Moby-Dick.* It is enough to say that throughout the last phase of Pierre's career his creator's imagination is enthralled by a cluster of embattled figures of the same substance with the indomitable Captain Ahab—Titan, Prometheus,* Satan, Lear, Timon, Cain, and Manfred, with images from *Isaiah* and the unChristian author of *Ecclesiastes* hovering in the background. At the center of this circle of heroic sufferers and malcontents, stands Byron in person, prototype of the Romantic genius, as celebrated by his biographer Thomas Moore. I refer especially to Moore's fervent defense of his thesis that Byron's "defects were among the elements of his greatness, and that it was out of the struggle between the good and evil

---

*The association of Pierre or of Ahab with Prometheus can hardly be justified, because, although both of Melville's heroes are *against* the gods, they are not *for* humanity. Having no beneficent cause to advance, they belong with Milton's Satan rather than with man's immortal champion.

principles of his nature that his mighty genius drew its strength." Moore's glowing tribute, combined with quotations from the poet's journals and letters, teaches the lesson that among the infallible symptoms of greatness are: an easily wounded heart, transitoriness of all joys, quick dissatisfaction with every human relationship, acute aversion to marriage, a bottomless well of grief (proof of wisdom), towering disdain of the world, interminable religious conflict. In brief—to exaggerate a little—the more miserable a man is on earth and the greater his detestation of humanity, the more certain we can be that he is superior—a fallen angel, a genius with a heaven-begotten soul. According to this creed a man who can not find his way out of the valley of death is superior to one who can.

Pierre's progressing inflation to the dimensions of a demi-god is interrupted now and again by periods of extreme deflation when, fatigued by his protracted mental efforts, he becomes abjectly depressed by the insufficiency of his state to his conceptions and loses confidence in his powers to attain their lofty goal. In him, he feels, the "thews of a Titan" have been "cut by the scissors of Fate." There is no redemption for an imperfect self. What Melville so heartbreakingly pictures here is the "expense of greatness," to use Blackmur's incisive phrase,[24] the private agony, we surmise, of the terminal *Moby-Dick* phase of his own career —the exhaustion, the self-distrust, the despondency, the eye failure, the fainting seizure, the insidious deterioration, the spreading enfeeblement. Such torments confirm Pierre in his conviction that greatness and grief are forever wedded and as author he becomes another apostle of affliction. Seeing no escape from his own miseries, he enviously damns, with his maker's collaboration, those intuitive philosophers whose solutions are in opposition to the Christian premise that sorrow is the divinely decreed law of life.

It is during these moments of dejection that the change in pattern of Pierre's relationship to Isabel is most apparent. Oblivious of her isolation, Pierre is now overwhelmed with compassion for his own. The object of his concern is no longer her mournfulness, but his. The word "heart" has come to mean a profound consciousness of his own distress. He succumbs to paroxysms of self-pity. He compares his soul to a pitiful "little toddler" who has no mother (society) or father (God) to hold its hand. The embracer is now longing to be embraced; but since Isabel is not yet prepared—having received little—to give much, Pierre becomes increasingly indifferent to her. In a short time he will be ready to concede that she is his "Bad Angel," and at the end, uncertain whether she is "saint or fiend," he will condemn her in words which tell symbolically what he has hungered for—"in thy breasts, life for infants lodgeth not."

Hawthorne portrays Hollingsworth's last condition in these words: "the powerfully built man showed a self-distrustful weakness, and a childlike or childish tendency to press close, and closer still, to the side of the slender woman whose arm was within his." This is the state that Pierre is now unconsciously approaching, and, so, when he receives an all-understanding and tenderly sympathetic letter from Lucy—a sublime expression of the Agape which he once thought was his—it seems as if an unarticulated prayer had been heard and answered. Lucy writes that she is resolved to come to him, to live with him and Isabel henceforth and forever, to serve them both, asking no questions and expecting no returns, because, says she, "I feel that heaven hath called me to a wonderful office toward thee . . . some terrible jeopardy involves thee, which my continual presence only can drive away." This letter serves to quiet the jealous agitations and sinister thoughts which were set in motion some time ago by the news that Glen Stanly had become the suitor of Lucy, and to hearten Pierre by testifying that a girl, the girl he has loved, is capable, "in this most tremendous of all trials," of acquitting herself "with such infinite majesty." Despite Isabel's reluctance to admit her, Lucy is welcomed in due course, "an essence direct from the universe of transcendental Being," as Watson has said, and within a short time her invulnerable and unobtrusive loving-kindness has pervaded the atmosphere of the household and even Isabel acknowledges that she is Pierre's "Good Angel."

Although both Lucy and Isabel are shadowy figures whom we readers can hardly see, the forces they embody are subtly communicated to us through their words and actions. In Melville's terminology, Lucy has "innate superiority" in "the absolute scale of being," because she is the incarnation of "angelicalness" (Agape) with "no vulgar vigor in it." Lucy is pure light and goodness, holy as the dove. Isabel is more complex. When we first met her she was almost wholly passive, undifferentiated, existing in utter darkness and without hope; a deep well of potentialities for both good and evil. She is the unconscious mind, she-who-must-be-brought-to-light, she-who-must-be-shaped. What she becomes depends upon how she is treated. Pierre's religious devotion awakens love in her, and we see goodness—not yet positive enough to be called "angelical" —emerging out of nothingness; but when Pierre's passion turns from her to his book and she is excluded from the enormous labor of constructing it and then Lucy joins them, other forces are engendered in her, forces with "vulgar vigor" in them—pride, possessiveness, jealousy, hatred of that "vile book." According to Melville's terminology, these dispositions springing from self-interest are "purely earthly." Thus, weighed in the scales of the New Testament, Lucy's worth is far greater than Isabel's.

But there is another way of comparing the two girls—in terms of their effect on the man they love. At Saddle Meadows Isabel, by presenting the ultimate challenge, called forth and unified all that was best and strongest in Pierre, gave him his supreme mystical experience. Thus she was his greatest benefactress. But this effect was momentary, neither of them knew how to interpret or perpetuate their experience; and she was incapable of holding him to his vows. Her failure in this respect was due in large measure, to an insufficiency, rather than to an excess, of "vulgar vigor." If she had had more of the stuff which several critics have deemed blamable in her she might have saved Pierre from the megalomania that is now eating up the last remnants of his humanity. Near the end of the novel there is an incident which suggests that Pierre's love for Isabel is susceptible of revival. At an exhibition of foreign pictures, the portrait of a stranger who resembles Isabel as much as did Mr. Glendinning in his chair-portrait excites feelings in Pierre (which are "entirely untranslatable into any words that can be used") along with a whirl of thoughts, the trend of which is to discredit the little evidence that exists of his kinship with Isabel, and, thus, to do away with the incest barrier.*

From the start Isabel's profoundest challenge to Pierre has been her profoundest threat—the death wish at the bottom of her nature, the retrogressive longing to return to the state of non-identity (experienced in the womb), to cease striving and to lose consciousness. Pierre's ultimate salvation and hers has been hanging all along on his power to reverse the direction of this underlying force, to generate and confirm in her the will to live. That Pierre's emotional desertion of Isabel was the course least calculated to effect this change is shown near the end when Isabel tries to throw herself into the ocean. (She had first crossed the Atlantic in her mother's womb.) Her abysmal desperation is transmitted to the hero and before sundown he is on his way to his own rendezvous with death. In the final scene Isabel names herself his murderess. Unwittingly she had lured him away from an enviably happy life to engage in a Quixotic experiment for which both of them were almost wholly unequipped.

If, as some critics have claimed, *Pierre* is a story of the career of Christian charity in the modern world, the novel has a heroine, Lucy Tartan, but no hero; and not the least of its ambiguities is the fact that this heroine who, in Pierre's estimation, is of "the highest essence compatible with created being" has a hurtful effect, if any, upon the hero. The first serious threats that come to Pierre from the external world— from Lucy's suitor, Glen Stanly, and her brother, Frederic Tartan—and the first serious threats from the internal world—his psychosomatic and psychotic symptoms—are direct consequences of Lucy's joining him at the Apostles'.

Lucy is a serene conserver, who lives, enjoys, promotes, and ministers to the reasonable values of her society; she represents the inherited, cultivated, civilized virtues of the land. To Pierre's "storm-tossed ship" she is the port that "would fain give succor; the port is pitiful; in the port

*Here the author tells us, for the first time, that Pierre now feels that his "transcendental persuasions" about Isabel were originally born *"purely* of an intense procreative enthusiasm." (Italics are mine.)

is safety, comfort, hearthstone, supper, warm blankets, friends, all that's kind to our mortalities. But in that gale, the port, the land, is that ship's direst jeopardy." Lucy, much as she loves Pierre, can have no spontaneous, unbidden sympathy for him as a critic of the sentiments she cherishes, as an exponent of new and seemingly irrational ideas, as a writer who may disturb the system in which she has been reared and antagonize people she respects. Consequently, she can not accompany him on his voyage of thought, even in spirit; all she can do is to stand by, hoping for his safe return. To him, unhappily, her mere presence is a perpetual plea to desist, if not a reproach, and, through his concern for her, a temptation to abandon the struggle of his life. And now that he has gone further from humanity and made a compact with the god of destruction, there is no possible common ground for them, and her serenity and gentleness can only serve to intensify his intolerable sense of isolation and to augment his guilt. These are two potent determinants of his physical and mental symptoms. Pierre treats Lucy as Hamlet does Ophelia, leaving her finally with cruel stinging words: "Dead embers of departed fires lie by thee, thou pale girl; with dead embers thou seekest to relume the flame of all extinguished love!"

Ever since the turning point of his career when he fell from Isabel Pierre has been undergoing a profound emotional regression which under somewhat different circumstances might have resulted in a transfiguring rebirth. But pride and other factors interfered, and, apart from the constructive achievement manifested in his book (about which we are told very little), almost all of Pierre's reactions are symptomatic of deterioration. He had prophesied correctly when he said, "If ever I fall from thee, dear Isabel, may Pierre fall from himself; fall back forever into nothingness and night!" Besides the emergence of a variety of infantile and youthful dispositions, the operation of a repressed homosexual component is most conspicuous. Melville devotes several pages to an account of the waning of Pierre's ardent "boy-love" for Glen Stanly and, in conformity with Freud's findings, of the gradual conversion of this sentiment into normal adolescent heterosexuality. But it would be evident to any psychiatrist that this transformation was not completed and that some residual energy remained, which, in conjunction with his enduring mother fixation, interfered with his full development. This accounts, to some extent, for the superdelicate quality of many of his social responses, his preference for almost sexless women, his identification with Christ, the ease with which he breaks off his engagement with Lucy (perhaps more truly, his flight from marriage), his choice of the physically unattainable Isabel, the rapid fading of his love for her, his final utterance to the two girls—"Pierre is neuter now"—the Enceladus vision, the paranoid trends, the recurrent expectations of a degrading physical assault, his final panic and his feverish suicidal homicide—"Oh, Glen! oh, Fred! most fraternally do I leap to your rib-crushing hugs! Oh, how I love ye two, that can make me lively hate, in a world which elsewhere only merits stagnant scorn!" This little must suffice, because any further analysis of the process of regression in Pierre and of the counteracting upsurge of delusional grandeur would require the use of technical conceptions unsuited to this context.

With a melodramatic flourish, Melville entrusts the abrupt ending of his tragedy to the swift and certain shears of death. Here he may have had in mind the final wholesale execution of the characters in *Hamlet* and, perhaps, more specifically (as Forsythe has suggested), a sensational event mentioned by him in "Bartleby the Scrivener" (1853)—the celebrated prison suicide of John C. Colt, murderer of Samuel Adams, which occurred in New York City in 1842.

The goal I set myself was the elucidation of certain critical points—in the development of the characters or of the plot of *Pierre*—which have been commonly overlooked or, as I see them, misinterpreted. Consequently, many significant features—those which are obvious to the average reader or which have already received sufficient critical attention—have been passed without comment. I am confident that the lop-sidedness of my account will be automatically rectified by the reader as he proceeds.

Equally neglected are those problems which, for their clarification, require a lengthy or deep or technical analysis, or call for considerable understanding of Melville's personality. Among questions of this class are: the author's interest in unique and immense sins—the Unpardonable Sin; *Pierre* as a thwarted catharsis of emotions pressing on the author; the incompleteness of the book as a confession of "sacred truth"—the possibility that the author withheld one secret, and therefore, at the end, his branding Pierre a liar and his leaving the reader with the words "ye know him not"; the writing of *Pierre* as an act of spiritual parricide and matricide; Melville's desire to bequeath in *Pierre* his "immortal curse" to the world, as Dante did "in the sublime malediction of the *Inferno.*" Here, as most pertinent to the maledictory (extrapunitive) current of this novel, allow me to make one observation: the hateful dispositions for which the hero blames and damns the once-beloved objects of his environment are precisely those which have been hitherto repressed with most difficulty in himself. Everything he condemns in the external world is a projection of his shadow self. This is proved, in due course, by his own actions: Pierre's incestuous inclinations are more sinful than his father's amorousness; his deception (of Lucy and of his mother) exceeds his father's; his pride ends by towering above his mother's; his juggling rationalizations are more fatal than the casuistry of Plinlimmon; he surpasses the world in heartlessness; his hostility goes to greater lengths than Glen Stanly's; and so forth. Thus Pierre's vision of the world shows less correspondence to the world of *his* day than it does to the contents of his unconscious, or, let me add, to the world of *our* day.

Pierre is a literary monster, a prodigious by-blow of genius whose appearance is marred by a variety of freakish features and whose organic worth is invalidated by the sickness of despair. It is a compound of incongruities and inconsistencies that is shocking to a nicely regulated intellect. Most readers instinctively protect their health from it by judicious revulsions or by unconsciously holding their minds back from the comprehension of its most devastating matter.

In form it is unquestionably a novel, but it is an anomalous one which defies precise classification. Though composed, to a surprising extent, of materials from other books, it is a unique combination, the product of an extraordinary season in the career of an extraordinary man. Its pedigree is still uncertain. On one side, a line of descent might be traced back through Cooper, with his New York State lords of the manor, to Scott, and finally to Fielding, and, another more distinct line through Benjamin Disraeli to Goethe's *Wilhelm Meister,* the ancestor of those novels which, like Bunyan's *Pilgrim's Progress,* are structured by the succession of spiritual dilemmas and transformations experienced by the hero. The strangeness of *Pierre* to the modern reader can be attributed, in part, to the fact that several of its lineaments were inherited from a family of gothic and of sentimental novels that are now virtually unknown, and, in part, to the conspicuous presence of qualities which seem natural enough on the stage but not in the context of a novel. *Pierre* is a dramatic novel, with the accent on "dramatic," its lineage being traceable through at least two centuries of the theatre to Shakespeare, if not to Seneca. Mostly from this side come its rapid tempo, its sensational intensity, its far-fetched stilted dialogue, its indifference to the actualities of everyday life.

The whole work seems to have been composed in a state of mind that requires some of the instrumentalities of poetry for its adequate expression. This is manifest very often in the imagery and not infrequently in the beat of the author's prose, which, as many critics have repeated, is reminiscent at times of Thomas Browne's majestic style and, now and then, of the flowing cadences of De Quincey. The influence of Carlyle is also unmistakable. But to date no one has given an adequate explanation of the miscellany of grammatical eccentricities, convoluted sentences, neologisms, and verbal fetishisms—not unlike schizophrenic speech—which sets *Pierre* off by itself as a curiosity of literature. A reader who can take these oddities in his stride will be repaid, and not infrequently, by coming to passages which will send shivers down his spine and which he will want to memorize and retain for life. It is precisely these amazements of figurative speech which lift this book above the common run of nineteenth century novels.

The pervading temper of *Pierre* is that of German romanticism. Witness the hero's subjectivity, his absolute abandonment to passion, his erotic mysticism, his over-reaching affectations—first of self-sacrifice and then of lofty solitary grandeur—his final negation of the world through the defeat of limitless aspiration. Note also the conjunction of opposites: Pierre the time-defeated pilgrim of eternity, the pitiless Christ, the falsifying apostle of Truth, the sex-crazed Galahad, the impotent demi-god, the arrogant democrat, the convention-subjugated scorner of convention. Throughout the drama, but more especially in the last act, the spirit of Byron—nobility of sentiment, sublime stretching, pride, defiance, revenge, contempt, and misanthropy—determines the course of events. Finally, in the savagery of his culminating disgust, the author qualifies for membership in that exclusive circle of which Swift is the acknowledged master. *Pierre* is the first of Melville's books in which the resilient humorist—a most relished and indispensable member of his company of selves —is incapacitated, crippled by tribulation. Weighed down by the burden of unrelenting moral seriousness, one cries out for a dash of joyful wickedness or levity.

These more or less repellent aspects of *Pierre* are balanced by some notable triumphs of craftsmanship. Although it is fashionable to say that Melville's *dramatis personae* are all pasteboard masks or puppets, I am inclined to except from this verdict one major personage, Mrs. Glendinning, and at least two minor ones, Mr. Falsgrave, and the generous-hearted, naively vain and garrulous Charlie Millthorpe, both of whom are "flat" characters but nonetheless alive and in every respect sufficient to their roles. Millthorpe will remind the reader of Dickens's conception of an American, say Colonel Diver, editor of the *New York Rowdy Journal,* in *Martin Chuzzlewit.* Besides these portraits, there are several scenes that are finely executed: Aunt Dorothea and little Pierre, the breakfast with Mr. Falsgrave, the harried author's solitary evening walks in the city and his fainting spell, the Enceladus vision, the visit to the picture exhibit. Melville's descriptions of the Memnon Stone and of the old Church of the Apostles are memorable. Much less successful is his attempt at a jocular treatment of the Apostles themselves. Cultists of such sorts (much more numerous in New York than in Concord) were wont to congregate at the Unitary Home[25] on East 14th Street, not five minutes' walk from Melville's house (1847–1850) at 103 Fourth Avenue.

Melville sustains his highest level of expression in describing Pierre's mental processes—the invasion of his mind by the impersonal unconscious, the operation of the anima image, his microscopic dissection of his mother's character, his descent into himself. In these passages he stands out from the bulk of his contemporaries as a seer among children, a forerunner of Henry James, Proust, and the whole modern school of psychological novelists.

In *Pierre* visualizations are weak, because appearances are not in focus. The author has given up his long-standing interest in "presentational immediacy" (as Whitehead would say) in order to concentrate on the essence of things. He has put aside his brush and palette; only "causal efficacy" matters to him. Furthermore, the scope of *Pierre* is markedly circumscribed, geographically and sociologically: outside of Saddle Meadows and a small area of the city the whole world is effaced as by a negative hallucination. Breadth is sacrificed for profundity, the observation of a variety of surfaces for intense interior penetration.

In *Pierre* Melville's greatness of range is confined to one dimension, that of depth, the distance he went down into himself; and this, in turn, is a measure of his antipathy to the human environment. He and his hero are as one in their complete repudiation of the world, in their desire to get out of it. Hence one can not understand the introverted orientation of the author or of the hero without reference to the culture of their day. But Melville does not present us with a pertinent spectacle or analysis of American society, nor does he state explicitly what forces of the culture are so inimical to his spirit that he and his hero are driven to condemn it *in toto.* Surely, so massive a reaction is not justified by anything we are told about Pierre's fellow citizens, the inhabitants of the city. This hiatus in emotional logic is one of the outstanding structural defects of the novel.

In descending into himself Melville was following the right course for a creative religionist whose function it is to conceive of myths and validate them in action; but being more of an artist than a religionist, an artist with unusual "negative capability," he did not take to the idea of action; he said NO! in thunder to everything without, and *yes* to everything within, and, like Pierre, gave himself up, "a doorless and shutterless house for the four loosened winds of heaven to howl through." A man does not do this, as he makes plain in this novel, "without additional dilapidations," dilapidations which would account for most of the weaknesses in *Pierre.* Thus both the best and the worst features of this novel are consequences of one thing: Melville's unconditional surrender to the forces of the unconscious.

Since the tragedy of *Pierre* is permissive of several formulations, each of which accords with Melville's sentiments, in all likelihood his own conception was, as usual, a composite one. *Pierre* may be viewed, first of all, as a tragedy of Fate, or Circumstance: the hero is confronted by an unmanageable situation. In this novel the hero's situation, like Hamlet's, calls for more immunity to disclosed evil, more Baconian wisdom and serpent's strategy, than can be expected of an inexperienced high-minded youth. Melville's phrasing—"The flower of virtue cropped by a too rare mischance"—is a modification of Bacon's abstract of the Memnon legend.*

*I am greatly indebted to my friend Professor Merton M. Sealts of Laurence College for referring me to Bacon's *Wisdom of the Ancients,* which contains a short interpretation of the Memnon fable.

Extend the idea of Fate to include the hero and you have the formula (best exemplified in *Billy Budd*) which Melville probably seized in reading Godwin's *Caleb Williams:* a sudden overwhelming situation forces an irresistible response which has disastrous consequences. In *Caleb Williams,* Mr. Falkland's tragedy is decided by an impulsive act, "a short-lived and passing alienation of the mind," which brings his years of delight to an abrupt end, and inaugurates a relentless sequence of afflictions. Godwin's necessitarian doctrine, by denying moral responsibility, annuls the most venerable concept of tragedy. It asserts that 1, the course of man's ethical development is a lottery, dependent on unpredictable and unmanageable conditions, 2, a single incident may initiate a sequence of events which will convert a virtuous man into a criminal, and 3, for this conversion the man can not be held accountable. Mr. Falkland, a spring of "heart-transporting benevolence," had entered upon his career with the purest intentions and the most "fervid philanthropy." In his early days he had imbibed "the poison of Chivalry," which had made him the "fool of honour and fame"; but his fortune had been "perpetually prosperous" until one momentary act of passion robbed him of all his joy and blasted the "blooming hopes" of his youth forever. Thus he was "changed by a set of circumstances into a gloomy and unsociable misanthrope!" "Honour, justice, virtue, are all the juggle of knaves!" he exclaims finally. "If it were in my power I would instantly crush the whole system into nothing." All this is certainly very suggestive of the language and general theme of *Pierre* and especially of one of its central ideas— "in the minutest moment momentous things are irrevocably done." It is possible, then, that Melville, in magnifying the compulsiveness of his hero's passion and in making him execute his life-binding resolution with such speed and fury, was intentionally molding the plot of his novel to Godwin's necessitarian design.

In *Pierre,* however, the hero's fateful compulsion is not aggressive and criminal, like Mr. Falkland's and Billy Budd's, but initially charitable; and this fact admits consideration of another formula: an idealistic, benevolent youth is crushed by the practical, non-benevolent world. The conflict, in this case, is not between the good and the evil but between the best (chronometrical truth) and the good (horological truth), the spiritual way (religious morality) vs the way of the world (natural morality).

This antinomy, derived from Socrates and St. Paul and exemplified by the tragedy of the Cross, should not be represented on the stage according to Aristotle, because the spectacle of innocent suffering is unbearable and the exposure of flaws in the moral order is blasphemous and unwise. Today it is not so easy to agree with the Stagirite on this point, since the moral order of our world, such as it is, does not compel respect, and what confidence we have is largely reserved for some vision of a future order to be reached mainly through the dedicated efforts of enlightened individuals. Even among Hellenic dramas exceptions to the famous ruling might be named. In the *Antigone* of Sophocles, for instance, the wholly admirable heroine, whose chronometrical soul keeps time with the eternal right of heaven, is destroyed by Creon, who, like the philosopher Plinlimmon, defends the horological justice of the existing culture.

Many critics have concluded that this is the formula on which the moral of *Pierre* is founded, that Melville's object was to show that Christ's truth is impractical, or, to state it another way, that consecrated idealism is folly since, by provoking the antagonism of the complacently moral public, it brings about its own defeat. But this statement can not be accepted in isolation from its opposite, because we can not disregard Pierre's conviction that were he to renounce Isabel, "In my bosom a secret adder of self-reproach and self-infamy would never leave off its sting," that is, if he had not acted as he did, he would have been tormented by his highest conscience. It is clear, furthermore, that the author's sympathies are with his hero from the start. Therefore, as I interpret this aspect of the tragedy, Melville's moral is that there is *no* moral, no satisfactory solution: it is impossible for a man "to reconcile this world with his own soul"; whichever course a chronometer (like Christ or Pierre) elects, he is condemned—on the one side by his conscience, on the other by the world.

Although knowledge of Melville's life leaves little doubt that this ambivalent conclusion was in his mind to stay, we should make certain that it is discriminately stated before applying it to this novel. For one thing, we must not associate Pierre's "own soul," as the author does, with Christ's truth; and, for another, we must not give room to the impression that the hero's action arrays "all men's earthly time-keepers against him." As it happens, the world is ignorant of the incriminating fact that Pierre is living with his sister. From *its* standpoint, young Glendinning is merely an impetuous young man who broke off his engagement with a rich girl and married a poor orphan in the face of his mother's opposition. Good democrats, if Pierre had only seen fit to make friends with them when he moved to the city, would have been more disposed to respect him than to condemn him for this action. The real battle, therefore, is not external at all, but internal.

It is difficult for a reader to avoid the Aristotelian formula in some form, because there are numerous conspicuous weaknesses in the hero, one or all of which could be justly held accountable for the tragedy. The most obtrusive of these is lack of head or prudence: Pierre's inability to hold passion in abeyance for a while, to analyze the situation and himself objectively, and to devise a workable and unhurtful strategy, based on realistic moral values. In contrast to Hamlet, Pierre is a tragedy of "reckless and unforeseeing impulsiveness," to quote Matthiessen's concise statement, or a tragedy of the "fatal precipitancy of youth," to use

Bacon's summary of Memnon's tragedy. Melville himself makes this point when he says: "That all-comprehending oneness, that calm representativeness, by which a steady philosophic mind reaches forth and draws to itself, in their collective entirety, the objects of its contemplations; that pertains not to the young enthusiast." It is clear from this and other passages that the author thinks of Pierre as a "rash boy," but that he does not regard this trait as a defect of character. On the contrary, in his mind, it is indicative of virtue, since a spontaneously generous heart and a shrewdly calculating head are incompatible in a boy of that age. As soon as a man hesitates and begins to reason, he is at fault; self-interest has become sovereign. This view conforms to one of Melville's favorite dichotomies: "the prompt-hearted boy" vs the matured man who is "very slow to feel, deliberate even in love, and statistical even in piety." "I stand for the heart," he informed Hawthorne. "To the dogs with the head!" When young Pendennis meets the supposed "fate" of his life, he announces that he must act immediately—"A delay implies a doubt, which I cast from me as unworthy." Arguing similarly, Pierre upbraids himself for taking as long as two days to come to a decision which will fix the entire course of his life. In short, Melville wants us to understand that Pierre's precipitancy is proof of his bountiful heart.

Another disastrous reaction of Pierre's, exhibited both in Saddle Meadows and in the city, is that of furious aggression; but Melville, in a fine passage beginning "all the world does never gregariously advance to Truth," defends this form of behavior as stoutly as he justifies impulsiveness. A seasoned philosopher might say that the two rules which would have saved the hero from his worst errors are contained in Christ's advice to his disciples: "Be ye therefore wise as serpents, and harmless as doves." But Melville associates this counsel with Pierre's pussyfooting opponent, Mr. Falsgrave. Presumably it is the very antithesis of enthusiastic virtue and nobility of soul.

A number of other relevant formulas jump to mind, several of which may be necessary for a comprehensive reconstruction of the plot, for example, *Pierre* is a tragedy of self-delusion: the hero believes he is motivated by Agape but, in truth, it is Eros that is impelling him; or he believes he is motivated by love and the will to uphold truth whereas actually this is but a veil of vapor overlying a volcano of pride and hate and the will to destroy falsehoods; or the hero is the infatuated victim of preposterous literary affectations, mountebank ravings of love and of misanthropy, which prevent his recognition and acceptance of the facts of human nature. Again, one might say that *Pierre* is a tragedy of moral conflict; in contrast to *Hamlet* (conflict before the deed), here we have conflict *after* the deed: the hero is equal to his action, but not to the idea of his action; he frees his body from prison, but can not free his mind. Finally, to mention one of numerous other possibilities, *Pierre* is a tragedy of the spirit: the hero gives up the governance of his mind and yields to the blast resistless until he becomes a "doorless and shutterless house" with no power to will the obligatory.

But these are no more than fantasies of mine, none of which lead to the author's intention. I say this because I think that the over-all impression one receives of Melville's attitude toward his hero, combined with what knowledge we have of his assumptions and sentiments in 1852, leads to the conclusion that he would have been reluctant to accept any statement which conformed to the Aristotelian pattern, that he would have exonerated his hero much as he did Fenimore Cooper in a letter written while he was in the midst of *Pierre:* ". . . it is certain, that he possessed no slightest weaknesses, but those, which are only noticeable as the almost infallible indices of pervading greatness."* Melville might possibly have admitted the slight criticism implied in Bacon's analysis of the Memnon fable and owned that Pierre was one of those "promising youths who, like sons of the morning . . . attempt things beyond their strength . . . and proving unequal, die in their high attempts," but I feel sure that he would never have acknowledged what is patent in his story, that it was the hero's strength of *heart* which was unequal to the thing that he attempted.

Pierre, in all truth, is deficient in heroic substance. Unlike Ahab, he does *not* "make a courageous wreck." His decline and fall begin immediately after quitting Saddle Meadows when he gives ear to the Evil One. A little later, half-siding with his enemies, he remorsefully recalls "all the minutest details of his old joyous life with his mother" and curses himself as an idiot fool for throwing away his noble birthright for a "mess of pottage." His reservoir of love is dry within a week; none of his sacred vows are fulfilled; his heart, "God's anointed," surrenders unconditionally to hate, disgust, and scorn, directed against himself as well as against the world; he succumbs to the castigations of a bad conscience and has no defense against the accusing countenance of Plinlimmon; he gives way to floods of self-pity, moans and whines over his humble quarters, his solitariness. Writing is a battle for him; but is he really so delicate? He damns his vocation, begrudges the energy he gives to his book. Having lost his own truth, he disparages all truth. Finally, traitor to the spirit, he goes over to the world, stabs his manuscript—"here will I nail it fast, for a detected cheat!"—and spits upon it. The only possession saved from the wreck of his whole character is his spurious pride of purity—a prime cause of the disaster. *Pierre* is "the undraped spectacle of a valor-ruined man."

The last words spoken in the novel sound another note, a note which initially encouraged me—mindful of Melville's habit of gathering

---

*Mr. Jay Leyda generously showed me his copy of Melville's original letter to Rufus N. Griswold (preserved by the Historical Society of Pennsylvania) in answer to an invitation to attend the memorial meeting to James Fenimore Cooper.

up and resolving his ambiguities in one compact, concluding utterance —to concentrate in this introduction on Pierre's dedicated love, brief as it indeed was. The words come from the lips of Isabel as she falls and dies on Pierre's heart and are addressed to his old companion Charlie Millthorpe and other bystanders—"ye know him not"—the simplest meaning of which may be expressed in phrases out of *Moby-Dick:* "ye, who have seen him outwardly know him not,—*I* only know his real self, because *I* only have seen him inwardly, in the ideal, 'so noble and so sparkling, such a grand and glowing creature' that for me his 'immaculate manliness . . . remains intact though all the outer character seem gone.' "

REFERENCES

1. Lewis Mumford. *Herman Melville,* New York, 1929, p. 196.

2. E. L. Grant Watson. Melville's *Pierre. New England Quarterly,* 1930, 195–234.

3. F. O. Matthiessen. *American Renaissance,* New York, 1941, p. 377.

4. Charles Olson. *Call Me Ishmael,* New York, 1947.

5. Raymond M. Weaver. *Herman Melville, Mariner and Mystic,* New York, 1921.

6. Robert S. Forsythe. Introduction to *Pierre,* (Knopf), New York, 1930.

7. William Wollaston. *The Religion of Nature Delineated,* London, 1722.

8. G. C. Homans. The Dark Angel: The Tragedy of Herman Melville. *New England Quarterly,* V (1932), 699–730, p. 701.

9. Henry James. *Moralism and Christianity; or Man's Experience and Destiny,* New York, 1850.

10. See footnote in Olson's *Call Me Ishmael,* p. 103. Cervantes writes: ". . . a knight-errant without a mistress is like a tree without leaves," and Melville adds: "or as Confucius said 'a dog without a master' . . . or a god-like man without a God."

11. William E. Sedgwick. *Herman Melville: A Tragedy of Mind,* Cambridge, 1944.

12. Edward Bulwer-Lytton. *Ishmael and Other Poems,* London, 1820. Ishmael was also a much discussed character in Cooper's *Prairie,* 1827.

13. E. Douglas Branch. *The Sentimental Years,* New York, 1934.

14. Herbert R. Brown. *The Sentimental Novel in America 1789–1860,* Durham, 1940.

15. Carl G. Jung. *Two Essays on Analytical Psychology,* London, 1928.

16. Justus Buchler, ed. *The Philosophy of Peirce: Selected Writings,* New York, 1940, "Evolutionary Love," p. 362.

17. Claude Bragdon. *More Lives Than One,* New York, 1938: "And should anyone ask me what else I imagine myself to be, I would have to confess to a secretly cherished belief that I am the Voice of Crucified Woman. By that I mean the defender of those women of the modern world who are derided, secretly persecuted, sometimes even incarcerated as insane, on account of the development in them of faculties and powers the very existence of which is so subversive of current materialist conceptions . . ." (p. 131).

18. For example, Morton Prince's "Sally Beauchamps," Freud's "Anna O.," and Jung's "Miss Miller."

19. S. Foster Damon. Pierre the ambiguous. *Hound and Horn*, 1929, *II*, 107–18.

20. For a detailed discussion of Eros (romantic enthusiasm, the source of which is the sex instinct) and Agape (compassion, charity, neighborly love), see M. C. D'Arcy. *The Mind and Heart of Love*, London, 1947.

21. See Dennis De Rougemont. *Love in the Western World*, New York, 1940.

22. See Carl G. Jung. *Two Essays on Analytical Psychology*, London, 1928.

23. Stanley Geist. *Herman Melville: The Tragic Vision and the Heroic Ideal*, Cambridge, 1939, p. 25.

24. Richard P. Blackmur. *The Expense of Greatness*, New York, 1940.

25. I am grateful to Mr. Van Wyck Brooks for telling me about this popular meeting place. See his book *The Times of Melville and Whitman*, New York, 1947.

19

BARTLEBY AND I

For some time now it has been *de rigueur* in some quarters for a writer to be tantalizingly obscure, unintelligible to all but the gifted few who are disposed to spend what time it takes to decipher his secret code of symbols. If his sentences are structured and coherent and their meanings unmistakable, he is a Square or squarish fellow traveler who is serving to perpetuate the basic cultural currency of the established order, the order that is headed for oblivion. In view of this, I shouldn't tell you who is meant by the "I" in the title I have chosen. I should weave around this first person pronoun an entangling spider's web of recondite allusions and insinuations, with unannounced shifts from one level to another. Initially you would naturally be led to think that "I" referred to the "I" in Melville's story, the only person who had a face-to-face relationship with Bartleby. Then you might come to the idea that I, the commentator, had myself in mind since, for better or for worse, whatever I say about the scrivener must be the result of an emphatic and cognitive transaction between him and me. Bartleby *per se* is meaningless so long as no reader can either discover or drive a bit of sense in him. In one respect at least it is not difficult for me to identify with Bartleby, since both of us have a wall to face: in my case it is that wall of legitimate aesthetic principles or laws—instead of Wall Street laws—which is there in some of you literary scholars to protect your domain against those who carry in their heads the weapons of analytical psychology. But the next minute you might be thinking, No, the "I" refers to Melville, since it is only he who knows to what extent, if any, the scrivener was consciously created in his own image. My identification with Melville is facilitated by the approximation of our initials, HAM and HM: to arrive at a momentary, sort of Christ-like state of mind, if that's what's necessary, I have only to delete the middle A, which stands for the Old Adam of original sin at the center of my nature.

At this point—if my paper were written with any particle of subtlety—some of you would undoubtedly become convinced that I, the commentator, was punning: the single letter "I" in my title must be a kind of camouflage for "Eye" in three letters, and you, ever-alert to esoteric

From H.P. Vincent, ed., *Bartleby the Scrivener.* Kent, Ohio: Kent State University Press, 1966, pp. 3–24.

significancies, might well surmise that the referent I had in mind was some all-seeing Eye; and from here on the opportunities for projection would be boundless. Might it not be the ominiscient Eye behind the pasteboard mask, the Eye whose incessant gaze was Melville's prime source of tribulation for so many years? or possibly the Evil Eye? or, let us say, the Eye of History? or the Eye of Criticism? or maybe the Eye of some special cult or doctrine—theosophy, Marxism, Freudian infantology, Jungian archetypology, existentialism, Zen Buddhism—whose penetrating rays could supposedly bring to light the locked-up secret that Bartleby took with him to the grave. But, of course, wherever you might locate the all-seeing, three-letter "Eye," you would have to include the single-letter "I" on this page, since willy-nilly it is I, the commentator, who, with all my liabilities to error, must be its mouthpiece for the length of this paper. And so, since some of you have classified me as a would-be biographer—one who, whenever urged to publish, baffles your good-will with a measly "I would prefer not to"—there is ground for the conjecture that one of the seeing Eyes that wants to use me as its mouthpiece is what could be called the Documentary Eye, say, of the biographer, of the critic or historian. Far more widely familiar to most of you than it is to me, the Documentary Eye may be defined as the power that resides in the knowledge of certain facts to make visible some previously invisible determinants of the mood, the themes, the episodes, the allusions, or the underlying meaning of a literary work. Finally, since certain features of Melville's mind can be seen in the vacillating mental processes of the attorney he created, we return to the point from which we started, the "I" of the imaginary narrator of the story. So you see I have ended by proving myself a veritable Square by dispelling all the mystery from my title. Now everything is clear. You have been introduced to most of my cast of spirit characters, the fantastic participants in the symposium to be reported here. The attorney has the floor.

THE ATTORNEY. "As I was being molded in the womb of my creator's mind I had certain disquieting premonitions as to the outcome of the on-going generative process; but not until I was delivered and could see the reflection of myself in the looking-glass of the novella, did I fully realize, after an initial shock of unrecognition, that my composer had intended from the start—and there must have been some malice sinewing that intention—to make a laughing-stock of me. For a week or so this distortion of my true nature rankled and festered in my heart. I kept thinking: if only I could wield a pen as *he* can, I would wreak my vengeance on him. But then I was reminded of Long Ghost and a score of other persons who had been similarly outraged by published caricatures of their peculiarities and conduct. The idea that we had all been sacrificed, one by one, on the altar of our creator's art engendered a sort of fellow-feeling which brought comfort to my wounded vanity. Later, hearing of the story's completely favorable reception—by the elder Richard H. Dana, for example—I began to feel a touch of pride that I was in it. This might be my only chance for immortality. After further thought, however, recalling Dana's two adjectives "ludicrous and pathetic," it became apparent that nobody could doubt that ludicrous applied to me and pathetic to my copyist. For a while I couldn't decide which was better: no life at all after death or life as a symbol of absurdity or sheer mediocrity. Anyhow, although it is against my grain to indulge in dangerous indignation (my creator was fair enough to admit that) I am still to this day nursing a grudge against him, mainly on one score: he confounded me with an insoluble problem. This is proved by the fact that for a hundred years, no critic, so far as I know, has come out with a definite statement as to what I should have done or what he himself would have done in my place."

THE PSYCHOLOGIST. "Let me interrupt you for a minute to make a bid for the distinction of being the first to say what he would have done in your place: call Bellevue Hospital."

THE ATTORNEY. "Well, Ginger Nut didn't hesitate to say that Bartleby was ' a little *luny,*' and eventually I too came to the conclusion that he was the victim of some 'innate and incurable disorder.' And so, in my own proper person I would naturally have thought of Bellevue or the Bloomingdale Asylum; but Mr. Melville did not offer me those tranquillizers of a bad conscience. The only available option of this sort was the city Tombs with all its associated images of brutality and misery. It is true that I could not bear the thought of consigning the defenseless Bartleby to the inhumanities of the existing penal system. That being repugnant to me, what resources did I have except the mental functions that constitute the basis of my profession, in fact the very basis of democracy? In other words, what could I do but trust to the power of reason? What else is there as a substitute for force?"

THE PSYCHOLOGIST. "In your day there was virtually nothing else. Most of the doctors who tried to cope with mental disorders used persuasion and suggestion very much as you did and with no greater success. The esteemed Dr. Brown at Bloomingdale, for example, was not able to liberate Mr. Melville's friend, George Adler, from paranoid schizophrenia. Hypnotism, or what was known to you as Mesmerism, had proved temporarily remedial in some cases; but Bartleby would never have permitted himself to succumb to that procedure."

THE ATTORNEY. "I welcome your support of my case against the author, which in summary is this, first, that he faced me, as I have said, with a problem that not even a trained psychiatrist could solve. Second, that he made Bartleby so meek and mild, that if I had forcefully ejected him from my chambers I would have gone down in literary history as just another striking proof of the heartlessness of the cold and wolfish world which my creator so thoroughly detested and would someday teach others to detest. Third, having limited me to unaided reason as an instrument of action, he caricatured and mocked the utter futility of all my well-meaning efforts. Fourth, although he endowed me with some propensity for sympathy, he made it evident that this was but one subordinate part of a calculating prudential philosophy, and that the spring of whatever benevolence I may have manifested was not a compassionate concern for the welfare of Bartleby, but dread of the suffering that a punishing conscience would inflict on me if I, on my own initiative, called the constables and had that inflexible irritant removed from my office. In other words, my creator was publicly announcing that so long as I didn't have to shoulder the abrasive burden of that amount of guilt, all would be nice and snug inside. Let the scrivener be handled—roughly if need be—by somebody who was not encumbered by my paralyzing scruples. That was not my business. Finally, when I visited my former employee in jail—it was kind of me to do so, wasn't it?—my maker went out of his way to unveil my dominating motive by having me too hastily announce my innocence: 'It was not I that brought you here, Bartleby.' But my profoundest, all-embracing grievance comes from an uneasy feeling, or suspicion, that Mr. Melville was out to flog me with the Sermon on the Mount, as if to say, you should have given the full measure of your love to Bartleby, all of it, every atom's atom of it, without reservations, qualifications, or reflections as to the consequences of so selfless a commitment of compassion. You should have sacrificed your profession, deserted your clients, set aside your duties to the High Court of Chancery, and taken Bartleby to live with you at home. Is not the author implying this and nothing less? If he is, I'd like to ask, what right has he to judge me from that unearthly and inhuman pinnacle of ethics?"

THE AUTHOR. "I will answer your question only so far as to assert that for me the Sermon on the Mount was the 'greatest real miracle of all religions. . . . This is of God! cries the heart, and in that cry ceases all inquisition.' In my youth I felt with my whole enthusiastic soul that those divine sentences 'embody all the love of the Past, and all the love which can be imagined in any conceivable Future.' From then on this was my topmost truth, the absolute standard which perpetually assured me that the world in which we live is 'saturated and soaking with lies.' This truth constituted my main justification for disliking 'all mankind—in the mass,' that is to say, the public, this generation of vipers, as distinguished from certain particular individuals. You, attorney, belong to the public in my mind, though you may be better than the vast majority of that class. You see, you're always playing safe, working your head in behalf of your conservative self-interests. You're the kind of man who would wince if he heard my bold declaration 'that a thief in jail is as honourable as General George Washington.' This declaration, like the Sermon on the Mount, is ludicrous to the head; and so I say 'To the dogs with the head! . . . I stand for the heart,' a heart which carries me but a step beyond the Sermon in ascribing a certain 'august dignity' to a prisoner in jail, even to 'the most mournful, perchance the most abased' of men. And so, when it came to Bartleby, I was sure that God would bear me out in it if I 'spread a rainbow over his disasterous set of sun.' "

THE ATTORNEY. "I protest. You have virtually admitted to an irrational prejudice against me in favor of the scrivener, just because I was reasonably well adjusted, responsible, and happy, and that lazy scrivener was maladjusted, irresponsible, and mournful. But look, it was not I who abased Bartleby, but Bartleby who abased me. My grievance is unalleviated."

THE AUTHOR. "Would it console you at all if I said that a man can truly sympathize only with another person in similar circumstances. I have been as full of grief as Bartleby ever since those early days when I was 'rubbed, curried, and ground down to fine powder in the hopper of an evil fortune.' You, on the other hand, having never actually experienced anything like the woe with which the scrivener was burdened, were in no position to proffer sympathy with grace. My story could not help but make this evident."

THE SCRIVENER. "Let me speak! I would prefer to. Who's got a better right? I'm the hero, ain't I? First I should tell you that I was a very ordinary fellow before Mr. Melville began the job of re-creating me. As you might suspect, I was about the unhappiest human being in the whole world with the idea of suicide almost continuously in mind, and Mr. Melville's heart went out to me with unquestioning and unerring understanding. His eyes expressed a tenderness that was more feminine than masculine. But he didn't act on it as Jesus would have done. Christ's fated role was to drive out devils, not to make books. That's the crux of the matter. What Mr. Melville did was to take me into himself to be reshaped with affectionate concern, and to give me a rebirth as a personage with far more drawing power than I ever had in real life. If in the flesh of my first birth I could have had a quarter of the sympathy I have received when presented to the world in the form of my second birth, I would never have landed in the Asylum with what they would call today, schizophrenia, catatonic type. There I refused to eat; but unhappily I was physically forced to submit to the indignity of being fed by stomach tube until a year or so later the Comforter came and terminated my soul's agony. Mr. Melville was truthful in ascribing to me a state of absolute misanthropy, or alienation, coupled with the hardihood to persist in affirming a sovereign nature in myself, amid all the institutionalized powers of society. But beyond that everything was of his invention. Look at the combination of strategies he gave me to defend the integrity of my being. First, silence combined with a stance of impassive immobility, the only effective tactic for a cornered person who is faced by the rage of a dangerous human being, mob, or beast. It was precisely this posture, combined with my pathetic look, which repeatedly dissolved the anger of my employer. Compared to a vehement No, my mild 'I would prefer not to' sounded as if it were no more than the expression of a personal choice, which in a democratic society is accepted as the inalienable right of every citizen. That was a very clever trick of Mr. Melville's. And, then, by having me withhold the reasons for my stubbornly held decision, the attorney was deprived of all possible points of entry for rational counter-arguments; and, furthermore, by having me refuse to answer his personal questions, I was able to frustrate his humane attempts to understand me. Indeed I cut him dead, spiritually speaking, virtually killed him so far as I was concerned, as a man unworthy of my trust, just another self-complacent member of that hateful world which I had totally and permanently rejected. By remaining mysterious, I implanted in the lawyer's mind a sticky riddle that called for some solution, a magnet to his thoughts; and partly by my meek exterior, but more especially by the disdain implicit in my unshakable refusal to converse with him, I gained an appreciable ascendancy over my employer, which so undermined what confidence he had in his own powers that a reversal of status was effected: I, the forlorn squatter compelled the legitimate owner to desert his own domain, leaving me, a little Bonaparte, as its solitary occupant. 'Blessed are the meek: for they shall inherit the earth.' "

THE PSYCHOLOGIST. "What were your innermost feelings through all those experiences?"

THE SCRIVENER. "As I have said, utterly misanthropic, a kind of hate-grief with pride to bolster it. Tired of everything, I had resigned myself to—well, a sort of death in life, and then to no life, the last resource of an insulted and unendurable existence. But yet, now that it's all over, I can confess to feeling a little lift of secret, spiteful enjoyment every time my employer laid down his arms before my wall of self-containment, my meekly voiced negation. I also derived some hidden pleasure from witnessing the disturbance I produced in the office, seeing to what extent I became the center of attention, and how, one after the other, they adopted my word 'prefer.' Nothing is sweeter than revenge, you know, and to tell the truth, my deepest satisfaction—rising in the very midst of my pervasive melancholy—came when I discovered how much guilt I could arouse in my employer. He had given me no good reason to abase him in his own proper person; but, seeing him as a pasteboard mask of the world that had humiliated me, I felt justified in making his conscience prick him till it hurt. And now looking back on the whole course of events I am very grateful to Mr. Melville's embracing sympathy in representing me as he did. I haven't been able to make out what there was in me—a very ordinary man as I have said—that fetched him."

THE AUTHOR. "Evidently, you haven't read my books. It was your sorrow: 'that mortal man who hath more of joy than sorrow in him, that mortal cannot be true.' And then your silence: 'Silence is at once the most harmless and the most awful thing in all nature. . . . Silence is the only Voice of our God.' And then your forlornness. That was irresistible to me. I used to call my favorite sister, Augusta, the Forlorn One. In short, I recognized in you a humble fellow-misanthrope."

THE PSYCHOLOGIST. "When did *your* misanthropy begin, Mr. Melville?"

THE AUTHOR. "When I wrote 'Bartleby' I was a confirmed misanthrope. But it was much earlier, about 1837—I'm not precise about dates—that I had my first acute and critical attack of it, at the time that my soul's ship, which I later called the *Pequod,* was irrecoverably sunk. But even before that, as far back as I can remember in my childhood, I was prone to melancholy moods. My father used to say I was morose."

THE BIOGRAPHER. "I have an overlooked document from the New York Public Library which may be pertinent at this point. Other biographers have started with Herman's birth, but I chose to start with his conception which, as it happens, can be definitely placed sometime during the first week in November, 1818, just after the Melvilles arrived in New York and took up lodgings at Mrs. Bradish's stylish boardinghouse on State Street. Mrs.

Melville was keenly looking forward to the grand dinners and parties for which this center of fashion was renowned. Family friends who had known her in Albany and were living in the neighborhood of State Street were notified of her arrival. But nothing happened, and less than a month later, when the future grief-stricken author of *Moby-Dick* was a sensitive three-weeks embryo within her body, Maria Melville wrote an unusually long letter to her brother Peter Gansevoort in Albany, which may be veridically abbreviated as follows:

> *'Dear Brother:*
>
> *'. . . I do think the inhabitants of New York, the most ungrateful, inasmuch, as many have been at our house partaken of our hospitality, & now that a return can be expected, feign not to know me, I am in a fair way of becoming a Misanthrope. . . .*
>
> *'. . . The Mayors Lady Visits every Lady that comes to the City, She has Given half A dozen large Parties, all go, invitations to all except us, Mrs. Bartley an actress is caress'd, visited, visited, invited, to the first houses in this City, while I am worse than forgotten, shuned, It is next to impossible that people, should not enquire and know who we are, altogether, this is a Selfish hateful Place. . . . I have too much pride to allow it to Mr. M—, but really the inhabitants of this Place, will not see merit they shut their Eyes, against everything but wealth, Wealth is their reigning God & if you have not wealth, you must have patience to put up with every slight, & many mortifications. . . .*
>
> *'Maria'*

"Here we have it in a nutshell: Everybody is invited to parties except me. I am worse than forgotten, shunned. This is a hateful place. The inhabitants must know who we are but they will not see merit. I have too much pride to admit it even to my husband, but I am in a fair way of becoming a misanthrope."

THE FIRST CRITIC. "This is the kind of thing that makes me boil! What has embryology got to do with the texture and structure of a work of art? Are you expecting us to take some purely hypothetical prenatal influence into account in our appreciation of Mr. Melville's consummate skill and poise in writing the superb story that we have before us?"

THE BIOGRAPHER. "I stand corrected. But before backing out, I should say first, that Maria Melville seems to have persisted in this attitude for many years, and second, that she was the most influential person in her son's entire life. Mr. Melville and his mother had a terribly profound reciprocal love-hate relationship almost, I would guess, from start to finish."

THE AUTHOR. "By the way, gentlemen, let's not stand on any ceremony here. It's proper for the characters I immortalized to call me 'Mister'; but you critics and biographers had better talk as you do when I'm not present. In view of the neglect I experienced in my lifetime, to be the center at this symposium of so much devoted attention and reflection is all that my scarred vanity requires to make it purr delightedly. The 'Mister' is superfluous."

THE FIRST CRITIC. "Thank you, Mr. Melville—oh, I should say Melville. Now, let's return to our proper province. So far none of the discussants have placed the novella in a historic literary context. No one has mentioned Dickens and Kafka and the comedy-of-the-absurd. And we haven't discussed the meaning of the story. We all know that most of Melville's stories have a hidden meaning."

THE SCRIVENER. "His meaning is hidden from me. I can only say that ever since my resurrection in this novella, most of my old sorrow has given way to a divine content. There is nothing like world-wide recognition and acclaim to cheer a fellow up. It seems that I have been virtually canonized as a kind of saint, because almost everyone has assumed that I am Herman Melville in disguise. By silencing me to the bitter end, he succeeded somehow in hanging a Christ-like halo over my head as if I had been crucified by society because I was too good for them. Actually I did no good to anybody and, as I've told you, my soul was chock-full of pent-up bitterness and hate."

THE BIOGRAPHER. "It's hard to avoid the inference that Melville had himself in mind to some extent when he turned you into the hero of his story. In the novella, remember, it is Bartleby himself who asks for the job of copyist. He is not forced to it; and there is not the slightest intimation that he is capable of greater works. This corresponds to the apparent fact that by 1853 Melville had written himself out—mostly in *Moby-Dick* and *Pierre* —just as he predicted to Hawthorne that he would. Those two No-in-thunder books were what he had most wanted to write, indeed had been impelled to write. But after two or three explosions of his volcano, he was left, like a burnt-out crater, with only a mild No to energize his composing a number of symbolic stories, pretty much as a copyist, we could say, of Hawthorne, whose No had never come with thunder, as Melville once said it did, but with mildness such as Bartleby's. Bartleby's preference for *not* correcting copy corresponds to Melville's preference for *not* correcting proof. Finally, analogous to the attorney's attempts to get the copyist out of his chambers, we have the efforts of Hawthorne and a score of lawyers, with Allan Melville in Wall Street as co-ordinator, to obtain a consulship for Melville—chiefly to get him *out* of the room in which he wrote at Arrowhead. These efforts were initially instigated by Melville's mother, who attributed her son's increasingly patent signs of mental illness to his 'constant indoor confinement—constant working of the brain & excitement of the imagination' (as we learn from our unexampled source book, *The Melville Log* by Jay Leyda). This gives us three rough correspondences between Bartleby and the Melville of 1853: both at first prefer to copy, both prefer not to correct copy, and both have lawyers trying to move them from their preferred location. Furthermore, both prefer solitude, both are suspected of being mentally unbalanced, and both are inclined toward suicide. We have, for example, as one of many bits of evidence, Sarah Morewood's account of a conversation with Melville in 1851 in which she says: I 'told him that the recluse life he was leading made his friends think that he was slightly insane—he replied that long ago he came to the same conclusion himself.' And, as for suicide, we have, among other things, Melville's admission in a letter to Samuel Shaw that: 'I once, like other spoonies, cherished a loose sort of notion that I did not care to live very long'; which sounds as if he had once been saying to himself: 'I would *prefer* not to live very long.' It all fits."

THE FIRST CRITIC. "Well, if that's it, if the story is just veiled autobiography, Melville is a lesser artist than I thought he was. According to my view the scrivener stands for the writer in America and Wall Street for the capitalistic system which had no use for him."

THE SECOND CRITIC. "That's looking at the story through the eyes of a twentieth-century writer. If *you* are right, Melville is a lesser artist than *I* thought, because as a parable or manifesto in behalf of the profession of letters it is a total failure. What capitalist could possibly get the idea that a young man who applied for the humble position of copyist and had nothing at all to say for himself was meant to represent a typical American writer or a great genius who was fuller than a city and capable of scaling great heights out of his present lowest depths? I don't believe that any living American author except Melville himself, or conceivably Hawthorne, would have seen any part of himself in Bartleby. Not Washington Irving, Cooper, Longfellow, Lowell, Thoreau, or Emerson certainly. Furthermore, the Wall Street lawyer is far more appreciative and benevolent than his copyist. If one condemns all forms of autobiography in literature, one must chuck out Shakespeare's sonnets and a hundred other great masterpieces."

THE BIOGRAPHER. "The question of better or worse is not the issue here. The primary question is, who or what did Melville have in mind when he shaped the character of Bartleby. According to my divining rod, the secret title of the Wall Street story is 'I and my Wall,' and it could stand as a companion piece to 'I and my Chimney,' for the perfect elucidation of which we are indebted to the intuition and scholarship of Merton Sealts. Without the knowledge which assures us that in 'I and my Chimney' Melville was representing the disturbance that was created in his household by what his mother took to be evidences of insanity in her son—without that knowledge-grounded intuition, a good deal of the charm, subtlety, humor, and pathos of the story would be wasted on us. I would wager that the spirit of Herman Melville, who always vainly hoped for worthy readers, fully and gratefully appreciates the perspicacity of Merton Sealts."

THE AUTHOR. "You're right there."

THE SECOND CRITIC. "But, even if we had the relevant autobiographic facts, this in itself would not define the meaning of the story; and since none of the rest of you seem to be disposed to tackle this problem, let me hazard these three related propositions in regard to Melville's conscious intention: first, to use today's terminology, it is a comedy-of-the-absurd marked by the surprising and unprecedented perversity of Bartleby's simple yet adamant refusal to perform his duties, in conjunction with the agitation and indecisiveness that is engendered in his baffled, conscience-ridden employer by the reiteration of this negative response to every one of his justified demands and by the frustration of each of his endeavors to reason this seemingly innocuous young man out of his unreasonable willfulness. Coupled with this continuously humorous aspect of the encounters between employer and employee is a tragic aspect which I shall call the second theme. This is determined by the impossibility of the attorney's empathetically comprehending the nature of Bartleby's entrenched grief. As Melville expressed it in *Pierre:* 'in the inexorable and unhuman eye of mere undiluted reason, all grief, whether on our own account, or that of others, is the sheerest unreason and insanity.' Here we might be reminded of Starbuck's attempt to dissuade Ahab from pursuing the White Whale: 'It will not fetch thee much in our Nantucket market.' To which Ahab replies: 'My vengeance will fetch a great premium here,' smiting his chest. Likewise with Bartleby inwardly considered. He is driven by a similar emotional necessity, and although his will is capable of executing the actions that have been chosen for him by that necessity, it is no longer free to choose and execute a different course of action. Finally, there is the theme of fortitude marked by Bartleby's adherence, despite everything, to the principle of self-sovereignty, the last stand of an oppressed ego. Given intense and irremediable suffering, there is nothing irrational about the act of suicide. It is irrational only to those who stand outside of it."

THE HISTORIAN. "At this moment that strikes me as a fitting summary of Melville's probable intentions in this novella. But there is a larger issue, namely that of the history of alienation in the West. Bartleby is a precursor of those fictional characters which have become predominant in recent years. It is all condensed in Malraux's dictum: 'Man is dead,' presumably because God is dead, as Hegel, Heine, Nietzsche, and Sartre announced. Melville was pretty close to this conclusion, wasn't he?"

THE FIRST CRITIC. "Bartleby is certainly as near to being dead, in this sense, as a man could be, more dead than alive: more dead than Camus's 'Stranger,' more dead than any of Beckett's non-heroes, for the scrivener has stopped talking, and there is no hint that he is waiting for any semblance of Godot. When we first meet him he has already committed social suicide and he is on his way to an organic suicide. The wall might stand for the meaninglessness of life, no future prospect or purpose to be seen."

THE SECOND CRITIC. "Let's ask Mr. Melville himself."

THE AUTHOR. "I'm not required to expose what I took pains to hide when writing 'Bartleby,' am I? Have you by any chance read my whaling story for boys? If you have, you will remember Captain Ahab exclaiming: 'To me the White Whale is that wall, shoved near to me. . . . How can the prisoner reach outside except by thrusting through the wall?' In that narrative, you may recall, Ahab fails in his attempt to kill the whale, that is, he fails to effect a breakthrough. So you find in the story you are now considering the very same wall shoved even closer to the hero. But in contrast to Ahab, Bartleby has concluded that the wall is impregnable and, acknowledging his defeat, is resigned to pallid hopelessness. He ends his career as an impotent, though noble, prisoner."

THE PSYCHOLOGIST. "Would you say, Mr. Melville, that the aggressive, destructive force which the sadistic Ahab directed outwardly at the whale is now directed inwardly at him, or what remains of him, namely, the partly masochistic Bartleby who is Ahab's shadowy antithesis or counterpart?"

THE AUTHOR. "If you like that kind of language, you can have it. I won't contradict you."

THE BIOGRAPHER. "My impression is that the majority of critics have pretty well agreed that the White Whale, besides being a real biological whale in the Pacific Ocean, represents the prohibiting and punishing Calvinistic and puritanical aspect of God that was implanted in Melville's soul at an early age. In short, the wall of the White Whale is the wall of an imprisoning, punishing, and mutilating conscience; and, if the Wall Street wall is of the same moral texture, the chances are that it represents those laws, in Melville's day, whose prohibitions and penalties reinforced the ordinances of Calvinism. In which case, Wall Street does not refer to the stock exchange and the economic system, but to the seat of the legal system, where Melville's brother, Allan, his friend Daniel Shepherd, and the scrivener's employer had their offices. We are dealing, then, with a wall buttressed by two formidable establishments: the Church and the Law. Now, when you consider the extreme degree to which Melville valued the open independence of his way, and consider that after his father's death his life was marked for nearly fifteen years by recurrent egressions—departures, escapes, flights, or whatever you choose to call them—from a confining space or job, you might surmise that in the late forties he found himself imprisoned to an intolerable extent in a way that he had never been before. He dropped out of school at twelve, a little later abandoned his job at the bank, then gave up working at Gansevoort's fur store, then left his uncle's farm at Pittsfield, then dropped the studies that were preparing him for teaching, then suddenly quit the Sykes School at Pittsfield, then dropped his studies at Lansingburgh Academy, then left home to be a sailor on a merchant ship to Liverpool, etc., etc., until he reached a total of seventeen egressions. Then in 1847—after starting *Mardi,* I would guess—he was married to Elizabeth Shaw, *period.* I would like to ask Mr. Melville whether or not marriage was his wall, his prison, in 1850, and, if so, why did he tantalize his readers with so many references to a wall without giving a few decipherable clues as to what it stood for."

THE AUTHOR. "Why should I put so private and delicate a matter before the eyes of a 'bantering, barren, and prosaic, heartless age,' a generation of censorious, nominally Christian hypocrites? To my world, with its pride of purity, marriage was a sacred, inviolable institution, guarded and walled-in by the most powerful moral sentiments. You people, with your permissive attitude toward sex and your lenient divorce laws, cannot possibly imagine what it feels like to be in the position I was in in 1850. Divorce was practically impossible. But since I had to be frank with *myself,* I could not omit the wall. Besides, I did give a few hints. For instance, I made it clear enough, for any knowledgeable reader, that passionate love for my gentle, innocent little wife dissolved within the first month of marriage. In *Mardi,* not long after I was married, speaking of Toji and Yillah, I wrote: 'For a time we were happy in Odo; Yillah and I in our islet. . . . Often I thought that Paradise had overtaken me on earth, and that Yillah was verily an angel . . . But how fleeting our joys. Storms follow bright mornings . . . Long memories of short-lived scenes, sad thoughts of joyous hours . . . Speed the hours, the days, the one brief moment of our joys . . . Oh Yillah, Yillah!' What could be more patent than this? And yet academic critics, whose heads are apt to suffocate their hearts, seem to have come to the conclusion that Yillah was meant to represent some transcendent entity, such as absolute truth or wisdom. They should pay more attention to the elucidation of that *Mardi* passage which I offered them in *Pierre* when I wrote of 'That nameless and infinitely delicate aroma of inexpressible tenderness and attentiveness which, like the bouquet of the costliest German wines, too often evaporates upon pouring love out to drink, in the disenchanting glasses of the matrimonial days and nights . . .' And then, in that novel, didn't I have the hero abandon his Lucy? I had them engaged instead of married, because I didn't think that the public would stand for a hero who deserted a devoted wife, and, as it turned out, the public's tolerance was much less than I anticipated: they condemned with blasts of moral indignation everything that my hero felt, and thought, and did. So you can see what I was up against. Besides, as I made plain in *Pierre,* my wife's 'sympathetic mind and person had both been cast in one mold of wondrous delicacy.' Her nature was permeated by 'what may be artistically styled angelicalness,' which, in my scales, is 'the highest essence compatible with created being.' I couldn't bring myself to hurt her any more than I did in that book."

THE BIOGRAPHER. "Didn't you rage at her occasionally in real life? I was told by a member of your family that once you clutched her by the throat and exclaimed: 'Now I know what a man feels like who wants to kill his wife.' And after that didn't she leave you and return to her family's house in Boston, taking her children with her?"

THE AUTHOR. "Yes, but I was overcome with remorse and pity and in a week or so—I don't remember how long it was exactly—I went up there and persuaded her to come back to me and try again. Nobody like you on the outside can possibly understand the anguish of those years for both of us. Do not judge, lest you be judged; and so the less said the better. 'Ladies are like creeds; if you cannot speak well of them, say nothing.' "

FIRST CRITIC. "I protest again, biographer. You have gone too far with your probings into the secret recesses of Melville's stricken heart. Numberless other artists, such as D. H. Lawrence and Eugene O'Neill, have attacked their wives with greater fury than Melville ever did. That's all too human. You may or you may not have hit on the best explanation of Melville's wall as cause of his own hopelessness, the state of mind which he portrays in Bartleby. But, whether right or wrong, this hypothesis is scarcely relevant to the work of art we are surveying, the basic theme of which is the inevitable opposition between the requirements of the on-going social system and the requirements of the individual with his innate need for autonomy. In Melville's narrative we have a miniature social system with its traditions and customs, laws and regulations, rewards and penalties, operating within the frame of the Protestant ethic and the utilitarian philosophy, in terms of which, as usual, rationality and sanity are defined. Buck the system, dissent, and you're 'straightway handled with a chain,' as Emily Dickinson has put it. The administrator of this system is a lawyer of good will who, believing 'that the easiest way of life is the best,' has chosen 'the cool tranquillity of a snug retreat' to perform his professional duties, confident that his two great virtues, prudence and method, will insure a smooth and regular routine of office work. But these peaceful expectations are destined—or, as the lawyer eventually concludes, *predestined*—first, to be shaken by his two clerks with their regular irregularities of conduct, and finally to be completely cancelled by the cadaverous Bartleby, who seems to be set on carrying Emerson's advocacy of nonconformity to the point of ultimate insanity as judged by the system he disrupts. Whatever principle or right Bartleby may be secretly defending, he prefers to die rather than to compromise and enjoy whatever scraps of pleasure would be then accessible to him. Since it can't be All (the wall prohibits it), it will be Nothing; and from that wall there will be retreat through him. That's the key to this superb story, perfectly wrought out of simple, realistic elements, a compact gem which embodies a whole world of complementary meanings, prophetic of much that will come later. Today we have the Squares and the Beats, another version of the archetypal situation."

THE SECOND CRITIC. "I agree with everything you've said; but before we leave the author and his wall, I would like to expound a little thesis which not only supports the biographer's emphasis on Melville's marital despair, but explicates the symbolism of the Dead Letter Office where Bartleby worked previous to his engagement as a copyist in Wall Street. My thesis starts with the observation that Melville's mental excitement usually reached its peak in conjunction with his writing of the last phase or chapters of a book; and, furthermore, as he progressed with the series of works that he wanted to write, those dictated by his daemon—*Mardi, Moby Dick,* and *Pierre*—his terminal agitation increased from book to book. Now, in late November, 1852—four months after the publication of *Pierre*—Melville informed Hawthorne with evident zest that he was about to begin the story of Agatha, that is, his fictional version of a true story about a Quakeress of that name, the details of which, as you all know, were obtained by Melville from a New Bedford lawyer on his trip to Nantucket in July. It must have been this work, then—since there is mention of no other possibility—which, as his mother put it, 'completely absorbed' Melville during the succeeding winter of 1853, and which, in the spring of that year, was said to be 'nearly ready for the press.' That Melville's agitation in finishing the Agatha story was even greater than it had been in finishing *Pierre* is suggested by his wife's note in her memoir of her husband, which reads: 'We all felt anxious about the strain on his health in spring of 1853,' as well as by the fact that it was at this time that his mother most urgently pressed her brother Peter Gansevoort, an Albany lawyer, to exert himself ('hoping that you will lose no time, as every day counts') in enlisting the support of influential friends, most of whom were lawyers, in procuring from President Pierce, Hawthorne's old friend, a consulship abroad for her son Herman. In short, what little evidence we have points to the conclusion that the writing of the Agatha story was attended by another—the last—outburst of Melville's existential daemon. Fitting this conclusion, as hand in glove, is the nature of Melville's material, the series of actual events and situations which awakened 'the most lively interest' in him and kindled his creative imagination. In other words, the history of the repeated desertions of the forbearing, patient, and permissive Agatha of Pembroke, Massachusetts, by her errant and erratic sailor-husband, combined with his two bigamous marriages, the second with Agatha's virtual consent—all this provided Melville with a compelling skeleton for one more last story of 'the intrepid effort of the soul' to break through her imprisoning wall and attain 'the open independence of her sea.' Among other things, Melville called Hawthorne's attention to the facility with which Robertson had first left his wife and then taken another one. Evidently the 'sense of the obligation of the marriage-vow to Agatha had little weight with him at first,' a moral condition which the former seaman Melville attributed to the likelihood that Robertson in his previous sailor life 'had found a wife (for a night) in every port.' Not until he had spent some years ashore did Robertson experience enough remorse to act on it to some extent. But I surmise, in agreement with Leon Howard, that what particularly appealed to Melville as something of profound significance was the wholly feminine, 'angelic' nature of Agatha, very similar to that of Pierre's selflessly devoted Lucy. As the New Bedford lawyer expressed it, it was Agatha's 'long continued & uncomplaining submission to wrong and anguish' which 'made her in his eyes a heroine.' This is about all I have to offer that is calculated not only to buttress the biographer's notion that the wall is Melville's marriage vow in the eyes of God and of the Law, but also to account for the author's excessive agitation in the spring of 1853."

THE FIRST CRITIC. "That's off the target of our main objective here. I've been paying attention to you all this time because I thought you were going to elucidate the passage about the Dead Letter Office in the sequel to 'Bartleby.' "

THE SECOND CRITIC. "Yes, to be sure. I'm glad you reminded me. My thesis is simply this: that since a 'new work' by Melville—and what could it be but the story of Agatha?—was said by his mother to be 'nearly ready for the press' on April 20th, 1853, and since no such story was ever published or found in manuscript form, the chances are it was destroyed, probably burnt by Melville himself in a moment of self-negating desperation. In any event, the melancholy fact that this product of a long winter of creative toil never reached a single reader is quite comparable to the fate of the dead letters which were assorted for the flames by Bartleby during his previous employment. Without stretching credulity too much we can imagine that the dead Agatha manuscript contained 'hope for those who died unhoping; good tidings for those who died stifled by unrelieved calamities.' My thesis ends here with the death of the two prime hopes of Melville's soul: the hope of embracing another love (represented by Isabel in *Pierre*) and the hope of writing another spirit-driven book. These two defeats account for the pallid hopelessness of Bartleby, the silent copyist."

THE BIOGRAPHER. "Not bad. And now, to return for a moment to the question of how much of the 1853 Melville is represented in the figure of Bartleby, I would like to remind you of a few more correspondences besides the three just mentioned and the six I listed earlier. Melville and Bartleby are similar insofar as both write all day long and, being seldom in the sunlight, Melville must have been nearly as pallid as his scrivener. It was thought that Bartleby had over-strained his eyes and impaired his vision much as Melville had; and both are unusually silent. In a letter to George Duyckinck, Mrs. Morewood reports that Melville, engaged in writing *Pierre*, frequently does not 'leave his room till quite dark in the evening—when he for the first time during the day partakes of solid food'; and the attorney tells us that Bartleby, 'ran a day and night line, copying by sun-light and by candle-light.' The much-traveled cosmopolitan, Maunsell B. Field, wrote of a drive with Darley in 1855 to see Melville 'whom I had always known as the most silent man of my acquaintance'; but later, when joined by Oliver Wendell Holmes, this most silent man opened up and became engaged in a discussion with the doctor 'which was conducted with the most amazing skill and brilliancy on both sides. . . . I never chanced to hear better talking in my life.' This shows that the always-silent Bartleby is no more than one aspect of Melville. A few convivial friends gathered in New York could count on a 'good stirring evening' whenever Melville arrived 'fresh from his mountain' in the Berkshires and 'charged to the muzzle with his sailor metaphysics and jargon of things unknowable,' as Evert Duyckinck, with his two-dimensional gentility of mind, characterized the abundance of his friend's thought. This gives us an enormous major difference and thirteen minor similarities between Melville and his scrivener. Finally, one more item that bears on the hypothesis that Bartleby-Melville is a copyist of Hawthorne, namely, the fact that initially Melville offered the Agatha material to his friend on the ground 'that this thing lies very much in a vein, with which you are peculiarly familiar . . . the thing seems naturally to gravitate towards you.' Having said to him, 'I think that in this matter you would make a better hand at it than I would,' the chances are that, when Hawthorne decided not to accept his offer, Melville carried out his treatment of the narrative with Hawthorne's vein and style prominently in mind, a step or transition, one might say, toward the Hawthornesque symbolism of his later short stories. But even when all this is said and done, the character of Bartleby remains a riddle."

THE PSYCHOLOGIST. "I have often been asked in what psychological or psychiatric category Bartleby belongs and I always answer that there is none made for him. Bartleby is unprecedented, an invention of Melville's creative spirit, the author's gift to psychology, a mythic figure who deserves a category in his own name. I see the scrivener as a composite of several very human dispositions, the first of which is silence, the refusal to speak; and here I could tell you of numerous cases of children as well as adults who, feeling insulted by something that was said to them by a parent or relative, vowed, in a vengeful spirit, never to speak to that person again, and some of these have stubbornly adhered to their vow for many years. But in such cases the verbal ostracism is specific; in Bartleby it is general, with occasional lapses as seen in patients with catatonic schizophrenia. Bartleby's absence of initiative, the immobility accompanying his wall reveries, is often indicative of an inhibiting dread of punishment or guilt, engendered by a surplus of pent-up hostility. It is related to the abulia one finds in some cases of obsessional neurosis and to the paralysis of will associated with severe depressions. The most accentuated of Bartleby's dispositions is an unswerving negativism which could be interpreted as a regression to the phase of normal development that commonly occurs in the latter half of the second year of life. The nay-saying characteristic of this stage marks the child's initial efforts to attain autonomy and self-sufficiency. Bartleby's refusal of food is indicative of regression to an even earlier stage, illustrated by those resentful and distrustful babies who pucker up their tightly closed lips when offered the bottle after being accustomed to the breast, I wouldn't put it beyond Melville—who had a 4-month-old daughter at the time—to have derived the name of Bartleby from bottle or bottle baby. Finally, let us note, that Melville had the scrivener end his life with his body huddled in the embryonic position at the base of the prison wall, with 'his head touching the cold stones,' which suggests a web of too many additional ideas for this symposium. That will do as a 5-cent sketch of what I have in mind on this topic. I will end by crediting Mr. Melville with the discovery of the Bartleby complex."

THE AUTHOR. "Is this meant to be a compliment? a prize for my remaining silent and unobtrusive throughout the length of your dissection of my heart and head? No ill-will; but I've had about as much as I can take today of that line of talk. Let's have some brandy and cigars, and reason of Providence and futurity."

I, THE COMMENTATOR. "All right, gentlemen, the meeting is adjourned. This fantasy has ended. All these I's, as I foretold you, were spirits, and are 'melted into air, into thin air.' They were 'such stuff as dreams are made on,' and now the time has come to rub our eyes, get up, and face the world of embodied actualities."

20

DEAD TO THE WORLD: THE PASSIONS OF HERMAN MELVILLE

This being the very first of the planned series of scientific lectures under these auspices, you have every reason to expect positive reinforcement of your locomotions to this place by hearing some authoritative intellectual news about suicide or its prevention. And so I start with fear and trembling lest the confidence you surely have in the judgment of the president of the Suicide Prevention Foundation be somewhat shaken by your encountering on this platform a nonauthority with a far-fetched title and subtitle, neither of which have any apparent relevance to the substance of your shared interests. For this, Dr. Shneidman is initially to blame, since it was he who, at an unenlightened moment a year and a half ago, invited me to address you on this occasion. I would attribute the invitation to his preternatural trust in the potentialities of his friends, which very occasionally inclines him to an act of folly—coupled with my inability to say No with a bang, or even with a whimper, when it comes to a request from him.

Fearing that you, being entirely unaware of its creative consequences, might focus on Dr. Shneidman's act of folly and hold it up against him, I have been prompted to preface this lecture with a very short true story, a kind of informative and inspiring parable, which will prove to you that your confidence in Dr. Shneidman's wisdom should be higher, rather than lower, than it has been. The moral of the parable can be expressed in a variety of ways. La Rochefoucauld's maxim that "a man who lives without folly is not so wise as he thinks" is pertinent but a little off-center. Closer to the gist of the matter would be: worthy of admiration is the man who can transmute the lead of folly into the gold of unexampled wisdom. You may choose your own wording after you have heard the story which begins more than a year ago at the moment that it dawned on Dr. Shneidman that for the opening lecture of this series

From E. S. Shneidman, Ed., *Essays in Self-destruction.* New York: Science House, 1967, pp. 7–29. This paper, in slightly modified form, was originally delivered by Dr. Murray at Bovard Auditorium, University of Southern California, October 6, 1963, as a Special Lecture sponsored jointly by the University and by the Los Angeles Suicide Prevention Center. On that occasion, Dr. Murray was introduced by his old friend, the late Dr. Franz Alexander.

he was saddled with a speaker whose scientific knowledge of suicide was confined to the writings of the staff of the Suicide Prevention Center. He saw the absurdity of my crossing the continent to bring honey to the very beehive from which it was extracted, and he saw me as entangled in a double bind from which I could neither withdraw with honor nor emerge with credit; and I even suspect that compassion, a professional compassion, was aroused in him by viewing me as a potential suicide, that is, as heading toward a suicide of whatever reputation I may laboriously have gained for talking out of knowledge more than out of ignorance. Faced by this predicament what do you think my dear old friend decided he should do? What would you have done? Nothing, I would wager, so unprecedented and so uniquely creative as *his* solution of the problem, which was to sit down and write, especially for my benefit, a substantial and exciting paper entitled "Orientations Toward Death,"[1] which consisted of two major parts, in each of which I was presented with an open route out of my dilemma.

In the first part Dr. Shneidman expanded the whole realm of the Foundation's concern by including a variety of phenomena whose relation or similarity to suicide or to a suicidal tendency had heretofore been overlooked, and, by so doing virtually permitted me to follow suit and choose as a topic certain other states, also analogous in some respects to suicide, which I am subsuming under my main title "Dead to the World." And then Dr. Shneidman, as if doubtful of my readiness to seize the suggestions he had proffered, wrote a terminal part to his paper which he called "An Example of an Equivocal Death." In this essay he invaded a region in which I had proprietary rights and provided the missing keystone to the arch which I had started a dozen years ago in the name of an old satanic friend of mine, the immortal Captain Ahab. Here he was saying in effect: "You see I am showing you, in case you can think of nothing else to talk about, that Herman Melville would be an acceptable topic to your patrons in Los Angeles." This explains my subtitle. In short, the timely publication of Dr. Shneidman's paper in two parts provided me with a frame reference for a lecture to be delivered here; and if you are not impressed by the creative intelligence and generosity involved in this resourceful act of his, you are not deserving of so great a president. So much for my preamble, a parable that may be more instructive than anything to come.

In the paper I have mentioned, "Orientations Toward Death," Dr. Shneidman stressed the importance of distinguishing between the wish for a permanent cessation of conscious life (a veritable suicide) and a wish for temporary cessation (or interruption) of conscious life. He pointed out that some people who have killed themselves and some who appear to have intended but failed to kill themselves did not actually commit suicide or attempt suicide, because in neither case did they deliberately intend an absolute termination of their lives. Their intention was no more than an urgently felt necessity to stop unbearable anguish, that is, to obtain relief by interrupting for a while the stream of suffering. In view of the existence of this motivational state, Dr. Shneidman suggested that attention to other forms of interruption, such as sleep, might provide "fresh leads and new insights into suicidal behavior." Aha! I said to myself at this point, if sleep would be a suitable topic for a talk at the Suicide Prevention Center, or SPC for short, why not some other related condition, such as a temporary or permanent cessation of a part of psychic life —the cessation of affect (feeling almost dead), for example—or the cessation of an orientation of conscious life—the cessation of social life (dead to the outer world) or of spiritual life (dead to the inner world), for example—or, instead of restricting oneself to two concepts—cessation (to stand for no life at all) and continuation (to stand for ongoing living processes)—it might be well to take account of different degrees and of changes of degrees of life—near-cessation (as good as dead) or a trend toward cessation (diminution).

When I chose the phrase "dead to the world," I was thinking of a variety of somewhat similar psychic states characterized by a marked diminution or near-cessation of affect involving both hemispheres of concern, the inner and the outer world. Here it is as if the person's primal springs of vitality had dried up, as if he were empty or hollow at the very core of his being. There is a striking absence of anything but the most perfunctory and superficial social interactions; output as well as intake is at a minimum. The person is a nonconductor. To him the human species is wholly uninviting and unlovable, a monotonous round of unnecessary duplicates; and since everything he sees and every alternative opportunity for action seems equally valueless and meaningless, he has no basis for any choice. In fact, to make even a small decision and to execute it calls for an exhausting effort. Sometimes, he unresistingly and automatically falls in with somebody else's decision; but he is more likely to respond to suggestions with a blanket No, keeping his thoughts hidden from others behind a deaf-and-dumb reserve, the impenetrable wall of a self-made prison.

I was thinking particularly of Melville's forty-year withdrawal from his society—the "Great Refusal" as Weaver called it[2]—and of a patient of mine who resembled Melville in this respect but whose cessation of affect was more total, suffering as he was from what we used to call the "feeling of unreality." His sensations and perceptions of nature and of people he encountered were unusually acute and vivid, but he did not experience other persons as animate beings: they resembled puppets, automatons, mechanical contrivances without any feelings or desires to which anyone could appeal. He saw eyes that were as bright as the glass eyes of a manufactured doll, but he received no intimations of a soul, or consciousness, behind these eyes. Primitive people and children spontaneously animate the inanimate—see a man in the moon who follows them on their walks, as Piaget has described; but here was a man who reversed the process; he inanimated the animate. All empathy was dead in him; he was inert as a stone, unmoved by any of the events or confrontations which moved others.

Then I thought of *The Stranger,* that landmark book by Camus in which the psychic condition of a man who is untouched by his mother's death is hauntingly portrayed. This condition of affectlessness—which has been expertly analyzed by Nathan Leites[3]—was almost immediately recognized as representative for our time, representative at least of the root mood of an articulate depth-sensitive minority, the Ishmaels of today. This brought to mind scores of other modern authors of whose views of the contemporary world Melville's writings were prophetic; their obsession with darkness, death, and leanings toward self-destruction epitomized in Malraux's affirmation: man is dead. But none of these seemed quite so revealing as Meursault, the nonhero of *The Stranger,* whose outburst of antitheistic rage near the end of the story showed that a volcano of resentful passion had been simmering all along beneath that crust of emotional inertia. What had once looked like an apathetic indifference to the surrounding world, an all-pervasive ennui, could now be more dynamically understood as an alternative to murder, namely ostracism of mankind contrived by an unforgiving heart that had been turned to stone by experiencing an intolerable offense.

At this point what psychoanalyst could resist coming forth with a battery of concepts to explain it all?—say, as nothing but a perseveration of the child's global reaction to his mother at a time when she quite literally constituted the child's whole known world and its culture. In the case of Camus as well as of Melville, for example, there is evidence that a virtually deaf-and-dumb, ostracising mother generated resentment in the child which was followed by a reciprocal, retaliative withdrawal. A conventional psychoanalyst would be likely to assume, if he were confronted by a patient in whom this state of being had persisted into adulthood, that it was his office to get his patient to look homeward, and like an angel melt with ruth. Once having reconciled himself to either his mother or his father, as the case might be, the patient would more readily become reconciled to the culture in which he was imbedded and less reluctantly adjust to it. But if the culture—society and its churches —was actually inimical to the realization of the fullest potentialities of an individual's personal life, as Melville and Camus believed it to be, the question is, should a man who saw the culture as the Enemy be persuaded by the implications of a seductive professional technique to throw in his sponge and surrender to it?

I have been talking about a diminution or cessation of feeling, one component of consciousness, on the assumption that this condition is somewhat analogous to a cessation of the whole of consciousness. If the cessation of feeling is temporary it resembles sleep; if it is permanent (a virtual atrophy of emotional life) it resembles death, the condition of the brain and body after the home fires of metabolism in the cortex have gone out. In a feelingless state the home fires are still burning but without glow or warmth. The implication here is that an intensive, detailed study of affective states in connection with suicidal phenomena should be fruitful in "fresh leads and new insights." This seems too obvious to require mention. For what is suicide in most instances but an action to interrupt or put an end to intolerable affects? But do we know all we need to know about the nature of intolerable affects? Is there not more to learn about the different varieties of feelings, combinations of feelings, and temporal sequences of feelings which are conducive to suicide on the one hand or, on the other hand, make suicide unthinkable?

As one standing-stone for my proposal let me quote from William James, whose books and letters abound in all sorts of uncommon common sense. "Individuality," he affirms, "is founded in feeling; and the recesses of feeling, the darker, blinder strata of character, are the only places in the world in which we catch real fact in the making, and directly perceive how events happen and how work is actually done."[4] Not very long after the avowal of this judgment, John B. Watson's swift invasion and conquest of a good deal more than half of the terrain of American academic psychology committed James to such an outcast state that one leading physiological psychologist announced—to the President of Harvard, of all people—that Professor James had done more harm to psychology than any man who had ever lived. But there are indications that the exile of James and of feelings as phenomena worthy of investigation was only temporary. They have recently named the Cambridge habitat of the behavioral sciences William James Hall, and throughout the country there have been an increasing number of studies of those negative affects —anxiety, anger, resentment, and guilt—whose vicissitudes and dynamics were revealed to us by Freud and his successors, Dr. Franz Alexander for one. And now, to do justice to some of the feelings and emotions omitted by psychoanalysis, we have the prospect of the completion in the near future of the intricate three-volume work by Silvan S. Tomkins, *Affect, Imagery, Consciousness.*[5] Besides, there is burgeoning in this country, as an antithetical reaction to strict behaviorism, an enthusiastic though still amorphous aggregate of phenomenological, existential, and humanistic psychologists who question the assumption that evolutionary processes fashioned human nature for the special advantage of technocratic behaviorists of this century, setting forth all its most important determinants on the surface and leaving nothing of any consequence inside. In short, a concentrated study of affects in relation to suicidal inclinations would have a sufficient array of facts and theories to start with and should break new ground, provided the investigators were prepared to make much finer distinctions than current terminology, or even the English language, permits, envisaging as an ideal, let us say, the power of an Indian (Hindu) language to differentiate, as we learn from Coomaraswamy, "three hundred and sixty kinds of the fine emotions of a lover's heart."[6]

We might start by asking what gross affects familiar to us all have been found to be associated with suicide? The results of one research will be sufficient for my present purpose. In a systematic statistical study of the case histories of neuropsychiatric male patients at Veterans Hospitals, of which 220 had committed suicide and 220 had not committed suicide, Farberow, Shneidman, and Neuringer found that the suicides were characterized by (1) more crying spells, (2) more fist fights and violent episodes, (3) more severe depressions, and (4) more periods of withdrawal and mutism. Furthermore (5) they escaped from the hospital more often.[7]

Of these SPC categories, the fourth—withdrawal and mutism—(best exemplified, perhaps, by a schizophrenic catatonic state) is evidently the closest to the concept of "dead to the world" as defined earlier, a correspondence that gives me sufficient provisional ground for the surmise that manifest affectlessness constitutes not only a partial interruption or cessation of social life but also a condition which predisposes its victim or initiator, as the case may be, eventually to terminate his life. With this hypothesis in mind, we might be well advised to look for whatever dynamic relationships may subsist between manifest affectlessness, or "dead to the world," and each of the other affective states that were found to be correlated with an intentioned suicide. What was the temporal sequence of these various emotional conditions and acts in each of the 220 cases? In ordinary life the order of experienced affects depends to a large extent on the unpredictable vagaries of fortune—the occurrence of events entirely outside a person's control, the kinds of situations he happens to encounter, whether because of good or bad luck he succeeds or fails in this and that endeavor, how he is treated by others, and so forth. But since a hospital environment is likely to be relatively stable and since the affects of a neuropsychiatric patient are more apt to be determined by his internal rather than by his external environment, it is possible that regularities would be found among short (micro) or longer (meso) processions of emotion in each subject, or in each type of subject, or even in the majority of subjects. A micro temporal study would be one in which expressions of emotion were recorded consecutively from moment to moment or from occasion to occasion; whereas a meso temporal study would concern itself only with the more striking changes that occur from day to day. A patient's entire stay in the hospital might be said to constitute a macro temporal unit. Since affects do not occur in vacuo but always in relation to an internal or an external confrontation (or *press*), or to a mixture of the two, an investigation of this sort would call for recordings of both aspects of each interior emotional transaction.

Now, in connection with this idea that very detailed studies be made

(first in a hospital setting and then in other settings) of the sequence of
affective states during free associations on certain selected or unselected
topics, as given by people who are suspected of entertaining suicidal
inclinations, it occurred to me that a roughly analogous study might be
made of micro, meso, and macro cycles of affective transactions in the
works of certain Romantic authors, authors whose credo encourages
them to give vent in apt and telling words to emotions of all sorts. I need
not tell you the name of my first choice among eligible authors. A comprehensive study of this sort would be a prodigious undertaking and even
a condensed report of the findings would take at least an hour to read.
So I decided on a crude macro survey of Melville's whole works and a
few micro analyses, restricting myself to the four negative affects and the
one action which the SPC had found to be correlated with suicide in
neuropsychiatric subjects—crying spells, fist fights and violent episodes,
depressions, withdrawal and mutism, and leaving the hospital. Out of
this, of course, came a very distorted impression of the range of feelings
in Melville's writings as well as in his personality, for in the early phases
of his career as an author he was a veritable hive of spontaneous positive
emotions—zest, mirth, affection, joy, admiration, and compassion. After
about three years of exuberant authorship, however, these brighter and
for him lighter states of being were invaded and submerged by a tide of
negative affects, roughly of the nature of those mentioned by the SPC.
Finer differentiations of the negative affects described in Melville's writings were not made, since my aim was to come out with categories which
seemed to correspond to those which the SPC had found to be correlated
with suicide in males.

The order of the negative (distressful, hostile, desperate, joyless)
emotional states which I found most characteristic in micro, meso, and
macro analyses of Melville's works is generally as follows:

1. *Pitiful forlornness, deprivation, distress, and grief* (which I am
taking as the nearest equivalent of the SPC's *crying spells* and maybe of
one form of the SPC's *depression*). The expressive prototype of pitiful
forlornness is the cry of the child at birth, forcefully expelled from its
comfortable habitation, and later, in its helpless state, when it is momentarily alone and hence deprived of what it hungers for: contact, food, and
love. In one way or another it is saying: "Poor me, I am suffering and
nobody I care for cares for me." Then as well as later the implication is
that the world (the mother, the beloved one, whoever "counts") is indifferent, cold, and heartless or that the one who counts is absent, dead, or
unattainable. Here we may be reminded of Shakespeare's "I all alone
beweep my outcast state. And trouble deaf heaven with my bootless
cries"; of Whitehead's "God the Void"; of Rilke's "Who, if I cried, would
hear me among the angelic orders"; and of Keats's sonnet to Fannie
Brawne, "I cry your mercy—pity—love! . . . in pity give me all, Withhold
no atom's atom or I die." Descriptions of various degrees of this affective

state are conspicuous throughout Melville's writings from the very first paragraph of his first book, *Typee,* to the last page of his posthumous *Billy Budd.*

Grief deserves a separate category; but for present purposes I am regarding it as an accentuation, deepening, and prolongation of deprivation (lack or loss) distress. It belongs to the family of depressed states which includes melancholy, that essential component of Romanticism dating from Rousseau, the "apostle of adversity," who, by way of Byron's poetry, had a lasting effect on Melville, which began in his adolescence. Melville distinguished a gradation of feelings running from pensiveness "whence comes sadness" (both of which were associated in him with more pleasantness than unpleasantness) through several degrees of melancholy and sorrow to the "far profounder gloom" of grief, or woe. Melville, who had been "rubbed, curried, and ground down to fine powder in the hopper of an evil fortune," firmly believed that "that mortal man who hath more of joy than sorrow in him, that mortal man cannot be true—not true, or undeveloped. With books the same. The truest of all men was the Man of Sorrows, and the truest of all books is Solomon's, and Ecclesiastes is the fine hammered steel of woe." Note that in this sentence Melville links Jesus, whose mission was to bring glad tidings of life after death, with the unchristian prophet-author (not Solomon as Melville assumed) of Ecclesiastes, who affirmed that belief in immortality is vain—"all is vanity." This opposition of dissonant figures, both venerated by Melville, manifests the force of his conviction that "there is a wisdom that is woe," and is made possible only by the image of Jesus, as the Man of Sorrows, hanging on the cross, the woeful worldly outcome of his unworldly wisdom. Even the atheistical "moody stricken Ahab" is described as standing before the officers of the *Pequod* "with a crucifixion in his face; in all the nameless regal overbearing dignity of some mighty woe." Generally speaking, woe is apperceived as sufficient justification for almost any form of conduct. In Ahab's case, however, we are warned that *his* woe is not the woe that is wisdom but the "woe that is madness." The woe that is madness takes us to my next category.

I have put the present category—which embraces a series of states running from a mild pitiful forlornness to a profoundly depressing sorrow —first in order, because in Melville's works sequences of expressed negative emotions most commonly start with affects of this nature. Characteristic is his description in *Redburn* of his melancholy mood when as a boy he left home for his first sea voyage. Perhaps his mother, he tells us,

thought me an erring and wilful boy, and perhaps I was; but if I was, it had been a hard-hearted world and hard times that had made me so . . . Cold, bitter cold as December, and bleak as its blasts, seemed the world then to me; there is no misanthrope like a boy disappointed; and such was I, with the warm soul of me flogged out by adversity.

But this same class of affects, as we shall see, is also prominent at the end of Melville's major books, indeed at the end of all tragic narratives. It includes the determinants of Aristotle's pity, the pity that is excited in a spectator's heart in the last act of a dramatic tragedy, a passion that may be intensified if the defeated hero gives vent to a heart-searing expression of his anguish, such as Mark Antony's "I am dying, Egypt, dying," and Christ's "My God, why hast thou forsaken me?"

2. *Extrapunitiveness* (blaming others), *anger, hate,* and *physical aggressiveness* (which is my nearest equivalent to the SPC's *fist fights and violent episodes*). This is a category that embraces the affects, words, and acts which in Melville's writings are most likely to follow, or even accompany, the cluster of feelings just described. The prototype of this fusion would be a child at birth or a very hungry child whose cries are more suggestive of an angry protest or furious complaint than they are of piteous helplessness. The transition from the first category to this, my second category, that is, from a forlorn "poor me" reaction to a howling rage, can be nicely illustrated by the opposition of two excerpts from Melville's works. The first comes from the opening paragraph of *Typee*, the very first lines that Melville ever penned and published in book form:

Six months at sea! Yes, reader, as I live, six months out of sight of land; . . . Weeks and weeks ago our fresh provisions were all exhausted. There is not a sweet potato left; not a single yam. Those glorious bunches of bananas which once decorated our stern and quarter-deck have, alas, disappeared! and the delicious oranges which hung suspended from our tops and stays—they, too, are gone!

After going on in this vein for two more pages, Melville tells us that the course of the "land-sick ship" has at last been shaped to the Marquesas. "Hurrah! . . . the Marquesas . . . Naked houris—cannibal banquets— groves of cocoa-nuts," and so forth. Now he is like a hungry but trustful child who is rendered patient by the confident prospect of close contact with the nurturant mother in the near future—a lovely houri and a cannibal banquet. But in one second a child's mood can change from this state of being into one of fierce intolerance, as is metaphorically represented in an excerpt from *Mardi* in which the author celebrates ecstasies of grief-rage as source of the greatest creativity:

He knows himself, and all that's in him, who knows adversity. To scale great heights we must come out of lowermost depths. The way to heaven is through hell . . . Howl in sackcloth and in ashes! . . . The lines that live are turned out of a furrowed brow. Oh! there is a fierce, a cannibal delight, in the grief that shrieks to multiply itself. That grief . . . pities all the happy.

When we come to *Moby-Dick*, the whole tragic conception of which was born out of a "furrowed brow," we find that the grief-rage which made its first appearance in *Mardi* (described in words that would be fitting for a hungry child momentarily howling for its absent mother) has become a consolidated, all-pervasive tragic state coupled with a dedicated, vengeful hatred that is ruling the personality of the proud, satanic Captain Ahab, for whom all evil, we are told, was:

visibly personified, and made practically assailable in Moby-Dick. He piled upon the whale's white hump the sum of all the general rage and hate felt by his whole race from Adam down; and then, as if his chest had been a mortar, he burst his hot heart's shell upon it.

Here is the essence of my second category carried by Ahab to an extravagant and irrational degree. The occurrence of such an intense, all-embracing, global emotion (not appropriate, as Starbuck pointed out, to the realities of the existing circumstance) is evidence of its origin in infancy when first the mother and then the mother and the father actually constituted their son's entire world and the apparent determinants of his fate. The same can be said of Ahab's antecedent state of mind, the consuming morbid grief which bred and seemed to justify his rage.

Considering the unparalleled abundance of oral imagery throughout Melville's works, his reference to Adam in the excerpt just quoted from *Moby-Dick* is consonant with the possibility that the boy-hero's first consequential trauma was that of weaning (at the age of twelve months) or its equivalent, a virtual expulsion from the paradise of his mother's embracing arms, up until then monopolized, this deprivation being dynamically related to an impatient, howling impulse to bite his mother's proffered apple-breast and eat of it with "cannibal delight." This hypothesis is supported by our knowledge that Herman had three teeth at the unusually early age of three months. What Melville described as "the half-wilful over-ruling morbidness at the bottom of his nature," I would attribute to this earliest of deprivations subsequently reinforced, time and time again, by his mother's all-too-obvious preference for his more promising older brother, her first-born child, and by her own seasons of unresponsive moody melancholy. "She hated me," Melville said in his old age. This is but a fragment of the evidence I have to offer to support the thesis that Melville was beset in his deeps by matricidal as well as parricidal inclinations and that the white whale upon which Ahab has been prompted to "burst his hot heart's shell" embodies the rejecting mother and the world she stands for, as well as the punishing father and the God *he* stands for, all of these being powerful and imperative components of the author's imprisoning conscience, or superego.

In view of the form of injury to which Ahab is reacting with such fury —the white whale's oral amputation of his leg—every good Freudian, I surmise, would identify the whale with the child's mythological images of the castrating father, generated by a terror of this punishment for incestuously possessing the beloved mother in his dreams. Since Herman Melville enjoyed and suffered from the most patent and protracted (overt as well as covert) Oedipus complex I have ever encountered in print or practice; and since his works, especially *Mardi*, are studied with castration imagery, I have no hesitation in agreeing with this orthodox formula, despite the fact that to me its ritualistic repetition in every case, however vaporous the evidence, has become almost unbearably banal. It happens that there is a remarkably close correspondence between psychoanalytic theories and the dynamic forms of Melville's imagination, almost as if Freud had had this amazing writer constantly in mind during the composition of his theoretical system. Nearly everything essential to the system is amply illustrated in Melville's life and works; and, further-more, it is apparent that in many instances Melville was conscious or half-conscious of the import, in a psychoanalytic sense, of what he was communicating.

As roots of the explosive fury which Melville eloquently expressed in a sublimated form while composing *Moby-Dick*, I have mentioned only the matricidal and parricidal dispositions of infancy, the overt actuation of which in any recognizable form was inhibited for many years, we can be certain, by the dread of losing love from a parent on whose affection the boy's security and happiness depended. There is evidence at hand which indicates that little Herman's inward development con-formed in most respects to Freud's conception of the usual sequence of events: the ambivalent (loved and hated) father served as a model for the development of a personified conscience which in its early stages was as punitive as the God of Calvinism. This brings us to my third category.

3. *Intrapunitiveness, remorse, guilt, depression, bad conscience,* and *need for punishment* (my nearest equivalent to the SPC's *depression*). This refers to any kind or degree of self-punishment subsequent to the actual or imaginal execution of a forbidden act. If a child has a nightmar-ish dream of being pursued, attacked, overpowered, or injured by a furious creature of some sort, man or beast, this is susceptible of various interpretations. But only one of these possible interpretations is relevant to the category I am discussing here, namely, the one which states that these assaults are guilt-bred imaginations of punishments coming at the termination of a dream, the first repressed strip of which portrayed the commitment of a forbidden act. In contrast to concealments of this na-ture, we are offered in the allegorical *Mardi* for the first time in Melville's writing the vivid spectacle of a crime perpetrated by the hero: the murder of a warlike old priest who was guarding a tent in which a beautiful maiden was held captive. Knowing that his father's name was Allan Melville, we prick up our ears first when the author refers to the priest as Old Aaron and then again when he tells us that his actual name is Aleema. The hero justifies his killing and his escaping with the maiden in his arms by saying that since Aleema was wickedly intending to sac-

rifice her to the gods, his own act was the virtuous one of "rescuing a captive from thrall." But then, suspecting his real motive, he is smitten with remorse, and for the rest of his journey among the islands of Mardi, he is pursued by the avenging furies in the persons of three sons of the old priest (Melville's three brothers?). I would suppose that this oedipal fantasy was derived from an early season of childhood near the onset of a period of tormenting conflict between an extraggressive instinct (category 2) and an intraggressive father figure (category 3). Evidently, this civil war within the boy's psyche was at least partially resolved by a change in the apperception and evaluation of the internalized father figure: God the enemy became God the friend. We gather that at seven years of age Herman was his devoted father's most "beloved son," a boy with "a docile and amiable disposition" who soon decided to follow in his parent's footsteps and become a merchant. We are told in the autobiographical *Pierre* that after his father's death when he was twelve, the author-hero was sustained in the conduct of his adolescent life by an exalted image of his departed sire enshrined in his soul's innermost retreat. "Not to God had Pierre ever gone in his heart, unless by ascending the steps of that shrine, and so making it the vestibule of his abstractest religion."

Here we have a striking example of the loving deification of a once partly hated father figure. In this instance it was chiefly as the immaculate exemplification of chastity and purity, a figure "without blemish, unclouded, snow-white, and serene," that the father of the author-hero of *Pierre* was raised to the status of a Christian saint. Here the important point is that by this conversion of feeling, the once ambivalent father figure became wholly univalent; and the conflict between instinct and conscience was brought to an end, because from then on, it would not be the boy's fear of punishment that would dictate his renunciation of instinct ("conscience doth make cowards of us all") so much as his ambitious resolution to be as perfect as his father. The dependence of the eighteen-year-old Pierre Glendinning (and of his creator, I am sure) on an unsullied image of his parent is sufficient explanation of the tumult Pierre experiences when he learns of the existence of an illegitimate sister, a premarital by-blow of his supposedly chaste father. Thus suddenly bereft of an exemplar to support the edifice of his character and give meaning to his life, Pierre feels that he has been deserted, struck down in a flowering season of his youth by father, Fate, and God, and his first reaction is one of utter desolation (category 1). And then Melville, announcing that a vigorous young man is "not made to succumb to the villain Woe," has his hero rise from the chair in which he has been sitting alone in his room, and murmur to the unhearing All:

"Myself am left, at least, With myself I front thee! Unhand me all fears . . . Fate, I have a choice quarrel with thee, thou art a palterer and a cheat; thou hast lured

me on through gay gardens to a gulf . . . I will be a raver, and none shall stay me!
I will lift my hand in fury, for am I not struck? I will be bitter in my breath, for
is not this cup of gall? . . . all piety leave me;—I will be impious, for piety hath
juggled me, and taught me to revere, where I should spurn. . . ." [category 2]

To understand the magnitude of this reaction we need, once again,
Freud's concept of "the return of repressed," in this case, the first explosive return in actual life of the long-submerged hatred whose genesis and
history in Melville I have already briefly traced in connection with its
second (more sublimated) return fourteen years later while writing
Moby-Dick. But, in addition to all this, it is important to recognize that
the collapse of young Melville's unifying, personified ideal resulted in a
diastrous regression to that state of obsessional conflict (categories 2 and
3) from which he had previously emerged and from which he would
never extricate himself completely. Thenceforth his self would be divided as Captain Ahab's body was divided by the livid scar which ran
down his skin from the top of his head. That Melville attributed the
genesis of this condition to the just-mentioned stunning disillusionment
of worship described in *Pierre*, and that his potent father, Fate, and God
were furiously blamed for inflicting it on him is indicated in the chapter
entitled "The Candles," where the hero Ahab, addressing the tripointed
trinity of flames in a tone reminiscent of the hero Pierre, exclaims:

"Oh! thou clear spirit of clear fire, whom on these seas I as Persian once did
worship, till in the sacramental act so burned by thee, that to this hour I bear the
scar; I now know thee, thou clear spirit, and I now know that thy right worship
is defiance . . . No fearless fool now fronts thee . . . Come in thy lowest form of
love, and I will kneel and kiss thee; but at thy highest, come as mere supernal
power; and though thou launchest navies of full-freighted worlds, there's that in
here that still remains indifferent. Oh, thou clear spirit, of thy fire thou madest
me, and like a child of fire, I breathe it back to thee . . . But thou art but my fiery
father; my sweet mother, I know not. Oh, cruel! what has thou done with her?"
[category 2]

So far I seem to have presented a superfluity of utterances illustrative of the return of Melville's long-repressed rage and extraggression
(category 2) and a paucity of examples of the intraggressive superego
forces that for years succeeded in repressing them (category 3). This
disproportion of space devoted to the two warring sides of our author's
divided self has been dictated by the fact that up to this point in Melville's
writings the extraverted forces have been vociferous and eloquent and
the intraverted forces relatively silent; and this being the case, demon-
strations of the potency of what was previously repressed provide us with
the best available measure of the strength of the united body of punishing repressors, symbolized by the unconquerable white whale. Later on
in *Pierre* there are numerous avowals of the anguish of guilt, and it

becomes apparent that Ahab's moody melancholy had been a depressing combination of grief (category 1) and a bad conscience (category 3). But in *Moby-Dick* and earlier, perhaps our best indication of the power of the compound of intraggressive forces in Melville's personality is the fact that all the really critical extraggressive intentions of his heroes are, as Shneidman made plain in Ahab's case,[8] patently suicidal or sacrificial. In other words, the idea of being killed is invariably linked with that of killing from the very outset, as when Melville says in *White Jacket* that "The privilege, inborn and inalienable, that every man has, of dying himself, and inflicting death upon another, was not given to us without a purpose. These are the last resources of an insulted and unendurable existence."

Characteristic transitions from one category to another are succinctly condensed in the famous opening paragraph of *Moby-Dick*. (*a*) Categories 1 and 2 (deprivation distress leading to grief-rage): "Call me Ishmael" ("whose splintered heart and maddened hand," Melville tells us, "were turned against the wolfish world"). (*b*) Category 3 (guilt, depression, need for punishment): "Whenever I find myself growing grim about the mouth; whenever it is a damp, drizzly November in my soul; whenever I find myself involuntarily pausing before coffin warehouses, and bringing up the rear of every funeral I meet." (*c*) Category 2 (anger, extraggression): "and especially whenever my hypos get such an upper hand of me, that it requires a strong moral principle to prevent me from deliberately stepping into the street, and methodically knocking people's hats off." (*d*) Category 4 (egression): "then, I account it high time to get to sea as soon as I can. This is my substitute for [category 3] pistol and ball. With a philosophical flourish Cato throws himself upon his sword; I [category 4] quietly take to the ship."

4. *Egression* and *desertion* (my nearest equivalent to the SPC's *leaving the hospital*). Physically considered, locomotion has two aspects: going some place and leaving some place. Although one of these two (attraction or repulsion) is ordinarily decisive and foremost in the consciousness of the locomotor, there may be times when the trend of his conduct becomes ambiguous even to himself, as when Ishmael was suddenly confounded by the impression that the *Pequod* was "not so much bound to any haven ahead as rushing from all havens astern." It is this second aspect of locomotion that I am stressing here and labeling "egression," which may be defined for present purposes as a person's intended departure from a region of distress, chiefly with the aim of terminating with relief the pain he has been suffering therein. In the last excerpt quoted from *Moby-Dick*, Melville gives us to infer that the distressing condition which in 1840 he, as Ishmael, hoped to terminate by going on a long whaling journey was that of an obsessional conflict between a diffuse homicidal rage and a suicidal depression (categories 2 and 3). That in Melville the simpler state of deprivation distress (category 1), engen-

dered by maternal indifference, was sufficient to instigate egression is exhibited in a juvenile effusion written in 1839, just prior to his first departure from home for a short voyage to Liverpool and back. In this story (with a distinctly Oriental flavor) the hero, after finally gaining access to the inner chamber of a resplendent, melancholy, queenly beauty, sinks on one knee and, bowing his head, exclaims: "Here do I prostrate myself, thou sweet Divinity, and kneel at the shrine of thy peerless charm." Receiving no response, he covers her passive hand with burning kisses and asks whether his passion is requited:

"Speak! Tell me, thou cruel! Does thy heart send forth vital fluid like my own? Am I loved,—even wildly, madly as I love?" She was silent; gracious God! What horrible apprehension crossed my soul?—Frantic with the thought, I held her from me, and looking in her face, I met the same impassioned gaze; her lips moved—my senses ached with the intensity with which I listened,—all was still, —they uttered no sound; I flung her from me, even though she clung to my vesture, and with a wild cry of agony I burst from the apartment!—She was dumb! Great God, she was dumb! Dumb and Deaf!

This is the way the story ends: deprivation distress, "agony" (category 1), with a touch of anger, "I flung her from me" (category 2), followed by a precipitous egression, "I burst from the apartment" (category 4). Two weeks after the publication of this fantasy in a local gazette, Herman left his widowed mother with whom he had been living in Lansingburgh, New York, and set forth in a troubled state of mind on the voyage dramatized in *Redburn*. His description of the behavior of the "sweet Divinity" is consonant with what I have said earlier about Mrs. Melville's inferable, customary attitude toward her adoring second son; and his hero's agonized reaction to it reminds one of Freud's statement that some people, especially narcissistic schizophrenics, hunger for such volumes of love that neutrality or indifference (deafness and dumbness) in another person is interpreted as hate, and hate is hated.

I have defined "egression," in the most general terms, as an intended departure from a region of distress, but more pertinent to our present topic is the genus of egressions that is marked by the outcrossing of the established boundary of a territorial, social, and/or cultural domain within which a person is conventionally expected or legally required to abide and play a role; and, therefore, by an egression of this import, the egressor runs the risk, maybe of pursuit and capture, maybe of punishment, maybe of social ostracism or at least of somebody's disapproval, and maybe, with or without one of these outcomes, a guilty conscience (in which case we have the states of category 3 following the action of category 4). The prototype of all these is "running away from home" in childhood.

Before he got himself married and tied down at the age of twenty-eight, Melville had a record of about seventeen egressions—from schools, jobs, home, country, and ships—but, as far as we know, veritable guilt was associated with none of them except, to a slight extent, with his desertion of the *Acushnet,* as described in *Typee,* and with his first temporary desertion of his home and mother, as described in *Redburn,* and, then, to a much greater extent, with his second, more absolute desertion of his home and mother when he left for New York in 1840 and later for the South Seas, a desertion for which he was severely criticized by at least one member of his family. Like many intended suicidal acts which involve the desertion of the perpetrator's closest, bonded persons, egressive desertions call for moral justifications or excuses of some sort, and these—as given, for example, in Melville's works—are no doubt susceptible to classification in terms of the species of logic that Dr. Shneidman has defined[9] and so should constitute suitable material for the exercise of his special talent in performing analyses of this type.

Melville's mode of thought, as he fictionally revealed it, is to have his hero become extrapunitive before he acts—to have him see the victim of his intended egressive (category 4) or aggressive (category 2) course of conduct as, in some respect, malevolent: The captain of the *Acushnet* is a tyrant who fails to provide enough good fodder for his crew; Aleema, the priest, is planning to sacrifice an innocent maiden he is holding in captivity; the mother is deaf and dumb to her son's affectionate entreaties; the white whale was prompted by malice when he devoured Ahab's leg (omitting the fact that Ahab was the original aggressor); Pierre's father is branded as an unpardonable sinner because of a single amorous affair four years before his marriage; and Pierre's haughty mother is said to be exiling him from his home ground to wander in a heartless world like an Ishmael without a maternal Hagar to console him (isolating the plain fact that Pierre has voluntarily expelled himself by an unexplained action which, so far as she could see, was both mad and cruel). By thus incriminating his opponent at the outset, the hero's urgent drive to action is not only made morally excusable but is rushed through the barrier of conscience on a wave of moral indignation. Not till after the deed is done does the other side of self come up with all the morbidly depressing dispositions of category 3. And then in *Pierre,* after this second, guilty phase has nearly run its course, Melville returns to the affectional state from which he started as a child—the desolation and piteous forlornness of category 1. Near the end of the novel, he speaks of the soul of the man who has radically egressed from home and faith as being born from the "world-husk," yet still craving for the sustenance it once enjoyed within the husk, "the support of its mother the world and its father the Deity." And then he tells us that the hardest and most grievous hour in the life of such a man comes, if it comes at all, when both the maternal world and the paternal God reject him and despise him. "Divinity and humanity then are equally willing that he should starve in the street for

all that either will do for him." Here Melville is virtually saying to his
mother and her world and to his father and his God: "Thou shouldst love
and honor thy son with all thy heart and with all thy mind; but instead
thou hast cruelly disowned him." In reply, the four targets of his indictment might have said in unison: "Out of your all-consuming, selfish
narcissism you demanded the impossible, a complete monopoly of love
and honor, *all* or *nothing;* and when you realized that you were not fated
to have *all,* you chose *nothing* as next best, and made certain that you
would end with *nothing* by madly disowning and detesting us." Granting
the validity of this interpretation, we can see that egression not only may
be, as it is in many cases, an expedient substitute for total suicide (insofar
as it results in a surcease of pain), but ultimately, in some rare cases, may
constitute a willful, partial suicide by taking the egressor beyond the
tolerance of his fellow men and of his own conscience, or, in other words,
to the point where he is as good as dead in the affections of the world
and of the "personified impersonal," and *they* are as good as dead in *his*
affections.

5. *Affectlessness* (one variety of "dead to the world," my nearest
equivalent to the SPC's *withdrawal and mutism*). This is a latecomer in
Melville. Not till after *Moby-Dick* do we get unmistakable premonitory
signs of its approach, especially in *Pierre,* where several profound experiences leading to affectlessness are perspicaciously and movingly communicated. By cutting the world dead and living entirely within his own
mind, a person may become emotionally dissociated from all the established values that regulate social interactions.

In those Hyperborean regions, to which enthusiastic Truth, and Earnestness,
and Independence, will invariably lead a mind fitted by nature for profound and
fearless thought, all objects are seen in a dubious, uncertain and refracting light.
Viewed through that rarefied atmosphere the most immemorially admitted maxims of men begin to slide and fluctuate, and finally become inverted . . . But the
example of many minds forever lost, like undiscoverable Arctic explorers, amid
these treacherous regions, warns us entirely away from them; and we learn that
it is not for man to follow the trail of truth too far, since by so doing he entirely
loses the directing compass of his mind; for arrived at the Pole, to whose barrenness only it points, there, the needle indifferently respects all points of the
horizon alike.

This passage could be taken as an anticipation of the state of mind
underlying today's widespread philosophy (if you will) of absurdity: everything is meaningless and purposeless, and hence there are no standards whatever in terms of which one can distinguish the better from the
worse; maybe what was once better is really worse, and what was worse
is really better, like Saint Genet. Another anticipation is the image of the
hollowness of modern man bereft of passion, faith, and aspiration. Melville's hero, Pierre, has been exploring his unconscious:

Ten million things were as yet uncovered to Pierre. The old mummy lies buried in cloth on cloth; it takes time to unwrap this Egyptian King . . . By vast pains we mine into the pyramid; by horrible gropings we come to the central room; with joy we espy the sarcophagus; but we lift the lid—and no body is there! —appallingly vacant as vast is the soul of a man!

Melville accounts for this state, in some measure, by saying that Pierre had been giving himself up, "a doorless and shutterless house for the four loosened winds of heaven to howl through," or, in psychological terms, he had been submitting to a flood of intoxicating passions and stirring archetypal images upsurging from the id, a succession of hot explosions which had ultimately left him cold and hollow as a "burnt-out crater," as if he had had in view from start to finish the passage in Revelation (3:16) which announces: "So then because thou art lukewarm, and neither cold nor hot, I will spew thee out of my mouth." Melville's image of a "burnt-out crater" could hardly be improved upon as a symbol of affectlessness, or dead to both worlds, a pathetic state which he touchingly set forth, as viewed from the outside, in "Bartleby, the Scrivener," a long short story composed in 1853, a year after the reception of a host of blockheaded and malicious feedbacks to the publication of his *Pierre.*

Since the concept of "dead to the world" has already been briefly expounded in this paper, and since, in another context,[10] I have communicated all that I have to say about "Bartleby," at this point I shall merely report, for the benefit of those who have not read it, that in this novella Melville presents us with an unforgettable portrayal of the near immobility and speechlessness of a forlorn young man whose spirit has been reduced to that last tenable position of individuality and pride, at which the embattled self insists on nothing but its inalienable right to say "No" to the whole world, or, in Bartleby's case, a mild "I would prefer not to." The attorney asks his clerk:

> "Will you tell me, Bartleby, where you were born?"
> "I would prefer not to."
> "Will you tell me *anything* about yourself?"
> "I would prefer not to."

And so it goes until the very end when Bartleby dies with his reticence unconquered and his privacy intact. The prototype of this condition of the soul is the morose, unresponsive apathy of a child, often an institutionalized child, who has been traumatically separated from his mother at a critical age, or of a child who has been severely deprived of maternal concern at home and on entering the hospital is given the diagnosis of FTT (failure to thrive) and the prescription of TLC (tender loving care) to be administered by the nurses. Still closer to the state depicted by Melville is that of schizophrenic catatonia coupled with the defiant No of the negativistic boy of about eighteen months. There is pride in it which seems to be saying to the mother with vengeful punitiveness: "Since you have been persistently, insultingly, and unforgivably deaf and dumb to my entreaties, I shall from now on be deaf and dumb to you in kind and may you suffer as I have!" In the specific case of the non-hero Bartleby, the conclusion is inescapable that both his passive social death (his refusal to engage in human reciprocities) and his passive total death (his final refusal to take nourishment) were intentional and willful, and, as it happens, it is only from this period of his life that we have an indubitable record of suicidal inclinations invading the stream of consciousness of Bartleby's creator.

The thread of fateful continuity that runs through the whole procession of negative states and emotions which we have been surveying is Melville's craving for the responsive, undivided, utter love of somebody whom he loves with his whole heart. Since this vision of affectional mutuality—the golden haven on the attainment of which his felicity depends—was never actualized for long enough to unify his being (because of internal and external impediments), what I have had to exhibit to you in this paper consists of hardly anything but a variety of reactions to the frustration of this craving in different situations, dating from childhood when love was fixated on his mother: piteous forlornness, desolation, grief-rage, fantasies of suicidal homicide, suicidal depression, egression as a substitute for suicide, egression as an intentional social suicide, and eventually, after several cycles of these grievous dispositions, a burnt-out crater, dead inside as well as outside. Not relevant to my topic were countless expressions of happier states—delectable humor, admiration or compassion for certain characters, celebrations of many shapes of beauty—which alternated with the doleful affects I have mentioned; and then—in this case not irrelevant to my topic but not mentioned in the SPC report—there was another state which succeeded the affectlessness portrayed in "Bartleby," and that was what I have called *disgust, bitterness, sardonic humor,* the temper of which the *Confidence Man* was wrought.

And now in ending, let me present to the members of the SPC for the exercise of their interpretive powers the following sequence of psychic states. The essence of Melville's outlook in *Mardi* (1849) can be credibly represented, I would say, in these words: "If I fail to reach my golden haven, may my annihilation be complete; all or nothing!" Two years later in *Moby-Dick:* "I foresee my annihilation, but against this verdict of Fate I shall hurl my everlasting protest." In *Pierre* (1852): "I am on the verge of annihilation but I can't make up my mind to it." In 1856, to Hawthorne in Liverpool: "I have pretty much made up my mind to be annihilated"; and in *Billy Budd* (1891): "I accept my annihilation." Did this last station of Melville's pilgrimage constitute a victory of the spirit, as some think? an ultimate reconciliation with God at the end of a lifelong quarrel? or was it a graceful acquiescence to the established morality and conventions of his world with Christian forgiveness toward those who had crushed him in their name? or a forthright *willing* of obligatory? or was it an acknowledgment of defeat? a last-ditch surrender of his long quest for a new gospel of joy in this life? or was it a welcoming of death?

> My towers at last! These rovings end,
> Their thirst is slaked in larger dearth:
> The yearning infinite recoils,
> For terrible is earth.

REFERENCES

1. E. S. Shneidman. Orientations toward death: a vital aspect of the study of lives. In R. W. White, ed. *The Study of Lives,* New York: Atherton Press, 1963.

2. R. M. Weaver. *Herman Melville, Mariner and Mystic,* New York: George H. Doran Company, 1921.

3. N. Leites. Trends in affectlessness, in C. Kluckhohn, H. A. Murray, and D. M. Schneider, eds. *Personality in Nature, Society, and Culture,* New York: Alfred A. Knopf, Inc., 1953.

4. William James. *The Varieties of Religious Experience,* New York: Longmans, Green & Co., Inc., 1902, p. 501.

5. S. S. Tomkins. *Affect, Imagery, Consciousness.* New York: Springer Publishing Co., 1963.

6. A. K. Coomaraswamy. *The Dance of Shiva,* rev. ed., New York: Noonday Press, Inc., 1957.

7. N. L. Farberow, E. S. Shneidman, and C. Neuringer. The socio-psychological matrix of suicide, unpublished report, Los Angeles: Central Research Unit, Veterans Administration Center, 1962.

8. Shneidman, *op. cit.*

9. E. S. Shneidman. Psycho-logic: a personality approach to patterns of thinking, in J. Kagan and G. Lessor, eds. *Contemporary Issues in Thematic Apperceptive Methods,* Springfield, Ill.: Charles C. Thomas, Publisher, 1961.

10. H. A. Murray. "Bartleby and I," *Kent State Melville Papers,* Kent, Ohio: Kent State University Press, 1965.

21

THE PERSONALITY
AND CAREER OF SATAN

To those members of the APA who are so strictly dedicated to the doctrine of immaculate Scientism that they must needs limit the compass of their professional attention to the simplest and purest of measurable phenomena, to those who with good reason pride themselves on having contributed to the historic emancipation of our discipline from the shackles of an outworn philosophy and theology, to these and perhaps to many others, the title of this paper provides ample cause for dismay or indignation. What will their reference group, the Olympian company of physicists, think when they hear that Satan was exhibited as an object for serious consideration at the annual meeting of their Association? By what deplorable slip of judgment did the Program Committee of Division 8 let the Devil—that shadow of a by-gone superstitious age—crash the gates of this emporium of genuine scientific commerce?

Here at the outset I must hasten to exonerate your Program Committee by reminding you that theirs was the power to accept or to reject every paper except this one, and, therefore, that mine is whatever blame there be for taking advantage of my over-privileged position to insert a topic which seems precisely calculated to affront the fastidious scruples of some of my most respected colleagues.

My front-line of defense runs as follows: first, that more knowledge about the major determinants of human behavior is one of the prime aims of the science of psychology; second, that one class of major determinants of behavior consists of products of the imagination (imaginations regarding causes and consequences, for example), these being not infrequently more powerful than percepts in their effects on a person's physiology, mood, emotions, decisions, and overt actions; third, that among the countless dynamic products of the imagination over the last two thousand years, the concept, figure, and deeds of Satan have been singularly influential, apparently surpassing in awesome potency, during certain periods in certain areas, the concept, figure, and deeds of God; and

From *Journal of Social Issues,* 1962, *28,* pp. 36–54. The paper was the presidential address given to Division 8, the Division of Personality and Social Psychology, of the American Psychological Association, at the 70th convention of the American Psychological Association on August 31, 1962, in St. Louis, Missouri.

fourth, since the amount of data bearing on the imagined personality and career of Satan down the ages is almost unique in volume and variety (my bibliography on the Devil consists of more than 150 titles), it would be hard to find a better case in which to test the plausibility of whatever hypotheses we may construct relative to the genesis, evolution, propagation, and survival of an enormously consequential inhabitant of the collective mind of Western man. Despite the fact that today it is not possible to observe the birth and development of this particular demon in a living mind, any more than an evolutionist can witness the rise and fall of the dinosaur, I hope that some of you, in view of these considerations, will concede that a longitudinal study of the Devil, if systematically conducted, may properly be given place within the boundaries of psychology as currently defined.

To what class of charismatic imaginal entities does Satan belong? Not to the class represented, say, by images of Alexander the Great; and not to the class represented by images of Hamlet or Don Quixote. Satan is similar to the members of both these only in one respect: he possesses a full complement of *anthropopsychic* properties, that is, he is described as perceiving, feeling, thinking, or intending as a human being does. Only occasionally is he endowed with solely *anthropomorphic* attributes. When he is portrayed in a nearly human form, he is almost invariably supplied with certain goat-like appendages, such as horns, a tail, and cloven feet. But more important than this he is an immortal being with supernatural powers at his command: he is capable of doing everything that children have always imagined doing in the furthest reaches of their wish-fulfilling fantasies. Being a pure psyche, or spirit, he is ordinarily invisible, can pass through walls of any thickness, and can invade and seize the will of any living creature. In this way he can take the shape of an insidious serpent as he did to seduce Eve, or that of a dragon at the jaws to Hell as he does in Breughel's canvases, or that of the dog who appeared in the laboratory of the fed-up scholar, Faust. In former days, we may presume, the Devil was more enchanting than God to some young boys because, with the wings of an angel he would fly from place to place without a gasoline motor and to any height, unencumbered by the elaborate apparatus of a science fiction hero, as he did, according to the Gospel of St. Luke, when he took Jesus "up into a high mountain" and later "set him on a pinnacle of the temple." These powers are comparable to those exhibited by countless heroes, gods, demi-gods, and demons of mythologies, sagas, and legends; and roughly speaking he belongs with them, but in a special class of supernatural entities whose exceeding potency depends on a vivid belief in their existence, and, further, in a sub-class of that class, composed of demonic entities, and in Satan's case, the source and ruler of all demons, indeed, in the Judeo-Christian tradition, the object of a monodemonism inter-related with the orthodox monotheism.

But here is the snag: people have always been disposed to think, on the one hand, that the supernatural anthropopsychic beings that play the leading parts in the dramatic mythologies and religions of all out-groups are purely imaginary, and, on the other hand, to be convinced that the *personae* of their own religious dramas (who were deeply planted in their psyches at the earliest age) are absolutely real and sacred beings, whose objective existence outside their minds has been unmistakably and irrevocably revealed. And so, seeing that Satan and God were the key figures in the sacred apocalyptic myth of both Judaism and Christianity, in one of which religions most of us were reared, it will be necessary if we wish to adopt our customary scientific impartiality in these matters to extricate ourselves from whatever constraining web of sentiments may still reside in us, and, taking the station of the man in the moon before the arrival of any missionary astronauts, look at the whole matter from afar in readiness for any sign of "usable truth," which Melville once defined as "the apprehension of the absolute condition of things as they strike the eye of the man who fears them not."

A Credo. The ground for this undertaking of mine, as well as for the hope that other psychologists will invade the abundant field of religious images and imagents, and grapple with one or another of its many mysteries, is a conclusion, or value judgment, I have come to, on the periphery of science, which might be termed a credo. It is the belief that the evidence set forth by anthropologists and psychoanalysts, particularly by Frazer and by Freud, in favor of the proposition that religions are products of human imaginations revised by rationality, is so massive and persuasive that it adds up to a veritable discovery, potentially the most consequential discovery since Darwin's theory of evolution. This discovery, as I view it, puts religion in the select company of science, philosophy, and art since these are also products of the best human imaginations revised by rationality. In fact, if one defines religion as *the* matter of ultimate concern, it gives religion the superordinate position. You can ask science for what? philosophy for what? and art for what? but not religion for what? because it is the function of religion to provide the best conceivable answers to all those "whats." To answer these "whats," to fulfil this basic function, as I see it, the propositions and stories of a religion should, first of all, be as true as they can be at any given time, that is, congruent with the deepest realities of human nature; and second, they should be as comprehensive and as self-consistent as they can be made; and third, they should comfort the distressed, and, by presenting visions of a realizable better future, engender hope, and encourage efforts to achieve this. Finally, a religious system should be applicable to the most critical problems of the day and aid in their solution, and hence, like science, should always be susceptible to correction and reconstruction. This is an ideal which was approximated by Christianity in the thirteenth century, at least as judged by most of the eminent intellectuals of that era as well as by the bulk of the population. But today only a minority of thoughtful people sincerely believe, in the marrow of their passions, that Christianity fulfils any of these functions to a consequential degree, and this failure, so evident to so many for so long, is in all likelihood the root determinant of the alienation and demoralization of large numbers of our fellowmen. And so the discovery I mentioned is both important and timely, for it means that religion, as a product of passionate human imaginations revised by rationality, can be sympathetically examined, analyzed, evaluated, revised, radically reconstructed, or built anew by people of sufficient depth and genius, just as art-forms and scientific theories have been periodically recreated down the centuries. Suspecting that Satan, the drama of the Good Father and the Bad Son, may be initially responsible in some degree for the fact that Christianity has not matured to the point of being equal to the dilemmas of our time, I shall turn to the question of the genesis and nature of this Bad Son.

Prologue. Essential to a genuine understanding of what I have in mind to say is a fifty-page prologue, which, of course, must be omitted. It deals with the application of contemporary anthropological and psychological theories to such fundamental phenomena as (1), the projection of anthropopsychic entities as powers immanent in natural objects, such as the earth and sun, and then their projection into space as transcendent powers outside of nature; and (2), the transition from the concept of a god as sheer power to that of a moral god who is both powerful and good; and (3), the evolution of a chaos of minor deities, by consolidation and crystallization, into a single god, highly magnified as to power and benevolence, or, as in Persia, the conception of two gods, coeval brothers of almost equal potency, one wholly good, known later as Ozmazd and the other wholly evil, known later as Ahriman; and (4), the social effect of the *cyclical* mythology of ancient India, portraying an eternal series of departures and returns with no progressions that endure, and Zoroaster's radical break with tradition by composing a dynamic *linear* mythology which announced that the age-old alternation of good and evil—first Ozmazd, the angel of light, truth, and virtue in control of things, and then Ahriman, the angel of darkness, lies, and vice—that this perpetual cycle would be terminated at an appointed future time, when Ozmazd and his good angels would utterly demolish the wicked Ahriman and his legions, cast him into the abyss, and establish a new and perfect world which would endure forever; and (5), the assimilation of the main features of this powerful apocalyptic myth and the composition of variant versions of it by the Hebrews during the second and first century B.C. (the once-called "silent centuries" between the Old and the New Testament), one in the book of Daniel and others in several non-canonical works, particularly the book of Enoch, which refers to the war in Heaven ending with the fall of the angels and visualizes another great war to end all wars between the powers of righteousness and wickedness; and (6), concomitant with this evolution of apocalypticism, the shaping, stage by stage, of the villain of the piece, out of a multiplicity of demons, minor devils, and more than one Satan. "Satan" is a word which in the Old Testament means "the Adversary" (of man)—not a particular person with a proper name, but a role played by a number of angels (like FBI agents) in the service of Jehovah, who have access to Heaven, as we see in the book of Job, and are evidently on good terms with the Almighty. All of this provides wonderful sources for studies of evolution on the mentational level, the emergence of innumerable variations which compete in a desperate struggle for survival.

From Dissonance to Consonance. Here I shall pause for a moment at the end of this summary of my prologue, because I have come to a body of material of exceeding richness and significance, mostly in the book of Enoch, which may be familiar to the next President of this Division; but if not, I would like to recommend it to him as just his meat. Whether he will be appetized or not, his is the theoretical digestive system which seems best fitted to give vital order to this plenitude of heterogeneous data. In agreement with the consensus of opinion of those scholars who are entitled to a serious hearing, a purely hypothetical model of the initial state of mind shared by the non-canonical writers of the last centuries B.C. might include the following: (1), a feeling of extreme distress engendered by the tribulations suffered by their peoples and by the perception of rewarded wickedness on all sides of them ever since the break-up of Alexander's empire; (2), an insistent need to find an explanation for this prevalence and these victories of iniquity, since it was no longer possible to view them as God's just punishment for their own sins; (3), a strong attraction to the Persian concept of Ahriman, first, because it *did* provide an anthropopsychic explanation of evil, and second, because of Ahriman's essential role in the inspiring and irresistible apocalyptic vision of the great war of supernatural beings that would end with the establishment of the Kingdom of Heaven on earth; and third, because it was comforting to have a single figure to whom all wickedness could be legitimately ascribed; (4), a state of dissonance resulting from the entertainment of this concept because, since Ahriman was a self-created god with powers almost equal to those of the good god, Ozmazd, this concept did not conform to their certainty that God was the creator of the universe, all powerful and all good; and (5), an antipathy to Ahriman because he was a foreign god never in any way related to Jehovah.

So much for this crude and over-simplified analysis of the initial condition of a hypothetical cognitive system. What an expert of Dr. Festinger's mettle might do, after revising my provisional formulation, would be to trace in the relevant non-canonical works the progression from this state of dissonance to that of relative consonance which was attained before the middle of the first century A.D., first, by giving the supernatural Ahriman the Biblical name of "Satan," second, by endowing this grandiose Satan with a large portion of Ahriman's evil powers, by admitting, in fact, that Satan was in control of the temporal and hopelessly vicious age of human history in which they were then living, an age in which the righteous were constantly tormented by his demonic and human agents; third, by announcing that the angel Satan had been created by God in Heaven but had fallen because of some unpardonable offense, and fourth, by stating that God, being omnipotent, had power over Satan, and being all good, would bring an end to the Devil's rule on earth in the near future as prophesied by the apocalyptic writers. Here endeth this prologue.

New Testament Satan. Here for the first time we encounter a fully formed and featured Satan, outcome of the just-described non-canonical imaginings revised by rationality: a fallen angel of the first magnitude, the Evil One, with supernatural powers, the implacable enemy of God's promised kingdom for the righteous. He is the being who in St. John is called the prince of this world and whom St. Paul names as the prince of the powers of the air. (Perhaps the architects of space programs should take note of this.) Satan's undisputed sovereignty on earth at that time is made known to us when he tempts Jesus by saying: "All this power will I give thee, and the glory of them: for *that is delivered unto me; and to whomsoever I will give it.* If thou therefore will worship me, all shall be thine." The presence of this hardly credible Satan in the New Testament has been an embarrassment to many modern theologians. But in the most recent book on the subject by Ling, it is argued that a supernatural antagonist is indispensable to the plot; that it was the extension of Satan's power on earth which brought forth the Christ to conquer hate with love, and to prove that the seductions of the prince of this world could be resisted, and that demons subservient to his vicious will could be exorcised from the souls of his unhappy victims. We need not be detained by this crucial issue. Suffice it to say that here was sufficient Biblical ground for a prodigious exuberance of imaginations about the Devil, which, in subsequent Christian centuries, exhibited him mostly as the arch tempter, the wily, cunning, and treacherous "old serpent," and more profoundly as the arch-hater, conspirator, destroyer of the faith, vindictively intent on marring God's fair work.

But these were popular legends for the most part and, my first duty being to discover the Christian party line respecting the personality of the Devil, I must turn to the struggles of the Church Fathers to construct a theory that did not contradict the orthodox premises they had inherited and that could be given scriptural support. Furthermore, since the problem was that of explaining the vicissitudes of a father-son relationship, the theory had to be psychologically plausible; and so, as we shall see at times, the reflections of these founding fathers of Christian theology resemble those of modern psychoanalysts. From the few specimens to be presented of the mentations of these theorists, you will also gain some impression of the difficulty of their task; which was that of producing consonance out of a cognitive model in which incompatible properties had already been implanted by projection. In subsequent rabbinical writings, Satan was the villain in many enthralling stories; but he never reached the monstrous proportions that he did in later Christianity. He was the tempter, accuser, and punisher, but not *the* principal of all evil.

What was the original state of the Devil? Here the basic premise was that since God is perfect, his celestial creations must be perfect, and hence the Devil must have been perfect on the day that he was made. But there was no Biblical support for this conclusion until Tertullian (*Adversus Marcionem, 2, 10*) encountered the famous prophecy in Ezekiel 28, 12, and decided (like many a dream interpreter of our time) that the King of Tyre to whom this passage is literally addressed was unquestionably a symbol of the Devil, and hence it was not the King but the Devil who was "full of wisdom and perfect in beauty . . . perfect in thy ways from the day that thou wast created, till unrighteousness was found in thee . . ." Tertullian's arguments were widely accepted and henceforth the Devil, in the first phase of his career, was known as Lucifer, the "Morning Star," the "Shining One," first and highest of the angels. Gregory of Nyssa (*ca.* 331–396) was of the same mind. St. Anselm (1033–1109) also assumed that Lucifer was perfect at the time of his creation, and St. Thomas (*ca.* 1225–1274) taught that he was one of the pure angels of God, probably "superior to all." That point at least was settled without much argument. The next question, however, brought forth a variety of answers.

What was the cause of the change in Lucifer's personality from the state of perfection to that of unrighteousness? There was peace in Heaven until Lucifer, out of a feeling of resentment, persuaded a large number of discontented fellow angels to join him in a revolution against the celestial government of his Almighty Father. What was the cause of the resentment which transformed Lucifer into Satan? The answers given can be ordered into two classes.

1. *Resentment engendered by jealousy and envy (dispositional determinants) provoked by the presence of another object of God's concern (situational determinant).* Justin Martyr (*ca.* 100–165) seems to have been the first to suggest that envy of Adam was the cause of the Devil's discontent. A little later we find Irenaeus (second century) affirming that the angel "became apostate and an enemy on the day when he became jealous of God's creature (man) and undertook to set him against God." To this thesis both Tertullian and Gregory of Nyssa were agreeable. But, according to Lactantius (fourth century), God first produced the Word (Christ) and then Lucifer, who was tainted with the venom of jealousy. "He was jealous of his elder brother, who, remaining attached to God the Father, obtained his affection." In short, these first explana-

tions of Satan's passage from good to evil are consonant with sound Freudian doctrine respecting the dynamics of so-called "sibling rivalry"; jealousy of the Father's preceding creation (elder brother) or of his succeeding creation (equivalent to a younger brother). The latter thesis is analogous to the story of the two other proud, vindictive (Satanic) characters in the Old Testament (e.g. Cain and Ishmael). Jealousy of this sort and of this intensity presupposes a high degree of *dependent narcism* (that is, the child's insistence on a monopoly of parental love), and, possibly, on the parent's too-obvious display of favoritism for the other sibling.

2. *Resentment engendered by envy of God's supreme position of power and glory and by a thwarted desire, coming out of pride, to ascend to God's elevated station.* It was the reverent doctor Origen (*ca.* 185–254) who proposed this hypothesis of *pride*, which was accepted by the great majority of subsequent writers. Having been exposed to Greek culture in Alexandria, Origen must have been familiar with the concept of *hubris,* so central to Hellenic thought. But he said he was persuaded to this idea by his conviction that the material world was created *after* the revolution of the angels (partly, indeed, to serve as a prison for these perverse spirits), and hence the jealousy-of-Adam theory was untenable. Also influential was the passage from Isaiah (14), in which the King of Babylon, who has just died and descended into Hell, is addressed by his royal predecessors:

Art thou also become weak as we? Art thou become like unto us? Thy pomp is brought down to hell . . . How art thou fallen from heaven, O day star, son of the morning! how art thou cut down to the ground, which didst lay low the nations! And thou saidst in thine heart, I will ascend into heaven, I will exalt my throne above the stars of God; and I will sit upon the mount of congregation, in the uttermost parts of the north: I will ascend above the heights of the clouds; I will be like unto the Most High.

Origen convinced his fellow theologians that these words could refer, not to any earthly king, but to Satan only; and henceforth the Devil became the prince of pride on whose brow was to be read: "I will be like unto the Most High." This puts Satan in a class which includes the giants who tried to scale Olympus and replace Zeus, as well as a host of other defeated defiant ascensionists, frustrated dictators, would-be deicides, regicides, and parricides.

In what precisely did Satan's pride consist? That Satan fell through pride was irrefutably established in the fourth century. It would have been perilous to tamper with that judgment. But the exact nature of the Angel's pride was still an open question, to the solution of which several eminent Church Fathers would direct their mentational powers as if they were so many clinical psychologists and psychiatrists discussing among themselves the dynamics of a single case, except that the ecclesiastical philosophers, being in a state of total data deprivation, had nothing but unaided rationality to carry them, and their exchange of logics and assured pronouncements lasted for a thousand years and led to no unanimous decision. Since there does not seem to be any vital conception of pride and its vagaries that has wide currency among the members of this Division, our private views, if any, on this neglected topic may be more discrepant than those of the Church Fathers, in which case a mere list of their conclusions as to the nature of Satan's sin might instigate some fruitful intellective activities in us:

1. Satan wanted to pass himself off as God, said Saint Gregory of Nazianzus (Lectures, 35, 5).

2. Satan tried to convince his fellow angels that he had created himself and then created matter out of his own body, announced Prudentius (*Hamartigenia,* 168).

3. Satan wished to shatter the bonds of his dependence upon God and to be his own master, asserted Saint Gregory the Great (*Morals* 34, 40).

4. Satan wished to obtain beatitude before the time appointed by his maker, argued Saint Anselm (*De casu diaboli,* 4).

5. Satan wanted the other angels to adore him as a self-created God, said Rupert (*De Victoria Verbi Dei,* 1, 8–12) in essential agreement with Prudentius.

6. Satan wished to derive his happiness from himself alone, instead of with the help of grace. This was the authoritative verdict of Saint Thomas (*Summa,* 1, 63, 3).

The differences between these six opinions, which entangled the fastidious intellects of the Church, could hardly detain the interest of a psychologist today. "To hell with these minutiae," he might say. "Satan wanted to be God, period." But not until the fourteenth century was a qualified version of this diagnosis literally set forth.

7. Satan could not have been so extravagant as to believe that he was capable of becoming God, but he could have felt a desire to possess the divine nature and could have regretted that divinity was beyond his reach, concluded Duns Scotus (*Sententias,* 2, 5, 1).

I shall not pursue this topic any further, since the controversy had no closure and the samples of psychological acumen I have given you will suffice as a basis for a summary statement of what the reverent doctors had to say about the Devil's sin, namely that it consisted in hardly more than a desire to be one grade higher on the heavenly scale of Being than he was at his creation, which meant the acquisition of a divine nature, since he already possessed every form of excellence but this.

In this day of non-authoritarian parents, of independence training, of the precocious emancipation of youth, and of teenage killers, Satan's ascensionistic hopes (perfect illustrations of the Adlerian craving for superiority) are not likely to be regarded as ample cause for everlasting ostracism and damnation. But of course this judgment of our time may be nothing but a consequence of the Devil's having pretty nearly realized his unswerving ambition to subvert our natures. In any case, we should remind ourselves that God was so unutterably and absolutely glorious in the sight of the Church Fathers that no filial fantasy of approaching the grandeur of his perfection could be considered as anything but monstrous. In view, however, of the abominable motives and enormities that they attributed to Satan from the moment he arrived on earth, we can scarcely say that they succeeded in identifying a form of pride that would explain both the utmost punishment that was meted out to him in Heaven and the malevolent course of his whole subsequent career. It is this mildness of their conclusions, as I weigh them, that has prodded me to seek a more sufficient answer, carrying on as they did with no facts, experiments, statistics, or computers to assist me. But before doing so, I must consider the most refractory of all the problems that confronted the Church Fathers.

What is the explanation of the emergence of evil dispositions in Lucifer's perfectly created personality? Of all those who have honestly endeavored to come to grips with this question, St. Anselm (1033–1109) is especially impressive. He assumes that the good angels who stood firmly in the truth did so because they had received from God the gift of *steadfastness.* Then he asks, did God fail to give Lucifer this gift or did he offer it but fail to transmit the necessary capacity or disposition to receive it? In either case, Lucifer-Satan must be judged blameless. St. Anselm's answer is that God gave Lucifer both sufficient power and sufficient will to be steadfast, but that the angel did not continue to exercise his will in the right direction to the end. No explanation is offered for the sudden weakening of the angel's disposition or power to be steadfast. Why was he deprived of this capacity? We are left with the assertion that God created a perfect spiritual being who became the epitome of imperfection. Let us consider three of several conceivable solutions.

1. God created Lucifer precisely in his own likeness (the very best that he could do), that is, he shaped a jealous personality liable to revenge ("God is jealous and the Lord revengeth"), who would insist on a monopoly of power and glory ("no other gods before me"), and give vent, when crossed, to horrific outbursts of wrath ("For behold, the Lord will come with fire, and with his chariots like a whirlwind, to render his anger with fury and his rebukes with flames of fire"). And then, having created these dispositions in his son, God closed the only possible avenue to their fulfilment by proclaiming himself the *everlasting* ruler of the universe. According to this interpretation, Lucifer acted much as his Father would have acted in his place, that is, if *relegated forever* to a subordinate

position. God's refusal to be succeeded, as other gods had been succeeded (*hubris* in a ruler), would be enough to account for the report that his once-admirable son has *never* been able to forgive him. This thesis would conform to the proposition that God was all powerful and possibly all good, but *not* all knowing, since he did not foresee that a replication of himself would eventually rebel, if all hope of any higher status were denied him.

2. If (by definition) God is omniscient and capable of foreknowledge, he must have *known* that he was not giving Lucifer (or Adam later) enough steadfastness for them to persevere in perpetual obedience, *known* that they would therefore disobey eventually, and *known* that he would punish each of them for this, despite the fact that he himself had planted the bent toward disobedience (the id tendency) and failed to imbed sufficient power to inhibit it (ego structure). One might surmise that God committed this grave injustice as the only possible means to a good end, namely, to provide mankind with an unforgettable object lesson of crime and punishment, which was to serve as the necessary forerunner of his later presentation of the possibility of redemption, as Christianity has affirmed. But this is hardly plausible, since if God were omniscient he would have realized that neither of these two object lessons would succeed in making mankind obedient, and that the day would come when people might suspect that he himself was responsible for the crimes he had punished so severely and unforgivingly.

3. In the case of Lucifer-Satan, God might purposely have endowed him with a preponderance of malice in order that he, Satan, might perform with gusto certain tasks which he, God, was reluctant to perform, such as in *Job* to test, by tribulation and torture, the limits of man's steadfastness in piety. By assigning all hateful functions to Satan, God could reserve all charitable functions for himself: if Satan was given freedom to seduce and to corrupt, then God could intervene with his gracious mercy and forgiveness. This thesis is in harmony with the widespread opinion that the glory of God is manifest not so much in sustaining a man in goodness as in converting a great sinner (e.g. St. Paul, St. Augustine, St. Francis, etc.), and with the judgment that a repentant sinner is closer to God than a consistently moral man.

Up to this point I have argued much as some of the Church Fathers argued, but with the addition of a few psychological hypotheses provided by recent studies of father-son relationships. The chief difference in bias is that *formerly* (perhaps since time immemorial) it was the children who were blamed for disobedience and rebellion ("Honor thy father and thy mother"), whereas *today* the parents are more likely to be blamed, the psychoanalytical commandment being: honor thy son and thy daughter.

But, in all earnestness, religious thought tends, or should tend, toward the ideal; and we are entitled to expect from it a story of a Father-

Son relationship in Heaven which will edify and inspire terrestrial fathers who are similarly confronted by a discontented son. But the truth is that hundreds of fathers of our own time display greater wisdom than was attributed to Diety in preparing their son for the advent of a younger sibling, or in transforming his enmity to affection. Many times, of course, they don't, and so we have in our midst numerous micro Satans, repressed Satanic personalities of minor scale and scope. Which brings me to:

An Abstract of the Satanic Personality. I say "Satanic personality" instead of "Satan's personality," because my goal is a theoretical formulation which is congruent not only with the Devil's character and career as represented to us by the scholastic theorists, but with the development of a compound of thematic dispositions which is manifested to a varying extent, covertly and overtly, by numerous persons of our own day, and which I have had the opportunity to investigate in a few cases. In attempting this, I shall be extending the speculations of the ecclesiastical theorists only so far as to propose, first, that absolute evil cannot be derived from a mild form of pride, but only from the most extreme form, which I shall call *absolute malignant pride,* or *malignant narcism,* and second, that the *potentiality* for absolute pride was necessarily present in Lucifer's personality from the day of his creation.

In briefest terms, my reconstruction involves the following familiar components: (1), an extravagant growth of four varieties of narcism originating and reinforced in the earliest years of childhood, at the core of which is the subject's tacit assumption that *his own supreme worth entitles* him to a *monopoly* (or at least the lion's share) of whatever goods, services, attention, adulation, honors, privileges, power, and prestige are to be had in his environment; (2), a series of shocks, frustrations, or punishments which are narcistically felt to be unforgivably malicious insults; (3), the transformation of the initial state of complacent self-esteem into a suspicious focal hatred of the insulting object, generalized into a diffuse misanthropy and distrust; and (4), a fixed determination to revenge the injury which, if unsuccessful, may lead to nihilism, self-hate, and suicide, the narcist against himself. I suggest that the first phase of narcistic expansion—illustrated, say, by Lucifer in his prime—is not malignant, but a possible precursor of malignancy, the development of which depends on whether the suffered narcistic wound is taken in good grace (impunitively or intrapunitively) or as an outrage to be avenged with extrapunitive fanaticism. All of this is congruent with orthodox belief regarding Satan's personality and career as given earlier.

The distinctive underlying characteristics of the Satanic personality, then, are (a) a secret feeling in the subject of having been harshly, treacherously, unjustly, or ignominiously deprived of his deservedly large share of benefits, rewards, and glory; (b) a basic state of alienation, resentment, and distrust; (c) a hidden envy coupled with expressed contempt of the notable achievements of others; (d) repression of guilt feelings; and (e) the adoption of one or another strategy—sly, slippery, and subversive or openly destructive—of giving vent to his self-consuming hatred. His negative characteristic, by which he is most easily identified, is the absence of any capacity to experience or express authentic selfless love, gratitude, admiration, or compassion.

Question. How is it that psychoanalysis has not emphasized malignant narcism, or Satanism, as a complex to be repressed? How is it that Oedipus reigns supreme as the epitome of evil in the id of Freudian theory? In Adlerian theory, to be sure, Satan's need for superiority, his envy and rage are adequately conceptualized; but not his invulnerable stockade of pride, as described in *Paradise Lost* or *Moby-Dick*, for example. Why is that? Or, to put it in another way, why did not the early religion-makers accuse Satan of lecherous excesses? It is true that some of them did consider for a while that concupiscence might have been the sin by which the Angel fell, and later, in the days of Witchcraft, hundreds of women, under torture, testified to the Devil's diffuse and inexhaustible libido; but more deadly than all that was malice coming out of pride. And yet today we have no psychology of pride.

Satan Down the Centuries. There is time here for no more than what you know already about Satan's seasons of ascendancy over the minds of men and women since the Dark Ages. A perpetually subversive agent, he was most influential in the Age of Faith, publicly as the inaugurator of the Black Mass and privately as the tempter and the interrupter of the prayers of the most devout, the "shadow," as Jung would say, of every monk and nun who strained for chastity and saintliness. Satan's victories were more spectacular, frightening, and obnoxious, however, in the overlapping and succeeding Age of Witchcraft, in which, as the acknowledged god of a persisting pre-Christian Pagan cult, he was the exciting cause of recurrent seizures of anxiety and panic leading to fanatic witch hunts, trials, tortures, and burnings at the stake. Since the Devil was blamed for all the neurotic and psychotic symptoms which today are attributed to the id, the published detailed records of witch trials which have come down to us constitute, as Freud discovered, a comprehensive compendium of the lurid psychopathology of that era, and hence of considerable professional interest to many of us. But this chapter in the religious career of Satan deserves an extensive treatment, as does his distinguished career in literature from the Faust-book and Christopher Marlowe down through Milton and Goethe to Rimbaud and Thomas Mann. The Devil's successes in each of these spheres of activity call for a separate volume, as does his relatively short but fiery upsurge into philosophy and politics from the late eighteenth century down to his total incarnation in the person of Adolf Hitler. But since these wonders and horrors are outside the possible scope of this paper, I shall turn to another phenomenon: the operation of a very dangerous propensity to the indulgence of which all of us are prone.

Projections of Satan in the Western World. To the primitive mind every opponent or enemy is bad by definition. But after the development and articulation of abstract ethical principles, by the Egyptians and Hebrews, for example, a person or group of people could be judged bad or good, regardless of whether he or they were friend or foe. This distinction, however, was rarely made in practice; and as all forms of wickedness became crystallized into a single fiendish Satan who, like a proliferating cancer invaded the susceptible collective minds of men, their projection of this malignant essence into their most formidable enemies became inevitable, producing as it did an encouraging inflation of their own sense of righteousness coupled with the conviction that the extermination of their enemies was their holy duty. Hence the inordinate brutality of religious wars. Christians, believing that theirs was the only "true" religion, were for centuries disposed to see Satan in the guise of each of their successive enemies: the entire Pagan world surrounding Roman Christendom, the infiltrating heresies—Mithraism, Manichaeism, and Gnosticism—the invading Huns and Moslems, the American Indians in New England, the deviant enthusiasms and cults arising in their midst, such as Romantic Love, Witchcraft, and the antitheistic French Enlightenment with its Goddess of Reason, and more recently, the self-proclaimed Antichrist Nietzsche and the atheist Marx giving shape to Communism. As a result of this dynamism of projection, it was possible for Catholics to see the Satanic spirit operating in their pre-Protestant and Protestant opponents, and for the latter, Savonarola and Luther, for example, to see Satan firmly ensconced in the Vatican at Rome, say, in the figure of Alexander VI, father of Cesare Borgia. Clearly the Capitalist plays the role of Satan in the apocalyptic thesis of Marx, which is extremely dangerous in this atomic age because it offers to those who are made gullible by misery the vision of an impossibly harmonious society without government, a society that is attainable only by a righteous war against the monodemonism of Capitalism.

Of course, it is a great error to assume that whatever system of ideas is once defined as optimally good and true will *always* be optimally good and true, and hence that every proposed change in the system must spring from an evil source, Satan in this context. This means that the creation of something new and the transformation of something old (the rarest and best of functions) are attributed in large measure to the Devil, often by the creator himself. For example, we find Blake, that admirable man, claiming that "every poet is of the Devil's party," and so, by degrees, Satan, hater of man, is endowed with some of the heroic virtues of Prometheus, lover of man, as Milton's Satan was endowed to some extent; and, in due course, "Devil's advocate" becomes a badge of honor, and all values are turned upside down, because Satan—at least according to the view presented here—is a wholly self-centered, envious, vindictive, nihilist without creative powers. In ancient Hindu mythology Siva, the destroyer, is not a nihilist, but the necessary fore-runner and initiator of the succeeding creative phase. According to one of several versions of his function, he is portrayed with a mighty lingam and ends his dance of destruction with a discharge of seed for the conception which originates the next period of construction.

Is the spirit of Satan operating in our midst? By the turn of the last century it seemed that Satan was no more than a vestigial image, a broken-spirited relic of a perished past, a ludicrous ham actor with no greater part to play in man's imagination than the vermiform appendix in his gut. The sweetness and light of reason had shown him to be a nightmarish product of moral indigestion, an horrendous superstition, which the human species—being set at last on the ascending path of progressive evolutions and feeling better every day in every way—had left dying in its rear. Improvements in the physical and social environment were gradually extinguishing whatever wicked dispositions had been manifest in less enlightened eras.

Such ill-bred complacency, of course, was fated for a fall; and after the shock of World War I there were lots of people conditioned to agree with Father Knox when he said: "It is so stupid of modern civilization to have given up believing in the devil when he is the only explanation of it." Somebody then suggested that precisely this was Satan's stratagem, as crafty as any in his long career, namely, to convince mankind of his decease and the inconceivability of his rebirth. In dealing with a scientist, for example, could Satan have devised a better tactic? To be sure the ruse of anonymity was not wholly new. It was the very first he chose. But in Paradise he was advantaged by the fact that Adam and Eve had never even heard of him, had not been warned of his foreseen intrusion, his wicked resolution and his wiles. Satan managed, somehow, to keep his name out of Genesis. To operate in the twentieth century, however, it was necessary first of all to get his bad name and deeds—centuries of sin —erased from the entablatures of man's brain. Then and then only could he achieve his end: to destroy man's serenity forever, or, possibly to terminate the entire human drama, by proffering an atom to be split, in the same seductive way as he had started it by proffering an apple. This might be one version of the Devil in our midst.

Another might be that he went underground for several generations to gather up his energies for an unparalleled display of nihilistic force and that since World War I he has been incarnate in a host of madmen, one, of course, particularly, who kindled the cruelest propensities in man's nature, and contrived detestable enormities on a larger scale than has ever been recorded in man's long history of criminality and martyrdom. In view of all this, some people have returned to the concept of original sin, or to a revised version of it, and the Devil has once again become an object of study, several books describing his nature and career having recently been published.

In a recent seminar on Satan at Harvard University which included several concentrators in literature and several in psychology, besides Professor Harry Levin and myself, there was an airing of diverse views as to what, if any, concept of the Devil as a force could have any significance for men with twentieth century minds. Since no unanimity was sought or approximated, I shall confine my concluding remarks to those tenable views which seem most pertinent to the theories and practices of psychologists.

Since the use of proper names derived from history (e.g. de Sade) or from mythology (e.g. Oedipus) to refer to certain definable human dispositions or complexes is an accepted convention in psychology today, the name "Satan" could be so used within a scientific framework. Precisely which nuclear disposition or compound of dispositions should be designated by the term "Satanism" or the "Satan complex" is a special problem that was not discussed in our seminar. Sufficient for our purposes was the idea that the Satanic spirit is marked by hate and a compulsion to destroy or to abase, both of which are born of a need to revenge a purely personal insult, as described so definitively and affectively by Captain Ahab, for example. As a corollary to this total vindictiveness would be an incapacity to love and an incapacity to create any variety of new forms that are valuable to humanity. This combination, let us say, would constitute an evil personality. But if the object of its hatred were something that was definitely harmful to man's welfare, a personality of this sort might perform a beneficial function. We are all familiar with the old adage to the effect that bad men may do good and good men may do harm. And so, in view of the original conception of the Devil, we should add that the target of the malevolent spirit of Satanism is man's conception of supreme worth, or excellence, and man's desire and resolution to abide by this conception and to approach it in his being and in his conduct.

I shall not stop to write a book in justification of this statement, but will simply call attention to the fact that if we assume that God, Satan's first and foremost enemy, was man's superordinate representation of superlative power and virtue, created in man's own image, then the Satanic personality is freed from its hereditary exclusive reference to a wicked figure in the mythology of Judeo-Christianity and becomes available for application in any context.

Since the modern world constitutes the context to be considered at this point, we should ask what conceptions of supreme wrath are dominant today. We think of Catholicism, Judaism, Mohammedanism, Buddhism, and Communism; and for those peoples who sincerely cleave to any one of these beliefs, the target of Satanic envy and destructiveness is unequivocal. But since for most of the rest of us there is no widely acknowledged comparable conception to guide our individual and social efforts and give some unity and superpersonal significance to our various unique purposes, we might reasonably surmise that the Devil's target in the case of pretty nearly the majority of men and women in the West consists of whatever dispositions and powers may reside in them to create conceptions of this nature: say, the conception of a better world composed of better societies of better persons and to strive to actualize it by self-transformations and social reconstructions. In other words, according to one tenable view, the Satanic aim is to prevent all developments in this direction by shattering man's faith in the existence of the necessary potentialities within himself and reducing him to cynicism and despair until the demoralization and abasement of his personality has reached a state beyond recovery and in one disgraceful debacle of genocidal fury he terminates the long, long history of his species.

And here is where our psychology comes in with the bulk of its theories, its prevailing views of human personality, its images of man, obviously in league with the objectives of the nihilist Satanic spirit. Man is a computer, an animal, or an infant. His destiny is completely determined by genes, instincts, accidents, early conditionings and reinforcements, cultural and social forces. Love is a secondary drive based on hunger and oral sensations or a reaction formation to an innate underlying hate. In the majority of our personological formulations there are no provisions for creativity, no admitted margins of freedom for voluntary decisions, no fitting recognitions of the power of ideals, no bases for selfless actions, no ground at all for any hope that the human race can save itself from the fatality that now confronts it. If we psychologists were all the time, consciously or unconsciously, intending out of malice to reduce the concept of human nature to its lowest common denominators, and were gloating over our successes in so doing, then we might have to admit that to this extent the Satanic spirit was alive within us. But personally I suspect that our abasements of man are consequences, first of all, of the established requirement for a Ph.D. degree, namely that we obtain, so far as possible, mathematically unequivocal results. And so, assuming there is some germ of truth in this, I shall leave you with the question of whether, by any chance, the current Ph.D. system is one of the Devil's cunningest contrivances.

22

AMERICAN ICARUS

If it were not for a dream of flying through the air on a maid's rump and an impromptu story of a modern Pegasus fertilizing from the sky a poor farmer's barren fields (and his cow to boot)—if it were not for these two exploits of the imagination, a psychologist might never have been goaded to delve in celestial myths and, with a selection of these in mind, to brood over the episodes of Grope's* terrestrial career and personality.

Could this short, dark-haired, loose-knit young man be a reincarnation of Tammuz, Attis, or Adonis? A fertility god or sky hero? Such questions would never have occurred to anyone who noticed him approaching on a campus path—collar open at the neck, unshaved most probably, and with a dazed look as if he had just got out of bed. "A typical adolescent," one might have thought in passing. There was little about him to impel a second glance.

As far as we could see, Grope's overt attitudes and behaviors were not far from commonplace. There is nothing unusual, surely, in an apathetic reaction to college courses, lectures, and required reading. Not rare, though less frequent, is withdrawal from competitive extracurricular activities. The only manifest attitude which seemed incongruent with the prevailing sociological portrait of today's American adolescent was Grope's reluctance to become engaged in any erotic ventures. An embarrassment in this sphere, however, is not so irregular as our magazines —*Life* and *Look,* say—might lead us to believe: in our files are numerous case records of college men who are Grope's match on this count. In short, when assessed in terms of overt reactions and proactions, our subject seems to belong to an unextraordinary class of college variants.

It is when weighed in the scales of imaginary activities that Grope

From A. Burton and R. E. Harris, eds., *Clinical Studies in Personality.* 2nd Edition. New York: Harper & Row, 1955, pp. 615–641.

*Grope, the hero of this story, was one of an aggregate of college students who volunteered to serve as subjects in a series of experiments and tests conducted at the Psychological Clinic, Department of Social Relations, Harvard University. The enterprise was financed by grants from the Rockefeller Foundation and from the Laboratory of Social Relations. For many of the findings included in this report I am indebted to my colleagues —Gardner Lindzey, Goodhue Livingston, Henry W. Riecken, Mortimer Slaiman, Robert N. Wilson, Esme Brooks, Tamara Dembo, Herbert Goldings, Josephine L. Murray, and Barbara Tuttle.

stands out as an unduplicated wonder. For these he had an abundance of free hours. Having rejected most opportunities to participate in real endeavors, he had little to interfere with his enjoyment of countless private shows of his excelling fitness for irreal endeavors, mostly of heroic scope. So pure, so unmodulated, so archetypal, were the majority of these dramas—exhibited in his dreams, reveries, story constructions, and most highly valued goals—that we could not escape the supposition that they had come all the way from childhood in their present shapes, with but slight revisions by negating or by counteracting tendencies. At our disposal there were no facts that contradicted this hypothesis, a good many that supported it.

The conclusion to be tentatively submitted here is that one highly influential covert part of Grope's current personality consists of a compound infantile complex, or unity thema, which approximates an ideal type.*

PROCEDURES

1. Autobiography and Interviews. Grope was given a brief outline of important topics to serve as guide in writing his autobiography; and then, after his autobiography had been delivered and read, he was interviewed three times (each for an hour), with items in this document serving as starting points for special lines of interrogation.

2. Questionnaires and Inventories. Grope filled out the following forms (an asterisk* indicating a form that is not yet published): (a) *Inventory of Overt Behaviors; (b) *Inventory of Abilities; (c) Extraversion-Introversion Questionnaire (Gray after Jung); (d) Four Functions Questionnaire (Gray after Jung); (e) Ascendance-Submission Test (Allport); (f) Study of Values (Allport and Vernon); (g) *Literary Knowledge and Interests (Wilson); (h) Psychosomatic Inventory (McFarland).

3. Projective Procedures. The unhappily named "projective" tests administered to Grope included: (a) MAPS (Shneidman); (b) Four Pictures (van Lennep); (c) Tri-Dimensional (Twitchell-Allen); (d) Dramatic Productions (Erikson); (e) Standard TAT (Murray); (f) *TAT No. 2 (Murray); (g) Rorschach; (h) *Musical Reveries; (i) Sentence Completion (modified); (j) *Sentence Construction; (k) *Similes; (l) Draw-A-Family; (m) Szondi; (n) *Mind-Reading; (o) *Psychodramatic.

4. Miscellaneous. Grope also acted as a subject in three special research projects: (a) Happiness Study (Goldings); (b) Facial Asymmetry Study (Lindzey); and (c) Study of Autonomic Reactions to Film of a

---

*An "ideal" unity thema, or "ideal" integrate of infantile complexes, is a convenient theoretical construct, or fiction, which may be defined as a constellation of clear-cut, interdependent themes (forms of dynamic interaction) coupled with evaluations, which is not adulterated or contaminated by irrelevant, inconsistent, or antithetical components.

Primitive Initiation (Mutilation) Ceremony (Lindzey, Ax, and Aas). Data pertinent to the assessment of Grope's level of mental ability were obtained from the college office: ratings on entrance examinations and course grades.

Since there is no space here to report the results of all these procedures, I shall select from our total collection of findings only those which seem most relevant to the formulation of the historic course of Grope's manifest personality and the formulation of his covert personality, or "unity thema," as expressed in his imagination. Although this circumscription of aim necessitates the exclusion of certain less related aspects of Grope's personality, it may be reassuring to know that it has not entailed the omission of any significant facts reported in his autobiography. The following is a reconstructed transcript of that document written, for the most part, in his own words.

PAST HISTORY, AUTOBIOGRAPHY

1. Family History. Grope was born near Springfield, Illinois, of a middle-class family in comfortable circumstances. His father graduated from a state university, worked his way from salesman to buyer in the shoe department of a large store, and, in middle age, organized a wholesale shoe distributing company of his own. His mother also had a college education. After graduation she did promotional work for a department store and later engaged in various civic enterprises. She gave birth to three children: Grope, our subject, another son born two years later, and fourteen years after that a daughter. During Grope's youth, the family lived mainly in two suburban homes, with a few summers spent in the country, near one of the Great Lakes.

2. Infancy and Childhood. Grope was a fat baby with curly hair. He believes that he was breast fed but has no idea at what age he was weaned. Weighing six and a half pounds at birth, he quadrupled his weight in the first year. Despite his rolls of fat, he learned to walk when he was twelve months old.

Grope's earliest memory is of dumping his supper on the floor. Seated in a high chair, he was asked by his mother if he wanted some string beans and, being in a bad mood, repeatedly said no, even though he usually liked string beans. She finally put the plate in front of him, and it was at this point that he upset it and pushed the beans on the floor. This, he writes, "was my first feelings of grief that accompany a sort of 'martyr complex' or 'cut off your nose to spite your face complex.' " (In an interview he defined the complex as a willingness to reject or throw away something he wanted or to fail in an enterprise if, by so doing, he could thwart and condemn, and thus aggrieve his parents. It seems that in his mind a suffering remorseful mother was the acme of sweet revenge.)

Grope has always been somewhat finicky about food. During his later grade-school years this finickiness was, in fact, the root of his most tempestuous quarrels with his mother. When he came home for lunch, he would sometimes run out of the house and back to school if he saw that turnips and cauliflower were being served. (Thus in one act did he deprive himself and condemn his mother.)

Several memories between the ages of 2 and 4 are of food: a cookie shop, a cookie given him by a lady, his mother saying, "What do you say?"; noticing a large display of fruit in a railroad station and being told by his mother that they were dates; receiving a "great big beautiful lollypop" at school and having his mother cut away all but a tiny piece of it.

Grope wet his bed and his pants quite frequently until he was 11. It was a daily issue at first which necessitated his carrying an extra pair of pants to nursery school. (He started nursery school at 3.). When he was wet he would cry so sorrowfully that the teacher would give him a cookie and then change his clothes. He tells us that his parents now believe that his enuresis persisted because he "didn't have enough affection." There may be some grains of truth in this, because both parents drove to work immediately after breakfast and were likely to be too tired when they returned in the evening to spend much time with their children. To their eldest, playing alone most of the day, the summers seemed "interminable." When night came he would not go to bed without a particular, highly valued knotted bundle of cloth, which he called "my Ewa." Today, he imagines that in a child's life such an object "takes the place of a doll, which in turn takes the place of a Deity or an omnipresent mother."

In his autobiography Grope devoted an unusual amount of space to an account of the toys of his childhood and of the course of his attachment to them. Whenever he was made to wait for something he had asked his parents for, his desire for that particular thing, and hence the value of it, in his mind's eye, would rise. But within a week or two of its arrival, the toy's appeal would begin to wane and before very long it was discarded, broken, or perhaps stolen. His Mechano set, his chemistry set, and his bricklaying set each had lost its luster by the end of the day it was presented to him. Only his painting set, his cap pistol, and his bicycle held his interest for any length of time. He tells of a toy auto he enjoyed until the day he sat his little brother in it and sent it rolling down a hill. Since the little fellow couldn't steer, the descent ended in a collision which bent the front axle. (There is no mention of the sibling's fate.) The auto was useless after that. Only once did Grope "very seriously" want something—a pocket watch, and his father, responsive as usual to his requests, bought him a good one which cost about five dollars. When last seen, it was lying in the snow with both hands broken and the crystal gone. "This sight of utter waste sorely disgusted me and the memory still makes me slightly angry." All of a piece with these experiences is Grope's summary statement: "Throughout my life I have found it very difficult to accept gifts properly. My appreciation is restrained and unenthusiastic." (This avowal was later confirmed by observing Grope's dead-pan response to an "experimental" gift.)

He learned to ride a bicycle when he was 7. His father would run behind him with his hand on the seat while he turned the pedals. One day he went thirty yards in one stretch but, on looking round and seeing that his father had stopped supporting him, fell off. ("Which shows what confidence will do.") He was quite proud that he was able to ride a bicycle when other boys his age could not. One night he left the bicycle outside and it was stolen.

Grope would sometimes "make up" knowledge and say something astonishing for a child of his years. Once, at the age of 6, at his grandfather's house he overheard a discussion about fire. He announced that "Fire is a yellow-orange gas from outer space." This utterance made such a hit that he was asked to repeat it over and over again until he got "sick of it."

Between the ages of 3 and 10 Grope was in the care of a German maid who tried to teach him how to read the clock. Each time he got it wrong she would slap him in the face, which only made him more flustered and her "more frustrated." But the maid appealed to him despite this treatment, or perhaps because of it.

3. School Experiences. Since he had gone to nursery school when he was 3, Grope did not have to attend kindergarten. He has few memories of his early years at primary school, except that he showed talent for drawing in second grade, and at home read and reread the Oz books (by L. F. Baum). In the third grade he overheard his teacher telling his mother that he was bright.

He acquired no athletic abilities until he moved to another school, just before entering fifth grade. Near his new home there were real woods which he enjoyed tremendously. He liked to climb birch trees and swing down again to earth, over and over again. He "shinnied up" practically every tree he could find. He developed a lot of strength this way, and one day after school he threw down, one by one, every boy in the class. He states that he soon became the best athlete in the school, the best football player, the best drawer, the smartest (with the highest mark on an achievement test), the first person to be elected president of the sixth-grade class, and the only person to be elected twice. The teacher kept telling him in front of the class that he was most likely to succeed. Besides, he was commander-in-chief of a club he formed, and "half a dozen girls" had a crush on him. He tells us that outwardly he was very modest, but inwardly he was convinced that no one surpassed him in all-around ability.

He enjoyed painting lessons in sixth grade and did quite a bit of this until his sophomore year in high school, when other activities took precedence; but he still had time for his drawing.

His "fall" began in sixth grade with loss of weight and sluggishness. He had many colds during that summer and when he went back to school in the seventh grade found that he hadn't grown an inch. The following winter he was in bed for two straight months. When he got well, his athletic career was "shot." He had lost his muscle and, what was more important to him, his courage. He feels that after this he was never much of an athlete. Today he plays only a fair game of ping-pong, tennis, baseball, and basketball. During his illness (seventh grade) he learned to play chess with such expertness that he beat all his relatives. He also learned to play bridge at this time.

Grope's account of his "fall" and subsequent lack of distinction at school is not wholly in accord with his list of high-school accomplishments. In his freshman year he won the bantamweight boxing title and in his senior year the middleweight title. Despite illnesses he played varsity tennis and junior varsity football. He was skillful in managing the campaign of the seventh-grade class president and the junior-grade vice-president, both of whom won. He was elected treasurer of his class sophomore year, and a member of the Student Council. Also, he was editor of the yearbook and an excellent comedian and master of ceremonies, talents which his classmates acknowledged by electing him "Biggest Joker" on graduation. In his studies he did well; he received the highest mark on a mathematics achievement test, was the only boy in his class to win a certificate on a nation-wide scholastic test, and passed the college board examinations with creditable grades. In his spare time he collected stamps, drew and painted, played chess and bridge.

He enjoyed building model airplanes.

His friendships were many but casual, never enduring. When he was a freshman in high school he was very close to a boy who lived on his street until a teacher happened to remark that familiarity breeds contempt. Both boys took this very seriously and their friendship deteriorated. At college he made no real friends until the end of his sophomore year. Currently he is extremely fond of one boy, a former member of his card-playing clique.

From eighth through tenth grade Grope suffered from halitosis, which, he believes, made him much less popular and thus gave rise to a distressing inferiority complex. He thought he could make himself less offensive by speaking with a minimal expiration of breath, and now, six years later, his voice is habitually so low that his words are not always audible.

4. *Sexual Experiences.* Grope's sexual potentialities were first aroused when he was about 8, the object of his "erotic tendencies" being the maid who was in charge of him. Seeing her breasts on one occasion started a sort of interior excitement which he did not think about or try

to define but the nature of which was indicated in a dream in which he rode through the sky on the rump of this maid. He began to get inexplicable erections before urinating and when he was angry or frustrated. One of his more bizarre fantasies was that of flying over a city and urinating on the buildings, all of which were constructed out of women's bodies. A little later, his sex education began informally. Learning "dirty words and dirty jokes," etc., he began to get a general idea "of what females were for." One of his chief misconceptions was that intercourse was achieved when the male inserted his penis into the female anus. As time went on, however, things became clearer and his curiosity was appeased by reading the more pertinent parts of Clendenning's *The Human Body.*

Outside of parties where Spin the Bottle and Post Office were played, he had nothing that approached an affair until he was 16, when he had a year-long romance with an 18-year-old girl. This affair petered out because he had "never heard or imagined of going beyond the leg-wrestling stage without making it actual intercourse." When he was 17 he "went steady" with a girl his own age, but they never got beyond the mutual masturbation stage and they finally separated, his reason being "too much sex."

He had never seen any reason for masturbating and believed that his friends did it merely to prove to themselves that they were virile. But at a summer camp where he was employed after graduating from high school he had occasion to discuss masturbation with one of the dishwashers. When asked by Grope why he masturbated, the young man replied, "Well, for the *thrill.*" This was news! Grope determined to start that very night. He has been masturbating frequently ever since. He suffers no remorse as he keeps reminding himself that the more sexually active he is now (according to Kinsey's findings), the longer he will retain his potency in later life.

At college this form of sexual outlet has taken the place of dating. He had only a few blind dates in freshman year, none since. He is looking forward to marriage and right now would settle for any girl who is "attractive, intelligent, non-argumentative, has large lips, wide hips, and is willing and able to bear me about half-a-dozen boys."

5. *Family Relationships.* Grope thinks that the relationship between his parents has been a "pretty good" one, despite occasional quarrels which are likely to terminate with his mother weeping. As for himself, Grope affirms that he has never loved either his mother or his father, his present attitude being one of confirmed indifference, mixed with a fair amount of "loyalty and respect." While working for his father's company last summer he gained some appreciation of this parent's business acumen; but his opinion of his mother is no higher than it was ten years ago. He thinks that her deficiencies of character outweigh her intellectual gifts. It is she who has disappointed him the most. Notwithstanding this, Grope insists that his parents have always been devoted and gener-

ous to him. They often tried to encourage him (with ill success) and were more thrilled than he whenever he was in any way outstanding. He is nonetheless disposed to believe that they must have made a lot of mistakes in rearing him, their first child.

When Grope's sister was born, a few years ago, his parents, "having read books on sibling rivalry," tried to heap an unusual amount of affection upon both him and his brother. This, he feels, was ridiculous, since by that time he had long outgrown any dependence on their love.

During his teens Grope had many fierce quarrels with his parents, ending by his plotting various schemes for revenge, such as a six-weeks silent treatment. He often imagined his own death and his parents' subsequent grief, one particularly gratifying fantasy being that of resurrection from the grave as a ghost and then of gloating unseen over his mother's remorseful grief.

Grope's brother was born when he was 3, but, he assures us, there was no sibling rivalry in those early years. In fact, he hardly ever thought of him. His brother was a nonentity until the age of 8, at which time the two boys began playing together and getting into fights. They became good friends in high school, when Grope began to appreciate him a little more. He states that he doesn't fight with his brother now, the latter being an inch taller, ten pounds heavier, and solid muscle.

6. *Ambitions, Goals, Values.* As a child Grope wanted to be an orange grower. Later, after reading a book on China by Pearl Buck, he "became incensed with the desire" to go there, "an industrially backward land," and build bridges. He also thought of becoming a painter. As his estimation of his own powers increased, he became "more and more inspired and confident" about his role in life.

His major recurrent fantasy was one of landing on a desert island in the Pacific with a band of followers, discovering an inexhaustible spring of fresh water and an abundant food supply, and then founding a new civilization with himself as king and lawgiver. He often dreamed and daydreamed of self-propelled flights and of jumping off a high place and floating gracefully and gently to the ground. But he was almost equally hospitable to less extravagant fantasies: he considered becoming a prize fighter, an actor, an army general, a millionaire, an inventor, a psychiatrist, and a teacher. "It would be a lot of fun working with kids, teaching them with a sense of humor, and having them think you are a 'good guy.'" He has imagined himself a famous tap dancer, a singer, and a movie comedian. He is attracted by the stage and has a tentative plan of enrolling in some school of the drama. His more immediate intention, however, is to enlist in the Air Corps and become a pilot. Although in his opinion world wars are preventable evils, he expects another one within fifteen years, which will destroy much or most of civilization. The two worst things that might happen to him are (a) to be maimed in the war and (b) to lose his self-confidence. Finally, he writes: "If I could remodel the world to my heart's content, I would establish a sound World Government and would like to be the dictator, a good dictator." He would be "most proud" of having his name "go down in history as a leader, or as an artist, or as a discoverer or inventor."

He thinks that his insight increased most rapidly during his early teens when he was embattled with his parents. It was then also that he began working out his philosophy, the chief tenet of which is that every person's goal in life is happiness. Another tenet is that happiness is attainable in a number of different ways, depending on the individual. In his own case, the major sources of prospective happiness, and hence the most valued goals, are money, power, glory, and fame. "These are the alternatives of most normal men." He has never been to church and states that he is "sure there is no sort of God or vital force."

At the moment Grope feels that he is spiritually becalmed. In the past, his development has always occurred in "spurts or cycles." "If I did something well, I would be spiritually elevated, that is, my spirits would become gay. In the last few years my spirits have been in equilibrium and my development has more or less stagnated." Today he does not seem to be able to decide anything. He will either try to turn over a new leaf academically or get a job some place, such as opening a snack bar with a friend. Concluding this topic, he writes: "I am just biding my time and waiting for the day when my 'soul' will ignite and this inner fire will send me hurtling (two rungs at a time) up the ladder of success."

7. Evaluations of Self and Others. Grope highly esteems "all other people." Everyone seems to him interesting and exciting (more or less); but he especially admires the personalities and achievements of supremely great men. He has had many heroes—da Vinci and Van Gogh in particular. At times, he tells us, he derives a lot of personal satisfaction from being gregarious, but he gets depressed if he is guilty of a *faux pas:* he "kicks himself mentally" for days.

Grope feels that the world's estimate of him is that he is a "pretty nice guy." As for his own estimate of himself, he used to think he was "pretty hot stuff," but now he "just agrees with the world."

COMPONENTS OF CURRENT MANIFEST PERSONALITY

In unfamiliar social situations Grope is keenly observant but shyly self-suppressed; he speaks little and with a very low voice. He waits for the alter to make the first move. Once his embarrassment has dissolved, however, he becomes relaxed, tensionless, responsive, and quietly jocose. In this phase he strikes one as an easygoing, good-natured fellow—a "good guy"—with a keen, ever present, satirical, though somewhat juvenile, sense of humor.

Grope reports that a few months after his arrival at Harvard he came to the conclusion that he was a "small frog in a big puddle," surrounded by many far superior competitors for athletic, social, and academic honors. No hope for glory. Since then he has made the minimum amount of intellectual effort. He studies very little and cuts many of his lectures, especially if they come before noon. As a result, he is on probation, ranking well below the scholarship level predicted for him—an "underachiever." He has joined no organizations, has accepted no roles or responsibilities, and dates no girls. This abstinence allows him to devote the maximum amount of time to sleep, relaxation, daydreaming, and playing bridge with a small clique of cronies. Of these the one he most liked has recently been flunked out of college. Except for this boy, he gives no evidence of affectional attachments.

Grope was rated (on a 1–6 point scale) by himself, by two of his acquaintances, and by six members of the Clinic assessment staff on a large number of manifest behavioral variables. Only those variables on which he was almost unanimously rated among the lowest 25 percent of our subjects (1 or 2), or on which he was almost unanimously rated among the highest 25 percent (5 or 6), will be mentioned here.

Grope was judged to be unusually passive (inactive, indolent, apathetic) under current conditions, though not incapable of considerable, though spasmodic, activity under more favorable conditions (need Passivity 5). There were no *objectifications* of ambition (need Achievement 1). These two ratings (high passivity, low achievement) are confluent with our subject's inability to start on his own steam and to keep going without coöperation or without anticipation of a close reward (need Autonomy, Self-Sufficiency 1, and Endurance 1).

All of a piece with these estimates was the high mark Grope received on need Exhibition, Recognition (5), which was clearly a very strong disposition of his personality, though manifested during the current period only when he found himself in a familiar, congenial, and appreciative social group, at which times this need was likely to be fused with Playmirth (6). He gained the attention he enjoyed by comical displays. It might be said that Expression, Exhibition was a part of Grope's overt *private* personality (behaviors manifested in intimate interactions with receptive, reciprocating alters), because in more public or less familiar situations this disposition was checked by his fear of committing a *faux pas* or "making a fool of himself" (need Infavoidance 5, coupled with a persisting Inferiority Complex).

Grope was also rated high (5) on need Excitance (enjoyment of novelty, excitement, thrills, spectacles, etc.) and high (5) relative to other undergraduates on need Sentience (appreciation or composition of artistic forms), despite the fact that his drawings were not "serious art" but more in the nature of satirical cartoons (Playmirth again predominating). Most questionable—in fact definitely wrong in retrospect—was the rating of 5 on need Affiliation, because, though habitually good-natured, smiling, and responsive, Grope had formed no firm and lasting friendships. He seemed to be existing without links, a free-floater in today's "lonely crowd," a passing acquaintance, with whom one is never seriously involved and on whom one can never seriously depend, a man of superficial contacts who does not attach himself for long to any one person and yet is dependent on everyone he meets. His self was open to friendliness—in no way distant, withdrawn, encased, aloof, resentful, or suspicious (need Rejection 2). He was rated below average on overt sexual behavior (need Sex 2) but rather high (5) on sexual and social curiosity (voyeurism).

Grope's room was always in a "mess"; he did not put his belongings in allotted places, and when he took off his clothes at night, he dropped them on the floor where they remained till morning. His appearance, handwriting, and written papers were all equally disorderly (need Order 1, and need Retention [conservation of possessions] 2). So much for the most striking of Grope's overt (manifest, or objectified) needs.

It was inferred on the basis of these and other evidences that Grope was very low (1) on degree of Ego Structuration and equally low (1) on degree of Superego Integration. He has very seldom, if ever, been concerned with moral questions and has no memory of ever feeling guilty or remorseful. No sociocentric interests or group identifications are apparent. His most valued goals—money, power, glory, fame—are perceived in a purely egocentric fashion. He has no religion. His dominant axis of evaluation is superiority-inferiority (of ability, wealth, social status, authority, and prestige); the ethical axis is absent or repressed, as it is in psychopathic personalities. This notwithstanding, Grope is guilty of nothing more hurtful or illegal than a few minor boyhood thefts. He seems to be free of vicious inclinations.

Grope rated himself high on Artistic Ability (6), Entertaining Ability (5), Social Ability (5), and Intuitive Ability (5), but very low on Self-Directive Ability (1) and Memory Ability (1).

Grope's responses on most of our questionnaires and inventories placed him in the middle range. He came out high (5), however, on Extraversion, and on the Studies of Values indicated more concern with Political issues than with the other five. On Level of Satisfaction he was low average and also low average in his estimates of the satisfaction level of other persons (supplementary self-projection).

INTERPRETATION OF CURRENT MANIFEST PERSONALITY

Since Grope showed considerable interest in athletics and scholarship at high school and was periodically quite energetic in organizing and promoting various social enterprises, we surmise that his current apathy, his lack of enthusiasm and will power, his submission to a sluggish id, is "situational," rather than unchangeably constitutional. The current situation is one of being outclassed in all spheres by more talented and/or more resolute associates. Evidently, he is not devoted to any form of athletics for its own sake, to learning for its own sake, or to any one of the numerous accessible extracurricular activities for its own sake; nor is he prompted by a need to learn some skill and to accomplish something for the sake of a resulting inner satisfaction or self-respect. It is glory he is after—praise, prestige, and fame—and since his present situation offers no prospects of these rewards, why should he exert himself?

Another significant attribute of Grope's current situation is the absence of parental support. During his school years in Illinois he had been constantly spurred on and, "whenever in any way outstanding," applauded by his for-him-ambitious parents; and among his classmates, furthermore, during at least one glorious period of his life, he had been the "best" at everything. But at Harvard unhappily no such encouragements were at hand, and without encouragement he had no confidence, and without confidence he was nothing. He had to learn his worth from the lips of others. This conclusion was confirmed by the finding that a few sentences of "experimental" praise set him going at his books for a week or more on two occasions.

Another confirmation comes from the story Grope composed for Picture 7 of the TAT: "A gray-haired man is looking at a younger man who is sullenly staring into space."

Here's a serious and intense young man, methodical, who the moment he entered Harvard knew he was going to be a pure physicist. He graduated Magna, Phi Beta Kappa, and went on to graduate school, where he was more or less a protégé of one of the great, good professors there, because he demonstrated unusual ability to learn, to grasp complicated theories as well as experiments in applied physics. Of course by this time, six years, he'd be in for a Ph.D. He is wondering if there is more to life than just studying. He's having his doubts about whether he can be happy being a physicist, working by himself instead of with others. This kind professor in the Graduate School sees the despondency of the last few weeks and decides to have a talk with him. He tries to encourage him at first, by saying, "If you want, I have a very good job set up for you with one of the big companies." This guy shrugs and finally decides to tell the scientist about what's been bothering him. He does, and this scientist is very understanding, and says, "Well, when I was your age I felt the same way." He had a lot of insight. He told him exactly what he was thinking about. He said that he felt the same way when he was his age, and that he must look for a purpose in life. It was just a psychological talk, kind of bolstered him. Well, anyway, the young man goes along with this. He just needed that extra push.

Among the internal conditions contributing to Grope's present slump in his weak, unintegrated, and immature ego system (already mentioned)—the absence of work habits and the insufficiency of will power, the inability, when bored or tired, to force himself to finish something he has undertaken. Another determinant is his low tolerance of failure, his fear of "falling." This might stem from a childhood supposition that his ambitious parents would not respect him if it were proved that he was not among the best. By not competing, by not trying, he can avoid the demonstration of this humiliating probability. But in the sphere of scholarship it is a different matter: how can he both abstain from effort and avoid the stigma of being expelled from college? At this point another factor begins to operate, Grope's "spite complex": failure can be used as a weapon of condemnation. He confessed that by flunking out of college he could prove that his father had erred in urging him to go to Harvard rather than to Illinois or to some smaller college where he might have been a "big frog."

One final all-important determinant of Grope's collapse at Harvard is the height, diversity, and inconstancy of his ideal self-conception (a fitful sequence of heterogeneous ego-ideal figures, some of whom—a self-propelled sky flier, the founder of a new civilization, the dictator of a world government, a famous inventor—are far beyond his present reach). With these glorious visions running through his head, how can he bend down to day-by-day pedestrian exertions in order to make for himself a little name at Harvard? He says that, although he used to think he was "pretty hot stuff," he has finally come round to the world's view that he is merely a good guy. This is what his intellect has decided; but the conflict is not thereby settled: to his soul a good guy is not nearly good enough. Hence, it is necessary for him to constantly refight the battle between his ideal self-conception and his real self-conception, as the following TAT story No. 8 makes evident. ("An adolescent boy looks straight out of the picture. The barrel of a rifle is visible at one side, and in the background is the dim scene of a surgical operation, like a reverie-image.")

This picture seems to show the imaginations of a boy. . . . The kid is a college student, leaning up against one of the pillars of Widener and thinking. He's a little frustrated by things at school—the competition, and the state of affairs, not only in school, but the fact that the world in his day is so much tougher. He feels that if he lived back in the days of, say, Aristotle he would certainly have thought up some of the fundamental concepts of physics or chemistry, or could have become a great doctor. If he wanted to be a pre-med student in this day, it would be very hard to achieve anything, any fame and glory. He takes time out to think back on the old days. Now he thinks he's a doctor on this warship, trying to perform an operation, using the light that comes through one of the portholes and a dim lantern. He thinks how people would look up to him the way he sterilizes everything, a practice not usually done then. . . . The reason he's doing these daydreams is because he doesn't feel he can get much glory in this age, this civilization. He needs to go back to an older one in his thoughts. He finally realizes that perhaps there were geniuses in the old days too. He would not have had any more chance then to achieve glory than he does now. He feels he must be satisfied with his time and position, and must get happiness out of some of the fundamental personal things in life, rather than getting his name in a history book. Anyway, he finally realizes his mediocrity. Before he went to school he thought he was good and he comes to school and realizes there are many others better than him, who have intellectual intelligence over him. He thinks that due to all this competition he will never get anywhere in a society like this, where there seem to be so few inventions left. He daydreams about a past where he would certainly have made a name for himself, there was so much room for growth. After two more years of study he realizes he isn't such a hot shot and has to be content with an average existence.

COMPONENTS OF COVERT PERSONALITY

1. Urethral Erotism. Grope recalls experiencing (during boyhood) erections just previous to urination, as observed by Halverson[1] in babies; and he entertained the idea that babies were made by urinating into a woman's rectum. In short, sex was apperceived in urinary terms. Also he manifested, in high degree, every other concomitant of urethral erotism, as defined by Freud and his followers: cathection of fire, "burning" ambition, exhibitionism, and voyeurism. Remember Grope's bright saying: "Fire is a yellow-orange gas from outer space." Even today he "gets a thrill" by lighting wastepaper in his tin scrap basket and seeing it flare up. There is a high incidence of pertinent fire imagery in his projective protocols. Finally, there is the association of persistent enuresis and urethral erotism (dreams of urination accompanied by ejaculation) which we and others have found in a number of personalities. Thus, the evidence for the presence and continued operation of this rather enigmatic infantile complex is about as complete as one can reasonably demand without a full-length psychoanalysis.

2. Ascensionism. This is the name I have given to the wish to overcome gravity, to stand erect, to grow tall, to dance on tiptoe, to walk on water, to leap or swing in the air, to climb, to rise, to fly, or to float down gradually from on high and land without injury, not to speak of rising from the dead and ascending to heaven. There are also emotional and ideational forms of ascensionism—passionate enthusiasm, rapid elevations of confidence, flights of the imagination, exultation, inflation of spirits, ecstatic mystical up-reachings, poetical and religious—which are likely to be expressed in the imagery of physical ascensionism. The upward thrust of desire may also manifest itself in the cathection of tall pillars and towers, of high peaks and mountains, of birds—high-flying hawks and eagles—and of the heavenly bodies, especially the sun. In its most mundane and secular form, ascensionism consists of a craving for upward social mobility, for a rapid and spectacular rise of prestige.

In Grope's case, ascensionism was fused—at the very start perhaps
—with urethral erotism. Recall his dream of flying through the air on the
maid's rump (in conjunction with his urinary theory of intercourse) and
his fantasies of urinating from the sky on the bodies of women. Then read
the following story told to one of the (unpublished) TAT 2 pictures ("Barn
surrounded by snow. A winged horse is flying across the sky. The head
of a bearded man is in right lower corner. In the snow is the dim outline
of a girl's face."):

An old hermit went out into the woods and built himself a farm. After thirty
years of living all by himself on the crops he produced, he got pretty tired of this
humdrum existence, so he decided that he wanted to re-enter the competitive
world and try to sell, was planning on selling his crops, planning to build some
sort of a fortune. So he worked for a few years, couldn't seem to get very large
crops, really good crops. They wouldn't grow. What he needed was more fertilizer, but he couldn't afford fertilizer in any quantity, so he was practically at his
wits' end, and one night he decided to turn to religion; and as miracles will
happen, the very next day Pegasus flew over and fertilized all his plants. Not only
that, but the cow in the barn bore him a daughter; something he had always
wanted. In the picture here, he is squinting in his happiness; feeling that life has
really been rewarding. So the picture is the spirit of happiness.

Grope reported many dreams and daydreams of rising in the air and
flying, sometimes in a car or in a horse-drawn chariot, like Apollo's. Other
fantasies were of shooting through space and landing on the planet Mars.

In his autobiography he proudly tells us that he learned to walk at
12 months and to ride a bicycle at 7 years; and he devotes a long paragraph to a detailed account of each stage of his baby sister's progress in
overcoming the pull of gravity. In addition to these items are Grope's
passion for climbing trees, swinging out and down, his fantasy of becoming a tap-dancer, the model airplanes he built, his admiration for Leo-
nardo da Vinci's flying machine, and his intention of enlisting in the Air
Corps, and the twelve or more flying creatures he saw in the Rorschach
blots: two butterflies, two flying bats, a flying dog, a horse's head with
hoofs emerging from a cloud bank, a pair of vultures being swooped on
from above by a pair of eagles and these attacked by a flock of jumping
woodpeckers. Asked by a hypothetical fairy godmother to make "seven
wishes," he listed Height as his fourth wish.

3. *Cynosural Narcism.* This strikes me as a suitable term (more embracing than exhibitionism) to denote a craving for unsolicited attention
and admiration, a desire to attract and enchant all eyes, like a star in the
firmament. It is first supremely gratified at that *epiphanal* moment of
babyhood when the grandparents and relatives arrive at the cradle, with
gifts perhaps, to beam with wonder at this new emergence of pure
potentiality, pure Being. No memory of this, of course, in Grope; but in
line with it is the grandfather's astonishment (at a later date) when the

child came out with his cynosural pronouncement about fire. The cynosural ego-ideal which Grope shaped for himself after he entered fifth grade and became the best at everything has remained to this day almost intact. In Draw-A-Family his self-portrait, twice the size of his father's and his mother's, was of a prodigiously strong athlete, corresponding in every way to his description of the image that came to mind when he was handed the blank card (No. 16) of the TAT:

> Well, I see a huge, powerful man. He is in the midst of throwing a shot-put. He weighs about 310 pounds and stands 6 feet, 6 inches high. He has no clothing except bathing trunks. There he stands with spectators all around him. He's about to win his third straight decathlon. Not only is he the most perfect physical specimen in all of Greece, but he is a nice guy, unspoiled. Everyone likes him. They practically worship him. He is a sensation; a wonderful box-office draw.

Already we begin to see a close, emotionally logical—indeed, an almost inevitable—connection, if not fusion, between ascensionism and cynosural narcism: the way to attract all eyes is to be very tall, to stand erect above the multitude, and best of all to rise in the air like a god. Remembering that in Grope's personality ascensionism was fused with urethral erotism and that urethral erotism ordinarily reaches its peak in the phallic phase of psychosexual development, we may surmise that we are dealing with an imagination in which an ascending cynosural phallus was transmuted into an ascending cynosural body, both being "pretty hot stuff" and possibly on this account associated with fire, to constitute, in any event, the kind of burning ambition which Grope portrays in his concluding sentence: "I am just biding my time and waiting for the day when my 'soul' will ignite and this inner fire will send me hurtling (two rungs at a time) up the ladder of success." Clearly this type of ambition depends on the carrying power of an unpredictable upsurge or excess of psychic energy (spontaneity, creative zest, self-confidence, enthusiasm), an excess which may someday be shown to consist of a quantum of sublimated erotic energy. In any event, little reliance is placed on will power, discipline, industry, conscientiousness.

Furthermore, since the youthful energy—passionate, romantic, fiery —that serves as motive power for this type of ambition is not likely to continue on a high level for very long without frequent reinforcements, its strategy entails a series of short, spirited, and spectacular achievements, never a long, slow, methodical, solitary, and inconspicuous, course of action.

The association of an ascending cynosural body and ascending fire is illustrated by Grope's story to Card 17 TAT ("A naked man is clinging to a rope. He is in the act of climbing up or down."). The fourth World War ended, he said, when a nation of supermen overran the globe, and now, in each conquered country, the victors are trying by means of strength tests to select other possible supermen with whom to start a new race. He continues as follows:

In this case this person elected to climb a rope; he was quite strong. The bottom of the rope was made of an inflammable—soaked in potassium chloride, I guess. They would set fire to the bottom of it and the flames would go at a certain slightly increasing rate. If the person failed to reach the top before the flames did, of course he was killed. This person starts out like fury and by fifty yards the rope is burned only about five yards from the bottom. . . . About seventy-five yards up his arms are like lead-weight. He doesn't feel that he can go any further. . . . He goes another five or ten yards and suddenly he slips back and barely manages to catch on five yards below. By now the flames are about half way up. Then he gets panicky, gets another tremendous burst, and goes about ten yards. He hangs on there and watches the flames increasing their momentum. . . . He goes on taking about a foot at a time, the flames getting nearer. He can't rest—very hard to rest hanging on to a rope. He finally gets about ten yards from the top, that's the last thing he remembers.

The end of this story suggests the next component.

4. Falling, Precipitation. "Falling" denotes an undesired or accidental descension of something (usually a human body or the status [reputation] of a person, but it may be feces, urine, or any cathected object). "Precipitation," on the other hand, means a consciously or subconsciously desired calamitous descension: the S allows himself to fall or leaps from a height (precipitative suicide), or he pushes another person over a cliff, throws something down, or purposely urinates or defecates on the floor. In one or the other of these two categories—it is often difficult to say which—fall a large number of items in Grope's case history: diurnal and nocturnal enuresis (eleven years of it), frequent micturition (checked on the Psychosomatic Inventory), several memories of fecal incontinence, fantasies of urinating and defecating from the air, the episode of throwing down a plate of string beans (his "martyr complex"), of dropping or throwing down his pocket watch, of shoving his little brother down a hill, of throwing stones down from a height on girls, of throwing down, one by one, every kid in his class, and recently, at college, his writing a comedy in which a rich man (father figure) is thrown by a huge gorilla down a water closet.

Finally, there is Grope's memory of falling off a bicycle and his statement that he often fell from trees, a resonance, perhaps, of earlier more traumatic falls during his learning-to-walk stage. The question of falling or not falling is central in the account he gives of his baby sister's efforts.

In all this we may dimly perceive an ascension-descension cycle on different levels: (a) fiery tumescence (ascension) of penis followed by detumescence (descension) with urination (precipitation of water); (b) ascension of desire for cathected toy followed by descension of cathection and precipitation of toy; (c) ascension of body followed by fall or precipitation (as in the story of rope climber and several other stories); and (d) ascension of status (prestige) followed by descension (the "fall" after his phenomenal sixth-grade success and now his "fall" at college). This is an archetypal thematic sequence against which we are warned by the ancient aphorism: "Pride cometh before a fall." Very probably the Adlerian formula is applicable here: Grope's ardent desire to ascend is a counteractive disposition excited by one or more experiences of descent—let us say, some unremembered locomotive accidents coupled with recurrent enuresis, intensified by several falls of status, beginning at 2 years with his displacement from the cynosural center by the birth of that "nonentity," his younger brother.

This ascension-descension sequence is also reminiscent of the great cycles of nature, especially the solar cycle and the myth of the solar hero, his superior origin, humble foster parentage, rise to glory, decline, death, and resurrection. The precocious, importunate, and extravagant character of Grope's ascensionism suggests that he belongs with the adolescent, overreaching, would-be solar heroes, Icarus and Phaëthon—father-superseding enthusiasts with unstructured ego systems.

Grope's early conflict on the physiological level between fire and water (heat and cold, erection and urination) was entertainingly projected into the weatherman on high in the story he told to Card 11 TAT ("A road skirting a deep chasm between high cliffs. On the road in the distance are obscure figures. Protruding from the rocky wall on one side is a long head and neck of a dragon."):

> This must be prehistoric times. A crowd of animals (live in this nice fertile valley). They are half baboon and half pig. And each year they have terrible weather. It would either be a drought, or a flood, extreme heat or extreme cold. So they all gather around and decide to send someone up to the weather maker's place. . . . When he got up there he found that the place was a combination of all the weathers. It seems there was fire from one side and rain up above. . . . "What do you want?" . . . This representative presented his case and asked why he had to send so many kinds of bad weather down on all this nice peace loving community. So this weather maker said, "Well, look at it this way, I have all weathers up here and I try to keep them all off you. I have hot weather, cold weather, wet and dry weather up here all at once. How do you think I feel about it anyway? Most of the time I keep at least three of these different kinds of weather up here. I only get rid of one of them. If I wanted to be mean I could send them all out."

Limitations of space forbid the printing of more than these few items out of our large collection of to-me-convincing evidences of the dynamic interdependence, in the mind of this young man, of fire (heat, passion) and ascension of body (rising, flying), of ascension and descension (falling, precipitation), of fire and water, and of descension and water (falling water or falling of body into water). One illustration of this last, truly Icarian association (precipitation into water) must suffice. It is the sixth story on Grope's MAPS protocol:

Well, the man in the striped tie, the Harvard tie, majored in physics (smiles). But he is not a good physicist. He doesn't work. He married a woman for the money she was capable of earning. (But the wife's rapid promotion aroused the envy and ire of the assistant buyer, her unsuccessful male rival at the department store. The buyer, armed with a gun, waylaid her one evening on the Cottage Farm Bridge.) He said to the woman: "Either you resign or I'll shoot you." "No, don't," she said and kept backing away, until she tripped and went over the railing into the river hundreds of feet below. (Two policemen arrive on the scene, followed shortly by the drowned woman's husband and son. The husband, realizing that he and his son have lost their one means of support, pushes the boy over the rail into the water, and then pushes one of the policemen after him.) The salesman sees his chance to make amends. So he shoots the husband, and turns to the other policeman and says, "Can't I go free? Have I paid my debt to society?" . . . The policeman shoots the man, but on the way back he is so drunk with delight that he stumbles over the rail. To this day, no one really knows what happened out there. (Six deaths, four by falling into water.)

Evidences of matricidal and patricidal fantasies (of an anal aggressive type), as well as of castration anxiety, are fairly plentiful; but these are common occurrences in the minds of young men and to stress them here would divert attention from the less conventional integrate of themas which constitutes the thesis of this paper.

5. *Craving for Immortality.* No doubt the narcistic core in every man yearns for perpetual existence; but of all our subjects Grope is unexampled in giving Everlasting Life ("I might settle for 500 years") as one of his seven wishes for himself. If everlasting life on earth is impossible, then one can conceive of resurrection of the body or the soul. As illustration we have Grope's fantasy of breaking out of his tomb, digging his way up, and hovering in phantom form over his parents' house. In three of his stories the hero dies and comes to life again. If resurrection (re-ascension) is not to be vouchsafed a man, there is the possibility of *replication,* which may be defined as the process whereby one or more persons are transformed in the image of the subject. It is the complement of identification, or emulation: the implanting of a memorable and impelling image of the self in the minds of others. This is the evolutionary significance of Grope's overreaching need for attention, worship, fame —glory in the highest. But if this is denied a man, there is still the possibility of immortalizing his likeness through reproduction. Grope was not invited by the idea of an enduring, stable marriage. For himself he prophesied divorce. What he did crave, however, was a number of tall sons with profiles somewhat better than his own. To Card 13 of the TAT ("A young man is standing with downcast head buried in his hands.

Behind him is the figure of a woman lying in bed.") he told the following story:

John, the man pictured here, liked children. When he went away to school, he used to think a lot about children. . . . As he liked them, he wanted to have his own, but he could never find a girl that he really wanted. So after he graduated, he came home, at night, and first he went into the maid's room—that's the room pictured here. He woke the maid up, and *she* said, "Oh, how good to see you again, John." John, who was not one for mincing words, said, "Listen, maid, I want children. Children mean a lot to me. How about it?" So the maid said, "No, no, John, no, I am already bespoken." So John said, "Well, in that case there is nothing for me to do." Well, I imagine the thought came to him that now that she was dead he couldn't have his children anyway. It suddenly hit him and he was quite peeved.

Other data reveal a profound concern with the possibility of impotence or sterility.

6. Depreciation and Enthrallment of Women, Bisexuality. Grope spoke contemptuously of his mother and cynically of women generally. Love was a never felt experience. But, as his projective protocols made plain, women were nonetheless important, if not indispensable, to him as glorifying agents: a female was (a) someone to be "swept off her feet," to be driven "sex-mad" by the mere sight of him; (b) someone to applaud his exploits; (c) someone with "wide hips" to bear him sons; and (d) someone to mourn his death. As one might expect in such a person, there were abundant evidences of a suffusing feminine component coupled with some degree of homosexuality. This is best illustrated by a story he told in the Tri-Dimensional Test. A king announces that he will give half his kingdom to the person who creates the most beautiful thing in the world. The last contestant (hero of the story) comes forward and says, "I have created a replica of myself." Whereupon the king says, *"That* is the most beautiful thing in the world, therefore *you* are the most beautiful thing in the world. Will you be my queen?" The king takes the hero as his male queen and gives this androgynous beauty half his kingdom (cynosural ascension of status).

INTERPRETATION OF COVERT PERSONALITY

1. Icarus Complex. This integrate might be defined as a compound of (a) cynosural narcism and (b) ascensionism, combined with (c) the prospection of falling. It seems to be derived, in its extreme form, from a fixation at the urethral-phallic stage of development, before object love has been attained. Consequently, it is associated with (d) the cathection of fire, and, if enuresis or incontinence becomes an issue, with (e) an abundance of water imagery. Furthermore, as offspring of this complex is (f) a craving for immortality (some form of re-ascension) as well as (g) a conception of women as objects to be utilized for narcistic gains.

I am inclined to the tentative opinion that the Icarus complex is the immature (perhaps perpetually adolescent) form of what might be termed the Solar complex, a complex which is characterized by the same genetical components but, in addition, by a relatively strong ego structure supported by tested abilities, which serves to constrain the reckless aspirations of youth within the bounds of realizable achievements, and thus to neutralize the dread of falling.

If tendencies for genital exhibitionism and arsonism are both suppressed, an Icarus or Solar complex might be objectified on the physical and technical levels by such cynosural and ascensionistic enterprises as high jumping, pole vaulting, discus throwing, high diving, fancy skating, circus acrobatics, ballet dancing, tree surgery, reckless mountain climbing, stunt aviating, or parachuting. On the verbal-social level one might think of singing or acting on the stage (becoming a Hollywood star), charismatic oratory and leadership, messianic enthusiasm and prophecy. But for the fullest expression of the complex one must turn to ardent romantic poetry (Byron, Shelley), to mythic philosophy (Socrates in *Phaedrus,* or Nietzsche in *Thus Spake Zarathustra*), or to some form of up-yearning (erotic) mysticism.

2. Predisposing Determinants. To explain the urethral-phallic fixation in this case, to explain the absence of emotional maturation to the stage of object attachment (oedipal love), one must go back in Grope's history to still earlier experiences and their chief resultant—a revengeful (almost implacable) rejection of the mother, because she, scrupulously following her day's dicta: (a) that children should be fed by the clock and (b) that maternal nurturance should be minimal, let the child cry, with his oral and affectional needs unsatisfied, much longer than is tolerable at his age. According to Sullivan[2] and others, such unrelieved intensity of need, combined with "desertion" by the mother, is likely to result in a kind of self-protecting apathy with rejection of both the giver and her gift when they do ultimately arrive—too late. This hypothesis would explain why Grope can give no reason, can remember no incident, which might account for his never having loved his mother, as well as for his food memories, his finickiness about food, his peculiar attitude toward gifts, and, most particularly, the incident of dumping the plate of string beans on the floor and his "spite complex." The hypothesis is further substantiated by Grope's mother's fairly full communication respecting her trustful adherence to the then-fashionable principles of John B. Watson.

Among Grope's story constructions there is one of a young man whose father shuts him up in total darkness. "No light ever entered the room. He could not perceive himself or anything around him." After thirty years of this, the hero "sort of lost his virility." In another story the boy hero dies in bed but regains life when his father brings him a cup of chicken soup. A somewhat similar story ends differently: The child hero goes to bed and calls for one and then a second glass of water. When he calls for a third, there is no response either from his father or his mother. "He was in bed a long time. He started yelling." But no one comes. Finally, the boy puts on his clothes, leaves the house, and lies down across the railroad track to be run over by an oncoming locomotive.

3. Unity Thema. The unity thema in this personality, as we have interpreted it, is a compound of the just-mentioned but not elaborated Mother Rejection complex and the less well known and hence more fully illustrated Icarus complex. Assuredly there were other constituents of Grope's covert personality—particularly those of an anal expulsive derivation—but here again, the prescribed space limits prohibit even the briefest exposition.

The surmise that Grope's overt personality during his college years —marked by apathy and withdrawal—was situationally determined is substantiated by his "conversion" into an enthusiastic, self-involved, hard-working, and coöperative fellow within a few weeks after leaving college when he found in a summer theater an admirable channel for his cynosural narcism.

REFERENCES

1. Halverson, H. M. Genital and sphincter behavior of the male infant. *J. genet. Psychol.*, 1940, *56*, 95–136.

2. Sullivan, H. S. *The Interpersonal Theory of Psychiatry.* New York: W. W. Norton & Co., 1953.

VI

Personology encompasses a wide range of concerns, from specific practical issues to human values and urgent global problems

One of Murray's most engaging intellectual characteristics is his pro-pensity for moving about into fields of inquiry both nearby and distant, what Murray himself refers to as his "sanguine surplus." In practice, these impulses involved him in a fair number of rather diverse activities: literary, scientific, political, military, theoretical, to name some. As ran-dom examples, in one rather full life, Murray volunteered to testify in the Alger Hiss trial; he supported the establishment of a Melville Room at the Atheneum (library) in Pittsfield, Massachusetts—a room where many Melville first editions and other memorabilia may be found; he was in charge of selection of "agents" to serve in dangerous assignments overseas for the Office of Strategic Services (OSS) during World War II; he was interested in the Broadway stage and had a theater of his own built on his farm at Topsfield, Massachusetts, where he and his friends and students performed psychodramas using, on occasions, a variety of masks which he had had constructed at the Metropolitan Opera; and, after he had obtained his medical degree and completed a surgical in-ternship, he spent a couple of years of his life at the Rockefeller Institute "peering through a microscope, through a little fabricated window in the egg's shell, spellbound as any libidinous voyeur, [where he] witnessed the procession of momentous transformations that mark the hours when the embryo is no bigger than an angel perching on a pin point."

Murray's published research includes studies on such topics as the effect of fear on estimations of maliciousness, the psychology of humor, reports of his OSS experiences—practical issues all—and he also wrote papers on the most profound of contemporary problems: on science and religion, on human values, and on world survival.

The "little paper" of 1937, cautiously called "A Note on the Possible Clairvoyance of Dreams," done with one of his graduate students, is peculiarly illustrative of his thinking style as a scientist-psychologist. It is not a study that stems from a large-scale theoretical system; it simply tests a rather common-sense question: Are dreams really predictive or clairvoyant? Murray conceived of this simple project while on a train when he accidentally overheard two women discussing their dreams in

relation to the then just recently kidnapped, but not yet found, Lind-
bergh infant. The brief study is imaginative in its design; it is proactive,
done before the fact of the outcome is known, rather than retroactive; it
is ingeniously simple, practically incontrovertible. All the past and cur-
rent stories and anecdotes and newspaper accounts and pulp magazine
stories of clairvoyance and psychics and prediction put together cannot
gainsay the straightforward evidence gathered from this study.

Between the first and third papers of this section (on a rough con-
tinuum of practical to worldwide issues) is an excerpt from Murray's
writings on his World War II experiences as chief for the assessment and
selection of agents for the Office of Strategic Services. His book (written
with other members of the OSS staff) Assessment of Men is the indispens-
able account of those practical-theoretical-idealistic achievements. Re-
produced in this section are the few pages from that book that relate to
the assessment of Chinese Army officers. Reading them, one can catch
something of the flavor of needing to do an important job as well as
possible under extremely trying and urgent circumstances, while keep-
ing in mind both guiding theories and practical necessities.

On August 6, 1945, when The Bomb was dropped on Hiroshima,
Murray was in China on an OSS assignment. He immediately grasped
the enormous implications of the change-in-the-world for the survival of
man, and in the two-year period from 1959 to 1961 wrote four extraordi-
nary essays "in the hope of arriving at a little clarity, order, dignity, and
vision" in relation to his deep concern over the possibility of world
destruction. "Two Versions of Man" was published in 1960. On the
surface, the issue in the paper appears to be that of the relationship
between science and religion—"the two worlds." Murray is a skilled
polemicist. First he turns the expected argument on its head by asserting
the superordinance of religion over science, then he turns it inside out
by stating that the core contemporary disputation is not between orga-
nized religion and physics or biology, but rather between religion and
psychology, and finally he carefully dissects the innards of the issue and
concludes that a radically new definition of religion (which he has pro-
moted) is an urgent universal requirement. While the essay—after touch-
ing on "the tremendous mental force of communism"—contains an im-
pressive survey of the psychological, mythic, creative, and evolutionary
history of the Judeo-Christian religion, its deeper message is that no
faith, myth, dogma, or religion which is fixed, parochial, or neglects man
as the center of things can be a viable world-saving force.

The final papers are two pieces, rather different from each other: a
short statement and a longish essay. The latter, "Beyond Yesterday's

Idealisms"—his Phi Beta Kappa oration in 1959—is an essay that Murray himself was especially keen to have included in this volume. In it he proposes a new "mythology"—worthy of our group adulthood—to get us beyond Judeo-Christian "mythology" and our current malaise, which he diagnoses as "a paralysis of creative imagination [and] an addiction to superficials." In the same way that Murray habitually avoids using a simple diagnostic psychiatric label as the description of a full human being, so he avoids writing a simplistic formula on a prescription pad to cure man's agues. Instead, he indicates the outline of a rather prolix elixir, a full book, no less, a book whose making and whose reading would constitute the re-education of the world that is so necessary. That book would, he says, have to be a supernational text, a world testament, "a synthesis of Eastern and Western wisdom." And Murray tells us how it might be created, what it might contain, and, most importantly, what its coming into being might prevent. His vision is based on his insistence on the importance—the necessity—of some world order. His exhortational address is also a testimonial of his faith in the power of the word, of language, of reason (tempered with appropriate passion) to change men's minds and to change their behaviors. Murray's vision for the world coincides precisely with the aspiration for this book: that it might serve to bring together biologically and psychodynamically oriented psychologists and other behavioral scientists to synthesize their wisdoms into what has never existed before—a science of psychology founded on methods and procedures indigenous to itself—and thus create a new era of the psychological study of man.

Now to turn to the shorter piece: In the mid-1930s Edward R. Murrow conducted a newspaper column called "This I Believe." Murrow asked celebrities of all stripes—politicos, tycoons, movie stars, athletes, intellectual leaders—to share (in no more than 500 words) their heartfelt beliefs with the American public. Murray was invited to contribute.

His piece contains several elements of his style of thought and expression which are deeply characteristic of much of his written work and, on those grounds alone, rewards a close examination.

Murray begins "This I Believe" by turning upon the key word in the title and—before he permits himself to spin off some list of beliefs—he examines the word itself. Thus, at the very outset, Murray shows us an important characteristic of his intellect: his penchant for careful definition, for detailed explication, and for comprehensive taxonomy. In relation to the word "belief," Murray notes that it has, like most words, various meanings; and then, in lofty and Biblical language—all the more subtly convoluted when we know his own private agnostic-atheistic religious beliefs—he warns us against the smugness of our beliefs, and then quickly fixes our minds—gently disturbing whatever superficial expectations we might have had for some simple set of platitudinous and comforting beliefs—on the "agues of our time," namely, the unsolved global life-threatening problems.

In the second paragraph, Murray indirectly tells us that he is forever embryologically and developmentally oriented: that all things—beliefs, religions, myths, political systems—are in a state of process, of change, and of flux. There is no fixation, no inertness, no final Truth. Further, Murray believes that a complete man should be capable of more than just talk; he should also be capable of action, based, of course, on ever-changing ideas, values, beliefs.

Then, Murray faces Murrow's assigned task indirectly: he lists a set of delights which engender beliefs: "mutual love, friendship, nature, travel, literature, and the vocation of psychology." By the last-named, he means the study of man for man's sake, not the mechanization of men either in concept or in act, by throwing out "mind" as the focus of study.

But, he continues, pious beliefs alone are obviously not enough to save a man or a civilization: they have not worked to date—again invoking a Judeo-Christian image and citing its being on the verge of "utter failure." The first order of business for anyone seriously contemplating his own beliefs must be "the global neurosis which so affects us," about which we had better do something drastic if we wish to survive. And then he states his basic premises: No freedom for any exuberant form of life without freedom from war; no freedom from war without a democratic world government and police force; and no world government without a dramatic re-education of thousands of people in light of a new synthesis of world wisdom.

However, he concludes, in the meantime we had better stay alert and "prepare our sinews for a long and protracted era of ferocity and anguish until our devils are subdued and our eyes opened." These are strong words. We can immediately see that his mind is focused—through his chosen vehicle of a man-oriented psychodynamic psychology—on the most horrendous life-threatening crisis the world has ever faced.

Today, in the 1980s, those earlier thoughts—clearly prophetic of the world's reality—sound more true and more urgent than ever.

23

A NOTE ON THE POSSIBLE
CLAIRVOYANCE OF DREAMS

(With D. R. Wheeler)

In March, 1932, a few days after the kidnaping of the Lindbergh baby, the Harvard Psychological Clinic had published in a daily newspaper a request for dreams relative to the kidnaping. The dreamer was asked to state his or her age, sex, marital status, and number of living or dead children. The request was copied by other papers throughout the country and in response over 1300 dreams were received from all parts of the United States and Canada prior to the discovery of the baby's body. The material yielded quantitative information pertaining to such matters as theme and outcome of dreams, as functions of age and sex. The present report, however, is concerned only with the accuracy of these dreams in representing the facts of the case as they were later ascertained.

The evidence in the case of State *v.* Hauptmann (115 N. J. L. 412) showed that the baby's mutilated and decomposed body was accidentally discovered in a shallow *grave,* in some *woods,* near a *road,* several miles away from the Lindbergh home in the adjoining county of Mercer, New Jersey. It was proved that the baby had suffered three violent fractures of the skull and that the *death* was instantaneous. Further, the child, when stolen, wore a sleeping garment, but there was no such garment on the body when it was found. Finally, Hauptmann, a German carpenter and ex-convict, was convicted of the crime.

In the search for any clairvoyant dreams among the 1300 which were submitted, it was these details which were kept in mind. It is interesting to note that many of the dreams contained references to "foreigners" or "men with foreign accents," which may be attributed perhaps to the popular notion that foreigners are "villainous" and to the repeated newspaper references to such characters as "Red" Johnson, the Scandinavian sailor. And innumerable dreams had the baby concealed on board a boat at sea, another popular newspaper hypothesis. None of the dreams, however, mentioned such relevant facts as the ladder, extortion notes, and ransom money.

From *Journal of Psychology,* 1937, *3,* pp. 309–313.

In only about five per cent of the cases did the baby appear to be dead, and only seven dreams, which follow, suggested the actual location of the body, its nakedness, and the manner of its burial.

MRS. J. K.: I thought I was standing or walking in a very muddy place *among many trees.* One spot looked as though it might be a *round, shallow grave.* Just then I heard a voice saying, "The baby has been *murdered* and buried there." I was so frightened that I immediately awoke.

MRS. K. J.: I seemed to be in a country that was cold, the *trees* were all bare of leaves and the ground was frozen. . . . Then I saw the Lindbergh baby. He was in a *shallow grave* lying on his back. His little body was covered either with frozen earth [by clods] or rocks, I could not tell which. His little face was exposed and the sun shining on his golden hair made a perfect halo around his head. I saw this only from a distance, and while I stood and looked a cloud or mist moved slowly over the grave and hid it from view.

MISS B. S.: I went into a strange country place and walked into what I thought was a back yard but there was no house. There were *two small trees* where the ground had been newly dug up and was not even. It was mostly clay. A shovel lay near by. I took it and tried to even up the dirt. While doing so I felt *something in the ground.* I took it out and it was the lower part of a baby boy's body. It was sticky and slippery and I flung it across the *road* into some *bushes.* Then I took another part out and it was the inside or the stomach. I put it back in the ground and called out, "Here is Lindbergh's baby." I then looked over the location. There was grass on one side, then a dirt road. On the other side of the road there was a *forest,* bushes and wild woods.

"A STUDENT OF PSYCHOLOGY" (widow of 56): In following this child in a dream or "vision" I find he passed to the great beyond six days after being kidnapped, of pneumonia. He had never travelled very far from home, being held at a cabin in the Sourland Mountains, and in a little new *grave* not very far from his home in the mountain he lies, while the world is searching in vain. Some day that little grave will be found. I have dreamed three times of him and each time I see him not in the hands of kidnappers now.

MRS. J. C. R.: I had a dream two nights after the baby was kidnaped that he would be found dead, lying on his back *naked.* The place where he was lying was down a valley and it was kind of hilly with marsh weeds all around.

MR. J. G. R.: I dreamt that a party of us found the baby in a muddy pool of water wrapped in some kind of cloth or sack. The baby evidently had been *dead for some time* as its face was swollen. The object when found could not be recognized as a baby until some kind of sticky substance was removed, then the features became distinct. The hair was blond and curly but had been clipped up the sides and back close to the skull.

MRS. M. T. G. (a colored woman of 50): I dreamed that I was walking up a country road in the early evening and I came to some *bushes* or undergrowth, and *just off the road* was a tiny *grave* and I exclaimed to my husband, "Oh there is the Lindbergh baby's grave." I turned to go back to inform someone, when I woke up. The grave was not flat but rounded on top. The road was in some *woods* that trees had just been cut out of and quite a bit of thick undergrowth had come up. The road was an abandoned one, possibly made for hauling out logs, slightly uphill, and the grave was on the left side going up, under some tall bushes.

In addition to these seven dreams, three others seem worthy of recording, not because of any outstanding fidelity to fact (in none of them does the baby definitely appear to be dead), but rather because in each case the writer states that the dream occurred *before* the kidnaping. We have, however, no objective confirmation of these assertions, and we cannot rule out later more or less conscious elaboration.

J. D. (a schoolboy): On the night that the Lindbergh baby was kidnaped I dreamed that two men who appeared to be foreigners had kidnaped the baby and put him in a box that seemed to be a large sugar box. They carried him through a small patch of woods until they came to a ditch that wasn't far from the Lindbergh home. In the ditch was an old bed that looked like a baby's bed. They put the box on the bed so the water wouldn't touch it. A bush stood near the place where the box was set in the ditch. One kidnaper walked along the edge of the ditch and the other walked in the ditch. Thirty feet down the ditch was a spot that appeared like blood that turned out to be a clue to the kidnapers. I later led three state troopers to the spot. I awoke out of my dream and told my mother that I had dreamed that Lindbergh's baby had been kidnaped, when the news came over the radio.

A NONYMOUS (a married woman of 40 with no children) [Dreamt the night before the kidnaping]: I was passing by a *roadside* and saw the body of a boy about a year old lying to one side with nothing but a diaper on. It was blue in the face and cold as ice and I tried to warm it by wrapping it in a baby blanket. Right at that point I woke up and it seemed so real that I began to worry about the children of my friends and relatives.

MRS. E. C. [dreamt the night of the kidnaping]: I dreamed an airplane went over the house and then the dream changed and I seemed to be reading a paper and the front page was covered with pictures of Mrs. Anne Lindbergh. Then the dream changed again and I seemed to be in a dark, damp, and dirty cellar-like room with a mud floor and one door. As I stood there a man and a woman entered. . . . I could not see the man's face plainly. Just as they hurried in he stooped and put down a small child on the floor. As he stood on his little feet I got the impression of a little boy. Then the man turned and hurriedly shut the door and taking a long wooden bar he fastened it from one side to the other. Then I dropped my eyes to the floor and I saw that there was only one step and on the step was a pile of human dirt. . . . The dream impressed me. . . . The next morning I told a number of my friends about it and at 1:30 in the afternoon I heard the news over the radio.

In seven of the seven dreams recorded above the child was found dead, and in five it lay in a grave, and in four it was located near trees or in a wood. Thus, only 4 out of 1300 dreams included the three items:

death, burial in a grave, location among trees. The possibilities in respect to such items are limited: the child must be (a) either dead or alive; and if dead it must be (b) either in water, above ground, or below ground; and if below ground it must be (c) either in a cellar, in an open space, or in the woods. We have not the data for estimating the probabilities in a kidnaping case of this sort, but if one considers only the possible combinations of listed items it appears that on the basis of pure chance one should expect a great many more dreams than were actually reported which combined the three crucial items.

There is a popular belief in the occasionally clairvoyant character of dreams. This belief has been entertained by many eminent men, but at present it seems to be less widespread than it was in former times. That it is still common is evidenced by the fact that many of our correspondents claimed to have predicted some great events of the past: the World War, the Titanic disaster, and so forth. As far as we know, this is the first time that a mass of dream material pertaining to a single event has been collected before the details of the event were revealed. The findings do not support the contention that distant events and dreams are causally related.

24

ASSESSMENT IN CHINA

In February, 1945, a cable was received in Washington requesting assessment personnel for a screening program in China. Paratroop commando units, formed from the Chinese Army, were to be trained by OSS and dropped behind the Japanese lines for combat, sabotage, and intelligence operations. They were to be led by Chinese officers with Americans as advisers under a joint Chinese and American strategic plan in connection with a forthcoming invasion of the China coast. Assessment was asked to help select several thousand troops.

Recruiting of assessment personnel for this task started immediately. In the United States, after a two months' search, the services of two qualified Chinese social scientists were obtained. In China, Dr. S. K. Chou, Professor of Psychology at the South-Western Associated University, Kunming, announced his willingness to assist in the program and to recruit graduate students if a need for them developed. Two senior members of the assessment staff in Washington were joined by one senior and one junior member of the Calcutta assessment staff, making a total of four Americans. The two Chinese from America participated in assessment at Station S [center in Fairfax, Va., where OSS personnel were selected and trained] while awaiting departure, and when in Kunming were part of a staff which finally included six other Chinese: Professor Siegen K. Chou and four well-trained graduate students—Mr. Fan Chun, Mr. Ma Chi-wei, Mr. Tien Ju-kang, and Mr. Tsao Jih-chang. Mr. Ting Tsan came over from Chungking, and somewhat later Miss Chao Wan-ho, an associate of Mr. Ting's at the National Institute of Health, Chungking, also joined us.

There were to be new experiences for assessment in China. Kunming, in southwest China, was a thriving frontierlike town, overgrown several times in size since the loss of coastal China. It was the gateway for supplies coming in over the Burma Road and the main air terminus for air-borne traffic into China. The Stilwell, or Ledo Road, and the fuel pipe line terminated at Kunming. American army units sprawled over the surrounding countryside. Training centers for Chinese troops dotted the side of roads, vying with the Chinese peasants for the land of China.

From Henry A. Murray (with staff), *Assessment of Men*. New York: Rinehart, 1948. Part of Chapter XI, Assessment in China, pp. 382–386.

Temples and schoolhouses, rich men's compounds and middle-class homes, and newly constructed buildings housed Chinese and American military units. Amidst this hive of activity, OSS established a training center for China's first parachute jumpers. Large numbers of troops were already in the process of commando training.

The assessment staff was now asked to select men for a replacement pool for the commandos already formed, and more urgently to select men for two "intelligence commandos," men who would not only be good commandos but would also be able to engage in intelligence activities. (It might be pointed out that a "commando" was used to refer to a unit of 135 men, as well as to a single soldier.) For two commandos, approximately 250 men were required; the officers and noncommissioned officers had already been selected. Where could these men be found? Any familiarity with recent Chinese events pointed to the difficulty of getting this number of physically and intellectually fit Chinese enlisted men.

The Chinese armies are somewhat unique in modern military annals. Hampered by ineffective staff work, and ridden with political appointees in high ranks, evolving slowly and showing little evidence of becoming a modern army, they struggled on, sometimes against the Japanese, sometimes merely to exist. Manpower was abundant, but of poor quality. There were no adequate records kept of personnel. While a draft law existed, those with influence, power, or wealth were able to avoid service. It was only the poor and illiterate farm boys who joined the Army, or stayed in after they were forcibly conscripted, for the sake of one bowl of rice a day. Once in the Army their lot was far from enviable. Runaway inflation made their meager salaries seem ludicrous. Medical attention was inadequate; trained doctors and medical supplies were not available in sufficient quantities. Diseases ranging from malaria to scabies were commonplaces. It was from this horde of ragged, dispirited, but long-suffering soldiers that assessment had to select 250 men suitable for intelligence and commando operations.

Official liaison between the American training units and the Chinese Army headquarters was generally satisfactory. The Chinese belonging to the already formed commando units were receiving excellent training in demolitions and combat tactics. Special equipment, extra pay, and the facilities usually accorded American military units had been granted. The men were honored in the district since they were the first in China to receive instructions in parachute jumping. Great fanfare and excitement attended the first jump of the first class trained in Kunming. As the composite American and Chinese officer cadre jumped out of the planes, a brass band played, reviewing generals cheered, and strings of firecrackers popped. Pride in the work increased as national interest became manifest. As assessment was an integral part of the commando program, consideration and cooperation were accorded that might otherwise have been difficult to obtain.

Arriving in Kunming and being informed that several thousand troops were available for recruiting, the assessment staff immediately set out to visit two pools in the hope of finding a quantity of literate men in reasonably good health. But even after modifying our definitions of "literate" and "reasonably good," the yield from these pools, and from two other pools visited the next day, was disappointing. Few of the men had had an education equivalent to that provided by an American primary school, and of those who could read, many were disqualified because of inadequate vision, poor health, or lack of strength. Since none was free from scabies, only those with the severest infestation were disqualified on this count. Nevertheless, at the end of two days 550 men who claimed some ability to read and appeared to be physically sound had been formed into columns and marched to the American training camp.

The site of the assessment was several miles outside of Kunming on a hillside overlooking a great plain of brilliant green paddy fields. There, on the edge of a little village full of children, adjacent to the training grounds of the parachute school, the assessment staff was allotted several areas. Its headquarters were set up in a small country house, which had a garden with an unused dirt tennis court and a swimming pool. On the court several tents were set up to serve as shelters for interviews and written tests; the pool was used for a bridge-building problem. Near by was a spacious temple where other tests could be conducted, and farther up the hill were two parade grounds and a mess hall available to us at certain times. A canyon on the side of one parade ground provided ideal conditions for situational tests and an obstacle course.

The test program may be divided into two parts: Part One was a one-day screening process the purpose of which was to eliminate the illiterate and those of distinctly low intelligence; Part Two consisted of one day of more exacting procedures designed to test energy, motivation, physical ability, leadership, and observational ability among those who had passed Part One.

Part One started in the morning with approximately 120 recruits who had just been selected from a larger number on the basis of a one-minute reading test. This reading test, conducted on the parade ground immediately after the recruits were assembled, was scored as it was given. Those who failed were permanently disqualified; those who passed were lined up, their names recorded, and an identifying numbered card to be attached in plain view to the jacket was issued to each man. After this, one half of the candidates were given a battery of tests to determine educational status, while the other half received paper-and-pencil intelligence tests. In an hour the two groups alternated. This ended the morning session.

The afternoon was devoted to a continuous round of tests, each of which could be administered to a group of 30 men in about forty minutes. In this battery were two outdoor group performance tests, several individual performance tests (the "quickies"), and a perception test. On the basis of the results obtained during the morning and afternoon sessions another elimination of the less suitable men was made.

Part Two began several days later and was applied to all men who had passed the first screening. Again the men were assembled on the parade ground and separated into groups of 30. This procedure was not so simple as one might expect, because the Chinese officers had no method of keeping track of their men. Consequently a portion of the morning period had to be spent in eliminating stray soldiers who had never been tested—as well as those who had been disqualified on Part One but had nevertheless rejoined their successful comrades—and in detecting substitutes who had been hired to assume the names of recruits who had passed Part One but, for one reason or another, had seen fit to quit. These substitutes could be identified by their signatures.

As soon as the bona fide candidates were grouped, a new roster was prepared and a numbered jersey issued to each man. While this was in process, each staff member attempted a quick over-all evaluation of each candidate on the basis of general appearance and reactions to instructions. These procedures followed: (1) Interview conducted by one of the Chinese members of the staff, or by an American assisted by an interpreter; (2) Bridge Building; (3) Obstacle Course; (4) Observation and Memory Battery. These, together with the procedures previously listed, are described in the succeeding section.

The next step in the program was to review the findings and formulate a recommendation. This was accomplished at a staff meeting where each case was discussed, not only in the light of the man's test scores, but also in terms of impressions not susceptible to numerical ratings. The final report prepared by the interviewer was an integrated evaluation of the candidate based on all the information available considered in connection with his future field operations.

Several considerations influenced us to adopt a three-point scale instead of the six-point scale employed in the States. The majority of the staff members were not accustomed to rating traits, particularly in complex social situations. And then, at the start of the program, norms had not been established for this population, and the concept, for example, of a high average as against a low-average performance was too indefinite to warrant making the distinction. Finally, in working with groups as large as these, the time spent in observing each candidate was too limited to justify fine discriminations. Every rating, therefore, was either Low, Average, or High.

In the following paragraphs, the procedures employed are briefly described. As will be noted, they follow the pattern of those used in

America, with modifications required by the necessity of screening large numbers in the shortest possible time.

Sign Reading. This test was devised to provide a rough measure of degree of literacy. Since it could be administered and scored quickly (one minute per man), it was used in the first rough screening of the recruits as they came from the replacement pool. Literacy sufficient to read a Chinese classic was, of course, too high a standard to require of simple soldiers. Even to demand the ability to read newspapers would have meant the elimination of too large a proportion of the men. Therefore a simple test was devised consisting of a series of key characters, a knowledge of which did not depend so much upon formal education as it did upon an acquaintance with signs which were part of the daily experience of every soldier.

Educational Level Battery. Since the purpose of the program was to select commandos suitable for intelligence operations, it was decided that the men should demonstrate some ability to count and to write as well as the possession of general information indicative of alertness to their social and physical surroundings. Each of the three tests was administered to groups ranging from 30 to 60 in number.

Arithmetic. This consisted of 25 simple calculations presented on a mimeographed sheet in both Arabic and Chinese characters. The candidates were to write the answers on a separate sheet of paper.

Writing. This required the filling in of a mimeographed form consisting of questions about personal history and interests. Space was provided for writing additional information.

General information. This consisted of 50 statements, on history, geography, politics, and so on, 27 of which were true and 23 false. The statements were read to the recruits, who merely had to indicate *true* or *false* on an answer sheet. Fifteen minutes were allowed.

Abstract Intelligence Battery. The tests constituting this battery were divided into two parts. Part 1 consisted of the Series Completion Test and the Block Counting Test (Non-Language Test: No. 22 of the Adjutant General's Office), both of which had been employed in Ceylon and India. Part 2 consisted of three short individual performance tests (the "quickies"): (a) a set of photographs which had to be arranged in a series according to the age of the subject; (b) a set of pictures which had to be sorted into two groups, males in one, females in the other; and (c) a geometrical form which had to be duplicated with a set of cards cut in different shapes (as in a jigsaw puzzle). One minute was allowed for each solution. The recruit was observed and scored as he worked.

Observation and Memory Battery. Three tests were used in this battery as indicators of a man's suitability for intelligence work.

DESIGNS. This measure of the ability to observe and recall accurately was also used to test two hypotheses. "Familiar" Chinese characters and symbols and "unfamiliar" English letters and symbols were drawn on a single sheet of white cardboard. This sheet was exposed for two minutes to a group of candidates who were then instructed to reproduce as many figures as they could recall. A slight imperfection (error or broken line) had been introduced in drawing each figure. The two hypotheses were these: (1) that the candidates would remember more of the familiar than of the unfamiliar figures, and (2) that they would overlook imperfections in the familiar figures more often than they would overlook them in the unfamiliar figures. The results will be discussed later.

SEARCH. This was similar to the Belongings Test in the program at Station S. The story invented for it was that of a Chinese captain who had been forced by the weather to camp in this place with his troops for the night. On departure he had left some of his possessions behind in the adjoining tent. The candidates, individually or in small groups, inspected the tent and after two minutes returned to the examiner, who asked them: What have you seen in the tent? Who was the captain who stayed in the tent? Why did he choose to stop in this place?

PERCEPTUAL ACUITY. This test measured speed and span of perception. Each figure was presented tachistoscopically at 1/10 second by a 35 mm. projector. The figures presented were a row of horizontal dots (from 3 to 7), Arabic digits, simple geometric figures, simple figures with a small gap somewhere in their contour, and so on. The men were required after each exposure to draw the figure seen. This test was designed in Washington and included in the battery chiefly for experimental purposes.

Group Practics Battery. These tests, three in number, were important for the data they provided on Effective Intelligence, Energy, Motivation, Cooperativeness, Physical Ability, and, to a certain extent, Daring. They corresponded, except in detail, to group field situations as used at other stations.

BRIDGE BUILDING. This required the construction of a bridge across the 27-foot width of the swimming pool. The recruits, ten at a time, were expected to complete this task in forty-five minutes. They were told to assume that the pool, which was full of water, was a river and therefore it was not possible to walk around it to the other side. Furthermore, the job had to be done without anyone wetting his feet. Two logs, 23 and 9 feet in length, heavy rope, planks, stakes, a sledge, and a pick were the materials provided.

FLAGPOLE. This called for the transportation of a long heavy log across a deep canyon by a group of ten men. The task called for energy and teamwork, and so provided a good opportunity to observe Leadership, Motivation, and Social Relations.

RAVINE. This involved the construction of a rope bridge across a canyon, two groups working cooperatively, one on each side of the canyon. After the job was finished the examiner called for volunteers to cross the bridge. This was considered to be a measure of daring.

Obstacle Course. This was constructed in a ravine located next to one of the parade grounds. The obstacles were arranged in a series in such a way as to require the recruit to cross back and forth over the stream as he worked his way up the canyon. The first obstacle was a log resting on the floor of the ravine and leaning at a 30-degree angle against the top of the bank. This had to be climbed to reach a horizontal rope stretching for 40 feet below the crest of the bank. Along this rope, hand over hand, the candidate would then make his way along the almost vertical wall. Here and there he could find some support for his feet. At the end he descended to the bottom via a vertical rope. Next was a 5-foot hurdle in the middle of the stream which he climbed to reach an 8-foot platform on the other side of the bank. From this elevation he jumped back across the stream and then recrossed once more on a horizontal log 10 feet above the water. This brought him to the last obstacle, a pair of parallel ropes suspended between trees 20 feet above the floor of the ravine. He reached these by a rope ladder, and with feet on the lower rope and hands on the upper, he worked his way over to the far side. When he reached the ground the course was completed.

The men were started one at a time at three-minute intervals. This course, easily viewed and scored from the top of the ravine, provided measures of daring, agility, and endurance.

Interview. Most of the interviews were conducted by two Chinese psychologists and by an American assisted by an interpreter. The interview was necessarily short, from five to fifteen minutes, but it was nevertheless important in view of its being the only face-to-face situation in the program. Frequently it was the deciding factor in settling the fate of recruits whose test scores were on the border line. Special emphasis was placed on the determination of Motivation and Emotional Stability. Ratings were made on all traits, however, and notes were taken on significant features of the man's past history and present attitudes. The method of interrogation, although subject to variations from interviewer to interviewer, was essentially the same as that used at other stations.

General Impression. This was undertaken as an amusing experiment to see how well the staff could predict the final over-all rating of each recruit on the basis of a few seconds of observation. When the recruits were lined up in the morning preparatory to engaging in the test procedures, each senior staff member rated each recruit as he stood in line. Usually at the moment the judgment was made the recruit was putting on a numbered jersey that had just been issued to him.

The following variables were rated (Low, Average, or High) on the final report form:

Educational Level, based on Sign Reading and Educational Level Battery. If the case was on the border line between two grades, the quality of handwriting, a talent highly esteemed among Chinese, was taken into account.

Effective Intelligence, based on Interview, Abstract Intelligence Battery, Observation and Memory Battery, and Group Practics.

Observation and Memory, based on the battery of three tests—Perceptual Acuity, Design, and Search.

Motivation, Social Relations, and Emotional Stability, three separate variables, each based on the Interview, Group Practics, and Obstacle Course.

Leadership, based on Group Practics.

Physical Ability, based on Obstacle Course and Group Practics.

Correspondence of the Procedures with the Final Over-All Rating at Kunming

TEST	NO DISCREPANCY (% of cases)	DISCREPANCY OF 1 CATEGORY (% of cases)	DISCREPANCY OF 2 CATEGORIES (% of cases)
Interview.	71	28	1
Sign Reading.	64	33	3
Educational Level Battery	63	35	2
Group Practics Battery. .	62	35	3
Observation and Memory Battery	60	37	3
General Impression. . . .	58	41	1
Abstract Intelligence Battery	54	43	3
Obstacle Course.	51	45	4

Since the final over-all rating was arrived at after an examination and discussion of the ratings on the separate procedures, it would be extraordinary if one found anything other than what is indicated in this table, namely, a rather high correlation between the test results and the final estimate of suitability. In the majority of cases the final rating was merely the average of all the other ratings.

The rank order of the different procedures [as shown in the table above] cannot be accepted as definite evidence of their relative merit, since a number of factors, some subjective and some fortuitous, were influential in determining the result. The Interview was clearly first, not only because this was a very revealing procedure, but because past experience had persuaded the staff that considerable reliance could be placed on an interviewer's judgment and also because the staff member who interviewed a candidate usually attained a greater degree of confidence in his ratings than that attained, let us say, by the staff member who observed him on the Obstacle Course. Consequently in the discussion of each case the interviewer was likely to be the one who argued with greatest conviction and was listened to with most respect.

Sign Reading stands high on the list because everyone who received a low rating on this test was automatically disqualified (i.e., received a low over-all rating). Of the seven ratings which appeared on the summary sheet presented to each staff member at the final discussion, four (Abstract Intelligence Battery, Educational Level Battery, Observation and Memory Battery, and Sign Reading) were estimates, direct or indirect, of cognitive functions. Furthermore, the interviewer was very likely to be influenced favorably by evidences of intellectual power. Consequently the average of the seven ratings was more representative of the candidate's intelligence level than it was of his physical energy, motivation, courage, leadership, team spirit, and so forth, which were covered by only two ratings on the summary sheet. This largely accounts for the fact that the Group Practics Battery and the Obstacle Course stand relatively low in the rank order. In this connection another point is perhaps worth mentioning: Chinese generally, and Chinese scholars (e.g., psychologists) especially, are inclined to value the intellect, even within the sphere of military enterprise, more than we Americans do. This helps to explain why the staff members, most of whom were Chinese, were usually more impressed by a high rating on the Educational Level Battery, for example, than by a high rating on the Obstacle Course.

The intercorrelations among the different procedures were relatively high compared to those found when comparable tests have been administered to American groups of similar age. This relationship probably means that some underlying general factor, such as motivational energy, was the chief determinant of excellence on all the tests in which the Chinese recruits engaged. According to this hypothesis the possession of a high degree of motivational energy (ambition) makes a boy more alert, and prompts him to exert himself not only at home, helping on the farm, but also at school; and as a result he will forge ahead of the more complacent majority in most lines of activity. In America, however, specialization begins earlier and is more widespread. A boy finds that he excels in athletics, or at mechanics, or in English composition, and before long we find that most of his energies are being canalized in this direction and in one or two others. Thus at twenty-five he has probably suceeded in developing himself beyond the average in certain abilities, but has fallen behind in others.

The relatively high correlation of General Impressions with final ratings is interesting, particularly since the scores on the former were not taken into account in deciding the latter. Fifty-eight per cent of the average of the staff impressions agreed exactly with the final ratings. The best estimates were made by one of the Chinese psychologists, and the next to the lowest by another. There was no appreciable difference between the averages of the American and the Chinese raters' scores.

In breaking down the scores on Designs into two parts, Chinese designs and American designs, it was found, in conformity with our hypothesis, that familiar Chinese symbols rather than unfamiliar American symbols were recalled better by the Chinese. Of the total number of correct responses, 68 per cent were to Chinese characters or symbols, and 32 per cent were to American. But the hypothesis that familiarity with the symbols would interfere with the observation of slight errors and omissions was not supported by the results. Instead of there being more incorrectly reproduced familiar designs (with the errors in pattern overlooked) there were more incorrectly reproduced unfamiliar designs. The figures were not presented tachistoscopically, however, and it is possible that the recruits, with two minutes to study the patterns, may even have been aided in the recall of the familiar by the special emphasis that these errors and omissions produced. Exposures of short duration might yield results to support the original hypothesis.

Just before the dropping of the first atomic bomb and the subsequent end of hostilities, it was decided that assessment in China should discontinue. Eight hundred men had been processed, 220 of them more intensively than the rest. Although the staff was prepared to assess more groups, suitable recruits were not to be found. Apparently there was nothing left to be done in the Kunming area.

Shortly before our departure, however, one more opportunity to get into action presented itself: the staff was asked by a Chinese general to give a demonstration of its methods by assessing a group of Chinese Army officers.

ASSESSMENT OF CHINESE ARMY OFFICERS

Heretofore assessment had operated under American auspices; now it was to be conducted in a wholly Chinese setting. Among the numerous agreeable discoveries to be made was the fact that convivial tea drinking, poetical wine toasting, and fine feasting were integral parts of the process of setting up a screening program. It was natural to engage in social activities of this hearty sort with considerable enjoyment and gusto, and within a day or two the Americans felt very much at home and in a mood to compromise on any issues that might arise. Although every step called for a sequence of courteous negotiations, in a few days all necessary materials and equipment were assembled, an obstacle course was constructed, and a schedule of procedures was arranged, several of which had to be improvised on the spot. The General, exceedingly cordial at all times, evidenced considerable interest in all our proceedings, and did everything in his power to facilitate preparations.

The group selected for processing consisted of thirty junior grade officers from various units, who had been transferred to main headquarters for a special training program under the General's supervision. Some of the men had engaged in combat in Burma; some had participated in "bandit suppression" expeditions before the Sino-Japanese War. They were all literate; the majority had had a junior high school education, and several were military academy graduates. Their motivation for the program was excellent, the General having exhorted them to cooperate to the limit. He was there to observe them during the whole program.

Four one-story-high school buildings, forming a square compound with a large court in the middle, were put at the disposal of assessment. Situated in the middle of a village about two miles from Kunming and close to the headquarters of the Fifth Chinese Army, the facilities left nothing to be desired. Across the road from the school compound a stream flowing swiftly between steep banks provided ideal conditions for a bridge-building problem. A half-built house near by was available for an obstacle course. Assessment does not depend upon a definite set of materials or conditions; the program can almost always be adapted in one way or another to local conditions. For instance, if, because of scarcity of materials in China, poles cannot be cut to size but must be borrowed and returned intact, then the problem becomes one of finding a spot that will fit the poles instead of the more usual one of fitting poles to a chosen spot.

There was no need for undue haste; only thirty men had to be assessed. Furthermore, we were not asked to decide the fate of each assessee, to accept or reject him. The program was designed merely to demonstrate our system of assessment to the Chinese General and other interested officers.

The staff remained unchanged except for the loss of two Americans who had left for Hsian, North China. It was augmented by the addition of three more Chinese graduate students and two experienced Chinese psychologists. These new members, three of whom were women, were eager to see assessment in operation.

Three series of tests were scheduled, A, B, and C, each of which lasted half a day. Series A, which took place indoors, consisted in filling out personal history forms and performing a variety of paper-and-pencil tests. Series B included outdoor field situations, individual and group, and an obstacle course. Series C was a sequence of indoor group procedures. The assessees were divided into three subgroups (I, II, and III) of ten men each. While Group I was taking Series A, Group II was engaged in Series B, and so forth. The three groups completed the three series in a day and a half. The interviews took place a few days later, after all tests had been scored and a preliminary sketch of each personality composed. As most of the procedures have already been described, a very brief account of them is all that is required here.

Personal Data Sheet. This was an abbreviated and slightly modified form of the sheet used at Station S.

Sentence Completion. Fifty of the phrases used at Station S were translated into Chinese with minor changes. Mimeographed sheets were presented to ten men (one subgroup) at a time.

Modified Thematic Apperception Test. Ten pictures, carefully selected from Chinese magazines, were divided into two sets, A and B, of five pictures each. While five of the candidates, seated round a table, were occupied with Set A, the other five at another table were busy with Set B. Each candidate was given one of the five pictures placed on his table and told to write a dramatic story in seven minutes for which the picture might be used as an illustration. When time was called, each man was instructed to pass his picture to the man sitting at his right. Thus in thirty-five minutes every candidate had written five stories. After an intervening test of another type, the two sets were exchanged and each man wrote five more stories.

This method of administration proved very successful. The stories, taken in conjunction with the responses to the Sentence Completion, yielded a great deal of pertinent information.

Series Completion and Cube Counting. These were the same as those used in the assessment of commandos.

Designs. The same test as that used in commando assessment.

Improvisations. As at Station S, the assessees belonging to one subgroup were taken in pairs, the members of each pair being told that they must imagine themselves involved in a certain situation (clearly described to them by the examiner) and that they must act as they would in everyday life. In accordance with these instructions, five different episodes (one by each pair) were enacted in front of the staff and the other members of the subgroup, five minutes being allotted to each episode. The situations chosen were close to the experience of these officers; they were not designed to check any special tentative formulation of each assessee's personality. The same five situations were used for all three subgroups.

Speech. Each man made a three-minute speech before his subgroup on a topic of his own selection. This procedure conformed to the traditional Chinese assumption that a leader must be a good public speaker.

Discussion. "Relations between the Army and Civilians" was assigned as the topic for an impromptu discussion among the ten members of each subgroup gathered around a table. Since there was a good deal of friction at the time between soldiers and civilians, this topic was both timely and provocative of emotion.

Bridge Building. Ten men were assigned the task of building a bridge across a 15-foot stream with banks 10 feet high. The problem was basically the same as that presented in commando assessment. This was called "group practics."

Obstacle Course. A half-built two-story house with rafters exposed, no floors laid, windows open, and roof unfinished served as a frame for the obstacle course. All that was needed was plenty of rope for climbing and swinging. Agility, daring, and strength could be readily estimated by the observers.

Assigned Leadership. Five outdoor situations, "critical emergencies," were invented, each at a different spot out of sight of the others; and every assessee was given five minutes to show how well he could direct the activities of a squad of four men in solving one of these situations. For this purpose each subgroup was divided into two squads of five men. Squad A started at the site of the first problem; Squad B at the site of the third. From then on the problems were taken in order, at each site a different man being selected to act as leader.

Individual Practics. Six low stone pylons (supposedly the remains of a blown bridge) placed at irregular intervals on the ground (the bed of an imaginary river) constituted the only supports for a bridge of planks and ropes which had to be constructed from one bank to the other in three minutes.

Sociometric. The form used at Station S was distributed to all the assessees at the end of the testing period. Since these men were members of a training class which had been living, working, and studying together for several months, everyone had had ample opportunity to observe the behavior of the others and so acquire sufficient basis for judgments of leadership traits and potentialities. Because of our ignorance of the standards that prevailed in the Chinese Army, the findings on this test were heavily weighted when we arrived at our final conclusions.

Interview. A few days after all the other procedures had been completed and the results analyzed and synthesized, each assessee was given an interview lasting from one and a half to two and a half hours. The advantage of this timing was that the interviewers had a good deal of information at their disposal to guide them to certain critical areas of each man's personality which required further exploration.

The report sheets used in this study were the same as those which had proved useful in commando assessment. There was the same list of variables rated Low, Medium, or High, and a typewritten personality sketch of the assessee (averaging two thirds of a page in length) written by the interviewer. In this final note an opinion was ventured as to the best use that could be made of the officer in question, whether, for example, he was better fitted for combat or for staff work.

Since the war came to an end a few days after the completion of the assessment period, there was no opportunity to evaluate the accuracy of our judgments. We never learned whether any of the assessees eventually engaged in combat against the Communists in the North. In the two weeks devoted to the enterprise we had added to our fund of knowledge as well as to our fund of intensely enjoyed experiences, and the General seemed pleased with what he had seen of the proceedings. This was the height of our expectations. The Chinese members of the staff had been astonishingly quick in grasping our methods and in learning to function effectively in a somewhat complicated schedule of procedures. To them belongs the bulk of the credit for the measure of success that was achieved.

Ar unfortunate sequel of the assessment process is not without interest. Our friend the General called together his headquarters staff, his training staff, and the thirty men who had been tested and publicly read each assessment report with the man under discussion standing at attention in front of the assembled group. Following each reading, the General lectured or praised the officer, depending on the content of the report, and saw fit to imprison at least one man in a dungeon "to reflect upon his bad moral character," and "rectify himself."

25

TWO VERSIONS OF MAN

Since I am not asked to report as an official or even unofficial representative of my profession, I assume that I am free to set forth whatever biological and psychological propositions and hypotheses seem to me both tenable and pertinent to our topic, whether the majority of my colleagues would agree with me or not. Also, I am trusting that you will tolerate the frank avowal, here and there, of certain beliefs of mine respecting science and religion, some of which are very questionable value judgments that may singe your ears or even upset your livers, but not seriously, I hope.

"Religion in the age of science." It should be opposite. Our topic states correctly the existing relationships of the two domains. But, as I see it, this relationship is the reverse of what it should be. That is to say, in my hierarchy of valued ends, the sphere of religion is *super*ordinate to that of science. Strange thing for a scientist to confess. But, let me add, I am not thinking of the Christianity that persecuted scientists, of Judaism, or of any other great religion, as it now stands. I am but dreaming of certain dawning possibilities, of a religion that is compatible with science and understands its aim and destiny.

Why do I believe that the sphere of religion should be *super*ordinate to the sphere of science? Because, as defined by men whose judgment in this matter I respect, the sphere of religion is the sphere of ultimate concern. That is, religion is, or should be, devoted to final values, beyond which no other values can exist. It is not hard to see what this means in the frame of the once-dominant Christian myth. A man's ultimate concern is whether he spends an eternity of years in the best place imaginable or in the worst place imaginable. Seventy multipleasured years on earth are of little worth when weighed against an endless age of sizzling in the underground; and a lifetime of vexation, misery, and woe are tolerable if after the fever of life is over one is destined to enjoy a trillion years of bliss.

But if one cannot believe this, apprehending the whole scheme as an effective stratagem of priests in suppressing misbehavior, useful as

From H. Shapley, ed., *Science Ponders Religion*. New York: Appleton-Century-Crofts, 1960, pp. 147–181. "Two Versions of Man" was given at a series of week-long summer meetings on the nature of man held on Star Island in New Hampshire in 1960.

well to rulers and to parents, if one cannot accept the Heaven-and-Hell alternative as a matter of ultimate concern, what can replace them? What is there in this world on earth of comparable value to the promise of another world? As you know, numerous answers to this question have been given, by ancient and by European authors, especially since the eighteenth-century Enlightenment. I suppose a portion of the answer I would give dates from the saying attributed to Protagoras: "Man is the measure of all things." Certainly in my scales the ultimate concern of man is man himself, the development toward perfection of his inner being, the development toward perfection of his interpersonal relationships, the development toward perfection of his societies, and eventually the creation and maintenance of a harmonious world community, in short, better personalities for a better life for a better world, the highest spiritual good of all men and women of this earth. This view accords with two of Alfred North Whitehead's memorable statements, first: "What should emerge from religion is individual worth of character," and second: "Religion is world loyalty." To put *in a nutshell* the science-religion relationship as I order it: It is the development of science for the development of man, rather than the development of man for the development of science.

I am suggesting here that religion should be defined not so much in terms of beliefs as in terms of aims.

Another way of defining its relative position is to say that science itself does not determine the ends to which its products will be used. The aim of science is valid knowledge, a theoretical system in terms of which events may be perceived, analyzed, formulated, explained, predicted within limits, and, as far as possible, controlled. Such knowledge is often a tremendous source of power, power to harm or power to benefit mankind. But which of these alternatives will be chosen? All scientists agree that the answer to this question lies outside their proper sphere; and because it does, the role of science, great as it surely is, will never be more than a subordinate or instrumental one in the enterprises of men and of societies.

If this is true, we are left with the question: In what sphere is it decided how scientific knowledge should be utilized? The down-to-earth answer is that scientific knowledge and techniques are utilized by those who want them and can afford to pay for them. There are countless individual decisions by the public as well as institutional decisions in the spheres of industry and of government. In the last analysis, of course, it is the government that decides. In Russia, for example, the government regulates to some extent which scientific theories will be announced and taught and which refused and suppressed. Happily, there are no crass interventions of this sort in these United States. But the influence of our government on the course of science—no doubt a necessary and proper influence within limits—is nonetheless enormous. With dazzling research grants as bait, it has hooked and landed a great number of physical, biological, and social scientists, and directed their imaginations and talents toward the solution of problems relevant to the successful prosecution of a global war, a war, the expert tells us, in which all we cherish might be shattered, might crumble and dissolve like Shakespeare's "insubstantial pageant faded, and leave not a wrack behind." I am not in any way condemning these practices of our nation, world conditions being as they are. I am merely pointing out that a large proportion of our scientists are being subsidized by the government in the name of might, and none, to my knowledge, in the name of right. Here we have science in an age of rampant nationalism and materialism.

But what is superordinate to nationalism and materialism? Nothing really influential so far as one can see. A widespread but vaguely apprehended moral standard, a diffuse yet fickle and unreliable goodwill, a great craving for security and peace; but as yet no clear vision of world unity, of the highest good for all men and women of this earth. Is it not apparent that this highest good is, or should be, a matter of ultimate concern to everyone? I would say, yes; and repeat that the sphere of ultimate concern is one definition, a fitting definition, of the sphere of religion. A multiplicity of militant nationalisms requires an inviting and evolutionary ideal of mutual embracement to subdue and unify them, the moral persuasion of a universal world religion. Today we have many religions in an age of science, science in an age of nationalisms, and nationalisms in an age of nothing, or nearly nothing, nothing in the West. Beyond the Iron Curtain, to be sure, there is the powerful ideology, the tremendous mental force, of Communism, like that of Islam in its day of vaunting strength; but in opposing Communism, we, unhappily, have no equally enthralling vision. There is no center of gravity that attracts, binds, and unifies the peoples of the free world, or even of the Western world. In the much quoted words of the poet Yeats:

> Things fall apart; the center cannot hold;
> Mere anarchy is loosed upon the world . . .
> The best lack all conviction, while the worst
> Are full of passionate intensity.

According to my dream, a transformed religion, a new religion, will ultimately occupy that center and hold the world together. Whatever may be the nature of this religion of the future, a good many of us believe that it will have to be compatible with science.

When people speak of the conflict between religion and science, they usually have in mind the Christian religion and the physical sciences: the Christian religion, because no other religion has so mightily and persistently gathered up its powers to oppose and suppress science on fundamental issues, and the physical sciences, because astronomy and physics were the first to collide with religion, and because these were the first to develop in a great way and today represent science at its best. But now the crucial conflict is not between Christianity and physics, or even between Christianity and biology; it is between religion and psychology. Here I am using the term "psychology" in a general sense to include all the young, groping would-be sciences of man—academic psychology, clinical and social, psychiatry and psychoanalysis, and, in addition to these, whatever facts and theories from cultural anthropology and sociology are relevant to an understanding of the emotional experiences, mental processes, and overt behaviors of human beings.

I am saying that the crucial conflict is between religion and psychology, because the focus of both of these disciplines is the same, namely, the nature and transformation of human feelings, evaluations, needs, beliefs, purposes, and actions. The Church can graciously withdraw from the domains of astronomy, physics, chemistry, and biology, without seriously weakening its foundations or its standing in the minds of men. It can readily give way to new scientific discoveries about the revolutions of galaxies, about the nucleoproteins of the living cell, or about bees, ants, and reptiles. But it can never abandon its concern with the vicissitudes of human personality, can never withdraw from the sphere of psychology, because *this* is its hereditary station. The Church Fathers were in no sense astronomers or biologists, but some of them—St. Augustine, for example—were eminent psychologists in their day, and during the succeeding centuries the Catholic Church accumulated—in large measure from intimate confessions—more knowledge about the tribulations of the human spirit than is dreamed of by academics of our day. And so, when Christianity is confronted, as it is today, by the findings and speculations of anthropologists and psychologists, there is trouble—not yet to any marked degree, but in the offing. Not yet, because nowadays the two disciplines are functionally separate, their currents of thought being almost wholly dissociated, neither of them knowing at what conclusion the other is arriving. Their social interactions are exceedingly amicable, but these rarely include intellectual communications on basic issues. The prevalent condition, as I see it, is one of peaceful, if not oblivious, coexistence, or, in some quarters, friendly collaboration in various practical endeavors. It's as if the members of both professions had tacitly agreed to put aside their differences in the name of sociability and composure.

In this genial company of compatible men and women, on this quiet island, in this mild weather, it seems that the part of decency and tact would be to tiptoe round the sleeping incongruities of faith and of aim between religionists and psychologists, and concentrate on what they have in common. Were I to choose this more agreeable and ingratiating policy, we might advance together smoothly and serenly to a happy ending, but we would have to leave several provoking problems in our rear, and these, sooner or later, would steal up on us and shatter our peace of innocence.

It is because I strongly feel that religion and psychology *should* and *will* eventually embrace each other, that I am adopting the opposite policy—disquieting today but soundest in the long run—of examining points of disagreement first, and later, if there is time, the broader area of agreement.

My plan is to submit to you a brief account of one version, one aspect or potentiality, of man's nature, a version, based on the theory of creative evolution, which is not without relevance to religion. At certain points I shall contrast this view with the traditional Christian view, and thereby call attention to certain differences between current assumptions of psychology and the age-old assumptions of this religion. Because differences on these issues constitute the present grounds for the functional separation of the two disciplines, these are the issues which must be settled if reconciliation is our serious and sincere intent.

Since I cleave to the principle that an adequate understanding of any living creature depends on the possession of sufficient knowledge of its history—its genesis, its past encounters with the environment, and its serial developments—since the truth of this principle has been verified over and over again in my experience, I shall start my characterization of man by considering the question of his origin. First, let us recall the biblical picture of the facts.

According to the Babylonian-Hebraic-Christian story, the first man was made by *the* supreme parent, the sovereign of the universe, in a single day and in his likeness. Then from this man's rib a woman was fashioned, and the pair, complete in mind and body, were assigned the selectest place in which to dwell in uninterrupted harmony and joy. Unhappily there was a flaw in each, an importunate and irrepressible need for freedom, freedom to explore and to experiment, to taste the never tasted and forbidden. The result was exile and a curse: from then on, life for the human race would be a load of pain, sweat, and grief, with perfection, paradise, and the tree of eternal life—the golden age of man —forever in the past.

Many centuries passed before another testament proclaimed that a new dispensation was forthcoming, and in due course it was concluded that paradise and the tree of eternal life had been transferred from earth to sky and the long-standing ban of exile was no longer absolute and unconditional. Thenceforth, the kingdom of heaven would be open to a number of elected people. As most authentically set forth by St. Augustine, confirmed by Calvin, and unanimously accepted in colonial New England, this revised conception states that all men, being inheritors of Adam's guilt, are born in sin and in the wrath, but that God has mercifully chosen some of them to be recipients of his indispensable, prevenient, irresistible, and indefectible grace, and by the operation of this grace—not at all by their own efforts—these will be saved from their depravity, redeemed, and so made fit for blissful living in the heavenly company of saints and angels. Down the centuries of Western history this still current view of the inherent nature of man, and of his possible mysterious transformation, has been tremendously influential in shaping the deep thoughts of men.

The points to be specially noted in this version are eleven in number: (1) the supreme male parentage of man; (2) man's creation in the image of God; (3) the omission, if not the denial, of sexual conjugation and the female's function—the absence of a Goddess, the procreation of life accomplished without her participation, the first woman being taken out of man; (4) creativity credited to the transcendent being outside of nature; (5) the great speed of creation; (6) the source of original sin—intellectual curiosity, the desire for wisdom, knowledge of good and evil; (7) the fall of man from an initial state of bliss; (8) a God-made perfect world, established in the past and then held up as the ultimate goal to be reached, if reached at all, in the far future, after death; (9) the depravity of human nature due to the inheritance of Adam's sin; (10) the possibility of transformation by the saving grace of God; and (11) the dictation of these statements by God and hence their absolute and undeniable truthfulness.

According to a more recent version of himself—the version I shall put before you—man is descended from the very humblest of parents, a purely fortuitous combination of chemical elements—such low-caste stuff as hydrogen, oxygen, carbon, and nitrogen. Instead of a day, it took two billion years or more to shape him. And instead of falling from his primordial state of being, he has risen—increasing his powers by periodic leaps as well as by more gradual acquisitions. Also noteworthy is the evidence that this wondrous evolution from the simple to the complex may be credited, in large measure, to the very propensity which in the Garden of Eden drama led to man's disgrace and fall, that is, the propensity of all organisms to explore and to experiment.

In the panorama presented to us by the theory of evolution, a better world—and we must avow that most religions are devoted to the idea of a better world, in one sense or another—a better world is neither a pre-made perfection that existed on this globe in pristine times, nor a pre-made perfection in the sky awaiting the elected few, but a condition that might, by concordant creative efforts, be achieved on earth in the very distant future.

Darwin's formula for the evolution of fishes, reptiles, birds, and mammals, man included, stresses two chief factors: (1) countless slight variations of structure, and (2) the survival of those organisms with variations that operated beneficially, concurrent with the elimination of those with variations which proved injurious.

When presented in the mid-nineteenth century, this conception of man's ascending career on earth was shocking to his self-esteem. The notion that he had moved up from the status of a monkey was somehow less congenial to his soul than the thought that he had backslid from the original gracefulness of Adam. The new theory was equally shocking to his intellect, in its abandonment of two long-cherished concepts: that of God's design—the operation of an unseen hand in the determination of events—and that of Aristotle's final cause or goal—something in Nature comparable to human purpose. According to Darwin, all the millions of variations which marked the path of evolution might be accounted for by purely accidental (and hence purposeless) physical changes.

When *we* do something accidentally, we commonly call it a mistake, or slip, and say that we are sorry. Could man, the paragon of animals, have been no more than a mistake, the end result of countless sorry slips? Not possibly, our pride assures us. Man is admirable, and when *we* do something admirable, we are apt to feel we purposed it, to claim we had the deed in mind before we acted, and to take full credit. God or Nature, therefore, must have planned for *Homo sapiens.* The advent of our breed must have been intended from the start. But, unhappily for vanity, the experts have repeatedly assured us there is no evidence of consciousness of goal in any of the structurations which led to the human species. At first blush, it looks as if the facts constrained us to the view that pure chance was the author of every variety of organism, even of so complex and remarkable an organism as that of the erect, tool-using tribal dreamer that we call man.

Despite Darwin's emphasis on accident, or chance, the theory of evolution was understood by some scientists as an encouragement to their faith that all biological phenomena, including human conduct, would eventually be understandable in terms of the physical and chemical properties of matter. The word they chose to symbolize their faith was "mechanism": human nature is nothing else than a machine of great complexity. This view of man is at the limit of self-depreciation, far more crippling to our aspirations than the theological assertion that man is born depraved. For, according to the mechanistic model, we humans do not even have the powers that might expose us to moralistic judgments: we are automata, first and last. And as mere automata we are unspeakably inferior to the best gadgets of today. Though savory to some tongues, this thesis has been rather hard to cram against the stomach of our knowledge that machines do not grow by feeding on their surroundings and constantly restructuring themselves, and do not habitually converse, embrace each other, multiply, nurse their young, and institute societies. But it did not become obvious that the word "mechanism" was a poor choice to designate this model of man's nature until classical mechanics was abandoned as a foundation for the sciences of physics and chemistry.

The error of supposing that the procession of organic variations could be represented in purely mechanistic terms might never have been launched had Darwin's terminology not concealed the crucial fact of creativity in nature, irreversible and hence unmechanical creativity. His theory, as we have seen, depends on the occurrence of variations of form; and what is a variation of form but a new configuration of elements, a unique pattern, that retains its structure for a while? And by these very words creativity is defined.

The original outline of the theory of creative evolution was Bergson's seminal contribution; but since its publication many profound thinkers have, in different and more or less radical ways, expanded and revised it.

Briefly, and most generally, this thesis states that the processes of nature have been constantly, though often very slowly and imperceptibly, formative and transformative. The transformations have been both integrative and disintegrative, evolutionary and involutionary; but the former have predominated, and among these—these products of integrative energy—some have been veritable creations, unparalleled in history. This applies on the chemical level to the compounding of new and more complex atoms, molecules, and crystals, and *hypothetically,* to the much later emergence of a living organism, say a few genes in an envelope of protoplasm; and then, on this supervenient biological level, to variant conjugations and permutations of genes, resulting in the development, through interactions with environment, of unexampled living forms, dispositions and abilities, of brains and animal intelligences. It applies with equal cogency, on the social level, to the establishment of groups and of exceptional systems of coordination among its members, and, on the symbolic-cultural level, to the creation of words, concepts, and germinal ideas eventuating through numberless expressions in collectively valued myths, beliefs, art forms, moral and legal codes, plans of action, technical designs.

This view of the natural course of events in no wise contradicts Darwin's formulation. In fact, it supplements it by pointing to those properties of things which might account for stable variations, not only as he described them on the biological and social levels, but on the chemical and ideological as well. We have only to conceive of the *movement* and hence inevitable approximation of different entities which are inherently attractive to each other—*attraction* being one of the great and constant forces in the universe—and then conceive of these attractions resulting in a multiplicity of structural *combinations* new to this planet, and, most importantly, conceive of the *coherence,* the sticking and staying power, and hence the relative stability and longevity of many of these unprecedented forms—organic compounds, genetic clusters, family relationships, governmental laws, religious creeds and rites. Since individual organisms are mortal, another power must be present on the biological, social, and symbolic levels, namely, the power of *propagation,* the ability to implant in others and hence to transmit and multiply the new variations from generation to generation. Furthermore, to survive in a competitive and dangerous environment, most entities must possess *combative strength,* defensive and offensive force. "Vary, multiply, and be strong" was one of the several pithy precepts drawn from Darwin's theory. Finally, one more property is required if an established form is to have further evolutionary value, namely, a certain *plasticity,* or flexibility, the capacity, that is, to play a part or to become involved in subsequent *transformations* or reconstructions. The picture is one of continuity through change. Only by losing its particular identity, by perishing as such, can a variation become a link, stage, or episode, in an evolutionary sequence, such as the one and only sequence that led to the human species.

Can we find evidence of purpose in all this?

For the production of chemical and biological variations no credit goes to purpose, or consciousness of goal. The creative transformations of nature, according to this theory, occurred blindly, without foresight of their ends. Furthermore, they were not necessarily, or even predominantly, beneficial: enormous numbers of them were useless or disadvantageous to the species in which they occurred, rendering its members more vulnerable to injury, less capable of resisting, circumventing, or coping with destructive forces from without. Thus, deleterious variations of form or behavior were, for the most part, extinguished and only those variations which happened to serve a vital purpose have survived. Consequently, almost all biological processes that are observable today are in the long run sustaining to the majority of individuals or to the race in which they occur, and so have a purposeful appearance. Without any consciousness of goals, they nonetheless attain them. For example, males and females of prehuman species may have been aware, in some fashion, of each other's fascinating qualities, but no members of a conjugating pair, we can be sure, were ever directed in their activities by the conscious aim of producing a variant that would advance the cause of evolution, and yet, in countless cases this was precisely what resulted from their unreasoning embraces.

Must all variations be attributed to accident?

Although no credit for these advances can be ascribed to purpose, only a portion of it, according to this theory, belongs to accident. We all agree that it is impossible to predict precisely which entities at precisely which stages of their careers will meet each other, or precisely which rearrangement of their components will occur at precisely what hour. Such synchronicities among events are affairs of chance and beyond our reckoning. For all we know, evolution might have taken a very different course and come out with a more amiable species than our own. But the occurrence of *some* form of evolution, the movement and mingling of different entities, magnetic and affectional, the enduring units that result —cohesive, cooperative, logical—and the reconstruction of these into larger and more accomplished units—events of this general character are no accidents but have been fated from the beginning by the inherent potencies of the universe. For us the crux of this version is the observation that the most outstanding heroes, or demigods, of the long epic of this earth—*movement, chance, attraction, combination, coherence, propagation, combative strength,* and *transformation*—are playing no less important parts today in the development of societies, of ideologies, and of personalities.

Such is the bare skeleton of a very general view respecting the more strategic component processes of evolutionary transformations. For the sake of brevity, several components have been omitted, as well as *all* details. Last year Professor Wald gave a beautifully ordered account of what facts and current suppositions are relevant to an understanding of evolution on the physicochemical and biological levels. This year Professor Emerson is certain to contribute a great deal to our knowledge of analogous processes on other levels. Last night we were informed by Professor Huntsman's admirable address. These disciplined observers of nature, these gifted theorists, I trust, will be my saviors, give meaning to the vagueness and diffuseness of my notions, by providing whatever substantial facts, whatever specificities and particularities, are essential to even a provisional acceptance of the view I am expounding. For better or for worse, I must confine myself to generalities, taking it for granted that you fully realize the tentative and hypothetical status of these concepts.

Now, assuming that the theory I have outlined is roughly consonant with the known facts, what additional conclusions pertinent to our topic can be drawn from it? At the moment, I shall restrict myself to four:

1. Creativity, the power to construct new and coherent forms, is a property of nature, of human nature especially, as I shall suggest later, of the deeper strata of the mind. This conclusion is contrary to the orthodox belief that creation is a special power and prerogative of a transcendent personality who like a master artisan manipulates natural objects from the outside. But it is not discordant with pantheism, the belief that God and nature are identical, or with the not uncommon inclination to deify creativeness in general or beneficent creativeness in particular.

2. Most of the more fundamental evolutionary processes occur so slowly—taking, in some cases, many thousands of years to run their course—that a Methuselah would be incapable of recording them. This is one of the major reasons why scientists for centuries, attracted first of all to the more static and stable aspects of nature, overlooked the crucial question of the *formation of the forms* they chose to study. Anyhow, we must confess that the biblical report of the creation of the universe in six days is a little out of line with the evidence that is now at hand.

3. The theory of creative evolution stresses the importance of the female role in sexual conjugation, reproduction, and child-rearing, as well as in other varieties of interpersonal relations, and by so doing,

opens our eyes, if by any chance they are still shut, to the several evidences of pathological prejudice toward women and toward sexuality in the Hebraic-Christian story of creation and in its story of man's first surrender to temptation. This prejudice was outspoken in the writings of the Church Fathers, and its virulence was contagious to subsequent generations, one result being that no spiritual form of erotic love has ever been offered us by Christianity.

4. Finally, the theory of creative evolution is death to the hope that any entity, any pattern, any production of the mind, can remain for very long both fixed and dominant. Infallibility is impossible in nature.

At this point, a few comments pertinent to evolution on the social level might serve to elucidate the view of human nature I am submitting to your judgment.

Surveying the evidences of man's development on earth, Darwin concluded: first, that the survival of the fittest is a principle which applies decisively *not* to individuals, but to rival groups—tribes, states, or nations —and second, that mutual sympathy, aid, and collaboration among members of a group are conducive to its solidarity, and hence to its combative power and survival. To put it another way, one of the critical variations established long ago was a clannish combination of families more powerful than any single person, a flexible yet stable social system with some differentiation of functions and consequently with an enhanced capacity to cope with various tasks and crises.

From the beginning, if we follow Sir Arthur Keith's composition of the evidence, every successful group has adhered to a double code of conduct, a Janus-faced morality: one face preaching submission to authority, reverence, cooperation, loyalty, good will, and generosity within the group; and the other more contorted face shouting with rage and murderous aggression toward members of opposing groups. Other things being equal, it must have been the clans or tribes which embodied this dual standard to the highest degree that triumphed and endured, and passed on to their descendants down to the present day the dispositions which sustained it.

This theory of group evolution helps us to understand why man is a social rather than a solitary, self-sufficient creature, and why, as a social creature, he is both humane and brutal. Illustrative of his *social* properties are such familiar facts as these: that the vast majority of men are reared in one particular society, a society that is prejudiced in its own favor, and are satisfied to be lifelong interdependent members of this society; that the bulk of their enjoyments come from interacting with its members; that they are at peace with themselves only when they feel and act in accord with its customs and ideals, and that, even in their furthest reaches of self-forwarding ambition, they choose for their most delectable final prize the applause of their fellow beings, and, after death, fame—"that last infirmity of noble mind." The dual morality of groups—tribes and nations—accounts, in some measure, for the failure, the halfheartedness and insincerity, of all attempts to abolish war, and for the fact that human beings have been generally so willing, even eager, to suppress their fears of self-extinction and fight for their country to the tragic end, as well as for the fact that a man who kills a hundred members of an enemy society is declared glorious, but is condemned to the severest punishment if he stops the life of a single fellow citizen.

It is supposed that the generally victorious groups were those which most fully incorporated and exploited the vaingloriousness and pride, the greed and will-to-power of their individual members. But what is the significance of the will to power? Power, intoxicating as it may be to some men and to some nations, is a *means* to something, not an end. Power for what? To this question the response of a creative evolutionist might be: power to construct ever larger and less vulnerable social units controlling ever larger areas of the earth's resources, or, in other words, power, spurred on by greed, to grow and to develop, by invading, conquering, subjugating, and assimilating weaker units, or, more peacefully and happily in some cases, by federating with other units. History reports a great number of such sequences: the integration of primal groups into clans, and of clans into tribes, and of tribes into small nations, and the integration of small nations into great nations that subsequently broke apart, the rise and decline, the evolution and involution, of mighty civilizations, as Toynbee has shown us, but as yet, unfortunately, no orchestration of state sovereignties into a world order, no political embodiment of that dream of universal fellowship which centuries of religious men have recommended to our hearts.

This curtailed abstract of evolutionary processes on the social and political level is clearly inadequate. Something should be said about the determining importance, first, of the family structure—the interrelations of father, mother, and offspring—and, second, of the total social structure, or form of government, of a group. Also necessary is some account of the role of religious beliefs and practices in the achievement and preservation of tribal and national unity. But the time allotted me does not permit even a brief discussion of these matters. Furthermore, this is not the place for it, since the evolution of human societies and religions has depended on the capacity for speech, and speech belongs to the symbolic-ideational level of creativeness, with which we have yet to cope.

Before proceeding, however, it might be stated that the theory I have been expounding gives comfort neither to the Augustinian judgment of total depravity at birth, nor to the judgment, most often attributed to Rousseau, that newborn babes are springs of sympathy and love. In my opinion, human infants are an aggregate of potentialities, potential drives to action and potential abilities, those which in the past have been most generally conducive to the evolution and survival of the social unit. Most of the potential drives, or dispositions, are in readiness to propel actions which aim at self-preservation and enjoyment, neither good nor evil in intent, and associated with these are dispositions conducive to the joy and well-being of other people as well as dispositions to fury and destructiveness. A sufficient study of the dreams and fantasies of little children, say four to six years old, will convince the most adoring mother that the human psyche, at this age at least, is predominantly and most excitedly engaged in inventing scenes of violence, death, and mutilation. But at present most psychologists believe that except for the instincts of the body, the bulk of the child's dispositions are no more than potentialities, and it largely depends on chance and the social environment—the parents and the surrounding culture—which among these various potentialities get stimulated, encouraged, and rewarded, and thus established as enduring components of the personality, and which *do not.* The theory of creative evolution draws special attention to the rhythms and stages of transformation which the structure of personality undergoes from birth to maturity, sometimes very slowly by imperceptible gradations and occasionally with striking rapidity; and also to the fact that the formative processes responsible for these changes go on unconsciously, for the most part, and, in their depths are scarcely more subject than the grace of God to man's deliberate direction. I assume that it is these transforming processes in human nature and their determinants which constitute the major focus of concern for the majority of religious men. But I shall say no more about them until I have discussed the top and last level of human evolution.

Consideration of the very earliest social systems—small colonies, let us say, of prehuman anthropoids—suggests another emergent variation in the course of man's genesis and development, this variation being one of the chief products of social life as well as the chief means of ordering and sustaining it. I am referring to symbolic language and to the mental capacity from which this kind of language stems, namely, the capacity to form concepts combined with some awareness of their meanings. It is the power of imagination and conceptualization linked with the power of symbolic representation and expression which distinguishes man most saliently from all preceding species. In the beginning was the Image and the Word.

This enormous step brought man to the ideational, the symbolic-cultural level of evolution. For the first time, the mind of a living creature could dissociate itself to a significant degree for a significant length of time from its immediate surroundings and conceive of things that were not then present to its senses, and even more, conceive of arrangements of things that had never been present to its senses. But this gift of abundant and far-ranging imagination had dangerous as well as fruitful possibilities. Spelled by its productions, on the one hand, and fearful of the external environment, on the other, a child might far prefer his inner world, come to live in it entirely, and remain an idle dreamer, or become a senseless visionary or victim of insanity. In short, lunacy is the dreaded peril and genius the coveted prize of this new power of thought and of verbalization, the power that lifted man out of the class of primates.

It is not without significance that the advent of this mental capacity was accompanied, on the one hand, by an unprecedented degree and duration of helplessness and dependency in the offspring, and on the other, by a corresponding increase of enduring maternal aid, devotion, and concern. Here, in this intimate symbiosis of primitive human mother and primitive human child, we might look for the first germ of religious compassion, the *agape* of Christianity, as well as for the first germ of ideational creativity.

Look at the human infant—of all creatures, objectively speaking, the most unfit to live, the most incompetent, endowed with no resources save the voice to cry for help. But there, encased within this body, as correlate of its complete impractibility, resides a mind, an imagination that is a veritable hive of promising possibilities to be realized in their season if chance consents—perhaps in middle-age or later—provided the child receives, during his good-for-nothing years, a due degree of maternal warmth and care.

If you insist on immediate efficiency and quick results, turn to the practical progeny of your animal neighbors, but if you require more efficiency than this and can check your importunity, turn to the impractical human infant, because this one is capable not only of learning a much wider variety of more efficient tricks but forming theories, theories which can be converted into actions of extraordinary practicality. Here is a truth this hasting world has not yet got hold of and digested. There is nothing so practical as a good theory.

Then look at the human mother, or mother surrogate, in close and constant proximity to her playfully dreaming child, teaching him to speak and applauding his every effort, encouraging his expanding spirit like a patroness of some unadjusted would-be artist, prophet, or philosopher.

The thesis I am submitting here is that the creativity of nature in general is manifested most clearly and most saliently by the creativity of human nature, by the formative mental processes of man; that novel ideas, charismatic ideas are the mutant genes of cultural evolution. Like countless wanton and wasteful experiments of nature, man's imaginings may run off the beam of progressive and beneficial developments and produce one or another variety of deformation—criminality, neurosis, or psychosis. But creative imagination at its best, cheered by sight of an ideal or valued end, and checked by rationality, is the fountain from which all inventive and regenerative currents flow. The ancients missed the point. Only recently, since the beginnings of romanticism in Europe, less than two hundred years ago, has the role of creativity in man become apparent to some people. Even now its role is not widely and sufficiently acknowledged, certainly not in the United States. It is not fully appreciated, to take one example, that our cherished democratic system, for the preservation of which so many men have lived and died, was derived from a formation of ideas that once took place in the heads of John Locke and of Rousseau. Nor is it fully appreciated in this country that all the fundamental hypotheses and theories relative to the atomic energy on which some think our mightiness depends came from minds in England, Germany, France, Denmark, Italy, Poland, and Australia. That the superior striking power, if not the continued existence, of an entire nation may hang on the unimpeded imaginations of a few theoretical scientists is today only too appallingly apparent.

But let us return for a moment to primitive man and the practical significance to him of his newborn power of imagination. When governed wholly by instinct, an organism can learn the specific ways and instrumental means to its goal only by overt trials, their failures and their successes, at the time the instinct is operating. But man, gaining a little liberty from instinct, became capable, by the mere play of fantasy, of conducting countless behavioral experiments in his head, conceiving of numerous alternative paths and tactics, evaluating them in his mind's eye, discarding the apparent worst and selecting the apparent best—all very much more rapidly than would be possible if every idea had to be successively acted out and tested by experience. And then, with the invention of language, consciousness of goal, or purpose, began to play an increasingly important role in social evolution. For language enables people to submit to each other's inner sight word-images of desirable ends, alternative strategies and rules, and through discussion to arrive at enough agreement to permit the execution of long-range collective enterprises. For these a consciously shared objective is indispensable. Language, furthermore, is the best means of introducing variations, since it empowers a person with a new idea, a new hope for the future, a new plan or tactic, or a new ethical conviction, to start it in the thoughts of others and keep it rolling there until familiarity argues for its acceptance.

In all likelihood, primitive man's creativeness was oriented almost entirely toward contriving means of physical survival—exploring for edible plants, for a suitable territory to occupy, building shelters, inventing pots and tools, and fashioning weapons for hunting and for war. Along the way, momentous discoveries were made: fire, agriculture, irrigation, the domestication and breeding of animals, stone, bronze, and iron. In the judgment of numerous historians, technical inventions have resulted in more drastic transformations of human behavior than any other kind of variation: a proposition that is verified most strikingly by the changes of habits that have occurred within our own lifetime.

Most relevant to the topic of this conference is the fact that as technology has advanced, first in this and then in that area of activity, religious beliefs and rituals have receded. Being largely dependent on the fertility of the earth, and hence concerned with the succession of the seasons, the heat of the sun, rainfall and the rising of their rivers, primitive man engaged in all manner of supposedly influential practices—sympathetic magic, supplications, propitiations, glorifications—directed toward the personified powers that were, in their beliefs, responsible for the required processes of nature. But in the West today such practices are almost obsolete. Christianity is to no extent preoccupied with the promotion of the crops. The same withdrawal has occurred in other fields, indeed to every field which the physical and biological sciences have invaded—medicine, for example, most people having come to the conclusion that the methods of trained physicians and surgeons are more generally efficacious than the ceremonies of the Church.

I have been talking about the creative processes of the mind operating in the service of physical well-being and survival, the well-being of individuals and, more often among primitives, the well-being of the whole society. Some of these imaginations, these novel ideas, have taken the form of purely physical or technological procedures, whereas others have been psychological in nature, symbolic postures, acts, words, and dramas, which might well have proved efficient if the forces of nature were veritable gods, such as Baal, Adonis, or Asclepius, with receptive psyches that were in sympathy with men's wants. A little while back, I also mentioned in passing the role of mental creativity in the development of effective governmental forms and the office of religion in maintaining the sanctity of the kingship and its code of morals, and thereby the solidarity and continuation of the social system.

The words "creation," "create," "creative," were limited at first to the operations of a divine agent. As Davies wrote in 1592, "To create, to God alone pertains." But as time went on, the usage of these terms expanded, and by the beginning of the nineteenth century they were being widely used to describe the mental processes and productions of poets, artists, and musicians, especially the works of romantic genius. Somewhat later people began speaking of eminent scientists as creative, those who had proposed and at least partially verified some all-embracing theory of great explanatory value. It is now allowed that some applied scientists and inventors are creative. Creativity in these two spheres, those of art and science, is at present generally acknowledged, and nothing I could say in a paragraph or two could be of service to us. Strangely enough the word "creative" is seldom applied to the mental processes of religionists. Why is that? As a psychologist apprehends it, man's imagination has gone to greater lengths, greater depths and heights, under the name of religion than under any other name. Think of the galaxy of primitive religions with their multiplicity of gods, myths, legends, beliefs, passions, solemn and wild rituals and orgies, bloody sacrifices, temples, idols, and sacraments. Whence all this, if not from the endless fecundity and spontaneity of man's mind?

Pertinent to this problem are two characteristics of creative processes: (1) their goal does not exist at first and hence cannot be visualized, and (2) they operate involuntarily and, to a large extent, unconsciously. The goal object, let us say, of the need for acquisition—be it food, a house, or some utility—is known to you: it exists somewhere in the environment and you must take it as it is. But the aim of creativity—say, a symphony, or a novel, or a scientific theory to explain a peculiar sequence of events, or a more effective foreign policy, or a better way of life—has no existence anywhere. It is necessary, first of all, to get a satisfying image or conception of it and, if fortune favors you with this, it is then necessary to embody your vision in a written work or course of conduct. A man may rack his brains throughout a lifetime without receiving the vision or idea for which he longs—say, a better form of architecture, a better theory, a better constitution for the United Nations—or, if he has the general idea in mind, he may labor for years without finding the way to expound it in a persuasive manner. That is to say, we are dealing here with energies of the human mind that do not respond directly to voluntary efforts. Voluntary efforts can influence their direction, defining, so far as possible, the target of their endeavor, but they cannot force them to render up the wanted form. Today it is pretty generally agreed that imaginations of any real consequence are generated outside or below the stream of awareness, during a more or less prolonged period of incubation, and they are apt to leap to consciousness abruptly at the most unexpected moments. Sometimes, like a dream, they seem to come from *without* rather than from *within* the mind. A vision is called a vision because it is a presentation, a present, a gift, to the inner eye, just as the heavenly constellations at night are a presentation, or gift, to the outer eye. We cannot *will* the rise of Sirius on the horizon, or the voyage of Jupiter across the sky. Nor can we dictate the emergence of an idea of great import to us or to society. These are extremely rare, and when they do come, they do not come from the conscious "I" in us, but from a deeper layer of nature.

The point I am getting at is that visions which appear as promised or possible fulfillments of a great craving, visions that hint of the resolution of a protracted conflict, visions of extraordinary beauty, visions that come—as did St. Paul's on the road to Damascus and St. Joan's at her home in Domremy—as a challenging invocation to one's innermost being, seemingly beneficent or coercive—spirit-lifting visions of this sort were for centuries attributed to superhuman force, to the gods, or to *the* God. And why not? Did the visionary consciously and deliberately compose this vision? No, it was engendered by autonomous forces, natural forces, a psychologist would say, yet forces which one might well call supernatural insofar as their product is an unexampled creation, a never yet conceived form or goal, something that was unpredictable by scientific laws, laws which announce only that which is statistically most probable as determined by recordings of past events. Since the vision does not conform to the regular laws of human nature, it is, by this criterion, unnatural, and since, in addition, the kind of vision we have in mind strikes the visionary as something of supreme worth, the most desirable, the most valuable thing he has ever contemplated, it is, in his estimation, not only unnatural, but supernatural, a veritable miracle.

We are all familiar with the passage in *Phaedrus* in which Socrates describes the four types of divine madness, "the source," he affirms, "of the chiefest blessings granted to man." Sustained by an array of evidence, he insists that inspired madness is a noble thing, that madness, being of divine origin, is superior to common sanity. The first kind of providential madness is associated with prophecy and the second with spiritual healing, a vision of deliverance from woe. The third kind is the madness of those who are possessed by the Muses, and the last the madness of erotic love. We hear an echo of this passage in Shakespeare's saying that "The lunatic, the lover, and the poet, Are of imagination all compact . . ." Shakespeare, however, does not ascribe the "fine frenzy" of his poet to a god, and Socrates, though sincere in his reference to the gods, does not insist that everything they tell him is absolute and incontestable truth for all men for all time.

Perhaps the most famous recent description of the state of creative possession is Nietzsche's account of how his *Zarathustra* was composed.

Can anyone at the end of this nineteenth century possibly have any distinct notion of what poets of a more vigorous period meant by inspiration? If not, I should like to describe it. Provided one has the slightest remnant of superstition left, one can hardly reject completely the idea that one is the mere incarnation, or mouthpiece, or medium of some almighty power. The notion of revelation describes the condition quite simply; by which I mean that something profoundly convulsive and disturbing suddenly becomes visible and audible with indescribable definiteness and exactness. One hears—one does not seek; one takes—one does not ask who gives: a thought flashes out like lightning, inevitably without hesitation—I have never had any choice about it. There is an ecstasy whose terrific tension is sometimes released by a flood of tears, during which one's progress varies from involuntary impetuosity to involuntary slowness. There is the feeling that one is utterly out of hand, with the most distinct consciousness of an infinitude of shuddering thrills that pass through one from head to foot:—there is a profound happiness in which the most painful and gloomy feelings are not discordant in effect, but are required as necessary colors in this overflow of light. There is an instinct for rhythmic relations which embraces an entire world of forms. . . . Everything occurs quite without volition, as if in an eruption of freedom, independence, power and divinity. The spontaneity of the images and similes is most remarkable; one loses all perception of what is imagery and simile;

everything offers itself as the most immediate, exact, and simple means of expression.

Note that even Nietzsche—who had recently announced with certainty that God was dead—could not completely reject the idea that he was the mere incarnation or medium of some almighty power. He does not intimate that this almighty power has a separate existence outside of him, and we can safely infer that he would have identified the creative force of which he, in his own proper person, was the instrument with a natural force, a force which happened to vent itself more powerfully in him than it did in other men. If this was his opinion, there would be few dissenting voices from the ranks of today's psychologists. It is the grandiose assertion that the source of such unleashed energy is an all-knowing and utterly truthful being in the sky which provokes dissent among my colleagues.

For the origin of historic and long-surviving assertions of this sort—dogmatic and unequivocal assertions of infallibility—one must turn to the Hebrew prophets, each of whom claimed to be in his day the one appointed mouthpiece of the omniscient Yahweh. Apparently, the imagination was not in any way involved. The prophet merely opened his ears and spoke the words of the Lord as they came down to him. The proud and vaunting certitude of these devout and dedicated men was, so far as I can see, the prime source of centuries of anguish. To speak as they did was no doubt natural to them and sanctioned, even demanded, by their society. In the light of a remark made by the eminent Jewish philosopher Spinoza, it was hardly more than a habit of speech. If Jews "desire anything," he tells us, "they say God has disposed their hearts towards it; and if they think anything, they say God has told them." This way of talking, of course, was carried to much greater lengths by the prophets, whose frantic utterances inevitably gave rise to the bitterest disputes. What could be said when scores of visionaries were in the streets, each insisting that his revelation was the sole authentic one? At one such time, the word of the Lord came unto Ezekiel saying: "Son of man, prophesy against the prophets of Israel that prophesy . . . out of their own hearts." That is to say, prophecies from a man's heart and mind are false and evil; all true revelations come from above, from the creative being who stands outside the order of nature. This conviction was fully accepted by the Church Fathers and passed down from generation to generation, the result being that no truly religious man, none of the great visionaries of Christianity, ever claimed to be, was ever officially thought to be, or allowed to be, creative. In short, the great religionists of the past reserved for themselves a separate category beyond the processes of nature.

Just here—if you will pardon a personal evaluation not flattering to the Church—just here is where religion eventually got stuck, in this blind alley, in this prison house which it invented and masoned for itself. The prison was built, it seems to me, by vanity and pride—ironically enough, the Christian Church's deadliest sin to be—the very human and understandable vanity and pride of those who insisted that they were the only selected spokesmen, the only genuine vehicles of the one and only God, that they had heard exactly what the omniscient Lord had said, remembered it and recorded it—"thus spake Yahweh"—without a flaw, and consequently everything that they wrote down was truth, absolute, infallible, and everlasting. Having compiled the writings of the chosen authors and bound them in a book, the high priests announced that *there*, between those covers, was the one sure repository of uncontradictable sacred truths. Later on, the Protestants were to agree with them completely, and so to become, in their turn, the "People of the Book." The Holy Bible is without doubt the most majestic creation of our literature, the greatest spiritual treasure that the West inherited from the East. But the nemesis of its majesty was this: Deity was imprisoned there and silenced. From then on, God could only repeat with minor variations or in different keys what he had said in Palestine, hundreds of years ago. He was not permitted to go further, to reveal more, to present men with any unprecedented vision, fitting and timely to their current situation.

In other words, the creative imagination was excommunicated and, beginning with the Renaissance, found in art, science, and public affairs far broader, freer, and happier domains for its exuberant and effective exercise. My thesis is that enchantment always keeps company with creative imagination, and what results from their combined play is evolution. Religion, by sitting pat in its citadel of solidified infallibilities, repelled the lovely goose that lays the golden eggs—the creativity in man —and thereby lost its charm, its lure, its magnetism, its spring of inspiration and renewal—the only source of veritable progress.

This is the rudest and crudest thing I have in my heart and mind to say about religion. Forgive me if you can.

Another important fact not generally acknowledged is that the Bible is poetry, in its best parts, magnificent and edifying poetry, and that without this poetic essence its spiritual efficacy would be negligible. Some devout Christians overlook the fact that the stirring and sustaining power of the Book they live by depends on the wonderous emotive language, the vivid imagery and figures of speech, with which its wisdom is transmitted. This is one of the major qualities by which a religion can be distinguished from a moral philosophy or system of ethics. If the New Testament, for example, had been written by a modern social scientist in the jargon of his profession, it would have died at birth, and Mithraism or Manichaeanism or Mohammedanism would have taken possession of the European mind. A religion is propagated by the aid of the aesthetic imagination, that is, in striking parables and metaphors that kindle or console our profoundest feelings. A code of morals, on the other hand, can appeal only to our intellects and to a few of our more superficial sentiments. This is but one reason why my discourse, couched as it is in commonplace referential language, cannot possibly touch your vital centers.

The playing down of the crucial import of the Bible's poetry has gone hand in hand with the playing up of its factual dependability, its historicity. The great fallacy of Christianity, Santayana has suggested, was:

The natural but hopeless misunderstanding of imagining that poetry in order to be religion, in order to be the inspiration of life, must first deny that it is poetry and deceive us about the facts with which we have to deal—this misunderstanding has marred the work of the Christian imagination and condemned it, if we may trust appearances, to be transitory. For by this misunderstanding Christian doctrine was brought into conflict with reality, of which it pretends to prejudge the character. . . . Human life is always essentially the same, and therefore a religion which, like Christianity, seizes the essence of that life, ought to be an eternal religion. But it may forfeit that privilege by entangling itself with a particular account of matters of fact, matters irrelevant to its ideal significance.

I have been assuming, all along, rightly or wrongly, that the focus of religious concern is the transformation, the conversion, of the personality at its very center. Something was said, a little while back, of its social development, from birth to maturity, the successful outcome of which is a well-adjusted person equal to the functions of the role he has elected. Religion is not uninterested in this process; but socialization does no more than fit a person for a particular society, in a particular place, during a particular period of history, and this requires the adoption of a great aggregate of conforming beliefs, sentiments, and tastes which are local and transient and, from a larger viewpoint, mere prejudices, restrictive of spiritual freedom. Furthermore, there are always countless individuals who have become alienated from their society—either by feelings of guilt, inferiority, and resentment, or by repulsion, a profound aversion to the values of the great majority. All such people—those who are stifled in the strait jacket of convention, those who are afflicted by neurotic symptoms, and those with superpersonal hopes and aspirations —all such people will be in need of some healing vision, of transformation and renewal. It is just here where religion, with its profound intuitive understanding of the tormented human soul, and psychology, with its new methods of investigation and of therapy, might most beneficently collaborate, provided they can come to some agreement respecting the aim of their endeavors.

Now it is time for a last reckoning, a summary of the story I have told so hurriedly, a final comparison of my short abstract of the once authentic Christian view of man's origin and destiny, and my abstract of the theory of creative evolution. To repeat what I have said before: According to the

latter view, man was not made from without and from above, like a pot
of clay by a master workman, but from within and from below. The great
God of creativity has been from the start and is today immanent in nature
and immanent in us.

Second, the creation of natural forms was not achieved all of a sudden, as the image of a tree, an animal, or a man can be instantly called
to mind by an act of will, but it proceeded gradually step by step over
millions of years. During the last centuries, however, it has been progressing very much more rapidly on the symbolic-cultural level than it
ever did on the physical-biological level.

Third, perfect chastity does not stand out as the highest ideal for our
time. On the contrary, sexual love, sexual conjugation, pregnancy, and
deliverance is the epitome, the very best paradigm, on the biological
level of the creative process. It proceeds like the Hegelian dialectic: the
male thesis embraces the female antithesis, and the result is a genetic
synthesis and the development of a new and unique being. Mutual erotic
love, erotic adoration, is the most natural religion, far stronger and more
natural than a son's adoration for his father, the father-son relationship
(with mother and daughter omitted) having been from the beginning the
mythic paradigm of Christianity.

Fourth, the newborn child is neither soaking in original sin nor
beaming with benevolence for all mankind. He or she is a composite of
manifold potentialities for promoting its own good, promoting the good
of others, or harming others.

Fifth, the course of a single life from its genesis, through its intra-
uterine existence, through childhood, adolescence, and its adult years is
marked by a continuity of formative and transformative processes, rapid
at first, on the physical level, and, with the passage of time, slowing down
and eventually coming to a stop, but advancing, in many persons, on the
dispositional and mental level until the age of maturity and beyond. The
theory of creative evolution stresses the fact that most of the formative
processes engaged in the development, the transformation, and conversions of personality, are not directly subject to the will, though the will
can indirectly influence their course; these divine creative processes of
nature occur autonomously, for the most part out of consciousness, and
chance plays a large part in determining their fortunes. This is roughly
comparable to the Catholic doctrine that the realization, or rather the
partial realization, of the ideal self-image is something that exceeds man's
voluntary powers and only through the operation of God's grace, with
the acceptance and cooperation of the will, can an individual approach
it.

Sixth, the conversion of personality from the old self to the new self
is only temporarily facilitated by forceful repression, say, the repression
of hatred, lust, greed, envy, and vanity. Harmful egocentric dispositions
of this sort must be transmuted and made to serve a nobler purpose. A

mass of evidence from the case histories of psychoanalysts goes to show that strong instinctual tendencies do not atrophy and die out when subjected to repression, but, living on in some subterranean region of the mind, are capable of no end of mischief. The puritan's sharp dichotomy of good and evil, of pure white and pure black, the obligatory *expression* of the white and the obligatory *suppression* of the black, is one of the major determinants of obsessional neurosis.

Seventh, Christianity's traditional method of dealing with evil *within* oneself by forceful repression is comparable to its traditional method of dealing with evil on the outside: evil persons, especially persons with deviant heretical beliefs, must be ostracized, persecuted, tortured, or burned at the stake, and, whatever may be their punishments on earth, committed after death to the most painful torments the imagination can contrive. The nearest approach to this in modern times are the gas chambers and lethal concentration camps of the Nazis. Such are the solutions of impatient adolescent sadists. The method of dealing with evil that is derivable from the theory of creative evolution is the exact opposite of this. It has never been more succinctly revealed, so far as I know, than by Henry James, senior. These are his words: "It is no doubt very tolerable finite or creaturely love to love one's own in another, to love another for his conformity to one's self: but nothing can be in more flagrant contrast with the creative Love, all whose tenderness *ex vi termini* must be reserved only for what intrinsically is most bitterly hostile and negative to itself." In the mind of America's most profound philosopher, Charles S. Peirce, this sublime sentence "discloses for the problem of evil its everlasting solution." Here is another way of putting it: Embrace the opposite. This applies, I would say, to opposing groups and nations, and to opposing theories and ideologies, just as well as to opposing individuals. This is evolutionary love, and its ideal products are deep, beneficent, and mutually creative harmonies, enduring continuities of relationship through change.

Eighth, a better world calls for the active imaginations and dedicated endeavors of peoples on this earth here and now and throughout many future generations. Transformations of personalities are certainly of prime importance, but these can be going on concurrently with efforts to improve society, to lure—shall we say?—this modern world out of the hollowness and dreariness of crass materialism.

Ninth, the Christian religion was not handed down from above in a perfect and unalterable form; but was produced, as art and science are produced, by the procreative powers of the unconscious mind of man, directed by the will to goodness and ordered by the powers of reason.

Tenth, the effective core of a religion is not historic facts, or theoretical speculations, or ethical propositions, but wondrous and awesome, comforting or inciting, edifying and transforming myths, legends, rituals, and precepts, poetically set forth. In its apprehension and utterance of the essence of a moral apperception, a religious parable or story, at its best, is a good deal nearer the wanted truth and surely far more efficacious than a matter-of-fact account of any historic episode, no matter how dramatic.

The moral of this tale, as I read it, is that the requirement of this dire moment in man's history is the religious imagination, the realization by religious men that the creativity of nature is within them, and, perhaps for the first time, with the assent and aid of a greater consciousness, free to stretch itself, to break the strangling bonds of an ancient allegiance, and bring forth the seeds of a new emergence of the spirit. If the religious imagination fails, where shall we be? Santayana suggests a gruesome possibility which I find challenging, and so with this in our mind's sight, I shall bring this discourse to a close.

"The greatest calamity," he writes, "would be that which seems, alas! not unlikely to befall our immediate posterity, namely, that while Christianity should be discredited no other religion, more disillusioned and not less inspired, would rise to take its place. Until the imagination should have time to recover and to reassert its legitimate and kindly power, the European races would then be reduced to confessing that while they had mastered the mechanical forces of Nature, both by science and by the arts, they had become incapable of mastering or understanding themselves, and that, bewildered like the beasts by the revolutions of the heavens and by their own irrational passions, they could find no way of uttering the ideal meaning of their life."

26

BEYOND YESTERDAY'S IDEALISMS

Mr. President, Ladies, and Gentlemen: The list of orators since the first performance of this rite in 1782, the blaze of famous names, was blinding to one who as an undergraduate was never on the Dean's list but often in his office, blinding to one who has been fumbling in the dark for many years, in the underground of mind, well below the level of luminous rationality sustained by members of this elite society. From the parade of annual orations one receives imposing views of the diversity of elevated thinking in America, challenging yet humbling, I would guess, to pretty nearly anyone your President might pick to add another theme to this medley of reflections.

Happily for a man in this predicament there are transfusions of courage to be had from a host of predecessors, especially, as you well know, from those wonderous emanations in 1837 of the Platonic Over-Soul of Ralph Waldo Emerson. To this apostle of self-confidence I attribute whatever stamina is required to speak freely to you today, some hundred and twenty years beyond his yesterday. Here my cue comes from Emerson himself, who reminded his enthralled audience that each age "must write its own books." "The books of an older age will not fit this."

Emerson's preoccupation was Man Thinking, or, to be more accurate, Mr. Emerson Thinking, serene and saintly, solitary and aloof, residing in his own aura without envy, lust, or anger, unspotted by the world and impervious to its horrors. My preoccupation will be a little different, a difference that makes all the difference: men and women thinking, privately and publicly, in the teeth of an infernal, lethal threat that will be here as long as our inhuman human race is here.

In the realm of thought, Sigmund Freud—who, on the question of innate, potential evil, concurred with St. Augustine—Freud marks the great divide which separates us irrevocably from the benign atmosphere of the untempted, unhurt, and unmolested sage of Concord. Also sepa-

Phi Beta Kappa Oration, Harvard Chapter, 1959, printed in *Views from the Circle: Seventy-five years of Groton School,* 1960, 371–382; also in C. Brinton (ed.), *The Fate of Man,* New York: Braziller, 1961; also in *Man Thinking,* by the United Chapters of Phi Beta Kappa, Cornell University Press; and partially reprinted as A Mythology for Grownups, in *Saturday Review,* January 23, 1960.

rating us from that tall, angular, gentle blue-eyed mystic, who saw evil
at such a distance that he could dismiss it and condone it, and who, in
so doing, as his admirer Santayana pointed out, "surrendered the category of the better and the worse, the deepest foundation of life and
reason"—separating us incurably from that justly venerated poet-thinker
are the blights and blasts of more than forty lurid years of enormities and
abominations perpetrated by our fellow men on the sensitive bodies and
souls of other men. Before the occurrence of this global epidemic of lies,
treacheries, and atrocities, most of us Americans were temperamentally
with Emerson, strongly inclined to optimism, and so to shun or to deny
the fact that human creatures were still capable of surpassing all other
species as callous and ferocious torturers and killers of their own kind.
But now that we have seen all this, the darker vision of the once-rejected
Herman Melville resonates with more veracity in some of us.

Would that I could offer, out of my well of joy, a nicer prospect, more
appropriate to this festive week! But were I, with bland, buoyant or
urbane ideas to indulge both you and me, I would deserve that label that
Melville, on second thought, attached to Emerson—Confidence Man.

You see there is still danger that out of shallowness and the desire
to be pleasant at all costs—two of our besetting sins—we may rid consciousness of the unflattering knowledge we have gained, and, by so
doing, cancel the possibility of ever reaching the conclusion that the
present degree and aim of certain of our dispositions and certain states
and aims of our various societies are definitely out of date, unsuitable for
survival. It looks to me as if we must transform or fall apart.

The inevitable decision is that the eminent Yankee seer was right:
the books of *his* age, his *own* books—imperishable as they surely are—
are not in all respects fitting to *this* age. The present age and your
coming age must write its own books.

I suppose that most of you, just-honored intellectuals, will necessarily
be occupied for the next years in thinking in a differentiated way, thinking as specialists—as lawyers, businessmen, doctors, scientists, historians,
educators. There is vigor and ample creativity involved in all of these
professions. But later, if not sooner, you will be pressured from within or
from without to think seriously once more about yourself and your relations with women and with men, to think personally and then imperson-
ally, to ask yourself embarrassing questions—knowledge for what? freedom for what? existence for what?—to think, in other words, as a
free-lance philosopher, or generalist, about matters of profound and superordinate concern: ways and ends of being and becoming, morals,
religion, the human situation, the world's plight. At such times each of
you will be, in Emerson's sense, Man Thinking, and your reflections may
beget a book or brace of books fitting to your age. Your capacity to write
a book—logical, critical, and substantial—has been accredited by the
conferring of the Key, symbolic of the fact that learning and transform-

ing what you learn may be the happiest of activities, and may, with luck on your side, lead to the solution of crucial problems, turn the lock and open the door to new knowledge.

Today the really crucial problems, as I hook them, are all deep, deep in human nature, and in this country with our long preference for appearances, for tangible, material realities, for perceptible facts, acts, and technics, for the processes and conclusions of conscious rationality, and for quick attainments of demonstrable results—with this native and acquired bent for things that one can plainly see, grasp, count, weigh, manipulate, and photograph, the probability of our solving or even seriously grappling with the strategic problems of our time does not appear to be encouragingly high.

Only if this appraisal is somewhere near the truth can I discern a single reason for your President's election of a depth psychologist as orator for this day. What could his reason be except to have the depth dimension stressed, with the accompanying hint that the key to the more perplexing problems might be lying in the dark. Pertinent to this issue is the old story of the London bobby who, in the blackness of one night, came upon a man half-seas-over stumbling in a circle within the lighted zone around a lamppost. "I am looking for my key," the man explained. "Are you sure you dropped it by this light?" the bobby asked. "No," the man replied, "I dropped it out there in the dark, but I can't see out there and I can see here."

What Freud discovered in the dark of the unconscious was what Puritan and Victorian morality suppressed as Sin, spelt with a capital. But now those floodgates are demolished and sexuality is conspicuously in the open, running loose among the young without benefit of form, grace, or dignity; and what is nowadays repressed, if my reading of the signs is not awry, are all the hopes, yearnings, claims, both dependent and aspiring, which down the centuries were comforted and directed by the mythologies and rituals of religion. Here I leave Freud and stand with Dr. Jung.

That a bent for the ideal is latent in the psyches of men and women of your age is not what I've been told by any confiding undergraduate, and it is about the last conclusion that a reader of modern literature would be likely to arrive at. For certainly most of the best poets, playwrights, and novelists, together with many psychoanalysts, behavioral psychologists, social philosophers, existentialists, and some angry others, seem to be conspiring, with peculiar unanimity, to reduce or decompose, to humiliate so far as they can do it, man's image of himself. In one way or another, the impression is conveyed that, in the realm of spirit, all of us are baffled Beats, Beatniks, or dead-beats, unable to cope as persons with the existential situation.

But tell me, what is the underlying meaning of this flood of discontent and self-depreciation? One pertinent answer comes from Emerson himself. "We grant that human life is mean, but how did we find out that it was mean? What is the ground of this uneasiness of ours, of this old discontent? What is the universal sense of want and ignorance but the *fine innuendo by which the soul makes its enormous claim.*" Yes, surely, "its enormous claim," and in the very midst of this American Paradise of material prosperity. The enormous claim of the sensitive, alienated portions of our society—artists, would-be artists, and their followers— comes, as I catch the innuendoes, from want of a kindling and heartening mythology to feel, think, live, and write by. Our eyes and ears are incessantly bombarded by a mythology which breeds greed, envy, pride, lust, and violence, the mythology of our mass media, the mythology of advertising, Hollywood and Madison Avenue. But a mythology that is sufficient to the claim of head and heart is as absent from the American scene as symbolism is absent from the new straight-edged, bare-faced glass buildings of New York.

An emotional deficiency disease, a paralysis of the creative imagination, an addiction to superficials—this is the physician's diagnosis I would offer to account for the greater part of the widespread desperation of our time, the enormous claim of people who are living with half a heart and half a lung. Paralysis of the imagination, I suspect, would also account, in part, for the fact that the great majority of us, wedded to comfort so long as we both shall live, are turning our eyes away from the one thing we should be looking at: the possibility or probability of co-extermination.

In his famous speech of acceptance upon the award of the Nobel prize for literature, Albert Camus declared as follows: "Probably every generation sees itself as charged with remaking the world. Mine, however, knows that it will not remake the world. But its task is perhaps even greater, for it consists in keeping the world from destroying itself."

Were this statement to be made before an auditory of our faculty and students—even by Camus himself, speaking with utter candor out of his embattled deeps of agony—I fear it would be met by a respectful, serious, yet stony silence, an *apparent* silence, for, coming from behind the noncommittal, uncommitted faces, all would be aware of the almost palpable, familiar throb of Harvard's splendid engines of sophisticated demolition.

We are as sick of being warned of our proximity to hell as were the members of Jonathan Edwards' congregation. Wolf! Wolf! How, in heaven's name, does Camus imagine that a league of artists and philosophers could possibly prevent the destruction of the world? The nearest that he comes to telling us is when he states that his "generation knows that, in a sort of mad race against time, it ought to re-establish among nations a peace not based on slavery, to reconcile labor and culture again, and to reconstruct with all men an Ark of the Covenant." These words —"re-establish," "reconcile," "reconstruct,"—suggest that in his mind the prevention of destruction does, in fact, call for a remaking of the world, the building of a new Ark of the Covenant as basis for re-union.

Here, reason might lead us to infer that Camus was thinking of the institution of world government, which as scores of enlightened men, from Woodrow Wilson to Bertrand Russell, have insisted is the only rational answer to global, social chaos, a central government being the sole means that man has ever found of securing and maintaining order. But framing a constitution for world government, as the competent Mr. Grenville Clark has done, is not in line with the special genius of Camus, and, furthermore, it is apparent that the concept of world government, though absolutely necessary, is gaining little popular or Federal support. Sanity is overmatched: deep, blind, primitive compulsions which bypass consciousness are towing us with a cable we have no knife to cut and driving us nearer and nearer to the verge of death.

At such a time, when hidden passions are deciding things, a legal scheme, no matter how commonsensical and logical, is not a magnet to large numbers of men and women: it chills them, leaves them frigid, uninvolved. Nor, at such a time, could something like Plato's plan for a Republic guided by philosophers arouse enthusiasm. But when Plato, envious of Homer's enormous influence in Greece, banished poets and myth-makers from his Republic, he deprived it of the springs of charismatic power, and so, when it came to a showdown with the masses, his beautifully reasoned books were plowed under by the passionate myths and images of the poet-authors of the Bible. The Bible proved to be *the* fitting book not only for that century but for many centuries to come. It seems highly significant to me that Camus, a firm opponent of the theism of Judeo-Christianity, should have reached into the fathomless well of the Old Testament to gain a potent image for his hope—Ark of the Covenant. It is there, among those images, that one can find the molds that shaped the deepest passions of the Western World, including Russia.

At this juncture I shall seize, with your permission, the remaining minutes of this proffered opportunity, with its cherished privilege of free speech, to submit a micro-sketch of a hypothetical book that I would write if I had been vouchsafed the necessary genius and resources. This hypothetical book would also be a sketch, though a far larger and more detailed sketch, of a book to come composed by other authors, a super-personal book, a book of books, that might be termed a testament, a world testament.

Before submitting this micro-sketch of a macro-sketch of a book for a new age, I should warn you that this imagined testament will carry us beyond the mythology of dependent and compliant childhood, the same as that of the dependent childhood of our society in colonial days, that is, the authoritarian father-son mythology of the religion we inherited, and also beyond the mythology of adolescence, the same as that of the adolescence of our Nation, the mythology of protest, rebellion, independence, rugged individualism. Both of these mythologies are still operative. In fact, the mythology of adolescence, stressing freedom without qualifications or conditions, constitutes our national religion. Please understand and hold in mind that in looking forward to a future that has moved beyond these idealisms of today and yesterday, I am not forsaking them. There is a helpless, suffering child and a frustrated, rebellious adolescent in every one of us, and always will be. I would say, there is a time and place for authority and the founding of character, and there is a time and place for liberation from authority and the development and expression of a self-reliant personality. But, as I see the human situation, we are in need of a mythology of adulthood, something that is conspicuous by its absence in Western literature, a mythology of interdependence and creation, not only on the level of imaginative love, marriage, and the forming of a family, but on other levels, especially that of imaginative international reciprocities. Have we not pretty nearly reached the age when we can well afford to go beyond the glorification of vanity, pride, and egotism, individual and national?

Well, now, to return to my sketch of a sketch. The essential features of the testament that now occupies my mind would be roughly these: it would be the product of the interdependent judgments and imaginations of numerous composers, drawn from different cultures and from different callings. The initial task of these presumably creative and judicious thinkers would be to select from the vast libraries of the world, arrange, and edit, whatever past and present writings in poetry or prose were suitable to the appointed purpose. Except for more abundant stores from which to draw their substance, a larger scope and longer span of time, these testament-makers would proceed, we may suppose, as did the compilers and editors of the canonical and non-canonical books of the Bible. They would certainly be advantaged by the example of those forerunners. Like the Old Testament, this new one would contain numerous variations of subject matter and of style: narratives, historical and biographical, stories, parables, legends, and myths, songs and poems, psalms of praise, codes and ordinances, premonitions and philosophical reflections.

Most difficult for the testament-makers would be the task of loosely integrating, as in the Bible, the selected parts in terms of a philosophy of social evolution—cycles of creation, conservation, decay, or induration —tending, in the long run, toward the fulfillment of that dream of human fellowship which centuries of deep and loving people have recommended to our hearts.

This testament would differ radically from the Bible inasmuch as its mythology would be consonant with contemporary science: its personifications would all refer to forces and functions *within* nature, human nature.

Also, it would differ radically from previous testaments of the Near East and West—the Bible, the Koran, and the Testament of Karl Marx

—by describing and praising, with even-handed justice, forms of excellence, achieved by each and every culture. There would be no bowing to special claims, made by any single collectivity, of unique superiority, of divine election, of infallible truth, of salvation for its members and damnation for all others. There would be no ovation for the apocalyptic myth, either in its ancient form—Persian or Judeo-Christian—or in its modern Communistic form; the myth of the inevitable and final Great Encounter between the all-good and the all-evil, resulting in an eternity of bliss for chosen saints or comrades, and death or everlasting torments for the enemy. There would be no acceptance of the necessity of inquisitions, persecutions, brain-washings, or concentration camps.

In a sense, the world testament would be a parable, a parable of parables, expressive of the universal need for peace, for interdependence, for fruitful reciprocations among those manifold units of mankind which are still proud and quarrelsome, still locked in clenched antagonisms. Its symbolisms would commemorate on all levels the settlement of hostilities between opposites, their synthesis, or creative union: man and nature, male and female, reason and passion, understanding and imagination, enjoyable means and enjoyable ends, science and art, management and labor, West and East. Its ultimate, ethical ideal would be the resolution of differences through mutual embracement and subsequent transformation.

Finally, in contrast to the unrelieved sociological language of the outmoded testament of Marx, this world testament, heir to the secret of the Bible's everlasting magic, would consist in its best parts of moving and revealing poetic passages. . . .

If, perchance, a world testament with the mythic qualities I have mentioned became an invitation to the feelings and thoughts of men and women, it would gain this influence only through its power to enchant, charm, clarify, edify, and nourish. There would be no agents of sovereign authority with threatened penalties to enforce compliance, and, in contrast to the testaments of our established Churches, it would be always susceptible to revisions, additions, and subtractions.

Everybody, I assume—especially on reaching the accepted age for the retirement of his brain—is entitled to a dream, and this is mine, heretical at certain points, but not so visionary as it sounds. Works of the magnitude of this imagined testament have been composed in the past, notably in India. Much of what is needed has been in printed form for years. Ample energy and genius is available—literary critics, historians, social scientists, philosophers, and poets—in different quarters of the globe. Enough money for the effort is in the keep of men who are aware of humanity's dire strait. A provisional first edition of the testament would not be very long in coming. Translated into all languages it might turn out to be the book this age is waiting for.

A war that no one wants, an utterly disgraceful end to man's long experiment on earth is a possibility we are facing every day. Events are hanging by a thread, depending on an accident, on some finger on a trigger, on a game of wits and tricks, of pride and saving faces. But ours is no momentary problem to be solved by this or that practical expedient. Does a mature nation sacrifice the future for the present? The day will come when small countries will possess enough lethal energy to eliminate a large country. Does a mature nation have the arrogance to believe that it can buy with dollars the permanent good-will and loyalty of other peoples? Has our government a long time-perspective, a philosophy of history, a world-view to guide its day-by-day and year-by-year decisions? If yes, only a few of us have heard of it.

It is such considerations that have pressured the generation of a vision of something which intellectuals like you and other members of the Phi Beta Kappa society might have a hand in shaping. Why not? Many times in the past, the direction of events has been affected by the publication of a single book. At the very least, the composition of this testament would constitute a brave, far-seeing try—no vulgar try—to kindle a little veritable light in a black world.

The one conversion requisite for those who would lose themselves in this demanding enterprise was long ago described in two famous, pithy sentences by a stubborn American patriot, contemporary with Emerson. No doubt many of you have had occasion to saunter down the elm-shaded path in the middle of Commonwealth Avenue and, arriving at the statue of William Lloyd Garrison, stopped to read these words: "My country is the world. My countrymen are all mankind."

27

THIS I BELIEVE

I believe that the word "believe" is, in its various meanings, slippery as a snake and, like the fabled snake, all too apt—in a bewildered age like ours—to lead us into evil, the evil of hypocrisy. The word comes as a temptation to retreat, for peace of soul, to some pious platitude of comforting banality, rather than brave the realization that we have not yet conceived a sufficient remedy for the agues of our time.

Experience has taught me to believe in no fixation of beliefs, but in the exciting process of perpetually reconstructing them in order to encompass new facts, experiences, and conditions. This, as I see it, is the essence and the responsibility of freedom. I am strongly inclined to shun inert ideas and cleave to live ones, born out of joy or tribulation, that demand embodiment in action.

As for personal history, I confess to constant gratefulness for the belief-engendering delights of mutual love, fellowship, nature, travel, literature, and the vocation of psychology. My faith in the potential value of psychology has never wavered. But I cast no vote for the omnipotence of science, and am appalled by the popular assumption that what is good for the machine is good for man.

I believe, of course, in the cardinal virtues of honesty, courage, charity, and dedication, and I am still trying to bring my Adam into line with them. But the reiteration of these verities is evidently not enough, since after more than two thousand years of earnest preaching, that large portion of the human race which appears, in its own eyes, most advanced in these respects is on the verge of proving itself an utter failure.

The gravity of the world's strait, in truth, has so overshadowed my own vibrations and fruitions, that I have come to believe that nothing is of signal significance today save those thoughts and actions which, in some measure, purpose to contribute to the diagnosis and alleviation of the global neurosis which so affects us.

There will be no freedom for any exuberant form of life, in my estimation, without freedom from atomic war; and no freedom from war without a democratic world government and police force; and no world

From Edward R. Murrow, ed., *This I Believe*, Copyright 1954 by Help, Inc. In the mid-1930s, Murrow conducted a newspaper column called "This I Believe," to which he asked celebrities in all fields to contribute 500-word essays on their beliefs.

government without a radical conversion and re-education of thousands of personalities in the light of a new conception, synthesis of Eastern and Western wisdom.

Many persons, from one angle or another, have envisaged the shadowy contours of such a faith: one which portrays the path of development through mutual affections and reciprocations—interpersonal, intercorporate, and international—as more gratifying, maturing, beneficent, and creative than the rewards of unitary ambition, conflict, and vainglorious superiority.

Present conditions, however, are so extremely unfavorable to an evolutionary advance of such scale and scope that we would be well advised to prepare our sinews for a long and protracted era of ferocity and anguish until our devils are subdued and our eyes opened.

CHRONOLOGY

Event	Year	Age	Selected Publications
Born, New York City	1893		
Graduated Groton School	1911	18	
A.B. in History, Harvard	1915	22	
Married (to Josephine Rantoul)	1916	23	
M.D., Columbia University College of Physicians and Surgeons	1919	26	
M.A. in Biology, Columbia	1920	27	
Daughter, Josephine Lee Murray, born	1921	28	
Surgical internship, Presbyterian Hospital, N.Y.C.	1924– 1926	31 33	
Embryological research, Rockefeller Institute for Medical Research, N.Y.C.	1926– 1927	33 34	21 articles on embryology and medicine (1919–1928)
Visited C. G. Jung in Zurich	1926	33	
Ph.D. in Biochemistry, Cambridge	1927	34	
Instructor, Harvard	1927	34	
Assistant Professor, Director, Psychological Clinic, Harvard	1929	36	
	1935	42	"A Method for Investigating Fantasies" (with Christiana D. Morgan)
Associate Professor, Harvard	1937	44	
	1938	45	*Explorations in Personality*
	1940	47	"What Should Psychologists Do about Psychoanalysis?"
Lieutenant Colonel, Office of Strategic Services	1942– 1946	49 53	
	1945	52	"A Clinical Study of Sentiments" (with Morgan)

Event	Year	Age	Selected Publications
Professor of Clinical Psychology, Harvard	1948	55	*Assessment of Men* and *Personality in Nature, Society and Culture* (with C. Kluckhohn)
	1949	56	"Introduction" to Melville's *Pierre*
Testified in the Alger Hiss trial	1950	57	
	1951	58	"In Nomine Diaboli"
	1959	66	"Beyond Yesterday's Idealisms"
	1960	67	"The Possible Nature of a Mythology to Come"
Josephine Rantoul Murray died	1961	68	
Emeritus Professor of Clinical Psychology, Harvard	1962	69	"The Personality and Career of Satan"
	1967	74	"Dead to the World: The Passions of Herman Melville"
	1968	75	"Components of an Evolving Personological System"
Married (to Caroline C. Fish)	1969	76	
	1977	84	"Indispensables for the Making, Testing, and Remaking of a Personological System"
The Henry A. Murray Research Center for the Study of Lives, established at Radcliffe College	1979	86	
Working on Melville	1981	88	

BIBLIOGRAPHY

ARTICLES AND CHAPTERS*

The development of the cardiac loop in the rabbit, with especial reference to the bulbo-ventricular septum. *Amer. J. Anatomy,* 1919, 26, 29–39.

Two unusual cases of melanocarcinoma. *Proc. of the New York Pathological Soc.,* 1919, XIX, 28–37.

Groton and adaptation. *Grotonian,* 1919, 31, 402–419.

With A. L. Barach. Tetany in a case of sprue. *J. of the A.M.A.,* 1920, 74, 786–788.

With G. King. A new blood coagulometer. *J. of the A.M.A.,* 1920.

With F. C. McLean and L. J. Henderson. The variable acidity of hemoglobin and the distribution of chlorides in the blood. *Proc. Soc. Exper. Biol. & Med.,* 1919–20, XVII, 180.

With A. B. Hastings and C. D. Murray. Certain chemical changes in the blood after pyloric obstruction in dogs. *J. of Biol. Chem.,* 1921, XLVI, 223–232.

With A. B. Hastings. Observations on parathyroidectomized dogs. *J. of Biol. Chem.,* 1921, XLVI, 233–256.

The bicarbonate and chloride content of the blood in certain cases of persistent vomiting. *Proc. Soc. Exper. Biol. & Med.,* 1922, XIX, 273–275.

With A. R. Felty. Observations on dogs with experimental pyloric obstruction. The acid-base equilibrium, chlorides, non-protein nitrogen, and urea of the blood. *J. of Biol. Chem.,* 1923, LVII, 573–585.

The chemical pathology of pyloric occlusion in relation to tetany. *Arch. of Surgery,* 1923, 7, 166–196.

Physiological ontogeny, A. chicken embryos. II. Catabolism. Chemical changes in fertile eggs during incubation. Selection of standard conditions. *J. gen Physiol.,* 1925, IX, 1–37.

Physiological ontogeny, A. chicken embryos. III. Weight and growth rate as functions of age. *J. gen. Physiol.* 1925, IX, 39–48.

With A. E. Cohn. Physiological ontogeny, A. chicken embryos. IV. The negative acceleration of growth with age as demonstrated by tissue cultures. *J. exper. Med.,* 1925, XLII, 275–290.

Physiological ontogeny, A. chicken embryos. VII. The concentration of the organic constituents and the calorific value as functions of age. *J. gen. Physiol.,* 1926, IX, 405–432.

Physiological ontogeny, A. chicken embryos. VIII. Acceleration of integration and differentiation during the embryonic period. *J. gen. Physiol.,* 1926, IX, 603–619.

Physiological ontogeny, A. chicken embryos. IX. The iodine reaction for the quantitative determination of gluthathione in the tissues as a function of age. *J. gen. Physiol.,* 1926, IX, 621–624.

Physiological ontogeny, A. chicken embryos. X. The temperature characteristic for the contraction rate of isolated fragments of embryonic heart muscle. *J. gen. Physiol.,* 1926, IX, 781–788.

*The titles in this bibliography are arranged chronologically.

Physiological ontogeny, A. chicken embryos. XI. The pH; chloride, carbonic acid, and protein concentrations in the tissues as functions of age. *J. gen. Physiol.*, 1926, IX, 789–803.

Physiological ontogeny, A. chicken embryos. XII. The metabolism as a function of age. *J. gen. Physiol.*, 1926, X, 337–343.

With A. E. Cohn. Physiological ontogeny. I. The present status of the problem. *Quart. rev. Biol.*, 1927. II, 469–493.

What to read in Psychology. *The Independent*, 1927, 118, 134.

A case of pinealoma with symptoms suggestive of compulsion neurosis. *Arch. neurol. Psychiat.*, 1928, 19, 932–945.

Abnormal psychology at Harvard. *Harvard Crimson*, 1929, Jan. 12.

With H. Barry, Jr. and D. W. MacKinnon. Hypnotizability as a personality trait. *Hum. Biol.*, 1931, 3, 1–36.

The effect of fear upon estimates of the maliciousness of other personalities. *J. soc. Psychol.*, 1933, 4, 310–329.

With H. A. Wolff and C. E. Smith. The psychology of humor. *J. abnorm. soc. Psychol.*, 1934, 28, 341–365.

The psychology of humor. II. Mirth responses to disparagement jokes as a manifestation of an aggressive disposition. *J. abnorm. soc. Psychol.*, 1934, 29, 66–81.

With C. D. Morgan. A method of investigating fantasies. *Arch. neurol. Psychiat.*, 1935, 34, 289–306. Reprinted in *Measuring Human Motivation*, (Eds.) R. C. Birney, R. C. Teenan. D. van Nostrand Co., Princeton, N.J.

Psychology and the university. *Arch. neurol. Psychiat.*, 1935, 34, 803–817.

The Harvard Psychological Clinic. *Harv. Alumni Bull.*, 1935, Oct. 25, 1–8.

Facts which support the concept of need or drive. *J. Psychol.*, 1936, 3, 27–42.

Techniques for a systematic investigation of fantasy. *J. Psychol.*, 1936, 3, 115–143.

Basic concepts for a psychology of personality. *J. gen. Psychol.*, 1936, 15, 241–268.

With R. Wolf. An experiment in judging personalities. *J. Psychol.*, 1936, 3, 345–365.

With D. R. Wheeler. A note on the possible clairvoyance of dreams. *J. Psychol.*, 1936, 3, 309–313.

Visceral manifestations of personality. *J. abnorm. soc. Psychol.*, 1937, 32, 161–184.

What should psychologists do about psychoanalysis? *J. abnorm. soc. Psychol.*, 1940, 35, 150–175.

Personality and creative imagination. *English Institute Manual*, 1942, New York: Columbia Univer. Pr., 1943, 139–162.

With M. Stein. Note on the selection of combat officers. *Psychosom. Med.*, 1943, 5, 386–391.

Assessment of the whole person. *Proc. Meeting Military Psychologists and Psychiatrists*, Univer. Maryland Pr., 1945.

With D. W. MacKinnon. Assessment of OSS personnel. *J. consult. Psychol.*, 1946, 10, 76–80.

Proposals for research in clinical psychology. *Amer. J. Orthopsychiat.*, 1947, 17, 203–210.

Time for a positive morality. *Surv. Graphic*, 1947, 36, 195.

America's mission. *Surv. Graphic*, 1948, 37, 411–415.

Research planning: a few proposals. *Culture and Personality*, (Ed.) S. S. Sargent and M. W. Smith. *Proc. Interdisciplin. Conf.* (Nov. 1947), Viking Fund, 1949.

Uses of the TAT. *Amer. J. Psychiat.*, 1951, 107, 577–581.

Toward a classification of interactions. In T. Parsons, E. A. Shils, E. C. Tolman et al. *Toward a General Theory of Action,* Harv. Univer. Pr., 1951.

World concord as a goal for the social scientist. *Proc. Internat. Congress Psychol.,* Stockholm, 1951.

In nomine diaboli. *The New England Quart.,* 1951, XXIV, 435–452. Reprinted in *Moby-Dick Centennial Essays* (Ed.) Melville Society, 1953; also *Discussions of Moby-Dick* (Ed.) M. R. Stern, Boston, 1960, and *Melville: A Collection of Critical Essays,* (Ed.) R. Chase, New York: Prentice-Hall, 1962; and *Theories of Personality,* (Eds.) G. Lindzey & E. S. Hall, John Wiley & Sons, Inc., New York: 1965, pp. 153–161. *Psychology Today,* 1968, Vol. 2, 4, 64–69.

Some basic psychological assumptions and conceptions. *Dialectica,* 1951, 5, 266–292.

Science in two societies. *The Contemporary Scene.* A symposium, Metropolitan Museum of Art, New York, 1954.

Versions of man. In *Man's Right to Knowledge,* 2nd series, Present Knowledge and New Direction, Columbia Univer. Pr., N.Y.: 1955. (An international symposium presented in honor of the 200th anniversary of Columbia Univer., 1754–1954.) Pub. by Herbert Muschel, Box 800, Grand Central, New York 17, N.Y.

American Icarus. In (Eds.) A. Burton and R. E. Harris, *Clinical Studies of Personality,* Vol. 2, New York, Harper, 1955. Reprinted in *Theories of Personality,* (Eds.) G. Lindzey, C. S. Hall, N.Y.: John Wiley & Sons, 1965, pp. 162–175.

With A. Davids. Preliminary appraisal of an auditory projective technique for studying personality and cognition. *Amer. J. Orthopsychiat.,* 1955, 25, 543–554.

Creative evolution, or a deity imprisoned in the past? *The Christian Reg.,* 1956, 135, 10ff. (abbreviated version of Two Versions of Man, below).

Theoretical basis for projective techniques. *Proc. Internat. Congress for Psychol.,* Brussels, 1957.

Drive, time, strategy, measurement, and our way of life. In (Ed.) G. Lindzey, *Assessment of Human Motives,* New York: Rinehart, 1958.

Notes on the Icarus syndrome. *Folia psychiatrica, neurologica, et neurochirugica Neelandica,* 1958, 61, 204–208.

Individuality: The meaning and content of individuality in contemporary America. *Daedalus,* 1958, 87, 25–47. Reprinted in *The American Style,* New York, 1958; and in (Ed.) H. M. Ruitenbeck, *Varieties of Modern Social Theory,* New York, 1963.

Vicissitudes of creativity. In (Ed.) H. H. Anderson, *Creativity and Its Cultivation,* New York: Harper, 1959.

Preparations for the scaffold of a comprehensive system. In (Ed.) S. Koch, *Psychology: A Study of Science,* Vol. 3, New York: McGraw-Hill, 1959.

With H. Cantril and M. May. Some glimpses of Soviet psychology. *Amer. Psychologist,* 1959, 14, 303–307.

Beyond yesterday's idealisms. Phi Beta Kappa Oration, Harvard Chapter, 1959, printed in *Views from the Circle: Seventy-five Years of Groton School,* 1960, 371–382; also in (Ed.) C. Brinton, *The Fate of Man,* New York: Braziller, 1961; also in *Man Thinking,* by the United Chapters of Phi Beta Kappa, Cornell Univer. Pr.; some of it (entitled A mythology for grownups) in *Saturday Rev.,* Jan. 23, 1960.

Two versions of man. In (Ed.) H. Shapley, *Science Ponders Religion*, New York: Appleton-Century-Crofts, 1960.

Historical trends in personality research. In (Eds.) H. P. David and J. C. Brengelmann, *Perspectives in Personality Research*, New York: Springer, 1960.

The possible nature of a "mythology" to come. In *Myth and Mythmaking*, New York: George Braziller, 1960.

Unprecedented evolutions. *Daedalus*, 1961, 90, 547–570. Reprinted in (Eds.) H. Hoagland and R. W. Burhoe, *Evolution and Man's Progress*, Columbia Univer. Pr., New York, 1962.

Commentary on the case of El. *J. proj. Tech.*, 1961, 25, 404–411.

Prospect for psychology. *Internat. Congress of Applied Psychology*, Copenhagen, 1961. Reprinted in *Science*, 1962, 136, 483–488.

Definitions of Myth. In (Ed.) Ohmann, R. M. *The Making of Myth*, New York: G.P. Putnam's Sons, 1962.

The personality and career of Satan. *J. soc. Issues*, XVIII, 1962, 28, 36–54.

Studies of stressful interpersonal disputations. *Amer. Psychologist*, 1963, 18, 28–36. Reprinted in *Theories of Personality*, (Eds.) G. Lindzey & C. S. Hall, New York: John Wiley & Sons, Inc. 1965, pp. 176–184.

Symposium on Morality. *American Scholar*, Summer, 1965.

Bartleby and I. In (Ed.) Howard P. Vincent, *Bartleby the Scrivener*, Ohio: The Kent State Univer. Press, 1966, p. 3–24.

Dead to the world: Or the passions of Herman Melville. In E. S. Shneidman (Ed.), *Essays in Self-Destruction*, New York: Science House, 1967.

Autobiography. (The Case of Murr). In *History of Psychology in Autobiography*, Vol. V., pp. 285–310, (Eds.) E. G. Boring, G. Lindzey, Appleton-Century-Crofts, New York, 1967.

Components of an evolving personological system. In D. Sills (Ed.) *International Encyclopedia of Social Science*, New York: Macmillan & Free Press, 1968, 12, 5–13.

Indispensables for the making, testing, and remaking of a personological system. *Annals of the New York Academy of Sciences*, April 18, 1977, 291, 323–331.

MONOGRAPH

With C. D. Morgan. A clinical study of sentiments. *Genet, psychol. Monogr.*, 1945, 32, 3–311.

BOOKS

With Staff. *Explorations in Personality*, New York: Oxford Univer. Pr., 1938.

With Staff. *Assessment of Men*, New York: Rinehart, 1948.

With C. Kluckhohn (Eds.). *Personality in Nature, Society, and Culture*, New York: Alfred A. Knopf, 1950.

With C. Kluckhohn and D. M. Schneider (Eds.). *Personality in Nature, Society, and Culture* (2nd ed.), New York: Alfred A. Knopf, 1953.

(Ed.). *Myth and Mythmaking*, New York: George Braziller, 1960.

PREFACES, INTRODUCTIONS, FOREWORDS

Introduction, *Contemporary Psychopathology*, S. S. Tomkins, Cambridge, Mass.: Harvard Univer. Pr., 1943.

Introduction, *Clinical Studies in Personality*, Vol. I, A. Burton & R. E. Harris, New York: Harper & Bros., 1947.

Introduction with footnotes (Ed.), *Pierre, or the Ambiguities*, H. Melville, New York: Farrar, Straus, Hendricks House, 1949.

Foreword, *An Introduction to Projective Techniques*, H. H. Anderson & Gladys Anderson, New York: Prentice-Hall, 1951.

Foreword, *Thematic Test Analysis*, E. S. Shneidman, New York: Grune & Stratton, 1951.

Introduction, *Clinical Studies of Personality*, Vol. II, A. Burton & R. E. Harris, New York: Harper, 1955.

Introduction, *Methods in Personality Assessment*, G. G. Stern, M. I. Stein, & B. S. Bloom, Glencoe, Ill.: Free Press, 1956.

Foreword, *Man Made Plain*, R. N. Wilson, Cleveland: Howard Allen, 1958.

Introduction, Myth and Mythmaking. *Daedalus*, Boston: American Academy of Arts and Sciences, 1959.

Foreword, *The Inner World of Choice*, Frances G. Wickes, New York: Harper & Row, 1963.

Prelude, *Melville and Hawthorne in the Berkshires—A symposium, Melville Annual 1966*, H. P. Vincent (Ed.), Kent State University Press, 1968.

Introduction, *Experiencing Others*, Franz From, Copenhagen, Denmark, 1971.

TESTS AND MANUALS

With Staff. *Thematic Apperception Test*, Cambridge, Mass,: Harvard Univer. Pr., 1943.

Thematic apperception test. *Military Clinical Psychology*, 1951. TM8-242-AFM160, 45, 54–71.

REVIEWS

Timon of America, Herman Melville, by Lewis Mumford, New York: Harcourt, Brace & Co., 1929. Reviewed in *Hound and Horn*, 1929, 430.

Herman Melville, by Lewis Mumford, New York: Harcourt, Brace & Co., 1929. Reviewed in *New England Quart.*, 1929, 523.

Mrs. Eddy: The Biography of a Virginal Mind, by Edwin Franden Daken, New York: Charles Scribner's Sons, 1929. Reviewed in *New England Quart.*, 1929, 341.

Pierre, or the Ambiguities, by Herman Melville, New York: Alfred A. Knopf, 1930. Reviewed in *New England Quart.*, 1930, 333.

The Conquest of Happiness, by Bertrand Russell, Horace Liveright. Reviewed in *Atlantic Monthly*, 1930, 12.

Civilization and Its Discontents, by Sigmund Freud, Cape and Smith. Reviewed in *Atlantic Monthly*, 1930, 14.

Not to Eat, Not for Love, by George Weller, New York: Harrison Smith & Robert Haas, 1933. Reviewed in *Harvard Crimson*, 1933, also in *Harvard Alumni Bull:* A novel about Harvard, 1933, 729–730.

Private Worlds, by Phyllis Bottome, Boston: Houghton Mifflin Company, 1934. Reviewed in *The J. Rev. of Literature*, Cambridge, Mass., April 21, 1934.

The Inner World of Man, by Frances G. Wickes, New York: Farrar & Rinehart, 1938. Reviewed in *The New York Times Book Review*, Dec. 4, 1938.

Psychological Foundations of Personality, by Louis P. Thorpe, New York: McGraw-Hill Book Co., 1938. Reviewed in *Amer. J. Psychol.*, 1939, 53, 493–94.

Fulcra of Conflict: A New Approach to Personality Measurement, by Douglas

Spencer, New York: World Book Co., 1939. Reviewed in *Amer. J. Psychol.*, 1940, 53, 161–162.

Personality and Problems of Adjustment, by Kimball Young, New York: F. S. Crofts & Co., 1940.

Mind Explorers, by John K. Winkler & Walter Bromberg, New York: Reynal & Hitchcock, 1940. Reviewed in *The New York Times Book Review*, Jan. 21, 1940.

Studies in Personality, by Lewis M. Terman, New York: McGraw-Hill, 1942. *Book Reviews*, edited by George L. Dreezer, Cornell Univer. Reviewed in *Amer. J. Psychol.*, 1943, 56, 307–308.

Personality: A Biosocial Approach to Origins and Structure, by Gardner Murphy, New York: Harper, 1947. Reviewed in *Surv. Graphic*, March, 1948.

The Trying-out of Moby-Dick, by Howard P. Vincent, Boston: Houghton-Mifflin Co. 1949. Reviewed in *The New England Quart*, 527–530.

Herman Melville: A Biography, by Leon Howard, Los Angeles: Univer. California Pr., 1951.

Melville's Early Life and Redburn, by William H. Gilman, New York: New York Univer. Pr., 1951.

Dynamic Psychiatry, by Franz Alexander & Helen Ross, Chicago: Univer. of Chicago Pr., 1952. Reviewed in *Psychol. Bull.*, 1953, 50, 304–306.

Freud: The Mind of the Moralist, by Philip Rieff, New York: Viking Pr., 1959. Reviewed in *Amer. Sociolog. Rev.*, 299–300.

Anthropology and the Classics, by Clyde Kluckhohn, Providence, R.I.: Brown Univer. Pr. 1961. Reviewed in *Amer. Anthropologist*, 1963, 65, 139–140.

The Psychology of Jung: A Critical Interpretation, by Avis M. Dry, New York: Wiley, 1961. Reviewed in *Contemp. Psychol.*, Dec. 1963, 468–469.

The Freudian Hawthorne. *The Sins of the Fathers: Hawthorne's Psychological Themes*, by Frederick C. Crews, Fair Lawn, N.J.: Oxford Univer. Press, 1966. Reviewed in *The American Scholar*, Vol. 36, 2, Spring, 1967, pp. 308–312, Reprinted in *Psychiatry & Social Science Review*, May 1967, Vol. 1, 5, pp. 11–13.

Tolstoy, by Henri Troyat, Doubleday. Reviewed in *The American Scholar*, Summer, 1968, p. 536.

SKETCHES, OBITUARIES

Dr. Morton Price, a founder of psychopathology. *Harvard Alumni Bull.*, 1930, Jan. 23, 490–495.

William Herman. *Boston Transcript*, about 1935.

Alfred E. Cohn. 2 unpublished addresses.

Sigmund Freud, 1856–1939. *Amer. J. Psychol.*, 1940, 53, 134–138.

Conrad Aiken, poet of creative dissolution. *Wake*, 1952, 11, 95–106.

Frank Wigglesworth. *40th Anniversary Report* of Harvard Class of 1915.

Morton Prince, sketch of his life and work. *J. abnorm. soc. Psychol.*, 1956, 52, 291–295.

Clyde Kluckhohn. (a) Memorial service, Oct. 1960; (b) minute on his life and services, read at a meeting of the Harvard Faculty, 1961.

Carl G. Jung. Address at Memorial Meeting in New York, Dec. 1962.

Leaves of green memories. Verses in celebration of the authors of *The Study of Lives* and other students of lives who attended the dinner at the Hotel Barclay, Philadelphia, Aug. 28, 1963 (privately printed).

Felix Frankfurter. The humanity of this man. In Festschrift composed in his honor, 1964.

Josephine Lee Murray 1894–1962. *Radcliffe Quarterly,* Feb. 1965, p. 9.

Ernest W. Hocking, 1967. Unpublished.

Edward Craighill Handy, Sept. 1967. Unpublished.

Frances G. Wickes: 1875–1967, a memorial meeting, Oct. 25, 1967, New York: Privately printed by the Ram Press, 1968.

Postscript: Morsels of information regarding the extraordinary woman in whose psyche the foregoing visions were begot. In C. G. Jung, *The Visions Seminars,* Zurich: Spring Publications, 1976, pp. 517–521.

SELECTED CHAPTERS AND PAPERS ABOUT HENRY A. MURRAY

Hall, Mary Harrington. Interview with Henry A. Murray. *Psychology Today,* Sept., 1968, 2, 56–63.

Haydn, Hiram. Portrait: Henry A. Murray. *American Scholar,* Winter, 1969–1970, vol. 39, no. 1, pp. 123–136.

Lindzey, Gardner. Murray's Personology. In C. S. Hall and G. Lindzey (Eds.), *Theories of Personality,* New York: John Wiley, 1957, pp. 157–205.

White, Robert W. Introductory essays in R. W. White (Ed.). *The Study of Lives: Essays on Personality in Honor of Henry A. Murray,* New York: Atherton Press, 1963.

———. Exploring personality the long way: The study of lives. In A. Rabin *et al.* (Eds.) *Further Explorations in Personality,* New York: Wiley-Interscience, 1980.

ACKNOWLEDGMENTS AND PERMISSIONS

Every printed book is a cooperative project involving, at the least, several willing minds and hands. In the preparation of this volume I have been particularly fortunate to have been helped by three extraordinary and enthusiastic people: a non-pareil agent-editor: Regina Ryan; a peerless editor at Harper & Row: Corona Machemer (and her capable aide, Liza Pulitzer); and at UCLA, a perfect assistant: Anita Navarra. I am also grateful to the students in the "Henry A. Murray" course at UCLA over the past several years.

Grateful acknowledgment is made for permission to reprint:

Drawing on title page by Henry A. Murray. Reprinted by permission.

"Preparations for the Scaffold of a Comprehensive System" by Henry A. Murray. Reprinted from *Psychology: A Study of a Science,* Vol. 3, pp. 7–54; edited by S. Koch. Copyright © 1959 by McGraw-Hill, Inc. Reprinted by permission of McGraw-Hill Book Company.

"The Case of Murr from *Autobiography*" by Henry A. Murray. Reprinted from *History of Psychology in Autobiography,* Vol. 5, pp. 285–310; edited by E. G. Boring and G. Lindzey. Copyright © 1967 by Irvington Publishers. Reprinted by permission.

Poem "George Crabbe" from *Children of the Night,* by E. A. Robinson. Copyright 1897 by Charles Scribner's Sons. Reprinted by permission of the publisher.

"In Nomine Diaboli" by Henry A. Murray. Reprinted from *The New England Quarterly,* December 1951, Vol. XXIV, pp. 435–452. Reprinted by permission.

Excerpts from *Explorations in Personality,* pp. 3–141; edited by Henry A. Murray. Copyright 1938 by Oxford University Press, Inc. Renewed 1966 by Henry A. Murray. Reprinted by permission of the publisher.

"Outline of a Conception of Personality" and "Personality Formation: The Determinants" by Henry A. Murray and Clyde Kluckhohn. Reprinted from *Personality in Nature, Society, and Culture,* Second Edition, Revised and Enlarged. Edited by Clyde Kluckhohn and Henry A. Murray, with the collaboration of David M. Schneider. Copyright 1948, 1953 by Alfred A. Knopf, Inc. Reprinted by permission of the publisher.

"Components of an Evolving Personological System" by Henry A. Murray. Reprinted from *International Encyclopedia of the Social Sciences,* 1968, Vol. 12, pp. 5–13. Edited by David L. Sills. Copyright © 1968 by Crowell Collier and Macmillan, Inc. Reprinted by permission.

"Indispensables for the Making, Testing and Remaking of a Personological System" by Henry A. Murray. Reprinted from the *Annals of the New York Academy of Sciences,* April 18, 1977, Vol. 291, pp. 323–331. Reprinted by permission of The New York Academy of Sciences.

"The Effect of Fear upon Estimates of the Maliciousness of Other Personalities" by Henry A. Murray. Reprinted from the Journal of Social Psychology, 1933, Vol. 4, pp. 310–329. Reprinted by permission of The Journal Press.

"What Should Psychologists Do About Psychoanalysis?" by Henry A. Murray. Reprinted from *Journal of Abnormal and Social Psychology*, 1940, Vol. 35, pp. 150–175. Copyright 1940 by the American Psychological Association. Reprinted by permission.

"Vicissitudes of Creativity" by Henry A. Murray. Reprinted from pp. 96–118 of *Creativity and Its Cultivation*, edited by Harold H. Anderson. Copyright © 1959 by Harper & Row, Publishers, Inc. Reprinted by permission.

"Psychology and the University" by Henry A. Murray. Reprinted from *Archives of Neurology and Psychiatry*, 1935, Vol. 34, pp. 803–817. Copyright 1935, American Medical Association. Reprinted by permission.

"Research Planning: A Few Proposals" by Henry A. Murray. Reprinted from *Culture and Personality*, edited by S. Stansfeld Sargent and Marian W. Smith; pp. 195–212. Copyright 1949 by Wenner-Gren Foundation for Anthropological Research, New York. Reprinted by permission.

"Techniques for a Systematic Investigation of Fantasy" by Henry A. Murray. Reprinted from *Journal of Psychology*, 1937, Vol. 3., pp. 115–143. Reprinted by permission of The Journal Press.

"A Method for Investigating Fantasies" by Henry A. Murray with Christiana D. Morgan. Reprinted from *Archives of Neurology and Psychiatry*, 1935, Vol. 34, pp. 289–306. Copyright 1935, American Medical Association. Reprinted by permission.

Introduction to Melville's *Pierre, or, The Ambiguities* by Henry A. Murray; pp. xiii–ciii. Published in 1949 by Hendricks House, Inc. Reprinted by permission of Hendricks House, Inc.

"Bartleby and I" by Henry A. Murray. Reprinted from "Bartleby the Scrivener," which appeared in the *Melville Annual 1968*, pp. 3–24; edited by Howard P. Vincent. Published by the Kent State University Press. Reprinted by permission.

"Dead to the World: The Passions of Herman Melville" by Henry A. Murray. Reprinted from *Essays in Self-Destruction*, pp. 7–29; edited by Edwin S. Shneidman. Published in 1967 by Science House. Reprinted by permission.

"The Personality and Career of Satan" by Henry A. Murray. Reprinted from *The Journal of Social Issues*, 1962, Vol. 18, No. 4, pp. 36–54. Reprinted by permission.

"American Icarus" by Henry A. Murray, pp. 615–641 in *Clinical Studies of Personality*, Volume II, edited by Arthur Burton and Robert E. Harris. Copyright © 1955 by Harper & Row, Publishers, Inc. Reprinted by permission.

"A Note on the Possible Clairvoyance of Dreams" by Henry A. Murray and D. R. Wheeler. Reprinted from *Journal of Psychology*, 1937, Vol. 3, pp. 309–313. Reprinted by permission of The Journal Press.

Excerpts from *Assessment of Men: Selection of Personnel for the Office of Strategic Services* by OSS Assessment Staff, pp. 382–386. Published in 1948 by Holt, Rinehart and Winston. Reprinted by permission.

"Two Versions of Man" by Henry A. Murray. Reprinted from *Science Ponders Religion*, pp. 147–181; edited by H. Shapley. Copyright © 1960 by Appleton-Century-Crofts, Inc. Reprinted by permission of Hawthorn Books, a Division of Elsevier-Dutton Publishing Co., Inc.

"Beyond Yesterday's Idealisms" by Henry A. Murray. Reprinted from *Views from the Circle: Seventy-Five Years of Groton School,* 1960, pp. 371–382. Reprinted by permission of The Groton School.

"This I Believe" by Henry A. Murray. Reprinted from *This I Believe,* edited by Edward R. Murrow. Copyright 1954 by Help, Inc. Reprinted by permission of Simon & Schuster, a Division of Gulf & Western Corporation.

INDEX

629